QUINTIN KENNEDY (1520-1564): TWO EUCHARISTIC TRACTS

PROMOTORES

PROF. T. A. BIRRELL,
PROF. DR. G. STORMS

QUINTIN KENNEDY (1520-1564): TWO EUCHARISTIC TRACTS

A CRITICAL EDITION

ACADEMISCH PROEFSCHRIFT

TER VERKRIJGING VAN DE GRAAD VAN DOCTOR IN
DE LETTEREN AAN DE KATHOLIEKE UNIVERSITEIT TE
NIJMEGEN, OP GEZAG VAN DE RECTOR MAGNIFICUS
T. A. BIRRELL, HOOGLERAAR IN DE FACULTEIT DER
LETTEREN, VOLGENS BESLUIT VAN DE SENAAT DER
UNIVERSITEIT IN HET OPENBAAR TE VERDEDIGEN OP
MAANDAG 15 JUNI 1964, DES NAMIDDAGS TE VIER UUR,

DOOR

CORNELIS HENRICUS KUIPERS, M.H.M.,

GEBOREN TE NOORDWIJKERHOUT

DRUKKERIJ GEBR. JANSSEN N.V. NIJMEGEN

PREFACE

Of the rather impressive list of *opera* attributed to abbot Quintin Kennedy by Thomas Dempster only few have so far been known to be extant, and even fewer have been available in print. That goes some way to explain why Kennedy's reputation as a scholar and ardent defender of the pre-Reformation church in Scotland has never been critically examined.

There is less justification for this neglect now that, in recent years, two of Kennedy's tracts have been discovered. A manuscript copy of his tract on the Mass, which had disappeared some hundred years ago, was found in 1952 by Dr. J. Durkan among a bundle of papers in the Catholic Archives of Scotland, then preserved at St. Mary's College, Blairs. And in 1960 a copy of his tract on the presence of Christ in the Eucharist made its unexpected appearance at a London sale. It was acquired by the Rev. William James Anderson, M.A., Keeper of the Catholic Archives of Scotland. The texts of these manuscripts have, furthermore, enabled me to identify incomplete copies of the same tracts belonging to A. J. B. fforde, Esq., of Brook, Surrey.

Exactly four hundred years after Kennedy's death the two tracts are now printed for the first time. Together they embody Kennedy's eucharistic teaching and easily constitute the most complete expository statement in Middle Scots of pre-Reformation doctrine on the subject.

Kennedy's writings cannot be adequately appreciated unless they are seen against the background of their time. Unfortunately, our picture of Scotland at the time of the Reformation is far from clear. And what is known about Kennedy from his writings and other sources not only throws light upon, but also forms part and parcel of, an all too obscure religious and literary situation. Nevertheless, the materials that could be collected and the discovery of his principal literary sources have warranted a first attempt to place Kennedy in the context of his time.

I consider it an honour to acknowledge my indebtedness to the various persons who, for different parts and at different stages of my work, have given me the advantage of their advice and/or assistance; particularly to the Rev. William James Anderson, M.A., Dr. J. Durkan, Mr. A. J. Aitken, M.A., editor of the *Dictionary of the Older Scottish Tongue*, who generously allowed me to make use of his unpublished notes on Middle Scots, the Rev. M. Taylor, D.D., of St. Peter's College, Cardross, who lent me his unpublished doctoral thesis on the theological conflict in mid-sixteenth century Scotland, and to Dr. Leslie J. Macfarlane, of King's College, Aberdeen.

As it has not seemed feasible to edit 'restored' texts, I have confined myself to an edition of the two complete manuscripts with due mention of textual variants in the incomplete manuscripts and of evidence in favour of particular readings. To the Rev. William James Anderson, owner of the first and custodian of the second complete manuscript, and to A. J. B. fforde, Esq., owner of the incomplete copies, my special thanks are due for permission to publish the texts in this way and to reproduce the illustrations.

In conclusion, I gratefully acknowledge grants from the *Dr. Nuyens Fonds* and the Netherlands Organisation for the Advancement of Pure Research *(Z.W.O.)*, which enabled me to visit Great Britain at two stages of my work.

CONTENTS

LIST OF ABBREVIATIONS

Ailsa Papers	MSS with inventory catalogued as GD. 25 at H.M. General Register House, Edinburgh.
AN	Anglo-Norman.
A.P.S.	*The Acts of the Parliaments of Scotland A.D. MCXXIV–MDCCVII*, edited by T. Thomson and C. Innes, 12 vols. in 13, Edinburgh, 1814–75.
Compendious Ressonyng	See p. 54.
Compendius Tractiue	See p. 49.
Crossraguel Charters	*Charters of the Abbey of Crossraguel*, edited for the Ayrshire and Galloway Archaeological Association by F. C. Hunter Blair, 2 vols., Edinburgh, 1886.
Davidson, *Answer*	*Ane Answer to the Tractiue set furth in the ʒeir of God 1558 be Maister Quintine Kennedy … Maid be Maister Johne Dauidsone, Maister of the Paedagog of Glasgw*, Edinburgh, 1563.
Essays	*Essays on the Scottish Reformation*, edited by David McRoberts, Glasgow, 1962.
Fisher, *De Veritate*	*Ioannis Roffensis Episcopi de Veritate Corporis et Sanguinis Christi in Eucharistia, adversus Iohannem Oecolampadium*, Cologne, 1527.
Hay, *Confutation*	*The Confutation of the Abbote of Crosraguels Masse, set furth by Maister George Hay*, Edinburgh, 1563.
Knox, *History*	*The History of the Reformation in Scotland* by John Knox (Laing's edition used).
Litil Breif Tracteit	See p. 51.
Laing, *Works*	*The Works of John Knox*, collected and edited by David Laing, 6 vols., Edinburgh, Wodrow Society and Bannatyne Club, 1846–64.
Mackenzie, *Lives*	G. Mackenzie, *The Lives and Characters of the most Eminent Writers of the Scots Nation; with an Abstract and Catalogue of their Works, their various Editions, and the Judgment of the Learn'd concerning them*, 3 vols., Edinburgh, 1722.
Mansi	J. D. Mansi, *Sacrorum Conciliorum Nova et Amplissima Collectio*, 31 vols., Florence, 1759 ff.
Maybole Ressoning	See p. 57.

viii

ME	Middle English.
Migne, *PG*	J. P. Migne, *Patrologiae Cursus Completus, Series Graeca*, 163 vols., Paris, 1857 ff.
Migne, *PL*	J. P. Migne, *Patrologiae Cursus Completus, Series Latina*, 221 vols., Paris, 1844 ff.
MSc	Middle Scots.
OE	Old English.
OF	Old French.
Oratioune	See p. 53.
Scand.	Scandinavian.
Smith, *Confutation*	Richard Smith, *A Confutation of a certen booke, called a defence of the true and Catholike doctrine of the sacrament ... sette fourth of late in the name of Thomas Archebysshoppe of Canterburye*, 1550.
Statuta	*Concilia Scotiae: Ecclesiae Scoticanae Statuta tam Provincialia quam Synodalia quae supersunt*, edited for the Bannatyne Club by J. Robertson, 2 vols., Edinburgh, 1866.
S.T.C.	A. W. Pollard and G. R. Redgrave, *A Short-Title Catalogue of Books Printed in England, Scotland, and Ireland, And of English Books Printed Abroad 1475–1640*, London, Bibliographical Society, 1946.
S.T.S.	Scottish Text Society.
The Scots Peerage	J. Balfour Paul, *The Scots Peerage, Founded on Wood's Edition of Sir Robert Douglas's Peerage of Scotland*, 9 vols., Edinburgh, 1904–14.
Wodrow Misc.	*The Miscellany of the Wodrow Society: Containing Tracts and Original Letters chiefly relating to Ecclesiastical Affairs of Scotland during the Sixteenth and Seventeenth Centuries*, selected and edited by David Laing, Edinburgh, 1844.

I. BRIEF CHRONOLOGICAL TABLE

1509–47	Henry VIII king of England.
1513	Battle of Flodden between England and Scotland.
1513–28	John Stewart, Duke of Albany, regent of Scotland.
c. 1520	Birth of Quintin Kennedy.
1525	First anti-Lutheran legislation in Scotland.
1527–58	Gilbert Kennedy of Dunure third Earl of Cassillis (eldest brother of Quintin Kennedy).
1528–42	Personal reign of James V, king of Scotland.
1534	Act of Supremacy passed in England.
1538	Marriage of James V and Mary of Guise.
1540	Quintin Kennedy a student at St. Andrews.
1542	Quintin Kenndy a student at Paris.
	Scots army routed by the English at Solway Moss.
1543–54	James Hamilton, second Earl of Arran, regent of Scotland.
1543–50	England's 'rough wooing' of Mary Stewart
1543–46	George Wishart's preaching in Scotland; John Knox one of his followers.
1545–47	First period of the council of Trent.
1546	Wishart executed for heresy; David Beaton, cardinal archbishop of St. Andrews and chancellor of Scotland, murdered.
1547–53	Edward VI king of England.
1547–59	Henry II king of France.
1547	Quintin Kennedy back in Scotland (possibly much earlier).
	Battle of Pinkie Cleuch between Scotland and England.
	Interim of Augsburg.
1548	Quintin Kennedy abbot of Crossraguel.
	Mary Stewart sent to France as prospective bride of the Dauphin.
1549–54	John Knox's preaching in England.
1549	National council of the Scottish church, convoked by John Hamilton, half-brother to the regent and archbishop of St. Andrews.
	First Act of Uniformity in England. *Consensus Tigurinus*.
1550	Knox's *Vindication of the Doctrine that the Mass is Idolatry*.
	Publication of Richard Smith's *Confutation* of Cranmer's *Defence*.
1551–52	Second period of the council of Trent.

	National council of the church of Scotland; publication of *Archbishop Hamilton's Catechism*.
1552	Second Act of Uniformity in England.
1553–58	Mary Tudor queen of England; England reconciled with Rome.
1554–59	Knox at Frankfort and Geneva (visit to Scotland in 1555–56)
1554–60	Mary of Guise regent of Scotland.
1555	Settlement of Augsburg.
1557	First 'Common Band' or 'Covenant' of the Scottish 'Lords of the Congregation'.
1558	Marriage of Mary Stewart and the Dauphin; Crown matrimonial of Scotland offered to Mary's husband.
	Publication of Kennedy's *Compendius Tractiue*.
1558–76	Gilbert Kennedy of Dunure fourth Earl of Cassillis (Quintin Kennedy's nephew).
1558–1603	Elizabeth I queen of England.
1559	National council of the church of Scotland.
	Unsuccessful arrangements for a debate on the Mass between Quintin Kennedy and John Willock. Treaty of Cateau Cambrésis. Acts of Supremacy and Uniformity in England.
	Knox's return to Scotland; beginning of the 'wars of the Congregation'.
1559–60	Francis II king of France.
1560	Open English intervention in favour of the Scottish revolt.
	The 'Reformation Parliament' in August accepts the *Confessio Scotica*, abolishes papal jurisdiction in Scotland, and passes anti-catholic penal legislation.
	Quintin Kennedy's *Litil Breif Tracteit* probably written this year.
1561–63	Third period of the council of Trent.
1561–67	Personal reign of Mary Stewart as queen of Scotland; she refuses to ratify the 'Reformation Parliament'.
1561–62	Quintin Kennedy's *Oratioune* and *Compendious Ressonyng*.
1562	Mary Stewart's campaign against the Earl of Huntley; 'Common Band' of the Ayrshire lords; three-days' debate at Maybole between Kennedy and Knox.
1563	Publication of Fergusson's *Answer*, Davidson's *Answer*, Hay's *Confutation* and Knox's *Maybole Ressoning*.
1564	Death of Quintin Kennedy.

II. THE SCOTTISH BACKGROUND TO
KENNEDY'S WRITINGS

It has been said that "Knox's attack on catholicism was not based on the scandalous lives of the Scottish Prelates, but on the allegation that the mass is idolatrous."[1] The Scottish Reformation, however, was a very complex affair, which is perhaps best described in the language of its supporters, viz. as "that same warre whiche God commanded Israell to execut aganis the Cananites."[2] Quintin Kennedy's definition that "ydolatrie is to ascriue Goddis glore to ony vther nor to God himself, or to werschip ony vther as God,"[3] was not accepted. Nor was his distinction between doctrine and practice, whether applied to the catholic clergy or to the reformed ministers.[4] For Knox, catholic sacrificial teaching was no isolated grievance. As a doctrine "broght in by Satan", the "perpetuall enimie to treuth and to ane honest life", it could not but produce "filthy liuing and ... filthie merchandrise in the temple of God". And like the "true Prophetes" of old, he felt that it was his mission in life to uproot the "adulterat and vsurped religion".[5]

Kennedy, who solemnly declared that he would never desist from the "just defence of the verite ... for bud not boist quhill that my tong ma steir," was painfully aware of the Reformers' association with the movement of revolt against the established civil authority.[6] But he was equally aware of the abuses in his church. From the point of view of an apologist these abuses would be all the more serious in that they placed a powerful weapon in the hands of his opponents. A defender of the divine character of the catholic church and its worship would naturally feel that evident abuses and immorality among the clergy would affect the persuasive force of his theological arguments.

Kennedy strongly advocated internal reform, and the way in which he did it admits of no doubt about his sincerity. But it is clear that his frank admission of what it would be useless to deny was at the same time an integral part of his method of defence. Unfortunately it is not known what he thought of Archibald Hay's *Gratulatorius panegyricus*,[7] of the deadly irony of Buchanan's early

---

[1] M. Mahoney, "The Scottish Hierarchy, 1530–65," in *Essays*, p. 40.

[2] Laing, *Works*, vol. i, p. 336.

[3] *Oratioune*, Laing, *Works*, vi, p. 159.

[4] *Maybole Ressoning, ibid.*, pp. 190f.

[5] See the editorial introduction and Knox's first speech of the *Maybole Ressoning* (*l.c.*, pp. 171 ff. and 187 ff.), from which these phrases are taken.

[6] This is clearly brought out in the *Oratioune*, here quoted (*l.c.*, p. 157).

[7] Paris, 1540. It was addressed to David Beaton on his elevation to the cardinalate.

3

poems,[8] of Lord Kilmaurs' *Epistle Direct fra the Holye Armite of Allarit, to his Bretheren the Gray Freires,*[9] or of Sir David Lyndsay's satires.[10] Kennedy was second to none in denouncing clerical abuses. But what, in this matter, distinguishes him from those writers is first of all his passionate appeal to the Nobility and the Crown – at whose request Buchanan had written his *Franciscanus* and which had on several occasions been entertained by Lyndsay's *Satyre of the Thrie Estaitis* – not to disclaim responsibility for the sad condition of the clergy. Kennedy did not excuse the clergy. He fully admitted that those who should preach were "(as sayis the Propheit) 'lyke dum doggis, quhilkis can nocht bark'", that those who should guide the people were "mair ignorante nor the simple pepyll self", and that those who should lead exemplary lives were in fact "oppin sclanderaris[11] of the Congregatioun (for the maist part)". He implored them to change their lives, "specialie quha occupyis the place of the Apostoles be office and authoritie". But he also denounced the hypocrisy of the Nobility and the Crown, the chief critics of the clergy but themselves responsible for the nomination of unworthy candidates to the ecclesiastical benefices: "and all for avarice, 'the rute of all vice'".[12]

It was not Kennedy's habit to mention names. But James V had been a notorious offender in this respect,[13] the regent Arran would be one of the persons in Kennedy's mind when he spoke of fatal nepotism,[14] and Mary of Guise's policy was not dictated by reforming zeal either.[15] On the contrary, she proved Kennedy right when, a few months after the appearance of the *Compendius Tractiue*, she requested the Primate of Scotland to convoke a national council.[16] And this was clearly the kind of thing Kennedy could not stand, one of the very few subjects which aroused his anger. If Crown and Nobility were sincerely concerned about reform, they had it in their power to 'unslander' the church. Like the council of 1549, Kennedy attributed the progress of the movement for radical reform chiefly to the ignorance and immorality of the

---

[8] George Buchanan, the humanist, was tutor to Kennedy's eldest brother, the Earl of Cassillis, in the early 'thirties and for several years stayed in the Kennedy household.

[9] Alexander Cunningham, Lord Kilmaurs, became Earl of Glencairn on the death of his father in 1547. He was a strong supporter of the Reformation movement from the 'forties onwards. The poem has been preserved in Knox's *History* (Laing, *Works*, i, pp. 72 ff.)

[10] *The Works of Sir David Lindsay of the Mount* have been edited for the S.T.S. by Douglas Hamer (4 vols., 1931–36).

[11] *i.e.* persons who bring reproach on the church by their conduct (Jamieson's *Etymological Dictionary*, with a reference to this place).

[12] *Compendius Tractiue*, ch. xiv, *Wodrow Misc.*, pp. 150 ff.

[13] Examples will be given in the following pages.

[14] Cp. M. Mahoney, *l.c.*, 51 ff.

[15] *Ibid.*, pp. 53 f. and 73 ff.

[16] See *Statuta*, ii, no. 255 (pp. 140 ff.).

4

clergy.[17] But he went on to say that this ignorance and immorality were, in their turn, the result of irresponsible lay interference with ecclesiastical appointments.

In a country where church and nation are co-extensive, where the life of the nation is permeated with the outlook and practices of that church, and where church officials are in various degrees at the same time civil administrators, it must of necessity be difficult to draw the dividing line between civil and ecclesiastical authority. By Kennedy's time the Scottish Crown had for a long time claimed the right to dispose of temporalities during episcopal vacancies. By an agreement of January 1449/50, in which bishop James Kennedy of St. Andrews had played a leading part, this right, together with the prelates' right to dispose by testament of their movable property, had been officially acknowledged by Parliament.[18] A papal indult of 1487 had granted the Crown the right of nominating beneficiaries of the rich monasteries and bishoprics, after first enjoying their revenues during vacancies.[19] It had excluded the capitular election which Quintin Kennedy considered a necessary condition of suitable appointments. After the disastrous Flodden campaign, which had been undertaken in support of France and in opposition to papal policy, Leo X had not renewed the indult. But the Duke of Albany, acting as Regent for his nephew James V, had deferred the traditional formal acknowledgement of the pope's authority until it had been confirmed and amplified in 1519.[20] It had been further amplified in 1535, within a year of England's final repudiation of Rome, and James V had not been slow to exercise his right of nomination.[21]

In defence of such royal control it might be argued that the First Estate constituted an important advisory body (which contributed such statesmen as James Kennedy, Elphinstone, Forman, the three Beatons, Gavin Dunbar and John Hamilton), were it not that the misuse of the power of nomination was too evident to be overlooked. In the winter of 1532/33 James V, aged 20, wrote an incredibly crude letter to Rome, in which he asked for legitimation of three natural sons and dispensation from the defect of birth and age, so that they might be promoted to orders and ecclesiastical benefices, including several of incompatibles and, in due time, bishoprics and archbishoprics; surely a pope called Clement could not refuse a petition prompted by paternal feelings.[22] As

---

[17] *Ibid.*, nos. 192 and 195 (pp. 97 and 99).

[18] See *A.P.S.*, ii, pp. 37f. Cp. *Statuta*, i, pp. c ff., and A. I. Dunlop, *The Life and Times of James Kennedy, Bishop of St. Andrews*, Edinburgh and London, 1950, pp. 112ff.

[19] See W. C. Dickinson, G. Donaldson and I. A. Milne, *A Source Book of Scottish History*, 2nd edition, London &c., 1958, vol. ii, pp. 88f.

[20] See *Letters of James V*, collected and calendared by R. K. Hannay, edited by D. Hay, Edinburgh, 1954, pp. 49–51, 68, 79.

[21] *Ibid.*, p. 285.

[22] See *Letters of James V*, pp. 237f.

affairs in England developed, the request was granted, and within a few years four of the king's natural sons were appointed to the five rich monastic establishments of Holyrood, Coldingham, Kelso, Melrose and St. Andrews. By act of Parliament it was subsequently ruled that the revenues were at the disposal of the Crown, "þe kingis gracis sonnis þame selfis being honestlie furnissit and sustenit ... quhill þai be of perfite aige." [23]

Such were the cases Kennedy must have had in mind when he wrote that extensive pastoral charges were entrusted to mere babes; and they were the persons who would in due time be expected to live exemplary clerical lives according to the norms of canon law.

A summary of the episcopal nominations during the three decades immediately prior to the Reformation speaks of those "of the personal rule of James V, when the dominant aim was exploitation of the church, for the financial benefit of the crown," those "during the regency of Arran, who attempted to make the church the appanage of the Hamiltons," and those "of Mary of Lorraine, which reflect her desire to obtain support for the Franco-Scottish alliance." [24] If this shows misuse of the right of nomination, it does not mean that the persons nominated were in every case the Crown's own or first choice. There was, indeed, every reason for a man like Kennedy to deplore the unreasonable demands of the nobility in the matter. The efforts of the Crown to form a stronger central power in the country, together with the strained relations with England, gave them an excellent opportunity to follow the example of blackmail set by James V. It was they who controlled the armed force of the country. Until a late date the majority was not against the royal decision to uphold catholicism, and support of Crown policy would less easily be withheld if it would at the same time advance their personal and family interests.

The result was that the First Estate, instead of forming a body of persons sincerely concerned and occupied with the religious life of the nation and the educational and social welfare work traditionally entrusted to them, largely reflected the political divisions and the moral weaknesses of the nobility. "About half of the incelibate bishops belonged to that influential, but generally unepiscopal, group who were sons of the greater nobles. Of seventeen of these bishops, twelve had illegitimate offspring; four of the two bishops and the three bishops-elect who defected were also of the same group. It may have been considered equitable that the nobility should have been strongly represented in the hierarchy, but such churchmen had usually little regard for the duties of

---

[23] *A.P.S.*, ii, p. 424.
[24] M. Mahoney, *l.c.*, pp. 46f.

the clerical state." [25] The same was true of the commendatory abbots, who were generally not in major orders and did not belong to the communities of which they enjoyed the revenues. "To have a member of the family appointed as commendator of an abbey or priory was a profitable device, and already some years before 1560 the office of abbot or commendator was in some cases becoming the perquisite of a particular noble house: thus Dryburgh tended to be at the disposal of the Erskines, Paisley and Kilwinning of the Hamiltons, Whithorn of the Flemings, Crossraguel of the Kennedies, Culross of the Colvilles and Jedburgh of the Humes." [26]

On a lower level the system of nomination did not materially differ. Nobility and gentry controlled the appointments to minor religious foundations which had been initiated by their pious ancestors or of which they had gained control in other ways. As in the case of bishoprics and abbeys, the normal method of endowing such foundations as collegiate churches and prebendal stalls in cathedrals had been to appropriate to them the revenues of one or more parishes. The incumbents of the benefices thus formed were at the same time parsons or rectors of those parishes and had to pay part of their income for the sustenance of vicars who did the parochial work. The percentage of parishes whose revenues had been diverted to other benefices has been estimated at seventy-five,[27] or even ninety.[28] Many of the vicars were underpaid, and this became worse when existing vicarages were in turn appropriated to new benefices and the pension of the actual parish clergy was accordingly diminished.[29] In such cases the parishioners would not only reluctantly pay their teinds to the agent of an unknown parson, they would also know that their own clergy belonged to the category which was not eligible for a better living.

Kennedy's strictures on negligent pastors and 'dum doggis' who were unable to preach, were very severe. It is known that in 1562 he started a series of instructions "within my Kirk of Kirkoswald",[30] one of the parishes belonging to his abbey of Crossraguel. And the fact that, for example, he and his uncle and predecessor, abbot William Kennedy, were generally respected, warns us not to exaggerate the implications of those strictures. On the other hand, the system which led to so many evils was far from unknown among the clerical Kennedys.

In 1371 one of Quintin Kennedy's ancestors had founded an oratory at

---

[25] M. Mahoney, *l.c.*, p. 57.

[26] G. Donaldson, *The Scottish Reformation*, Cambridge University Press, 1960, p. 39. Also see M. Mahoney, *l.c.*, pp. 57 ff.

[27] W. Croft Dickinson, *Scotland from the Earliest Times to 1603*, London &c., 1961, p. 126.

[28] Denis McKay, "Parish Life in Scotland, 1500–1560", in *Essays*, p. 86.

[29] See G. Donaldson, *o.c.*, pp. 12 f., and sources quoted.

[30] *Maybole Ressoning*, Laing, *Works*, vi, p. 185.

Maybole for a priest and three chaplains, which had become a collegiate church with a provost on March 1st, 1383/84. In 1501 the patronage of the provostry and a prebend is included in a list of Kennedy property. From this period till his death in 1532 the provostry is actually held by Gilbert, fourth son of John, second Lord Kennedy.[31] A reference, in 1530, to Walter Kennedy of Glentig as provost of Maybole must be a mistake. He was a canon of Glasgow, who had succeeded his father, the poet Walter Kennedy, to the parsonage of Douglas, which he continued to hold till his death in the winter of 1561/62.[32] Meanwhile a John Kennedy had filled the prebendal stall at Maybole between the early 'twenties and early 'forties, a James Kennedy had been vicar of the collegiate church, and the vicarages of Dunscore and Penpont had been associated with persons of the same name.[33] The last-mentioned benefice was subsequently held by Thomas Kennedy, from whom it passed to his younger brother Quintin, who already held the clerkship of the rich[34] parish of Colmonell, which he resigned in favour[35] of his younger brother Hugh when he received the abbacy of Crossraguel, which had for nearly thirty years been held by his uncle William Kennedy, who had at the same time been perpetual commendator of the abbey of Holywood.[36]

That nepotism was not restricted to individual cases is perhaps best illustrated by an act of council on the eve of the battle of Pinkie. It was announced to the army that if any churchmen should die in battle, their nearest of kin would have the right of "presentatioun, provisioun and collatioun" of the benefice to the nearest of kin most qualified for it.[37] It seems to have been in virtue of this ruling that Quintin Kennedy succeeded his brother Thomas as vicar of Penpont.[38]

With respect to ecclesiastical property, Crown and nobility had played into each other's hands in yet a different way, viz. in the matter of clerical taxation, which, in its turn, was closely connected with the political situation and the suppression of heretical opinion. In order to solve its financial problems the Crown naturally turned to the church, the wealthiest body in the country. Since it needed the continued political as well as the financial support of the clergy, it

---

[31] See *Ailsa Papers*, section i, nos. 11f., 19, 130, 179ff., 184, 187, 270, 316.

[32] *Ibid.*, nos. 240, 299, 301, 496, 557, 604f. No. 240 suggests that the poet Walter Kennedy lived till 1518; cp. Dunbar's *Lament for the Makaris* (1507–8), lines 89–91.

[33] *Ibid.*, nos. 274, 281, 291, 356, 360, 376, 413; 288, 305, 307, 316, 334, 360; 291, 326. John is referred to as provost in November 1532 (no. 316).

[34] See *Accounts of the Collectors of Thirds of Benefices, 1561–1572*, edited for the Scottish History Society by G. Donaldson, 3rd series, vol. xlii, Edinburgh, 1949, p. 21.

[35] *Resignatio in favorem* was a method of ensuring succession; cp. *Statuta*, ii, no. 218f. (pp. 115f.)

[36] See *Ailsa Papers*, i, nos. 367, 476, 479 and below, p. 26.

[37] *A.P.S.*, ii, p. 599f.

[38] See p. 26 below.

resorted to the method of taxation for the alleged purpose of maintaining the position of the church. The clergy, on the other hand, needed the support of civil authority, and was forced to turn to the nobility for cash to pay its taxes.[39]

Faced with a possible defection of Scotland, the pope could only comply when, in 1531, James V requested a huge sum from the revenues of the church in Scotland for the foundation and upkeep of a College of Justice. The Scottish prelates protested. James was willing to allow modifications of his demands, but simple references to the English example were sufficient to enforce regular and recurrent extra taxations. Henry VIII repeatedly tried to make Scotland an ally in schism. Sir Ralph Sadler, the envoy he sent to Edinburgh in 1540, had clear instructions in this respect. But when he proposed that James should confiscate the wealth of the monasteries, he was answered that taxation was the much more efficient method.[40] It "meant the possibility of tapping the Church's wealth, without destroying the reservoir from which it flowed." The regents Arran and Mary of Guise continued the practice, so that "by 1560 clergy taxes were regarded as a proper source of income for an impecunious government."[41]

The problem for the clergy was how to raise the necessary money. Their income was largely in kind, and one after another was forced to resort to the old forbidden practice of tacking and feuing ecclesiastical property. By a tack, or lease, they could, for a stated period, transfer the right of teinds and the onus of their collection to the local nobility or gentry in return for a fixed rent. Similarly, by feu charters they could grant lands in return for a fixed payment once and specified annual feu-duties. But as a result of the large scale on which feu charters were being granted for long terms, and even heritably, in the last decades before the Reformation, the nobility got a firm hold of ecclesiastical landed property. The Kennedys of Dunure were neither inactive nor unsuccessful in this respect, controlling the properties of the abbeys of Glenluce and Soulseat as well as Crossraguel by the early 'sixties.[42] The young Earl of Cassillis, head of the Dunure branch and chief of the entire clan, would gain by either the continuance of the old system or by its radical overthrow. He, and many other noblemen with him, would lose by a drastic internal reform of the pre-Reformation church. This danger was not a very real one, however, and

---

[39] On this matter see W. Stanford Reid, "Clerical Taxation: The Scottish Alternative to Dissolution of the Monasteries, 1530–1560," in *The Catholic Historical Review*, xxxiv (1948), pp. 129–153.

[40] See *The State Papers and Letters of Sir Ralph Sadler*, edited by A. Clifford, 2 vols., Edinburgh, 1809, vol. 1, pp. 29f.

[41] W. Stanford Reid, *l.c.*, pp. 135 and 150.

[42] See *Ailsa Papers*, i, nos. 451, 589ff., 599, 643, and G. Donaldson, *Thirds of Benefices*, pp. 21 and 296.

within a few more years he realized that the political tide had definitely turned in favour of the overthrow of catholicism.[43]

Down to the middle of the sixteenth century Scotland, in order to protect its independence in the British Isles, had for many years been politically allied to France. To be sure, the 'auld alliance' had not been considered the ideal policy by every Scot,[44] but the imperious claims of Henry VIII over Scotland, accompanied as they were by his 'rough wooing' in the 'forties, led to a strengthening of anti-English feeling instead of a furthering of his interests, Meanwhile, however, the established church had become inevitably committed to the proFrench policy of the government – at least in as far as it was anti-English –, whilst the political as well as the religious opposition naturally turned to England for readily offered support. There is some irony in the circumstance that the catholic interregnum of Mary Tudor combined with the too-French policy of Mary of Guise to strengthen the Scottish opposition; in fact, the regent needed some sort of an alliance with the protestant nobility against Arran, whom she had supplanted as regent in 1554, and his Hamilton faction.[45] But when the inherent danger of the French alliance became too imminent through the marriage of Mary Stewart with the Dauphin in April 1558, and Elizabeth, on her accession towards the end of that year, was not only confronted with an impending league of the catholic powers, but also with Mary Stewart's openly expressed claims to the English throne,[46] it was only a question of choosing an opportune moment for a self-constituted calvinistic 'godly magistracy' to take over the government with English support.

In another respect the earlier regime had been rounded off in April 1558, when Walter Myln, an aged priest who held heretical opinions and had contracted marriage, was tried and burned at St. Andrews. Thirty years earlier the first Lutheran martyr had been burned in the same town. But it is significant that when Knox came to write his *History of the Reformation in Scotland*, he traced the beginnings of the increasingly victorious movement beyond early Lutheranism to fifteenth-century Lollardy, notably the trial of the 'Lollards of Kyle'.[47] He thus established an historical link between his own opinions and a

---

[43] Cp. W. Law Mathieson, *Politics and Religion. A Study in Scottish History from the Reformation to the Revolution*, 2 vols., Glasgow, 1902, vol. i, p. 29.

[44] Note, e.g., the influential John Major's *Historia Majoris Britanniae* (1521).

[45] See W. Law Mathieson, *o.c.*, i, pp. 42ff., and J. H. Burns, "The Political Background of the Reformation, 1530–1625," in *Essays* (pp. 1–38), pp. 13ff.

[46] There had been marriage negotiations between Philip II and Elizabeth of France in February 1558/59 (see, e.g., *Cambridge Modern History*, vol. ii, p. 566). The treaty of Cateau Cambrésis was signed on April 2nd. Also see J. H. Pollen, *Papal Negotiations with Mary Queen of Scots, 1561–1567*, Edinburgh, Scottish History Society, 1901, p. xxxviii, for rumours about secret treaties between catholic powers.

[47] See Laing, *Works*, i, pp. 7ff.

long tradition of revolt against an ordained priesthood whose lives, in the eyes of these opponents, showed too clearly that they could not be dispensers of salvation and who answered criticism with repressive measures. Not that Knox denied civil authority the right to suppress heresy. On the contrary, the principle was incorporated in the *Confessio Scotica* of August 1560, which said of civil magistrates that "not onlie thay ar appointit for ciuile policie, bot alswa for mantenance of the trew religioun and for suppressing of Idolatrie and super- stitioun quhatsaeuer."[48] But the emphasis on the intolerable situation that 'false prophets' should receive official support for their 'abominations', whilst the 'preaching of the Evangel' was suppressed, formed a substantial element of his appeal and was ultimately based on his fundamental views of justification.

Of course, Knox could hardly be expected to weaken the force of his appeal by referring to efforts at internal reform in the pre-Reformation church.[49] Similarly, Kennedy was out to show the necessity of reform to his co-religionists, and he may well have felt that his language was more forceful when, instead of making much of holiness in his church, he generalized about deserters to the opposite camp:

"Is it nocht thocht that the preist, monk, or fleschelye forloppin freir, followis treulie the verray doctryne of St Paule, quhilk is rynnegat fra his religioun, and makis ane monsterous mariage, and it wer[50] with ane non; and zit he wyl sweir and saye, that all that he dois is for the glore of God and the libertie of the Evangell."[51]

Knox was more voluble, when he replied to this sort of accusation that Kennedy, "ioyning with him the whole rable of the horned Bischoppes," could non convict the reformed ministers of being

"adulterers, fornicators, dronckards, bloodscheders, oppressors of the poore wedow, fatherles, or stranger, or yet, that do idilly liue vpon the sweat of other mennes browes. And how many of them from the hiest to the lowest, are able to abyde an assyse of the forenamed crimes?"[52]

Knox's language is a kind of climax of the anti-clerical feeling of the previous period, and he carried it against Kennedy in the end.

The distinction between different degrees of anti-clericalism and clearly heterodox opinion is not easy to draw during the reign of James V; more

---

[48] *A.P.S.*, ii, p. 534.

[49] See, e.g., A. Ross, "Some Notes on the Religious Orders in Pre-Reformation Scotland," in *Essays*, pp. 185–244, and the decrees of the sixteenth-century councils in Robertson's *Statuta*, vol. ii.

[50] even if.

[51] *Compendius Tractiue, Wodrow Misc.*, p. 150.

[52] *Maybole Ressoning*, Laing, *Works*, vi, p. 190.

precisely, it cannot be ascertained how far Lutheranism had spread by the end of his reign: about its presence in the country there can be no doubt. An act of Parliament of July, 1525, amplified in September, 1527, had forbidden the introduction of heretical literature into the ports of Scotland under pain of forfeiture of the ships and imprisonment of the culprits.[53] 1528 had seen the trial and burning of Patrick Hamilton, member of one of the most influential Scottish families and author of a small Lutheran treatise on faith and good works generally referred to as *Patrick's Places*.[54] In the 'thirties the government demonstrated recurrent zeal to proceed against heresy as James needed money from the clergy or papal favours.[55] Among those who fled the country were John Gau, whose *Richt Vay to the Kingdome of Heuine* was printed at Malmö in 1533,[56] Alexander Alane, or Alesius, who was soon to engage in a literary dispute with Cochlaeus on the expediency of spreading a vernacular version of the *New Testament* in Scotland (from which it appears that this had been forbidden by the hierarchy[57]), George Wishart, who was to translate the *Confessio Helvetica* of 1536,[58] John Willock, an Ayrshire man, who was to become chaplain to the duke of Suffolk under Edward VI,[59] and George Buchanan. The last three persons were in due time to return to Scotland and to play prominent parts in its further history. Among the victims was a young Ayrshire Kennedy with poetic gifts.[60]

Mention has already been made of the arrival, in 1540, of Henry VIII's envoy Sir Ralph Sadler. James first agreed to meet his uncle at York, then was prevailed upon by the clergy and the prospect of a considerable sum of money not to go, had nine acts passed about church affairs in the parliament of March 1540/41, and asked Rome why the extra grant of money had not yet been confirmed.[61] Notable among the acts were the prohibition, under pain of death and confiscation of all goods, against denying the pope's authority, the prohibition

---

[53] See *A.P.S.*, ii, p. 295. For earlier acts against heresy, see *A.P.S.*, i, p. 211 and ii, p. 7.

[54] See Laing, *Works*, i, pp. 20 ff.

[55] See the wording of the act of May, 1532 (*A.P.S.*, ii, p. 335), passed when James wanted money for the College of Justice, and the repeated letters to Rome requesting legatine powers for Cardinal Beaton, which coincided with the prolonged heresy-hunting towards the end of the 'thirties (*Letters of James V*, pp. 349, 358, 377, 384, 400, 405 and 422).

[56] Edited for the S.T.S. by A. F. Mitchell, Edinburgh & London, 1888.

[57] See G. Christie, *The Influence of Letters on the Scottish Reformation*, Edinburgh & London, 1908, pp. 28 ff.

[58] Printed after his death under the title *The Confescion of the fayth of the Sweserlandes* (*Wodrow Misc.*, pp. 7–23).

[59] See Kirkwood Hewat, *Makers of the Scottish Church at the Reformation*, Edinburgh, 1920, p. 132.

[60] See Laing, *Works*, i, pp. 63–66.

[61] See *A.P.S.*, ii, pp. 370 f., and *Letters of James V*, p. 183.

against organizing or allowing discussions on Scripture, and the act 'For reforming of kirkis And kirkmen', which admits that "þe vnhonestie and misreule of kirkmen baith in witt, knawlege And maneris Is þe mater and causs þat þe kirk and kirkmen ar lychtlyit and contempnit."

James died in December, 1542, just after the battle of Solway Moss, which had been the result of his anti-English policy, and a week after the birth of his daughter. James Hamilton, second Earl of Arran, was proclaimed regent and for a brief spell showed reforming and pro-English tendencies. For this he could count on the support of such persons as the Ayrshire Earls of Cassillis and Glencairn, who had been taken prisoner at Solway but, after due indoctrination, had been released under hostages after the death of James, pledged and paid to promote a match between Mary Stewart and Edward VI.[62] The parliament of the following March agreed to the marriage arrangement and, in spite of the prelates' request to wait till a provincial council had discussed it, permitted the general use of Scripture in the vernacular.[63] This latter act meant that the Tyndale Bible, which had so far been one of the forbidden books stealthily smuggled into the country, was now allowed to be read, at least until the church should produce a new translation.[64]

However, before a year had passed the situation had changed completely. In September Arran and cardinal Beaton were reconciled, Beaton became Chancellor, and the English policy was reversed. In December Parliament passed an act ordering the hierarchy to set up an inquiry into the presence of heretics in their territories, because "heretikis mair and mair risis and spredis within þis realme sawand dampnable opinionis Incontrar þe faith and lawis of halykirk, actis and constitutionis of þis realm;" the prelates could apply for the assistance of the secular arm if necessary.[65]

An act of the Privy Council, issued half a year earlier, gives more information, because it forbade the production and ordered the suppression of "slanderous

---

[62] Cp. *Acts of the Privy Council of England*, edited by J. R. Dasent, new series, London, H.M. Stationery Office, 1890 ff., vol. i (1542–47), pp. 67–69, from which it appears that Quintin Kennedy's brother, the Earl of Cassillis, was considered the chief prisoner and that he was entrusted to the care of no less a person than Archbishop Cranmer.

[63] See *A.P.S.*, ii, pp. 415 and 425.

[64] A MS copy of a Wycliffite bible, belonging to an Ayrshire family, has been edited for the S.T.S. by T. Graves Law (*The New Testament in Scots*, being Purvey's Revision of Wycliffe's Version, Turned into Scots by Murdoch Nisbet, c. 1520, 2 vols., Edinburgh & London, 1901 & 1903), and more copies may have been used among the 'Lollards of Kyle'. For the early introduction of the Tyndale version, cp. C. Anderson, *The Annals of the English Bible*, 2 vols., London, 1845, vol. ii, p. 409. Knox suggests that in 1543 the Bible could be found "lying almaist upoun everie gentilmanis table" (Laing, *Works*, i, p. 100). As far as is known the catholic translation never came off.

[65] *A.P.S.*, ii, p. 443.

bills, writings, ballates, and books ... daily made, written, and prentit to the diffamation of all estatis, both spiritual and temporal."[66] This contains undoubtedly an early reference to *The Gude and Godlie Ballatis*, associated with the names of James, John and Robert Wedderburn, of Dundee, and circulating in broad-sheet form from about this time onwards.[67] A 1567 collection[68] shows that they consisted of metrical psalms, hymns and 'bawdie songs' turned into 'godlie rymes'. The criticism of the pre-Reformation clergy contained in this last group is illustrated by the following lines from a ballad beginning "The Paip, that pagane full of pryde":

> The blind Bischop he culd not preiche,
> For playing with the lassis;
> The syllie Freir behuffit to fleiche,
> For almous that he assis;[69]
> The Curat his creid he culd nocht reid,
> Schame fall the cumpanie:
> Hay trix, tryme go trix,
> Vnder the grene wod-tree.[70]

The implications of such criticism were expressed in the *Swiss Confession*, which Wishart brought with him when he returned to Scotland in July 1543: the church of Christ is "the congregacion and eleccion of all holy men," among whom the authority "to preache Goddes Worde ... shulde be committed onely to them that are mete therfore." The end of this preaching is to inculcate "that we are safe onely by the marcie of God, and merite of our Sauiour Christ," "refusing utterly all other meane of lyfe and saluacion." The congregation gathers in church "so that fyrst, chefely, and before all thynges, the worde of

---

[66] Quoted in *Statuta*, ii, p. 294.

[67] The Wedderburns had fled the country about the year 1540. John went to Germany, where he became acquainted with Lutheran hymnology. He was back in Scotland in 1543, but soon fled to England (D. Calderwood, *The History of the Kirk of Scotland*, edited for the Wodrow Society by Th. Thomson, 8 vols., Edinburgh, 1842–49, vol. i, pp. 141–143; cp. vol. viii, p. 147).

[68] *A Compendious Book of Godly and Spiritual Songs, Commonly Known as 'The Gude and Godlie Ballatis'*, edited for the S.T.S. by A. F. Mitchell, Edinburgh & London, 1897.

[69] asks.

[70] The tune was indicated by the first lines in the following curious specimen:
> "Johne, cum kis me now,
> Johne, cum kis me now;
> Johne, cum kis me by and by
> And mak no moir adow.
> The Lord thy God I am,
> That Johne dois thé call;
> Johne representit man,
> Be grace celestiall."

God be preached to the people ... And that by the Holy Supper of thankes, called Howselynge, the faithe of the godly be ofte exersysed, and that they shulde be contynually in prayer for all men, and for the necessities of all men. But the rest of ceremonies which, as they are unprofitable, so are they innumerable, as vescels, garmentes, waxe, lyghtes, alters, golde, sylver, in so moch as they serue to subuerte the trewe relygion of God: and chefely Idols and Images, that stande open to be worshyped." [71]

Wishart was the first regular preacher of the Reformation in Scotland. His work at Dundee was soon stopped by cardinal Beaton, but he escaped to the Ayrshire districts of the Earls of Cassillis and Glencairn, where he could count on the support of these magnates. John Knox became one of his followers when he afterwards preached at Haddington, in East Lothian. He was apprehended in the winter of 1545/46, tried, and burned on March 1st. Cardinal Beaton was assassinated three months afterwards. [72] A year later a French fleet reduced the castle of St. Andrews, where the murderers and those who had rallied round them had entrenched themselves. They were carried off as prisoners, John Knox among them. More substantial French aid arrived in Scotland after the defeat of the Scottish forces at Pinkie (September, 1547). Its presence in the country was gradually to put an end to the 'rough wooing'; in fact, the seal had been set upon the 'auld alliance' after Mary Stewart had been sent to France, in July, 1548, as the prospective bride of the dauphin.

The anonymous author of *The Complaynte of Scotlande* was probably only one among many educated catholics who anticipated that this would be the beginning of the restoration of peace in the realm. [73] Yet he is fully aware that Scotland has to set its own house in order, for the national calamities that have befallen the country are the result of national sins, as he argues in the first five chapters. In the remaining part he watches the dawn of a glorious new day and describes a peaceful pastoral scene in rural Scotland, [74] after which he sees Dame Scotia in a dream as she is in reality. Her mantle, once beautifully adorned with emblems representing a valiant and strong nobility, a spirituality devoted to learning and charitable work, and an industrious commons, is now all torn and ragged. One after the other she upbraids her three sons for their unpatriotic

---

[71] *Wodrow Misc.*, pp. 16, 17, 15 and 20f. respectively.

[72] A Wishart, though not necessarily the preacher, was implicated, with Cassillis, in an earlier plan to murder Beaton. See A. Lang, *John Knox and the Reformation*, London, 1905, p. 16.

[73] Edited for the E.E.T.S. by J. A. H. Murray, London, 1872. It was first printed in 1549; the "Epistil to the Qvenis Grace" (i.e. Mary of Guise, widow of James V) contains a reference to Mary Stewart's departure for France.

[74] Including a large number of ballads not made 'godlie' (E.E.T.S. edition, pp. 64ff., lxxxvii ff.)

vices, she exhorts them to lay aside their discords and to unite against the 'ald enemies of Ingland' after the manner of true Christians.[75]

The author's nationalist, anti-English sentiments are predominant throughout, also in the nineteenth chapter, which, in rather general terms, contains the indictment of Spirituality. The clergy must reform their lives as a necessary condition for national unity and successful warfare against England. But Dame Scotia was undoubtedly right when she exhorted her son:

"correct thy self of thy lang abusione, that is to say, thou suld gyf gud exempil in thy conuersatione, conformand to thy professione and to thy doctryn. ... doutles thy abusione ... is the special cause of the scisma and of diuers sectis that trublis al cristianite."[76]

And she was not less wise when she added that persecution by an unreformed church would continue to be useless.[77]

It is interesting that, in Dame Scotia's opinion, the clergy should have known better because they had the advantage of their learning,[78] whilst the church council which convened at Edinburgh in November, 1549, referred to clerical immorality "*cum bonarum literarum artiumque omnium crassa inscitia*" as the two chief causes of heresy. It shows that there was both ignorance and learning among the clergy, and is a reminder that the council issued its disciplinary decrees from pastoral motives.[79] The deliberations of the council have not been preserved, but the decrees sufficiently express their general aim, viz. the reformation of morals and the extirpation of heresy, with special emphasis on the clergy because their ignorance and moral laxity were realized to constitute a chief cause of the spread of heresy as well as evils in themselves.[80]

The decree *De Concubinariis* of the council of Basle is followed by a number of statutes respecting the behaviour of the clergy, exempt as well as non-exempt, and measures to ensure their observance. A prohibition against alienating ecclesiastical property through long-term leases, except with express episcopal permission in case of necessity, aims at providing a source of income for a resident clergy. It thus serves as a link with the next group, in which Tridentine regulations regarding instruction and preaching are followed by a long string of more detailed statutes. Finally, there are a few decrees on ecclesiastical

---

[75] In the author's opinion the answer to the question "quhidder that inglismen be sarrasyns or christin men" is self-evident (p. 164).

[76] pp. 158 and 160.

[77] p. 160.

[78] pp. 157f.

[79] On learning in pre-Reformation Scotland see, e.g., J. Durkan and A. Ross, *Early Scottish Libraries*, Glasgow, 1961, and J. Durkan, "The Cultural Background in Sixteenth-Century Scotland," in *Essays*, pp. 274–331.

[80] Cp. *Statuta*, ii, p. 81 and decree no. 222 (p. 118).

16

courts and a decision to meet again in August, 1550.[81] Of particular interest is a list of sermon subjects to which inquisitors must pay special attention during their visitations. It includes the sacraments, the Mass, traditional ceremonies and the authority of general councils in matters of dogma. John Knox had strongly expressed his views on these subjects in 1547, they formed the substance of the charges against Adam Wallace, a native of Failfurd, in Kyle, who was tried in 1550, and ten years afterwards they formed the principal subjects of Quintin Kennedy's writings.[82]

Nothing is known of a council in 1550, but the prelates assembled in January, 1551/52, about the time when, together with the Nobility, they found it necessary to forbid "bukis concerning the faith, ballatis, sangis, blasphematiounis, rymes alsweill of kirkmen as temporall and utheris, tragedeis alsweill in Latine as in Inglis toung."[83] This parliamentary act shows that the council must not be interpreted too strictly, when it inserts a statement in its own decrees to the effect that the heresies which have latterly sprung up in various parts of the country have now been practically suppressed.[84]

The decrees of the earlier council, notably those concerning the ministry of the word, had not been everywhere observed. They were re-affirmed, and it was duly observed that the people's attendance at Mass and sermons had left everything to be desired. Since, generally speaking, the parochial clergy lacked sufficient learning to give sound catechetical instructions, it was now decreed that a catechism was to be compiled in the vernacular, from which – after due preparation, so as to avoid stammering – the clergy were to read to the people for half an hour before Mass on Sundays and holy days. They were to restrict themselves to reading, and on no account to engage in discussion.[85]

The *Catechism* was published at St. Andrews in 1552,[86] having in all probability been chiefly composed by Richard Marshall, an English Dominican, who

---

[81] *Ibid.*, nos. 171–186 (pp. 86–94), 187 (p. 94), 188–227 (pp. 95–121) and 228–237 (pp. 121–127) respectively. It may be noted here that no Scottish prelate attended any of the sessions of Trent, at least if Robert Wauchope, a Scot who had become archbishop of Armagh, is left out of consideration.

[82] See *Statuta*, ii, no. 225 (pp. 119f.); cp. no. 221 (p. 117).
On Knox's disputation at St. Andrews in 1547 see Laing, *Works*, i, pp. 193ff., and A. Ross, "Some notes on the Religious Orders in Pre-Reformation Scotland," in *Essays*, p. 199; on Wallace's trial see Laing, *Works*, i, pp. 237–41 and 543–50.

[83] *A.P.S.*, ii, pp. 488f.

[84] See *Statuta*, ii, no. 253 (pp. 135f.).

[85] *Ibid.*, nos. 238–242 (pp. 128–130), 245 (pp. 131f.) and 253f. (pp. 135ff.) respectively.

[86] *The Catechisme: That is to say, ane commone and catholik instructioun of the christin people in materis of our catholik faith and religioun, quhilk na gud christin man or woman suld misknaw: set furth be þe maist reuerend father in God Johne Archbischop of sanct Androus Legatnait* [i.e. Legatus natus] *and primat of þe kirk of Scotland, in his prouincial counsale haldin at Edinburgh the xxvi. day of Januarie, the 3eir of our Lord 1551, with the aduise and counsale*

had fled to Scotland in 1536.[87] It shows a number of detailed resemblances with John Gropper's *Enchiridion*, and in addition "the compilers ... have embodied in their exposition of the first article of the Creed at least one extract from the *Longer Catechism* of Luther, and in their explanation of 'the sacrament of penance' two or three from King Henry VIII's *Necessary Doctrine and Erudition for any Christian man.*" Mitchell, who discovered these literary relations,[88] also noted the absence of any mention of the pope and the absence of, for a catholic catechism, due mention of the Mass.

The *Catechism* cannot, in fact, be classed as polemical literature. It is a simple, conciliatory and remarkably irenic exposition of doctrine, written at a time when compromising opinions were being voiced on the continent, and clearly calculated to draw the doubting back to Roman allegiance when the movement for radical reform appeared to be out of the running in Scotland.[89] As Mitchell remarked, "the doctrine which is put throughout in the foreground is that of the authority of the external Church as represented in General Councils lawfully gathered, to determine all questions and controversies in religion, and the necessity of remaining in the communion of this external Church, having unbroken succession of bishops, in order to share in the benefits of the death and mediation of our Lord Jesus Christ."[90] In this respect the *Catechism* anticipated the fuller statement of Kennedy's *Compendius Tractiue*. The absence in the *Catechism* of clear statements on the sacrificial nature of the Mass may at least be partly explained by the postponement of further discussions on the subject after the arrival of envoys from the protestant German princes at the council of Trent, in January, 1552.[91] In the changed situation about the year 1560, Kennedy evidently felt that he could not wait for the next Tridentine session to issue its decrees. In any case, Knox's conviction of the idolatrous character of catholic worship was impervious to conciliatory language.

Early in 1549 Knox had been released from French captivity. He had gone to England and had been appointed by the Privy Council to preach at Berwick,

---

of the bischoppis and uthir prelatis with doctours of Theologie and Canon law of the said realme of Scotland present for the tyme. – Type-facsimile edition (140 copies) by A. F. Mitchell, Edinburgh, 1882; edited for the Bannatyne Club by T. G. Law, Oxford, 1884.

[87] See J. Durkan, "The Cultural Background in Sixteenth-Century Scotland", in *Essays*, pp. 301f. and 326–329.

[88] *The Catechism set forth by Archbishop Hamilton, together with the Two-Penny Faith*, Edinburgh, 1882, pp. xiii f.

[89] Cp. J. Durkan, *l.c.*, pp. 301f.; M. Taylor, "The Conflicting Doctrines of the Scottish Reformation," in *Essays*, pp. 253f., and M. Mahoney, *l.c.*, pp. 65f.

[90] *O.c.*, p. xvi.

[91] See *Concilium Tridentinum. Diariorum, actorum, epistolarum, tractatuum nova collectio*, 13 vols., Freiburg (Görres Society), 1901ff., vol. vii, pp. 465–475.

where he had at once departed from the rubrics of the *Prayer Book* by making his congregation sit at communion. Summoned before the Council of the North for Public Affairs in April, 1550, he had publicly defended his assertion that the Mass is idolatry,[92] and subsequently he had been associated with the insertion of the 'Black Rubric' into the *Prayer Book*.[93] On the accession of Mary Tudor he fled to the continent. He visited Calvin and Bullinger, putting before them the problem which was to engage his mind till, in 1558, he would at last be clear on the answer, viz. the problem of active resistance to princes who maintained idolatry in their territories.[94] He acted as preacher to the English exiles at Frankfort, but the arrival of a less Puritan group under Cox made his position there impossible and he returned to Scotland in the autumn of 1555.

He found the situation considerably different from what it had been on his departure. Arran had been supplanted as regent of Scotland by Mary of Guise, the Earl of Cassillis replaced the ex-regent's half-brother, archbishop John Hamilton, as treasurer. From the new regent's point of view, the political situation required delicate handling. In order to oust Arran, she had needed the support of the protestant nobles. If the accession of Mary Tudor had appeared to make them comparatively harmless, her marriage with Philip of Spain had greatly complicated matters. Mary of Guise had to consider the interests of France. She was all the more in need of support because both her clerical taxation[95] and the appointment of Frenchmen to high offices – including the chancellorship – were very unpopular.

In any case, Knox found that he could freely associate with such persons as John Erskine, Laird of Dun, the Earls of Argyle and Glencairn, Lord James Stewart, afterwards Earl of Moray, and the protestant lairds of Kyle and Cunningham. All these persons clearly felt themselves in a strong position. Wherever he went Knox persuaded his hearers no longer to associate with 'idolaters' and 'idolatrie'. He met John Willock, who was doing similar work during his visits to Scotland in the interests of the Duchess of Friesland. And when, at the end of ten months, the catholic protests became too strong for him to remain in the country, part of his work was continued by William Harlaw.[96] Knox himself returned to Geneva to become one of the preachers to the English

---

[92] See Laing, *Works*, iii, pp. 33–70.

[93] See P. Lorimer, *John Knox and the Church of England*, London, 1875, pp. 98 ff.

[94] See J. H. Burns, "The Political Ideas of the Scottish Reformation," *Aberdeen University Review*, vol. xxxvi (1956), pp. 253–263, and "John Knox and Revolution," *History Today*, vol. viii (1958), pp. 565–573.

[95] See J. H. Pollen, *Papal Negotiations with Mary Queen of Scots, 1561–67*, Edinburgh (Scottish History Society), 1901, pp. 19, 30, 429, 522 ff., 530.

[96] See Laing, *Works*, i, pp. 245–54.

refugees. However, he left his Scottish sympathizers *A most Wholesome Counsell* on how to regulate their gatherings as well as their private devotions,[97] and he was to remain intimately involved in Scottish affairs.

As early as March 10th, 1556/57, four of the protestant lords requested Knox to return to Scotland, declaring that they were prepared to hazard their lives for the Reformation cause.[98] But when he arrived at Dieppe in October, there were letters informing Knox that the moment was not yet opportune for him to enter Scotland. Knox exhorted them that "the Reformatioun of religioun, and of publict enormities, doith appertene to mo then to the Clargie, or cheaf reularis called Kingis." and his *History* suggests that the protestant lords and lairds were induced by his letters to sign the 'Common Band' of December 3rd, 1557.[99] In this document it was solemnly promised that they would "with all diligence continually apply our hole power, substance, and our verray lyves, to manteane, sett forward, and establish the most blessed word of God and his Congregatioun; and shall laubour at our possibilitie to have faythfull Ministeris purely and trewlie to minister Christis Evangell and Sacramentes to his people." They further pledged opposition against "all wicked power that does intend tyranny or truble against the forsaid congregatioun," and enmity to "the congregatioun of Sathan, with all the superstitious abominatioun and idolatrie thereof."[100]

It is from this period that Knox reckoned "our weak begynnyng" when he wrote the first part, now Book Two, of his *History*.[101] Whilst postponing open revolt against the regent's authority, the lords protected the zealous preachers who became active in various parts of the country. "The greatest fervencie appeared in the Mearns and Angus, and Kyle, and Fyfe or Lothian; but cheifely the faithfull in Dundie exceeded all the rest in zeall and boldnes, preferring the true religion to all things temporall. But in Edenburgh their meeting wes but in privat houses."[102] In the mean time Knox had returned to Geneva, from where he forwarded his theoretical justification of a revolution: Mary of Guise, like

---

[97] *Id.*, iv, pp. 129–140.

[98] See Laing, *Works*, i, pp. 267f.

[99] *Ibid.*, pp. 272f.

[100] *Ibid.*, pp. 273f. Note that, as ally of France, Scotland had declared war on England in November. Not only Arran, now Duke of Châtelherault, and Huntly, who had lost the chancellorship to a Frenchman, but also such protestants as Cassillis and Argyle, who generally supported the regent's policy, refused to invade England in the interests of France.

[101] *Ibid.*, pp. 297ff.

[102] Anonymous *Historie of the Estate of Scotland from July M.D.LVIII to April M.D.LX.*, in *Wodrow Misc.* (pp. 53–85), p. 54. Cp. Laing, *Works*, i, pp. 276ff. and 300f. On the iconoclasm in 1558, see D. McRoberts, "Material Destruction Caused by the Scottish Reformation," in *Essays* (pp. 415–62), p. 428.

Mary Tudor, had no right to obedience, and it was the duty of nobility, gentry and commons to resist "the tyrannie of those raging beasts", i.e. "the whole rabble of the Papistical Clergie" and their idolatry.[103]

Mary Tudor died in November, 1558. Her half-sister Elizabeth, who was so deeply interested in a defeat of French influence in Scotland, succeeded to the throne at the very moment when the Scottish Parliament was granting the crown matrimonial to the Dauphin, who had married Mary Stewart in April. It took some manipulation on the part of the regent to have the act passed, because the Duke of Châtelherault, as heir presumptive, would naturally object.[104] But she secured protestant support by allowing the 'Lords of the Congregation' to read a protestation of which it has been said that "in fact, they aver that they will not only worship in their own way, but prevent other people from worshipping in the legal way, and that the responsibility for the riots will lie on the side of those who worship legally."[105]

Towards the end of December archbishop Hamilton summoned the chief preachers – John Willock, John Douglas, William Harlaw, Paul Methuen and John Christison – to appear before him on the second of February. The 'Congregation' "caused informe the Queene Regent that the said preachers would appear with such multitude of men professing their doctrine, as wes never seene befor in such like cases in this countrie."[106] Moreover, on January 1st the *Beggars' Summons* was affixed to the gates of the Edinburgh friaries, in which, in the name of all the poor of Scotland, it was announced that, with the assistance of the 'Congregation', the friars would be expelled from their houses before Whitsunday.[107] The regent told archbishop Hamilton to postpone the hearing of the preachers, but at the same time changed her conciliatory policy. And she could well use the money which the catholic hierarchy offered her.[108]

The church, which thus continued to depend on a government which was rapidly losing control in the country, held its last provincial council in March-April following. The prelates read and discussed a number of "Articles proponit to the Quene Regent of Scotland be sum [catholic] temporall Lordis and

---

[103] Laing, *Works*, iv, pp. 517 and 515. *The First Blast of the Trumpet against the Monstrous Regiment of Women*, the *Appellation to the Nobility of Scotland* and the *Letter Addressed to the Commonalty of Scotland* were printed at Geneva in the early summer of 1558.

[104] See *A.P.S.*, ii, p. 507.

[105] A. Lang, *John Knox and the Reformation*, London, 1905, p. 90; see Laing, *Works*, i, pp. 312ff.

[106] *Historie of the Estate of Scotland, Wodrow Misc.*, p. 55. John Willock had returned to Scotland in October, 1558; John Douglas was chaplain to the Earl of Argyle and is not to be confused with the person of the same name who was provost of St. Mary's College, St. Andrews, and one of 'the six Johns' who drew up the *Confessio Scotica*.

[107] See A. Lang, *o.c.*, pp. 90ff.

[108] See *Historie of the Estate of Scotland, Wodrow Misc.*, pp. 55f.

Barronis, and sent be hir Grace to the haill Prelatis and principallis of the clargie convenit in thair Provincial Counsall in Edinburgh." This memorandum referred to the resolutions on clerical reform in the parliament of 1541 and the provincial councils of 1549 and 1552, of which "nan or litill fruict" was to be seen as yet. It further made particular recommendations concerning such subjects as frequent preaching, examination of candidates for the ministry in doctrine and intellectual acquirements, brief exhortations before the reception of the sacraments, prayers in the vernacular, and measures against those who departed from traditional doctrine and practice concerning the sacraments. This last point is of special interest not only as a reference to subjects treated by Kennedy, but also for its implication that the hierarchy, with the backing no doubt of the government, would still be in a position to control the movement for reform. The lords suggest

> "that na manner of person within this realme pretend to usurp sic hardiment as to dishonor or speik irreverently of the sacrament of the blissit Body and Blude of our Saviour Iesus Christ, bot that the samin be haldin in sic reverence, honour, and worship as efferis Christin men to do, and is commandit be the law of God and Haly Kirk, and that nane dishonour the Divine Service of the Mess nor speik injuriouslie nor irreverentlie tharof.
>
> Item, that na man pretend to use the sacraments and ceremonies of Marriage, Baptism, and blessit Body and Blud forsaid, nor suffer the samin to be ministrat, bot in sic manner as is aforesaid, and be sic persons as that ar admittit deulie, and ordanit to the administration tharof." [109]

The council was more realistic in this respect when it ruled that the clergy were not to retain any persons in their households who held heretical views. [110]

In general, however, the recommendations of the lords were accepted. The legislation against the incelibate clergy again received a prominent place, the two archbishops being singled out for special admonition; episcopal sons were no longer to be presented to ecclesiastical benefices and daughters were no longer to receive dowries from the patrimony of the church; the visitation of dioceses and monastic houses was to be strictly carried out and any abuses corrected. [111] As in the case of the earlier councils a second large section of the statutes deals with preaching and instruction. Dioceses and monasteries were to see to it that they had qualified theologians; frequent preaching was prescribed, and the preachers were to explain to the people the traditional doctrine of the church on such points as the real presence and adoration of Christ in the Eucha-

---

[109] See *Statuta*, ii, no. 258 (pp. 146–151; passage quoted on p. 150).
[110] *Ibid.*, no. 265 (p. 156).
[111] *Ibid.*, nos. 261–264 (pp. 153–156), 269–273 (pp. 158–161).

22

rist, the sacrificial nature of the Mass and the sacramental priesthood in the church; in accordance with the lords' memorandum it was decided to provide the clergy with short printed exhortations, which were to be read out before the celebration of Mass and the administration of certain sacraments; ecclesiastical traditions and practices were to be held in honour by the clergy and to be explained to the people, although mortuary fees and Easter offerings were not to be insisted on in the case of persons who could not afford to pay them.[112]

The Scottish hierarchy was to meet again in February 1559/60, but the events of the intervening months made this impossible. These events can be briefly summarized. Knox arrived in Scotland on May 2nd. A few days afterwards he was at Perth, from where the protestants meant to proceed to Stirling with the preachers who had been summoned to appear there on May 10th. However, they changed their minds and stayed in Perth. On May 11th Knox preached on the 'idolatrie' of the Mass, and the town was purged of such 'idolatrie' as a result.[113] Before the end of the month Glencairn was at Perth with an army of 2500 men, which remained active from then onwards and became larger as the weeks passed. In the beginning of August Knox, on behalf of the 'Congregation', was negotiating for English aid.[114] With reinforcements for the regent's army coming from France, such aid was indispensable. On October 21st the "Nobilitie, Barrones, and Provest of Burrowes", acting as "borne Counsallouris", "sworne protectouris and defendaris" of the country, and therefore "In name and authoritie of our Soverane Lord and Lady", suspended Mary of Guise from the regency and constituted themselves Great Council of the realm.[115] The treaty of Berwick between England and the rebelling Scots in the following February did not mention the religious issue; among the signatories were two abbots and three commendators.[116] Similarly, the peace treaty of Edinburgh in July, a month after Mary of Guise's death, whilst stipulating the withdrawal of the French as well as the English forces from Scotland, left the religious question to be solved by a parliament in August.[117]

As the August parliament approached, notice was given not only to "all sick as by law and ancient custome had", but also to those who "mycht clame to

---

[112] *Ibid.*, nos. 274–279 (pp. 161–166), 281 (pp. 167f.), 285 (pp. 171f.), 290 (p. 173) and 293f. (pp. 174f.). – One of these brief exhortations, viz. the one to be read out before communion, has survived; see W. J. Anderson, "Some Documents of the Scottish Reformation," in *Essays*, pp. 359ff.

[113] Cp. Laing, *Works*, i, pp. 321ff., vi, p. 23, and *Historie of the Estate of Scotland*, *Wodrow Misc.*, p. 57.

[114] See Laing, *Works*, vi, pp. 56ff. Note that Henry II had died in July and that Mary Stewart laid claim to Elizabeth's throne.

[115] *Id.*, i, pp. 444–449.

[116] *Id.*, ii, pp. 46–53.

[117] *Ibid.*, pp. 73–83.

have vote thairin." The result was that there was a large number of lairds who would not normally be seen in parliament, whilst "sum, alsweill of thame that be callit Sprituall as Temporall Lordis, contemptuouslie did absent thame selffis." [118] At the parliament itself "thay that are callit the Clergye" were accused of "living in huredome, adultery, defloring virgeinis, corrupting matronis, and doing all abominatioun, without feir of punischement;" of being "all thevis and murtheraris, yea, rebellis and tratouris to the lauchfull authoritie of Empriouris, Kyngis, and Prenceis; and thairfor unworthy to be sufferit in any Reformeit Commonwealth." [119]

Indeed, the zeal of the Reformers contrasts sharply with the absence of any organized activity on the part of the catholic hierarchy. The fact that of the twenty abbots and priors present no less than fourteen were lay commendators symbolizes its paralysis. [120] It goes far to explain the attraction of a church with the true preaching of the Word, the right administration of the sacraments and strict ecclesiastical discipline as its avowed marks. But what Kennedy considered the principal cause of the religious revolt also prevented radical reform from being carried through in 1560. The 'Reformation Parliament' could pass the *Confession of Faith*, forbid the celebration of and attendance at Mass and abolish papal jurisdiction in Scotland, [121] it was not permitted to discuss the *First Book of Discipline*, which the Great Council had commissioned the Reformers to draw up in April. The fact that the material interests of so many influential nobles were involved prevented the reformed church from supplanting the pre-Reformation establishment. What Kennedy deplored as the cause of the disaster actually enabled him to remain in the country and to continue the defence of catholicism.

[118] *Ibid.*, p. 88; the *sederunt* is in *A.P.S.*, ii, p. 525.
[119] *Ibid.*, pp. 90f.
[120] See J. Hill Burton and D. Masson, *The Register of the Privy Council of Scotland*, Edinburgh, 1877 ff., 2nd series, vol. i, p. cvii.
[121] See *A.P.S.*, ii, pp. 525–535 and Laing, *Works*, ii, pp. 93–125.

III. KENNEDY'S LIFE

Quintin Kennedy was the fourth son of Gilbert Kennedy of Dunure, second Earl of Cassillis and Chief of the Kennedy clan, and of Elisabeth Campbell, daughter to the second Earl of Argyle.[1] The family to which he belonged had gained increasing prominence ever since, in 1405, James Kennedy had married the princess Mary Stewart, second daughter of king Robert III. The match had brought the Dunure Kennedys the hereditary bailiary of Carrick, earldom of the Bruces. Of James and Mary's sons, Gilbert had become the first Lord Kennedy in 1457, whilst James had been bishop of St. Andrews, founder of St. Salvator's College and distinguished statesman in fifteenth-century Scotland.[2] One of Sir Gilbert's sons had been the Walter Kennedy of Glentig, parson of Douglas, who had duly claimed royal blood in *The Flyting of Kennedy and Dunbar*. David Kennedy, Sir Gilbert's grandson and abbot Quintin's grandfather, had been created first Earl of Cassillis in 1509. He had died at Flodden[3] and had been succeeded by Quintin's father, who, in consequence of a quarrel with Sir Hugh Campbell of Loudoun, sheriff of Ayr, was ambushed and murdered near Prestwick in 1527.[4] Of the two subsequent Earls, who were to be deeply interested in the affairs of Crossraguel abbey, Quintin's eldest brother Gilbert has already been mentioned as High Treasurer in the 'fifties, whilst Quintin's nephew, also called Gilbert, was in due time to be styled 'King of Carrick'.

Quintin Kennedy was born about the year 1520.[5] Of his early life nothing is

---

[1] Information on Kennedy genealogy may be gathered from the *Ailsa Papers*, and the anonymous *Historie of the Kennedyis* (edited by Robert Pitcairn as *Historical and Genealogical Account of the Principal Families of the Name of Kennedy*, Edinburgh, 1830). The information of these and other sources may be found in *The Scots Peerage*, vol. ii, pp. 443–502, J. Kevan McDowall's *A Genealogical History in Cartographic Form Pertaining to Galloway and its Ancient Division of Carrick*, Glasgow, 1938 (chart, 9' × 2'8"), and his *Carrick Gallovidian*, Ayr, 1947, esp. pp. 62f.

[2] See *Ailsa Papers*, section i, nos. 29, 45, 52 and 73. McDowall (*Carrick Gallovidian*, p. 38) holds that the Kennedys descended directly from Henry Kennedy (Cinneadais or Cinnidh), younger brother of kings Malcolm IV and William the Lion, and, in the female line, from the Lords of ancient Galloway. On bishop James Kennedy, see A. I. Dunlop, *The Life and Times of James Kennedy, Bishop of St. Andrews*, Edinburgh and London, 1950.

[3] See *Ailsa Papers*, i, nos. 222 and 233.

[4] See R. Pitcairn, *Criminal Trials in Scotland*, Edinburgh, 1833, pp. 136f. and 242.

[5] The *Ailsa Papers* (nos. 403 and 419) and the *Historie of the Kennedyis* (ed. Pitcairn, p. 7) prove that there were seven sons, born in the order Gilbert, Thomas, David, Quintin, Archibald, Hugh and James. The latter source further mentions two daughters *(ibid.)*, whilst McDowall has found references to yet two others (*Carrick Gallovidian*, pp. 62f. and *Genealogical History*). Gilbert was born in 1515 (*The Scots Peerage*, ii, p. 468) and the father died in 1527.

known, although he may well have benefited by Buchanan's prolonged presence in the Cassillis household in the 'thirties.[6] In 1540 he matriculated at St. Salvator's College,[7] where John Major was provost, and afterwards continued his education for the church at Paris university – to all appearances at the College of the Sorbonne. Twenty years later both John Davidson and George Hay remembered the friendly terms on which they had lived with Kennedy during their Paris years.[8]

By the summer of 1547 Kennedy was back in Scotland,[9] but the date of his return is unknown. His uncle William Kennedy, abbot of Crossraguel, died at this time,[10] and was not improbably to have been succeeded by Quintin's elder clerical brother Thomas. But Thomas, "according to some accounts,"[11] died in the battle of Pinkie (September 10th). This would explain why Quintin succeeded his brother as vicar of Penpont.[12] At the same time he became the family candidate for Crossraguel. Archbishop Hamilton, acting as abbot of the older Cluniac foundation of Paisley, confirmed his nomination on January 1st following. Kennedy resigned the vicarage of Penpont and the clerkship of Colmonell parish to the Crown and the dean and chapter of Glasgow as the respective patrons, and was put in possession of the abbey on February 1st.[13]

---

[6] See J. M. Aitken, *The Trial of George Buchanan before the Lisbon Inquisition*, Edinburgh and London, 1939, p. xvi.

[7] See J. Maitland Anderson, *Early Records of the University of St. Andrews*, Edinburgh, Scottish History Society, 3rd series, vol. viii (1926), p. 245.

[8] "Quintinus Kennedy nobilis Glasquensis [sic] diocesis" occurs in the manuscript *Acta Rectoria* of Paris university for the period December 13th–Easter 1542/43, during the rectorship of William Cranston (information received from Dr. J. Durkan). For Hay's studies at Paris, see "A Memoir of Fr Edmund Hay S.I.", in *Archivum Historicum Societatis Iesu*, vol. viii (1939), pp. 84f. In his answer to the *Compendius Tractiue* Davidson speaks of "the aulde Parisiane kyndnes that was betuix us" (*Wodrow Misc.*, p. 257). Hay refers to "an withered and intermitted amitie, yea althogh it were neuer so strait and deare" (Hay, *Confutation*, p. 4r. Similar references on pp. 2r and 3r). He speaks of Kennedy as "this sophister, new start vp out of Sorbone," and "our new Sorbonist", who talks "all Magistraliter et Sorbonice" (pp. 5r, 52r and 41r respectively). Perhaps this is to be interpreted as abusive language solely, rather than a specific reference to Kennedy's college.

[9] See *Ailsa Papers*, i, no. 501.

[10] See R. K. Hannay, *Acts of the Lords of Council in Public Affairs 1501–1554:* Selections from the *Acta Dominorum Concilii*, Edinburgh, 1932, in which abbot William is referred to as living on May 23rd, as dead on June 16th (pp. 566 and 575). Cp. *Crossraguel Charters*, i, p. 108, footnote 3.

[11] *The Scots Peerage*, vol. ii, p. 465 (p. 466 omits the restriction). Thomas was alive on July 6th (*Ailsa Papers*, i, no. 497); his death is mentioned in the *Register of the Privy Seal of Scotland* (ed. M. Livingstone, and others, 1918 ff.), vol. iii, no. 2478).

[12] See p. 8 above. The vicarage was in the gift of the Crown, so that he would not automatically have succeeded in normal circumstances.

[13] See the *Protocol Book of Henry Prestoun*, MSS., H.M. General Register House, Edinburgh, fos. 202–204 (abstracts by Sir James Fergusson in *Ayrshire Archaeological and Natural History Society Collections*, 2nd series, vol. iii (1950–54), pp. 46–64) and *Register of the Privy*

The Cluniac abbey of Crossraguel[14] had been founded by Duncan, Earl of Carrick, in 1244. King Robert the Bruce, whose father had acquired the earldom through his marriage with Duncan's granddaughter and heir, had been one of the abbey's main benefactors. By a Crown Charter of 1324 he had erected its possessions into a free barony. Robert III had amplified this in 1404 by a grant to the abbot and convent and their successors "in liberam regalitatem seu regaliam ... in feodo et hereditate ac in puram et perpetuam elemosinam ... cum furca fossa sok sak tholl theme infangtheif outfangtheif et cum quatuor punctis spectantibus ad coronam."[15]

In 1548 the abbey itself numbered, apart from the abbot and sub-prior, nine monks, which appears to have been its normal number.[16] But the abbey's income was far from inconsiderable and included the teinds and offerings of the parishes of Kirkoswald, Straiton, Dailly, Girvan and Ballantrae, as well as the revenues of territorial estates extending over practically the whole of Carrick and of such special sources as coalpits, mills and woods. The editor of the *Crossraguel Charters* concludes that the abbots were the greatest personages in all Ayrshire, greater therefore than such temporal lords as the Earls of Cassillis, Glencairn and Eglinton.[17]

It was to be expected that, in accordance with the custom of the age, the Kennedys of Dunure would try to continue and strengthen their connections with the abbey in their immediate neighbourhood. And in the 'forties it was equally to be expected that the government would anxiously guard the power of a man with Cassillis' English sympathies. In May, 1544, he had been implicated in a plot against the regent.[18] The following winter had found him in England, where he received a letter from abbot William of Crossraguel mentioning that

---

Seal of Scotland, vol. iv, no. 106. – I have not found evidence for the assertion that Kennedy also held the vicarage of Girvan (cp. *Charters of Crossraguel*, vol. i, p. xli). He never was prior of Whithorn (cp. Mackenzie, *Lives*, vol. iii, p. 57), and there is no reason for assuming that he did not belong to the secular priesthood (cp. Kirkwood Hewat, *Makers of the Scottish Church at the Reformation*, Edinburgh, 1920, p. 136, where he is stated to have been a Franciscan).

[14] The name is of Gaelic origin and appears in many different forms in the late Middle Ages. For its etymology, see *Crossraguel Charters*, i, pp. lxvi ff. and J. Kevan McDowall, *Carrick Gallovidian*, pp. 196f. *Monasterium Crucis Regalis* is a late interpretation.

[15] *Crossraguel Charters*, i, p. 38; the other documents are on pp. 3f and 15f.

[16] See *ibid.*, pp. 40, 107, 118, 120f. and 122.

[17] See *ibid.*, pp. lvi ff., with references to the various charters and a map of the abbey regality. For a brief survey of Ayrshire feudal relations, see W. J. Dillon, "The Origins of Feudal Ayrshire," *Ayrshire Aarchaeological and Natural History Society Collections*, 2nd series, vol. iii (1950–54), pp. 65–85. On the fifteenth-century Crossraguel mint, see G. MacDonald, "The Mint of Crosraguel Abbey," *Proceedings of the Society of Antiquaries of Scotland*, vol. liv (1920), pp. 20–44.

[18] See *Ailsa Papers*, section i, no. 524.

he was "evill luifit be my lord Governour and diwers noblis of the realme for zour deperting aganis in Ingland."[19] He had returned with English presents as well as his Scottish hostages and soon afterwards, in May, had proposed a plan to the English government for murdering cardinal Beaton, chancellor of Scotland and main obstacle to Henry VIII's Scottish policy.[20] On November 22nd, 1546, abbot William and Cassillis had, in the presence of Arran and the Lords of Council, signed a document whereby the abbot was not to lease abbey property to his nephew.[21]

It has been suggested that after he had apparently refused to take part in the military operations which led to the battle of Pinkie, Cassillis transferred his allegiance to Arran as "a result of the heavy casualties suffered by his kinsmen and neighbours in the battle, which included not less than seven Kennedy lairds killed."[22] It appears, however, that the change had taken place at an earlier date. For on July 10th, 1546, Arran promised his daughter Jean Hamilton – together with a huge dowry – in marriage to the young Master of Cassillis.[23] This agreement, six weeks after Beaton's murder, must obviously be seen as a political move on the part of the regent, who needed all the support he could get, particularly in the south.[24] But there is no reason to suppose that, after the generous offer, he could not be sure of Cassillis. And the abbey property of Crossraguel may well have constituted an extra incentive.

After abbot William's death the sub-prior and monks, "*non sine magno desiderio*", had requested Cassillis to protect the abbey and its property during the vacancy. Apparently, they too trusted him, even though the request may have been suggested by the Earl himself. In any case, it gave him an actual hold on the abbey property, which he did not release until the installation of his brother on February 1st.[25] By that time neither the regent nor his brother, the abbot of Paisley and nominee for the primatial see of St. Andrews, could have objected to the new abbot, for in January Cassillis had assisted Arran in expelling the English invaders.[26] In April Kennedy was admitted to the temporal-

[19] *Crossraguel Charters*, i, pp. 60 f.

[20] See *The Scots Peerage*, vol. ii, p. 469. Cp. *A.P.S.*, ii, p. 460 (October, 1545): "... now in tyme of weir na scottisman sall sitt vnder assurance of þe Inglismen ... vnder þe pane of tynsale of lif, landis and guidis."

[21] See *Crossraguel Charters*, i, pp. 101 f.

[22] J. Fergusson, *The White Hind and Other Discoveries*, London, 1963, p. 36 (cp. pp. 14 and 19). Similar interpretation in *The Scots Peerage*, ii, p. 470.

[23] See *Ailsa Papers*, section i, no. 475.

[24] Abbot William's election as a member of the Privy Council gains in significance when seen in the same light. He would be an extra check on Cassillis. (See J. H. Burton & D. Masson, *The Register of the Privy Council of Scotland*, 1st series, i, p. 33).

[25] See *Crossraguel Charters*, i, pp. 102 ff.

[26] *The Scots Peerage*, ii, p. 470.

ities of his abbey by a precept under the privy Seal.[27] Less than a month later the abbey was in "urgent mister and necessity". If this was because Arran had made financial stipulations, as was so often done at the time, Cassillis was the man who benefited by it, because the abbot had to feu part of the abbey property to his brother as a means of obtaining cash.[28]

Kennedy is said to have been three times present at the Privy Council in 1548, but the sources quoted in justification of this statement show that he has been confused with abbot William, who was three times present in 1547.[29] In fact, there is no indication that Kennedy ever aspired after a political career. The only parliament he is known to have attended was that held at Edinburgh on April 12th, 1554. And on that occasion he may well have been induced to attend by his brother, who did have political aspirations. In December, 1548, Cassillis had been appointed Lieutenant of the South, an office which he had held till after the peace of Boulogne (March, 1549/50).[30] From that time onwards he had transferred his support from the Hamiltons to Mary of Guise. The parliament of April, 1554, assembled to appoint the queen-dowager regent in the place of Arran, whilst Cassillis was to succeed archbishop Hamilton as treasurer.[31] In the absence of sufficient information it is risky to interpret Kennedy's motives. But any interpretation will have to take into account that Crossraguel had always had to defend its independence against the claims of Paisley abbey to control the affairs of the younger Cluniac foundation,[32] that John Hamilton, archbishop of St. Andrews and abbot of Paisley, organized the reform councils in Scotland but remained one of the "oppin sclanderaris of the Congregatioun",[33] and that at least in 1559 Kennedy was very "hamelie" with James Beaton, occupant of the rival archiepiscopal see of Glasgow and a person who could not thus be classed.[34]

"*Quintinus abbas monasterii Crucis Regalis*" is mentioned as having been present at the provincial council which met in Edinburgh on November 27th,

---

[27] M. Livingstone, and others, *Registrum Secreti Sigilli Regum Scotorum*, vol. iii, no. 2736.

[28] See *Crossraguel Charters*, i, pp. 105 ff.

[29] *Ibid.*, p. xli, and *The Scots Peerage*, ii, pp. 466f. Both refer to *The Register of the Privy Council*, i, pp. 60–67 (*Crossraguel Charters* actually refers to vol. ii, which must be a printer's error). These pages cover 1546–47, and in one of the three cases the abbot actually signed 'W. Abbot off Corsragwell' (p. 60). Moreover, there is no Privy Council Register for the period August 22nd, 1547 to March 25th, 1550.

[30] See *The Register of the Privy Council of Scotland*, first series, vol. i, pp. 98 f.

[31] See *A.P.S.*, ii, p. 603. The marriage between Arran's daughter and the Master of Cassillis never took place, not improbably as a result of Cassillis' desertion of the Hamiltons.

[32] See *Crossraguel Charters*, pp. xxiiiff., xxixf., xxxv and charters referred to.

[33] *Compendius Tractiue, Wodrow Misc.*, p. 151.

[34] Cp. Kennedy's letter to Beaton, *Wodrow Misc.*, p. 267.

1549,[35] but nothing is known about any role he may have played there. With regard to the subsequent councils it can only be said with certainty that he did not attend that of 1559.[36] A letter of assedation of the teinds and offerings of Straiton parish to the Earl of Cassillis, dated March 10th, 1552/53, is the only further piece of information about his activities until he emerges from obscurity in 1558.[37]

It has been suggested that "he was too busily engaged with his theological studies to pay much attention to affairs of State," and that "for the ten years which preceded the Reformation, he was almost constantly engaged in refuting Protestant principles." Another author is of the opinion that Kennedy "seems to have spent the greater part of his life in the same neglect of professional duty which characterized his brethren," and that "he was roused from his inactivity by the zeal and success of the Protestant preachers, who, in the years 1556 and 1557, attacked the Popish faith, and inveighed against the idleness and corruption of the Clergy."[38]

The question of Kennedy's literary activity at this period will be discussed in the next section. Meanwhile, it may be observed that his *Compendius Tractiue* printed in 1558, refers the readers to Bunderius' *Detectio Nugarum Lutheri*, a work which had appeared in 1551.[39] In the dedication to his nephew, the Master of Cassillis, Kennedy says that his *Tractiue* was the outcome of private discussions with this young man, who had asked his uncle to amplify his answers and arguments and to publish them as a tractate. And in his preface to the reader he writes that he has been specially moved to publish his book for the "releif of my awin conscience towart sic as I have charge of, conforme to my vocatioun."[40] This may mean that it had not been his habit to trouble himself about his pastoral office, although it is no necessary inference. In the autumn of 1562 he instructed his people on the sacrifice of the Mass,[41] but it is not known whether or not he preached in the 'fifties, or saw to it that it was done by others. Again, he possessed a guide for canonical visitation[42] which a worldly prelate

---

[35] *Statuta*, ii, no. 168 (p. 83).

[36] See pp. 33f. below. There are no lists of those attending the councils after 1549.

[37] See *Crossraguel Charters*, i, pp. 117f.

[38] *Crossraguel Charters*, i, p. xlii, Michael Barrett, O.S.B., *The Scottish Monasteries of Old*, Edinburgh & London, 1913, p. 117, and Thomas M'Crie, *Life of John Knox*, 5th edition, 1831, vol. ii, p. 60 respectively.

[39] Ioannes Bunderius (Jan van den Bundere), *Detectio Nugarum Lutheri, cum declaratione veritatis catholicae & confutatione dogmatum Lutheranorum*, Louvain, 1551. Cp. *Compendius Tractiue*, *Wodrow Misc.*, p. 159.

[40] *Wodrow Misc.*, pp. 97f.

[41] See below, appendix II.

[42] J. F. de Pavinis, *Baculus Pastoralis ad dirigendos in viam pacis pedes visitantium et visitatorum, cum sit lucerna quaedam pedibus eorum. Quem omnis in Domini sortem electus diligenter*

would not bother to acquire, but there are no means of knowing when he acquired it; and even if he had had it at an early date, the question would still remain in how far he carried out its rules and the decrees of the Scottish councils. The council of 1549 had ruled that Crossraguel was to have one theologian [43] and Kennedy may have shouldered the task himself, but that raises the question as to how he interpreted that task before 1558. John Knox made a relevant remark at the Maybole disputation, but it is rather difficult to make out what he meant to say of Kennedy personally:

"As for my self I nothing dout but the great perturbation, controuersie, and debate, laitlie stirred vp in all christen realmes, for cause of religion, is the cause that my Lorde abbote hath bene of lait dayes troubled with vnaccustomed laubores. For if the supersticion, idolatrie, pride, vaine glorie, ambition, vniust possessions, superfluous rentes and filthy liuing vsed and manteyned heretofore by suche as clame the name and authoritie of the Church had not bene openly rebuked and a parte thereof in dispyte of Sathan supresed, it may be thoght that my Lorde in this his impotent age could haue contented him self with the self same ease and quietnes that in his yonger age and better habilitie he enioyed. But now the trompet soundeth dampnation to all negligent pastors, and thereof is my Lorde afrayed, and therefore to discharge his conscience he will take the paine to instruct his flock, and to warne them to be ware of fals teachers." [44]

It is not without significance that the personal accusation is limited to "ease and quietnes" in the matter of preaching. This was bad enough in Knox's eyes, and it argues against pastoral zeal on the part of the abbot. It must be remembered, however, that the council of 1549 had prescribed a minimum of four sermons a year to be given personally by the benefice holders. [45]

In any case, by 1558 Kennedy felt that something had to be done to stop the growing revolt against the church and he decided to do it himself. His *Com-*

---

in dextera gerere debet, ad arcendam luporum, carnis videlicet, mundi, et dyaboli truculentam rabiem, in gregis consolationem, vt mereatur illum audire canentem canticum prophetae: virga tua et baculus tuus ipsa me consolata sunt. Last page: *Explicit tractatus Visitationum domini Iohannis francisci de pauinis, cui Baculo pastorali (si auctori creditur) nomen est, adamussim per Iohannem Chappuis in iure caesareo licentiatum reuisus. ... In sole aureo vici sorbonici Anno domini Millesimo quingentesimo tertio die vero xxviij Novembris.* A nineteenth-century owner of the copy now in Durham University Library wrote on a front flyleaf that "the book was formerly the property of Quentin Kennedy, Abbot of Crossraguel," presumably because his initials had been on the original covers. See J. Durkan & A. Ross, *Early Scottish Libraries*, Glasgow, 1961, p. 120.

[43] See *Statuta*, ii, nos. 197f. (pp. 101ff.).

[44] *Maybole Ressoning*, Laing, *Works*, vi, pp. 188f.

[45] See *Statuta*, ii, no. 195 (pp. 99f.).

pendius Tractiue, in which he fully admitted the principal abuses prevailing in the Scottish church but at the same time defended ecclesiastical authority in matters of faith and worship, was dedicated to 'Gilbert maister of Cassillis', who became Gilbert fourth Earl of Cassillis on the death of his father, November 18th, 1558,[46] (although he sat in parliament as Master of Cassillis on November 29th, 1558.[47]). Consequently, Kennedy will have taken his tract to the press before the news of the Earl's death reached Scotland.

The tract may well have influenced the conservative line taken by the young Earl of Cassillis, who was one of the two temporal lords to vote against the Confession of Faith in August 1560.[48] Bishop Tunstal of Durham apparently praised it,[49] and Ninian Winzet spoke highly of it as "a werk commendit be sindry cunning men as weil of Ingland as of Scotland." It is strange, however, that he should only have heard of it himself,[50] whereas John Davidson admitted that

"thare hes bene many movit to continew still in thare auld superstitione and idolatrie, throw the reasonis contenit in the same, quha had imbracit the sincere and trew Religione of Christe or thir dayis, and it had bene supprest in its infancie."[51]

Not long after the publication of his *Compendius Tractiue* and before John Davidson joined the Reformers, Kennedy heard that the publication of a reply was being contemplated.[52] Possibly fearing that his opponents might cavil at at immaterial details, or perhaps merely in order to defy them, he composed a

---

[46] See W. Law Mathieson, *Politics and Religion*, vol. i, p. 48. Cp. W. Croft Dickinson's edition of Knox's *History*, 1949, vol. i, p. 13, footnote 4, where November 14th is given as the date of the Earl's death. The exact date seems uncertain.

[47] See *A.P.S.*, ii, p. 503. Cp. *The Scots Peerage*, ii, p. 472.

[48] See Randolph's letter to Cecil of August 19th in J. Bain, *Calendar of State Papers relating to Scotland and Mary Queen of Scots, 1547–1603*, Edinburgh, H.M. General Register House, 1898ff., vol. i, p. 467, and J. Stevenson, *Calendar of State Papers, Foreign Series, 1560-1561*, p. 241 (cp. pp. 166, 258 and 312). His motives appear to have been mixed. He refused to subscribe the *First Book of Discipline* and objected to the granting of manses and glebes to the reformed ministers on the alleged ground that manses were of great quantity in his district (W. Croft Dickinson, *o.c.*, vol. i, pp. cii f., 344, footnote 5, vol. ii, p. 305). In September, 1566, he married the daughter of the Earl of Glamis and became a protestant by her persuasion, although he fought in Mary Stewart's army at Langside.

[49] See Randolph's letter to Cecil, dated February 28th, 1561/62, in Bain, *o.c.*, vol. i, p. 609.

[50] See *Certain Tractates, together with the Book of Four Score Three Questions and a Translation of Vincentius Lirinensis*, by Ninian Winzet, edited for the S.T.S., 2 vols., Edinburgh, 1888 & 1890, vol. ii, pp. 9–11.

[51] Davidson's *Answer, Wodrow Misc.*, p. 186.

[52] See *ibid.*, p. 256. For Davidson's early and sudden conversion, see J. Durkan, "The Cultural Background in Sixteenth-Century Scotland," in *Essays*, p. 330. On Davidson as Principal of the College of Glasgow, see J. Cooper, "The Principals of the University of Glasgow before the Reformation", *The Scottish Historical Review*, vol. xi (1914), pp. 252ff.

summary of his fundamental thesis and main arguments. He sent a copy to his old friend Davidson, Principal of the College of Glasgow, with the request to pass it on to archbishop James Beaton.[53] The real addressees, however, were his "Deirly belovit Freindis and Nychbours" whom, in an accompanying letter, he challenged to refute 'ony part of this breve rehears of our Buik be Scripture, Reasone, and Authority, conforme to the doctrine of Ancient Fathers."[54] The statement that Davidson's *Answer*, which was not written until the winter of 1562/63, was composed at the Earl of Glencairn's urgent request, repeatedly made over a period of several years,[55] suggests that Kennedy had been principally thinking of Glencairn and the 'Gentilmen of Kyle and Cunynghame'.

John Willock, ex-friar of Ayr, returned to Scotland in the autumn of 1558 and, protected by Glencairn, preached openly at Ayr that winter. When his trial was postponed and he continued his sermons,[56] archbishop Beaton of Glasgow requested the prior of the Dominicans at Ayr to preach against Willock. But although the prior "did his pairt as become him to haif done in all sortis, and that rychte manfully ... he wes alluterlie dissobeyit, and culd haif na entres in the Peroche-kyrke." Apparently Beaton then appealed to the more influential abbot of Crossraguel, who "passit on Pasch evin till Ayr, and thair remainit aught dayis,"[57]

On Easter Sunday, March 26th, Kennedy sent Willock an official challenge to a semi-public disputation on the Mass, with an audience of twelve persons on each side. Willock accepted the challenge and proposed to hold the disputation in St. John's church, Ayr, on the following Sunday, and Kennedy readily agreed. But the disputation never came off.

It appears that, contrary to the condition stipulated by Kennedy and accepted by Willock, the latter made his appearance on the scene of the debate accompanied by the Earl of Glencairn and "above four or five hundred to fortifie him." On his part, Kennedy might have called to his assistance the Earls of Cassillis and Eglinton with "all thair freindis and servandis," who were ready

---

[53] See Davidson's *Answer*, *Wodrow Misc.*, pp. 187 and 256.

[54] *Ibid.*, pp. 255f.

[55] *Ibid.*, p. 186.

[56] See pp. 20f., above.

[57] Kennedy's first challenge is dated March 26th, one of Willock's letters "this Wednesday the penult day of Marche" and the final notarial instrument – drawn up on the day referred to as "Sounday nixt to cum" and "Sounday last wes" – April 2nd (*Wodrow Misc.*, pp. 268, 271, 269, 266 and 276 respectively). Willock evidently made a mistake when he dated his letter on the Wednesday (cp. A. Giry, *Manuel de Diplomatique*, Paris, 1894, p. 203). – The day of Kennedy's arrival at Ayr is a different question. In Wycliffe's Bible translation and its Scots version by Murdoch Nisbet 'pasch evin' corresponds to Vulgate *Parasceue* (see T. M. A. Macnab, "The New Testament in Scots," *Records of the Scottish Church History Society*, vol. xi (1951–53), pp. 89f.).

33

to enter the town if required. But he preferred to decline the debate under these circumstances, "for gif I had done utherwyse, it had not failzied cummyr." Instead, after Willock had gone to the parish church and had proceeded to preach to his following, Kennedy sent one John Blair of Middle Auchindrane, accompanied by a notary public and witnesses, to repeat his challenge in public and to protest solemnly that it was due to Willock that the debate did not take place and that, therefore, he had failed to accept the abbot's challenge.[58] No doubt he was aware that the Reformers had repeatedly demanded a fair trial of the truth and that repressive measures had given them an easy opportunity of exploiting this demand.[59] In his *Compendius Tractiue* he had already tried to explain a number of the traditional beliefs. When he missed the chance of an open debate on the vital point of the 'idolatrie' of the Mass, he evidently felt that what he needed was official proof that he had not shirked the enterprise.

Meanwhile, the last provincial council of the church had opened on March 1st. There seems to have been an adjournment from the third week of March till April 6th,[60] not likely in connection with the Holy Week ceremonies. On the day after the reopening Kennedy was still in Ayrshire, where he received two letters from archbishop Beaton, the one apparently summoning him to a synod to be held in Glasgow that same month, the other asking particulars about his dealings with Willock. Kennedy at once sat down to write the report and promised that he would be present at the synod.[61] Unfortunately he reserved for that meeting information which would probably have thrown much extra light on his plans for saving his church:

> "Eftir my opinioun, this cuntre may be easilie helpit, quhilk to wryte to zour Lordschip war owr prolixe; thairfoir I referr it to out meitting, as said is. Nottheles, thair is sum thingis quhilks wald be presently done, (and that in ane verray secreit maner,) as zour Lordschip sall persaif on the uther syde of the leafe."[62]

What these last, more urgent 'thingis' were, the reader is likewise left to guess, because the original letter has not survived. He may have suggested a

---

[58] See *Wodrow Misc.*, pp. 266 and 276f.

[59] See, e.g., Laing, *Works*, iv, pp. 480 *(Appellation to the Nobility and Estates)* and 525 *(Letter to the Commonalty)*.

[60] See Thomas Winning, "Church Councils in Sixteenth-Century Scotland," in *Essays*, pp. 346f.

[61] See *Wodrow Misc.*, p. 265. Beaton was at the Edinburgh council, as Kennedy asked him to "commend my hertlie service to my Lord of Sanct Androis, and lat his Lordschip knaw sic novellis as ar amang us and the brethir in this cuntre" *(ibid.*, p. 267). On the Glasgow synod, see Thomas Winning, *l.c.*, pp. 354f.

[62] *Wodrow Misc.*, p. 266. Kennedy informs Beaton that he has also sent a report to Mary of Guise, perhaps in connection with Scottish legislation against religious disputations (see p. 13 above).

request to the government that the anti-heretical laws be executed, although it remains a mere guess. A year and a half afterwards, when the tables had been turned, this method was applied against him.

Kennedy did not attend the 'Reformation Parliament' of August, 1560; his reasons for absenting himself are not known. His *Litil Breif Tracteit*, as will be argued on a subsequent page, may have been written at this period. And it is not impossible that he had been commissioned by the Glasgow synod to write a clear statement and defence of the traditional doctrine of the presence of Christ in the Eucharist.

What is certain is that he did not acquiesce in the legislation against the Mass. On December 27th, 1560, the first General Assembly of the reformed Kirk decided to

"aske at the estates of parliament and lords of secreit counsell ... that sharp punishment may be made upon the persons underwritten ... whilk sayes and causes messe to be said and are present thereat within the places following: ... In Kyle, Carrick, and Cunninghame: The Erles of Eglintoun and Cassills ... The Abbot of Crosraguell. The parochiners of Mayboill, Girvan, Oswald, and Dalay, within the kirk whereof messe is openly said and mantained."[63]

As far as is known the request passed unheeded, but it shows that Kennedy, backed by his nephew, ignored the new laws. No doubt, the young Earl's influence was not the only reason why he could do so with impunity. During the interval between the death of Francis II (December 5th, 1560) and the anticipated return of Mary Stewart the lords were unwilling to enforce an act which the queen had declined to ratify. Nevertheless, the second Assembly, which convened in May, 1561, had more success when there had been signs of catholic attempts to resume control. The ministers presented "ane humble Supplicatioun" to the Secret Council to the effect that, among other things, "Idolatrie, and all monumentis thairof, suld be suppressit throwout the haill realme; that the sayaris, heiraris, mayntenaris, and usaris of the Messe, suld be punischit according to the Act of Parliament." This time an army was despatched to the west of Scotland. It burned the abbey of Paisley and 'cast down' Failford, Kilwinning and a part of Crossraguel.[64] It is not recorded why the work was left uncompleted in the case of Kennedy's abbey; perhaps the Earl of Cassillis intervened.

On August 25th, 1561, six days after her arrival in Scotland, the queen issued a proclamation in which she directed that, as long as the religious question had

---

[63] *Acts and Proceedings of the General Assemblies of the Kirk of Scotland from the Year M.D.LX*, 3 vols., Edinburgh, Bannatyne Club, 1839, vol. i, p. 6.

[64] Laing, *Works*, ii, pp. 156–168. On 'casting down', see D. McRoberts, "Material Destruction Caused by the Scottish Reformation," in *Essays*, p. 420.

not been definitely settled by the Crown and parliament, no one was either privately or publicly to attempt anything against the situation as she had found it on her arrival.[65] In Knox's opinion this meant the re-introduction of the Mass in Scotland;[66] it certainly meant legal recognition of the existing situation in the Kennedy area.

For Knox "one Messe ... was more fearful ... then gif ten thousand armed enemyes war landed in any pairte of the Realme, of purpose to suppress the hoill religioun.", and he afterwards regretted that he had not demonstrated more zeal at this juncture.[67] His followers among the nobility, however, showed even more hesitation in pushing the matter to a head. The ministers tried in vain to convince the protestant lords of the necessity of opposing the queen, but at the third meeting of the General Assembly, December 1561, Knox had to admit that there was open disagreement between the politicians and the enthusiasts.[68]

In fact, there had been a fundamental disagreement for a long time, precisely because purity of religion was not the only – or, for that matter, even the most weighty – consideration which dictated the nobles' course of action. It had come to the fore at the time when the acceptance of the *First Book of Discipline* had been discussed. Knox said of them that "thair was none within the Realme more unmercyfull to the poore Ministeris then war thei whiche had greatest rentis of the Churches." On January 27th, 1560/61, the Book's plans for reform had at last been approved by "a great parte of the Nobilitie", but on condition that benefice holders who joined the reformed party would be allowed to enjoy the revenues for life if they supported the active ministers.[69] This, too, proved impracticable, and the endowment of the reformed ministry was to remain an unsolved problem for many years to come.

However, in their *First Book of Discipline* the ministers had offered "publict disputatioun to all that list oppung any thing affirmed" by them.[70] And if an attempt was to be made to win the country back for Rome, the autumn of 1561 might well be considered the least unfavourable moment.

On November 19th René Benoist, the queen's French chaplain, challenged Knox and the other ministers to a disputation, either orally or by interchange of letters. The letter, written in Latin, was translated into Scots, but the challenge was not accepted at the time.[71] A few weeks later, on December 10th, the same

---

[65] See *ibid.*, pp. 272f.

[66] See *ibid.*, vol. vi, pp. 129ff.

[67] *Ibid.*, vol. ii, pp. 276f.

[68] See Laing, *Works*, ii, pp. 265f. and 291ff.

[69] *Ibid.*, p. 129.

[70] *Ibid.*, p. 187.

[71] David Fergusson, minister of Dunfermline, finished his reply on April 26th, 1562, but it was not published until May 7th, 1563: *Ane Answer to ane Epistle written by Renat Benedict,...*

Benoist published his *Necessarius atque certus modus tollendae Religionis Discordiae*. Like the earlier letter, it asked for a dispassionate and charitable discussion of the disputed matter, but again without result, except that his efforts may have stimulated two native writers to join him.[72]

On the 15th of February Winzet addressed his *First Tractate* to the queen, asking her for permission to enter upon a written controversy with the Reformers. The request appears to have been granted, for a week afterwards he sent Knox three of his eighty-three questions which were by then circulating in manuscript, and challenged him to reply to them.[73] Randolph was mistaken when, in a letter dated February 28th, he attributed the *Buke of Four Scoir Thre Questionis* to "the Abbot of Corserogell, the lypperie Abbot,"[74] but the mistake testifies to the fact that Kennedy, too, was active.

---

to Iohn Knox and the rest of his bretheren ministers of the word of God, made by David Feargussone, minister of the same word at this present in Dumfermling, Edinburgh, 1563 (*S.T.C.*, no. 10819). Edited for the Bannatyne Club by J. Lee in the volume entitled *Tracts by David Fergusson* (Edinburgh, 1860). It divides the Scots text of the letter into four parts, replying to each part in turn. The Bannatyne Club volume also gives the Latin text of the letter: *Renatus Benedictus, Verbi Dei Professor, disertissimo Ioanni Knox atque aliis eruditissimis viris apud antiquitatem nobilem Scotiae vocatis Ministris* (pp. 83–87). – On Benoist, see E. Pasquier, *René Benoist, le Pape des Halles (1521–1608)*, Paris, 1913.

[72] The *Necessarius atque certus modus* was printed in Paris, 1562. Benoist strikes a rather different note in two other compositions, written in Scotland (i.e. before September 1562) but not known to have circulated. The *Stroma de obedientia vere fidelium et rebellione infidelium haereticorum*, an ingenious argument purporting to show that the catholics should take pride in the nickname *Papistae*, bears the date *15. Calend. Ianuarij, 1561*. In the undated *Stroma de Idololatria Coenae Caluinicae* (written *contra fidei hostes in nobilissimo Scotiae regno ... cum illic cum optima regina degerem*) he argues that not the catholics but the calvinists are blasphemous idolaters, because they call God an idol and attribute salvation to creatures. Benoist had these two brief pamphlets printed as an appendix to the 1575 edition of his *Locorum praecipuorum sacrae scripturae ... conquisitio, et Catholica expositio*, printed in Paris. (The pages of this appendix are not numbered).

[73] Winzet repeated his challenge in letters to Knox dated March 3rd, 10th and 12th. On March 31st he wrote what was subsequently to be called his *Third Tractate* to oppose discriminatory measures against Edinburgh catholics. The following May these minor writings were printed in one volume entitled *Certane tractatis for Reformatioun of Doctryne and maneris, set furth at the desyre and in þe name of þe afflictit Catholikis, of inferiour ordour of Clergie, and layit men in Scotland* (Edinburgh, May 21st, 1562). The publication of *The last blast of the trompet of Godis worde aganis the vsurpit auctoritie of Iohne Knox and his Caluiniane brether intrudit Precheouris, &c.*, was prevented on July 31st. Winzet fled to the continent on September 3rd, in the company of Goudanus, the papal legate. His Scots writings have been edited for the Maitland Club by J. B. Gracie (*Certain Tractates for Reformation of Doctrine and Manners in Scotland, by Ninian Winzet, MDLXII–MDLXIII*, Edinburgh, 1835). and for the S.T.S. by J. King Hewison (*Certain Tractates, together with the Book of Four Score Three Questions and a Translation of Vincentius Lirinensis, by Ninian Winzet*, 2 vols., Edinburgh, 1888 & 1890).

[74] J. Bain, *Calendar of State Papers relating to Scotland and Mary Queen of Scots, 1547–1603*, vol. i, p. 609.

The *Oratioune* is explicitly ascribed to "þe zeir of Gode 1561", which lasted till March 25th. An allusion in the text – with a more direct marginal reference – to a sermon preached by Knox on the 10th of August, 1561,[75] limits the time of composition to the latter half of the year. In addition, it mentions the *Compendious Ressonyng* as on the point of being published,[76] and Randolph's report at the end of February that Kennedy had 'latelye' published a book was in all probability occasioned by the last-mentioned tract. In his opening speech at the Maybole disputation Kennedy was to recall that the previous February he had sent to Knox his scriptural argument for the sacrificial character of the Mass which had as yet not been answered. And that argument occurs only in the *Compendious Ressonyng*.[77] Kennedy's defence of the Mass, contained in the same tract, may well have been welcomed by many catholics. His *Oratioune*, an appeal to the nobility not to let themselves be deceived by the preachers, is not known to have had any results.

On February 15th that same winter it was ruled that the thirds of benefices were to be paid to the Crown, partly for Crown needs and partly for distribution among the reformed ministers.[78] Considering the demands of the *First Book of Discipline* this financial settlement must have come as a kind of relief to many endowed prelates and interested nobles. Quintin Kennedy, however, seems to have been one of those who disagreed with the arrangement. He refused to pay and was "ordourelie denunced rebell and put to the horne." But even that did not change his attitude. On one occasion he "plainlie deforced" the collector sent to declare his goods confiscated.[79] That he could do this in Carrick with impunity is in sharp contrast with the general picture painted by Goudanus, the papal legate who was in Scotland from June till the beginning of September.[80]

According to Knox, Kennedy was present at a secret convention of arch-bishop Hamilton and a few leading catholics which was held at Paisley in

---

[75] See Laing, *Works*, vi, pp. 158 and 160. Perhaps the sermon is the same as the one assigned by Knox to a Sunday later in August, after the queen's arrival (*id.*, ii, p. 276).

[76] *Ibid.*, vi, 161. Of course, the title page of the *Compendious Ressonyng* implies that it was written before the end of March.

[77] Cp. Laing, *Works*, vi, p. 186 and *Compendious Ressonyng*, p. 163, below. – At the end of Kennedy's first speech at Maybole Knox replied to the "Abbottes oration" (*l.c.*), which is interpreted by Hugh Watt (*John Knox in Controversy*, London, 1950, pp. 57f.) as referring to the *Oratioune*. But the argument cited does not occur in the *Oratioune*, and the "Abbottes oration" is Kennedy's opening speech.

[78] See G. Donaldson, *Accounts of the Collectors of Thirds of Benefices, 1561–1572*, Edinburgh, Scottish History Society, 1949, pp. x ff.

[79] See *Crossraguel Charters*, i, p. 126 and Donaldson, *o.c.*, p. 142 (cp. pp. 20, 34, 38, 41, 62, 69, 74, 113, 135, 139 and 165).

[80] See W. Forbes Leith, *Narratives of Scottish Catholics under Mary Stuart and James VI*, London, 1889, pp. 63–79.

June–July, 1562. They are said to have been joined by an envoy from the Earl of Huntly, with whom they discussed the possibilities of a catholic rising in the south simultaneous with that in the north.[81] At the same time the General Assembly of the reformed Kirk was planning a new campaign to increase its influence in the south-west of Scotland: John Knox was to go to Kyle and Galloway, George Hay to Carrick. Hay's work is shrouded in obscurity, but for Knox's activity we have his own words. He warned his sympathizers of

"the dangearis that he feared, and that war appearing schortlie to follow; and exhorted thame to put thame selfis in sic ordour as that thei myght be able to serve the authoritie, and yit not to suffer the ennemeis of Goddis treuth to have the upper hand. Whairupoun a great part of the Baronis and Gentilmen of Kyle and Cunynghame and Carrik, professing the treu doctrine of the evangell, assembled at Ayre; and after exhortationis maid, and conference had, subscrivit this Band. The tennour whairof followis: We ... do promesse ... that we, and everie ane of us, shall and will manteane and assist the preaching of his holy Evangell, ... and also will manteane the ministeris of the same against all personis, power, and authoritie, that will oppone the self to the doctrin proponed, and be us receaved. ..."[82]

By these and similar means, Knox says, he prevented what he feared. But the Earl of Cassillis had not been one of the signatories of the covenant, and this meant that Quintin Kennedy was still relatively safe. Nevertheless, an encounter between him and Knox became inevitable when the latter, with a following, entered Carrick during Cassillis' absence in the beginning of September and proceeded to the place where Kennedy was to preach. Kennedy declined an encounter under these circumstances, but at the same time expressed his eagerness for an orderly disputation. A correspondence between them eventually resulted in a public debate at Maybole on the scriptural warrant for the Mass. It lasted three days and ended in a complete deadlock.[83]

Knox's *History* has only a surprisingly brief allusion to the Maybole debate. He adds that Kennedy "farther presented him self to the pulpit, but the voice of Maister George Hay so effrayed him, that efter ones he wearyed of that

---

[81] See Laing, *Works*, ii, pp. 346f. For a criticism of Knox's account and a different interpretation of the facts, see A. Lang, *John Knox and the Reformation*, pp. 220ff.

[82] Laing, *Works*, ii, pp. 347ff. (cp. *Acts and Proceedings of the General Assemblies*, Bannatyne Club edition, pp. 17f.). In his letter to Knox of September 7th Kennedy refers to vain attempts on his part to arrange debates with Willock and Hay. When Knox published the text, he commented: "Maister George Hay offered vnto you disputation but ye fled the barras." (*id.*, vi, p. 179). If this comment is correct, it is strange that Hay is silent about it, although he alludes to charges of cowardice against his person (Hay, *Confutation*, pp. 3r f.).

[83] See *Appendix* II, below, for a more detailed account.

exercise."[84] Other evidence, however, shows that the efforts of the Reformers did not result in the success they had anticipated, that catholics boasted about Kennedy's triumph at Maybole, and that he continued to be an influence to be reckoned with. At the instance of the Earl of Glencairn John Davidson at last undertook to write his *Answer* to the *Compendius Tractiue* during the following winter, George Hay was commissioned to write his *Confutation* of the *Compendious Ressonyng*, and, in order to counteract the rumours of Kennedy's alleged victory, Knox himself edited the documents relating to the disputation at Maybole.[85]

Meanwhile Mass continued to be said in the various catholic centres, apparently – and not unreasonably – with an appeal to the queen's proclamation of August, 1561. "The brethren ... aspying that the Quene, by hir proclamationis, did but mock thame, determined to put to thair awin handis." About Easter 1563 several priests in the south-west of Scotland were apprehended. Kennedy and others were notified that the protestants would no longer complain to the queen, but that they would themselves "execute the punishment that God has appointed to idolateris in his law, by such means as thei mycht, whairever thei should be apprehended."[86] It appears, however, that the government stepped in before the 'Congregation' could take the law in its own hands. A letter by Randolph, dated May 20th, reports:

"The Bishop of St. Andrew's arraigned; so was the Prior of Whithorne, and the Abbot of Corserogall should, but could not be taken ... The abbot of Corserogall was summoned, and for his absence shall be put to the horn."[87]

The names of those who had been tried before the Court of Justiciary on the previous day, May 19th, do not include that of Kennedy. But since the charge was, among other things, for attempting to restore popery at Kirkoswald and Maybole, it is clear that he was very much involved.[88]

If at this time Kennedy was still in reasonable health, his physical condition

---

[84] Laing, *Works*, ii, p. 352.

[85] Like Fergusson's tract against the letter of René Benoist, these three publications appeared in 1563. For further particulars, see below, pp. 216ff. – In the *Confutation* there is no hint of Kennedy's supposed discomfiture at Hay's preaching. It is not impossible that Kennedy soon stopped preaching for reasons of health.

[86] Laing, *Works*, ii, pp. 370f.

[87] J. Bain, *Calendar of State Papers relating to Scotland and Mary Queen of Scots, 1547–1603*, vol. ii, p. 9. There is no evidence for the assertion that Kennedy "was put prisoner in 1562 for saying of Mess" (Richard Augustine Hay, *Scotia Sacra*, MSS, 1700, National Library of Scotland, p. 278).

[88] See R. Pitcairn, *Criminal Trials in Scotland*, Edinburgh, 1833, vol. i, pp. 427*ff.– Most of the persons mentioned were committed to ward, soon to be released. According to Knox it was a put up affair in connection with the parliament due to convene on the 20th, but postponed till the 26th (Laing, *Works*, ii, pp. 397f.).

very soon deteriorated. There are indications that his health had been rather poor for a considerable time. The previous September Knox had spoken of Kennedy's "impotent age",[89] which cannot have referred to old age because he was in his early forties. In July 1563 he was expected to die,[90] and it is not impossible that he "could not be taken" and had not been tried in May on account of his critical condition.

It is not known when and in how far he recovered. In view of his illness just at that period, it must be considered most unlikely that he was presented to the queen when she stayed at Dunure castle on the 4th, 5th and 6th of August in the course of her 'progress' through the west of Scotland.[91] A few charters bear witness to the fact that he sufficiently recovered to administer the temporal affairs of his abbey. There was, however, little administration for him to do. In 1559 he had made his nephew heritable bailie of the regality of Crossraguel, and apparently he had leased the entire patrimony of his abbey to the Earl that same year.[92] Four months and a half before his death this latter contract was renewed for another five years, and as late as June 2nd, 1564, the abbot was told by the Lords of Council to live up to these contracts.[93] Perhaps the adherence to the catholic religion of all his monks[94] gave him more satisfaction than his last financial transactions.

A letter from Pius IV, dated June 13th, 1564, in which he was exhorted to persevere in the Roman faith,[95] probably never met his eye, for he died on the 22nd of August.[96] Randolph reported his death to London, adding one of its effects:

"The abbot of Corsrogall is dede, and the Kenedies reddie to fall by the eares for his good. Mr. George Bouchanan hathe geven unto hym by the Quene the whole temporalities of that Abbacie: with spiritualities he wyll not

---

[89] Laing, *Works*, vi, p. 188.

[90] See Hay, *Confutation*, pp. 3v ff. (in the dedication to the Earl of Moray, dated "the penult day of July, 1563"). His health must have been in a reasonable condition at the end of April, for on the 29th of that month he had been one of the two judges asked to arbitrate between the Earl of Cassillis and James Kennedy of Ochtrelure (*Ailsa Papers*, section i, no. 631).

[91] See D. Hay Fleming, *Mary Queen of Scots*, 2nd edition, London, 1898, p. 524 *(Itinerary)* and J. Fergusson, *The White Hind and Other Discoveries*, London, 1963, p. 49.

[92] See *Crossraguel Charters*, i, pp. 130 ff. The assedation to the Earl of the entire benefice is proved by a letter to the tenants, dated July 9th, 1560, preserved among the *Ailsa Papers*, but not included in the *Crossraguel Charters*.

[93] *Crossraguel Charters*, i, pp. 137 ff.

[94] G. Donaldson, "The Parish Clergy and the Reformation", in *Essays*, p. 138.

[95] See J. M. Rigg, *Calendar of State Papers, Relating to English Affairs, Preserved Principally at Rome, in the Vatican Archives and Library*, London, H.M. Stationery Office, 1916 ff., vol. i, p. 165.

[96] See *Crossraguel Charters*, i, pp. 139 f. and 177 f. – According to Dempster (*Menologium Scoticum*, Bologna, 1622, p. 20) Kennedy died "*lento veneno consumptus, corruptoque san-*

meddle, bycause he can not preache. ... At Edenbourge, the xxiiiith of October 1564." [97]

In fact, Kennedy was the last preaching abbot of Carrick. In due time, and after various manipulations, the Earl of Cassillis managed to consolidate his position as 'King of Carrick' by the acquisition of the abbey possessions. [98] The surviving monks were permitted to die in peace, after which the abbey itself was allowed to dilapidate. [99]

guine". Nine years later David Chalmers, *alias* Camerarius, interpreted this as "*ab inferni asseclis medicato poculo sublatus*" (*De Scotorum Fortitudine*, Paris, 1631, p. 168). But Dempster's words, probably based on information from abbot Gilbert Brown of Sweetheart, are better interpreted as referring to a wasting disease during the last years of Kennedy's life. Dr. Durkan has suggested to me that, in view of the designation 'the lypperie Abbot', Kennedy may have suffered from some kind of crippling illness. A remark made by Kennedy at the Maybole debate corroborates this suggestion: "I haif my life and my feit louse" (Laing, *Works*, vi, p. 183; cp. "not withstanding my great inhabilitie" and "swa that the habilitie of my bodie will serue ony wise," pp. 185 and 217 respectively).

[97] J. Bain, *Calendar of State Papers relating to Scotland and Mary Queen of Scots, 1547–1603*, vol. ii, p. 88. Buchanan, tutor to the Earl of Cassillis' father at an earlier period, was tutor to the queen at this time and therefore personally known to Randolph. – One of the Reformers commemorated Kennedy in an *Epitaphium Abbatis Crossagvel* [sic.]:

"*Vae mihi quod Papae dederam nomenque fidemque*
Vae mihi quod Christi strenuus hostis eram:
Vae vobis Papistae omnes, nisi tempore vitae
Vos Christum amplexi Pontificem fugitis."

(Patrick Adamson, *De Papistarum Superstitiosis Ineptiis*, 1564, fo. 7v f.; reprinted in his *Poemata Sacra*, London, 1619, p. 64v.). The opposite opinion, that Kennedy was canonized on his death (see Crawfurd, *The Peerage of Scotland*, Edinburgh, 1716, p. 76 and A. Agnew, *The Hereditary Sheriffs of Galloway*, 2nd edition, 2 vols., Edinburgh, 1893, vol. i, p. 384), is probably to be traced to Dempster: "*Augusti XXII ... Monasterio Crucis Regalis obitus Beati Quintini Kenneddii ...*" (*l.c.*). Alexander Boswell suggested that he had been confused with S. Kinetus Eremita, a sixth century saint (Advertisement to his edition of the *Oratioune*, Edinburgh, 1812, p. vi; the same opinion was adopted by the editor of the *Crossraguel Charters*, vol. i, p. xlv, footnote 8, and in *The Scots Peerage*, vol. ii, p. 466).

[98] Cassillis purchased the Crossraguel lands in January, 1575/76 (J. Maitland Thomson, *Registrum Magni Sigilli Regum Scotorum*, vol. iv, p. 668).

[99] See J. Fergusson, *The White Hind and Other Discoveries*, London, 1963, pp. 54 ff.

IV. KENNEDY'S WRITINGS

A. THE WRITINGS ATTRIBUTED TO KENNEDY

The catalogue of writings attributed to Kennedy in Thomas Dempster's *Historia Ecclesiastica Gentis Scotorum* may well have been the reason – or part of the reason – why Thomas Innes extended Kennedy's life into the seventeenth century,[1] and that the Rev. James Scott of Perth, aware that Kennedy had died as early as 1564, wrote that by March–April 1559 he "had long been celebrated for his controversial writings and great learning."[2] Kennedy's own reference to "my awin buke" in his report on the events described by Scott suggests a more modest literary reputation.[3] Indeed, the context makes it clear that the *Compendius Tractiue* is meant; but if he had written more tracts by that time, he might justifiably have been expected to mention it by name. The words with which he had prefaced this earlier tract had likewise not been those of a writer with an established name:

> "I am assurit, (benevolent Redare,) quhen thow dois mark and consider the tytle of our lytle Tractive, thairefter persavis quha is the furthsetter and author of the samyn, thow wyl wounder gretlie and mervell, that I (quha am ane man void of all eloquence, rude of ingyne, and jugement) durst be sua baulde, as to attempt sua heych ane purpose; specialie in this miserable tyme, quhair into thair is sua gret diversitie of opinioun amangis swa mony pregnant men of ingyne."[4]

Kennedy refers to his writings in a few more places. In the *Oratioune* he speaks of "our little werk, quhilk is all reddy to be set furth, concerning the sacrifice of the mess," and of "our litill werk concerning the real presence of our Lordis body in the sacrament of the altar."[5] The context of the *Oratioune* leaves no room for doubt that the *Compendious Ressonyng* and the *Litil Breif Tracteit* are meant. And it has already been pointed out that at the Maybole debate Kennedy quoted an argument from the *Compendious Ressonyng*, the same argument which he had sent to Knox the previous February. So far, therefore, nothing is postulated beyond the four tracts which have in fact survived. And of

---

[1] See W. J. Anderson, "Narratives of the Scottish Reformation, II: Thomas Innes on Catholicism in Scotland, 1560–1653," *The Innes Review*, vol. vii (1956), p. 118.

[2] *A History of the Protestant Reformers in Scotland*, Edinburgh, 1817, p. 61 (cp. p. 68).

[3] *Wodrow Misc.*, p. 268

[4] *Ibid.*, pp. 97f.

[5] Laing, *Works*, vi, pp. 161 and 164.

these four tracts the *Oratioune* takes up less than nine pages in Laing's edition of *The Works of John Knox*. In one of his letters to Knox, however, Kennedy alludes to the "warkes set furth be me".[6] Since this letter was written in September, 1562, it does not necessarily postulate additional tracts, but it might be construed into a confirmation of external evidence for a larger literary output.

Kennedy's contemporaries cannot be said to provide such evidence. Of those who might be expected to mention his works, Winzet knows the *Compendius Tractiue* through Davidson's *Answer*,[7] Knox practically ignores him in his *History*, Davidson is silent on Kennedy's work except the one tract he is intent on refuting, whilst George Hay's testimony is too vague. He is also unreliable in as far as it is his purpose to magnify the figure of the "proude and wyde blowing Goliath" so that the fall will be the greater. On the one hand he says that

"this our Abbote hath continually barked from the beginning of this mercy-full visitation of our God, and reformation in Scotland, yea, and set forthe some thinges that be plainely red, and euerie where to be found, that the rest of his workes which be no less pernitious be neglected, and this onely hath bene iudged worthy of answer"

but on the other

"that before this boke wes deliuered to me, I neuer had sene none of his workes, yea, and I beleue that the most part of his writtings be ether vnsene to the rest of my brethren, or at least, they that they haue sene, they haue iudged vnworthy of any answer."[8]

Bishop John Lesley, another contemporary, though writing several years after Kennedy's death, says that the latter

"duos, praeter alia opuscula, edidit libros exquisitissima Doctorum Concilio-rum Scripturarum doctrina refertos, unum de Conciliorum auctoritate al-terum de publico Ecclesiae Sacrificio. E quibus illum Ioannes Davidsonus hunc Georgius Haius sectarii ministri ita refutarunt, ut catholica veritas inde magis diluscescat iis quorum mentes haereseis malitiaeque tenebris plane non fuerint obvolutae."[9]

The names of Kennedy's opponents prove that the two works specified are the *Compendius Tractiue* and the *Compendious Ressonyng*.

Kennedy's name does not figure among the writers listed by Bale and Gesner,

---

[6] *Ibid.*, p. 179.

[7] See *Certain Tractates together with the Book of Four Score Three Questions and a Translation of Vincentius Lirinensis by Ninian Winzet*, edited for S.T.S. by J. King Hewison, 2 vols., Edinburgh, 1888 and 1890, vol. ii, pp. 9f.

[8] Hay, *Confutation*, preface, pp. 1r and 2r (cp. p. 3v).

[9] *De Origine, Moribus et Rebus Gestis Scotorum*, Rome, 1578, p. 540.

or in the "General catalog of the writers of Scotland" appended to Francis Thin's continuation of Holinshed's *Scottish Chronicle*.[10] Nor does it occur in David Buchanan's *De Scriptoribus Scotis libri duo*.[11] And this failure to take notice of Kennedy would have been most reprehensible if he had been the author of the works attributed to him by Thomas Dempster in 1627. Dempster's entry deserves to be quoted in full:

"Quintinus Kennedius, comitis Cassiliae frater, Crucis Regalis abbas, ingens literatorum fautor, magno et nobili animo haeresi in Scotia nascenti familiaribus colloquiis ac scriptis restitit, nihil omittens quo Catholican fidem strenue propugnaret. Ejus sunt opera, Joanne Leslaeo auctore:

De Conciliorum Auctoritate	lib. I.
De publico Ecclesiae Sacrificio	lib. I.
Contra Errores Germanorum	lib. I.
Fidei Capita quatuordecim defensa contra Georgium Sophocardium	lib. I.

Atque haec typis vulgata, inedita vero sunt:

Responsio ad Joannis Davidsoni opus	lib. I.
De vetitorum Ciborum Abstinentia	lib. I.
De illicito Presbyterorum Matrimonio	lib. I.
De Cultu Imaginum	lib. I.
Palinodia Willoxio reddita xxix. Martii MDLXII	lib. I.
Querimonia super Knoxii Fraude et Impietate	lib. I.
Oratio pro Obedientia supremis Potestatibus, habita die ultima Augusti MDLXII	lib. I.
De Praesentia Corporis in Sacramento Altaris dicitur prodiisse	lib. I.

Florebat anno MDLXIV. obiit autem die xxii. Augusti eodem anno."[12]

Concerning this catalogue, which appears to have been largely responsible for the exaggerated literary reputation that has been ascribed to Kennedy, it may be remarked in the first place that, apart from the proceedings of the Maybole debate, published by Knox, the *Compendius Tractiue* is Kennedy's only tract known to have been printed in the sixteenth century.[13] Another

---

[10] *Index Brittanniae Scriptorum quos ... collegit Ioannes Baleus*, edited by R. L. Poole, *Anecdota Oxoniensia*, Oxford, 1902; *Bibliotheca instituta ... a Conrado Gesnero ... amplificata per Iohannem Iacobum Frisium Tigurinum*, Zürich, 1583; the 1587 edition of Holished's southern version of Bellenden's *History and Croniklis of Scotland* (itself a translation of Hector Boece's *Scotorum Historiae*) was reprinted in 2 volumes at Arbroath, 1805: *The Scottish Chronicle, or, A Complete History and Description of Scotland*, the 'Catalog' by 'Francis Boteville commonlie called Thin' occurring in vol. ii, pp. 465–479.

[11] Written about 1627, first printed by the Bannatyne Club (ed. D. Irving), Edinburgh, 1837.

[12] *Historia Ecclesiastica Gentis Scotorum: sive, De Scriptoribus Scotis* (Bologna, 1627), Edinburgh, Bannatyne Club, vol. ii, pp. 422f.

[13] Cp. *S.T.C.*, nos. 15074 and 14932.

obvious observation is that Dempster would have given the opening words of the first chapters, if he had had access to these alleged writings.

The first two titles are from the passage in Lesley's *De Rebus Gestis* which has been quoted above. As this book mentions no other works by Kennedy, Dempster, after first copying these two descriptive titles *Joanne Leslaeo auctore*, may have come across similar references in other books or from private information and uncritically have added them as titles of distinct works. Thus *Querimonia super Knoxii Fraude et Impietate* and *Oratio pro Obedientia supremis Potestatibus* would both do for descriptions of Kennedy's *Oratioune;* the date *die ultima Augusti MDLXII* would then be wrong, and *habita* would be an unwarranted interpretation.[14]

If this is correct, it becomes less fanciful to point to the following passage from the thirteenth chapter of the *Compendius Tractiue* as the possible source of three other titles:

"Thair is sum mair rigorus, and rasche of jugement, affirmand planelie, that thair is divers constitutionis of the Kirk, quhilkis may na way stand with the Worde of God; sick as is the constitutioun of Fastyng at certane tymes appoyntit, Invocatioun to be maid unto Sanctis, Mariage forbiddin to Preistis."

But although Kennedy subsequently goes to some extent into the question of the invocation of saints and deplores the moral laxity of the clergy, he had not written any tracts on these subjects at the time and evidently did not consider it necessary. The following words occur a few lines after those just quoted and refer to the three subjects there mentioned:

"To make the Redare sufficientlie to understand how thir, and mony utheris Scripturis, ar falslie and impropirlie allegit, and interpretit agains the Kirk, presentlie, wer ovir prolixt; and als thair is divers utheris, quhilkis hes habundantlie tretit thir purposis in the Inglis toung."[15]

Dempster's corresponding titles may be based on information that Kennedy had denounced the views of the Reformers on these points, or perhaps the word 'presentlie' gave rise to the conclusion that he would certainly write on these subjects on a later occasion.

Of a reply by Kennedy to Davidson's *Answer* nothing is known. If it is unfair to surmise that it was considered fitting that he should have written it, the only

---

[14] Knox preached a violent sermon against the queen on Sunday, August 31st, 1561. If we assume that the *Oratioune* refers to this occasion and that through a scribal or printer's error the marginal date was altered to August 10th in the printed edition, we may well be on the track of Dempster's date. See p. 38 and note 75, above.

[15] *Wodrow Misc.*, p. 147.

thing that remains is to suspend judgment.[16] The date of the *Palinodia Willoxio reddita* suggests that it refers to one of the arguments of the *Compendious Ressonyng*, each of which was addressed to a particular reformer.[17] It has already been said that Kennedy certainly sent Knox the argument allotted to him, and it is quite possible that he did this in each case.

The last work listed by Dempster may safely be identified with the *Litil Breif Tracteit*. This leaves numbers three and four, which have not yet been considered so far. Dempster may have found somewhere that Kennedy had written "*contra errores Germanorum*" and interpreted it as a title, although, as will be shown presently, some subsequent writers have combined it with the next title in the catalogue. In this latter supposition it would be bound up with the interesting question raised by the fourteen chapters against Sophocardius, i.e. Wishart. The interest derives from the fact that the first fourteen chapters of the *Compendious Tractiue* form a distinct unit rounded off by one of Kennedy's characteristic summaries. This literary aspect of the question will come up for discussion on a later page. For the time being it may be remarked that here we may have external evidence of an earlier and shorter edition of the *Compendius Tractiue*.

Although George Mackenzie was of the opinion that "Dempster, from Bishop Leslie's Words, [had] made five Books out of two,"[18] he gave Dempster's list twice over, once in English and once in Latin. In both cases, however, he gave the full Scots title of the *Compendius Tractiue* instead of Lesley's Latin reference. In the English list, unlike the Latin one, he assigned the *Challenge given to Willox* to March 25th, 1562, and in the Latin catalogue he reduced the number by one, viz. by listing a work *Contra errores Germanorum in Fidei capita quatuordecim defensa contra Georgium Sophocardium*.[19]

The editor of the *Crossraguel Charters* copied the Latin catalogue from Mackenzie. Although he called it "a complete list" of Kennedy's writings, he went on to state that Kennedy wrote an additional "learned work on the 'Judge of Controversies' in eighteen chapters, giving a detailed history of the Church Councils from early times."[20] From a subsequent footnote[21] one infers that he identified this supposed work with what Lesley had called "de Conciliorum auctoritate" and that he found it "printed in Mackenzie's *Lives of the Scotch Writers*."

---

[16] A tract of any length would seem to be excluded by Kennedy's poor health during the last fifteen months of his life.

[17] See pp. 151f, below.

[18] *Lives*, vol. iii, p. 63.

[19] *Ibid.*, pp. 58 and 62.

[20] *Crossraguel Charters*, i, pp. xlii f.

[21] *Ibid.*, p. 130, footnote 1.

Apparently he was misled by a curious procedure on the part of Mackenzie. After translating Dempster's catalogue into English, Mackenzie had continued as follows:

"His Book upon the Judge of Controversies contains 18 Chapters, ... his main Drift is to show the many Inconveniencies that would arise from making the Scripture the Judge of Controversies, or our own private Judgment and Opinion. ... for fear of increasing the Bulk of his Book too much, he proceeds no further than the first four General Councils, and then proceeds to common Topicks used in the Controversies betwixt the Papists and Protestants; but we shall only trouble the Reader with the List of the General Councils after our Author's Method." [22]

Mackenzie had then given a list of twenty-one general councils, including Trent, in the manner in which Kennedy might have treated them but, for all Mackenzie knew, never had done. [23]

For completeness' sake it may be added that Spottiswoode attributed a "faith" to Kennedy, [24] i.e., in the interpretation of Richard Augustine Hay, "a Booke against the Protestant confession of faith," [25] or, in that of Mackenzie, "a Catechism." [26] From the context in Spottiswoode one gathers that this 'catechism' can be traced back to the 'artickles' of which there is frequent mention in the documents relating to the Maybole debate, viz. the propositions of Kennedy's catechetical instructions. Some of these 'artickles', viz. those on the Mass, were committed to paper and delivered to Knox, so that they would have a starting-point for the debate. [27]

Briefly, although the first fourteen chapters of the *Compendius Tractiue* may have circulated as a separate tract before it was amplified for the printed edition, there is no evidence for attributing more tracts to Kennedy than those which have in fact survived.

---

[22] *O.c.*, p. 58. – Mackenzie had himself been beaten by Lesley's Latin, viz. when he had interpreted him as attributing to Kennedy two works, "the first against John Davidson, and the other against George Hay." (*ibid.*, p. 61; see Lesley's words on p. 44, above).

[23] Mackenzie's Latin list is also reproduced in A. Bellesheim's *History of the Catholic Church of Scotland*, translated, with notes and additions, by D. Oswald Hunter Blair, O.S.B., 4 vols., Edinburgh and London. 1887–1890, vol. ii, p. 254, footnote 1. In this case there is an attempt to improve the Latin: *Contra errores Germanorum in fide: capita quattuordecim defensa contra Georgium Sophocardium.* Other authors refer for Kennedy's *oeuvre* to the list in Dempster, Mackenzie, or *Crossraguel Charters* (*e.g. The Scots Peerage*, ii, p. 466, *D.N.B.*, *s.v.* Kennedy, Quintin).

[24] J. Spottiswoode, *History of the Church of Scotland*, Spottiswoode Society edition, 3 vols., Edinburgh, 1851, vol. ii, p. 15.

[25] Richard Augustine Hay, *Scotia Sacra*, MSS 1700 (National Library of Scotland), p. 278.

[26] *Lives*, iii, p. 57.

[27] See *Maybole Ressoning*, Laing, *Works*, vi, pp. 175 ff.

1. *Ane compendius Tractiue conforme to the Scripturis of almychtie God, ressoun, and authoritie, declaring the nerrest, and onlie way, to establische the conscience of ane christiane man, in all materis (quhilkis ar in debate) concernyng faith and religioun.* Set fvrth be Maister Qvintine Kennedy Commendatar of the abbay off Crosraguell, and dedicat to his derrest, and best beluiffit Nepuo, Gilbert maister of Cassillis. In the ʒeir of God, Ane thousand fyue houndreth fifty aucht ʒeris.[28]

The title page has no place or printer's name, but the woodcut, also used for Ninian Winzet's *Certane Tractatis*,[29] shows that it came from the press of John Scot, either at Edinburgh or St. Andrews. By the eighteenth century the book had become so rare that Keith printed chapters twelve and fourteen by way of specimen.[30] The entire tract was reprinted in the *Miscellany* of the Wodrow Society (pp. 97–174).

The text is divided into eighteen chapters, without headings, preceded by a brief dedication to the Maister of Cassillis and a preface to the reader. Kennedy's aim is to show that there is only one way towards cessation of all religious controversies, viz. to agree on a judge with authority to discern between the right and the wrong interpretation of God's mind and will, and that it is clear from Scripture, history and reason that only the church can be such a judge. Scripture, to be sure, embodies the divine truth, but that makes it a witness, not the authoritative judge necessary to discern between different interpretations. That Scripture might be its own judge is an illusion and a pretext for private, unorthodox opinions. Heretics all through the ages have appealed to Scripture, and the various Reformers still attempt to base their mutually exclusive views on what each conceives to be its correct interpretation.

Kennedy stresses that Scripture does not derive its truth from the church. The church decides which books belong to Scripture, but that is because, inspired by the Holy Spirit who remains with it until the end of time, it cannot but testify to the divine truth which it discerns in Scripture. Thus the church is

---

[28] *S.T.C.*, no. 14932.

[29] See the reproduction of the title page in J. King Hewison, *Certain Tractates, &c. by Ninian Winzet*, S.T.S., vol. i, opposite p. cxx.

[30] R. Keith, *History of the Affairs of Church and State in Scotland, from the Beginning of the Reformation to the Year 1568,* (1734), reprinted for the Spottiswoode Society, 3 vols., Edinburgh, 1844, vol. iii, pp. 400 ff. – MSS leaves comprising chapters sixteen, seventeen and the first half of chapter eighteen of Kennedy's tract are, together with other MS material (including Benoist's letter to John Knox and the other reformed preachers) inserted at the back of the copy of William Manderston's *Bipartitum in Morali Philosophia* listed on pp. 69 and 80 of J. Durkan and A. Ross, *Early Scottish Libraries*. The sixteenth-century hand has not been identified. (The existence of these leaves was pointed out to me by Dr. J. Durkan).

judge, not of the truth, but of the true meaning of Scripture. And for the same reason the church can never be said to appropriate to itself the glory which belongs to the Word of God.

The next question is how this works out in practice. The church, says Kennedy, is the universal congregation of all those united by baptism in one faith and forming a mystical body of which Christ is the head. Just as the various members of a body perform different tasks for the good of the entire body, so some members of this mystical body have been appointed leaders of the church. When assembled in properly convoked general councils, they constitute as it were the eye of the body and as such represent the church's power to discern the correct meaning of God's Word. And it would be foolish as well as disastrous for the rest of the body not to follow the judgment of the eye.

This is Kennedy's main line of thought, principally dealt with in the first four chapters but frequently recalled on subsequent pages. In the next ten chapters he tackles the objection that, in this matter, there is a distinction between apostolic and post-apostolic times. These chapters include sections on the vexed questions of disedifying behaviour among the clergy and the authority of councils to regulate christian worship and life by means of non-scriptural but not anti-scriptural constitutions. After a general summing up at the end of the fourteenth chapter he returns to this latter question in the remaining chapters, making much of the differences in 'faith' as well as 'religioun' among the various continental Reformers.[31]

2. *Heir followis ane schort rehears, quhairin is contenit the hale substance and effect of the tractiue set furth be M. Quintine Kennedy, Commendatoure of the abbay of Crosraguell, &c.*

This is not a separate tract, but a summary of the principal line of argument of the *Compendius Tractiue* sent to the Reformers about April 1559. The text is preserved in *Ane Answer to the Tractiue, set furth in the 3eir of God. 1558. be Maister Quintine Kennedy, Commendatar, Abbote of Crosraguell, for the establisching of ane Christiane mannis conscience (as he alledgis) the Forth and strenth of his Papistrie, and all vthers of his Sect, as appearis weil be his Epistle direct to the Protestantes, and Prentit in the last part of this Buik:* Maid be

---

[31] "I cal materis concernyng Religioun, ceremonyes, civile ordinances, or lawis maid be the Kirk, gevand Christin men occasioun (as I schew thé of before) to be the mair habyll to keip the law of God. I cal materis concernyng Faith, interpretatioun of the Word of God, specialie that is necessare to be knawin, and usit for ane Christiane mannis salvatioun, as ar the Sacramentis." (*Wodrow Misc.*, p. 155).

Maister Johne Dauidsone, Maister of the Paedagog of Glasgw.[32] Like Kennedy's *Compendius Tractiue*, this work was reprinted in the *Miscellany* of the Wodrow Society (pp. 183–258).

The Kennedy text is divided into eight parts separated from each other by Davidson's replies. Kennedy's accompanying "Epistle, directit to the Brethren Protestantes", in which he had challenged them to reply to his arguments, is followed at the end by a personal answer, in which Davidson appeals to his old friend to abandon the human inventions of the Roman church and embrace the true religion of Scripture.

Kennedy's 'Epistle' is the only thing not found in his *Compendious Tractiue*. Unfortunately it is not complete, the last part, including the date, being summed up in "&c.". Of the arguments themselves, the first sentence is a general introductory statement. The rest of the text consists of passages from the first, second and sixth chapters of the earlier tract.[32]

3. *Ane litil breif tracteit maid be master Quintine Kennidy, abbot of Corsragal,*
   prevand cleirlye þe real body of Iesu Crist to be present in þe sacrament of þe
   altare, contrar þe vickit opinione and heresy of Ecolampadius and oþeris diuerss in
   þir miserabil dais falslye deniand þe sammyne.

The manuscript from which this title is taken is the only complete copy of this tract known to be extant. It was copied on August 3rd, 1561, by Alexander Wood, a chaplain in Old Aberdeen. A name on the *recto* of f. 1 suggests that in the sixteenth century it belonged to one "Gilbertus Murray, monachus Deirensis". Four pages written by Archibald Constable, Edinburgh, February 15th 1809, and inserted into the present binding, mention that the MS had been in the library of Sir Robert Gordon of Gordonstoun, son of the fifteenth Earl of Sutherland. In 1803 it had been acquired by Constable. He had it restored and bound, and offered it to the Marchioness of Stafford – of the Gordon family – in 1809.[33] In 1960 it turned up at a London sale.[34] It was purchased by the Rev. William James Anderson, M.A., Keeper of the Catholic Archives of Scotland.

A copy of the *Compendius Tractiue*, at present owned by A. J. B. fforde, Esq., of Brook, Surrey, and on deposit in the National Library of Scotland,[35] con-

---

[32] Edinburgh, 1563 (S.T.C., no. 6320).

[32] Cp. *Wodrow Misc.*, pp. 189f. with 100 + 117f., 210f. with 118, 220f. with 118f., 229f. with 119f., 235ff. with 104f., 240 with 105, 241f. with 105f. and 246f. with 106.

[33] See Appendix I, below.

[34] Christie's, November 28th, 1960, lot no. 79.

[35] Catalogued T.D. 313; a complete set of photostats of the manuscript pages has shelf-mark Acc. 2682. – The volume is listed among Greenlaw's books in J. Durkan and A. Ross, *Early Scottish Libraries*, p. 107. The statement that it contains part of "an unknown treatise

tains the incomplete text of the same tract on manuscript pages inserted after the printed text. It was at one time in the possession of John Greenlaw of Haddington. The Campbell escutcheon with underline in the book shows that at a later date it belonged to "The Honourable Archibald Campbell Esqr. 1708". Subsequently it must have passed into the possession of the chief of the Kennedys, for a more recent notice states that it was "purchased from the Marquis of Ailsa, with many other books, by Mr R. MacLehose, Bookseller, Ayr, (my uncle) and by him given to my Father, James MacLehose," i.e. the father of the better-known printer and publisher of the same name.

The *Litil Breif Tracteit* is for the first time printed in the present volume. Although Kennedy refers to it in the *Oratioune* and although Dempster's catalogue contains a corresponding Latin title, the tract has in fact been quite unknown. In its nine chapters Kennedy defends the doctrine of his church concerning the presence of Christ in the Eucharist against the opinions of those who deny it, notably Oecolampadius and Calvin. The opening lines of the first chapter recall the general thesis of the *Compendius Tractiue:* the normal way of settling disputes on the Eucharist would be to have recourse to the doctrine of the church, which must *a priori* be in conformity with the Word of God contained in Scripture. But since the church's doctrine is said to contradict Scripture, Kennedy will argue the matter.

In the first part of the tract, which covers the first five chapters, he distinguishes between two opposed views: that the real body and blood of Christ are present in the Eucharist, and that it contains only a sign of his body and blood. He confronts each with the scriptural accounts of the institution of the Eucharist and answers a number of objections to the church's interpretation. After first adducing scriptural arguments for a real presence of Christ, he thus has an opportunity of explaining that it implies no contradictions. Presence of a body does not necessarily mean presence after the normal manner of a body. The answer to the problem of how Christ could be contained in a small quantity of bread and wine is that a better way of expression would be to say that he is present under the forms of bread and wine. In the Eucharist Christ does not occupy place, because he has the qualities of a spirit; and for the same reason he cannot be touched or seen.

In chapter six, the second part of the tract, Kennedy considers which of the two opposed interpretations contributes most to the glory of God and the profit

---

of Kennedy on the Eucharist copied by Greenlaw" needs qualification. The leaves contain parts of the *Litil Breif Tracteit* and the *Compendious Ressonyng*, the latter in Greenlaw's hand, the former in a different and unknown hand, but with interlinear and marginal corrections and additions by Greenlaw.

of the recipients. He argues that the Reformers refuse to recognize the most wonderful act of God's omnipotence and that it is more profitable to receive Christ both spiritually and really than spiritually only.

Having thus completed the plan proposed at the beginning of the tract, Kennedy adds a third section in which he compares the sixteenth-century Reformers with the early Christian heretics. His conclusion is that, for distorting the Word of God, Oecolampadius and Calvin are every whit as guilty as Arius and Nestorius.

4. *Ane Oratioune in fauouris of all thais of the Congregatione, exhortand thaim to aspy how wonderfullie thai ar abusit be thair dissaitfull prechouris*, set furth be Master Quintine Kennedy, Commendatour of Corsraguell, the ȝeir of Gode 1561.

This is not known to have been printed till the beginning of the nineteenth century, when it appeared in black-letter type, edited by Sir Alexander Boswell from an original manuscript in the Auchinleck library.[36] It was reprinted in Laing's edition of *The Works of John Knox*.[37]

In the brief dedicatory *Epistol to the Nobilite and Principalis of the Congregatione* Kennedy explains that, in view of the reforming zeal of these lords, who are so concerned about the true Word of God, he wishes to help them to form a balanced judgment about and against the "railling ressoning" of the protestant preachers. The *Oratioune* itself consists of three parts and a concluding paragraph. In the first part he attacks Knox's argument for the idolatrous nature of the Mass, referring his readers to the *Compendious Ressonyng* – "quhilk is all reddy to be set furth"– for a more detailed treatment of the matter.[38] In the second part he appeals to the lords to consider the results of the seditious sermons of the Reformers, stressing especially the material destruction and the disorder in the country. He asks them to have pity on the common people and to remember that the blame for the sad religious condition in the country has lain principally with their social class, because, as patrons of the ecclesiastical benefices, they have failed to provide qualified pastors. In the third part he passes on to the presence of Christ in the Eucharist. If, as the Reformers hold, there is no change of the bread and wine, the sacramental species may indeed be considered mere signs. For then, Kennedy says, they give as little spiritual refreshment as the sign of a tavern gives bodily refreshment. In

---

[36] Edinburgh, 1812.
[37] Vol. vi, pp. 157–165.
[38] The *Compendious Ressonyng* also contains Knox's argument; see p. 154, below.

the Eucharist, however, the forms of the bread and wine not only signify, but also contain Christ's body and blood, in much the same way as a loaf in a baker's shop indicates that bread is sold there and at the same time is itself bread.

For more details on this matter Kennedy refers his readers to his *Litil Breif Tracteit*. He ends the Oratioune with a challenge to the protestant preachers either to refute his arguments or to recant and return in obedience to the church of God.

5. *Ane compendious ressonyng, be þe quhilk is maid manifest, treulie, and propirlie, conforme to þe scripturis of almychtie God (bayth new testament and auld), þe mess to be Institute be Iesu Christ oure salueour in þe latter supper, incontrar þe ralling ressonyng of all sic as dois affirme þe mess to be Inventit be the brayne of man.* Set furth be Maister Quintyne Kennedy, commendatour of þe abbay of Corsraguell, In þe ȝeir of God ane thousand fywe hundreth threscoir ane ȝeiris.

After a table of twenty-nine theses with page references, there follows a preface *To the redar in generale, and in speciall to Knox, Willock, Wynrame, Gudeman, Dowglas, Hereot, Spottiswod, Athenis, and all þe laif of the famows precheouris to the congregatioun.* The text proper bears the heading *Ane familiar ressonyng of þe misterie of þe sacrifice off the mess betuix tua brethir, Maister Quintyne Kennedy, commendatour of Corsraguell, and Iames Kennedy of Vcht-wallure.*

David Laing extracted and printed the title, preface and the first page of the text proper from a manuscript copy owned by the Rev. George A. Griffin, catholic priest at New Abbey, Galloway.[39] From these extracts and Laing's summary description it appears that it is the copy which is at present in the Catholic Archives of Scotland.[40] In 1952 it was discovered at Blairs by Dr. J. Durkan. Since the removal of the Blairs Archives to Edinburgh, it is kept at Columba House, Edinburgh, c/o the Rev. W. J. Anderson. It is the only complete copy of the tract known to exist.

A free rendering of what in this manuscript is simply called *Appendex*, written in Greenlaw's hand and entitled *Ane appendix In maner off collocutione and resoning betwyxe Quhintyne, commendator off Corsraguell, and his browthir Iames Kennate: set fwrth be þe sayd commendator*, is inserted among the manuscript pages in Mr fforde's copy of the *Compendius Tractiue*. Numerous and

---

[39] See Laing, *Works*, vi, pp. 155 and 166 ff. – In the introduction to his edition of the *Oratioune* Alexander Boswell had mentioned a less perfect copy in the Auchinleck library.

[40] Father Griffin had been on the staff of Blairs College. The MS probably went to Blairs on his death.

quite extensive quotations from the *Compendious Ressonyng* exclusive of the *Appendex* may be found in George Hay's *Confutation* of the tract.[41] Boswell's remark, in the introduction to his edition of the *Oratioune*, that "a MS of the work [*i.e.* Kennedy's] is said to be now in the library of the Marquis of Stafford" is probably based on inaccurate information about the tract presented to the Marchioness in 1809.[42]

Apart from the passages extracted by Laing, the *Compendious Ressonyng* has never been printed. The full text presented in this volume is that of the MS in the Catholic Archives of Scotland.

The tract takes the form of a dialogue between Kennedy and his youngest brother, James Kennedy of Ochterlour, who plays the part of the protestant until he is convinced by his brother's arguments. Even before that time, however, James merely puts in the right questions and objections at the appropriate moments, enabling Quintin to develop his reasoning. James begins by pronouncing the Mass idolatry, quoting Knox – without mentioning the name – in his support. As in the *Oratioune*, Kennedy shows the weak points of the argumentation. He then proceeds to prove that the Mass is a commemoration of Christ's passion and death, in which, in conformity with Christ's institution, bread and wine are changed into the body and blood of Christ, offered to God and received by the faithful as spiritual food.

To the objection that Christ was once for all offered in sacrifice on Calvary, so that the Mass cannot be a sacrifice, Kennedy answers that the Mass implies no new redemption, independent of the one perfect sacrifice of Calvary. But just as medicine, however good, remains ineffective unless it is applied to the body, so the salutary fruits of Christ's passion and death must be applied to us by means of the Mass.

After the various arguments for his main thesis and its speculative explanation Kennedy argues that, in view of Christ's promise of the divine Spirit, it is impossible to maintain that the church should have committed idolatry for fifteen centuries, and that the recent attack upon the Mass should represent

---

[41] Published at Edinburgh, 1563 (*S.T.C.*, no. 12968). Boswell *(l.c.)* and A. C. Southern (*Elizabethan Recusant Prose, 1559–1582*, London & Glasgow, 1950, p. 436) are hesitant about the identity of the tract which drew forth Hay's *Confutation*. Also Laing, in *Works*, vi, p. 155, although he had had no such hesitation when he had edited the *Miscellany* of the Wodrow Society (p. 94). But even a superficial comparison of the two tracts is sufficient to see that there cannot be the slightest doubt.

[42] Dr. J. Durkan has drawn my attention to the following entry in the *Catalogue of the Library of the late John Scott of Halkshill* (Sotheby, March 27th, 1905): MS 1129. "Treaties of the Mass, Original Autograph Manuscript *on paper (40 ll.) incomplete and several ll. defective, all inlaid on modern white paper*, ... c. 1562. ... on reverse of leaf 23 *'finis qd. Q.K.'*" My efforts to trace this MS have been without result.

the correct interpretation of Scripture. In the *Appendex* James then returns to a question which he has already raised in the body of the tract, viz. that of the unscriptural ceremonies of the Mass. Kennedy repeats his principle that these things have been left to the church to regulate and that adding to Scripture is not the same thing as contradicting Scripture. When he has traced the origin, or supposed origin, of a number of ceremonies, given explanations of the vestments and defended the use of Latin, James asks whether the Mass forgives mortal sin. Kennedy recalls that Christ's death is the only medicine for sin, that the sacraments of baptism and penance have been instituted for the application of this medicine towards the remission of original and mortal sin, but that the grace received through the Mass disposes man to penance and helps him to resist sin.

In the preface, clearly written after the tract itself, Kennedy again states the fundamental teaching of his *Compendius Tractiue*. In proving that the Mass, far from being idolatry, has been instituted by Christ, he bases himself on Scripture as interpreted by the early Fathers and councils of the church. He has selected eight arguments from his tract and defies the eight Reformers named in the heading of the preface to refute the particular argument which, with a curious kind of irony, he assigns to each as appropriate.

6. *Letter to Archbishop James Beaton of Glasgow*, dated April 7th, 1559, re-
   porting on Kennedy's recent efforts to arrange a disputation on the Mass with John Willock, together with *five letters to Willock*, dated March 26th, 30th (three letters) and 31st.

"These letters formed part of the Collection of Archbishop Beaton, which he bequeathed to the Scottish College at Paris. Copies of them were communicated to Keith, who fortunately published them in the Appendix to his *History*, as it is more than doubtful whether the originals are still preserved." In 1844, the year in which Laing introduced his own edition of the correspondence with the above words,[43] Keith's work was itself reprinted for the Spottiswoode Society.[44] Both editors also printed Willock's six letters to Kennedy and the notarial instrument drawn up at the latter's instigation on April 2nd.

Willock had maintained in his sermons that both Scripture and the early church Fathers prove the idolatrous nature of the Mass. Kennedy replied that, on the contrary, Willock stood condemned as a heretic by the Fathers' inter-

---

[43] *Wodrow Misc.*, p. 263 (the correspondence fills pp. 265–277).
[44] R. Keith, *History of the Affairs of Church and State in Scotland, from the Beginning of the Reformation to the Year 1568*, 3 vols., Edinburgh, 1844, vol. iii, pp. 393 ff.

pretation of Scripture and that he, Kennedy, was prepared to demonstrate it. Willock then desired to be judged by Scripture, but Kennedy maintained that it would be necessary to have a judge to arbitrate between their interpretations. Willock, however, made it clear that he would submit to the judgment of God's Word only, admitting the authority of the Fathers in as far as they agreed with the express words of Scripture.

In spite of this fundamental disagreement they agreed on a debate in the end. In his report to Beaton Kennedy noted that he had forced Willock to come out with his unreasonable demands.

7. *Heir followeth the Coppie of the Ressoning which was betuix the Abbote of Crossraguell and John Knox, in Mayboill concerning the masse, in the yeare of God, a thousand fiue hundreth thre scoir and two yeares.*

This work, which will be discussed in Appendix II, was published by Knox.[45] It is entitled to inclusion in the present list on account of its contents. It contains a lengthy introduction by the editor; Kennedy's first letter, of September 6th, 1562, with Knox's answer to it; Kennedy's second letter interspersed with editorial comments by Knox; the Earl of Cassillis' letter to Knox with the latter's answer to it; Kennedy's third and fourth letters; a note that other letters have been omitted as of less importance; a contract signed by Kennedy and Knox by which they express their agreement on the conditions of the debate; their speeches and arguments during the three days of the disputation with numerous marginal comments by Knox; a brief account by Knox of how the disputation broke up; a somewhat similar account by Kennedy together with a protestation of his willingness to continue in the queen's presence at Edinburgh; the syllogism handed by him to Knox at the end of the third day; and finally Knox's subsequent reply to this syllogism combined with a general conclusion from his point of view.

A black-letter reprint, from an original copy in the Auchinleck library, was edited by Sir Alexander Boswell together with his black-letter edition of the *Oratioune*.[46] The text is also included in the last volume of Laing's *Works of Knox*.[47]

---

[45] Edinburgh, 1563 (*S.T.C.*, no. 15074).
[46] Edinburgh, 1812.
[47] Vol. vi, pp. 169–220.

V. KENNEDY'S LITERARY DEFENCE OF CATHOLICISM

It cannot be reasonably called in question that Quintin Kennedy had strong religious convictions, that he was aware of the involvement of his church in a highly complex social and economic structure, that he was all in favour of reform within the established church of Scotland and that he had a hatred as well as a dread of disorder. The combination of these qualities made it *a priori* impossible for him to range himself on the side of the radical reformers. What Knox considered the just war of the 'Congregation of God' against the 'Congregation of Antichrist' was in Kennedy's eyes a dreadful rebellion against established ecclesiastical and civil authority, in their own spheres each of divine right. Knox's reform, including his claim to the support of a 'godly magistracy', was attempting to revolutionize the existing order to an extent and in a manner which went completely against Kennedy's strongest convictions.

Kennedy's attitude towards the religious situation in his time is perhaps best expressed in the following sentence: "Off all the vices that evir thou sall reid punischeit be God, thou sall fynd twa in speciale, ane is, the dissobedience of the subjectis, the uther, the necligence of thaim quha ar in authoritie, quhilkis dois not thair dett and dewtie to thair subjectis conforme to thair vocatioun." [1] Kennedy's view of the situation was quite simple. The nobility, moved by greed, had their own scions appointed to the rich ecclesiastical benefices. The resulting neglect of clerical duty and laxity of clerical discipline bred contempt of ecclesiastical authority and even heresy, not to mention the social unrest. Given this situation, the remedy, too, was quite simple, at least in principle. The clergy, notably the hierarchy, must mend their ways, the nobility and Crown must see to the appointment of qualified prelates and the faithful in general must join Kennedy in prayer that the nobility and the clergy would live up to their duties,[2] "Thus suld Christin men seik reformatioun, (and that be ane ordour,) and nocht plane distructioun and confusioun, as men dois in thir dayis." [3]

The great guiding principle is that "al authoritie quhilk is of God cumis be ane ordour." [4] The result will only be the more disastrous when self-constituted

---

[1] *Compendius Tractiue, Wodrow Misc.*, p. 142.

[2] See esp. *Compendius Tractiue*, ch. xiv (*Wodrow Misc.*, pp. 150–53) and *Compendious Ressonyng*, p. 171, below.

[3] *Wodrow Misc.*, p. 147.

[4] *Ibid.*, p. 120. It may be remarked here that chapter 7 of the *Compendius Tractiue* (pp. 120 ff.) contains all the elements for Winzet's later challenge to Knox to prove the lawfulness of his vocation *(Second Tractate)*.

58

reformers want to take the matter into their own hands.[5] The protestant ministers, therefore, are 'pestilent preachers' who, though without any authorisation, claim to know better than the whole church of Christ. They not only preach heretical doctrines, but also subvert society. Kennedy is quite prepared to admit the deplorable irresponsibility of the nobility and hierarchy – the two classes to which he himself belonged – but this irresponsibility does not give any person the right to make things worse by rebellion against lawful authority.[6] In fact, although Kennedy expressly admits a causal relation between the abuses in his church and the origin and success of the unorthodox reform, there is not a single sentence in his writings which might be quoted to show that he also admitted the possibility of genuine doubts about the divine mission of the catholic church. Those who were not persuaded by the evidence could only be accused of 'induritnes', 'blindnes', 'furie and wodnes'.

For Kennedy, it was *a priori* impossible that his church could be wrong in matters of faith or that its cause could be lost. Widespread as heresy might be, the gates of hell could not in the end prevail against the church of Christ.[7] This dogmatic attitude was a matter of fundamental principle. His willingness to argue the matter and to pay particular attention to the earliest patristic writings and church councils implied no willingness to subject his convictions to a critical examination. And his eagerness for disputations where the truth was to 'come to the trial' constituted no exception either. His avowed primary aim was to show that there was no reason for any doubts in matters of faith, and to restore tranquillity through submission to the teaching of the church.[8]

This assertiveness went hand in hand with a refusal to take explicit notice of his immediate opponents, to an extent which naturally raises the question in how far he was aware of the progress of the protestant movement in Scotland and in how far his writings were topical.[9] As a member of the Ayrshire nobility

---

[5] "Thair sal mair inconvenientis follow on al thyngis quhilkis ar done by [i.e. without] ane ordour, nor to thole the abuse, to the tyme God provide ane remeid be ane ordour" (*ibid.*, p.147).

[6] *Ibid.*, pp. 134 ff.

[7] See, *e.g.*, *Litil Breif Tracteit*, last paragraph of ch. v (p. 134 below).

[8] Cp. the title page of the *Compendius Tractiue*.

[9] Scotland and the Scottish Reformers are ostensibly ignored in the *Compendius Tractiue* and the *Litil Breif Tracteit*. Knox is mentioned in the *Oratioune* (Laing, *Works*, vi, pp. 158 ff.) and Willock, Winram, Goodman, Douglas, Heriot, Spottiswoode "and all the rest", are added in the margin (*ibid.*, p. 165). To these names is added that of Alexander Gordon, titular archbishop of Athens, in the preface of the *Compendious Ressonyng* (p. 152 below), but the tract itself again ignores them, even when James quotes Knox. In the *Compendius Tractiue* Kennedy refers slightingly to "sum factius men" (*e.g. Wodrow Misc.*, pp. 100 and 118; similarly, *Litil Breif Tracteit*, p. 126, below). At other times he refers, in a ringing sentence which he repeats in the *Oratioune*, to an "arrayit hoiste" of heresies (*Wodrow Misc.*, p. 100, and Laing, *Works*, vi, p. 158). It is extremely difficult to decide, however, when he is thinking of Scotland and when of the general situation in Europe.

he cannot have been ignorant of the 'Common Band' of the previous year when he wrote his *Compendius Tractiue* in 1558. It would have been strange if the Cassillis family had not been approached on the subject. For all that is known his brother may have been one of the signatories.[10] Glencairn definitely signed, and so did Argyle and his heir. Thus, although a treatise on the authority of Scripture and the church would have been topical at any time in the age of the Reformation,[11] it must be presumed that the tract is more than topical in the most general sense. No details are given of the oral discussions between Kennedy and his nephew which had preceded the written tract.[12] But the abbot would obviously be concerned to keep the heir to the Cassillis title from espousing the protestant cause, all the more so since the young man's father had had definite protestant leanings. In a sense, the dedication of the *Compendius Tractiue* was an announcement that the house of Cassillis had been won back to catholicism through the arguments contained in the tract, and it thus symbolized what Kennedy anticipated, viz. that the nobility would discontinue their support of the Reformation. Even if it may not be so in the case of the *Compendius Tractiue*, this symbolic meaning is quite clearly conveyed by the literary form of the *Compendious Ressonyng*. In the course of the debate the theologically less informed brother is gradually instructed and persuaded by Quintin, until in the end he expresses his regret that the entire country has not heard the abbot's arguments.[13] In a similar way Gilbert had asked his uncle to publish the arguments by which he had himself benefited. Some months later Kennedy had sent a summary of his first tract to his relatives and neighbours, i.e. principally the Ayrshire nobility and gentry. And when he wrote the *Oratioune*, he showed that he was still aware of how much the continued succes of the reform movement depended on the continued support of the lords. By that time, of course, he also knew that his own comparatively unimpeded stay in the country depended on his connections with the catholic Earl of Cassillis.

That Kennedy should devote so much attention to the civil power is but natural. It was supposed to maintain the established religion and by 1558 part of the nobility had been transferring its support to the radical Reformers.

---

[10] *i.e.* he may have been included in Knox's *Et cetera* after the first five names (Laing, *Works*, i, p. 274). But Cassillis' earlier protestantism may have been affected by his appointment to high office under Mary of Guise.

[11] Cp. P. Polman, *L'Élément Historique dans la Controverse religieuse du XVIe Siècle*, Gembloux, 1932, esp. pp. 284–309. Kennedy's teaching on authoritative interpretation of Scripture echoes Trent's phrase "...*Ecclesia, cuius est iudicare de vero sensu et interpretatione Scripturarum*" (Mansi, vol. xxxiii, col. 23).

[12] See *Wodrow Misc.*, p. 97.

[13] p. 171, below.

During his visit to Scotland in 1555–56 Knox had preached in and around Ayr. Not long before leaving Scotland he had, at the instigation of the Earls Marischal and Glencairn, written a *Letter to the Queen Regent*, which had been presented to Mary of Guise by Glencairn. Knox had requested freedom of worship for the protestants, since it would probably be beyond her power to forbid catholicism, and in the preface he had appealed to a lawfully assembled general council of christendom in which radical reform might be carried through.[14] After Knox had fled the country he had written his *Appellation to the Nobility of Scotland*. In this appeal from his condemnation by the catholic hierarchy he had not only given a summary of his teaching in Scotland, but he had again expressed himself in favour of a council where the various disputants would humbly submit to what he considered the plain command of God's Word.[15] In general, however, it was an appeal to the nobles to abandon the prelates and promote the Reformation.

The *Compendius Tractiue* gains in significance when seen as a reply, at least in part, against these writings of Knox and against the attitude of persons like Glencairn, who were partly responsible for them. The *Appellation*, to be sure, was not printed till the summer of 1558, but it had been circulating in manuscript. On account of his earlier association with George Wishart, as well as his influential position towards the end of his life, the Earl of Cassillis would have been one of the principal addressees. It is, therefore, not unreasonable to suppose that a copy of the *Appellation* had found its way to the Kennedys. Its contents would in any case be in the air. The connection would all the more explain Kennedy's insistence on the maintenance of law and order and his implicit appeal to the nobility not to respond to persons who were trying to sow sedition.

This is not to deny the general and impersonal character of the *Compendius Tractiue*. But it appears that that was merely a question of method, probably dictated by considerations of prudence.[16] Kennedy's aim was to demonstrate that there was no theological foundation for rebellion against established authority, temporal or ecclesiastical, because God had provided all the necessary means for an orderly settlement of doctrinal disputes and an orderly adjustment of abuses. Writing in the mid-sixteenth century, Kennedy would

---

[14] See Laing, *Works*, i, pp. 251f. The letter is printed in vol. iv.

[15] *Ibid.*, iv, pp. 489, and 518ff.

[16] Open attack would have meant the public exposure of magnates like Glencairn and Argyle – and perhaps his own brother – which would probably have further antagonized them.

find plenty of literature to draw upon.[17] He selected what he wanted, adapted it as he thought fit and for the rest left it to the circumstances of its appearance to make clear what he was referring to. As it happened, the publication of the *Compendius Tractiue* must have occurred about the time when the protestant party protested in parliament that their demands for freedom of worship and official support against catholicism proceeded from religious motives only and that, if violence were to ensue, this would be the responsibility of those who refused to grant their demands.[18] This illustrates how well Kennedy had sensed what had been in the air, for this had been precisely the sort of thing he had written against. In how far he had been just in ignoring the possibility of genuine motives on the part of the protestant lords is a different matter. Modern historians tend largely to agree with him.[19]

One advantage of Kennedy's impersonal treatment of current subjects was that he could implicitly include the Scottish Reformers in his attack without explicitly attributing particular doctrines to them. In as far as the Scottish Reformers were at one with the continental protestants in denying the teaching authority of the catholic church, the implied inference of the *Compendius Tractiue* that the former were included in Kennedy's strictures on the latter was valid. But even in the *Compendius Tractiue* Kennedy tended to over-simplify matters, as when he assumed that all protestants allowed "every man to tak quhat opinion he plesis."[20] The danger of refuting doctrine which was not being taught at all in Scotland was much greater, however, in a tract on the Eucharist, because there were various views among the protestants themselves, all more or less hotly disputed. Briefly, although Calvin 'and all the others' are often mentioned in one breath with Oecolampadius, the *Litil Breif Tracteit* selects the latter for special attack, and Kennedy's defence of the catholic doctrine on Christ's presence in the Eucharist consists largely of the refutation of a single alternative, viz. that the bread and wine are "bot ane syng and takin only" and that Christ's words at the last supper were "spoken be ane figure and simili-

---

[17] There are obvious relations between the *Compendius Tractiue* and Cochleus' *Dialogus de tollenda in fide et religione discordia per concilium generale* (1535), printed in his *In causa religionis miscellaneorum libri tres, in diversos tractatus antea non editos ac diversis temporibus locisque scriptos digesti*, Ingolstadt, 1545. But Kennedy may have known Cochleus' teaching through another author, e.g. Bunderius.

[18] See Laing, *Works*, i, pp. 312–314. The parliament opened on November 29th, so that Kennedy cannot have written his tract after the protestation.

[19] See esp. J. H. Burns, "The Political Ideas of the Scottish Reformation", *The Aberdeen University Review*, xxxvi (1955–56), pp. 251–268. Cp. J. Stevenson, *Calendar of State Papers, Foreign Series, 1560–1561*, p. 166, for rumours about the impending landing of a French army on the Ayrshire coast in the summer of 1560, at which Cassillis was to assist. In his case too, there is no reason to suppose that religious motives were the only ones dictating his actions.

[20] *Wodrow Misc.*, p. 99 (also in the conclusion, p. 174).

tude".[21] Though this simplification might be justified for a presence of Christ outside communion, it did not do justice to the Calvinistic teaching on the reception of Christ and this once again raises the question as to whether Kennedy was sufficiently familiar with protestant teaching in Scotland. The 'six Johns' who composed the *Confessio Scotica* of 1560 may well have wished to repudiate Kennedy's suggestion that they could be classed with Oecolampadius, when they solemnly protested: "whosoever sclandereth us, as that we affirmed or beleved Sacramentis to be onlie naiked and bair signes, do injurie unto us, and speak against a manifest treuth."[22]

It does not appear certain, however, that Kennedy would have written a different tract after 1560. In the *Oratioune* he actually imputed the same general interpretation to his opponents,[23] and Winzet did the same thing, adding that the Reformers were far from clear in defining the presence they held.[24] No doubt this difficulty in pinning down the precise eucharistic views of the Scottish Reformers partly explains why Kennedy grouped them with Oecolampadius. At the same time, it is far from certain that reformed opinion on the subject was uniform, either before or after the *Confessio Scotica*.[25] There is no reason to suppose that the earlier Zwinglian, or moderately-Zwinglian, views had disappeared, if for no other reason then at least because the average Scotsman would find it more difficult than Kennedy and Winzet to distinguish between Wishart and Knox, or, more relevantly, between Willock and Knox. Willock's

---

[21] p. 113, below.

[22] *Cap.* xxi (Laing, *Works*, ii, p. 115). Their positive teaching is added to a similar repudiation on the previous page: "we utterlie dampne the vanitie of those that affirme Sacramentis to be nothing else but naked and bair signes. No, we assuredlie beleve ... that in the Supper, rychtlie used, Christ Iesus is so ioyned with us, that he becumis the verray nurishement and foode of our saullis. ... this union and communioun which we have with the body and bloode of Christ Iesus in the rycht use of the sacraments, is wrocht by operatioun of the Holy Ghost, who by trew faith caryes us above all thingis that ar visible, carnall, and earthlie, and maikis us to feid upoun the body and bloode of Christ Iesus, whiche was ones brokin and schedd for us, whiche now is in the heavin, and appeareth in the presence of his Father for us."

[23] Laing, *Works*, vi, pp. 163f.

[24] *The Buke of Four Scoir Thre Questions*, qu. 20 (S.T.S. edition, vol. i, p. 86; cp. qu. 13, *ibid.*, p. 81).

[25] It may be pointed out here that, quite unlike the words of the council of Trent in 1551 (Mansi, xxxiii, col. 80f.: ... synodus, in Spiritu Sancto legitime congregata ... interdicit ne posthac de sanctissima Eucharistia aliter credere, docere aut praedicare audeant, quam ut est hoc praesenti decreto explicatum atque definitum."), the preface to the *Confessio Scotica* rather invites criticism, so that it may be refuted or used for correction of the text (Laing, *Works*, ii, p. 96).

"sympathies were more with Zurich than Geneva," [26] and as early as March 1559 (*i.e.* more than a year before archbishop Beaton left Glasgow and Willock became superintendent of the West), he was said in Ayrshire to have been "chosin Primat of thair religioun in this realme." [27] The prominent position of Willock in S.W. Scotland may well go far to explain Kennedy's interpretation of Protestant eucharistic teaching.

But there may have been other reasons. In the *Compendius Tractiue* Kennedy speaks of "Oecolampadius quhais opinioun men in thir dayis praysis sua hichlie." [28] Unfortunately, he does not say by whom. But if it does not mean more, it means at least that Oecolampadius's classic work on the Eucharist was being quoted. [29] And Kennedy would know that there had been quite an anti-Oecolampadian tradition in English catholic apologetics. As early as 1527 John Fisher had written an extensive reply, [30] to which Kennedy refers in a manner which presupposes that he knew it. [31] After the death of Henry VIII, Cranmer had invited a number of continental Reformers to England. One of them, Peter Martyr Vermigli, had lectured on the Eucharist at the university of Oxford. He had distinguished between the catholic, Lutheran and Swiss interpretations and had unambiguously declared himself in favour of the Swiss teaching. [32] That same year Bullinger, Calvin and Farel had signed the *Consensus Tigurinus*, [33] which appears to have satisfied the English reformers more and more with the years. [34] Cranmer's own views seem to have been uncertain at this period. [35] But when he had written his *Defence of the True and Catholic Doctrine of the Sacrament of the Body and Blood of our Saviour Christ*, 1550, [36] he had to defend himself against accusations of Zwinglianism. Both Richard Smith and Gardiner

---

[26] J. Durkan, "The Cultural Background in Sixteenth-Century Scotland," in *Essays*, p. 313.

[27] Kennedy's letter to Beaton, *Wodrow Misc.*, p. 267. Cp. Keith, *o.c.*, vol. iii, p. 10.

[28] *Wodrow Misc.*, p. 159. On the early presence (1540) in Scotland of at least one work by Oecolampadius, see D. Calderwood, *The History of the Kirk of Scotland*, Wodrow Society edition (8 vols., 1842–49), vol. i, p. 116.

[29] *De genuina verborum Domini 'Hoc est corpus meum' iuxta vetustissimos auctores expositione liber*, Basle, 1525.

[30] *De veritate corporis et sanguinis Christi in Eucharistia adversus Joannem Oecolampadium.* Cologne, 1527.

[31] *Compendius Tractiue, Wodrow Misc.*, p. 168.

[32] See the prefatory chapter of *De sacramento Eucharistiae in celeberrima Angliae schola Oxoniensi habita tractatio* (1549), Zurich, 1552.

[33] See B. J. Kidd, *Documents Illustrative of the Continental Reformation*, Oxford, 1911, pp. 652 ff.

[34] See C. W. Dugmore, *The Mass and the English Reformers*, London, 1958, pp. 141–175.

[35] See F. Clark, *Eucharistic Sacrifice and the Reformation*, London, 1960, pp. 159–168, and literature quoted.

[36] Edited by C. H. Wright, London, 1907.

made extensive use of Fisher's work in their replies[37] to Cranmer. Tunstal composed a treatise against the *Tigurini* and Oecolampadius without ever mentioning England or Cranmer,[38] and Gardiner did exactly the same in his further reply to Cranmer.[39]

This is precisely what Kennedy does in his *Litil Breif Tracteit*. It will be shown afterwards that he mainly used Smith's *Confutation*, and that he probably had Tunstal's work. Whether he took his method from Tunstal or Gardiner must remain an open question as long as it cannot be proved that he had Gardiner's *Confutatio*. In any case, he knew that both Knox and Willock had been in England at the time of this controversy, and as official preachers of the Edwardian church.[40] Unfortunately Willock has left no writings, so that it cannot be ascertained to what degree Kennedy had him particularly in mind, to what degree he simplified the variety of eucharistic views among the protestants of Scotland, and to what degree he slavishly followed his English models. When he does mention the protestant preachers, he does not refer to different views among them. Like the *Compendius Tractiue* and the *Compendious Ressonyng*, the *Litil Breif Tracteit* appears primarily to be an exposition of traditional doctrine and only secondarily a refutation of other views.

If it cannot be doubted that Kennedy's eucharistic writings presuppose the English controversy on the subject, it is not certain that it determined his outlook. It would appear that a more fundamental influence had been exercised by John Major, the provost of St. Salvator's College when Kennedy was a student at St. Andrews. For Major, as for Kennedy, the Reformers' opinions on the Eucharist were the revival of the condemned heresies of Berengarius and Wycliff; transubstantiation was the doctrine of Scripture and the church Fathers, even though the term might be of more recent origin; the practice of bestowing

---

[37] Richard Smith, *A Confutation of a certen booke, called a defence of the true and Catholike doctrine of the sacrament ... sette fourth of late in the name of Thomas Archebysshoppe of Canterburye*, 1550; Stephen Gardiner, *An Explication and Assertion of the true Catholic Faith touching the Blessed Sacrament of the Altar, with confutation of a Book written against the same* (1550), printed in *Writings and Disputations of Thomas Cranmer ... Relative to the Sacrament of the Lord's Supper*, edited for the Parker Society by the Rev. J. E. Cox, Cambridge, 1844 (viz. as incorporated in *An Answer by the Reverend Father in God Thomas Archbyshop of Canterbury ... Vnto a crafty and sophisticall cauillation deuished by Stephen Gardiner ... Wherin is also, as occasion serueth, answered such places of the booke of D. Rich. Smyth, as may seeme any thyng worthy the answeryng*, originally published at London, 1551).

[38] *De ueritate Corporis et Sangvinis Domini nostri Iesu Christi in Eucharistia*, written 1551, printed at Paris, 1554 (a second edition, with index, appeared that same year).

[39] *Confutatio cavillationum quibus sacrosanctum Eucharistiae sacramentum ab impiis Capharnaitis impeti solet*, Paris, 1551.

[40] c. 1566 Willock left Scotland to accept a living in the Church of England, only to return a few times to officiate as Moderator of the Scottish General Assembly (see Kirkwood Hewat, *Makers of the Scottish Church at the Reformation*, Edinburgh, 1920, p. 135).

ecclesiastical benefices on unworthy candidates was highly objectionable; reform of the church was a matter of deplorable necessity, but deviation from its doctrine constituted pestilent heresy.[41] And Kennedy, like Major, appears to have been a conciliarist of the moderate type.[42] He may mention early authorities who "succedit in the place of Peter",[43] but he attributes decisive authority to duly constituted general councils without ever referring to contemporary popes or their personal prerogatives. He insists, it is true, that they must be 'dewlie conuenit' – a phrase which he never explains – but the obvious meaning of the *Compendious Tractiue* is that they do not derive their authority from the Roman pontiff but from the fact that they represent the universal church.[44]

Major was a staunch scholastic thinker, not uninfluenced by humanism but in his later years definitely anti-humanist in sympathy.[45] The same might be said of Kennedy. He must have known Buchanan, the tutor of his brother, and he speaks of Erasmus as "the excellent clerk".[46] Moreover, it has been said that the ringing phrases of his *Oratioune* "owe a large debt to the humanistic concern with precision of language."[47] But Kennedy was no humanist himself. It exemplifies his attitude that in the opening sentence of the *Compendious Ressonyng* he allows James to monopolize 'the new learning' and that he proceeds to prove that the traditional learning is sounder after all. Similarly, in the *Compendius Tractiue* he argues that the reading of Scripture is "commendabyll and godlie" if the reader seeks spiritual guidance. But he does not leave the topic until he has implored "every privat man" to "flee curiositie".[48]

In 1559 Kennedy wrote somewhat triumphantly to Beaton that he had forced Willock to the confession that he would accept no patristic testimonies which did

---

[41] A. J. G. Mackay, *Memoir of John Major of Haddington ... 1469/70–1550*. A Study in Scottish History and Education, Edinburgh, 1892, pp. 65 f.

[42] Cp. J. H. Burns, "The Conciliarist Tradition in Scotland." *The Scottish Historical Review*, vol. xlii (1963), pp. 100 f.

[43] *Compendious Ressonyng*, p. 175, below.

[44] It may be noted here that in 1561 archbishop Guerrero of Granada requested the council of Trent "in titulo addi synodus universalem ecclesiam representans, etsi fateatur Pontificem esse caput concilii et etiam supra concilium esse," and that the request was not granted (*Concilium Tridentinum. Diariorum, actorum, epistolarum, tractatuum nova collectio*, Görres Society, Freiburg, 1901 ff., vol. viii, p. 330; cp. vol. ix, pp. 1124 ff.).

[45] J. Durkan, "The Beginnings of Humanism in Scotland," *The Innes Review*, vol. iv (1953), p. 7.

[46] *Compendius Tractiue*, *Wodrow Misc.*, p. 162; *Compendious Ressonyng*, p. 162, below.

[47] J. Durkan, *l.c.*, p. 17.

[48] *Wodrow Misc.*, p. 133. Kennedy goes on to define: "I call curiositie to ony privat man on lyfe, to seik ane uther understanding of thir secretis [*i.e.* the sacraments, predestination, free will and justification] nor the generale Counsalis hes all reddy techeit ws, quha in declaratioun of materis doutsum, necessare, or expedient to be knawin for all Christin mannis salvatioun, assuritlie hes nevir errit" (*ibid*).

not agree with the plain word of Scripture.[49] One feels, however, that Kennedy's appeal to Erasmus savoured of a similar opportunism. To a certain extent he defended the principle of the development of authentic christian doctrine and worship, but in his case that was an *a priori* theological assumption rather than anything else. If his church taught transubstantiation, there could not be any contradiction or conflict between transubstantiation on the one hand and the words of Scripture or the teaching of the early Fathers and councils on the other.[50] He cannot be said to have applied himself to a serious study of early christianity if George Hay could ridicule his ignorance of Greek in attributing the term *Missa* to Ignatius of Antioch and *theothitos* to the council of Nicea.[51] Similarly, he does not show any awareness that there was a controversy going on concerning the authenticity of the testimonies of Denis the Areopagite or those in the *Decretum Gratiani*.[52] It made him a vulnerable opponent of George Hay, who sneeringly remarked that the *Appendex* of the *Compendious Ressonyng* was not worthy of an answer.[53]

Fundamentally, Kennedy's weakness as a controversialist was his failure to realize that he argued in the first place from the certainty of his own faith. He may instinctively have felt – though not nearly as much as Winzet – that the best method was to put the onus of persuasive proof on one's opponents. But Kennedy went on to employ his exposition of the catholic faith as proofs in a controversy. One feels that his tracts would confirm those who were already of his opinion, but his opponents would find many weak points in his argumentation. The first page of the *Litil Breif Tracteit*, for example, can be reduced to the following reasoning: in view of the teaching of the church there can be no doubt about the meaning of Scripture, but since certain persons refuse to accept it, I shall prove the church to be right; the interpretation of the church is the obvious meaning of Scripture; the unanimous teaching of the church Fathers and councils confirms that it is in fact the correct interpretation. Clearly, this

---

[49] *Wodrow Misc.*, p. 266.

[50] For Kennedy, transubstantiation was a convenient and suitable term for the miraculous change of the bread and wine, just as it had been for the council of Trent in 1551 (Mansi, vol. xxxiii, col. 80–84). It was in this sense that he attributed it to the Fathers, not in its full scholastic explanation. See pp. 134 and 196, below.

[51] *Confutation*, pp. 10v f. (referring to *Compendious Ressonyng*, p. 155, below). With the orthographic confusion of *c* and *t*, Hay might have read *theothicos* instead of *theothitos*. But the forms *theothycus* and *theoticos* in the *Litil Breif Tracteit*, and again *theoticos* in the *Compendious Ressonyng* do not suggest that Kennedy's originals had *theotokos*. As a former fellow-student Hay would probably know that Kennedy's education had not included Greek.

[52] On this matter, see P. Polman, *o.c.*, pp. 62f. and *passim*, and the same author's "Religieuze Polemiek en Historische Kritiek in de XVIe Eeuw," *Studia Catholica*, x (1933–34), pp. 421ff. Cp. Fisher, *De Veritate*, lib. iv, cap. xxviii and lib. v, cap. xxiii.

[53] *Confutation*, p. 95r.

kind of logic was hardly calculated to persuade persons like Willock and Knox, whose pre-conceived convictions were equally as strong as Kennedy's.[54]

Unlike his sixteenth-century sources, Kennedy does not quote the *Decretum de Consecratione*, but it need not be doubted that he used it. He preferred to give marginal references to the *Histories* of Eusebius, Cassiodorus and, on one occasion, Platina,[55] and he frequently cites the Fathers. Hay insinuated that this was merely a pseudo-critical attitude, because Kennedy copied his quotations from "scabbed treaties of Eccius, Cochleus, Hosius Stanislaus youre new start vp Campion, and of such of your faction."[56] And it cannot be denied that the patristic texts in Kennedy's writings can be found in the controversial manuals of his time. On the other hand, there is sufficient evidence that Kennedy's acquaintance with the Fathers went beyond such selective reading, even though the cart-load of patristic tomes he is supposed to have brought to Ayr for his disputation with Willock[57] must be an exaggeration. Kennedy reported to Beaton that Willock had appealed to the teaching of Irenaeus, Chrysostom, Hilary, Origen and Tertullian. He had at once "persavit the craft of the knaif, quha belevand to haif gottin na recountar, allegeit sic doctoris, belevand thair workis had nocht bene in this cuntre, quhairthrow he mycht apply thame as he pleasit." As it was, however, Kennedy "had all the doctoris he alledgit, and diverse uthers, quha treittis *quod coena* is *sacrificium*."[58] Who these 'uthers' were, is suggested by one of his letters to Willock, in which he proposed that they would test their own teaching by that of Cyprian, Gregory of Nazianzen, Jerome, Ambrose, Augustine, Theophilact, John Damascene and those already

---

[54] Cp. Appendix II, below. – Dr. J. Durkan drew my attention to the following New Testament commentary in King's College Library, Aberdeen, formerly on Kennedy's shelves: *Clarissima et facillima in quatuor sacra Iesu Christi Evangelia, necnon in Actus Apostolicos scholia, ex praecipuis tam Graecorum quam Latinorum sententiis selecta, Ioannis Benedicti theologi cura emendata. Authore Ioanne Gagneio Parisino Theologo Christianissimi Francorum Regis Francisci Ecclesiaste, ac primo eleemosynario*, Paris, 1552. It has *M Q K* gold-tooled on both covers. It has numerous references to the *Decretum de Consecratione* – rather than to particular places in the Fathers – but it would obviously constitute a useful manual for an apologist.

[55] Battista Platina, *Opus de vitis et gestis summorum pontificum*, Venice, 1479 (several times reprinted before Kennedy's time). – It may be added here that Kennedy also possessed Polydore Virgil's *Historia Anglica* (Basle, 1534; reprinted 1546 & 1555). I am indebted to Dr. J. Durkan for the following reference in the *Supplement to a Catalogue of Books Now on Sale, at the Prices Affixed, by Wm. & D. Laing, 49 South Bridge Street, Edinburgh*, January 1824, p. 9, item 8794: "Polydori Vergilii Historia Anglica Historia [*sic*.], with M.S. notes, Basil. 1546. ... This volume is supposed to have belonged to Quintin Kennedy, Abbot of Crosraguel, at the time of the Reformation. It has the initials M.Q.K. stamped on the boards."

[56] *Confutation*, p. 18v.

[57] J. Scott, *A History of the Protestant Reformers in Scotland*, Edinburgh, 1817, p. 62.

[58] *Wodrow Misc.*, p. 265.

mentioned.[59] Similarly, in one of his letters to Knox previous to the Maybole disputation, Kennedy stipulated a limited audience to guarantee a scholarly conference: "gif we cum to the iust tryall of the treuth, thair man be conferenee of mony buikes, quhilk can not be done in publick audience."[60]

This is not the language of a man who merely depended upon a number of patristic anthologies. George Hay's designation of Kennedy as a "wyde blowing Goliath"[61] rather suggests a person who would try to impress opponent and audience with heavy volumes;[62] it would certainly be in keeping with his rhetorical bent. That, on the other hand, Kennedy should have made use of the works of contemporary authors, is but natural and plausible. In chapter XV of the *Compendius Tractiue* he mentions two of those works. John Fabri's *Malleus in Haeresim Lutheranam*[63] is a rather surprising title in a book which itself ignores the papacy. Actually, Kennedy only refers to it for proof that Luther had contradicted himself. For the same purpose he refers to the *Detectio Nugarum Lutheri* of the Dominican Bunderius,[64] a more recent work which he would not have mentioned if he had not personally been acquainted with it. It may not be irrelevant to add that Andrew Leich, prior of the Dominicans at Ayr, possessed another work by Bunderius.[65] Perhaps Kennedy and Leich exchanged books. For a correct treatment of the Fathers' teaching on the Eucharist, he proposes the reading of Fisher's *De Veritate*.[66] This was a particularly useful book in that it not only defended the catholic doctrine, but also gave and refuted Oecolampadius' objections to it. Accordingly, when Kennedy decided to write a tract against Oecolampadius, he freely drew upon Fisher, as the notes to the text will show. And "the intriguing feature" of Kennedy's *Compendious Ressonyng*, that it preceded by a year the council of Trent's definitions on the sacrificial nature of the Mass,[67] becomes less intriguing when

---

[59] *Ibid.*, p. 271.

[60] Laing, *Works*, vi, p. 180.

[61] *Confutation*, p. 3v.

[62] Nothing is known about the Crossraguel library. Richard Augustine Hay, quoting Dempster, mentions one Micheas, "qui ex sacerdote saeculari monachus in Caenobio Crucis Regalis factus, erudita multa posteris mandavit, vixit 1530," and John Mure, Kennedy's subprior, "vir doctissimus, qui multa scripsit et obijt 1585" (Scotia Sacra, MSS 1700, p. 278). Contemporary records appear to be silent about their literary work.

[63] Cologne, 1524; edited in *Corpus Catholicorum* by A. Naegele, 2 vols., Munster, 1941 & 1952.

[64] *Detectio Nugarum Lutheri, cum declaratione veritatis catholicae et confutatione dogmatum Lutheranorum*, Louvain, 1551. On Bunderius, see J. Quetif and J. Echard, *Scriptores Ordinis Praedicatorum Recensiti, Notisque Historicis et Criticis Illustrati*, vol. ii, Paris, 1721, pp. 160f.

[65] See J. Durkan & A. Ross, *Early Scottish Libraries*, Glasgow, 1961, p. 180. Leich was the person who was unable to silence Willock in 1559 and then brought Kennedy to Ayr.

[66] *Compendius Tractiue, Wodrow Misc.*, p. 168.

[67] M. Taylor, "The Conflicting Doctrines of the Scottish Reformation," in *Essays*, p. 265.

Kennedy's tract is compared with Fisher's.[68] It would have been rather strange if Kennedy had departed from Fisher's teaching.

According to George Hay Kennedy's argument from the *Commonitorium* of Vincent of Lerins "is drawn out of Tunstallus, Bishop of Durame, howsoeuer this glorious diuine decketh it vp in an other and new apperell."[69] Hay may have had information that Kennedy had Tunstal's *De ueritate Corporis et Sangvinis Domini nostri Iesu Christi in Eucharistia.* Kennedy's mention of the 'Vincentian canon' certainly does not presuppose it.[70] From 1528 onwards, when it appeared in Sichardus'*Antidotum*,[71] the *Commonitorium* had numerous editions and there is no reason apparent why Kennedy should know it from the brief quotation in Tunstal's work. This is not to deny, however, that Kennedy had it. Although so much of the argument had become common property by 1560, the striking similarity of the following appears to imply direct indebtedness:

"Nonnulli uolunt obiicientes dicere, quod signum, siue munomentum alicuius rei, et res ipsa, non possunt esse eadem, sed semper sunt diuersa, sicut corona hederae, pendens apud ostium tabernae, indicans uinum uenale, et uinum in taberna, diuersa sunt. ... Panis in signum in fenestra pistoris prostans, et signum est ibi haberi panum copiam, et ipse panis prostans esui est aptus. ... Per haec facile quiuis intelligere potest, in sancto Eucharistiae sacramento simul et signum, uel sacramentum esse posse, et naturale Christi corpus iam spirituale."

In the first lines of the following quotation Kennedy refers to the eucharistic doctrine of the Scottish protestants:

"Treulie the breid and wyne, beande ministrat and ressauit efter this maner ... ma weil be callit and thocht ane simple signe in deid, or ellis na thing bot as vther commone breid and wyne, quharby ane Cristiane manne is alsemekill refreschit in his saull as ane thristie manne in his body, goande by ane taverne behalding the sying of the samyne. ... breid in ane baxtaris buyth wyndo signifys breid to be saulde, and is brede the self quharwith menne ar corporalie refreschit: sua the blissit sacrament of the altar is nocht onelie ane

---

[68] Esp. book v, from cap. vii onwards. Of course, Fisher never considered his teaching novel: "Quoniam illud altaris sacrificium nobis Christi mortem repraesentat, et est ipsius mortis sacramentum, ideo colligit Augustinus hoc ipsum ... recte a nobis immolationem vocari posse" (cap. xxiv). On pre-Reformation Mass theology, see F. Clark, *o.c.*, pp. 73–99.

[69] *Confutation*, p. 89r. The reference is to *Compendious Ressonyng*, pp. 172f. below.

[70] Cp. the passage in the *Compendious Ressonyng* with Tunstal, *o.c.*, 2nd edition, Paris, 1554, pp. 120f.

[71] *Antidotum contra diversa omnium fere seculorum haereses seu sanctorum Patrum tractatus varii polemici in unum congesti*, Basle, 1528. – A Scots translation by Ninian Winzet was published at Antwerp in 1563: *Vincentivs Lirinensis of the Natioun of Gallis, for the antiquitie and veritie of the catholik fayth, aganis þe prophane nouationis of al haereseis &c.*

signe of the Lordis body, bot als the Lordis body is realie contenit therein."[72] It shows that Kennedy was able to convert an analogy into a vivid image.

The principal source for Kennedy's eucharistic tracts was, however, the *Confutation* of the Oxford theologian and controversialist Richard Smith, who had fled to Scotland under Edward VI and had been associated with the council of 1552 and the compilation of *Hamilton's Catechism.*[73] Unfortunately it cannot be ascertained to what extent his writings circulated in Scotland,[74] so that it cannot be established in how far Kennedy was continuing a kind of tradition when he wrote his eucharistic tracts. But at least there cannot be any doubt about the similarity and the indebtedness. At the end of his prefatory apology to the readers of his *Confutation* Smith had written: "*Multo melius est vera rustice, quam falsa diserte proferre. Hieronymus in expositione primae visionis Esaiae.*"[75] Greenlaw wrote the same words on the title page of his copy of Kennedy's *Compendius Tractiue*, and he may well have wished to indicate the connection between the two authors.

Kennedy's indebtedness to Smith's *Confutation* is especially clear in the patristic texts, because there Kennedy simply copies the translations, with minor adaptations to the northern dialect and at times minor clarifications in the translation. One example, which is of particular interest, may here be given by way of illustration.

"Annunciantes enim secundum carnem mortem unigeniti filii Dei, id est Iesu Christi, et resurrectionem eius, et in coelos ascensionem pariter confitentes, incruentam celebramus in ecclesiis sacrificii servitutem. Sic etiam ad mysticas benedictiones accedimus, et sanctificamur participes sancti corporis et

---

[72] Tunstal, *o.c.*, pp. 15v f. and *Oratioune*, Laing, *Works*, vi, p. 164.

[73] See J. Durkan, "The Cultural Background in Sixteenth-Century Scotland," in *Essays*, pp. 301 f. and 326 ff. – Dr. Durkan first suggested to me that there might be literary relations between Smith and Kennedy.

[74] John Lesley is known to have possessed one of his books (J. Durkan & A. Ross, *o.c.*, p. 170) and Greenlaw was clearly acquainted with them, for in his copy of the *Compendius Tractiue* he wrote the following inventory of works by Smith (topmost line cut away by a subsequent binder):
"...
fwrtht in Inglyss
ane confutatione of a certane bowk callid a defence of the trewe and catholike doctryne of the sacrament set fwrtht in nayme of thomas archebyschope of canterbury
Item ane bowk of traditiones
Item the bowklair of faytht
Item the bowk of vnvryttin weriteis
Item contrair petir martir, in sacramento altaris, ane vder bowk."
It seems certain that Greenlaw used *A bryefe treatyse of the sygne of the Crosse, and of the Crucifyxe*, contained in the first part of *A bouclier of the catholike fayth of Christes church*, for his version of the *Appendex* of the *Compendious Ressonyng*; see p. 213, below.

[75] fol. 1v.

pretiosi sanguinis Christi omnium nostrum redemptoris effecti, non ut communem carnem percipientes (quod absit), nec ut viri sanctificati, et verbo coniuncti secundum dignitatis unitatem, aut sicut divinam possidentis habitationem, sed vere vivificatricem, et ipsius verbi propriam factam."[76]

"We do offre an vnbloudie wourshipinge of a sacrifice, and so we do also come vnto the holie sacrament, and are made holie, beinge partakers of the holie bodie, and precious bloud of Christ, which was made the redeamer of vs al, not receauinge it as common flesh (God forbid that), nor as the fleash of a man made holie, and ioyned vnto the sonne of God, by an vnite of worthynes, or els as beinge a mansion of God, but as that which verilie geueth lyfe (to mans soul), and was made propre vnto Goddes owne sonne hym selfe."[77]

"We do offer ane vnbludy sacrifice. Alsua we cum onto þe halie sacrament, and are maid halie beand part takaris of þe halie body and blude of Iesus Christ, quhilk was maid redemar of vs all: nocht ressaiffand It as commwne flesche (God forbid þat), nor as þe flesche of ane man maid halie and Iwnit onto þe Sone of God be ane vnite of worthines or ellis as being ane mansioun of God, bot as þat quhilk veralie geifis lyf onto mennis saull and was maid propir onto Goddis awin Sone him self."[78]

If Kennedy did not know Greek, he would at least have had easy access to the Latin translation of the *Decretum de Consecratione*, either in that work itself or in Fisher's *De Veritate*.[79] But he simply copies Smith's English version, further simplifying the truncated text by leaving out Smith's rendering of *servitutem* and adopting Smith's bracketed explanation of *vivificatricem* as part of the original text.[80] The quotation is enlightening in various respects. For one thing, it shows that Kennedy can hardly have read Cranmer's reply to Smith's *Confutation*.[81] It illustrates that the rather frequent quotations in his writings do not in themselves prove him to have been a patristic scholar. It also reveals a basic weakness in his eucharistic theology. In the preceding exposition he

---

[76] Cyril of Alexandria's letter to Nestorius. Latin text taken from Gratian's *Decretum de Consecratione*, Migne, *PL*, vol. clxxxvii, col. 1773 (cp. Mansi, vol. iv, cols. 1090 and 1075f.).

[77] Smith, *Confutation*, p. 2r f.

[78] *Compendious Ressonyng*, p. 169, below.

[79] Fisher deals with it extensively (*lib*. iv, *cap*. xxix), citing *De Consecratione*.

[80] In Hay's *Confutation* (pp. 85r f.) the brackets are likewise absent.

[81] "Now in the beginning of the very preface itself, when this great doctor should recite the words of Ephesine council, he translateth them so unlearnedly, that if a young boy, that had gone to the grammar school but three years, had done no better, he should scant have escaped some schoolmaster's hands with six jerks. And beside that, he doth it so craftily to serve his purpose, the he cannot be excused of wilful depravation of the words." (*The Answer ... against the false calumniations of Doctor Richard Smith*, appended to *An Answer ... vnto ... Stephen Gardiner*, in *Writings and Disputations of Thomas Cranmer ... Relative to the Sacrament of the Lord's Supper*, Parker Society, Cambridge, 1844, p. 369.)

dwells on the Mass as the representation of Christ's death. In his commentary on the text he says that it proves at once the sacrificial nature of the Mass and the real presence of Christ, but he fails to connect these two elements of the Eucharist. In the *Litil Breif Tracteit* he insists on the identity of the Christ who is in heaven and the Christ who is in the Eucharist. In the *Compendious Ressonyng*, on the other hand, he concentrates on the relation between the Mass and the historical sacrifice of Christ. There is a gap between the two tracts which he fails to bridge. Whether he does not give too much abstract theology already is a different matter, which will be considered in the section on his style. The point here is that on the one hand he does not stop at the mere affirmation of either Christ's presence or the sacrificial nature of the Mass, whilst on the other he does not give the attentive reader a satisfactory synthesis of his principal affirmations. A fuller rendering of Cyril's text and Fisher's commentary would have given him the opportunity.

Of course, Kennedy found himself in a difficult situation. He wrote for "sick as ar of mair sobir knawlege and understanding nor we ar."[82] It has already been shown that he had especially the nobility and gentry in mind. They had had at least some education and they were the persons who had the money to buy books. They thus had at least an elementary acquaintance with the arguments of both sides, and Kennedy shouldered the task of providing them with further positive exposition. This implied at the same time criticism of his opponents; but his principal aim was clearly to build up what could still be built up, anticipating that a better insight into catholic doctrine would secure submission to the church. As it was, however, catholic theology was largely a matter of scholastic reasoning in a highly technical Latin. No doubt, there was also the popular pulpit tradition.[83] But Kennedy had to go beyond that. He also enlivened his tracts, though not often enough, with passages which clearly belonged to the tradition of colloquial Scots.[84] Again, his appeal to order and common sense contains a strong element of social and political philosophy, a subject in which the Scots language had already been explored by John Ireland.[85] Popular theology as such was nothing new. But for Kennedy there was clearly a difference between his general mental background and the specific task with which he saw himself confronted. Called upon to answer the particular

---

[82] *Compendius Tractiue, Wodrow Misc.*, p. 101.

[83] See, *e.g.*, the homiletic language of *Litil Breif Tracteit*, ch. II, pp. 117f. below.

[84] *e.g. Compendious Ressonyng*, pp. 171, below.

[85] The first two books of *The Meroure of Wyssdome* (1490) have been edited for the S.T.S. by C. Macpherson, Edinburgh, 1926. On Ireland, see J. H. Burns, "John Ireland and *The Meroure of Wyssdome*," *The Innes Review*, vi (1955), pp. 77ff. and Brother Bonaventure, "The Popular Theology of John Ireland," *The Innes Review*, xiii (1962), pp. 130ff.

challenge of the moment he said: "Trewlie, gude Redare, ... it is verray difficile to expresse and declair the samyn planelie and ordourlie, (as the mater requiris, and is of worthynes,) specialie in our language, and at the leist, to ane man of my sobir understanding."[86] There was a gap, which he found difficult to bridge, between the technicalities of his theology and its popular exposition.

Perhaps that is the reason why he drew so much upon contemporary English authors who had written polemical treatises before him. It certainly cannot be said that Kennedy's tracts are original. He read a number of contemporary works to qualify himself for his task, but he lacked the familiarity with simple expository Scots of a schoolmaster like Winzet. On the other hand, the statement that he was "distinguished as a historian, a theologian and a scholar,"[87] does not find sufficient corroboration in his writings.

---

[86] *Compendius Tractiue, Wodrow Society*, pp. 116f.
[87] *Crossraguel Charters*, i, p. xl.

VI. KENNEDY'S LANGUAGE

Kennedy wrote in what is known as Middle Scots, the literary language of his country. In origin this was the dialect of the Anglian occupants of Northumbria, with a strong admixture of Scand. from the Viking settlers. As the centuries had passed, this Germanic tongue had gradually extended its boundaries into the Lowlands and farther northwards along the eastern coast of Scotland. The Gaelic speech of Carrick and Galloway[1] had resisted the advance of 'Inglis'[2] until the end of the fifteenth century and was not finally superseded until about a century later.[3] By that time, however, the former Anglian dialect had behind it a long period of development, first as part of what is known as Northern English and afterwards, as England developed its own literary language, as the means of literary expression in an independent kingdom. To be sure, it has been rightly said that "from a very early period Scotsmen, in calling their language 'Inglis', had recognised that they spoke what was substantially the same language as that of the Southern kingdom."[4] On the other hand, the differences were far from inconsiderable, even though they were undoubtedly exaggerated by Winzet when, in 1563, he wrote to Knox that he was not acquainted with the latter's 'Southeroun'.[5]

These differences were not restricted to the phonemes and spelling conventions. While generally coinciding with that of ME, MSc vocabulary developed new meanings or retained older words which ceased to be used in the Southern language. Other words differed in frequency of use, and MSc had quite a number of borrowings which did not exist, or not in the same form, in contemporary English. In addition, differences in accidence and syntax, though less numerous, formed distinctive features of the Scots language.

When speaking of literary MSc, it must of course be borne in mind that

---

[1] Galloway was not finally annexed to the Scottish throne till 1455.

[2] The normal designation of the Germanic speech, to distinguish it from the Gaelic 'Scottis' or 'Ersch'. The southern variety of English was called 'Sudroun' or 'Southroun'. The first writer known to have used 'Scottis' for the Lowland tongue and 'Inglis' for 'Sudroun' was Gavin Douglas, in the prologue to the first book of his *Eneid* (S.T.S. edition by D. F. C. Coldwell, vol. ii, 1957, p. 6).

[3] See the historical introduction in J. A. H. Murray's *The Dialect of the Southern Counties of Scotland*, London, 1873, pp. 1–93.

[4] M. A. Bald, "Contemporary References to the Scottish Speech of the Sixteenth Century," *Scottish Historical Review*, vol. xxxv, p. 163.

[5] *Certain Tractates*, &c., S.T.S. edition by J. King Hewison, vol. i, p. 138.

'Older Scots'[6] comprised various spoken dialects and that the literary language might in various degrees approach dialectal speech. In the case of Kennedy's tracts, however, it would be extremely precarious to draw conclusions about peculiarly Carrick elements.[7] From their nature they contain a very large percentage of Christian terms, which were either in general use or adapted from the language of theology according to the normal rules of borrowing. Moreover, Kennedy's rhetorical style is far from colloquial and, last but not least, it cannot be ascertained to what extent scribes may have tampered with the original spelling. And in any case, the texts are in the first place samples of literary MSc, and the primary aim of the following pages will be to describe them as such.

A. Phonology and Spelling[8]

1. Unaccented Syllables

From OE times onwards there had been a general weakening and partial disappearance of the sounds, especially in the endings. Loan-words were subject to the same tendency, after being adjusted to the native system of accentuation.

Final unstressed -e was a mere spelling convention in MSc or a device to indicate the long quantity of a preceding vowel.

Meaningless in *according(e)*, *adorit(e)*, *among(e)*, *ascendit(e)*, *befoir(e)*, *bluid(e)*, *becaus(e)*, &c.; with an orthographic function in *adore*, *affore*, *appreue*, *blude*, *declare*, *dispare*, &c.

---

[6] *A Dictionary of the Older Scottish Tongue* (edited by W.A. Craigie and, since fasc. xvii, A. J. Aitken, 1937–) registers the Scots vocabulary up to 1700.

[7] Cp. *The Flyting of Dunbar and Kennedie*, lines 110–112:
"I tak on me ane pair of Lowthiane hippis
Sall fairar Inglis mak, and mair parfyte,
Than thow can blabbar with thy Carrik lippis."
(p. 8 in W. M. Mackenzie's edition of *The Poems of William Dunbar*, London, 1932).

[8] The summary analysis of the following pages is meant as an introductory description of Kennedy's prose. The phonological observations apply principally to the sound system of the Central Scots area, which formed the basis of literary MSc. The symbols enclosed in slanting lines represent the main phonemes and do not take account of possible allophones. The division and history of the phonemes rest mainly on the following authorities: J. A. H. Murray, *o.c.*; K. Lenz, *Zur Lautlehre der französischen Elemente in den schottischen Dichtungen von 1500–1550*, Marburg, 1913; K. Luick, *Historische Grammatik der englischen Sprache*, Pt. I, Leipzig, 1921; R. Jordan, *Handbuch der mittelenglischen Grammatik*, 2nd ed. rev. by H. Ch. Matthes, Heidelberg, 1934; E. Dieth, *A Grammar of the Buchan Dialect*, vol. i (phonology-accidence), Cambridge, 1932; K. Brunner, *Die englische Sprache: ihre geschichtliche Entwicklung*, vol. i, Tübingen, 1960; and unpublished notes on MSc by A. J. Aitken, M.A., which the compiler generously allowed me to use. – The examples given are illustrative and their number is generally not exhaustive. References to the texts may be found in the glossary, but certain peculiarities of the MSS have been indicated as follows: A stand for Fr. Anderson's copy of the *Litil Breif Tracteit*, F for Mr. fforde's copy of the same tract, B for the copy of the *Compendious Ressonyng* in the Catholic Archives of Scotland and G for Greenlaw's version of the appendix to this latter tract.

The sibilant suffix of the present indicative of verbs and the possessive and plural forms of nouns, normally written -is, -ys, less often -es or -s, remained syllabic after sibilants, with the quality of the vowel-sound somewhat obscured. The suffix was presumably weakly voiced after voiced consonants and perhaps also after vowel-sounds.

Verbal suffix: *allegis, alleges, gois, has*, &c.; possessive suffix: *Christis, Christes, Goddis, Goddes, Peters*, &c.; plural suffix: *apostlis, apostles, beis, ennimeys, formys, others, otheris*, &c. The same holds for the old possessive ending when used in an adverbial function: *aganis, anis, alvais, elss, ellis*, &c.; the Southern excrescent -*t* does not occur in such words.

The dental suffix of the preterite and past participle of weak verbs was generally written -*it* or -*yt*, less often -*et* or -*ed* through English influence, in a few cases -*t* or -*d* through loss or absorption of the inflectional syllable. The quality of the vowel-sound must have become obscured where it remained.

The various forms are illustrated by *allegit, alleget, avansyt, changit, changed, felit, feild, maid, hard, blessit, blesset, blessed, blist, puft vp, poysont, assuirtly, spred, sched*.

Verbs ending in -*at* or -*ut* did not normally take an extra dental suffix. But -*at* was also used as a participial ending, though most participles in -*at* were directly borrowed from the corresponding Latin forms in -*atus*. These endings would retain secondary stress and the quality of the vowel would correspond to that of earlier /ā/ in open syllables.

Thus A *communicat*, past part., B *communicate*, inf., and *commwnicate*, pret.; other forms include A *resolut*, part., B *statute*, pret., and *institute*, pret. and part., and the participles *prefigurate, consecrate, repudiat, dilatate, vendicat, perturbate, dedicate*, all in B. The participle *baptizate* corresponds to the infinitive *baptize*, both in B, and F has a participle *seuerat* where A has *separate*. Substantival *tracteit* suggests raising of the vowel sound, though it may be a scribal error for *tractait*.

The gerundial ending was usually -*ing*, sometimes -*in* or -*en* as a result of the loss of the velar element in the pronunciation, so that it had become the same as that of the *in*-ending of the strong past participles. Each of these two endings could also easily be confused with -*and* of the present participle, in which the *d* had ceased to be pronounced and the vowel had developed an obscured quality. In addition, through French influence the ending -*ant* sometimes occurs as a variant of -*and*. The ending of the strong past participle had in a few cases disappeared.

Gerund: *ressonyng, kneylling*, &c., but also A *chaungene, spekin*, B *gangin, lyftyn*, G *misknawin*, &c. Past participle: *approvine, approvyne, spokin, spoken, sein, sene*, &c., but also a form like G *approving*. Present participle: *pertenand, sayand*, &c., but *euerlestyng* as well as *euerlestand*, and also such forms as A *vritin*, G *twychin* ('touching') and B *succedant*. Similarly, A has *aboundand* and *aboundantlye*.[9]

---

[9] In F Greenlaw once corrects an earlier *Magdaling* into *Magdalene*.

The endings of the comparative and superlative forms of adjectives and adverbs were *-air/-ar/-er/-ir* and *-ast/-est/-aist*. The very variety shows that the quality of the vowel had become obscured. The same can be said of the endings of the *nomina agentis*. Those of the *ar/er*-type must have been phonetically indistinguishable from the comparative endings of adjectives. When borrowed as *nomina agentis* from French or Latin they normally retained the spelling *-our*, but this suffix had lost its original emphasis and was probably well on the way towards levelling with *-ar/-er*.

Comparative: *better, bettir, forder, ferther*, G *farthair, latter, lattir, letter, lettar, rather*, G *raythair*. Superlative: *gretast, laittest, nerrest*. Nomen agentis: *begynnaris, crear* ('creator'), *criaris* ('those who cry'), *gospellaris, redar, reader, redemar*, G *redemair*, &c.; *ambassatouris, authour, doctour, pelour, saluiour*, &c. The weakening of *our* is illustrated by *bletour* (of native origin), *ordour, chaptour* (both from OF *re*), and by the use of *our* in a word like *scriptour* (OF /ü/).

The phonetic value of the large number of MSc suffixes not yet mentioned was subject to the same general weakening of unstressed final syllables. In Latin and French loan-words the quality of the vowels was still unstable. In poetry they could even be used with their original accentuation, apparently without violence to linguistic feeling, but the general tendency remains incontestable.

The following features of the spelling deserve to be noted. Native *litil* and *mekil* often appear as *litle* and *mekle*. Conversely, variants such as the following are common: *apostle, apostil, article, artikil, aggreable, aggreabil, damnable, damnabil, miserable, miserabil, symple, sympil*, &c. A has spellings like *allegeans, presens, ramemberans* as well as *allegeance, presence* and *rememberance*. There is no indication in the spelling that the suffixes *-ian* and *-ion* had become monosyllabic in pronunciation. That the OF ü-sound in *-ure* and *-ude* had not resulted in a diphthong may to some extent be inferred from the spelling *scriptour* instead of *scripture* or *scriptuir*.[10] The weakening of final *-ous, -us* is indicated by the spellings *effectuislye* and *superflowis*, both in A. OF final *-té* appears regularly as *-te* or *-tie*, plural *-teis*: *authorite, authoritie, verite, veritie, propirtie, propirteis, obscuriteis, qualiteis*, &c. Similar spellings occur in such words as *ennimeys, fure, herese, heresy*, plural *heresis* and *hereseis, mistery*, plural *misteryis* and *mistereis*, and in verbs like *certify, certifeit, certifyet, satifeit, satifyet, pacifeit, signifyit*, A *mare* and *mareit, occupeand, occupeit*. The native *bureing* in B proves that the e-spelling did not imply /e/ and suggests a weakened i-sound for all these cases. The e-spellings do not occur in verbs where the vowel had remained stressed and where it had been diphthongized: *apply, appliand, applyit, denyand, denyit, cryit, tryis*.

With respect to unstressed prefixes MSc tended on the one hand to use aphetic forms, on the other to give its words a Latin appearance.

Thus B *suage* is an aphetic form, whilst B *reparaling* ('apparel') and *appreif* (in the meaning of 'prove') and G *accuregit* represent unetymological Latinizations. OF *e* before 'impure' *s* remains in *establisit*, but has disappeared in words like *scornit, scriptour, scurge, sklenderly, space, special, spreit, stait*.

The vowel-sounds of medial unstressed syllables tended likewise to be

---

[10] This can also be said of the spelling *plesour*, even though the ending is not etymologically correct.

obscured and to be represented in different ways. Obviously, sentence stress too had much to do with the phonetic quality of sounds and words. Thus, the personal pronouns had strong- and weak-stressed forms, not distinguished by particular spellings. The *l*-sound in *suld* and *wald* had been lost through weakening. Spellings like *was, wes, war, wer, haif, hef, has, hes, had, hed* point to full and shortened pronunciations.

Earlier medial vowels have disappeared from words like *chaptour* and *mokrie, remembrance* occurs by the side of *rememberance*, A has *anciant* and *saluiour*, B *anceant* and *salueour*, and unetymological letters occur in *beneualent, ceromonies, chesabill* and *prymatywe*.

2. The Consonants

The OE long consonants had ceased to exist. As far as gemination had any phonetic significance, it indicated the short quantity of a preceding vowel, but it is no infallible guide.

/b/   The sound had been lost in the combination *-mb*, except where it had developed as a non-etymological glide consonant between *m* and a liquid.

The different sources of the sound are illustrated by *abone, beir, better, bluid, body, bosoume, bot, but; abhominable, beistis, breif, table, vengebel; bayth, birth; bardis.* The sound has disappeared from B *cummyr*, A *lam*, though B has *lamb*, from A *humilye*, B *hwmillie*, G *humlie*, A *nowmer* and B *dwm*. It does not appear in A *doute*, B *douttit*, G *wndowtitlie*, but has been introduced into *subtyle* from the Latin original. It appears as a new glide consonant in A *skambles*.

/p/   A glide consonant, in many cases already existing in OF, often appears between *m* and *n* or other combinations with *m*.

The sound is of OE origin in *apone, cropin, lippis, put* &c.; of OF/Latin origin in *appere, capacite, people, part, pwir*, &c. A has *damnacione, condamnit, condamnable*, but *redempcione*, B *condemp, condempnis, damnatioun, dampnatioun, contempnis, hympne, solemniteis, solempnitlie*, G *cowmpt. Psalme* is a latinization.

/d/   Post-nasal /d/ in weak-stressed syllables had been unvoiced or lost and final /d/ in other unaccented syllables had generally been unvoiced. Before *r* it often appears as *th*. In this position the pronunciation was "intermediate between d and th – say dth."[11] OE *cuþe* had become *cude* through analogy with the weak preterites in *-de*, and was normally spelled *culd* in MSc through analogy with *suld*.

The different sources of the sound are illustrated by *ald, day, deyth, do, durris, maid, syde, ȝeid; dawin; according, adduce, adoire, considder, declair, dewly*, &c. Post-nasal *d* still appears in words like *bondage, spendynge, vand, vindokkis* and *vonder*. The past participles *bound, funde* and *onderstand* probably represent assimilation of the nasals of

---

[11] G. G. Smith, *Specimens of Middle Scots*, Edinburgh & London, 1902, p. xxii.

stem and ending after the loss of the *d*-sound.[12] The spelling G *abundlye* is probably to be explained in the same way.

Before *r* the following spellings occur: B *broder*, *brother*, *brethir*, A *brether*, *fader*, *father*, *forder*, B *ferther*, *gaddir*, A *gadderit*, *hitherto*, B *hidderto*, A and B *moder*, A *other* ... *nother*, B *older* ... *nolder*, A *quhidder*, F *quhether* and *quhethir* (once for A *quhy dar*, a scribal slip presupposing a *d*-like sound), A *to gidder*, G *vderes*, B *vtheris*, A *vorthely*, F *wordelye*. A *ferde*, B *feirdlie* and F *fourt* show similar variation after *r*.

An unetymological *d* appears in B *advansis* (A *avansyt*) through incorrect latinization. In *seruand* the native participial ending has been substituted for OF *-ant*.

/t/   The sound had been lost in final position after /p/ or /k/. An excrescent *t* frequently appeared after final *th* and *ch*, and an etymologically correct *t* was frequently omitted after *ch*. This omission resulted from the strong pronunciation of the preceding fricatives, whilst the traditional *t*-spelling in these cases probably occasioned the excrescent *t* in other cases.

The different sources of the sound are illustrated by *betuix*, *craft*, *gilty*, *it*, *litil*, *oft*, *quhat*, *teche*, *to*, *tre; lyft*, *tak*, *traist*, *at*, conj.; *alteracione*, *antiquiteis*, *celestial*, *certifie*, *consecrat*. The sound had developed from earlier final /d/ in the dental suffix of weak verbs and in *tovart*, *eftervart*, *brygant* (post-nasal; cp. the spelling *seruand*); from earlier /þ/ become final in *fift(-lie)*, *saxt*, *sextlie*, *sevint(-lie)*, *auctht*, *nint*.

The loss of /t/ after /k/ is illustrated by A *adieckit*, *astrickand*, *colleckit*, *subieke*, *respeckis* and by the unetymological *t* in B *attentict* (by the side of *attentik*). The latinized spellings are more common: *collect*, *collectit*, *instructit*, &c. The latinization of other words involved the insertion of a non-phonetic *c*: B *appoynctit* (G *appontit*), *fructe* (G *fructfull*) and *sanct*, A *inwnctit* (F *inontit*). The loss of /t/ after /p/ is not indicated in B *acceptis*.

Excrescent *t* occurs in A *deitht*, *truetht*, *tharthrocht*, B *althocht*, *throucht* and frequently after final *th* in F and G. Conversely, A has *auch*, vb., *noch*, *sich*, *thouch*, vb., by the side of *aucht*, *licht*, *nocht*, *rycht*, *sicht*, *thocht*. An excrescent *t* also appears in A *peruerstly*, *peruersit* and *prolixit*.

/g/   OE final post-nasal /g/ had been lost, leaving a velar nasal sound in stressed syllables and an alveolar nasal sound in unstressed syllables.

The variety of sources is illustrated by *agane*, *gadderit*, *gilty*, *God*, *goist*, *grete*, *guid*, *hungyr; gange*, *gef*, vb., *gif*, conj., *gift*, *begine*, *gapyng; aggreable*, *argument*, *glore*, *langage; begilit*, *disagysing*, *garmontis*, *regard* (OF /g/ corresponding to Germanic /w/).

The sound had been lost in *among*, *kingdome*, *lange*, *thing*, and in the unaccented gerundial ending.

/k/   Through separate developments in the Northern dialect, as well as through Scand. influence, this sound occurred in many words where the OE palatal stop had become /ts/ in the Southern English dialects. The sound had been lost in the preterite *made*, from which a new infinitive *ma* had been formed by the side of *mak(e)*. An analogous *ta* came likewise to be used by the side of *tak(e)*.

---

[12] See E. Dieth, *o.c.*, p. 124.

The different sources are illustrated by *ask, cald, clene, eik, kneis, knokking, sik, quhilk, think; according, artikil, attentik, colleckit, exame* (/ks/), *antiquiteis, equal, questione* (/kw/); *cal, kirk, skyne, tak, vaik.* The Northern French stop appears in *roik* and *cloik.* In A *vindokkis* the sound had resulted from the unvoicing of Scand. final /g/.

The sound is represented by *ch* in *Christ,* by the side of earlier *Crist,* and *paschal.* Latinization of words like *profet, appontit, inontit, delytit,* &c. had led to the introduction of *c* in words like A *inwnctit,* B *amict, appoynctit, fructe, sanct.* Both A and B have the past participle *tane.*

/v/ The sound was variously represented by the spellings *f, ff, u, v, w.* In addition to words like *has, had, heid, lady, laird, lord* and *woman,* where /v/ had been lost at an early date, earlier post-stress intervocalic /v/ had been vocalized before syllabic *l, n, r.* Full spellings, however, remained common, and it cannot be established to what extent there may have been alternative pronunciations. The vocalization had given rise to a diphthong /ǫu/ (e.g. *our*) and the long vowels /ī/ (e.g. *euil, giuen*), /ę̄/ (e.g. *euer*) and /ū/ (e.g. *abone*).

The sound is of OE origin in *beleuand, beluffit, fywe,* &c.; of OF/Latin origin in *beneualent, conuertit, obserwit, salueour, verray, voce,* &c.

Vocalization is shown by the spellings *abone* (by the side of *aboue* and *abuyf*), *attour, our, ourcumin* and *puyr; euer, neuer, devill, evin, discouerit,* &c., retain the traditional spelling.

/f/ Earlier final /f/ in unaccented syllables and weak-stressed monosyllabic words had presumably been voiced. OE medial voiced *f,* subsequently unvoiced in final position through the loss of the earlier ending, will have been voiced before syllabic inflections. – Initial *ff* was used for capital *F.*

The main sources are illustrated by *befoir, craft, fader, fall, feit, folovand, fouth, vif; afferme; fallowis, fra, lyft.* The sound is represented by the digraph *ph* in *phrais, triumphe, Theophilact* and *Telesphorus.*

The sound had presumably become voiced in unaccented *of.* On the other hand, the earlier voiced sound would be unvoiced in stressed final position, as in *beleif,* sb., *abuyf, luf,* sb., *preiffe,* sb. In the case of verbs the inflected forms will have influenced the pronunciation of the uninflected forms; the spellings are unstable: *beleif, beleue, gif, gef, geue, haf, hef, haue, appreif, appreue, persaif, persaue, persaw, perceaue* (all in A).

G *lesum,* unlike B *leifsum,* shows loss of *f* before *s.* The spelling does not indicate loss of the sound in *self.*

þ *(th)* The OE and Scand. initial voiceless thorn had become voiced in pronouns and adverbs, presumably also finally in unaccented syllables and monosyllabic words. In stressed syllables the earlier voiced intervocalic thorn had been unvoiced after the loss of the ending. The voiced sound had become /d/ in *culd,* the voiceless sound /t/ after voiceless fricatives *(fift).* The sound has disappeared from *sen* and *syne,* adv.

The use of the thorn, indistinguishable from *y,* is restricted to the first letter of pronouns and adverbs and the word *oþer,* although *th*-spellings are equally frequent in these words. The voiceless sound occurs in *deith, fouth, mouth, thyng, thre, thoill, thorne, throte; birth, hundreth*. It cannot be determined from the texts whether *authoris, authorite* and *marthir* (influenced by contemporary Latin *th*-spellings) had spelling pronunciations. The variants *auctorite* and *martyr* suggest the contrary.

The spelling *claythis*, plural of *clayth*, does not show loss of the sound. In the verb *cleith* it would normally be voiceless, but voiced before syllabic endings and this may have influenced the pronunciation of the uninflected form. It was probably also voiced in weak-stressed *with*.

F *mychthe* reflects assimilation of the plosive to the preceding fricative. The final *d* in *deid*, sb. (by the side of normal *deith*) appears to represent East Scand. *d* for Icelandic thorn.[13] In *faith* the digraph represents the OE suffix *-þu* (as in *fouth*), although its real origin may have been the *d* of *feid*.

/z/   The letter *z*, i.e. the same scribal symbol as the yogh which represented /j/,[14] was generally used in words of Greek origin. Normally *s* was used to represent /z/ as well as /s/. Speaking generally, the voiced sound occurred in intervocalic position, in weak-stressed *his, is* and *was*, and in numerous instances of the sibilant suffix of nouns and verbs.

The sound is represented by *z* in *zeill, baptize* and *baptizate;* by *s* in *bosoum, mesure, esaly, miserable, plesis, poysone, vsyng, dois,* &c.

/s/   MSc initial /s/ had the tendency to become /š/, possibly through Gaelic influence.[15] At the same time there was a tendency for unstressed /š/ to become /s/, as in *sal* and *suld*.[16] Apart from *s(e)*, the sound was represented by *ss* and *c* before front-vowels.

The various sources and graphic representations of the sound are illustrated by *ansuer, ask, seik, cursit, goist, house, lesse, sa, sik, send, sone;* sua (Scand. *svá*), *skyne, traist; cace, case, caiss, croce,* G *croyss,* B *crocesing, counsall* (Latin *concilium* and *consilium*), *difficle, medycyne,* A *mencione,* B *mentioun,* G *mensione, scisme.* /s/ instead of AN /tš/ or /š/ appears in *reherse, seirsynge, aboless,* B *diminiss* and, with latinized spelling, A *diminucis, establisit, finissit, obliss, periss,* G *vincust* ('vanquished'). The sound does not occur in *baptyme* and *satifeit;* B *satisfeit* is a latinization.

/ž/   As OF /ū/ did not become a diphthong /iu/ in MSc, words like *mesure* retained the blade-alveolar fricative.

OE *-cʒ-* had MSc equivalents with affricate /dž/ or, through Scand. influence, plosive /g/. Infinitives like *say* and *lye* had been formed from inflected forms in which the sound had been lost at an early date.

The OF/Latin voiced affricate remained in MSc, written *i, g, ge,* or *dg.*

---

[13] See R. Jordan, *o.c.,* no. 207, *Anm.* 3.

[14] The scribal *ʒ* was represented by *z* or *y* in printed books.

[15] So J. A. H. Murray, *o.c.,* p. 126. The explanation, not the tendency itself, is repudiated by G. G. Smith, *Specimens of Middle Scots,* p. liii.

[16] MSc *-is(s)* in verbs is explained by Lenz (*o.c.,* nos. 157–161) as due to OF *-iss-*, by Jordan (*o.c.,* nos. 208f. and 299) as due to Northern English weakening of AN /š/.

Although the spelling does not indicate it, lip-protusion would have been the normal development in *occasione*. Affricate /dž/ occurs in a large number of words of OF/Latin origin: *aige, allege, angellis,* G *bauge* ('badge'), *euangell, dangerous, generall, generat, gentyll, gorgeous, ingine, Image, iniures, Iuge, Ionit, Iowis, Ihone, Iesus, Iob, Iust,* &c.

The word *clengit* has a voiced affricate for OE /z/, possibly under the influence of words like *chengit*. In *knawlege* the OE affricate has been voiced in unstressed final position; the spelling will have been influenced by OF *-age* as in *bondage, langage, heretage, mariage*).

/š/   This sound was generally spelled *sch* in MSc, although English *sh* was not uncommon. Spellings with simple or geminated *s* show that it tended to become /s/ (see above). The voiceless affricate /tš/ was represented by the spelling *ch*.

> OE /š/ remains in words like *bischope, flesche, sched,* vb., *schew, schortly, schutis, schynand, wische* ('washed') and *devillische;* also in *mischeant, punischement* and *punishment,* of AN origin. The spellings do not reveal development to /š/ in *anceant, sufficient, ascensione, diffinitioun, inspiracione,* &c.[16a]
>
> In *scho* the sound had arisen through the contraction of opening consonant and following vowel, in *schir* through the Northern tendency to raise the main body of the tongue when pronouncing /s/. Affricate /tš/, from OE palatal *c,* occurs in *speche, teche, wichecraft, wrechit;* also in the loan-words *chalice, chaptour, cheif* (but G *capitane*), *cherite, chesabill, preacheouris, tuichit,* &c. The *ch*-spelling in *rachys* suggests that the Scand. word had been borrowed from AN.

/j/   The unstressed OE prefix ȝe- had disappeared or had at least been reduced to an obscured vowel sound. Apart from this exception, the OE initial ȝ remained as /j/ in MSc, although there were a number of Scand. borrowings with /g/. The earlier medial palatal ȝ had been vocalized.

> The earlier prefix had disappeared from the past participles. It remains as a vowel sound in *anew* ('enough').
>
> /j/ remains initially in stressed syllables: *ȝe, ȝea, ȝeid, ȝeir, forȝet, ȝettes* ('gates'), *ȝit* and *ȝow*.

/w/   OE /w/ had been lost in a few words in post-consonantal position. It remained in initial position, although it appears to have had a *v*-like quality in early Scots. *v*-spellings remained common in the sixteenth century and were phonetic before *r*.

MSc vocabulary has AN initial *w* as well as Central French *g(u)*. OF/Latin /kw/ is normally represented by *qu*, OE /kw/ by analogy. The corresponding voiceless consonant, represented by *hw* in OE, was spelled *quh* in MSc. The English *wh*-spelling was especially common in the early printed texts.

> The sound is of OE origin in *betuix, duellis, quickly, vas, vardle, vil, vith, wemen, witnes, worschippit,* &c.; of Scand. origin in *vaik, vindokkis, want, sua;* of OF/Latin

---

[16a] Cp. H. Kökeritz, *Shakespeare's Pronunciation*, Yale University Press, 1953, pp. 293f.

origin in *equall, quantite, questione, perswade, suage*, &c. The sound had disappeared from *ansuer*, B *anser, as, sa* (of OE, not of Scand. origin), *sik;* it was pronounced in *twa*. AN initial *w* for Central French *g(u)* appears as *v* in *revarde*.

The voiceless consonant occurs in *quha, quhair, quhat, quhilk, quhen, quhidder, quhill, quhow* (B *how*), *quhy*. G *Quhintyne* instead of *Quintine* must be a scribal error. A *for* instead of *quhair* is an early witness of the North-Eastern labialization of the fricative element.

Initial *v*-spellings are particularly frequent in A.

/x/   OE /x/ remained in MSc in final position and before final *t*. The corresponding voiced sound had been vocalized in intervocalic position.[17] The normal MSc spelling for /x/ was *ch*, though *gh* became more common as English influence increased, especially in the printed texts and in a writer like Knox.

The sound occurs in *althouch, aucht*, num. and vb., *nocht, thocht*, vb., and sb., *throuch, vrocht, brocht.*

/ç/   OE palatal /ç/ remained likewise in final position and before final *t*, whilst the corresponding voiced sound had been vocalized in intervocalic position. The sound was represented by the same digraphs as the velar sound.

The sound occurs in *heycht, hiechtlie, licht, michty, nycht, richt, sicht, wechtie*. A *mich, mych*, vb., may have to be transcribed *mith, myth*, i.e. as early witnesses of the modern North-Eastern sound in this word.

/h/   The OE initial antevocalic aspirate remained in MSc. Antevocalic *h* in OF loan-words of Latin origin was silent (and often absent in the spelling).

The OE aspirate appears in *hail, haly, hart, hellis, hill, hirdis, house, hyid*, &c.
The silence of OF initial *h* in words of Latin origin is shown by the spellings *able, hable, erbis, exort, exhortand, abhominable*, A *Helias*, F *Eleas*.

/l/   Earlier preconsonantal /l/ had been lost in weak-stressed *as, sik, suld* and *wald*. In stressed syllables it had been vocalized when preceded by short /a/ or /o/ and in many cases when preceded by short /u/. The letter *l* was often retained in the spelling and came to be used as a means of indicating the *u*-element of /au/ and /ǫu/ and the long quantity of /ū/.[18] The

---

[17] This explains the existence of doublets like *enewe* and *eneuch*. The latter word represents the earlier uninflected form, in which the fricative was final and voiceless, the former the earlier inflected form. The same holds for the palatal sound, as in *he* and *heich, neir* and *nixt* (with /çs/ assimilated to /ks/).

[18] Before this sound-change took place stressed short /a/ before -*ld* had been diphthongized to /au/ with retention of the following /l/. In words like *auld, bauld, cauld*, also spelled *ald, bald, cald*, there was, therefore, no longer a short back vowel at the time of the general *l*-vocalization.

84

similar OF *l*-vocalization was frequently ignored in attempts at latinized spellings.

OF *l-mouillé* appears in MSc as *lʒ* (i.e. /lj/) or as simple *l*.

The main sources are illustrated by *allanerlye, beleif, feill, gilty, lam, lippis, luke, sal* (not vocalized because unstressed), *saull; fallowis, law* ('law' and 'low'), *lyft, til; allege, applaude, establisit, laick, laudable, repellit*, &c.

In A *fault*, B *falte*, G *foirfaltit*, G *soldior* and in *saluiour* the *l* has been reintroduced by way of latinization. The sound has become /u/ in native words like *all, call, fall, hald, small* and stressed *als*. Vocalization is clearly shown by the spelling in *fouth* ('fulness') and *caand*, whilst the sound-change is presupposed by the introduction of unetymological *l* in B *older* and *nolder*, where it stands for /u/.

OF *l-mouillé* appears as simple *l* in A *prevaile, merualit*, B *railling*; as *lʒ* in G *wail-ʒeantlye* and *tewlʒae* ('toil'). A *vardle*, unlike B *warld*, has metathesis of *ld*.

/r/   The sound generally remained, whatever its origin. Metathesis was fairly frequent in MSc.

The different sources are illustrated by *affore, ar, barkand, braine, buir, dar, far, rest* ('peace'), *rowme; birth, fra, hundreth, kirk, traist; bardis; abhorrit, adore, breif, degre, peruerstly, sobyr, rest* ('remainder'); and, of Dutch origin, *vproir*.

Metathesis occurs in A *thre* and *third*, B *thridlie, thrist* (OE *þirst*), *throuch* (OE *þurh*), A *vork*, vb., and *vrocht*.

A has both *(in-)contrar* and *(in-)contra*, the latter spelling probably being a latinization of a dubious sort.

/m/   This sound too, whatever its origin, remained in MSc, except of course where it has disappeared as an element of earlier inflection.

The main sources are represented by *am, cum, hym, may, mak, man*, vb., *mister; affirmand, commaund, communicat, determyt, imparfit, simpil*.

Absence of assimilation, as in B *conmwnicate*, occurs only when the prefix is written at the end of a line.

/n/   OF *n-mouillé* was represented in MSc by simple *n* (alveolar nasal), *ng* (velar nasal), *nʒ* (/nj/) or *gn* (presumably pronounced in any of the other three ways). The OE velar nasal consonant remained in MSc, with the exception of the fronted variety, which had become /n/ before /d/, /t/ or /þ/, and of the weak-stressed gerundial ending, where it had likewise become /n/. In stressed final *-ing* the earlier /g/ had ceased to be pronounced, but it probably remained in medial position.

OE /n/ remains in *and, ansuer, begine, can, end, evin, in, mony, na, nor, takin*, sb., &c.; OF/Latin /n/ in *anceant, benefice, confund, ennimeys, expone, nature*, &c. Apart from the gerundial and participial endings, an inflectional *n* remains in *eyne*, A *almychtyne* and *sam(m)yn(e)*. B *condemp*, inflected form *condempnis*, A *condame*, inflected form *condamnit*, show loss of post-consonantal final *n*.

The word *messingeris* has an intrusive *n*. The confusion between *dar* ('dare') and *darn* ('hide'), as in F, occurs more often in MSc. The second *m* in *manteyme* is not uncommon.

OF *n-mouillé* appears as simple *n* in *constreine* and *disdanit*; as *ng* in *rengis* and *ryngis*, pret. *rang, Impung, syng*; as *gn* in *sygne* and *repugnant*; as *ngn* in G *Angnus Dej* (which suggests that it was pronounced as a velar nasal). The velar nasal further occurs in *drink*, *distinct, thankis, think; hungyr, langage, distinguit; among, kingdome, lange, soung*, vb., *thing, toung*.

3. *The Vowels in Stressed Syllables*

/a/ The principal sources of this sound were OE *æ, ea* (except in *-eaht*) and *a* in closed syllables. Apart from weak-stressed *ony* and *mony* there had been no rounding before nasals.

Before *-ld* the sound had become /au/ and in other words it had formed /au/ with a following /l/. There was also a tendency towards fronting and lengthening of /a/ before a covered *r*. Shortened OE /ā/ as well as Scand. and OF/Latin /a/ in closed syllables had formed additional sources of the MSc sound. Before a covered nasal the French sound was, however, often represented by *au*, and after /tš/ it tended to become /e/. It was not rounded after /w/. The Scots form of *after* is *efter* or *eftir*.

The sound derives from OE *æ, ea, a* in *at*, prep., *craft, last, quhat; dar, vax, mark, tovart; am, ansuer, can, fand, gadderit, hand, lange, man, sangis*, &c.; from Scand. short *a* in *at*, conj., *gange, tak* (unlengthened through early loss of the ending); from OF/Latin short *a* in *antiquiteis, avansyt, damnable, faccione, impassible, tracteit*, &c.

A *among*, unlike B *amangis*, has Southern rounding. *au*-spellings before covered *n* appear in A *anciaunt* (also *anciant*), A *appearaunce* (also *apperance*), A *chaunge* and *chaunged* (also *changit* and *chengit*) A *perchaunce* (also *perchance*), A *rememberaunce* (also *rememberance*). By the mid-sixteenth century these spellings cannot have been phonetic for the weak-stressed instances; in the stressed instances they may have represented some degree of rounding.

Fronting after /tš/ appears in *chengene, chengit, cheptour* (also *chaptour*) and *cherite*. Spellings like *barne, part*, &c. do not indicate fronting or lengthening before covered *r*.

The sound derives from OE/ā shortened before two consonants in *ask*.

/e/ The principal sources of this sound were OE *e* and *eo* in closed syllables, with the exception of *-eoht*. After /w/ the Southern rounding often appears. There seems to have been a tendency to lower and retract the sound to /a/ in the combination *er*, but the results of this change had probably been undone by Kennedy's time, when the tendency towards fronting of /a/ before covered *r* had probably become stronger.[19]

At an early date /e/ had been lengthened before *ld*, but it is not certain whether this had been general.

Shortened OE *ǣ, ē, ēa* and *ēo*, and Scand. and OF/Latin /e/ in closed syllables formed additional sources of the sound.

The sound derives from OE *e* in closed syllables in *better, ellis, end, duellis, forʒet, hellis, inmest, rest* ('peace'), *send, set*, &c.; from Scand. /e/ in *ken;* from OF/Latin /e/ in

---

[19] Cp. J. Wright, *The English Dialect Grammar*, Oxford, 1905, nos. 37 and 56.

affermand (with latinized *affirmand*, both in A), *certane*, &c.; from shortened long sounds in *bekking, blessed, clenget, flesche, less, sched, cled, held, spred*.

Earlier lowering and retraction before *r* may be indicated by the spellings A *barkand*, G *arthtly* (A *earth*, B *erth*), A *far*, G *farthair* (B *fer* and *ferther*), A *hart*, A *hard* (shortened from OE /e/), A *vark* (also *verkis* and B *werk*), B *marvellous* (A *mervalous*). The precise spelling is often left to the student, because the identical sign of abbreviation is used for *er*, *ar*, and *air*.

Southern retraction and rounding after /w/ is shown by the spellings A *vordle* (also *vardle* and B *warld*), A *vork*, B *work* (also A *vark* and *verkis*, B *werk*), A *vorth*, B *worschippit*, B *suorde*.

The digraph in A *seirsyng* indicates lengthening before covered *r*, but the spelling is not normally digraphic.

/i/   OE *i* and *y* in closed syllables and Anglian *-eht* formed the principal sources of this sound. It had been lengthened before *-ld*, but generally remained unchanged in MSc. Scand. and OF/Latin *i* in closed syllables and shortened OE /ī/ had been levelled with it and thus formed additional sources.

The sound derives from OE *i*, *y* and *e(ht)* in *begine, biddis, blindnes, did, drink, first, fulfill, gilty, hill, hirdis, mich, his, hym, in, is, it, quickly, nychtis, sicht*, &c.; from Scand. /i/ in *birth, kirk, lyft, skyne, till, vindokkis*; from OF/Latin /i/ in *astrickand, distinguit, insticcione, invincible, pictour, prince, resistit*, &c.; from earlier /ī/, /ȳ/ shortened before consonant clusters in *fift* and *visdome*.

The variants *rengis* and *ryngis* illustrate phonetic approximation of /e/ and /i/. The nouns *giftis* and *geftis* (both in A), are probably of OE and Scand. origin respectively as far as the vowels are concerned. The spelling *this* ('thus') is normal in MSc.

/o/   OE /o/ in closed syllables generally remained in MSc; /o/ in closed syllables of loan-words had been levelled with the native sound, just as earlier native /ō/ if shortened before consonant clusters at an early date.

The sound derives from OE /o/ in *for, God, morne, schortly, thorne*, &c.; from OF/Latin /o/ in *abhorrit, concord, conforme, exort, possesse, scornit, sort*, &c. In *costlye* it is of Dutch origin. Shortening of /ō/ before /xt/ has taken place in *brocht, thocht;* in *mot* the earlier long sound has been shortened through loss of the ending combined with lack of emphasis, in *gospellaris* through the following consonant combination.

The word *nocht* had developed from OE *nawiht*. There is no spelling evidence for lowering to /a/ in words like *of, oft*.

/u/   The MSc *u*-sounds were represented by *u, v, w, o* (esp. in the neighbourhood of *u, v, w* and nasals), *ou, ow*, and *ul*. The last digraph was exclusively, *ou* and *ow* were principally, used for the long sound.

OE short /u/ in closed syllables remained in MSc, also before *-nd*. The study of sixteenth-century rhymes shows unstable length of the *u*-sound in words of French/Latin origin, also in closed syllables.[20] No doubt this was

---

[20] See K. Lenz, *o.c.*, nos. 40–43.

partly due to the fact that the two varieties did not differ in quality, partly to the largely literary character of many of these words.

Words with OE /u/ are *bound*, past part., *cursit, dwm, furth, funde*, past part., *ground*, vb., *groundit* and *grundit, hunder, hungyr, lustis*, sb., *monkis, put, sone* ('sun'), *soung*, past part., *sum, toung, vonder*. The different spellings for /u/ in OF/Latin loan-words are illustrated by *cuntre, cowpe, cupe, cwpe, coupe, customes, mwrmwr, nowmer, suppar, returne, triumphe*.

/ā/   OE /ā/ had not been rounded in the North. By Kennedy's time it had, together with Scand. /a/ and /ā/ resulting from lengthening in open syllables, from monophthongization of /au/ (from earlier *aw*, *āʒ*, *aʒ*, *al*, *a* before *ld*, foreign *au*) and /ai/ (from earlier *ēʒ*, *eʒ*, *ǣʒ*, *æʒ*, OF *ei* and *ai*, Scand. *ei*), been fronted to open /ę̄/. In several districts, however, the immediate neighbourhood of a labial consonant had prevented this fronting. These districts included the Kennedy area and the Aberdeen district (where A was copied), whilst both pronunciations appear to have been possible in Greenlaw's native Haddington.[21]

The absorbed *u*-element in /a/ from monophthongized /au/ formed an inhibiting influence to fronting. It cannot be said in how far it caused rounding. Southern *o*-spellings for OE /ā/ were far from uncommon in MSc.

MSc words with /ā/ from earlier /au/ include the following from Kennedy's tracts on the Eucharist: *furthschaw, knaw(-lege), saull, savine, saw* (pret. of 'see'); *avin, law* ('low'), *lawe* ('law'), *drawin; caus, authoris, awn* ('ass'); *auld, baulddie, cauld, hald, all, cal, fall, false, small*. Words in which the fronting of /ā/ was regionally inhibited by a labial include *quha, quhais, twa, sua, vater, fader, qualiteis* and, if /ai/ had been monophthongized, *vay, avay, vaik*. For the copyist of A, however, the *v* in *avin, knavin* and *savine* may well have represented /v/.[22]

/ę̄/   This sound had resulted from the fronting of earlier /ā/, whatever its origin, except that resulting from the monophthongization of /au/ and those instances in which fronting had been inhibited by a neighbouring labial consonant.

The large number of words in which the sound occurs includes *allanerlye, anis, gaist,*

---

[21] See the map on p. 117 in A. McIntosh, *Introduction to a Survey of Scottish Dialects*, Edinburgh, 1961, and Dieth, *o.c.*, p. 31. It may be added here that as a result of the monophthongization of /ai/ and the other MSc *i*-diphthongs in the central Scots area *i* and *y* came to be employed as length-marks. On the monophthongization of /ai/ and /ei/, see O. T. Williams, "The development of ai and ei in Middle Scotch," *Transactions of the Philological Society*, 1907–10, pp. 285 ff.

[22] Monophthongization of /au/ in unstressed syllables is indicated by the spellings B *attentik* and *attentict*, F *Agustine* and *Agustinus*, and G *actorisit*. F has once *ayld* instead of *auld* or *ald*. On *avin*, &c., in North-Eastern Scotland, see E. Dieth, *o.c.*, p. 116.

[23] *Examine* also occurs in MSc. Apparently *-ine* was associated with inflection.

graipe, hail, haly, ma ('more'), *mair, na, rais, sa, takin,* sb., *fra, gapyng, laitlie, name, maid, tane; adoracione, ayge, cais, debate, exame, fauour, grace, laick, phrais, place, suage; brane, daly, ganestude, ma,* vb., *said, traist; consauit, disdanit, dissauit, maister, ordanit, paine, perceaue, plane, praye* ('prey' and 'pray'), *prevaile, railling, remane, vane.*

Southern *o*-spellings occur in *boith, bonis, goist, knowand, most, no, one, quho, quhome* (the normal form in MSc), *so, two.* The spelling *they* in A, instead of *tha* or *thai,* is also due to Southern influence.

The verbs *haf, mak* and *tak* had short forms due to early loss of the final syllable (i.e. before lengthening in open syllables took place). Long forms, suggested by the spellings *haue* and *haif,* were easily introduced from the inflected forms.

/ī/ Before the end of the sixteenth century earlier /ę̄/ had in the great majority of words in which it occurred coalesced with earlier /ē/, which had for some time been raised to /ī/.[24] The main sources of the open e-sound had been OE *ēa*, Scand. *æ*, and earlier /e/ in open syllables; those of the close e-sound OE *ēo* and (Anglian) *ē*, Scand. *ē, ei* from *eʒ-*, OF *ē* if the stress remained on this sound, OF *ié* and *ué*, and earlier /i/ in open syllables.

Although the quality of the sounds cannot be adequately ascertained, it may at least be said that the spelling of Kennedy's tracts is the same for the words of those various origins and that in general it is consistently distinct from that of fronted earlier /ā/: *cleith,* vb., *deill,* vb., *leif,* vb., *leiffis,* sb., *menyng* and *meanynge, lerit, lene,* vb., *see* ('sea'), *techis, ʒea, breid* and *bread, deid* ('dead'), *deith* and *death, dremis, gretar* and *greater* (B *grit,* with the shortened vowel of the OE comparative), *hede* and *heid* ('head'), *beir,* vb., *eit* and *eate, meit,* sb., *spekis* and *speakis, appeir, beistis, eiss* ('ease'), *freir, pleis, preche,* and *preacheouris, releif,* vb., *succedit, zeill, eyne, neir, sene, deid* ('deed'), *feyr, rede* and *reade, be,* vb., *beleif,* vb., *beseik, beis,* sb., *breist, feill, feirdlie, feit,* sb., *eik, frelie, freyndis, hede* ('heed'), *here* and *heir,* adv., *keip, seiknes, thre, weiping, ʒeid, ʒeir, levand* and *leiffit* ('lived'), *mekil, speir* and *spere, steir, spreit, redemar, people, preif, reprevis, aggreable, breif, cheif, cleirly* and *clearly, manteinaris, obtene, pertenis, sustenit,* &c.

F *continet,* past part., will be a latinization. The *ea*-spellings in A (in words with earlier /ę̄/) are anglicizations. The *a-* and *ai*-spellings in B *dissaitfull,* A *dissauit,* G *wndesawabill,* &c., represent OF *ei*, early Scots *ai*, and are therefore normal. This cannot be said of A *plaege* ('pledge'), F *havin* and G *radyness* and *ʒae.* Here the spelling indicates levelling of earlier open *e*-sounds with fronted *a*-sounds.

The long vowels in B *geif, geiffin* may be explained as lengthened /i/ in open syllables (for the uninflected form at least by analogy).

/ǭ/ This sound derived from earlier /o/ lengthened in open syllables and from monophthongized /oi/; it had also been the sound represented by the Southern *o*-spellings for OE /ā/, but by Kennedy's time this had become /ou/.

The sound occurs in *before, befoir, cropin, adore, adoire, brokin, cloik, closit, deplorit, explodit, decoir, hoist* (Latin 'hostia'), *loving* ('praise'), *note, roik,* A *spokin* (B *spokkin,* in which the geminated consonant indicates a short vowel), *stoill, thoill, throte,* &c. The word *glore* may derive from AN *glorie* or OF *gloire.*

___

[24] Cp. J. Craigie's study of William Fowler's language, S.T.S. edition of *The Works of William Fowler,* vol. iii (1940), pp. lviff.

/ū/   OE /ū/ remained unchanged in the Scots language. The sound also remained in the large number of French/Latin loan-words in which it
occurred. Earlier *ūʒ-*, *uʒ-* and stressed *-ul* formed further sources of the
sound. It was graphically represented by *ou, ow, ul* or *u*.

> It derives from OE /ū/ in *doun, house, kow, now, our, out, mouth, quhow, rowme, thow;*
> from OE *uʒ-* in *sow* and *throw* (also *throuch*); from earlier /ul/ in *fouth;* from OF/Latin in
> *doute, counsall* and *cunsal, floureseis, aboundand, abundance, boundis,* sb., *recours, pro-
> nuncit,* &c.

/ǖ/   OE close /ō/, after being shifted to /ȫ/, had been levelled in Scotland
with OF /ǖ/. Unlike unchanged /ō/ of Midland English, this sound was
not affected by the great vowel shift. Additional sources of the sound were
earlier /u/ in open syllables, OF close /ō/ and monophthongized OF /ui/.

> The sound derives from OE /ō/ in *bluid, do* (G *dowes*), *fude, broder, ganestude, guid,
> luke, moder, vther, scho, schutis, vodnes;* from Scand. /ō/ in *tuik;* from OF /ō/ in *approvine,
> mowis, puyr, discouerit, Rome;* from OF /ǖ/ and /ui/ in *assurit, fure, refuise, mature, rude,
> tuichit, vse,* vb. and sb., *fructe, appoynctit, inwnctit, Ionit, poysone;* from earlier /u/
> lengthened in stressed open syllables in *aboue* and *abone, beluffit, dure,* sb., *hwny, luf, son*
> ('son').
>
> The sound is variously represented by *ui, ue* (in F), *u, o* (especially in the immediate
> neighbourhood of *u, v* or nasals), *ow* (in G) or, when derived from /ui/, *oi* or *oy.* The
> infinitive *cum,* which will have remained short through early loss of the ending, and the
> past participle *cumin* are distinguished in spelling from the preterite *come.*

/iu/   The sources of the diphthong were OE *ǣw, ēow, iw* and *ōʒ-* (through the
unrounding of the first element in /ǖu/) and OF *ęu, eau* and final *ęu.*

> The diphthong occurs in *anew* ('enough'), *new,* B *renewit* (A *renow*), *schew, threw,
> trew* and *true, treuth* and *trueth; dewly, dewite, Mathow, Iowis, retenewe, vertue.*

/ei/   Earlier /ī/, from OE and Scand. /ī/ and /ȳ/ and OF /ī/ if it had remained
stressed, had been diphthongized to /ei/ in the great vowel shift. The long
i-sound which had resulted from OE final unstressed *-īʒ* or *-īʒ* had been
shortened before this change had taken place.

> The diphthong derives from earlier native /ī/ in *by, byd,* vb., *hyid,* vb., *lif,* sb., *lyis*
> (from OE inflected *liþ*), *lyk,* vb., *lykwyse, my, nyne, quhy, ryise, schynand, tyme, vine,
> wyte,* sb., &c.; from earlier /ī/ in OF/Latin loan-words in *apply, baptize, begilit, cryit,
> declynit, deny, delytit, desyr, deuidit, diffidis, diffinit, disciple, dispyt, fyne,* sb., *pryise,* sb.,
> *requiris, sufficis, tryit,* &c.

/ǫu/   This diphthong had its origin in the vocalization of intervocalic *v* and
ʒ and post-vocalic final *w.*

> It occurs in *grow, our, attour, ourcumin* and in the weaker-stressed syllables of *fallowis*
> and *folowis.*

/ai/, /ǫi/, /ui/   The sources of these diphthongs have already been indicated.
They were not universally monophthongized in MSc.

The following spellings imply monophthongization of these three diphthongs and show the use of *i* and *y* to indicate the long quantity of (original) monophthongs: A *daly, voce, Ionit, maid, cloik, tuik;* B *brane, croce, fructe, laitlie, stoill, abuif*. It must be remembered, however, that a copyist might follow the spelling of his originals or that of the Central Scots area.

B. GRAMMAR AND STYLE

With the weakening of unaccented syllables, the MSc preference for aphetic forms, the greatly increased use of prepositional phrases to express relationships of linguistic units and the introduction of numerous words of foreign origin, it is not surprising to find that the OE prefixes had lost much of their earlier importance. On the other hand, the Latin prefixes could not yet be used as freely as in modern literary English. Nevertheless, there remained a number of fixed combinations with no longer productive, and often reduced, prefixes; other prefixes – though few in number – continued to be productive and could also be used for hybrid formations; and MSc had various kinds of compound vocables, which added to the continuing importance of composition as a means of forming semantic units.

Reduced prefixes remain in words like *abone; aganis, ansuer; anew; affore, effore, among, avay, now adayis, alikvise. Inlikmaner* and *inlikvise* are later formations; *on-* remains in B *on lyf* but has disappeared from B *lykwyse*, just as *of-* from *doun*. The prefix *be-* remains in words like *befoir, begine, beleif, beluffit, betuix*, but also in the hybrid formations *becaus* and *begilit*. The first syllable in G *foirfaltit* may have been associated with the native prefix in *forbeid, forgeif* and *forʒet*. But the clearest example of a still productive native prefix is *un-:* *vnbludy, vndeserwit, vngodlie, ontruely* and *one truely, one defendit, onpropirlye* by the side of *impropirlye*. The verb *set furth* occurs by the side of *furthsetter* and *furthschaw*. Similarly, A has *agane saynge*, F *say aganis*, and *ganestude* is spelled as two words in G *gayne stud*. This latter inconsistency is very common in compounds, as in *all wayes, alwayes, euerlastand, evir lastand, insafer, in safer, part takar, parttakaris, partakaris, quhairof, quhair of, vther wayes, vderwyss*. Noun-with-noun combinations are rare: *day licht, almous deid, Obet Mess, thankis gevin, meit offering;* the first nouns in *my hand wryte* and *þe sone rysing* may represent old genitives, as is more clearly the case in *markispoinct*. B *wichecraft* and *lyftyme* are written as single words. The plural forms of two different types of compound nouns are represented by *criaris oute* and *mess claythis*.

Most of the Latin prefixes had been borrowed via OF, though they often appear in a latinized form, not infrequently indicative of faulty etymology. Hybrid formations with these Romance prefixes were rare in MSc; aphetic forms were very frequent.

Words like *according, afferme, appere, apply, appreif, commandit,* &c., are of OF origin but have latinized gemination of the consonants. OF *en-* remains in A *ennimeys*, is represented by *on-* in *onforce*, has been assimilated to *ac-* in G *accuregit* and has been latinized in such words as B *inimeis*, A *intend, ingine, incontrar, inwnctit*. Similarly, OF *de-* remains in *declair, deliuer, dependens*, &c., but appears as *di-* in *dispar, distres, dissauit, dissaitfull, dispyt, diffinitioun, diffinit*, in several cases with misleading gemination of the consonants.

OF *des-* appears as *dis-* in *disdanit, dysseuer, discouerit, disput,* whilst OF *me-* may have been confused with native *mis-* in *mischeant* and *mischeif.* In B *dissagysing* a native prefix has been added to latinized OF *des-.* Latinization does not occur in the earlier borrowings *counsal, cunsal, cuntre, custome* (by the side of *consuetude*), *purpos, purchasingis, rahers, rasaif, ramemberance.*

A *renou* and B *renewit* deserve to be noted as hybrid formations, B *suage* as an aphetic form.

The remaining OE suffixes were much more important than the remaining OE prefixes. The ordinary noun-, adjective- and adverb-forming suffixes were all of native origin; the large number of Roman suffixes in MSc, which had been borrowed with the words in which they occurred, were rarely used in new formations with native elements.

OE *-þu* remains as /þ/ in *fouth* and *strenthit,* but *-nes* was much more frequently used to form abstract nouns, also from recent borrowings: *aggreabilnes, besyness, blindnes, Induritnes, pesefullness, quietnes,* &c.; OE *-hæd* and *-dom* are restricted to early formations: *godheid, manhede, preistheid, kingdome, christindome, visdome.* The same can be said of OE *-scipe,* even though it occurs with a Scand. element in *falloschipe.* On the other hand, through the levelling of OE *-ere,* Scand. *-are,* AN *-er* and to some extent even later *-our,* there are many *nomina agentis* of foreign origin with the native suffix: *Inventaris, iustifear, offendar, redemair, takaris,* &c. The OE adjective-forming suffix *-ful* occurs in *vonderfull* and *leifful,* but also in *faithfull; -ig* in *haly, michty, ony; -leas* in *rakless* and *lawless; -sum* in *hailsoume* and *leifsum,* but also *doutsum.* It is somewhat different with *-ly,* which was at the same time an adverb-forming suffix with high frequency; but it remains as an adjective-forming suffix in the hybrid *costlye.* The suffix *-lyk* occurs only in *helplyk.*

Kennedy's tracts contain a large number of words with Romance suffixes, such as *-age (langage, bondage), -al (brutale, originall, real), -ance* and *-ence (abundance, allegeans, difference, presens), -ant* and *-ent (constant, pregnant, expedient, pestilent), -aire (contrar, familiar, necessar), -able* and *ible (abhominable, laudable, corruptible, vengebel), -é (pouerte, propirtie, vtilite), -ein (certane), -eil (counsall,* Latin 'consilium', *mervalous), -ice (benefice, sacrifice), -ie (fure, heresy), -ier (mare, certifie),* OF *-iere,* AN *-ere (maneir, mater), -ion (questione, diffinitioun), -il (counsall,* Latin 'concilium', *evangell), -ment (arrayment, garmontis, vestimentis), -our (authour, fauour), -os, -eus (curiouslye, monstruous, preciouse), -ude (multitude, serwitude), -ure (euentuir, figure, mesure).* The spellings A *corruptable,* G *Immovabill* and *inextinguabill* suggest association with independent adjectival *(h)able.* The suffix in B *bletour* may be explained as a mere spelling adaptation. Similarly, adverbial G *wonderus* is a corruption of ME adverbial *wonders,* G *rychtuslye* of ME *rightwis,* so that there is no question of new compounds.

MSc borrowed verbal forms might reflect OF or Latin infinitive or participial forms. There was clearly considerable freedom in the choice of different forms, and there was a vague preference for non-English forms.

Thus *suppone, disponand* and *expremit* are normal MSc forms. B has both *disposit* and *proponit,* past participles, *argwne* and *argumentis,* G has both *promittand* and *promisset.* A *distinguit* and *vnit* correspond to MSc infinitives *distingue* and *uny,* which do not occur in the texts. Similarly, *contenit, obtene, pertenis, sustenit* and *(ap-)preif, reprevis,* do not represent a phonetic development but a derivation which differs from that of the normal Standard English forms.

The inflection of nouns had been drastically simplified since OE times but, such as it was, remained important for expressing notional relationships. The only productive inflectional ending, the sibilant suffix, was used for plural, possessive and adverbial forms.

A remnant of the old instrumental dative sg. may be seen in *na thinge strange*. The *n*-plural survives in *eyne*, the mutation plural in *feit, men, wemen* and *brethir* (which has the vowel from the old dative sg.). The *s*-plural is also used for words which did not originally have it, as in *faderis, ʒettes, bonis, dedis* ('deeds'), and in loan-words. The word *scoir* has no plural form; *ʒeir* may have a plural meaning, but *ʒeiris* is more common: *threscoir ane ʒeiris, thretteyn hundreth ʒeir*. For A *all the aige, ʒeire* and *tymes* B has *all ageis, ʒeiris* and *tymes*. G *gallois* is a 'plurale tantum'; B *claythis* has a sg. form *clayth*. The collective meaning of a sg. form may be illustrated by B *gorgeous and costlie reparaling quhilkis war*....

The possessive suffix occurs principally in proper names and nouns referring to persons, but not exclusively: *Cristis, Goddis, sanct Iohnis, sanct Paullis, sanct Peters, Polycarpus* (with the suffix absorbed in the final sibilant); *halie kirkis, hellis, mannis, our lordis*. Mutation plurals take the sibilant suffix for the plural possessive, for other words it is the ordinary plural form: *cristiane mennis saluacione, his disciplis feit, our bodyes flesche*.

The suffix has an adverbial function in A *alvais* and *na vais*, by the side of *alvay* and *na vay, sume tymes*, by the side of *sumtyme, oft tymes*, B *in sumpartis*, by the side of *(in) sumpart, besydis, in þe myddis*. It is also added to non-substantival words: *aganis*, prep., by the side of A *agane, anis, amangis*, by the side of A *among*, and B *amang, ellis*. It does not occur in *tovart* and *sene*, where Southern English had it, and the Southern excrescent *t* is never added.

With the exception of *it*, which did not have a possessive form, the MSc personal pronouns had subjective, objective and possessive forms: *I, me, my; þow, þe, þj; he, him, his; scho, hir, hir; it, it, -; we vs, our; ʒe, ʒow, ʒour; þa(i), þa(i)m, þa(i)r*.

Objective *it* was rarely used. The reflexive pronouns were formed as in modern English, but emphatic identity was indicated by *sam self*, not by *selfsame* (except through Southern influence).

Instead of a possessive form of *it* the article is used in A *of þe avin nature*, B *in þe awin forme*, F *of þe awin wertew* (cp. *be his awin powar*); in B *perfyt in þe self* the last two words represent a substitute for a reflexive form of *it*. The regular substitutes for a possessive form of *it* are *of it, þairof* and *of þe sammyne*.

Objective *it* occurs with the verb *think* in *þow thinkis it strange* and *gif the reader thinkis it ane superflowis persuasione*, but is absent in *quhy thinkis þow impossible* and F *þow ... thinkis strange*. A frequent substitute for objective *it* is *þe sammyne*. It is not used as 'provisional subject' in *restes to considder, gif sa var þat* and *this may be cleirlye persauit*.

The way of expressing emphatic identity is illustrated by *þe same selffe bodye, þe samyn self redemptioun* and *at þat sam verray tyme*.

The MSc demonstrative pronouns were *þis* and *þat* for the singular, *þir* ('these') and *þa* or *þai*, by the side of *þais*, ('those') for the plural, *sick* and *ʒone* for either singular or plural. Their use roughly corresponded to that of their equivalents in modern English. Demonstrative *þai* (from OE þa) cannot always be clearly distinguished from the personal pronoun *þai*, especially when used in a determinative function. The definite article occasionally had demonstrative force.

The pronoun *ʒone* does not occur in Kennedy's tracts. As in modern English, the demonstrative pronouns may have an emotional connotation *(þir grosse gospellaris)* and, in conjunction with *and*, anaphoric *þat* may have an indistinct backward reference *(and þat be ane supernatural maner*, corresponding to Latin 'idque modo supernaturali'). But *þat* and *þa* may also have a distinct reference to an antecedent in the singular or plural: *and þa impropirly and peruerstly thrawin*. The definite article has demonstrative force in B *þe day ... þe morne*. Plural *þais* is common in B, but does not occur in A.

The interrogative pronouns were *quha*, *quhais* and *quhome*, only used for persons, *quhat* and *quhilk*, used for persons and things, and *quhethir*, which was principally used with its correlative *or* to introduce alternative questions. Their use corresponded to that of their modern English equivalents.

The MSc relative pronouns were *quha*, *quhais*, *quhome*, *the quhome*, *quhilk*, *the quhilk*, *quhilkis*, *the quhilkis*, *þat*, *at* and, after determinative *sick*, *as;* indefinite sense was normally expressed by *-saever*, *-sumever*, or simply *-ever* added to *quha* or *quhat*. *Quha* referred only to persons, the other relatives could refer to persons or things. *Quhilk* and *quhilkis* did not necessarily refer to antecedents in the singular and plural respectively; the other relatives were always used irrespective of number. *Quhais* occurred only in adjectival use, *quhilk(is)* in adjectival and substantival use, *quha*, *quhome*, *þat*, *at* and *as* only in substantival use. The use of the definite article with the relative pronoun was comparatively rare and appears to have been optional.

Antecedent and relative pronoun are frequently separated from one another, at times by several lines, as in the last sentence of ch. II of the *Litil Breif Tracteit*, where *quhais* refers back to *þe anciaunt fatheres*, and in G *all sic within þat towne quhair þe plage was to cum as lamentit* .... The relative pronoun may express cause, as in *þan had our saluiour bein contrarius to hyme self, quha said ane litil befoir* ....

In A, unlike B and F, *quhilk* and *quhilkis* are made to refer indiscriminately to antecedents in the singular or plural. Constructions like *Quhilkis wordis gif ...* are probably modelled on corresponding Latin constructions ('Quae verba si ...'). *Confer þe scriptouris quha plesis* (whoever); *reid all þe evangell quha pleissis* likewise recall Latin syntax.[25]

Relative *at* does not occur in Kennedy's tracts. Contact clauses are rare: *þare vas na creature mych disseuer theme, he is ane evill Iuge condempnis or he knawis*.

The indefinite article was *ane*, less often *a*, each also used for the number 'one'. Its negation was *na*, less often *nane*. Indefinite number or quantity was further expressed by such words as *all*, *ane man*, *certain*, *every*, *diuers*, *ilkane*, *ony*, *ony ane*, *other*, &c.

All frequently has the meaning of 'every', as in *al cristiane mannis saull;* *sum* may likewise have singular or plural meaning, as in *sum other part*, *sum chief testimonyis*. Substantival *otheris* may be preceded or followed by modifying *diuerss*: *oþeris diuerss*, *diuerss oþeris*.

---

[25] e.g. *Percurre cuncta quae nobis credenda traduntur, et perspicies ...* (Fisher, *De Veritate*, lib. ii, cap. iii) and *Graeca autem [verba] qui volet leget* (Gagneius, *o.c.*, p. 179v.). Note the similar native construction discussed in A. A. Prins, "Loke who, what, how, when," *English Studies*, vol. xliii (1962), pp. 165 ff.

Adjectival *other* has a plural *otheris*, frequently employed to make it agree with a noun in the plural number: *operis scripturis, others dedis.* It is not always clear whether there is question of adjectival *otheris* agreeing with, or of substantival *otheris* standing in apposition to a following noun: *diuerss operis damnable heretikis, vtheris godlie fatheris, all vtheris godlie interpretouris, vtheris maners of wayes, vtheris Innumerable commoditeis;* the singular form in *all vther faythfull ministeris* suggests that it was felt to be an adjective in all these cases.

The indefinite article is regularly *ane*. Emphatic *a* occurs by the side of emphatic *ane: there is bot ane God; twa natures in a persone; godheid ... vnit to his manheid in ane persone.* The use of the definite article differs from that of Standard English in minor details: *onder þe paine of, in maner abone rehersit.* The earlier instrumental case remains before the comparative forms of adjectives: *nochtþeles, þe mair easelie.* The article replaces *to* in B *þe day, þe morne, þe gidder.*

MSc adjectives frequently took plural inflections so as to agree with nouns in the plural. Post-position of adjectives often occurred in literary MSc. Adjectival forms might have the function of adverbs, though adverbs were normally formed by means of the suffix *-ly*. Periphrastic comparison by means of the adverbs *mair* and *maist* was often used with monosyllabic adjectives and regularly with adverbs in *-ly*. The comparative particles were *than* and *nor*.[26]

With the exception of *vtheris*, already mentioned, adjectives do not take plural inflection in Kennedy's tracts. Post-position occurs normally when the adjective is followed by an adjunct *(all thingis necessar for ...)*, but also when this is not the case: *þe concell Nicene*, G *þe pillair Immovabill and grwnd off trewth wndesawabill*, B *without command of God express* by the side of *without express command of God*. Such post-position is avoided by the A scribe, who changes *concell Nicene* into *counsal of Nece;* three out of four times he also omits the definite article before *Mary Magdalene*.

The comparative form has absolute meaning in *þe lettar suppar* and *þe letter day;* the superlative is used for the comparison of two alternatives in *for the maist part. Planar vordes* is used by the side of predicative *mekil mair plaine and propir.* This adverbial *mair*, from OE adjectival *mara*, corresponds to adjectival *ma*, from OE adverbial *ma*: A *thretty sax... or ma*, B *ony may sacrifices.*

A has *all reddelye* for B *all reddy*, but *baldye* for B *bauldlie*. Since A has metathesis of *-ld* in a word like *vardle*, it may also have occurred in the pronunciation of *baldye*, but the omission of the *l* may be due to the preceding *ld*. The suffix is also absent after syllabic *-l* in other cases, although it is not always easy to distinguish the words concerned from predicative adjectives: A *his power to pase throw þe multitude of the Iowis invisible, trowbles the vordle so miserable, is contenit invisible* (B *Is contenit invisiblie*), B *offerit vp ... in þe awin forme, visible and sensible;* A *to be explodit and cryit out one boith equall* (F *equalie*) may perhaps be similarly explained. The word *expres* occurs without the adverbial suffix in B *expres aganis þe scripture, expres contrar to þe command of God;* in A it occurs with or without the suffix: *expreslye ... contrar þe opinione, expresly contenit in scripture, it is expresse agane the vorde of God, expresse aganis the first and principall article.* To the large number of suffixless adverbs belongs also *wrang:* B *ȝe think all wrang* and *ȝe rehers the text wrang.*

Comparison of adverbs in *-ly* is normally periphrastic *(mair plainly, mekil mair aboundant-lye, mast feruentlye)*, but A also has the form *gretarlye*. A uses *forder*, B *ferther* in the sense 'furthermore'.

Noteworthy is the construction *na (nocht) ... mair than (nor)* in the sense 'no more ...

---

[26] Cp. F. Holthausen, "Negation statt Vergleichungspartikel beim Komparativ," *Indogermanische Forschungen*, vol. xxxii, pp. 339f.

than': *it ... occupeis na place in the sacrament mair then quhen he enterit ...; his ... body occupeit na place ... mair nor it hed bene ane spreit.*

After an opening adverb subject and verbal predicate frequently occur in inverted order: *Here may ve persaw, schortly sal ve rahers, impropirlye cal they to remembrance, this may þow cleirlie persaif* (also: *this ʒe may perceaue*).

MSc had two simple tenses, present and past. Other time-relationships were expressed with the help of auxiliary verbs and adverbs, and *do* was frequently used to form periphrastic present and past tenses.

Since the use of an inflectional suffix for the second person plural of the imperative had fallen into desuetude, the present tense forms differed from the infinitive only in certain cases of the indicative, viz. when they took a sibilantic suffix. The verb *will* and the verbs belonging to the old class of preterite-presents never took the suffix; *be* followed rules of its own, to be outlined below; *do* and *go* and the ordinary classes of weak and strong verbs took the suffix according to the following norms: it occurred invariably in the second and third persons singular; in the first person singular and in all persons of the plural when the subject was not a personal pronoun immediately preceding or following the verbal predicate. When the linguistic unit separating a personal pronoun from the corresponding verbal predicate was of negligible length or importance, the verb might occur with or without the suffix.[27]

The verb *be* had several forms of, or substitute forms for, the present indicative, all different from the infinitive form: *am, ar, is, art, bene.* The last two forms, for the second person singular and for the plural, were due to Southern influence; *bene* was rare, the use of *art* tended to increase with Southern influence. *Am* was used for the first person singular, *is* for the third person singular, *ar* for the second person singular and the plural, although *is* tended to be used in all positions where other verbs would have the sibilantic suffix.

The non-indicative moods of the present had only one form, identical with that of the infinitive.

The verbs *can, dar, man, may, mot, sall, wait* ('know'), *aucht* and *will* never occur with the sibilantic suffix in Kennedy's tracts. It must be added, however, that they do not occur in all the positions where other verbs would have the suffix. The use of the suffix for the main body

---

[27] The use of the suffix may be illustrated by the following classification of subject-predicate combinations:

a. personal pronoun with predicate immediately preceding or following (e.g. *I do, do I*);

b. personal pronoun with predicate not immediately preceding or following (e.g. *I ... dois, I do ... and dois*);

c. subject other than a personal pronoun with predicate either or not immediately preceding or following (e.g. *I quha dois, ʒour lordschippis dois, mony dois*).

Usage may vary in pattern b, when subject and predicate are separated by a unit of negligible length or importance.

of verbs is in accordance with the above norms: *I haue, I am contentit and acceptis, I renunce ... and takis, I geif ... and douteis, I am ... and thinkis; þow hes, thinkis þow, O lorde God quhilk has; he makis, it obscuris and diminucis, God quha hes, quha eittis ... and drinkis; ve haue, ve rasaue ... and restis, we teche ... and commandis; ȝe haif, think ȝe, ȝe ... dois, ȝe ... communicatis, of ȝou þat thinkis, of ȝou ... þat callis, ȝe quha vsis, ȝe kirkmen has; þa leif, thay differ, they obscure, hyid and diminucis, they baith allege, they merite and deseruis, al anciant faderis ... þat euer hes beine, men ... quha doise, thais of þe new learnyng has Inventit,* &c.

A has once *þow art; bene* does not occur as a present tense form. The different syntactical combinations in which the other forms of *be* occur are exemplified by *I am, I quha am, þow ar, ar þow,* F also *is þow, he is, he sittis ... and is, this quhilk is, ve ar, ar we, I and þe Father ar boith ane, ar ȝe, ar þa, nother sal they mare ... bot ar, þir ar, þe scripturis ... ar, þe breid and wyne quhilkis ar, quhairby þe fructis of Christis deyth and passioun is daylie renewit and applyit, quhairby ar applyit ... þe fructis of his deyth and passioun, in þe sacrament ... is contenit realy þe body and bluid, þe reall body and bloude of Iesus Christ ... is verraly contenit, þe substance of breade and vyne ar chaunged;* 'introductory' *þair* is regularly accompanied by *is* when followed by a subject in the plural, but the verb may also agree with the plural subject: *there is diuerse heretikis; þai ar sum prophane precheouris þat thrawis þe scripture.*

The past tense of weak verbs was formed by means of the dental suffix, that of strong verbs by means of vowel mutation. The verb *be* had two forms, *was* and *war*, for the singular and plural respectively.

The form of the past participles of weak verbs was the same as that of the preterite, that of strong verbs differed from the corresponding preterite by the addition of the *in*-ending and, generally, a different stem-vowel. The ending had been lost, however, in several participles.

With the exception of a few verbs which had become weak, the strong verbs were those which had survived of the different classes of strong verbs in OE, although a few loan-words had been added to their number. Those verbs were weak which had been weak in OE and practically all verbs which had been borrowed from other languages. The vowel of the strong preterites was, generally speaking, that which had developed from the OE first and third persons singular.

Brocht, thocht and *vrocht* have a different vowel in the preterite; the preterite of *teche* is *techit.* Shortening had regularly taken place in A *left,* B *spred* and *cled.* Apart from the verbs ending in *-at(e)* and *-ut(e),* mentioned before, the dental suffix is also absent in *set, put* and *interpreit,* pret. The different classes of vowel-gradation in strong verbs are represented by *ryise, rais, rissin; fynd, fand, funde; beir, buir* (with the vowel of the OE sixth class), *borne; gif, gef* (B *gaif*), *gevin; onderstand,* B *vnderstude, onderstand* and F *vnderstanding (* also weak A *onderstandit*): *thraw, threw, thrawin.* Schew and *schawin,* corresponding to the present tense form *schawis,* have become strong through analogy. The loan-words *appreif, approvine, ryngis, range,* and *tak, tuik, tane* have the vowels of the old second, third and sixth classes respectively. A *forbeid* (OE *beodan*) occurs in the same sense as B *forbid* (OE *biddan*) which has a regular preterite *forbad.* The participles *spokin, cropin* and *brokin* have the vowel of the old fourth class. The suffix has disappeared in *funde, bound, soung, onderstand, ganestand* and *cum* (by the side of *cumin*).

The MSc present tense may be said to have had a special form for the subjunctive in those cases where the indicative would have the sibilantic suffix. The forms *be* and *war* were used for the present and preterite subjunctive of the verb *be*. Mood, aspect, passive voice and time-relationship were further expressed by means of contextual features, notably auxiliaries and adverbs or adverbial adjuncts, in very much the same way as in modern English.

The use of *do* as a periphrastic auxiliary is unstable; it was not felt to be necessary in questions *(Quhy diffidis þow ...? Think ʒe þat ...?)* and frequently occurs in positions where it would not be used in modern English *(þai ... quhilkis did affirme; there is na authoritie quhilk dois perswade the errour of Arrius to be ongodlye bot þe sammyne dois perswade ...).* On the other hand, the distinction between the past and perfect tenses agrees with that of modern English: *the same authoritie ... hes at all tymes condamnit þe vickit heresye of Ecolampadius and Calvyne as dide condame the errour of Arrius; his natural body, quhilk he tuik of þe virgine with þe tyme; his godheid, quhilk he hes tane of his Fader ... before al tyme.*

Concord of tense frequently appears to reflect attempts to express the content of Latin verbal forms: *they expone the vordes ... to haue bene spoken; ... allegis þir vordis ... to be spokin; þair is na ressone ... quhairfor it suld be thocht þat þe vordis ... suld be spokin; quha belewit þat our saliuour wald hef giffin his flesche to hef beine couponit.* On the other hand, the Scots omission of *haue* between another auxiliary and a past participle occurs only once in A: *than suld the heresy of Arrius hed place rather nor ....*

A notable feature of Kennedy's extensive use of the present participle is the repetition of the subject both before the participle and when the main structure of the sentence is resumed. Here too, however, practice varies: *our saluioure beand inwnctit be Marye Magdalene said ...; our saluiour, he beand apone þe hill, he passet throuch þe multitude; ane potent prince beand of purpose to send ..., he geiffis ...* The same feature occurs also with appositions and subordinate sentences: *sua Iesus Chryst oure potent prince he left ...; our salueour quhen he institute þe sacrament of baptyme, he commandit ...; þe godly vark and myracle and it mich be comprehendit be natural reasone, it var na ... miracle.* The practice appears to represent a too meticulous translation of the personal endings of Latin verbal forms. The parenthetic character of such constructions adds to the rhetoric of Kennedy's style and links them closely to absolute constructions: *þis confutatioun beand maid sufficient to all oure confirmatiouns, I oblis myself ...; lyk as, ane perfyte medycyne beand applyit be diuers instrumentis proper þairfoir, þe instrumentis dois ..., sua ...; lyk as, ane tre haiffand þe leiffis dilatate and spred, þe sone schynand þairapon, everie leif of þe tre castis ane vmbre ..., Sua It is þat ....* Also compare: *To geif ʒou iust occasioun to consider þe samyn, I will ...; to geif ʒou ferther persuasioun, ʒe sall ....*

The gerund occurs with both noun-modifiers and verb-modifiers, according as the stress is on the substantival or the verbal character: *þe sayingis of þe auld wrytaris; for þe mair perfite vnderstanding of ...; þe resauynge of þis sacrament vorthely.*

MSc had various paratactical, co-ordinating and hypotactical means of expressing notional relationship. A number of prepositions and conjunctions were not, or not with the same frequency, used in Southern English, but special syntax was principally determined by the circumstances of a text or the style of its author.

Apposition occurs not only in *Quintine Kennidy, abbot of Corsragal,* where the class-noun further identifies the proper name, but also in such groups as *godly men his ministeris, heretykis his Instrumentis, þe auld anceant fatheris Interpretouris of þe scripturis,* where the modifiers express non-identifying functions of the persons concerned. The case where the nominal subject of a sentence reflects the appositional character of the Latin nominal subject, has already been mentioned. Of special interest is the apposition in *bayth God and man, twa natures in a persone*, which acquires an all but absolute nature in *he is þe fwid of our saull, realy contenit in þe blesset sacrament, twa natures in ane persone.*

Non-introduced clauses occur in *I wald ȝe maid ȝour sayingis mair plane; It apperis to me ȝe rehers the text wrang; I think ȝe quha vsis þe mess dois nocht ...; &c.* Grammatical co-ordination may express notional dependence, as in *thais of þe new learnyng has Inventit certane oratiouns and cerimoniis to decoir þair commwnioune and Is* ['although they are'] *nocht of þe substance and effect of þe commwnioun.*

Far from limiting himself to standard expressions like *oft and diuers tymis* (or to the native multiplication of negatives, as in *is nocht nor ȝit can noch be*), Kennedy makes the Renaissance mannerism [28] of using pairs of synonyms a distinct feature of his rhetorical style. The second word may supply the necessary interpretation of a vernacularized loan-word *(subrogate and ordanit); often only the conjunction of the two words expresses the contextual meaning (cp. declaracione and onderstanding, declaracione and doctrine, doctryne and Interpretatioun);* but equally often the second word does not modify the meaning of the first and is equally well-known or equally foreign: *syng and takin; plaine and manifest; figure and similitude; contentacione, contenment and satisfaccione.* At times Kennedy is capable of employing this practice with great effect, as when he combines it with alliteration in the concluding paragraph of the *Litil Breif Tracteit,* where he speaks of *pestilent precheouris ... subuertand, subornand and circumuenand the symple people.* [29]

A number of prepositions and prepositional phrases deserve to be noted: *be* ('by'), *by* ('beside, beyond'),[30] *but* ('without'), *conforme to* ('in conformity with'), *(in)contrar, contrarius to* and *contrar to* ('contrary to, opposed to'), *fra* ('from'), *in* and *into* (both used for 'in' and 'into'), *quhill* ('till'), *till* ('to'), *tovart* and *as tovart* ('concerning').

Parallelism and correlation are common features in Kennedy's tracts. The correlatives of the comparison of equality occur very frequently and in different combinations: *alse ... as* ('as ... as'); *as ... In þis sammyne maner; lik as ... swa* ('just as ... so ...'); *lyk as ... Evin sua; lyke as ... Inlykvise; in lik maner ... as* ('suchwise ... that'). The comparative of parallel increase is represented by *A þe mair vonderful þat it is, the maire it is to þe glore of God.*

Other notable conjunctions and conjunctional phrases are: *and* ('if'), *at* ('that'), *bot gif* ('unless'), *gif* ('if'), *gif sa var þat, geifand þat, in cais þat, in euentuir* ('lest perchance'), *lesse nor* ('unless'), *nocht the les þat* ('although'), *nocht ... without first* ('not ... until'), *quhill* ('until'), *sua beand þat* or simply *swa* ('if'), *to þe effect þat* ('that, so that, in order that'). Condition may be expressed by the mere inversion of the normal order of subject and predicate: *vil þow mark ... thow sal esaly persaif ....* Condition is expressed by *þat* in *þat I haif vsit ... hypocrisie ..., in þat case I renunce Goddis mercy.*

The syntax of the tracts differs from that of modern Standard English in many minor details, partly to be indicated in the notes to the texts. One common feature may be pointed out here, viz. the unstable position of adverbs: *to be in this blissit sacrament really; quhairin is contenit Christis flesche realy; quhilk inseparatly is Iounyt to his humanite; quhilk ... suffi-*

---

[28] The Renaissance mannerism consisted in the choice of the words and the extent of the practice, rather than in the practice itself; see L. Kellner, "Abwechselung und Tautologie: zwei Eigenthümlichkeiten des alt- und mittelenglischen Stiles"; *Englische Studien,* vol. xx (1895), pp. 1–24.

[29] From the repeated collocation *substance and effect* it appears that Kennedy uses the latter word in the sense of the scholastic 'effectus formalis'; cp. *þe effect* [i.e. of the Mass] *and It þat is signifeit be þis terme* [i.e. 'Mass'], one of the cases where *and* stands for 'that is'.

[30] The difference between MSc *be* and *by* is clearly illustrated by the sentence quoted on p. 59, footnote 5. The phrase *by ane ordour* is equivalent to *misordourlie* (which occurs in the immediate context of the sentence), whilst *be ane ordour* would be equivalent to *ordourlie.* The use of *by, quhairby, þairby* in MSc texts was due to Southern influence.

ciently hes declarit; þe mess hes bene vniuersalie approvin; þat It be approvin vniuersalie; God hes moir sclendirly furthschawin his benevolence; quhilk is familiar euer in þe scripture; quhilk cursit curiositie now in thir dais constrenis men; &c.

This last example contains one of the instances of successful alliteration in Kennedy's tracts. The most notable passage in this respect occurs in the *Compendious Ressonyng*,[31] where he inveighs against such *monstruous ministeris* as the *bletour - bischop*, the *awn - abbotte*, the *pultroun - priour*, the *pelour - persone*, the *veill - vicar*, the *kow - curate*, and again: *pestilent precheouris - pastouris, Ignorant awns - abbottis, prowd pultrouns - priowris*, unconcerned about the ruin of the church *sua thai may suage thair insaciable sensualite*. This sort of language is clearly in the tradition of the 'flyting', in which one of Kennedy's kinsmen had been a master. If more of its vividness had entered his tracts, they would have been considerably more attractive from a literary point of view. As it is, the emotional force of the sounds and imagery of that passage cannot be said to be typical of Kennedy's work as a whole.

Much more characteristic of his style is the appearance in that same passage of familiar ringing collocations like *pestilent precheouris, monstruous ministeris, blindit in Ignorance* and *drownit in lustis*. The occasional reappearance of these and other phrases in different contexts and of similarly structured rhetorical periods is suggestive of the habitual speaker. Kennedy is directly concerned with the positive exposition of what he considers the real points at issue between catholicism and the radical reformers, but rhetoric remains an integral means of persuasion. Not only does he show a distinct preference for certain turns of phrase, his language also contains many rhetorical units. *I dar bauldlie say þat* has the value of 'surely', 'undoubtedly', and the phrase *þis may þow persaif þat*, which occurs on nearly every page of the *Litil Breif Tracteit*, with or without minor modifications, may generally be replaced by 'therefore'.

What Kennedy's average style is like, is perhaps best seen when a particular passage is compared with what may be presumed from the close similarities to have been its immediate source.

OEcol. *Ante omnia ne tam crassum quiddam de coena Dominica sentiamus, verbum Domini: Spiritus viuificat, caro nihil prodest, tanquam angelus igneo gladio armatus obsistit.*

Roff. *Si locus is adeo manifestus est atque tu praetexis, iam et Christus frustra suscepisset carnem. Nam si non omnino frustra susceperit carnem, profecto caro quicquam profuit. ... Audient ergo lectores principio Chrysostomum in commentariis huius loci super Iohan. Homil. 46. ... Sic enim in eiusdem loci expositione super Ioannem Augustinus ait: O Domine magister bone, quomodo caro non prodest quicquam— ... Caro non prodest quicquam, sed quomodo illi intellexerunt.*

Now vil we – as it vil pleis God to gif ws grace – to mak þe redaris to onderstand quhow þe rest of þe scripturis allegit be Ecolampadius and oþeris in þir dais inlikvis ar impropirly applyit to fortify þair vickit opinione tovart þe onderstanding of þis mistery of þe blissit sacrament of þe altare.

Ane of þe cheif argumentis quhilk þa apply in contrar þe godly doctrine of þe kirk is þe vord of our saluiour quhair he sais: "It is þe spreit þat giffis lif, þe flesche profitis na thyng." Of þir vordis infer þa þat þe body of our saluiour is nocht realy contenit in þe sacrament, becaus it is þe spreit þat giffis lif. And in caiss, sa þa, þat Cristis body var realy contenit in þe Sacrament, it iss onprofitable, becaus Crist hyme self Sais þat þe flesche profitis na thyng.

Treuly, þis inferrens is verray impropir and seruis of na thyng to þair intent. And to þat effect þat þow ma cleirly persaif þe sammyne, ve vil mark to quhome þir vordis var spokin,

---

[31] Below, p. 171.

Carnem quippe sic intellexerunt quomodo in cadauere dilaniatur aut in macello venditur: non quomodo spiritu vegetatur. Perinde sic dictum est: caro non prodest quicquam: quomodo dictum est: scientia inflat? Iam ergo debemus odisse scientiam? absit: et quid est: scientia inflat? sola, sine charitate. Ideo adiunxit: charitas vero aedificat. Adde ergo scientiae charitatem, et vtilis erit scientia, non per se, sed per charitatem. Sic etiam nunc caro non prodest quicquam, sed sola caro. Accedat spiritus ad carnem, quomodo accedit charitas ad scientiam, et prodest plurimum. Haec ille. Et paulo post subdit: Spiritus ergo est qui viuificat, caro non prodest quicquam, sicut illi intellexerunt carnem. Non sic ego do ad manducandum carnem meam. Haec Augustinus. ...

OEcol. *Etenim breui illo dicto non minus a carnali manducatione abducimur, quam Nicodemus, ne carnalem regenerationem animo suo conciperet, quum diceretur ei, quod ex carne est, caro est.*

Roff. *A carnali profecto abducimur manducatione, si carnalem ita accipias, vt Capernaitae nimis quam crasse secum cogitarunt, hoc est sicut Augustinus ante dixit; quomodo in cadauere dilaniatur caro, aut in macello venditur* ....

and swa sal it be esaly persauit quhow impropir is þis inferrens.

Thir vordis war spokin be our saluiour to ane certane of his discipulis quhilkis var vaik and imperfit, and quha lenit to þe Iugement of þe flesche, outwart vittis and sensis, as mony dois in þir dais, and nocht to þe Iugement of þe spreit: quha belewit þat our saluiour wald hef giffin his flesche to hef beine couponit and diuidit as flesche deuidit one þe skamles and eittin. Treuly, þe flesche deuidit fra þe spreit efter þis maner according to þair fleschly beleif profeit na thing: quhilk can neuer be said propirly of Cristis flesche, becaus it is neuer deuidit fra þe spreit. For quharsumeuer Cristis flesche is, þair is his diuinite, quhilk is þe spreit þat giffis lif. Thairfor mark þe vordis of our saluiour. He sais indifferently: "þe flesche profitis na thyng." He sais nocht: "my flesche profitis na thing," for þan hed our saluiour bein contrarius to hyme self, quha said ane litil befoir: "he quha ettis my flesche and drinkis my bluid hes euerlestyng lif."

To mark þe vordis of our saluiour, Sayand: "Þe flesche profitis na thing, it is þe spreit þat giffis lif," And þat þa ma be mair esaly onderstand, ve sal confer þe testimonyis of scripturis with oþeris scripturis, conforme to þe exempil of anciant authouris. The apostil S. Paul, vritin to þe Corinthianis, sais one þis maner: "Science makis men proud, cherite edifyis." Þow ma persaif þat science without cherite is onprofitable, bot cherite Iunit to science edifyis and makis science profitable. Sua flesche only without þe spreit, as flesche is þat is deuidit one þe skamles, is onprofitable for mannis saluacione. Bot flesche Iunit to þe spreit quhilk is God, as Cristis flesche is, can nocht be bot verray profitable.[32]

Unlike his practice elsewhere, where he copies patristic quotations from Richard Smith, Kennedy here merely refers to *anciant authouris*. He freely uses Fisher's information on what Oecolampadius had taught, adds the *oþeris in þir dais* and renders the gist of St. Augustine's commentary. The result is a fine combination of argument and homily, in which *Capernaitae* is significantly rendered by *ane certane of his discipulis quhilkis var vaik*. The relative simplicity of Kennedy's style is obvious. Its lucidity is perhaps best appreciated when it is compared with Greenlaw's prose in the last part of what we have

[32] Fisher, *De Veritate*, lib. v, cap. xxvii; cp. lib. iii, cap. iv. Kennedy's version occurs at the beginning of ch. II of the *Litil Breif Tracteit*.

called MS G. To a much greater extent than Greenlaw's, Kennedy's prose is a synthesis of traditional pulpit oratory and Renaissance rhetoric.[33]

It is not, however, always of the same quality. His long periods often tend to be overcrowded with prepositional phrases, as in ... *impropirly applyit by the godlye menynge of the sammyne incontrare the godlye doctrine of the kyrk tovart þe onderstandinge of this most excellent mistery of the blesset sacrament of the altare*. Again, his frequent parentheses tend to make his sentences complicated. Thus the concluding passage of the *Litil Breif Tracteit* consists of one long period which, when reconstructed and provided with proper punctuation, proves to be a fine piece of rhetoric combining well-chosen imagery and alliteration with the accumulation of the words. But the corrupt text in A shows that it was too much for at least one copyist. And when Kennedy subsequently adapted it for the final passage of his *Oratioune*, it became a strange admixture of appeal and invective, with an abrupt change to the concluding formal prayer.[34] Again, Kennedy tends to be much too abstract in the presentation of his eucharistic teaching. It may be supposed that the circumstances of controversy secured sufficient interest in a work like the *Litil Breif Tracteit*. But one feels that even his contemporaries would not read it for its concrete presentation of theology. The dialogue form[35] of the *Compendious Ressonyng* meant a real improvement in this respect. Not that this latter tract is a perfect example of its kind. It is not devoid of emotion, but it is no dramatic debate, even though, with an apparent allusion to Erasmus, Kennedy once calls it a *colloquium*.[36] The comparison only serves to emphasize the relative naivety of the literary form in Kennedy's case. It is amusing that, for example, he now gives his customary recapitulations only at the request of James. Indeed, the improvement effected by the literary form does not consist in any dramatic persuasiveness, but in the less abstract character of the tract.

The *Appendex* treats mainly of liturgical ceremonies and vestments, subjects not belonging to the principal matter of the tract proper and not referred to in the table of propositions at the beginning. It is noteworthy that the last three chapters of the *Litil Breif Tracteit* contain a somewhat similar addition not mentioned in the outline of its opening pages. And in the same way the first fourteen chapters of the *Compendius Tractiue* round off the treatment of church authority before Kennedy proceeds to *utheris questionis movit in the contrar of our purpose*.[37] It has already been remarked in connection with Dempster's mention of a supposed work by Kennedy in fourteen chapters that this may point to an earlier separate existence of the first part of the *Compendius Tractiue*. This question cannot be decisively answered. In chapter viii, after stating that Luther and Oecolampadius contradict one another in their eucharistic

---

[33] On this matter, see G. R. Owst, *Preaching in Medieval England*, Cambridge University Press, 1926, and *Literature and Pulpit in Medieval England*, Cambridge University Press, 1933; also R. W. Chambers, "The Continuity of English Prose from Alfred to More and his School." pp. xlv–clxxiv in the E.E.T.S. edition of *The Life and Death of Sir Thomas Moore, Knight, ... by Nicholas Harpsfield, L.D.*, London, 1932.

[34] See Laing, *Works*, vi, p. 165; on the whole, however, the *Oratioune* is a better literary product than the *Litil Breif Tracteit*.

[35] A discussion of sixteenth-century polemical dialogues may be found in C. H. Herford, *Studies in the Literary Relations of England and Germany in the Sixteenth Century*, Cambridge, 1886, pp. 21–68.

[36] p. 168, below.

[37] *Wodrow Misc.*, p. 154.

doctrine, Kennedy adds: *as efterwart salbe declarit*.[38] This is actually done in chapters xv–xviii, so that they cannot have been added to an unrevised earlier tract.[39] The mere number 'fourteen' in Dempster's catalogue is weak evidence for an earlier edition of the *Compendius Tractiue*, if it was Kennedy's habit to let first things come first and then to deal with connected questions by way of 'appendix'.

---

[38] *Ibid.*, p. 130.

[39] The title of Greenlaw's version of the *Appendex* presupposes the title of the *Compendious Ressonyng* proper, just as the opening lines presuppose the earlier pages. Apparently, Greenlaw was interested in a defence of customs and devotions which were subject to particular attack and ridicule. There is no reason to suppose that Kennedy himself had caused the *Appendex* to circulate by itself.

VII. THE MANUSCRIPTS

MS A.   *Ane litil breif tracteit*, &c., owned by the Rev. William James Anderson, M.A., Keeper of the Catholic Archives of Scotland, Edinburgh. *Copy*, written by Alexander Wood, chaplain at Old Aberdeen, August 3rd 1561. Paper; 22 leaves including title page (numbering in pencil, by a later hand); all loose leaves, water marks hand with star and two parallel lines (perhaps originally two gatherings of twelve leaves, with final blank leaves now gone), inlaid and bound in boards (spine and corners leather) under the supervision of Archibald Constable, *c.* 1803, Constable's explanatory letter being inserted before, and the original vellum wrapper (Latin liturgical text with musical notation) after the tract. The inlaid title page measures 110 mm. × 102 mm., the other inlaid leaves varying from 124 mm. × 170 mm. to 150 mm. × 187 mm. Several corners torn off; small holes in title page, leaf no. 5 and the last four leaves (increasing in size towards the last leaf: see *Plate I*). A writing area of 107 mm. × 157 mm. is marked off with clearly visible single lines on ff. 2r–7r, that of the remaining pages is not marked off and varies in size from 120 to 135 mm. × 160 to 173 mm. The title page contains seven lines of writing, the number of lines on the other pages varies from twenty-five to thirty-two to a page (25–28 on the first seven leaves, 28–32 afterwards).

The manuscript, clearly written with great rapidity, is in a free, running and non-ornamental sixteenth-century hand. The writing is continuous throughout each chapter, with larger interlinear spaces and bolder writing at the beginning of a new chapter and before the concluding paragraph of the tract. The lines frequently describe concave curves. Capitals occur at the beginnings of the title and the chapters and occasionally within the text, notably to indicate the beginning of an important clause after one or more dependent clauses, but not as a rule at the beginning of a new sentence. The punctuation consists mainly of slanting lines, often, but not always, longer for the more important pauses. A double dot is occasionally employed to indicate a full stop. Double slanting lines, usually somewhat shorter than the others, are used at the end of a line to indicate division of words. (See *Plate I*).

There is a change in the spelling from the *verso* of f. 7 onwards, consisting in the frequent use of *th* instead of *þ* and a greater variety of spellings for the same words than before (e.g. *presence, scriptouris,*

Christ, made. bene, clear, bloud, bread, sall, bodie, bodye, -lie, -lye by
the side of previously regular *presens, scripturis, Crist, maid, bein, cleir,
bluid, breid, sal, body, -ly*).

For the history of the MS, see above, p. 51.

MS B. *Ane compendious ressonyng,* &c., preserved in the Catholic Archives
of Scotland, Edinburgh (c/o the Rev. William James Anderson, M.A.)
Copy, written by an unknown scribe, 1561 or soon after. Paper,
32 leaves, water marks hand with star (not identical with that of MS A)
and two parallel lines, three gatherings, viz. of eight, sixteen and again
eight, not coinciding with foliation: iv (title page, table and preface,
not foliated) + 23 (*Ressonyng* and *Appendex*; foliation partly or, in the
case of a few leaves, entirely cropped in the *Ressonyng,* completely
absent in the *Appendex,* which begins about the middle of the *verso* of
f. 18) + 5 (blank, though ruled for writing). The leaves measure
150 mm. × 180 mm. and have been recently bound in brown morocco,
with the name *Quentyne Kennedy* printed in gilt on the front. The lower
parts of the present vertical edges are worn and have brown stains due
to much fingering. The writing area of the pages, marked off by firmly
drawn lines, measures from 102 to 105 mm. × 140 to 145 mm. Notices
in the outer margin are separated from the text by a second line, at a
distance of about 5 mm. from the text. The original edges have been
cropped and many marginal entries are incomplete. The text of the
title page is divided over nineteen lines. f. 20v has thirty-four, f. 21r
thirty-three, the ordinary pages have from twenty-eight to thirty-two
lines of writing.

The manuscript is written in a neat court hand, with a more formal
style of writing for the Latin quotations. There are frequent ornamental
flourishes and numerous capitals have been touched up with red ink.
The title page (the first letter of which is decorated with a bearded face),
table, preface, first page of the *Ressonyng* (facsimile in *Essays,* facing
p. 400) and the title of the *Appendex* have more or less profusely
decorated initials in red, whilst red ink is also used throughout to set
off the initials *Q* and *I* of the two brothers, the names of church fathers
and Mass vestments, and such introductory words as *First, Secundlie,*
&c. Whereas the writing is continuous, the use of the red ink serves to
pick out the different subordinate sections. The marginal cross-re-
ferences to the table of propositions are likewise in red ink. Where it
is used in greater quantity, the red shows through on the other side of
the leaves (see *Plate II*).

The punctuation consists of commas, dots and occasional marks of interrogation. Commas are very frequent by modern standards. Double slanting lines are used at the end of a line to indicate division of words.

The spelling is much more consistent than that of MS A. Among the distinctive spellings – at least in the frequency of their occurrence – are: *-lie, -tioun, samyn, vnder, grit, doctryne, amangis, evir, worde, haif, dayes, how* (A *-ly, -cione, sammyne, onder, grete, doctrine, among, euer, vord, haue, dais, quhow*).

For historical information on the MS, see above, p. 54.

MS F.   [*Ane Litil Breif Tracteit*]: incomplete *copy*, without title page or name or author, owned by A. J. B. fforde, Esq., Brook, Surrey, and at present on temporary deposit at the National Library of Scotland, Edinburgh *(T.D. 313)*. Written by an unknown copyist, possibly one called John Dunbar, with corrections and additions by John Greenlaw of Haddington (d. 1566). Paper; 30 leaves extant, not foliated; at least four leaves lost, viz. at least one (probably not more than one) which preceded the present first leaf, one which came between the twenty-first and twenty-second extant leaves and two between the twenty-fourth and twenty-fifth extant leaves. Inserted in Greenlaw's rebound copy of the *Compendius Tractiue*, immediately after the printed text, and cut at the edges to 140 mm. × 180 mm. so as to fit the size of the small quarto volume. The writing area, which measures from 100 to 110 mm. × 160 to 165 mm., is not marked off. Marginal entries by Greenlaw, often separated from the text of the tract by roughly drawn lines, have been partly cropped at the outer edges or cannot be integrally read at the inner edges through the tight binding.

The present binding of marbled boards with leather spine and corners is nineteenth century. It cannot be ascertained whether all the contents of the present volume, which include a letter by one Robert Callanwood, dated June 4th, 1597, had been gathered in one earlier binding. MSS F and G certainly belonged together before the nineteenth century, since they are written on one and the same set of leaves. The common water marks are hand and star, with the letters *RB* (possibly *RR*) on the wrist of the hand, and parallel lines. The binding cord between extant leaves ten and eleven as well as the water marks indicate a first gathering of twenty-two leaves (on the supposition that only one leaf is missing at the beginning). The water marks suggest that there must be a second binding cord (the presence of which cannot be ascertained through the tightness of the binding) between extant leaves thirty-one and thirty-two. On the same earlier supposition that only one leaf was lost at the beginning and taking into account the other three lost leaves, this would mean a second gathering of twenty-six leaves, the last seven – presumably blank – leaves of which would be lost. In any case, MS F extends far into the gathering which contains MS G.

The end of MS F is marked by the words *Finis coronat opus*. The remaining open space of the last page is filled up with the following verses in a more formal style of writing but in what would appear to be the same hand. The name of the versifier, John Dunbar, may well be that of the copyist:

> *Beleue Is ane wonder*
> *quhilk ressone nocht can*
> *Quhow maid wes ane mothir*
> *and god wes ane man*
> *Leif þow thy ressone, belewe in þe wondre*
> *Belewe Is abone, and ressone Is vndre*
> *cedit ratio fidej in misteriis diuinis*
> *Anteferenda fides, victa ratione quod vna*
> *virgo simul genitrix, et deus extet homo*
> *Esto suprema fides, victa ratione relicta*
> *hec superest victrix: victa sed illa subest*
> *Tantillj versus si queras quis fuit author*
> *Dunbar Iohannes, tale epygramma dabat.*

The tract is written in an informal court hand. The writing is continuous, larger and with fewer words to the line than in MSS A and B. Normally there are from twenty-five to twenty-seven lines to the page, but two pages have twenty-four lines, two twenty-eight, one twenty-nine and one, the last, eleven.

The punctuation consists of commas, dots, double dots and occasional marks of interrogation. All these signs, however, are extremely sparingly used, especially towards the end of the tract. Word-division at the end of a line is not indicated by any sign. Among the spelling habits of the copyist are the use of capital *R* at the beginning of words, the frequent use of *w* for /v/, the use of *ie* instead of *ei* in *clierlie*, of *continet* instead of *contenit*, of *attoir* by the side of *attour*, of *ue* as a variant of *ui* for the long *ü*-sound, and the frequent excrescent *t*'s after final *th*.

The leaf following upon the last one of Kennedy's *Litil Breif Tracteit* has more versification, first in the same hand and then in that of Greenlaw. The latter's signature occurs at the bottom of the recto (see *Plate III*). On the next leaf Greenlaw's hand, distinctive in spelling habits as well as form, continues with MS G.

MS G.   *Ane appendix in maner off collocutione*, &c. 6 leaves, not foliated, of the same size as the above. Normally from twenty-three to twenty-six lines to the page, but twenty-nine on the verso of the third leaf and fourteen on the last page. The text stops rather abruptly in the middle of a recto.

The writing area of the pages measures from 100 to 110 mm. × 160 mm. It is not marked off except by occasional rough lines which separate the text from additions in the margin and at the foot of the page (see *Plate IV*). The text is written in an informal hand, with several writing mistakes and without any attempt at neatness. The punctuation consists of commas, dots, double dots and occasional marks of interrogation, but is often absent. Words and groups of words which stand out in red ink in MS B are roughly underscored in G. Among the peculiarities of Greenlaw's spelling are the gemination of final *f*, the use of *ow* for the long *u*- and *ü*-sounds, the frequent excrescent *t*'s after final *th* and the preference for *-air* whatever the origin of the ending in a particular word.

The first six pages follow the first part of the *Appendex* of MS B more or less closely. From the end of the *verso* of leaf three onwards, however, the text digresses on the subject of the sign of the cross and does not again take up the thread of the B text.

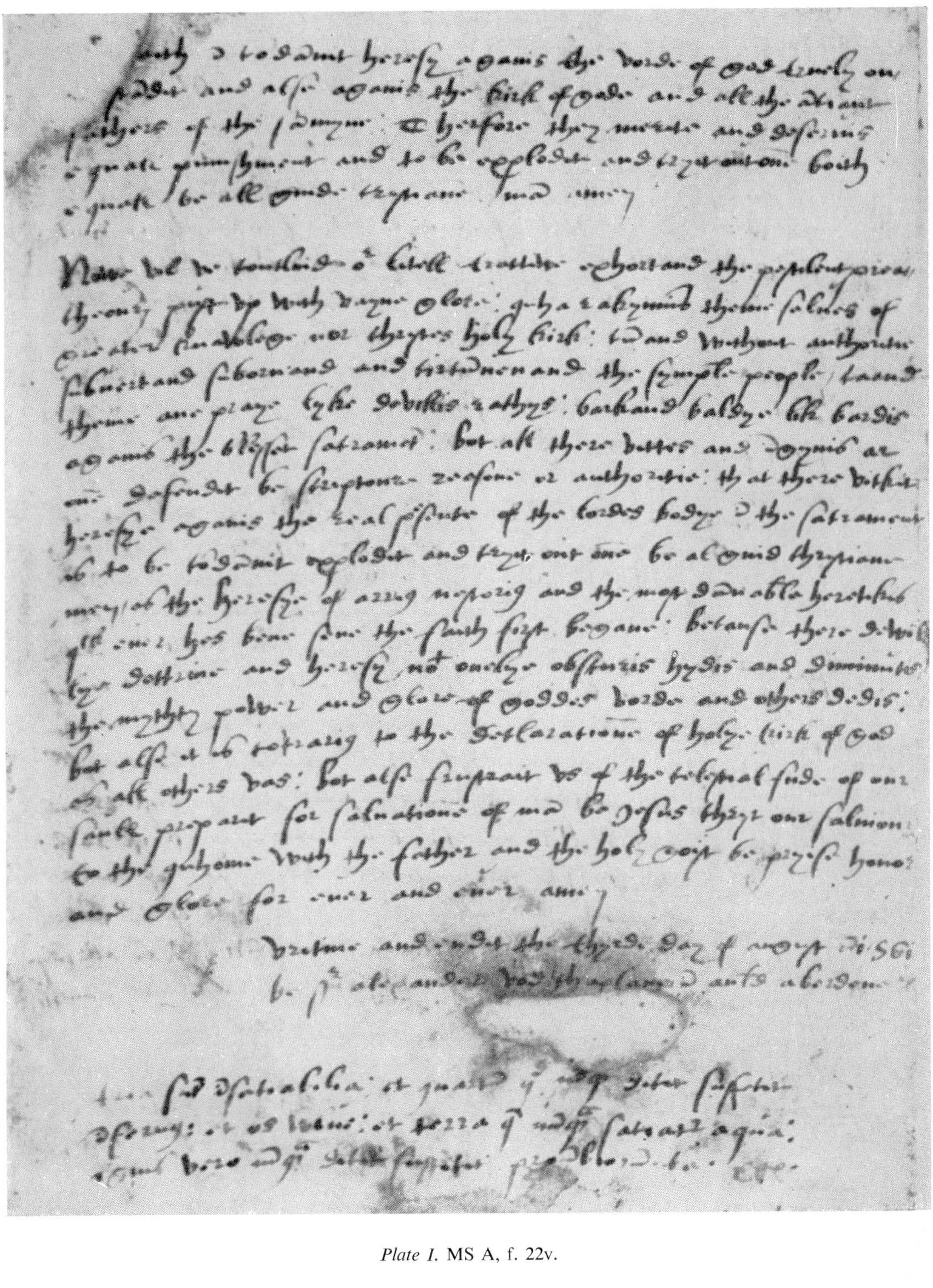

Plate I. MS A, f. 22v.

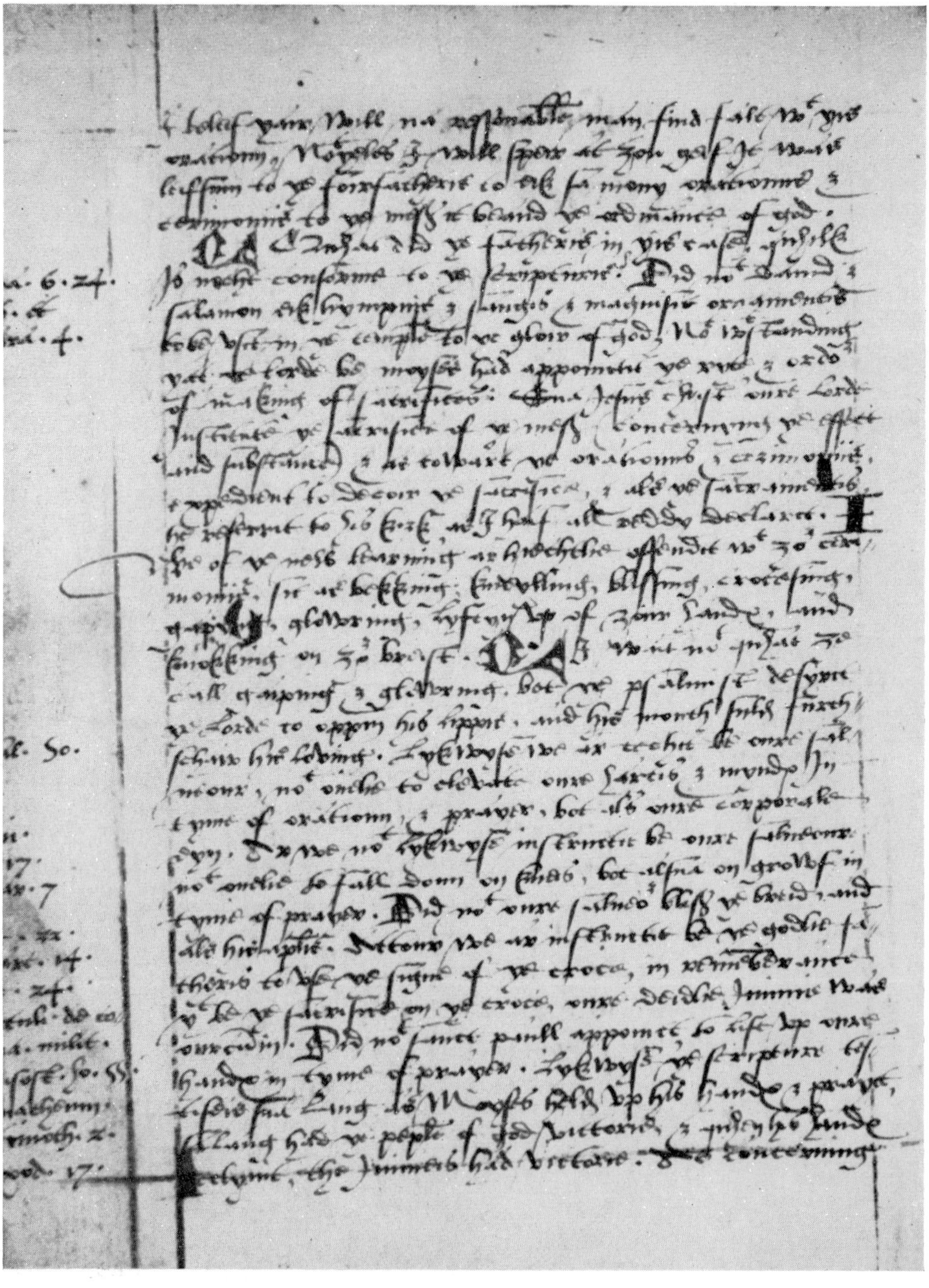

Plate II. MS B, f. 20v.

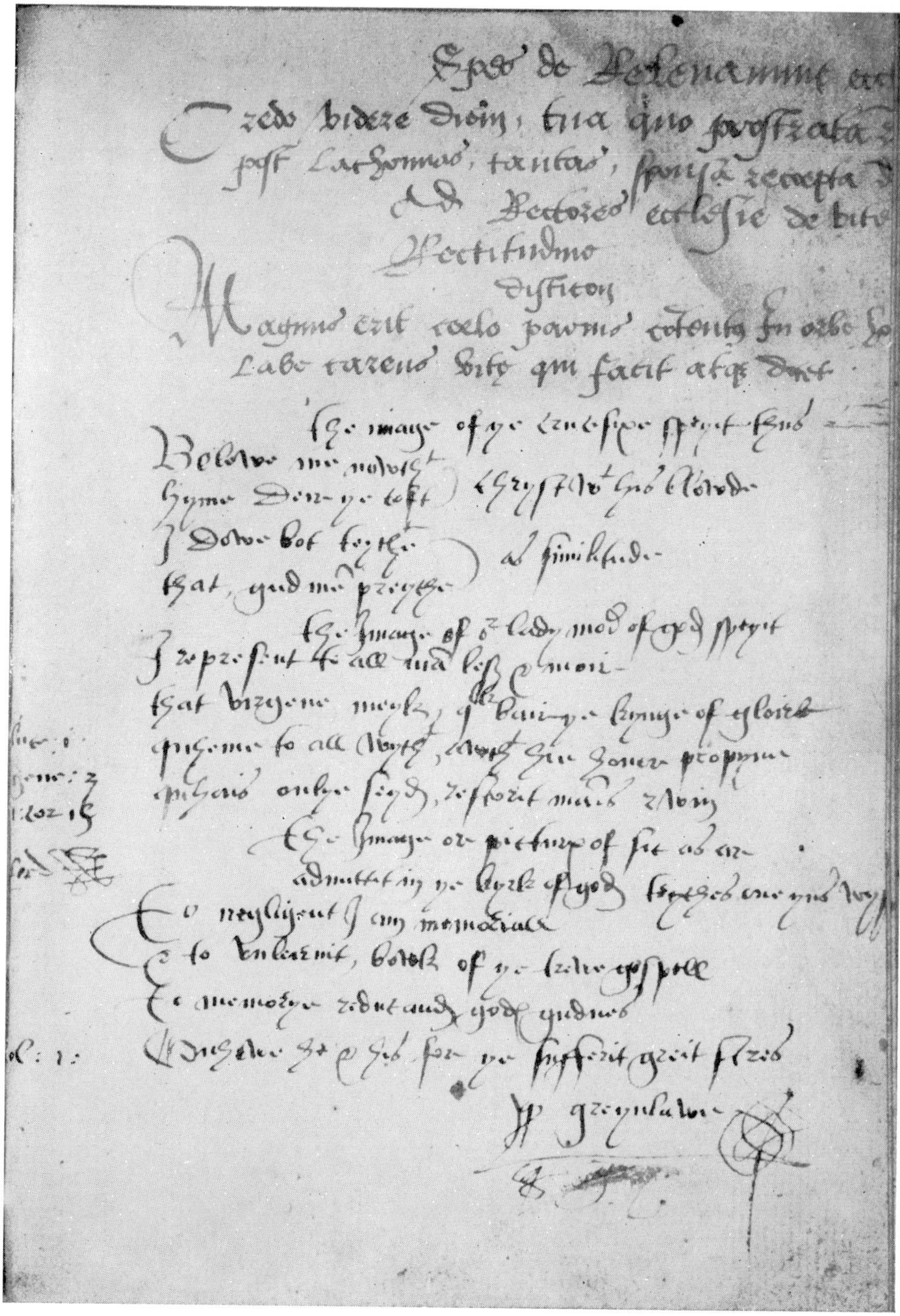

Plate III. Greenlaw's Signature.

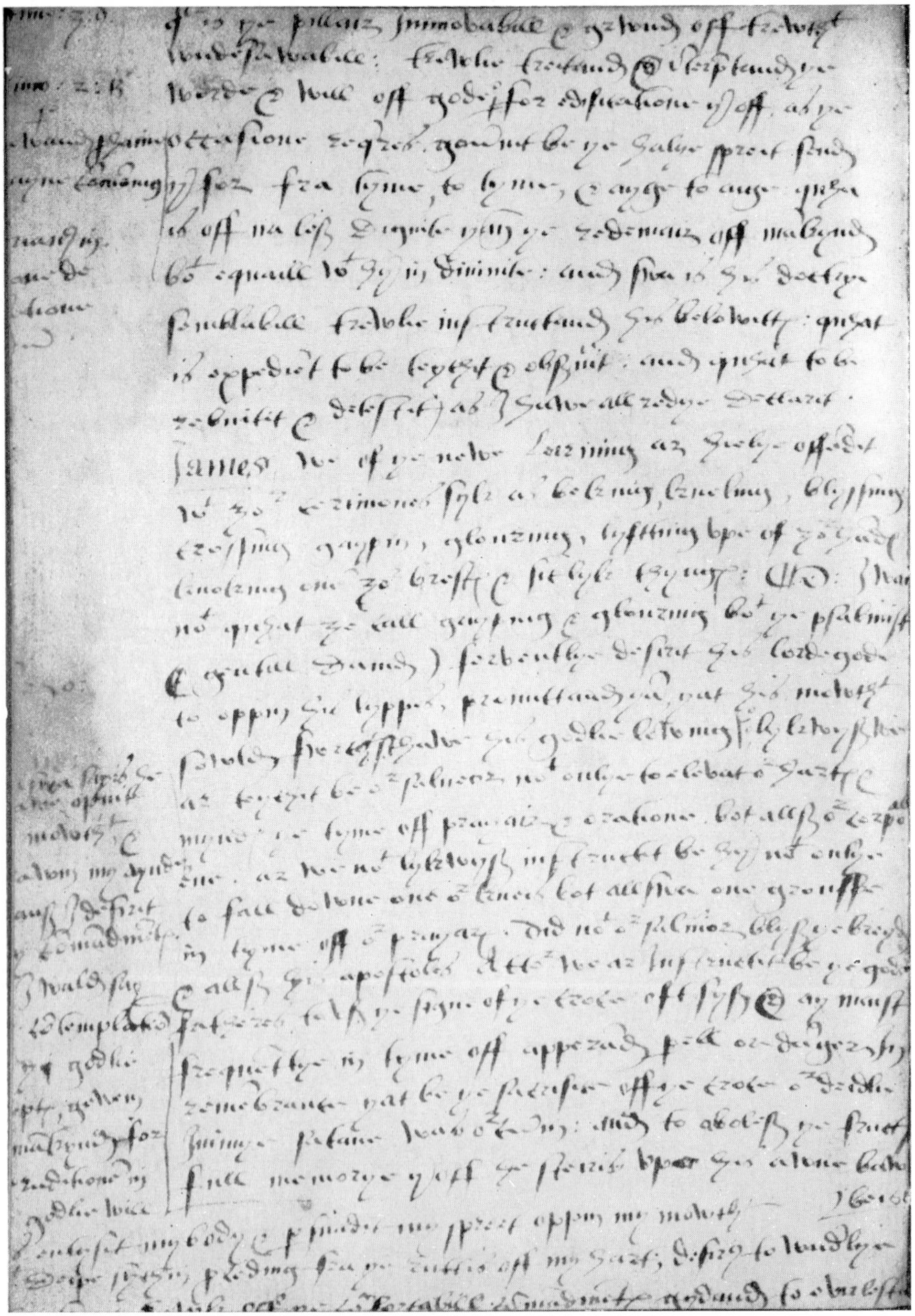

Plate IV. MS G, f. 3v.

VIII. METHOD OF EDITING

The printed texts are those of the two complete manu
register the textual variants of the other manuscripts, but
variants. Commentary is relegated to the subsequent *Note*
cases the numbers refer to the numeration of the lines, wl

The scribal $\mathfrak{z}$ is printed as z where it represents /z/, as $\mathfrak{z}$ \
The *þ* is also retained, but for all other letters the ordinary
The elaborately formed *s* which looks somewhat like Germ
Other different forms of the same letters are disregarded.
in words where either symbol would be acceptable has b(
parison with other words and by considerations of consis!
-cione in A, *-tioun* in B).

The capitalization of proper names and the opening wo
been adjusted to modern practice, the punctuation also as fa
type is used for letters or words which in various degrees s
normal script, ordinary italics for the more formal hand o(
MS B and for expanded contractions. The abbreviation $\mathfrak{d}$
the sign for *-is/-es* as *-is*, that for *ar/air/er* in the form which
or in the immediate context. Final superscript *u* is indicat
but other contracting superscript letters have not themsel
(e.g. no^t = no*c*ht, w^t = w*ith*, þ^t = þ*at*, q^{lk} = q*uhi*lk). Me:
are disregarded in the printed text.

Rounded brackets represent the brackets used in the MS!
have been introduced into the text within pointed brackets:
additions and corrections within reversed pointed brackets
numerous marginal and interlinear additions by Greenlaw i
which can in no way be attributed to Kennedy, have been disr
additions are enclosed within square brackets.

[fo. 1v., title page]

Ane litil breif tracteit

maid be mast*er* Qui*n*tine Kennidy, abbot of Corsragal,

prevand cleirlye

þe real body of Iesu Crist to be present i*n* þe sacrament of þe altare,

contrar þe vickit opinione and heresy of Ecola*m*padius

and oþ*er*is diu*er*ss

i*n* þir miserabil dais falslye deni[an]d þe sa*m*myne.

The nerrest and only vay, benevalent [redar], to be establisit and satifeit
in conscience tovart þe rycht onderstanding of þe profund mistery of þe
blissit sacrament of þe altare – and al oþer misteryis contenit in þe scripturis
5 necessar to be knavin for cristiane mennis saluacione –, is to haue recours
to þe doctrine of þe kirk of God, Quhilk oft *and* diuerss tymis sufficiently
hes declarit þis mistery, treuly conforme to Goddis vord, as ma, aucht, and
suld be to þe contentacione, contenment, and satisfaccione of al guid
cristiane men.
10 Nochtþeles, be ressone þat þe declaracione of þe sammyne conforme to
þe doctrine of þe kirk is thocht contrarius to þe trew onderstanding of
Goddis word be ane callit Ecolampadius, *and* oþeris quhilkis ar villing to
renow condamnit heresis, We vil ressone þe mater sumpart, and in lik
maner – God villing – as al gud cristiane man sal hef Iust occasione
15 conforme to Goddis vord to rasaif þe approvine doctrine of þe kirk tovart
þe trew declaracione and onderstanding of þis mast excellent sacrament.
And to þat effect ve sal breifly collect resonyng in twa hedis, and þat be
continual conferrens of scripturis.
In þe first heid <caput 1.> ve sal mark þe declaracione and doctrine
20 of þe kirk tovart þe onderstanding of þis sacrament to gidder with sum
[f. 2v] [cheif testi]monyis of scripturis allegit and applyit be [þe ki]rk til
appreue þe sammyne. Thairefter ve sal mark [þe o]pinione *and* interpretacione of Ecolampadius in contrar þe godlye doctrine of þe kirk. And als þair
with sum cheif testimonyis allegit and applyit be hyme. <...is maner ...
25 appreif his [vi]ckit opinione.> Thane sal we diligently considder and note
quhilk of þe twa interpretaciones is maist propir *and* aggreabil with þe
plaine text of þe scripture.
In þe secund heid <caput 2m.> ve sal mark quhilk of þe twa interpretaciones is maist to þe glore of God *and* to þe veil *and* profeit of þe haly
30 congregacione, and þat conforme to Goddis vord. For without dowt þat
interpretacione quhilkis is maist to þe glore of God *and* þe veil and profeit
of þe haly congregacione – beand propirly colleckit of þe scripture (and
nocht of mannis Imaginacione) – is alvais to be rasauit.
As tovart þe first heid, þow sal onderstand þat it is þe doctrine of þe kirk

---

31. *þe veil and profeit*] F weill. 32. *haly*] F haill.

of God *and* of al anciant fad*er*is of þe sa*m*myne þat eu*er* hes beine co*n*forme
to Godd*is* vord, That i*n* þe sacrame*n*t of þe altare is co*n*tenit þe verray real
body and bluid of Iesu Crist o*ur* saluio*ur*, and þat be ane sup*er*natural
man*er*, co*n*forme to þe vord of o*ur* saluio*ur* vritin i*n* þe evangelis S. Matho*w*
5   <26>, S. M*ar*k <14>, *and* S. Luk <22>, Sayand: "þis is my body,
q*uhi*lk salbe giffin for ʒo*w*; This is my bluid of þe new testame*n*t" – And
alss co*n*forme to þe vord*is* of þe apostil vriting to þe Corinthyis, quhair
he makis me*n*cione of þe blissit sacrament, Say - [fo. 3r]and þir vord*is*:
<1 Corin. 11.> "Quhene he hed giffin tha*n*k*is*, he b[r]ak þe breid and
10 said: tak ʒe and eit, þis is my body, q*uhi*lk salbe giffin for ʒo*w*. And eft*er*
þe sa*m*myne man*er* he tuk þe cwpe, eft*er* þat he hed swpit, Sayand: 'þis
cwpe is þe new testame*n*t i*n* to my bluid. Do þis sa oft as eu*er* ʒe drink i*n* to
my rame*m*berans'. Quho*w* oft þat eu*er* ʒe sal eit of þis breid and sal drink
of þis cwpe, ʒe sal fur*t*hscha*w* þe deid of þe lord q*uhi*ll he cu*m*. Quhasum-
15 eu*er* sal eit of þis breid and drink of þis cwpe onvorthely, he salbe gilty
of þe body and bluid of o*ur* lord. Lat ane ma*n* exame hyme self, and swa
lat hym eit of þis breid and drink of þis cwpe. For he þat eitt*is* and drink*is*
onvorthely, he eitt*is* and drink*is* his avin da*m*nacione, becaus he makis
na difference of þe body of þe lord."
20   Diuers testimonyis of scriptur*is* beand left q*uhi*lk*is* ar co*n*forme to o*ur*
purpos, we vil rahers þe opinione of Ecola*m*padius tovart þe onder*stan*ding
of þis sacrame*n*t, q*uhi*lk is þat i*n* þe sacrame*n*t of þe altare is bot a*n*e syng
and takin only of þe body and bluid of o*ur* saluio*ur*, Sayand i*n* his last suppar: "þis is my body", ar spokin be ane figure and similitude.
25   To preif þe sa*m*myne i*m*propirly callis he to rame*m*berance þe vord*is* of
þe apostil, Sayand: "Crist vas ane roik" <1 Corin. 10.>, and als þe vord*is*
of o*ur* saluio*ur*, Sayand: "þe flesche profit*is* na thing, it is þe spreit þat
giff*is* lif" <Ioan. 6.>, and i*n* ane oþ*er* place: "ʒe sal haf þe puyr wi*t*h ʒo*w*
for eu*er*, bot ʒe sal [f. 3v.] no*ch*t haue me wi*t*h ʒo*w* for eu*er*" <Math. 26.>:
30 he sitt*is* at þe ry*ch*t hand of þe Fader and is to returne agane one þe lett*er*
day to Iuge levand and deid. Of þir testimonyis of scriptur*is* i*n*ferr*is* Eco-

1. *þat*] F and.   2. *is*] F ar.   4. *vord*] F wordes.   4. *S. Mathow*] F of sanct Mathow.   6. *testament*] F testament, q*uhi*lk salbe sched for ʒow *and* mony.   8. *þe blissit sacrament*] F þis blisset
sacrament.   9. *Quhene*] F And quhen.   10. *and eit*] F eit ʒe.   11. *efter þat*] F eftir.   11–14. *þis
cwpe ... he cum*] omitted in F.   14–15. *Quhasumeuir*] F qhatsumeuir.   15. *cwpe*] F coup of þe
lord.   16. *our lord*] F þe lord; *exame*] F thairfor examyn.   19. *body of þe lord*] F lordis body.
20. *scripturis*] F scriptuir.   21. *we vil rahers*] F now schorlie will we rehers.   22. *quhilk is*] F
quhilkis.   23. *saluiour*] F salueo*ur*, and þat þe wordes of o*ur* salueo*ur* in his latter supper.
26. *ane*] F þe.   28. *and in ane oþer place*] omitted in F.   29. *with ʒow*] omitted in F.   31. *to Iuge
levand and deid*] omitted in F; *scripturis*] F þe scriptuir.

lampadius þat þe verray body and bluid of Iesu Crist our saluiour ar nocht
realy contenit in þe blissit sacrament of þe altare.

   Mark diligently, gud redar, and þow sal esaly persaue þat þe scripturis
allegit be þe kirk ar mekil mair plaine and propir to preif þe real presens
5 of þe body and bluid of our saluiour in þe sacrament of þe altare nor ar þe
scripturis allegit be Ecolampadius to preif þe contrar. For quhy þe
scripturis allegit be þe kirk ar sa plaine and manifest, declarand þe
real presens of þe body and bluid of our saluiour in þe sacrament of þe
altare, þat þa leif na place of dowt til al sik as vil nocht peruerstly thraw
10 þe scriptur contrar þe godly menyng of þe sammyne. For quhat planar
vordis culd our saluiour hef said to certify ws of þe real presens of his
precious body and bluid in þe sacrament nor þir quhair he sais: "This is my
body, quhilk salbe giffin for ӡow", and "þis Is my bluid of þe new testament, quhilk salbe sched for ӡow and mony"?
15   Treuly, ve ar compellit be þir vordis to sa þat Cristis real body and bluid
ar contenit in þe sacrament, or elss it vas nocht Cristis real body and bluid
quhilk vas giffin and sched for vs one þe croce.

   Inlikvis mark þe vordis of þe apostil, Sayand <1 Corin. 11.>: "Lat
ane man exame hyme self, and [f. 4r.] swa lat hyme eit of þis breid and
20 drink of þis cw[pe]. For he þat eittis and drinkis onworthely, he eittis and
drinkis his avin damnacione, becaus he makis na difference of þe lordis
body." Quhilkis wordis gif þow vil mark diligently, þow salbe compellit to
say þat in þe sacrament of þe altare is contenit realy þe body and bluid
of Iesu Crist our saluiour. First he biddis ane man exame hym self affor he
25 be part takar of þis blissit sacrament, and þat onder þe paine of damnacione, quhilk vas neuer requirit affor þe vsyng or rasauyng of ony sacrament, it beand bot ane syng or takine only. Quhairfor it is manifest þat
it is þe lordis real body quhilk þe apostil biddis ws sa ernistly prepair our
selfis to rasaue, and nocht only ane syng *and* takin of þe lordis body. The
30 circumstance of þe text schawis þe caus quhairfor ane man suld exame
hyme self sa rigourislye affor he rasaue þe sacrament, Sayand: "quha eittis
þis breid and drinkis þe cowpe of þe lord onvorthely,he is gilty of þe body
and bluid of þe lord." *And* it folowis þat "he eittis and drinkis his damnacione becaus he makis na differens of þe lordis body."

9. *til*] F to. 11. *vordis*] F word. 12. *nor þir*] F nor þir ar. 14. *quhilk*] F þat. 16. *or elss*] F or
ellis þat. 17. *quhilk vas*] F quhilkis war. 19. *exame hyme self, and swa lat hyme*] omitted in F.
20. *he eittis*] F eatis. 22. *quhilkis*] F quhilk. 24. *affor*] F afoir þat. 25. *þis*] F his. 29–30. *The circumstance of þe text*] F Thaireftir he. 31. *þe sacrament*] F þis sacrament; *quha*] F he quhilk.
32. *þe cowpe*] F of þis coup. 32. *he is*] F is. 33. *And it folowis*] F Mark, þe apostole sayes
he is gilteous of þe lordis body and bluid. And it followis; *his* F his awin.

114

Gud redar, quhat planar vord*is* culd þe apostil hef said to declair þe
real presens of *our* lord*is* body and bluid to be realy *in* þe sacrame*n*t nor
þir ar? I vil ask at þe, quhat artikil of *our* beleif is mair plainly and expresly
co*n*tenit *in* scripture þa*n* þis is? Sua ma þo*w* cleirly *per*saue þat þe scrip-
5 tur*is* ar plain and manifest q*uhi*lk*is* þe kirk dois allege to preif [f. 4v.] þe
real presens of þe body and bluid of *our* saluio*ur* *in* þe sacrame*n*t of þe
altare.

Be þe co*n*trar, m*ar*k þe scriptur*is* allegit be Ecola*m*padius and oþer*is*
quha denyis þe real presens of *our* lord*is* body and bluid *in* þe sacrament
10 (contrar þe godly doctrine of þe kirk), and þo*w* sal no*ch*t *per*saue ane plaine
nor manifest text allegit be þa*m* propirly to preif þair vickit opinione, bot
al scriptur*is* of *in*ferrens, and þa *im*propirly and *per*uerstly thrawin contrar
þe *in*terpreta*c*ione and Iugeme*n*t of al godly me*n* q*uhi*lk*is* euer hes beine *in*
þe kirk of God. And to þe effect þat þo*w* ma cleirly *per*saue þat þe scrip-
15 tur*is* allegit be Ecola*m*padius and diuerss oþer*is* *in* to þir miserable dais ar
*per*uerstly thrawin contrar þe godly menyng of þe Sa*m*myne and doctrine
of haly kirk tovart þe ond*er*sta*n*ding of þis sacrament, schortly sal ve
raherss þe cheif testimonyis of scriptur*is* allegit be þa*m*, and þairthroc*h*t to
mak þe redar cleirly to ond*er*stand (God willing) quho*w* *per*uerstly and
20 *im*propirly þa ar applyit to preif þair vickit opinione.

It is vritin *in* þe eva*n*gelis, quhair me*n*cione is maid of þe lett*ar* suppar
of þe lord, þat he blissit þe breid and gef to his discipulis, Sayand <Math.
26, M*ar*c. 14, Luce 22>: "þis is my body, q*uhi*lk salbe giffin for ʒo*w*";
and *in*likvis þe cupe, Sayand: "þis is my blud of þe new testame*n*t, q*uhi*lk
25 salbe sched for mony". Ecola*m*padius and diuerss oþer*is* allegis þir vord*is*
of *our* saluio*ur* to be spokin only be ane similitude and figure. And to
[f. 5r.] fortify þair vickit and *per*uersit allegeance and t[hra]wine *in*terpreta*c*ione *im*propirly cal þa to rame*m*be[rance] þe word*is* of þe apostil,
Sayand <1 Corin. 10>: "Crist vas þe roik", and þe vord*is* of *our* saluio*ur*,
30 Sayand <Ioa*n*. 10, Io. 15>: "I a*m* þe du[re]", "I a*m* þe wine tre", allegeand þat lik as *our* saluio*ur* vas no*ch*t ane roik, ane dure, nor vine tre *in*
deid, bot be ane figure and similitude, Swa þe breid q*uhi*lk he blissit *and*
gef to his discipulis at þe lett*ar* suppar was bot ane figure only of his body,
and no*ch*t his real body.

1. *Gud redar*] F Lord God (guid reader). 2. *to be realy*] omitted in F. 4. *scripture*] F þe
scriptour; *þan*] F nor. 5. *quhilkis*] F q*uhi*lk. 14. *persaue þat*] F perceaue quhow. 15. *in to*] F
in. 18. *þairthrocht to mak*] F mak. 20. *preif*] F appreue. 22. *gef*] F gaif it. 24. *inlikvis*] F
lykwys. 25. *for mony*] F for >ʒow *and* < mony. 27. *vickit and*] omitted in F. 29. *þe roik*] F
ane Rock; *and*] F And als. 31. *ane dure*] F. dure. 32. *figure and similitude*] F similitude only.
32–34. *Swa ... body*] F Sua (sayes men gewin till wicked opinioun in þir dayes) þat it was bot ane
similitude only of his body, and no*ch*t his reale body, q*uhi*lk *our* salueo*ur* gaif to his disciplis.

Treuly, þis conferrens of scripturis is verray Inpropir, and seruis of
nocht to þair intent. For quhy, þe scripture spekis nocht ay bot sumtyme be
similitude. For gif sa var þat it spak in al places be ane similitude, our
fayth war confundit. As be ane exempil, in þe evangel of S. Mathow it is
5   vritin, the voce of þe Fader vas hard, Sayand "þis is my beluffit Son, in
quhome I am veil complesit". And S. Petir said to our saluiour <Math.
16>: "Þow ar Crist, þe Sone of þe leving God". And S. Ihone inlikvis
sais <Io.1>: "Þe vord (þat is to say þe Son of God) was maid flesche". Is
it nocht ane reddy vay to confund our hail fayth, gif ony man vald say – as
10   diuerss vickit heretikis did – þat þir testimonyis of scripturis abone rehersit
ar spokin be ane similitude and figure?

And treuly, þair is na ressone nor caus giffand ony Iust occasione
quhairfor it suld be thocht þat þe vordis of our saluiour, Sayand "þis is my
body", [sul]d be spokin be ane [f. 5v.] [fi]g[ure] or similitude, mair nor þe
15   vordis of þe Fadir, Sayand "þis is my Sone", suld be spokin be ane figure
or similitude. For þair is na dependens of scripture, nother befoir nor ȝit
þat efter folowis, giffand ony maner of apperance quhairfor þe ane suld
be spokin be ane similitude and figure mair þan þe oþer – quhilk is familiar
euer in þe scripture, and ane rewil til onderstand quhensumeuer ane thyng
20   is spokin be ane figure or similitude. For vil þow mark ernistly þe vordis of
þe apostil, Sayand "Crist vas þe roik", and als þe vordis of our saluiour,
sayand "I am þe dure", "I am þe vine tre", Thow sal esaly persaif þat þe
plaine text precedand and efter folovand declaris manifestly þir testimonyis
of scripturis last abone rahersit to be spokin be ane figure and similitude.
25   Swa ma þow cleirly persaif quhow vickitly, falslye, and impropirly dois
Ecolampadius and al oþeris quhilkis denyis þe real presens of our lordis
body and bluid to be realy in þe sacrament of þe altare, thrawand þe scripturis as did Arrius, Marcione and diuerss oþeris damnable heretikis, aganis
þe godly menyng of þe Sammyne, to fortify þair damnabil herese and
30   opinione.

For lik as Ecolampadius and diuerss oþeris in þir dais allegis þe vordis

---

1. þis] F þir. 2–8. *For quhy … flesche*] F For quhy, albeit þe scripture speikis sumtyme be ane
similitude, It argumentis nocht þat it spekis ay be ane similitude. For gif sua wer, than war
our haill fayth confundit. As be exempil, It is writtin In þe evangill þat þe Fader sayis: "þis is
my Soune", and als þat sanct Petir said … lykwayis þat sanct Ihone sayis "the word was maid
flesche". 9. *reddy*] F plane. 10. *þir*] F þe. 10. *scripturis*] F scripture. 11. *and*] F or. 14. *or*] F
and. 17. *þat*] omitted in F; *giffand*] F and gifand. 18. *similitude and figure mair þan*] F figure
or similitude mair nor. 19. *and ane rewil til onderstand*] omitted in F. 19–20. *ane thyng is*] F
ony thing*is*. 23. *precedand*] F proceding. 26–27. *our lordis body and bluid to be realy*] F þe
body and bluid of our salueour. 27. *thrawand*] F thraw. 28. *damnable*] F deplorit. 29. *fortify*]
F satifee.

116

of our saluiour Sayand "þis is my body" to be spokine be ane figure *and* ane similitude, Sua did Marcione allege þe vordis of S. Ihone, Sayand <Io.1> "þe vord vas maid fles[che", *and*] inlikvis Arrius allegeand þe vordis of þe Fader, sayand "þis is my Sone", to be spokin [f. 6r.] be ane
5 figure and similitude, as eftervart – God villing – salbe mair cleirly declarit. This ma þow cleirly persaif þat it hes beine euer familiar till heretikis at al tymis to thraw þe scripture to þair avin appetitis, contra þe godly menyng of þe Sammyne *and* doctrin of haly kirk.

Sum argumentis and sais þat þe sacrament of þe alt[are] is ane figure of
10 our lordis body, giffin be hyme in þe lettar suppar in ramemberance of his deitht; quharfor it can nocht be þe lordis body in deid.

This argument seruis of nocht. For quhy, ve ar assurit be þe apostil <Heb.1.> þat our saluiour is þe figure of þe substance of þe Fader, and nocht þe les he is verraly God, ane with þe Fader in substance. Ans als he is
15 þe Image of þe invisible God, and nocht þe less he is þe invisible God, equal and ane with þe Fader. Sua in þe sacrament is þe figure of þe lordis body <þe formis of breid *and* vine>, and als þe sam self body is realy contenit þairin. For gif þe sacrament of þe altare var na thing bot only breid *and* vine, as Ecolampadius and oþeris giffin to þis vickit heresy in þir
20 dais dremis, Than hed þe paschal lam beine ane mair propir figure of Cristis body nor breid or vine, be ressone þat þe innocence of þe lam signifyit þe innocence of Crist, þe deith of þe lam þe deith of Crist, *and* als be ressone of þe oblacione of þe >lame < in sacrifice, þe quhilk hed gretar similitude with þe offering of Cristis body nor has þe breid or vine.
25 Þis ma þow persaif þat in þe sacrament is nocht only þe figure of þe lordis body, bot als þe sam self body, conforme to þe vo[rdis] of our sal- [f. 6v.] uiour, Sayand "þis is my body".

The secund chaptour.

Now vil we – as it vil pleis God to gif ws grace – to mak þe redaris to
30 onderstand quhow þe rest of þe scripturis allegit be Ecolampadius and

---

1–2. *ane figure and ane similitude*] F figure and similitude. 3. *and inlikvis Arrius allegeand*] F to be spokin Be ane figure and similitude, and in lyk wayis Arrius allegit. 5. *salbe mair cleirly*] F mair largelye salbe. 9. *þe sacrament*] F in þe sacrament. 10. *our*] F þe; *ramemberance*] F þe rememberance. 12. *apostil*] F apostole sanct Paulle. 14. *verraly ... substance*] F God with þe Father. 15–16. *he is ... Fader*] F he is God with þe Father. 16. *þe sacrament*] F þis sacrament. 22-23. *and als*] F þe bluid of þe lambe þe bluid of Christ, And als. 23. *þe quhilk hed*] F be þe quhilkis it had. 25. *þe sacrament*] F þis sacrament. 29. *to gif*] F till gif; *to mak*] F. mak; *to*] F till.

oþeris in þir dais inlikvis ar impropirly applyit to fortify þair vickit opinione
tovart þe onderstanding of þis mistery of þe blissit sacrament of þe altare.

Ane of þe cheif argumentis quhilk þa apply in contrar þe godly doctrine
of þe kirk is þe vord of our saluiour quhair he sais <Ioan. 6.> : "It is þe
5 spreit þat giffis lif, þe flesche profitis na thyng." Of þir vordis infer þa þat þe
body of our saluiour is nocht realy contenit in þe sacrament, becaus it is
þe spreit þat giffis lif. And in caiss, sa þa, þat Cristis body var realy contenit
in þe Sacrament, it iss onprofitable, becaus Crist hyme self Sais þat þe
flesche profitis na thyng.

10 Treuly, þis inferrens is verray impropir and seruis of na thyng to þair
intent. And to þat effect þat þow ma cleirly persaif þe sammyne, ve vil mark
to quhome þir vordis var spokin, and swa sal it be esaly persauit quhow
impropir is þis inferrens.

Thir vordis war spokin be our saluiour to ane certane of his discipulis
15 quhilkis var vaik and imperfit, and quha lenit to þe Iugement of þe flesche,
outwart vittis and sensis, as mony dois in þir dais, and nocht to þe Iugement
of þe spreit: quha belewit þat our saluiour wald hef giffin his flesche to hef
beine couponit and diuidit as flesche [f. 7r.] deuidit one þe skamles and
eittin. Treuly, þe flesche deuidit fra þe spreit efter þis maner according to
20 þair fleschly beleif profeit na thing: quhilk can neuer be said propirly of
Cristis flesche, becaus it is neuer deuidit fra þe spreit. For quharsumeuer
Cristis flesche is, þair is his diuinite, quhilk is þe spreit þat giffis lif. Thairfor
mark þe vordis of our saluiour. He sais indifferently: "þe flesche profitis na
thyng". He sais nocht: "my flesche profitis na thing", for þan hed our
25 saluiour bein contrarius to hyme self, quha said ane litil befoir <Ioan. 6> :
"he quha ettis my flesche and drinkis my bluid hes euerlestyng lif".

To mark þe vordis of our saluiour, Sayand: "þe flesche profitis na thing,
it is þe spreit þat giffis lif", And þat þa ma be mair esaly onderstand, ve sal
confer þe testimonyis of scripturis with oþeris scripturis, conforme to þe
30 exempil of anciant authouris.

The apostil S. Paul, vritin to þe Corinthianis <1 Corin. 8.>, sais one

1. *inlikvis ar*] F ar Inlykways. 3. *Ane*] F and; *quhilk*] F quhilkis. 4. *is þe vord*] F as the wordis.
6. *our saluiour*] F þe lord. 8. *onprofitable*] F imposeabill. 11–12. *ve vil ... spokin*] F we sall
mark þe wordis of our salueour, to quhome þaj wer spokin, the tyme and þe occasion quharfor
thay wer spokin. 12. *esaly persauit*] F easye to perceaue. 15. *imperfit and*] F imperfyte in þe
fayth. 17–18. *hef beine couponit and diuidit as flesche deuidit*] F be eattin, cowponit and dewydit
as flesche is dewydit. 18–19. *and eittin*] omitted in F. 19. *þe spreit*] F spreit. 25. *quha*] F
quhilk. 26. *quha*] F quhilk; *euerlestyng lif*] F the ewirlesting lyfe. 27. *To mark þe vordis*]
F till mak þir wordis. 28. *And þat þa ma be mair esaly onderstand*] F to be þe mair easely vnderstanding; *sal*] F will. 29. *þe testimonyis*] F þis testimonye; *scripturis*] F of scriptoure. 30. *anciant
authouris*] F þe anceant fatheris.

þis maner: "Science makis men proud, cherite edifyis". Þow ma persaif
þat science without cherite is onprofitable, bot cherite Iunit to science
edifyis and makis science profitable. Sua flesche only without þe spreit, as
flesche is þat is deuidit one þe skamles, is onprofitable for mannis salua-
5 cione. Bot flesche Iunit to þe spreit quhilk is God, as Cristis flesche is, can
nocht be bot verray profitable.

For forder considdering of þis profund mistery þow sal mark and considder in our saluiour thre thingis. Þe first is his natural body, quhilk he
tuik of þe virgine with þe tyme be operacione of þe haly Goist. The secund
10 is his saul, quhilk [f. 7v.] vas creat be þe blissit trinite Ionit to his bodie.
Thayrbye þow sal considder his godheid, quhilk he hes tane of his Fader
without begynnynge and before al tyme, quhilk beand Iunit to his manheid
makis hyme to be bayth God and man, twa natures in a persone.

Now sal thow consider, lik as it vas nocht þe manlie nature of our
15 saluiour – in so far as he vas þe sone of þe virgine – þat vas þe cheif caus of
our redempcione, bot his godheid Iwnit to his manheid vas þe cheif causs
of all mannis redempcione, Inlikmaner as it is nocht þe flesche nor manlie
nature quhilk our saluiour tuke of þe virgine Marie (resauit realie in þe
sacrament) þat of þe avin nature gyfis lif to þe Saull, bot þe diuine nature
20 quhilk is inseparatlye Iwnit to his flesche. Swa þat quhensumeuer thow rasauis
þe flesche of our lord Iesu Christ in þe blissit sacrament, þow art part takar
of his diuine nature, quhilk is Iwnit inseperatlie to his flesche and is þe
spreit þat giffis liff to al cristiane mannis saull.

This may þow cleirlie persaif quhow profitable is þe real presens of
25 Christis flesche in þe blissit sacrament – contra þe vickit opinione of vane
men in þir dais –, quhilk is þe instrument quharby we ar partakaris of þe
diuine nature, Sua þat be þe resauynge of þis sacrament vorthely, quharin is
contenit Christis flesche realy, ve ar made þe tempil and duellinge place of
þe lord, conforme to his vord saynge <Io. 6> : "he þat eatis my flesche and
30 drinkis my bloud duellis in me and I in hyme."

Attour þow salbe assurit þat þe diuinite and humanite of our saluiour

1. *persaif*] F perceaue be þir wordis. 4. *þat is*] *omitted in* F. 8. *Þe first is*] F first. 9. *virgine*]
F virgine Marie; *operacione*] F þe operatione. 9–10. *The secund is*] F Secoundlie. 10. *creat*] F
Ionit to his body and creat. 11–12. *Thayrbye ... tyme*] F Threidlie Sall þow consider his godheid Is generat of þe Father withoutin tyme. 13. *makis hyme to be*] F he Is. 14. *considder*] F
consider þat. 15. *þe virgine*] F man. 15–16. *þat vas ... redempcione*] F that Redemit ws on
þe croce, bot In sa far as he quha sufferrit was þe Sone of God, Sua þat his godheid Ionit to
his manheid was þe cheif cause of our Redemptioun. 17. *as*] *omitted in* F. 19. *þat*] F quhilk;
avin nature] F awin wertew. 20. *is inseparatlye Iwnit*] F Inseperatlye Is Ionit. 21. *flesche*]
omitted in F. 22. *is Iwnit inseperatlie to his flesche and*] *omitted in* F. 23. *to*] F till. 26–27.
þe diuine nature] F his deuine nature.

beand anis Ionit to gidder var neuer separate, [f. 8r.] nor ʒit of ony maner
of vay cane be separat, ʒea nocht þe tyme of his deth. For Christis death vas
nocht be separacione of his diuinite fra his humanite, bot be separacione
of his saull fra his body, as þe scriptoure plainlye techis ws; becaus he hed
5   nocht corporal liffe be ressone of his godheid, bot be resone of his saull.
Forder ve ar assurit be Goddis vord þat he rais one þe thyrd day be his
awin powar, and þat be verteu of his godheid quhilk inseparatly is Iounyt
to his humanite. Als ve rede þat he beand in his mortale liff he ves subieckit
to hundyr, thrist, and cald, and his Godheid euer remanand with his
10 manhede in al sik calamiteis and miseries, lik as in his death. For at all
tymes Christ vrocht þe misterye of mannis redempcione In twa natures beand
vnit to gidder in ane persone, lyke as he is þe fwid of our saull realy contenit in þe blesset sacrament, twa natures in ane persone.
This may þe redare clearly persaue the vordis of our saluiour, sayand:
15 "it is þe spreit þat giffis liff: the flesche profitis na thynge", nocht to mak
derogacione to þe real presens of Christis flesche in þe sacrament of þe
altare. Bot þat vas said onlye to supprese þe fleschlye Iugement of his
disciples quhilkis vas vaik in þe faith, and al oþeris quhilkis our saluiour to
gif his flesche to be eaten as flesche diuidit one þe skambles, Albeit Christ
20 meanit na thinge lese bot þat he vas to gif his naturall flesche to be eaten
as spirituall fuid of our saul, and þat be ane supernaturall maner (as eftervard, God villynge, abounddantlye salbe declarit).
It is nocht vnknawyne to me quhow þair is diuerse men in þir dais quha
dois afferme þe testymonyis of scriptour contenit in þe saxt chaptour of
25 S. Ihone, allegit be vs for con[f. 8v.]firmacione of our purpose, to be
spokine allanerlye of þe spiritual manducacione of Christis flesche. Nocht
þe les ve haue funde þe anciaunt fatheres apply þir scriptouris as ve haue
done, Sik as Chrisostom, Homelia 46 super Ioannem, Augustine, tractatu
26 super Ioannem, Hilarius, li. 8 De Trinitate, Cirillus, super Ioannem
30 sexto, Theophilactus, super Ioannem 6, Ambrosius, li. 6 De Sacramentis ca.
primo, Gregorius, super Ioannem ca. 6, Ciprianus, super Exposicione
Oracionis Dominice, Origenis, Homilia 7 super Numeros, Ireneus, li. 5
Aduersus Hereses, – Quhais Iugementis, aggreand al in ane, ar to be

---

1. *separate*] F seuerat; *of ony maner*] F in na maner.   2. *separat*] F seuerat; *þe tyme*] F in
þe tyme.   3. *bot be separacione*] F bot þe separatioun.   7. *inseparatly*] F Inseperablye.   9. *hundyr*] F hunger; *remanand*] F Remanit.   11. *redempcione*] F saluatioun; *In twa natures*]
F his tua naturis.   15. *þat*] F quhilk.   15–16. *nocht to mak derogacione*] F to mak na derogatione.
18. *vas*] F war; *quhilkis*] F quhilkis belewit.   20. *to be eaten*] F realye to be eating   21. *saul*] F
saulis.   23. *quha*] F quhilk.   27. *anciaunt*] F ayld anceante.   28. *Homelia 46*] F Homilia 48.
17. *super Ioannem*] F super Iob.   32. *Homilia 7 super Numeros*] F super Numeros 7 Homilia.

preferrit to þe opinione and Iugement of priuate facciouse men sayand þe
contra in þir dais.

The third chaptour.

Here ve vill cal to ramembrance ane other special testimonye of scrip-
5   toure quhilk vas applyit be Ecolampadius and oþeris diue[rs] (alikvise
*im*propirly) to fortifye þair vickit opinione. Our saluioure beand inwnctit
be Marye Magdalene said one to Iudas (quha disdanit þe spendynge of þe
costlye vnctment apone our saluiour) <Math. 26>: "ʒe sal haue þe pwire
with ʒow for euer, bot ʒe sal nocht haue me with ʒow for euer." Ecolam-
10 *padius* and oþeris inferris of þir vordis of our saluiour þat his bodye is
nocht realye in þe sacrament.
For þe onderstandinge of þe sammyne þow sal considder that, albeit þe
preciouse bodye of our saluiour be nocht in þe sacrament to be handlet,
grapit, and inwnctit, as he vas be þe Marye Magdalene, Nocht þe lese it is
15 þe same selffe bodye in substance quhilk is in þe sacrament and þat quhilk
vas inwnctit be Marye Magdalene, conforme to his vordis, sayand: "This
is my bodye".
To þe effect þat þe redare ma mair easalye onderstande þe sammyne, We
vil ʒit as of befoire confere þir testimonyis of scriptouris with oþeris scrip-
20 touris.
The apostil S. Paul, vritynge to þe Corinthianis, quhair he makis
mencione [f. 9r.] of þe resurreccione, sais <1 Corin. 15.>: "Flesche and
bluid sal nocht possesse þe kyngdome of heawine". Thir vordis apperis
strange, considderrynge þat it is beleuit be al christiane men þat our bodyes
25 flesche and bloude sall possesse þe kingdome of heawyne be þe mercy and
grace of þe lorde, conforme to the saynge of S. Paul <1 Cor. 15.> that
"that corruptable bodye sal cleith incorrupcione, and þat mortal bodye
sall cleith immortalitie", And conforme to þe sainge of þe godlie father Iob
<Iob 19.>: "I knawe treulye þat my redemare luffis, and I am to ryise
30 one þe lettar daye and salbe clede with my skyne, and in my flesche I sall
se God".

_____

4. *ve vill*] F will we; *to*] F till.   5. *vas*] F is; *oþeris diuers*] F diueris vþeris; *alikvise*] F lyk
wayis.   7. *Marye Magdalene*] F þe Marie Magdaling.   9. *with ʒow*] *second time omitted in* F.
15. *bodye in substance*] F substance of body; *and þat*] F þan.   18. *To*] F And to.   19.
þir testimonyis of scriptouris] F þis testimonye of scriptoure.   21. *to*] F on to.   24. *be*] F of;
men] F man.   25. *þe mercy*] F mercie.   26–28. *conforme to... immortalitie, And*] *omitted in* F.
28. *Iob*] F Iob sayand.   29. *luffis*] F lewis.   30. *clede*] F claid agane.

Treulye, þe flesche and bloude sal possesse þe kyngdome of heawine,
And þe flesche and bluid sall nocht possesse the kyngdome of heawine:
quhilkis ar baith trew efter diuerse respeckis and consideraciones. Flesche
and bloude subieckit to fleschlye imperfecciones as it is in þis mortale
5   liffe – >as< to vice and syne, and alse hungyr, thrist, and caulde, and last
of all to deith and corrupcione –: Treulye, efter þat maner flesche and
bloude sal nocht possesse the kyngdome of heawine. Bot quhen þe sammyne flesche and bloude quhilk vas corruptible and mortal, salbe clede
with incorrupcione and immortalitie, subieckit to na kynde of fleschlye
10   imperfecciones, þat flesche and bluid sal possesse þe kyngdome of heawine:
the sam selff flesche and bloude in substance quhilk vas in þis mortall liffe,
nochtþe lese it sal nocht haue þe sammyne qualiteis (as I vald say), noch
subieckit to fleschlye imperfecciones of vice and syne, to hungyr, thrist, and
cauld, deith, and sik oþer calamiteis and miseryes. Sua in lik maner þat
15   albeit þe bodye of our saluiour quhilk is contenit realye in þe blissit sacrament be nocht subieckit to [f. 9v.] hungyr, thrist, calde, and deith, hauand
sik qualiteis as it hed in þis mortall liffe quhen he vas Inwnctit be Mary
Magdalene, nocht þe les it is þe same selff substance of bodye.
    <Aliud argumentum> ȝit remanis ane cheiffe argument applyit be mony
20   in þir dais incontra þe godlye doctrine of the kirk tovart þe onderstandinge
of this mast excellent mystery, Sayand þat our saluiour Iesus Christe
ascendite to the heawyn and sittis at þe rych hand of þe Father, and is to
returne agane one the letter day. And of this þaj infer that þe blessed body
of our saluiour is nocht nor ȝit can noch be realy in þe sacrament, becaus it
25   is aganis þe artikil of our beleif.
    Truely, albeit it be repugnant to manly ressone (as ar al þe artikles of our
beleif) þat þe body of our saluiour suld be in hewine and realy in the sacrament, it is no vays repugnant to the vordes of God, nor ȝit to þe almychty
power of God. For quhy, Goddes vorde is true saiand þat Iesus Christe
30   our saluiour ascendit to þe hewine and sittis at þe rych hand of the Fa-

---

1. *Treulye, þe flesche*] F Trewþt it is þat flesche. 2. *þe flesche*] F flesche. 3. *quhilkis ... consideraciones*] F quhilk is to be vnderstanding eftir diuers respectis and considerationis. 5. *as*]
F Syk as; *thrist*] *omitted in* F. 8. *mortal*] F it þat was mortall; *salbe*] F Is. 9. *incorrupcione and*]
omitted in F; *subieckit*] F as sayis þe apostole, and Is maid glorifeit, subiect.   10. *þat*] F
Than. 11. *sam selff*] F samyn. 12. *nochtþe lese*] F nocht the les þat; *sal nocht haue*] F hes nocht;
noch] F Is nocht. 13. *to ... syne*] *omitted in* F. 13–14. *thrist and cauld*] F cauld and. 14.
oþer] F vþeris. 14–15. *Sua in lik maner þat albeit*] F Sua albeit. 15. *realye*] *omitted in* F; *þe
blissit sacrament*] F þis blisset sacrament. 17–18. *Mary Magdalene*] F þe Marie Magdalene.
23. *And*] *omitted in* F. 24. *noch*] *omitted in* F. 25. *artikil*] F articles. 27. *realy*] *omitted in* F.
28. *vordes*] F word; *almychty*] F mychthe.

ther, And Goddes vorde is true sayand "This is my body, q*uhi*lk salbe
giffin for ʒow", quharbe ve ar certifyet þat in the sacrame*n*t is þe same
selff bodye i*n* substance q*uhi*lk is in hewine, be þe vertue of his vorde,
q*uhi*lk is o*mn*ipotent.

5   And ʒe vill diligentlye considder quhat phrais and maner of spekynge
menis þir vordes, sayand þat Iesus Christe o*ur* saluio*ur* sittis at þe rich hand
of the Father, it salbe easalye persauit þat the doctrine of þe kirk tovart þe
onde*r*standinge of þis mistery is mekil mair propir and agreabill with þe
articles of o*ur* beleue nor is the contrar opinione. For quhy, quhat menis
10   þir vordes, sayand "Iesus Christe o*ur* saluio*ur* sittis at þe rych hand of the
Father" bot þat he is equall with þe Father in diuine power? Tha*n* – he
beand equall with þe Father i*n* diuine power – it folowis mekil bet*ter* to þe
doctrine of þe kirk þat his preciouse bodye is no*ch*t astrickit to ony ane
place, bot þat he may be, and is really, i*n* the blessed sacrame*n*t co*n*forme
15   to his vord, [f. 10r.] or quar eu*er* he plesis: no*ch*t that his body is astrickit
and cane no*ch*t be in diuerse places quhe*n* he pleasis and quhair he pleasis,
considerand he is equall with the Father i*n* diuine pover.

Truelye, vill þow considder þis vickit i*n*ferrens – q*uhi*lk is no*ch*t co*n*tenit
i*n* þe scriptour, nor agreabil þarwith – astrickand þe body of o*ur* saluio*ur*
20   to remane i*n* hewine onlye quhill þe lett*ar* day, þo*w* sal cleirlye persaue þat
no*ch*t it obscuris and diminucis the michty power of o*ur* saluio*ur* – quha
is o*mn*ipotent becaus he is equall with þe Father –, but also it is expresse
agane the vorde of God.

To preife þe sa*mm*yne þo*w* sall ma*r*k þe vordes of S. Paul, quhar he dois
25   plainlye certifye al christiane me*n* be his epistle vriten to þe Cori*n*thianis
<1 Cori*n*. 15> That Iesus o*ur* saluio*ur* vas sene be hyme efter þat he vas
sene be þe rest of the apostles and disciples. Ve ar co*m*pellit to say be þis
text that it vas þe very reall body of o*ur* saluio*ur* q*uhi*lk S. Paul saw i*n*
earth efter his ascensio*n*e, becaus he preuis be þe sich q*uhi*lk he saw of o*ur*
30   saluio*ur* his corporall resurreccio*n*e. Truely, gif he hade sene o*ur* saluio*ur*
be ane sp*irit*uall visio*n*e and no*ch*t corporally (as did the laif of þe ap*ost*lis),
it vas no*ch*t sufficient preiffe of his resurreccio*n*e to say þat he saw hyme

---

1. *vorde is*] F wordis. 1–2. *quhilk salbe giffin for ʒow*] *omitted in* F. 3. *hewine*] F þe havin;
vertue] F powar. 5. *And ʒe*] F Gif we; *phrais*] F þis phrais. 6. *þir vordes*] *omitted in* F; *sayand
þat Iesus Christe our saluiour*] F trewlie saying þat o*ur* salueo*ur* Iesus Christ. 11–12. *Than …
power*] *omitted in* F. 12. *to*] F according to. 13. *to*] F till. 14. *really in the blessed sacrament*]
F in þe blisset sacrament realye. 15. *or quhar euer*] F and owir all quhair; *nocht that*] F nor
þat; *astrickit*] F astrictet to ane place. 19. *þe scriptour*] F scriptour. 20. *onlye*] F alanerlye.
21. *nocht*] F no*ch*t onely. 25. *epistle*] F apostole. 26. *Iesus*] F Iesus Christ. 29. *earth*] F þe
ertht; *þe*] F þis. 31. *be*] F onelie be. 32. *it vas*] F becaus It was; *resurreccione*] F corporall
resurrectioun.

be ane sp*irit*uall visione. This may be cleirlye persauit be þe reader þat þe
expresse doctrine of S. Paull is aganis all sik tretaris of the bodye of o*u*r
saluio*u*r to be *in* heavin allan*er*lye sene his asc*en*sione, and na vais realy
and corporally *in* ony other place one to þe lett*ar* day.

5   Atto*u*r, quhair it is said þ*at* o*u*r saluio*u*r asc*en*dit to þe heawin and sittis
at the rich hand of the Father, þo*w* ma*n* remowe all sik fleschlye Iugements
to think þat God þe Father, q*uhi*lk is ane spreit, hes other richt or left hand.
Bot be þis phrais and maner of spekynge ve ma*n* onderstand the equalite
of þe Sone with þe Father in [f. 10v.] diuine power be ressone of his godheid,
10   q*uhi*lk inseparatlye is vnit to his manheid in ane persone. Quharbe ve may
be assurit þ*at* he is *in* hewine and als *in* the sacrament, co*n*forme to his
vorde (q*uhi*lk is o*mn*ipotent), sayand "This is my bodye."

     Forder þo*w* sal considder quhowe agreable is þe doctrine and Iugement
of auld a*n*cia*n*t fathers vith þe playne text of scriptour*is* and doctrine of
15   holy kirk, affirmand þe body of o*u*r saluio*u*r to be in diuerse places at a
tyme.

     S. Augustine <Psal*m*. 89> vritis in this maner: "Thair vas neuer ma*n*
þ*at* buir hyme self in his awin handes bot Iesus Christ in þe letter supper,
q*uhen* he tuke þe breade and gef it to his disciples, sayand 'This is my
20   bodye'." Here may ve persaw be þe plaine text of þe scriptour, accordinge
to þe int*er*preta*cio*ne of this godlye docto*u*r, þat Christ*is* bodye vas in
diuerse places *in* ane tyme. Trueht it is, S. Augustine *in* ane other place
vritis one this maner: "One to þe end of the vardle the lord is aboue" –
q*uhi*lk be na vay is repugna*n*t to þe doctrine of þe kirk, as mony me*n* in þir
25   dais vald perswade. For quhy, It is no*ch*t þe doctrine of þe kirk þat þe
body of o*u*r lord, quhilk is *in* hevine, levis þe hevine, bot þat þe same self
body is *in* hevin and als *in* þe sacrame*n*t: q*uhi*lk is co*n*forme to þe scriptour*is*, as ve haue al reddelye declarit.

     Accordynge therto vritis þe a*n*ciant godlye father Chrisostome <to. 5.
30   Hom. 50 ad Populu*m* Antiochenu*m*>, saynge: "Helias ascendand left
truelye his cloik to his disciple, The Sone of God ascendand left to vs his

---

1–2. *This … doctrine*] F This may þe Reader clierlye p*er*ceaue quhow expres þe doctrine.
2. *tretaris*] F as tractis.   3. *heavin*] F þe havin.   6. *man*] F may.   7. *to*] F as to; *richt*] F ry*ch*t
hand.   10. *inseparatlye*] F inseperablelye.   11. *als*] *omitted in* F.   14. *auld anciant fathers*] F þe
auld anceant father*is*; *scriptouris*] F scriptoure.   15. *in*] F at.   17. *in*] F on.   18. *in þe letter sup-*
per] F buer himself in his awin handis In þe lettar soupar.   19. *tuke þe breade*] F blisset bread;
it] *omitted in* F.   22. *in ane tyme*] F at ane tyme.   24. *be na vay is*] F Is na wayis; *mony*] F
vane.   26. *our*] F þe; *hevine*] F þe havin.   27. *hevin*] F þe heavin; *als*] *omitted in* F.   28. *reddelye*]
F reddy.   30–2. *Helias … samyne*] F Eleas þe prophete ascen*d*ing wp leift his mantill vnto
his disciple, bot þe Sone of God, ascendit wp to þe heavin, hes left ws his awin flesche. As for
Eleas lewand his ma*n*till vnto his disciple, leift It fra him self; bot o*u*r salueo*u*r Christ hes
baitht leift his flesche w*ith* ws and alsua hes takin it w*ith* him self in his ascentione.

124

flesche. Bot Helias discouerit; Christ truely left his flesche vith vs and ascendit vith þe samyne." O lord God, gude reader, quhat planar vordes culd be spokine conforme to þe scripture of almichty God and doctrine of holy kirk incontrare þe vanite of faccious priuat men in þir dais!

5   Truelye, [f. 11r.] it is to be mervalit quhat menis men in thir dais to dispar and to be in doute þat Christis veray reall body is in þe sacrament and in hevine, considderynge þat Christis awin vord techis vs boith þe ane and þe other so plainlye. Nochtþeles þat it is agane þe ordour of nature, as ar all the articles of our beleiffe, Is it nocht als far aganis þe ordour of
10   nature to beleiff þat þe Sone is generat of þe Father, equall with the Father in diuine power, two parsonis in a godhede, as þat ane persone salbe in two places at ane tyme, considderynge þat it is þe same self persone and glorifyet bodye of hym quha is boith God and man? Truely, the vordes of our saluiour, saiand "This is my bodye", ar as true as the vordes saynge
15   <Io. 10.> "I and þe Father ar boith one". And þe ane is als far aganis the ordour of nature as þe other.

    Bot alvay I dar baldely say it is na vay þe dewite of ane christiane man to luke for þe ordre of nature in þe profunde misteryis concernynge our faith, as S. Gregore ansuerynge to þis questione mowit be hyme self <Hom.
20   super Ioannem, 20 cap.>: "Quhow vas it þe verray reall body of our lord efter his resurreccione þat enterit in þe hows amonge his apostlis, durris and vindokkis beand closit?" His ansuer is this, "that þe godly vark and myracle and it mich be comprehendit be naturall reasone it var na mervalus and miracle. For faith hes na merit, for naturall reasone giffis experience.
25   Bot quhen the mervalous verkis of our saluiour can nocht be comprehendit in þame seluis, than ar þa to be considderit and wyit be ane other of his vorkis more mervalouse, quhilk sal mak vs to beleue þe mervalous vork. The real body of our saluiour efter his resurreccione enterit in to þe house amonge his apostlis, durris and vindokkis beand closit, The quhilk in þe
30   tyme of his most blessed birth come forth to þe licht of þe vardle, the bosoume of the blesset [f. 11v.] virgine Marie remanand closit." And conforme to þis said þe anciant byschoppe and doctour of godlye learnynge and guid liff S. Ambrouse: "Quhy dois þow seik heir in þe sacrament þe

---

2. O] omitted in F. 3. culd] F can; scripture] F scriptouris. 4. faccious] F factionis. 6. to be] F be. 7. hevine] F þe heavin. 8. þe other] F vthir; Nochtþeles þat] F nochteþeles nochtwithstanding þat. 9. as] F lyk as. 14. saiand ... saynge] F ar als plane saying "þis Is my body" as ar þe wordis of our salueour saying. 17. alvay] F alwayis; na vay] F na wayis. 18. þe profunde misteryis] F profund misteryis; our] F ane. 19–31. as S. Gregore .... closit] omitted in F. 31–32. And conforme to þis] F þairfor. 32. anciant] F excellent. 33. S. Ambrouse] F Ambrose.

ordour of nature in Christis bodye, seand that Christ our saluiour vas borne
of the virgine aganis the ordour of nature?"

The ferde chaptour.

As hes pleasit God to gif vs grace, ve haue schawin gud vill to mak the
5   reader truelye to onderstand quhow þe scriptouris allegit be Ecolampadius
and diuerse others in thir days ar impropirly applyit, by the godlye
menynge of the sammyne, incontrare the godlye doctrine of the kyrk tovart
þe onderstandinge of this most excellent mistery of the blesset sacrament
of the altare, swa þat þe readar may be assurit þat þe scriptures allegit be
10   þam to fortifye þair thravin interpretacione seruis of nocht to þair vickit
intent. Sene therfor þair is na scriptour playne and propyre for þe confirmacione of thair vickit opinione, It is to be considderit – or rather to be
merualit – quhat blindnes, quhat ignorance, fure and vodnes is þis, quhilk
is cropin and ryngis in the hartes of men in thir miserabil days, quhilk
15   mowis them to refuise þe godlye doctrine of þe kirke of God and all
anciant fathers of the sammyne tovart þe true onderstandinge of this most
excellent sacrament, And to subieke þam selues to þe peruersit Iugement of
sum priuat faccious fallowis cumand vithout authorite, nocht knowand
quhair fra þa come nor be quhat ordour.
20   Truely, gud readar, vill þow diligentlye mark and considder, þow sal
perceaue þat it is the same Ignorance and fure quhilk mowit the Iowis to
dispare of þe diuine nature of our saluiour, That mowis theme in thir dais
to dispare of þe reall presens of þe preciouse body and bloude of our
saluiour to be in the sacrament, and to think þat it Is onely bot ane figure
25   and taken of the lordes bodye and bloude. For quhat mowit the Iowis to be
so indurite, thinkand þat our saluiour vas nocht boith God and man, bot
they onderstude nocht þe scriptoure, and lenit to þe Iugement of þe flesche,
thair [f. 12r.] outvart vittes and senses, seand our saluiour efter ane pwir
and simpil maner vse daly among theme nocht hauand – as he sais hyme
30   self – ane place till incline his hede to? Than they thouch: "quhow cane þis
man be God, redemar of the vardle, quhilk is in sik miserye and pouerte",

---

1. *seand*] F sen. 8. *onderstandinge*] F trew vnderstanding. 10. *vickit*] *omitted in* F. 11. *and*]
F nor. 13. *merualit*] F mervelit vpone; *fure*] F quhat furie; *þis*] F that. 14. *is cropin*] F hes
croppine. 15. *all*] F all þe. 16. *true*] *omitted in* F; *this*] F þe. 17. *to subieke*] subiect. 18. *faccious*
fallowis] F factionis followis; *vithout*] F but. 21. *quhilk*] F quhilkis. 22. *theme*] F men.
23. *body and bloude*] F blued and body. 24. *to be*] *omitted in* F. 25. *and bloude*] *omitted in* F.
26. *bot*] F bot þat. 28. *thair*] *omitted in* F. 29. *simpil*] F seyllie. 30. *to*] F Into.

126

nocht considderand his vonderfull miracles and quhow he villingly sustenit
his misery and pouerte to vork the misterye of mannis saluacione. Swa
doise men in þir dais, quha doise mesure þe profunde mistery of the sacrament be thair outvard vittes and senses, lenand to þe Iugement of the
5   flesche and nocht to þe mychty power of Goddis vorde, thinkand: "quhow
is it possible þat God and mane may be reallye contenit onder þe forme of
sik ane sobyr quantite of breade and vine".

Bot vil þow lene to þe mychty power of Goddis vorde, truely onderstandand the sammyn, þow sal think it na thinge strange þat þe reall body
10   and bloude of Iesus Christ our saluiour is verraly contenit in the blesset
sacrament of þe altare. For quhat vonder or miracle is techit be þe kirk to
be in þis sacrament of þe altare bot it þat Christis avin vordes beres vitnes
to and is conforme to þe scriptour: that þe substance of breade and vyne ar
chaunged in þe bodye and bloud of our saluiour? I vil aske at þe: quharfore
15   ar þow mair offendit therwith nor with Moyses, quho – beand ane sympil
seruand of the lordis – chaunged ane vand in ane serpent? And als our
saluiour hyme self chaunged þe vater in vyne – quhais pover is als sufficient
to chaunge bread and vyne in his avin body and bloude be þe vertue of his
vorde, quhilk is omnipotent.

20   Quhy diffidis þow of þe mychty vord of God, quha hes geffin to þe beis
sik instinccione and craft to chaunge the sukkin of erbis and substance of
diuerse floureseis and mony other thinges in hwny and vax? Quhy thinkis
þow impossible þat almychty God, þat hes giffin sike instinccione and craft
to sa small beistis to chaunge ane substance in ane other, may nocht
25   chaunge bread and vyne [f. 12v.] in to his avin bodye and bloude, conforme
to expresse testimony of his vorde, sayng: "This is my body, quhilk salbe
giffin for ʒow"? The fleschly Iugement is offendit to thynke quhow þe
bodye of our saluiour salbe in diuerse places at ane tyme. Quharfore ar
þow mair offendit therwith nor þat our saluiour ʒeid apone the see vith
30   his verray natural body, and als þe scriptour techis þe sammyne <Math.
14.>. And it is alse far aganis þe ordour of nature þat S. Peter, quha hed
ane mortal bodye, sulde gange apone the see, as þat þe preciouse body of our
saluiour, quhilk is immortall, glorifyet, and vnit to his godhede in ane per-

3. quha] F quhilkis. 3–4. þe sacrament] F þis sacrament. 6. may be reallye] F realye salbe.
8. þow] F we; truely] F and trewlye. 9. þow] F we. 10. verraly] omitted in F. 11. quhat vonder
or miracle is] F quhat Is þe wonder or miracle; 12. þat] F quhilk; vitnes] F ws. 13. scriptour]
F scriptouris; ar] F is. 15. mair offendit therwith nor with] F offendit þarwith mair nor;
ane] F bot ane. 16. in] F In to. 17. in] F Into. 18. in] F Into. 20–26. Quhy diffidis ... of his
vorde] omitted in F. 27. is] omitted in F. 30. als] F als sanc Petir; þe sammyne] F the ane
als plane as þe othir. 33. immortall ... persone] F ane Immortall glorifeit body, and þat þe
body of him quhay Is baith God and man.

sone, suld be in diuerse places at ane tyme. And quhare þow thinkis it
strange, ȝea, *and* impossible, þat the body of *our* saluiour, q*uhi*lk is co*n*tenit
in þe sacrament, cane be co*n*tenit *in* sa litle ane qua*n*tite of bread *and* vyne,
Thow sal co*n*sidder þat þe body of *our* saluiour q*uhi*lk is contenit *in* þe
5   blesset sacrame*n*t is ane sp*irit*uall glorifyet bodye, hauand flesche, blude,
and bonis, and is the body of hyme quha is boith God and man, godhede
and manhede Iounit to gidder *in*separatlye, and occupeis na place *in* the
sacrame*n*t more nor it var ane sprite, no*ch*tvithstandynge þat it is his verray
reall body þat is there present. And to þat effect that þow sal no*ch*t thynk
10   þat this is ane vayne i*n*ue*n*tit thinge be Imaginacio*n*e and braine of ma*n*,
I (God villinge) sal declare *and* preife it plainly be diuine scriptour*is*.

To onderstand þe sa*m*myne, first quhare it is said þat it is ane sp*irit*ual
body – hauand flesche, bluide, and bonis – q*uhi*lk is contenit *in* þe blissit
sacrame*n*t, þow may no*ch*t thynke that þe lordes bodye *in* þe sacrame*n*t is
15   chau*n*ged *in* þe nature of ane sprite, bot þat þe lordes body is cled vith
sp*irit*uall giftes. M*ar*k quhow þe apostle S. Paul vritis on this maner: "It
q*uhi*lk is savine ane naturall body sall ryise ane sp*irit*uall bodye." S. Paul
callis *our* bodeis ef*ter* the resurreccione sp*irit*uall bodeis, no*ch*t cha*n*git in
sprites, bot clede with sp*irit*uall giftes and qualiteis.
20   Conforme to this ve rede *in* þe eva*n*gell þat þe Sadduceis, quha denyit þe
resurreccione, sperit at *our* saluio*ur* quhais vif scho suldbe efter þe resurreccione quha hede mareit sevin brether. Our saluio*ur* a*n*suerit and said
<Math. 22.> þat *in* þe hevin [f. 13r.] nother sal they mare nor be giffin til
mariage, bot ar lik to þe angellis of God. Here may ve perceaue þat ef*ter*
25   the resurreccione ve salbe lik onto the angellis in sp*irit*uall qualiteis *and*
perfeccion as hes the angellis in hevin, and salbe made *in* þis maner
sp*irit*ual.
Quhow mekil mair is þe precious body of *our* saluiour ane sp*irit*ual
body, q*uhi*lk is cled with sp*irit*ual geftis and qualiteis far aboue þe angellis,
30   as the scriptour plainly techis vs. Quharbe ve may be assurit þat þe preciouse bodye q*uhi*lk is co*n*tenit realye *in* the sacrame*n*t, is na vay subieckit

---

1–4. *And quhare ... considder*] F Is þow offendit and thinkis strange þat þe body of *our*
salueo*ur* salbe co*n*tinet realye vnder the forme of sa lytle quantite of breid and vyne? For
vnd*er*standing þairof þow man co*n*sider. 6. *and is*] F and; *quha*] F quhilk. 7. *and occupeis*] F
q*uhi*lk Is subiect To na fleschelye distresse nor calamiteis, and he be his godlye powar occupeis.
9. *þat is there present*] omitted *in* F; *þat effect*] F þe effect. 10–12. *þat this is ... þe sammyne*]
F þis manlye Imaginatioun, we sal co*n*ferre þe scriptou*ris* and mak þe clierlye and easely (God
willing) To vnderstand þe samyn. 15. *þe lordes body*] F þe lord*is* body þairin. 16. *quhow*] F
þow as be exemple. 17. *ane naturall body*] F is ane naturall body and. 18. *the*] F þair;
nocht] F ar. 19. *bot clede*] F (God forbeid þat) bot þat *our* bodyis salbe claid tha*n*. 20. *quha*] F
quhilk. 23. *til*] F to. 24. *to*] F onto. 25. *the resurreccione*] F *our* resurrectioun. 26. *in þis*
maner] omitted *in* F. 30. *þe*] F his. 31. *sacrament*] F blisset sacrame*n*t.

128

to fleschly calamiteis and distres mair nor þe angellis in hevin or glorifiet bodies efter þe resurreccione. And albeit it be dalye vsit and communicat, it sufferis na iniures, chengene, alteracione, nor is diuidit mair nor quhen Thomas put his hand in his syde, becaus the lordes body vas and is at al
5   tymes in þe sacrament – be þe pover of his vorde – impassible, occupeand na place therin. As be ane exemple, ve ar assurit of the euangell þat þe preciouse body of our saluiour enterit in þe house quhair his disciples var, durris and vindokkis al beand closit; and ʒit he sufferit na distres in his passyng in. And als ve ar assurit þat his preciouse body occupeit na place
10   in his passyng In mair nor it hed bene ane spreit, nochtvithstandinge þat it vas his verray real body, flesch and bonis. Therfor, quhen þe apostlis vonderit quhow þat our saluiour vas cum In there – beleuand þat it hed bene ane spreit and noch his real bodye: lik as men vonderris now in þir dais, quhilkis ar our fleschly in Iugement, quhow þe real body of our
15   saluiour suld be in the blessed sacrament – he said plainly to þame þat "ane spreit hes nocht flesche and bonis, as ʒe se me haue".

This, vil þow consider the propirteis of ane glorifyet body, and speacialye of his preciouse body, quhilk is boith God and man, thow sal nocht thynk it strange albeit his reall bodye be contenit onder þe formes of
20   breade and vyne – nocht the lese be ane spiritual maner –, becaus it is glorifyet and occupeis na place in the sacrament mair then quhen he enterit in [f. 13v.] the house quhair his disciples var, durris and vyndokkis all beand closit. Truely, is as sufficient to do þe ane as the other. And it is alse necessar þat þe congregaciones quhilk ar mantemares of Iesu Christ be
25   confortit be þe blist body of our saluiour resauit realy in þe sacrament, as it vas necessar til his apostlis to be confortit be þe faith of þe sammyne, conforme to þe vordes of our saluiour sayand: ,,and ʒe eate nocht þe flesche of þe Sone of man and drinke of his bloude, ʒe sal nocht haue liff in ʒow. He þat eatis my flesche and drinkis my bluid hes euerlestynge liffe."

30   **The fift chaptor.**

Perchance thow vil spere, quhat is the cause þat ve se nocht þe body and

---

1. *nor*] F than. 2. *þe resurreccione*] F þair resurrectione. 3. *chengene, alteracione, nor is diuidit*] *omitted in* F. 5. *impassible*] F impassable body. 6. *ane*] *omitted in* F. 9. *passyng in*] F passage; *his preciouse body*] F þis precious body. 10. *passyng In*] F passage. 12. *cum In*] F cummine. 13. *real*] F verray reall. 13–14. *now in þir dais*] F nowadayis. 14. *our fleschly in Iugement*] F of fleschelye Iugement. 16. *and*] F nor. 18. *quhilk*] F quhay. 19. *formes*] F forme. 21. *then quhen*] F than nor quhan. 23. *is*] F his pouer Is; *And it is*] F and his word testifeis to ws als planelye the ane as þe othir, and It is. 24. *congregaciones quhilk*] F congregatioun quhilkis. 26. *it vas necessar til his apostlis to be*] F his apostolis wer; *faith*] F seicht. 28. *drinke of*] F drynk. 29. *euerlestynge liffe*] F þe ewirlesting lyfe. 31 *and*] *omitted in* F.

flesche of our lorde in þe sacrament as did the apostlis quhen he enterit in þe house quhare they var, durris and vindokkis beand closit. I vil gif the ane ansuere to this questione, sik as I haue learnit of Damascen, Theophilactus, and others of the anciant fathers.

5 Iesus Christ our saluiour, of his infinite gudnes and visdome knavand the grete vtilite and profeit þat men vas to haue of this sacrament – and that christiane men suld nocht be frustrat of this grete benefice throuch there fleschly imperfecciones and vaiknes, quha naturally vald haue ab-horrit to se and eat þe body of ane man –, villingly of his infinite mercy, 10 power, *and* grace conuertit *and* chengit the substance of breade and vyne into his reall bodye and bloude, quhilkis ar nocht necessar to be handelit, grapit, nor ʒit sene with our corporal eyne, bot onely be faith in þe forme and quantite of bread and vyne, *and* is resauit and remanis still: quhilk is most agreable to þe daly vse of men.

15 Attour, ve ar assurit in þe evangell <Luce. 4> þat Christ Iesus our saluiour, he beand apone þe hill, he passet throuch þe multitude of the Iowis in his verray natural bodye, quhilk vas than mortal. Nochtþelese it vas nocht feld, grapit, nor seyne sa lange as he plesit. Quhy vil þow nocht inlikvise beleif þe body of our saluiour to be really in þe sacrament, albeit 20 it be nocht therin feild, sein, nor grapit, consydderinge þat Goddes vord hes alse plainly declarit the [f. 14r.] ane as the other? And his power is as sufficient to make his body invisible and insensible in the sacrament hauand ane immortal and glo>ri<fyet bodye, as vas his power to pase throw þe multitude of the Iowis invisible and vithout persauynge of there senses 25 and vittis, hauand ane mortall body.

Forder I vil speir ane questione at thir grosse gospellaris, quha vill nocht beleif the body of our lord to be in this blissit sacrament reallye lesse nor they se hym, feill hym, and graipe hyme: Quhy dar they beleue þam selues to haue immortal saulis? I traist there be nane of theme sa rude bot he 30 beleuis hyme selff to haue ane immortall saul; than vill I speir quharbe he

---

1. *flesche*] *omitted in* F; *in þe sacrament*] F *and* felis It nocht In þe sacrament. 5. *gudnes and*] *omitted in* F. 6. *and*] *omitted in* F. 9. *ane*] *omitted in* F. 11. *and bloude*] *omitted in* F; *quhilkis ar*] F quhilk Is. 12. *ʒit*] *omitted in* F; *with our corporal eyne*] F In þat berand with oure imperfectione; *in*] *omitted in* F. 13 .*quantite*] F qualite; *and is*] *omitted in* F; *remanis*] F Remane; *quhilk is*] F quhilkis ar. 15. *in*] F be; *Christ Iesus*] F Iesus Christ. 16. *he*] *both times omitted in* F; *hill*] F heycht of þe montane. 17. *in*] F with; *of the Iowis*] *omitted in* F; *Nochtþelese it*] F and. 18. *grapit nor seyne*] F sene nor grapit be ony man. 19. *our saluiour*] F the lord. 20. *therin*] F pairinto. 21. *declarit*] F declarand. 22. *to make his body*] F to be. 23. *immortal*] F mortall [*subsequently erased*]. 24. *of the Iowis*] *omitted in* F. 24–25. *vithout persauynge of there senses and vittis*] F insensible. 25. *mortall*] F Immortall *(first two letters subsequently erased)*. 27. *this*] F be. 28. *and*] *ommitted in* F; *Quhy dar*] F Quhethir. 29. *immortal saulis*] F immortall saulis or nocht. 30. *vill I*] F I will.

knawis þat he hes ane immortal saull. He neuer feld, grapit, nor saw his
saull. And there is na vay to knaw þat ane man hes ane immortal saul mair
þan beistis assuritly bot in sa far as Goddis vord techis ws. Quhy vill þow
nocht beleif than Christis reall body and bloude to be in the sacrament,
5 considderinge his awin vordes techis it alse plainlye as ony passe in all the
scriptour techis vs ane man to haue ane immortal saul? As the saul may nocht
be seine nor felit becaus it is ane spreit, Sua þe body of our lord, quhilk is
contenit in the sacrament, can nocht be felit nor seine because it hes the
propirteis and qualiteis of ane spreit – as I haue all reddelye deciarit –,
10 and is invisible and insensible at þe vill of the lord quhen and quhair he
plesis, quhais power and visdome, as sais þe apostle <Rom.11.>, is
incomprehensible.

Truely, gude reader, there is na vay to be satifyet and to be at þe rest
of our conscience with þis mistery – and all other mistereis pertenand til
15 our faith – bot gif ve refuise þe Iugement of the flesche, outvart vittis and
senses, and lene to þe mychty power of the vorde of Gode, Conforme to
þe godlye counsall of the godlye father Chrisostome, vritand one this
maner: "Lat vs beleif in God euery thynge and nocht agane saynge hyme.
ȝea, althouch the thynge þat he say nocht appere and be inconuenient to
20 our senses, boith thouch and onder- [f. 14v.] And do also excede our senses
capacite and reasone; lat vs, I beseik ȝow, beleif in his vorde in al thingis,
and cheifly in the sacrament of þe altare, nocht lukand onely apone they
thinges quhilk lyis before vs, bot alsua considder his vordes, for be his
vordes ve can nocht be dissauit. His vordes can nocht be false, our senses
25 ar verray oft tymes begilit and made false. Quharfore, sene Christ hes said
'þis is my body', lat vs na thinge doute therof, bot beleif and perceaue it
with þe eyne of our onderstandynge." Hitherto vritis this godly bischope
and doctour, 1100 and more ȝeres sene.

I pray God þat euery christian man vald imprent this hailsoume and
30 godlye doctrine in his hart and mynd, quhilk is vorth euerlestand memorie.

1. he knawis] F knawis he; grapit] omitted in F. 2. saull] F awin saule; ane man] F ony
man. 2-3. mair þan beistis] omitted in F. 4. and bloude to be] omitted in F. 5. vordes] F word;
techis it alse plainlye] F techis als planelye the samyn. 6. vs] omitted in F; immortal] omitted
in F; may] F can. 7. our] F þe. 8. can nocht be felit nor seine because it] omitted in F. 9.
propirteis] F perfectione; reddelye] F reddy. 13–14. to be at þe rest of] F be at rest In. 14.
other] F vthyris; til] omitted in F. 17. godlye father] F anceant father. 18. in God euery thynge]
F God In ewerie thing; agane saynge] F say aganis. 19. say] F sayis; nocht] F do; and
be] F ane. 19-20. to our senses boith] F bath to our sensis. 20. onder-] F vnderstanding. 21.
beleif in] F beleue. 22. and] F bot; of þe altare] omitted in F; they] F thays. 23. quhilk] F
quhilkis 24. dissauit] F dissauit, bot our sensis ar verray easelye to be dissauit. 25. begilit and]
omitted in F. 28. 1100 and more ȝeres sene] F xij hundreth ȝeiris syne Or neirby. 30. in]
F Into; vorth euerlestand memorie] F euerlesting worthy of memorie.

Thane suld ve nocht efter ane fleschlye maner be so curiouse in seirsynge
out of Goddes vord, quhilk cursit curiositie now in thir dais constrenis
men, one þe maner, throuch imperfeccione of faith to make ane atome of
þe preciouse body and bloude of Iesus Christ our saluiour in þe blissit
5   sacrament.

    Benevalent reader, gif thow vil diligently mark and considder our hail
disputacione abone rehersit, þow may cleirly persaue the godly doctrine of
the kirk tovart þe real presence of the body and bloude of Iesus Christe our
saluiour in the sacrament mekill mair propir plainly and aggreable vith
10   þe text of þe scriptoure, than is þe vickit heresy and false opinione of
Ecolampadius and diuerse others be scripturis peruerstly applyit and
impropirlye vald preiff þe contrar. Als þow sal perceaue the doctrine of the
anciant fathers agreable therwith, quhilkis all heir to reherse var our
prolixit. Nochtþelese, sum vil ve in special adduce.
15   And first vil ve begine at þe anciant father and holy bischope S. Augustine,
vritand one this maner one the 89. psalme one this verse: adorate scabellum
pedum eius, spekand of the flesche of our saluiour quhilk he tuke of the
gloriouse virgine in his mast blessed incarnacione: "He tuke his flesche,
and þe same selffe flesche he gef vs to eate til our saluacione. Lat na man
20   eate of this flesche without first he adoire it; for ve sine nocht adorand þat
flesche, bot ve syne [f. 15r.] and ve adore it nocht."

    Mark quhow expreslye þis doctour and bischoppe is contrar þe opinione
of men in þir dais. Nocht onelye dois he afferme the real presens of the
lordes body in the sacrament, bot alse the sammyne to be adorit. Truely,
25   quhair sum euer Christe is (as he is assuirtly in þe sacrament) thair is boith
God and man, and quhair sumeuer God is, he is to be adorite: nocht þat
christiane men giffis Goddes glore to þe formes of breade and vyne
quhilkis they se with there corporale eyne, nor ʒit to Christis flesche bot in
sa far it is Iounit inseparatlye to his godheid in vnitie of persone and is
30   contenit invisible onder the formes of breade and vyne and is seine with
the eyne of our faith and onderstandyng, as Christis avin vord techis vs,

---

2. of] F of þe secreittis of. 3. atome] F anatomie. 7. disputacione] F disputatioun and ressoning.
8. and bloude] omitted in F. 9. mekill mair propir plainly and] F to be mekle mair plane, propir,
and. 10. than] F nor; false] omitted in F. 11. diuerse] F all; be] F quhay be. 11–12. and impropirlye vald] F wald impropirlye. 12. Als] F and als. 14. adduce] omitted in F. 15. vil ve] F we
will; at] F to; and holy bischope] omitted in F. 16–18. one the ... incarnacione] F vpon þe
psalmes, spekand of our salueour, of þe flesche of þe virgine Marie. 19. til] F to. 20. without
first he] F bot gif he first. 20–21. for ... nocht] F for nocht allanerlye we syn nocht be giffin
adoratione till It, bot we syn and we gif nocht adoratioun till It. 27. formes] F forme. 28–30.
nor ʒit ... contenit] F bot to þe blisset body of þe lord, quhilk is contenet. 30. formes] F forme.
31. onderstandyng] F belewe.

132

sayand: "This is my bodye, quhilk salbe geffin for ʒow". Lik as the thre
vise men quhilkis come fra þe orient gef nocht adoracione to our saluiour in
spreit in respect of his manhede, quhilk they saw onely vith there corporall
eyne, bot be ressone of his godhede, quhilk they saw be faith vnite withhis
5 humanitie.

It is nocht onknavin to me quhow þair is sum þat allegis the vordes of
S. Augustine schortlye folouand, *and* peruerstly applyis them by þe true
menynge and contrar the doctrine of the kirk, sayand: "ʒe sall nocht eate
this bodye quhilk ʒe se, nor drink þe bluid quhilk they ar to sched þat cruci-
10 fyis me". Trueth it is, ve sal neuer eate þe bodye of þe lord nor drinke his
bluide efter þe sammyne maner as his bodye vas seine and his bluid vas
sched hauand sik qualiteis. Nocht the lesse, it is the same bodye and bluide
in substance, as I haue schavin þe ofbefore, resauit efter ane other maner.
And this is þe true menynge of thir vordes, as þe hail sentence precedand
15 and efter folovand plainlye declaris.

Now vil ve cal to rememberance sum other part of ald anciant fathers.
Chrisostome vritis one this maner: "It is nocht ane man þat makis our
lordes bodye and bluid of the thynge set furth apone þe table [f. 15v.] to be
consecrat, bot it is Christe, þat vas crucifyet. Thir vordes ar pronuncit of
20 ane preist, and þe breade and vyne ar consecrat be Goddes vord." Damascene vritis one this maner: "The breade and vyne ar noch ane figure of
Christis bodye and bloude (God forbeid þat), bot it is made the lordes
bodye it self Iounit to his godhede, our lord hym self vorkand be his vord
'this is my bodye', pronuncit be þe preiste." Theophilact, vritand one this
25 maner: "The breade is nocht onely ane figure of Christis bodye, bot it is
chaunged in þe same self body of Christ. The lord sais: the breade quhilk
I gyfe is my flesche; he said nocht: it is ane figure of my flesche." S. Ambrouse vritis in this maner: "Affore þat it be consecrate it is breade, bot
efter þat Christis vordes be cumin till it, it is Christis bodye." Cipriane
30 vritis one this maner: "The breade quhilk the lord gef to his disciples beand
changed, nocht efter þe outvart forme bot as concernynge þe nature, be the
almychty power of the vorde it is made flesche."

---

2. *gef*] F and gaif. 4. *they saw be faith vnite*] F be faytht thay saw cleyd. 7–8. *þe true menynge
and*] F his trew menyng. 10. *sal*] omitted in F. 13. *haue schavin*] F schew. 14. *þe true menynge*]
F ane trew menyng. 16. *sum … fathers*] F sum vthyris of þe ald doctouris. 19. *crucifyet*] F
crucifeit for ws. 20. *ane preist*] F þe preist; *vyne*] F the wyne; *Goddes*] F þis. 21–22. *of Christis
bodye and bloude*] F of blue dand body of Chryst. 22. *bot it is made*] F bot. 23. *Iounit to*] F Ionit
on to. 23–24. *vorkand … preiste*] F sayand 'This Is my body'. 24. *vritand*] F wrettis. 25. *onely
ane figure*] F ane figure onelye. 27. *he said … flesche*] F he said: It Is nocht ane figure of my
flesche, bot It Is my flesche. 28. *in*] F on. 29. *till it*] F þarto. 30. *The breade*] F this breid.
31. *efter*] F as towart; *þe nature*] F nature. 31–32. *be … flesche*] F Is maid flesche be þe
almychthing power of þe word.

Mark, gude reader, quhow agreable ar þe saingis of the anciant fathers
vith þe plane text of the scriptoure and godly doctrin of haly kirk, boith
tovart þe reall presence of the preciouse bodye and bluide of Iesus Christ
our saluiour in the sacrament, And als tovart the transsubstanciacione and
5 chaungene of the substance of breade and vyne in the bodye and bluid of þe
lord. Nocht onely this is and euer hes bene the doctrine of the anciant
fathers of the kirk, bot alsse the sammyne doctrine is plaine and manifestlye set furth be þe sicht of þe most speciall ennimeys of the kirk of God
in þir days: Of the quhilk I vald mak the readaris to knaw ane notable pur-
10 posse.
        Luther in al his vorkes apprevis þe real presence of the lordes bodye in
þe sacrament, bot he denyes transsubstanciacione. And Ecolampadius
denyes the reall presence; nocht þe lesse, vritand aganis Luther he reprevis
the Iugement and doctrin of hyme þat apprevis þe real presence and denyes
15 transubstanciacione, and preuis be plaine authoritie of scriptour, and
invincible argumentes and [f. 16r.] reasones, that giffe thare be þe real
presence of the body of our lord in the sacrament, onforce there man be als
transsubstanciacione. Sua there is na man settis furth transsubstanciacione
mair quickly nor doise Ecolampadius. Be the contrar, Luther as ernistlye
20 as ony man in thir dais settis furth þe real presence contra Ecolampadius,
and denyes transsubstanciacione, Sua þat the ane for þe real presence and
the other for transsubstanciacione settis out manifestlye þe true catholike
doctrine of the kirke, baith tovart the real presence and transsubstanciacione, nochtvithstandynge þat they ar repugnant the ane to þe other and
25 alsua to þe kirk.
        This ʒe may perceaue quhow vonderfullye God tryis þe trueth of his
vorde, nocht onely be godly men his ministeris, bot also be vicket instrumentes: to there grete confusione and manifestacione of there intolerable
Ignorance and Induritnes, And plain confirmacione of the godly doctrine
30 of his kirk, aganis the quhilkis hellis ʒettes quhilk is haresy, vice, and syne –
cane nocht prevaile.

The saxt chaptour.

Sene ve haue hed Iust occasione conforme to þe scripturis of almychty
Gode tilbe resolut and satifyet vith þe first hede and part of our disputa-

---

1. *the*] F þir.   2. *haly kirk*] F þe haly kirk.   3. *bodye and bluide*] F blued and body.   4. *tovart the*] *omitted in* F;   5. *bodye and bluid*] F blued and body.   6. *Nocht onely*] F and nocht alanerlie.
7. *bot*] *omitted in* F; *plaine*] F planlye.   8. *þe sicht of þe*] F syk as hes bene; *ennimeys of*] F ennimes to.   9. *readaris*] F redar.   11. *his*] F þir; *lordes bodye*] F body of þe lord.   12. *And*] *omitted in* F.   13. *reprevis*] F apprewis.   14. *hyme þat apprevis*] F Luther þat dois apprewe.
15. *authoritie of scriptour*] F scriptour, authorite.

134

cione tovart þe true onderstandynge of this most excellent mistery of the blissit sacrament of the altare – quhare questione vas quhidder þe doctrine of the kirke or þe opinione of Ecola*mpadius* vas maist agreable with the plain text of the scriptoure –, Now restes to considder quhidder þe doctrine
5   of the kirk affermand the real presence of the body of our saluiour in the sacrament, or the opinione of Ecola*mpadius*, quha denyis þe real presence of the lordes bodye in the sacrament, giffis ony vay glore, estimacione, or prise to God and his vord conforme to þe scriptour, as dois the godlye doctrine of the kirk, becaus impropirlye and ontruelye and ongodlye they
10   expone the vordes of our saluiour, sayand "This is my body", to [f. 16v.] haue bene spoken be ane figure and similitude; be þe quhilk vristit inter-pretacione they obscure, hyid, and diminucis the most vonderfull vorke of almychty God, makande litle difference betuix this sacrament and sacrifice And the sacramentes and figures of þe auld lawe, quhilkis vas bot
15   similitudes and figures onelye, Sua þat the beleif of þe sammyne is litle or na thynge to þe glore of God. Quhat grete mater is it to beleif, and quhare in is Goddes glore avansyt to say, þat the breade and the vyne ar onelye ane figure and taken of Christis bodye? This may þow cleirlye perceaue quhow þis vickit opinione obscuris, hyddis, and dyminucis þe vonderfull vorke of
20   almychty God.

    Be þe contra, mark þe godlye doctrine of the kirk, and þow sal cleirly perceaue þat it declaris þe vonderfull vork of almichty God conforme to his vorde. For like as Iesus Christ our saluiour vas consauit abone ordour of nature in þe bosume of the virgine Marie, godhede and manhede vnit
25   to gidder – twa natures in ane persone –, And as he enterit in to þe house quhare his disciples var, durris and vindokkis al beand closit, with his verray hail reall bodye hauand flesche, bloude, and bonis, and occupeit na place in his passynge – and þat far abone þe ordour of nature –, Sua, be his godlye power far abone the ordour of nature, he is contenit realye under
30   the formes of bread and vyne, godhede and manhede vnit to gidder in ane persone hauand flesche, bloud, and bonis, and occupeis na place therin. This is and euer hes bene the godlye doctrine and vonderfull beleif of the kirk of God and al the anciant fathers of the sammyne; And þe mair vonderful þat it is, the maire it is to þe glore of God, considderinge the
35   sammyn is nocht consauit of mannis Imaginacione bot of Christis avin vordes, quhilk is omnipotent, sayand: "This is my body".

---

23. *ordour*] F þe ordour. 26. *disciples*] F apostolis. 27. *hail*] *omitted in* F. 28. *passynge*] F passage. 29–30. *realye onder ... vyne*] F vnder ... vyne Realye. 32. *the godlye doctrine*] F ane godlye doctrine. 33–34. *And ... glore*] F þe mair wonderfull þe mair to þe glore.

Attour, þow sal onderstand þat the godlye doctrine and beleif of the kirk tovart þe onderstandynge of this profunde mistery is mekil mair profitable to þe resauar nor is the contra opinione. For quhy, quha sa euer resauis this blissit sacrament vorthely hes nocht onely profeit be [f. 17r.]
5 reasone of his faith, bot also be reasone þat he rasauis [Chris]tis real bodye, godhede and manhede vnit to gidder insepara[tlye], sua þat ve rasaue mekil mair aboundantlye þe grace of God and [rest]is gretarlye assurit of Christis fauour tovart vs resauand Christis bodye boith spiritually and reallie, as his vordes plainlye techis vs, nor to resaue the lordes body
10 spiritually allanerlye or be ane figure and sygne.

And to þe effect þat þow may mair easaly onderstand the sammyne, þow sal considder þat there is diuersse maneris of the resauynge of Christes body, and mair aboundand grace in the ane nor in the other: lik as, in þe resauynge of the giftes of the holy Spreit, ve ar assurit þat þe apostlis
15 resauit the giftes of þe holy Spreit diuerse vais at diuerse tymes, and maire aboundantlye at ane tyme nor at ane other. For truelye, þe apostlis resauit þe giftes of þe holy Spreit vithout doute mair aboundantlye efter his gloriouse ascensione þan of before, boith in til grace of onderstandynge and visdome of al veritie – conforme to his godlye promesse spekand of his
20 blissit Spreit þat þe apostlis vas to resaue efter his ascensione, said: "Quhen he cumis, he sal teche ȝow al verite" –, And als anent the fouth of grace infundit in there saulis, quharbe þa var clengit fra syne and confermit in the luff of God, Sua that they mich haue al said with S. Paul þat þare vas na creature mych dysseuer theme fra the luf of God, as they ver disseuerit
25 in þe tyme of his passione, boith corporally and spiritually, nochtvithstand-ynge þat they hed resauit þe gift of the holy Spreit effore þe Sammyne. Swa sume tymes ve resaue þe bodye of the lord spiritualye onelye be faith and deuocione, Sum tymes boith spiritualye and reallye, as quhen ve vorthelye resaue þe blissit sacrament of þe altare, quharin is contenit þe invisible gift
30 of grace quhilk is Christis reall bodye – vnit with his godhede as said is –,

---

1. onderstand] F consider. 3. nor] F conforme to þe scriptour, nor; quha sa euer] F quhat-sumeuir. 4. hes] F he hes; profeit] F proffet for þe part of þe ressauer. 5. be reasone þat he rasauis] F for þe part of the self sacrament, quhairin Is contenit. 7. aboundantlye] F abund-ance of. 7–8. restis gretarlye assurit] F far gretar assurite. 8. Christis] F Goddis. 9. vordes] F word. 10. be] omitted in F. 12–13. there is... lik as] F þar Is greys In þe Receawing of þe lordis body, lyk as. 14. Spreit] F Gaist. 15. giftes] F gift; Spreit] F Gaist; and] omitted in F. 16. at ane other] F ane vthir. 17. giftes] F gift. 17–28. vithout doute ... spiritualye and reallye] F notheles þar Is na doubt bot þe apostolis ressauit þe gift of þe haly Gaist mair abundantlye eftir þe ascentione of oure salueour be ane visible figure. Sua sum tymes we ar parttakaris of þe body of þe lord bath spiritualye and Realye. 29–30. þe invisible gift of grace] F invisible grace. 30. vnit with his godhede as said is] omitted in F.

136

quharbe ve resaue mekil maire abundance of grace nor resauand it spiritualye or be ane sygne or figure allanerlye.

Thys [f. 17v.] may the reader cleirlye perceaue þat in þe cace þe scriptour
gef equal apperaunce of the interpretacione of Ecolampadius and Calvin
5 tovart the onderstandynge of this profunde misterye as for þe interpretacione of the kirk (quhilk is alse false as God is true), ȝit alvais þe interpretacione of the kirk is rather to be folowit, becaus it is mekil mair to þe
glore of God and profeit of the resauar, as I haue al reddelye declarit conforme to Goddes vordes.
10 Lord God, quhat vengebel vodnes is this, quhilk rengis in þe christiane
hartis of men in thir dais, quha hed rather thraw þe scriptoure by Goddes
menynge of the Sammyne, sekand ese and contenment of thair fleschly
Iugement and natural reasone, nor truely till onderstand the sammyne,
albeit it be contrar natural reasone as ar all maters of faith for the glore of
15 Gode and thair avin saluacione. Becaus þe vickit interpretacione of Ecolampadius and Calvin is mekil mair agreable to our outvart vittes and
manly reasone tovart þe interpretacione of this mistery – as commonlye al
hereseys ar – nor is the godly interpretacione of the kirk, Therfor men in thir
dais quhilkis ar fleschly in Iugement ar miserable subieckit to this vickit
20 heresy of Ecolampadius and Calvine, contrar the godlye doctrine of þe
kirk, to quhome it pertenis to tak ordour in misteryis pertenand our faith.

Lord God, may nocht euer ane christiane man perceaue and onderstand
quhow þis vickit and thrawine interpretacione denyand the real presens
of the lordes bodye in þe sacrament euellis and alteris the hartes fauour and
25 godlye disposicione quhilk the apostle requiris of ane christiane man before
he receaue þe blesset sacrament? Dois nocht S. Paul expresly commaund
al christiane men affore they be parttakaris of this sacrament to exeme
them selues, and þat onder þe payne of damnacione? Quhow sal it be
possible þat ane christiane man sal dispone and exeme hyme self efter þis
30 rigorouse maner quhilk thinkis in his conscience (and þat fleschlye) þat
he is to receaue bot bair breade and vyne beand in ane figure only and

---

1–2. *nor ... allanerlye*] F as said Is, nor be ane bair signe alanerlye. 3. *þe cace*] F in cace. 4.
of the] F for þe. 8. *reddelye*] F reddy. 9. *vordes*] F word. 10–11. *christiane hartis of men*] F hartis
of christiane men. 11-12. *Goddes menynge*] F þe godlye menyng. 12. *of*] F to. 13. *Iugement*]
F Iugementis; *till*] F to. 14. *natural*] F þar manlye; *for*] F to. 15. *and*] F to. 17. *reasone*] F
ressonis; *interpretacione*] F interpretationis. 19. *fleschly in Iugement*] F of fleschelye Iugementis. 20. *contrar*] F In contrar. 21. *it pertenis*] F onelye It appertenis; *misteryis*] F all
misteryis. 22. *euer ane*] F euery. 23. *interpretacione*] F interpretatione of Oecolampadius and
Caluine and vthyris. 24. *euellis*] F annoillis (*with v-sign above quite clear first i*); *hartes*] F hart.
26. *þe*] F þis; *S. Paul*] F Paule. 27. *men affore they be parttakaris*] F man afor he be partakar.
28. *them selues*] F him self. 30. *fleschlye þat*] F falslye. 31. *in*] *omitted in* F.

similitude of the lord*is* [f. 18r.] body? Quhat christiane ma*n*nis hart cane
be sterit vp to s[ik] fauour and feyr to receaue þe pictour and similitude of
h[is] lord and mast*er*, as gif he thouch i*n* his co*n*science – þat truely conforme to Goddes vorde – þ*at* he is to receaue his lord and master, crear and
5   redemar?

    No*w* vil I hu*m*ilye and ernistlye exort þe reader to be equal Iuge, and
considder q*uhi*lk of thir twa int*er*pretaciones – the ane affermand the real
presence of the lordes bodye i*n* the sacrame*n*t, The other affermand the
Sacrame*n*t to be ane signe onely of the lordes body – mast feruentlye
10   disponis o*ur* hartes to þe rigour requirit be S. Paull affore ve be partakar*is*
of þe blissit sacrame*n*t.

The sevint chaptor.

    According til o*ur* promesse i*n* þe begynnyng of this tracteit ve haue
schavin gude vil – as it hes plesit God to gif vs grace – to declair quhidder
15   the int*er*preta*c*iones of Ecola*m*padius, Calvin, and others diuerse in thir
dais ar most propir and agreable with the plaine text of the scriptour*is*.
Therefter ve haue reasonit and declarit q*uhi*lk of the twa int*er*preta*c*iones
is maist to the glore of Gode and veil of þe resauars, co*n*forme to þe scriptour*is*.
20   No*w* vil we co*n*cluid and reasonynge be co*n*ferrens of this vickit heresye
and opinione of Ecola*m*padius, Calvin, and others denyand the real presens
of the lordis body i*n* þe sacrament vith the most detestable and abhominable hereseis q*uhi*lk euer hes bene sene the i*n*carna*c*ione of Iesus Christ, be
the q*uhi*lk – God villinge – ve sal mak the reader cleirly til onderstande this
25   heresye of Ecola*m*padius and Calvin abone rehersit to be ane of the most
deplorit and co*n*damnable hereseys þat eu*er* hes bene sene the faith begane,
and to be rekkynnit with the first, and that efter this maner and co*n*forme
to þe procedynge. I vil speir at ony ma*n* pregnant of i*n*gine quha hes adieckit
and [f. 18v.] subieckit them selues determinatlye to þe opinione of Ecola*m*-
30   *padius* and Calvyne and the rest: be quhat scriptour*is* propirlye and truely

---

2. *to sik fauour*] F be syk feruor; *and similitude*] F or similitude.   3. *thouch*] F think; þat
truely] F and trewlie.   4. *and master, crear*] F maister, creatour.   6. *ernistlye*] F hartlie.   10.
our hartes to þe rigour] F the hart of ane christiane ma*n* to exa*m*me him self according to
þe rigore.   13. *til*] F to; *tracteit*] F tractiue.   15–16. *interpretaciones … ar*] F interpretatione
of Oecolampadius Is.   16. *scriptouris*] F scriptoure.   18. *resauars*] F receauer.   20. *and*] F ane.
21. *Calvin and*] F and Caluin and all.   23. *quhilk*] F q*uhi*lk*is*.   24. *til*] F to.   27–28. *conforme to
þe procedynge*] F forme of proceding.   28. *adieckit*] F addictet.   29. *them selues*] F þame self.
30. *scriptouris*] F scriptoure.

138

allegit, or be quhat authoritie or reasone, vil they preif and perswaide the
opinione of Ecolampadius and Calvine to be resauit and approvyne true
and godlye doctrine, And the opinione of Arrius, Macedonius, Nestorius,
and others of þe most deplorit heretikis quhilk euer hes bene, to be refusit
5 and repellit as one true and ongodlye doctrine – and the doctrine of
Ecolampadius and Calvyne to be resauit as true and godlye doctrine, bot
becauße they allage diuerse testymoniis of scriptoure for theme.

    This sammyne argument perswades þe opinione of Arrius and Nestorius
mekill mair to be resauit. For quhare euer Ecolampadius or Calvyne alleges
10 ane testimony for confirmacione of thair opinione, Arrius alleges thre,
quhilk easaly may be persauit gif thow vyl reade þe vark of Hilarius
<Hilarius> vritand aganis Arrius, and alse the vorke of Athanasius
<Athanasius>, quha vas in þe tyme of Arrius ane godly byschope quha
resistit til his errour.

15   Wil thow say þat the scriptouris alleget be Ecolampadius and Calvyne
ar truely and propirlye allegit, and the scriptouris alleget be Arrius ar one
truely and onpropirlye alleget? I dar baldye say, nochtvithstandynge þat
they baith allege the scriptouris peruerstlye by þe godlye menynge of the
sammyne, lat ony man of Iugement diligentlye considder all þe testimonyis
20 of scriptouris alleget be theme baith, he sal fynde and perceaue the scriptouris alleget be Arrius to gif gretare apperaunce (besid þis, þat is, ther is
far mair of them) nor dois the scriptouris alleget be Ecolampadius and
Calvine, quhilkis and ve var curiouse to confer it ver easy to preif.

    Bot ve vil nocht curiouslye do the sammyne, in euentuir fleand ane
25 inconuenient ve sal fall in twa, nocht þe lese þat þe reader sall nocht thynk
þat it is said of plesour and effeccione, sene in special ve vill conterfate þe
craft of learnet men medicinaris quha, persauand ony man intoxicat or
poysont, be contra poysone curis þe pacient: lik as ve intend – God
villynge – be conferrynge of thir errouris to con- [f. 19r.] streine the ane
30 to expell the others, one this maner.

    It is v[ri]tyne in the evangell, for mencione is made of the supper of the
lorde, þat he blessit þe breade and gef to his disciples, sayand: "This is my
bodye". Ecolampadius and Calvine, incontrar þe true meanynge of the
scripture and godlye doctrine of haly kirke, exponis thir vordes to be
35 spoken be ane similitude. To fortifye there thrawine interpretacione impropirlye cal they to remembrance the vordes of the apostle, sayand:
"Christ vas the roike", allegeand lik as our saluiour vas nocht ane roike in
deid bot be ane similitude, swa sais Ecolampadius and Calvyne that it vas
bot ane similitude of his bodye – and nocht our saluiouris reall bodye –
40 þat he geue til his apostlis.

Truelye, þis confferrens of scriptouris is verray impropir, as I haue al reddelye declarit in the first chaptour. For quhy, albeit þe scriptouris speakis sumtyme be ane similitude, it argumentes nocht þat it speakis euer be ane similitude. For gif sua var, our hail faith var confundit, as thow sal
5 cleirlye persaue.

The kirk to confund the vickit opinione of heresy of Arrius, allegeand the vordes of our saluiour, sainge: "I and þe Father ar boith ane". Arrius, quha denyit the Father and the Sone in godhede to be boith ane substance, alleget þir vordes of our saluiour folouand to be spoken be ane
10 similitude and figure (as dois Ecolampadius >and< Calvin to fortifye there errouris be scriptouris impropirlye applyit), and, to preif the sammyn errour to be true, alleget þe vordes of our saluiour quhare he dide praye to þe Father of heawine for þam þat euer vas to beleue in hyme, Sayand: "Holye Father, keip theme in þj name quhome þow hes geffin to me, þat
15 they ma be ane as ve ar ane". Arrius inferrit of thir vordes þat like as they quhome for our saluiour prayit var nocht ane in substance, bot be concord of mynd and vyll.

This it ma be persauit, gif regard var hed to fals and vickit applicacione of scriptouris, than suld the heresy of Arrius hed place rather nor þe heresy
20 of Ecolampadius and Calvyne, because [f. 19v.] this text of scriptoure – and þe rest, as þow sal schortly perceaue – hes far greater apperaunce for confirmacione for Arrius errour and vickit opinione. Gif our saluiour hed said: "This is my body as I am the roike", lik as he sais: "I pray the Fader þat they be al ane as ve ar ane", Thane vald Ecolampadius, Calvin, and
25 otheris haue thouch they had mater to triumphe aganis þe kirk.

The auctht chaptor.

Ane other cheiffe argument þat Ecolampadius, Calvin, and all others þat fauowris there faccions, vsis to cause there heresy to seme godlye aganis þe true doctrine of þe kirk, sais that þe interpretacione of þe mistery of þe
30 supper of the lord conforme to þe doctrine of the kirk may nocht stand with þe articles of our beleif: for it is said þat our saluiour ascendit vp to hewyne and sittis at þe rich hand of the Father, and is to returne agane one the letter day.

I vil speir at the: quhat sais Ecolampadius and Calvyne and all others

---

29. *sais*] F Is, sayand. 31. *for*] F as Quhair. 34. *speir*] F ask.

140

þat fauouris there vickit opinione *and* faccione *in* þis *p*art bot as said Arri*us* and þe rest þat fauourit his faccione? Said no*ch*t Arri*us* plainlye þat the int*er*pretac*i*one of þe scripture conforme to þe declarac*i*one of the kirk tovart the mistery of þe diuine nature of *our* saluio*ur* vas expresse aganis
5 the first and principall article of *our* beleue, q*uhi*lk*is* is to beleue *in* ane God? For quhy, said Arri*us*, gife there be God the Father and God the Sone diuidit *in* twa personis, quho*w* ca*n* þe first article of *our* beleiff be of veritie, Saiand: "There is bot ane God"?

Truelye, it is alse far aganis the ordo*ur* of nature þat there suld be twa
10 personis *in* ane substance, as þat ane persone suld be in twa places at ane tyme. I dar baldye say þat it is no*ch*t ane phraise nor maner of spekin agreable nor propir for ane christiane ma*n* to speir quho*w* Christes bodye ca*n* be in diuerse places at ane tyme. Or quho*w* ca*n* there be twa distinguit personis *in* ane godhede? It sufficis þat Christes vord techis vs, q*uhi*lk all
15 christiane ma*n* auch to beleue *with*out reasonynge quho*w* sik thinges may be. There is no*ch*t ane article *in* all hail *our* beleiff q*uhi*lk cane be perceauit be ma*n*lye reasone.

Ane other cheiff argument q*uhi*lk is applyit be Ecola*m*padius, Calvyne, and others, *in*contrar þe [f. 20r.] godlye doctrine of the kirk tovart the
20 ondersta*n*dinge of this profunde misterye of the sacrame*n*t of þe altare is þe vord of ou[r] saluio*ur*, sayand: "It is the spreit þat giffis lif; the flesche profitis na thynge" <Io. 6>. Tak hede, gude reader, and þo*w* sal perceaue þat, lik as Ecola*m*padius and Calvyne applyis thir vordes of *our* saluio*ur*: "This is my bodye", *in*contrar þe true doctrine of the kirk tovart þe real
25 presence of the bodye of þe lord *in* the sacrame*n*t, Sua dois Arri*us* impropirlye apply þe vordes of *our* saluio*ur*, sayand: "The Father is mair nor I", *in*contra þe doctrine of the kirk tovart þe ond*er*standynge of þe diuine nature of *our* saluio*ur*, becaus, sais Arri*us*, quhare there is mair and lese ca*n* no*ch*t be equalite. Truelye, hauand respect to þe godhede of the Father
30 and ma*n*hede of the Sone onelye, there is no*ch*t equalite; bot gif ve vil haue respect to þe godheid of þe Sone, he is al vais equal with þe Father. Sua, lyke as þe Father and the Sone ar equal and no*ch*t equall efter diuerse respeckis and co*n*siderac*i*ones, Inlykvise þe flesche diuidit fra þe spreit is

---

1. *the vickit opinione and faccione*] F þat wicket factione; *as said Arrius*] F as þe said Arrius.
5. *quhilkis*] F q*uhi*lk. 9. *suld be*] F salbe. 10. *substance*] F substance of godheid; *suld be*] F salbe. 11. *dar baldye*] F dar*n* baldlye; *nor*] F or. 13. *can be*] F suld be; *Or quhow can there*] F or quhow þar salbe; *distinguit*] F distinct. 15. *thinges*] F thing. 16. *There*] F for ther; *perceauit*] F persuadet. 21. *vord*] F wordis; *sayand*] F quhair he sayis. 23. *applyis*] F impropirlye applyis. 24. *"this is my bodye"*] *omitted in* F. 29. *can*] ther can. 33. *Inlykvise þe*] F for quhy.

no*ch*t profitable for saluac*io*ne of ma*n*; bot þe flesche Iounit to þe spreit
q*uhi*lk is God – as Christes flesche – is euer profitable, as I haue all reddelye
declarit. This may þe reader perceaue þ*at* efter þe sa*mm*yne sort and maner
as Arri*us* vickitlye int*er*preit and threw þe scripture, by the godlye meanynge
5   of þe sa*mm*yne, to fortifye his vickit heresy and opinione, Sua dois Ecola*mp*adius and Calvyne to preif there errour*is*.

Attour, confer þe scriptour*is* quha plesis, they sal na vay perceaue þe
opinione of Ecola*mp*adius and Calvyne to be godly be conferrens and
allegeans of the scriptour*is*, bot þe sa*m* vay they sal perceaue rather þe
10   opinione of Arri*us* to be godlye, q*uhi*lk is playne h[e]resye aganis þe faith.
Giff I vald be als curyouse as perchaunce I mych be, ʒit culd I call to
reme*m*beraunce thretty sax testimonyis of scriptour*is* or ma allegit be
Arri*us* i*n*contrar þe doctrine of þe kirk of God, of þe q*uhi*lk*is* ony ane
[f. 20v.] giffes alse grete apperaunce for co*n*firmac*io*ne of his vickit
15   opinione as the maist propir text allegit be Ecola*mp*adius or Calvyne i*n*-
contra þe kirk dois to fortifye there vickit heresye and opinione. Therfore
ve mane be assurit þat þe allegeance of scriptour*is*, q*uhi*lk*is* euer hes bene
at all tymes famyliar til al heretik*is*, persuadis na vais the opinione of
Ecola*mp*adius, Calvyne, and þe rest, to be approwyne mair nor the opinione
20   of Arri*us*, bot rather lesse.

Nowe, sene ve ar assurit that there is na scriptour*is* q*uhi*lk ca*n* be propirlye allegit for co*n*firmac*io*ne of the opinione of Arri*us*, it is to be considderit be quhat authoritie ony ma*n* fauourand þe faccione of Ecola*m*-
padius and Calvyne ca*n* perswade þat there opinione aucht to be resauit
25   and þe opinione of Arri*us* conda*m*nit. Vil þo*w* say þat the godlye generall
counsall of Nece <co*n*siliu*m* Necenu*m*>, quhar into vas dewlye co*n*uenit
thre hundreth auchtene fathers, Iustlye co*n*damnit the heresy of Arri*us*?
There vas mony fathers of godlye lernynge and gud liffe – beand gadderit
of al the partes of christindome – dewly co*n*uenit i*n* ane general counsal
30   <co*n*silium Lateranen*se*>, quhare naturally and sufficientlye disput þe
heresy of Ecola*mp*adius, q*uhi*lk vas sterit vp first be ane callit Berengari*us*
and vas Iustlye conda*m*nit be this cou*n*sal of Rome and diu*er*se others.

---

1. *þe flesche*] F flesche.   2. *as Christes flesche*] F as Chrystis flesche Is; *reddelye*] F reddy.
4. *vickitlye interpreit and threw*] F deid vicketlye *interpret* and thraw; *scripture*] F scriptouris.
4–6. *by the godlye meanynge … errouris*] F to fortife his haresye, sua deid Oecolamp*adius* and
Caluin thraw þe scriptoure by þe godlye meni*ng* of þe samyn to fortife þair wicket heresye
and opinione.   7. *they*] F and þaj.   8. *be conferrens*] F for co*n*ferrence.   9. *þe sam vay they sal
perceaue*] F be þe samyn way sall thay persuade.   15. *propir*] F impropir.   17. *mane*] F may.
18. *at all tymes*] omitted in F.   21. *scriptouris*] F scriptoure.   24. *can*] F will.   26. *of Nece*] F
Nicene; *quhar into*] F quhairin þair.   28. *mony*] xiij hundretht.   29. *al the*] F all.   30. *quhare*]
F quha.   31. *callit*] omitted in F.   32. *of Rome*] omitted in F.

142

Attour, gif the reader think*is* it ane superflowis persuasione þat this
vickit heresye of Ecola*m*padius, Calvyne, and other denyand the real
p*r*esens of the lordes body i*n* the sacrame*n*t, is sa effectuislye co*n*damnit
with sik nowmer of godlye fathers þat it is to be cryit out one be al chris-

5 tiane ma*n*, as the heresye of Arri*us*, Thow sal onde*r*stande that this
sa*m*myne cou*n*sall of Nece q*uhi*lk dyde co*n*dame the heresy of Arri*us*,
the sa*m*myne counsal i*n* effect dide co*n*dame the heresy of Ecola*m*padius,
And sa far as it plesit God to steir vp the hartes of the a*n*ciant fathers quha
dewlye conuenit i*n* the laudable cou*n*sall of Nece to site anent the mist[ery

10 of] this blissit sacrament co*n*forme to þe int*er*pretaci*o*ne and doctrine of the
kirk tovart the reall p*r*esence of the body and bloude of *our* saluio*ur* i*n* þe
sacrame*n*t determyt as efter folowis: "Disponand our selues one to þe
godlye [f. 21r.] table, lat vs no*ch*t luke sklenderly apone the breade an[d]
cwpe set before vs, bot lat vs lyft vp *our* myndis be faith, on[der]standand

15 in that haly table to be þe lame of Gode takar avay the synnes of the
vardle, offerit be þe preist without bluid. And ve, resaua*n*d veralye his
p*r*eciouse bodye and bloude, aucht to beleiffe theme to be þe plaege of *our*
resurreccione." Hithertil the counsall.

Mark quho*w* agreable is the declaraci*o*ne of this godlye counsall with

20 þe doctrine of the kirk tovart the ondersta*n*dynge of the real p*r*esence of
Christes body and bloude i*n* the sacrame*n*t of the altare – and alse tovarte
the offerynge vp of the lordes bodye be the preistes i*n* sacrifice. This counsal
of Nece vas the first counsall generall efter þe counsall co*n*uenit i*n* the tyme
of the ap*ost*lis of Iesus Christe, And hes bene approwine in all ayges, ȝeris,

25 and tymes. Sua sal þo*w* perceaue þat the same authoritie, and alse the grete
authoritie, hes at all tymes co*n*damnit þe vickit heresye of Ecola*m*padius
and Calvyne as dide co*n*dame the errour of Arri*us*. And this may þo*w*
cleirlye onderstand þat there is na authoritie q*uhi*lk dois perswade the
errour of Arri*us* to be ongodlye bot þe sa*m*myne dois perswade inlikvise

30 the errour of Ecolampadi*us* *and* Calvin to be alse ongodlye.

1. *gif the reader thinkis it ane*] F to gif þe reader. 2. *other*] F vthyr*is*. 3-4. *is sa … þat it*] *omitted
in* F. 5. *this*] F þe. 6. *Nece*] F Nicene. 7. *dide condame*] F comdamnet. 8. *And sa far*] F
Insafar. 9. *of Nece*] F Nicene; *to site anent*] F for þe declaratione of. 11. *body and bloude*] F
blued and body. 12. *determyt*] *omitted in* F. 14. *myndis*] F mynd. 15. *takar*] F takand. 16.
preist] F preist*is*. 18. *Hithertil*] F Hethir to. 19. *declaracione*] F diliberatione. 20. *the onderstandynge of*] *omitted in* F. 23. *of Nece*] F nicene; *þe counsall conuenit in*] *omitted in* F.
25. *perceaue*] F ewir perceaue; *the grete*] F gret. 28. *quhilk*] F þat. 29. *inlikvise*] F Inlykwayis.

The nint chaptor.

Sene ve ar certifyet þat there is na scriptour nor authorite quhilkis perswades the opinione of Ecolampadius, Calvyne, and all others denyand the real presence of the lordes bodye in the sacrament, to be godlye, and
5 the opinione of Arrius, Nestorius, *and* the most condamnable heretikis quhilkis euer hes bene, to be ongodlye, restes to considder be quhat reasone ony man may be persuadit þ[at t]he a[ne] opinione is to be resauit as ane godlye doctrine, a[nd th]e other to be repellit as ongodly doctryne.

Vill ve say þat þe opinione of Ecolampadius and Calvyne is to be resauit
10 becaus there is mony christiane men in thir dais [f. 21v.] [quhi]lk dois fortifye and applaude to the sammyne? I dar baldy say: [quhar] euer there is ane applaudand to þe opinione of Ecolampadius *and* Calvyne, [d]enyand the reall presence of the lordes body in the sacrament, ther var neir ane hunder boith lerit and lawit quhilk dide applaude, fortifye, and mateyme
15 (ʒea, evin to þe deth) the vickit heresy of Arrius denyand the equalite of the Father and þe Sone in diuine power. For quhy, ve rede þat þe gretast part of the hail vardle vas subuertit to the vickit heresy of Arrius (and þat ane lange tyme).

Attour marke, gud reader, all the aige, ʒeire, and tymes sene þe heresye
20 of Ecolampadius and Calvyne first begane contra the reall presence of Goddes bodye in the sacrament, thow sal neuer fynde ony nowmer of learnit men conuenant and concludand all in ane opinione of Ecolampadius and Calvyne. Ve reide at fiwe hunder learnit men conuenit all in ane day and concludit all in ane opinione conforme to þe opinione of the most
25 deplorit heresy of Arrius! This may þow cleirlye perceaue that there is na apperaunce nor reasone quhilkis persuades the opinione of Ecolampadius and Calvyne to be godlye doctrine bot the sammyne persuades mekil mair the opinione of Arrius to be godlye, quhilk but doute it condamnit to be heresy aganis our faith: and sua ar they boith, As Goddes vorde truely
30 onderstand (to gidder with Iust declaracione of holy kirk) certifyes al christine men.

---

2. *quhilkis*] F quhilk. 3. *Calvyne*] F and Caluin. 6. *to be*] *omitted in* F. 7. *be persuadit*] F persuade. 8. *doctryne*] *omitted in* F. 9. *ve*] F þow. 10. *quhilk*] F quhilkis. 11. *to*] F on to; *dar baldy*] F darn baldlie; *quhar euer*] F quhar sum ewir. 12. *applaudand to*] F applaudis of. 13. *the lordes*] F our lordis; *ther var neir*] F thay war ewir. 14. *lerit*] F lernit; *quhilk*] F quhilkis. 16. *the Father and þe Sone*] F þe Sone and þe Father. 16. *gretast*] F gret. 19. *marke, gud reader*] F mark; *the aige, ʒeire*] F aegis, ʒeiris. 20. *contra*] F incontrar. 22. *in ane opinione of*] F In ane opinione conforme to þe opinione of. 24–25. *the most deplorit heresy of Arrius*] F Arrius. 26. *quhilkis*] F quhilk. 27. *godly doctrine*] F godlie. 28–29. *it condamnit to be heresy*] F Is condamnet heresye. 31. *men*] F man.

144

I cal to rememberaunce þir antiquiteis of the heresy of Arrius of sik
purpose, to gif all christiane men Iust occasione to be constant in þe true
faith and beleif, resauit be the kirk of God be inspiracione of the holy
Goist, tovart the onderstandynge of this profunde misterye of þe sacrament
5   of the altare, nocht douttand bot as almychtyne God of his infinite gudnes
with tyme deliuerit and clenget his faitfull kirk and congregacione fra þe
vickit heresy of Arrius, quhilk range so lange and a[pprovin be so mo]ny
baith learnet and onlearnet, he and law degre, In þis sammyne maner the
gude lord sall deliuer his faithfull kirk and congragacione fra the vickit
10   heresy of Ecolampadius and Calvyne and there faccionaris denyand the
real pre-[f. 22r.]sens of our lordes bodye in þe blissit sacrament, quhilk
n[ow trow]bles the vordle so miserable, appliand sa falslye th[e scrip]touris
contra the godlye meanynge of the sammyne and approvyne doctrine of
the kirk.
15   ȝit restes to considder, lik as there is diuerse heretikis in þir days denyand
the real presence of the lordes bodye in the sacrament quha fyndis fault
with the godlye doctrine of the kirk, sayand þat the kirk hes offendit
inuentand new termes, – sik as þis terme, transsubstanciacione –, sua did
Arrius fynd fault with þe godlye doctrine of the kirk, sayand þat the kirk
20   inuentit this terme, homousyon, quhilkis vas noch expreslye contenit in
scripture. <in þe cunsal of Nece trinitas vas callit homusyon, þat is of ane
substance.> And inlik maner Nestorius fand fault with þe doctrine of the
kirk, quhilk inuentit þis terme, theothycus, declarand the blessit virgine to
be moder of God and man incontra his vickit heresye and opinione.
25   Truelye, it is na fault to inuent termes for þe manifestacione of the mysteryis of our faith quhilkis ar agreable with þe scripture and propyrlye
colleckit for þe sammyne, as ar all þaj abone rehersyte.
    Thys may þe reader perceaue quhow vickit heretikis in all tymes hes bene
euer contrarius to the godly doctrine of the holy kirk. And alse it is mani-
30   fest be our conferrens abone rehersit þat there is na scriptoure, reasone,
or authoritie, quhilk persuades the doctrine of Arrius, Nestorius, and þe
most condamnable heretikis quhilkis euer hes bene contrar þe kirk, to be
ongodlye, bot the sammyne persuades the opinione of Ecolampadius,

1. *sik*] F set. 2. *men*] F man. 5 *as*] F lyk as. 6. *tyme*[F þe tyme; *clenget*] F changeit. 7. *approvin*]
F wes approwin.   8. *onlearnet*] F lawit; *he and law degre*] F he degre and law.   9. *the*] F þis.
10. *and there faccionaris*] *omitted in* F. 12. *appliand sa falslye the scriptouris*] F the scriptoure
falslye applyit. 14. *the kirk*] F haly kirk. 15. *considder*] F consider þat. 16. *quha*] F quhilkis.
18. *termes*] F termis quhilkis ar nocht expreslye continet In scriptoure. 20. *quhilkis vas*] F quhilk
is.   21. *scripture*] F the scriptoure.   23. *virgine*] F vergen Marie.   25. *to*] F till; *manifestacione*] F mair manifestatione.   27. *for*] F of; *as ar all þaj*] F as all thir ar.   29. *to*] *omitted in*
F; *holy*] *omitted in* F. 31. *or*] F nor; *quhilk*] F quhilkis. 32. *quhilkis*] F quhilk.

Calvyne, and al others denyand the real presence of the lordes body in the sacrament to be alse ongodlye: Swa þat be all scriptoure, reaso[ne,] or authoritie the sammyne Iugement and punishment auch[t and suld] procede one Ecolampadius, Calvyne, and all others steraris [vp] and man-
5 temaris of there vickit heresy and opinione, quhilk aucht and suld procede one Arrius, Nestorius, and steraris vp of there faccione, because they ar equiualent and [f. 22v.] [alik b]aith in condamnit heresy aganis the vorde of God truely on[der]standit, and alse aganis the kirk of Gode and all the anciant fathers of the sammyne. Therfore they merite and deseruis equall
10 punishment, and to be explodit and cryit out one boith equall be all guide cristiane man. Amen.

Nowe vil ve concluid our litell tractiwe exhortand the pestilent prea-cheouris puft vp with vayne glore – quha rakynnis theme selues of greater knawlege nor Christes holy kirk, cumand without authoritie, subuertand,
15 subornand, and circumuenand the symple people, caand theme ane praye lyke devillis rachys, barkand baldye lik bardis aganis the blesset sacrament: bot all there vittes and ingynis ar one defendit be scriptoure, reasone, or authoritie – that there vickit heresye aganis the real presence of the lordes bodye in the sacrament is to be condamnit, explodit, and cryit out one be
20 al guid christiane men, as the heresye of Arrius, Nestorius, and the most damnable heretikis quhilk euer hes bene sene the faith first begane: because there dewillye doctrine and heresy nocht onelye obscuris, hydis, and diminucis the mychty power and glore of Goddes vorde and others dedis, bot alse it is contrarius to the declaracione of holye kirk of God – as all
25 others vas –, bot alse frustrait vs of the celestial fude of our saull preparit for saluacione of man be Iesus Christ our saluiour, to the quhome, with the Father and the holy Goist, be pryise, honor, and glore for euer and euer. Amen.

---

2. or] F and.   3. *Iugement and punishment*] F punischement and Iugement.   4. *one*] F of; *Calvyne*] F and Caluin; *and mantemaris*] *omitted in* F.   5. *quhilk*] F þat.   6. *Nestorius*] *omitted in* F.; *there*] F his   9. *deseruis*] F desseruit.   10. *explodit and*] *omitted in* F; *boith equall*] F equalie.   11. *Amen*] *omitted in* F.   13. *quha*] F quhilkis.   14. *holy*] F haill; *without*] F but.   15. *caand theme ane*] F ceirsand þar.   16. *devillis*] F þe deuillis; *the*] F þis.   17. *bot*] F to preiffe; *ar one defendit*] F and defend.   19. *is*] F Is nocht.   21. *damnable*] F deplorit; *quhilk*] quhilkis.   21. *first begane*] F begane.   22. *dewillye*] F deuillische.   23. *and others dedis*] F as all vthyris did.   24. *bot alse it*] F and als; *declaracione of*] F deliberatione of þe.   25. *frustrait*] F frustratis.   20. *the quhome*] F quhome.   27. *the holy Goist*] F haly Gaist; *pryise*] F prays.   28ff. '*Amen*' *and the following lines do not occur in* F.

146

Vritine and endit the thyrde day of August a*n*. 1561 be s*chi*r Alexander
Vod, chaplane i*n* Auld Aberdene.

Tria su*n*t i*n*saciabilia, et quartu*m* qu*o*d nu*m*qu*am* dicit suffecit: i*n*fern*us*, et
os wlue, et terra q*uae* nu*m*qu*am* saciat*ur* aqua; ignis vero nu*m*qu*am* dicit
5   sufficit. Prou*er*bioru*m*, ca. xxx.

Ane Compendious Ressonyng,

be þe quhilk is maid manifest,

treulie, and propirlie,

conforme to þe scripturis of almychtie God

(bayth new testament *and* auld),

þe mess to be Institute be Iesu Christ oure salueour

in þe latter supper,

incontrar þe ralling ressonyng of all sic

as dois affirme þe mess to be Inventit

be the brayne of man.

Set furth be Maister Quintyne Kennedy,

commendatour of þe abbay of Corsraguell,

In þe ȝeir of God

ane thousand fywe hundreth threscoir ane ȝeiris.

Si ex deo est consilium hoc aut opus, non poteritis dissoluere,

ne forte et deo repugnare videaminj,

< Act. 5. >

[f. i v.] **Ane** table
declarand (conforme to þe ordoure of þe leyffis)
þe maist notable heidis and purposis
contenit in þis litle werk.

5 **1.** The diffinitioun of þe mess declarand þe samyn: fo. 2.B.

2. Oure salueour institute in þe latter supper ane sacrament, and als the sacrifice of þe mess: fo. 8.A.

3. The prophet Malachie prophecit of þe sacrifice of þe mess: fo. 4.B.

4. The preistheid and oblatioun of Melchisedech prefigurate þe preistheid
10 of oure salueour and þe sacrifice of þe mess: fo. 5.A.4.

5. The paschale lamb was nocht onelie ane figure of þe sacrifice of þe croce, bot als ane mair expres figure of þe sacrifice of þe mess: fo. 9.B. et fo. 10.B.1.

6. The figuris of þe auld testament ar sufficient confirmatioun of materis of
15 fayth concernyng þe new testament, specialie of þe mess: fo. 10.B.2.

7. We ar certifeit be Invincible ressouns, aggreable with Goddis worde, þat thais quhilkis war disciplis to þe apostlis had the trew vnderstanding of þe profund misteriis of þe scripture necessar to be knawin for all christiane mannis saluatioun, specialie of þe supper of þe lorde, quhairapon Is treulie
20 and propirlie gadderit and collectit þe sacrifice of þe mess: fo. 11.A.

8. The sacrifice of þe mess is sufficientlie provin be plane testimonie of scripture, bayth auld testament and new, according to þe interpretatioun, doctryne, and Iugement of thais quhilkis war disciplis to þe apostlis and martyris for þe fayth of Ihesus Christ our salueour in þe prymatywe kirk:
25 fo. 11.B.

[f. ii r.] **9.** The sacrifice of þe mess is sufficientlie provin be þe plane testimonie of scripture, accordyng to þe interpretatioun and deliberatioun of þe maist anceant generale consellis quhilkis evir has bene sen þe tyme of Iesus Christ our salueour to thir dayes: fo. 14.A.

30 **10.** It is treuth þat oure salueour was offerit vp anis in sacrifice apon þe croce, and nevyr to be offerit vp agane eftir þat maner: fo. 5.A.1.

11. It is treuth þat oure salueour is offerit vp daylie in þe sacrifice of þe mess, sua þat ane verite makis nocht ane vþer verite fals, eftir diuerss respectis and consideratiouns: fo. 5.A.2.

35 **12.** The sacrifice of þe mess dois na wayes obscure, nor diminiss þe gloir of þe sacrifice of þe croce (as vane men in þir dayes dreymis), bot rather advansis: fo. 5.B.3.

13. The caus of þe sacrifice of þe croce, callit þe sacrifice of redemptioun: fo. 5.B.1.

14. The caus of þe sacrifice of þe mess, callit þe sacrifice of commemoratioun: fo. 5.B.2.

15. The sacrifice of þe croce *and* þe sacrifice of þe mess In sump*art* aggreis *and* in sump*art* differis: fo. 5.A.3.

16. It is expedient *and* necessar þat þair be diu*erss* cerimoniis vsit in ministratioun of þe sacrame*ntis*, *and* als in þe sacrifice of þe mess, quhilk*is* ar no*cht* co*n*tenit in scripture: fo. 6.B.

17. This terme 'Missa' was vsit be þe disciplis of þe ap*ost*lis, according to þe instructioun had be þe ap*ost*lis: fo. 3.A.

18. The sacrifice of þe mess is to be worschippit with all men: fo. 12.A.2.

19. The lorde is delytit w*ith* þe sacrifice of the mess: fo. 12.A.1.

20. The preistis of þe new law ar to be honorit throu*ch* the sacrifice of þe mess: fo. 13.A.1.

[f. ii v.] **21.** The mess is profitable for thais q*uhi*lk*is* ar depart*it*: fo. 13.A.2.

22. Obet Mess was obserwit *and* vsit in þe kirk of God thretteyn hundret*h* ȝeir syne, *and* mair: fo. 13.B.

23. The mess has all p*ro*pirteis requir*it* to ane godlie institutioun and doctryne: fo. 17.B.1.

24. The wickit opinioun aganis þe mess hes nevir ane propirte aggreand w*ith* ane godlie doctryne: fo. 18.A.1.

25. Quhat is þe cheif caus of þis grit variance quhilk Is rissin now laitlie amang*is* christiane men for þe sacrifice of þe mess *and* all vther materis co*n*cernyng fayt*h* *and* religioun: fo. 15.B.

26. The wo*r*dis of þe consecratioun war institute be oure salueo*ur* in þe lattir supper, sayand: "This is my body": fo. 3.B.

27. The mess hes beyn evir approvin *and* vsit at all tymes, in all regiouns, be all natiouns professand þe fayt*h* of Iesus Christ: fo. 17.B.2.

28. The first þat evir ganestude þe mess was ane callit Wicleiff: fo. 18.A.2.

29. Luther was þe nixt þat ganestude þe mess, affirmand þe mess to be Idolatrie, quha sayis þe devill forbad him to vse þe mess: fo. 18.A.3.

[**30.**] To affirme þe mess Idolatrie >is< als fals as God Is trew, co*n*forme to Goddis worde, bayt*h* auld testament *and* new: fo. 17.A.

Finis.

150

[f. iii r.] **To** the redar in generale,
and in speciall to Knox, Willock, Wynrame, Gudeman, Dowglas, Hereot, Spottiswod, Athenis, *and* all þe laif of the famows precheour*is* to the congregatioun.

5   **Haifand** co*m*miseratioun *and* piete of ane grit parte of þe subiectis of þis realme, quhilkis wondirfullie and miserabillie hes beyn þis lang tyme bypast circu*m*venit and abusit be ȝoure dissaitfull doctryne – persuadand wickitlie and falslie the Mess to be Idolatrie Inventit be þe brayn of man –, We haif, be Goddis grace *and* favour, set furt*h* ane litle werk quhairby
10 (God willing) salbe maid manifest to all thais of þis realme treulie, according to þe scripture of almyc*h*tie God, The mess to be institute be Iesus Christ oure salueour in þe latter supper.

    To preif þe samyn, we ground vs apon þe new testament *and* auld testament, [f. iii v.] according to þe doctryne *and* Interpretatioun of þe
15 anceant fatheris – specialie thays quhilk*is* war disciplis to þe ap*ost*lis *and* m*a*rtyris for þe fayt*h* of Iesus Christ in þe prymatywe kirk –, to gidder wit*h* þe deliberatioun *and* declara*ti*oun of þe maist anceant *and* notable generale co*n*sellis quhilk*is* evir hes beyn sen þe fayth of Iesus Christ first began, to quhom It appertenis (dewlie co*n*venit) to tak ordo*u*r towart þe
20 trew vndirstanding of þe obscuriteis *and* misteriis of Godd*is* worde: Quhair of we haif gadderit aucht co*n*firmatiouns to preif þe mess institute be Iesus Christ – **Prayand** ȝou aucht famows precheour*is* In speciall, and all þe rest, to mak aucht co*n*futatiouns sufficient incontrar oure co*n*firmatiouns, or ellis to recant ȝo*u*r railling ressonyng *and* Intollerable mokrie
25 *and* dispyt aganis þe mess.

    And first I will desyr Schir Iohne Knox (quia est sacerdos Dei altissimj secundum ordine*m* Caluini) to mak ane co*n*futatioun incontrar our confirmatioun groundit apon þe preistheid *and* oblatioun of Melchisedech.

    Secundlie, I will desyr father Willock (quia multa contingebant illi in
30 figuris quhen he was ane freir) To mak ane confutatioun to oure co*n*firmatioun groundit on þe figuris of þe paschale lamb.

    Thridlie, I am assurit þat Mag*iste*r n*oste*r Wynrame (Quha Is wonderfullie learnit, bayt*h* in þe new testament, auld testament, *and* mekle mair) will mak ane co*n*futatioun to oure co*n*firmatioun *and* co*n*clusioun groundit
35 on þe auld testament, new testament, and ane notable doctryne of Vincentius Lirinensis.

    Feirdlie, I will desyr docto*u*r Gudeman to mak [f. iv r.] ane confutatioun contrar þe confirmatiouns of all gude men allegeit be ws to preif o*u*r purposs.

Fiftlie, I haif na dout bot doctour Douglas (Qui de nulla non re dubitat) will mak ane confutatioun to oure *con*firmatioun groundit apon þe prophecie of Malachie.

Sextlie, I will desyr Hereot (Qui adhuc hesitat) to mak ane confutatioun
5   to oure *con*firmatioun groundyt apon þe testimoniis of þe new testament, to preif þe figuris of þe auld testament sufficient pruyf of materis of fayt*h* concerning þe new testament.

Sevintlie, I will desyr Spottiswod (becaus he is superintendent of Lowdeane) þat he tak no*ch*t þat spot to him (he beand sua *pro*fundlie learnit in
10   þe misteriis of þe new testament) bot he mak ane confutatioun to oure confirmatioun of þe sacrifice of þe Mess gru*n*dit on þe misterie of þe supper of þe lorde.

Last of all, I will hwmyllie desyr my lorde of Athenis, ass maist honorable to go hindmest in þis famous processioun, That it will pleis his lordeschip
15   (becaus he Is mature and constant in all his deliberatiouns *and* consellis) to mak confutatioun to oure *con*firmatioun grundit apon þe deliberatioun of þe maist anceant generale consellis.

And þis confutatioun beand maid sufficient to all oure *con*firmatiouns, I oblis my self be þis my hand wryte to renu*n*ce my religioun *and* subiect my
20   self to ȝoure factioun, quhilk I rekkyn na less in my conscience nor to renu*n*ce my God and subiect my self to evir lastand deyt*h and* dampnatioun, [f. iv v.] – fra þe quhilk þe lorde God mot preserwe ȝou *and* me, and all christiane man, for evir *and* evir. Amen.

Orandum pro Inimicis.

Hodie si vocem domini audieritis nolite obdurare corda vestra.

152

Ane familiar ressonyng
of þe misterie of þe sacrifice off the mess
betuix tua brethir,
Maister Quintyne Kennedy, commendatour of Corsraguell,
and
Iames Kennedy of Vchtwallure.

Quintinus   **Iacobus**

I. Broder, gif It may stand with ȝour favouris, I wald be glaid to ressone
sum purposis quhilkis ar in contrauersie and debate (specialie concerning
þe mess), Providand all wayes þat I may frelie cleyth me and tak apon me
(without ȝour offense) þe place and personage of thais callit now of þe new
learnyng. [f. 1v.]

Q. Broder, I contentit and acceptis þe conditioun with all my harte.

I. Afoir þat I will entyr in ressoning with ȝou, I will protest and requyr
þat ȝe defend nocht ane iniust caus, preissand ȝour wit and ingyne to
circumveyn me with sophistrie, logik, or oratrie, Bot treulie to declair þe
treuth according to ȝour iugement, as ȝe will anser to þe hie Iuge: for þe
cuntre sayis ȝe can do bettir and ȝe will.

Q. As to þe vngodlie mwrmwr and Ignorant Iugement of þe cuntre
vndeserwit, I stand nocht þairby; bot þat I haif vsit older in worde or wryte
(in materis concerning fayth) hypocrysie, craft, or dissimwlatioun according
to my vnderstanding, in þat case I renunce Goddis mercy and takis me to
his iugement, Nochtwithstanding I knaw my self ane offendar vther wayes,
as ony wrechit synnar In erth.

I. Treulie, ȝour acquittance is sua rigorous þat I geif ȝow gude traist, and
douteis nocht bot ȝe will declayr þe treuth according to ȝour vnderstanding.
Thairfor lat ws go to þe purpose, and certifie me quhat ȝour monstruous
mess menis: For we rekkin It to be plane Idolatrie, sorcerie, and wichecraft.

Q. I dar bauldlie say, þair will na man think þe mess to be Idolatrie or
wichecraft bot gif It be sic Ignorant peple, led with þe spreit of errour, as þai
war quhilkis did affirme our salueour to be possessit with þe devill <Io.
8.>, and ascriuit þe workis of þe apostolis to be sorcerie and wichecraft
<Act. 17.>.

I. I marvell of ȝou þat thinkis nocht þe mess Idolatrie.

Q. <fo. 2.> I marvell mekle mair of ȝou, and mony hundreth vtheris of ȝour sect, þat callis þe mess Idolatrie, *and* ȝe knaw nolder quhat þe mess nor Idolatrie menis. He is ane evill Iuge condempnis or he knawis.

I. I will preif þe mess Idolatrie.

Q. ȝe haif tane mair on hand nor all ȝour sect may iustlie *per*furnys.

5   **I.** I will preif the mess Idolatrie on þis maneir:

All worschipping of God Inventit be þe brane of man *with*out >expres< *com*mand of God Is Idolatrie. The mess is Inventit be þe brayn off man *with*out >expres< *com*mand of God. Thairfoir It followis weill þat þe mess is Idolatrie.

10   **Q.** As to þe first parte of ȝour argument, quhair þat ȝe say That all worschipping of God Inventit be þe brane of man *with*out expres *com*mand of God Is Idolatrie: It is expres aganis Goddis worde. For þe scripture planelie techis vs þat Abraham *and* diuers vtheris Inventit wayes and meynis to worschip God, *with*out expres *com*mand of God <Gen. 22., Gen. 4.,

15   Gen. 8.>. Bot it is no*ch*t vnknawin to me, how þai ar sum *pro*phane precheo*uris* þat thrawis þe scripture by þe godlie menyng of þe samyn, to fortifie þair wickit opinioun: As quhair þe scripture makis mentioun how king Saull maid sacrifice thinkand to do ane acceptable werk to God, And als preserwit Agag þe king fra deyt*h* <1. Reg. 15., 1 Reg. 13.>,

20   quhais work in deid was vngodlie becaus It was expres aganis Goddis *com*mandiment; quhairby we may persaif þat it is ane grit difference (and þe zeill appeir nevir sa gude) to do ony work expres aganis Goddis *com*-mandiment, be to do ane gude work of godlie zeill *with*out *com*mand of God [f. 2v.] express, as þe scripture planelie techis vs. For we reid <Act.

25   10.> þat Cornelius centurio, beand ane gentyll, did diuers gude workis quhilkis war acceptable to God *with*out express *com*mand of God. Quhairfoir we may persaif þat þis subtyle ressonar has no*ch*t diligentlie markit þe scripturis in consideratioun of diuersite of werkis done on gude zeill expres contrar to þe *com*mand of God and werkis done on ane gude

30   zeill *with*out express *com*mand of God. For þe ane may nevir stand *with* þe scripture, þe vther aggreis with þe scripture, bayt*h* auld testament *and* new, as we haif all reddy declarit.

    As to þe secund parte of ȝour argument, sayand: "The mess was Inventit be þe brane of man", ȝe sall consider þat þe effect *and* substance of þe mess

35   was institute onelie be Iesus Christ <B.>. For we call no thing propirlie þe mess bot <diffinitioun of þe mess.> þe sacrifice of þe lordis body, realie co*n*tenit vnder þe formys of breid and wyne, Institute be Iesus Christ in þe latter supper in reme*m*berance of his deyt*h* and passioun <Math. 26., Marc. 14., [L]uc. 22.>. Treuth it is, þe ap*os*tlis and þair disciplis *and*

40   diuers vtheris godlie fatheris be successioun of tyme maid certane oratiouns,

aggreable with þe worde of God, to decoir þe laudable sacrifice of þe mess, quhilkis ar nocht of þe effect and substance of þe mess, quhairwith be ressone ȝe will find na falte. For thais of þe new learnyng has Inventit certane oratiouns and cerimoniis to decoir þair commwnioune, and Is

5   nocht of þe substance and effect of þe commwnioun, nor ȝit contenit in þe scripture.

I. How ar ȝe able to preif þe mess to be þe institutioun of Christ, considerand þair is nocht sic ane terme in all þe new testa-<fo. 3.>ment as the Mess? Thairfor it apperis ane terme laitlie inventit be þe brayn of

10 man.

Q. <A.> Treulie, we reid þis terme 'Missa' vsit be Clemens <Epistola 3. ad Iacobum fratrem Dominj.>, quha was sanct Peters disciple, And lykwyse be Ignacius <Epistola ad Smirnenses.>, quha was sanct Iohnis disciple, quhairby we may persaif þat þis terme 'Missa' is nocht laitlie

15 Inventit.

And ferther, geifand þat þair war nocht sic ane terme In þe new testament, and þat it war Inventit be man, It argumentis nocht bot þe effect and It þat is signifeit be þis terme is contenit in þe new testament. Sua þe effect is to be markit, and nocht þe terme. As be exemple, The godlie consell

20 Nycene, declarand þe misterie of þe diuine nature of oure salueour, Inventit þis terme 'homousion' incontrar þe wickit errour of Arrius <Hist. Trip., lib. 5., ca. 42.>. Lyk maneir þe kirk Inventit this terme 'Theoticos', declarand þe blissit virgyne Marie to be moder of God and man incontrar þe errour of Nestorius <Platina, Vigili p.>. And als it is ane familiar terme

25 in oure langage 'Trinite'. And ȝit nevir ane of þir thre termes is expreslie contenit in þe new testament. Nochtþeles he war ane evill christiane man þat wald deny þe effect of þir termes to be aggreable, and contenit in þe new testament. Sua albeit þis terme 'Mess' war nocht contenit in þe new testament, It argumentis nochtþeles bot þe effect is contenit in the new

30 testament, as – God willing – I sall preif sufficientlie bayth be auld testament and new.

I. I persaif, and oure ressonyng tak effect, we man cum to þe declaratioun and vnderstanding of þis terme 'Mess'.

[f. 3v.] Q. As to þe vnderstanding and declaratioun of þe mess: I vnder-

35 stand þe mess to be ane commemoratioun and rememberance of Christis deyth and passioun into þe quhilk þe breid and wyne ar consecrate according to Christis Institutioun <Luc. 22., Marc. 14., Math. 26.>, and þe body and blude of Iesus Christ (vnder þe formis of breid and wyne) ar offerit to þe Father of hevin and ar ressauit as þe hevinlie fude of oure

40 saull.

I. Ar ʒe hable to iustifie *and* appreif ʒour vnderstanding and declaratioun be scripture?

Q. Or ell*is* I wald think my laubo*uris* in vane. And for þe mair p*er*fite vnderstanding of þis interpretatioun *and* declaratioun ʒe sall mark þe
5 wordis of oure salueour in þe latter supper, sayand <Luc. 22., Marc. 14.>: "Do this in rememberance of me", be þe quhilk*is* word*is* he co*m*mandit his ap*ost*lis to consecrate þe breid *and* wyne as he did, sayand: "This is my body" <B.>. And sua he institute þe consecratioun; *and* be þe *con*-secratioun þe verray body and blude of Iesus Christ oure salueour ar
10 contenit vnder þe formis of breid *and* wyne be þe powar of þe lordis worde, q*uhi*lk Is om*n*ipotent.

According to þis þou sall mark þe godlie anceant saying*is* of Chrisos-tome wrytand on þis maner <Chrisostom., Homil. 48. In Ioahan.>: "It is nocht man þat mak*is* þe lord*is* body and blude of þe breid and wyne set
15 furth apon þe table to be consecrate, bot It is Christ þat was crucifeit for vs. Þe word*is* ar pronu*n*cit of þe preist, *and* þe breid *and* wyne ar co*n*secrate be Godd*is* worde *and* grace. He said: 'This is my body'. Þe breid *and* wyne q*uhi*lk*is* ar set furt*h* ar consecrate be þis worde." Hidderto Chrisostome.

And no*ch*t onelie said oure salueo*ur* <Lucas. 22.>: "This is my body",
20 quhairthrow he Institute þe consecratioun, bot als he eikit þir word*is*, <fo. 4.>, sayand: "quhilk is geiffin – and brokin – for ʒou", be the q*uhi*lk*is* wordis presentlie at þat sam verray tyme he declarit his body to be ane vnbludy sacrifice to be offerit be þe ap*ost*lis, *and* all o*þer*is ministeris of Christis kirk to þe end of þe warld, in reme*m*berance of his dey*th*, sayand:
25 "Do þis in rememberance of me".

According to þis wrytis þe p*ro*phet Malachie <Mala. 1.>: "I haif na pleso*ur* of ʒou, sayis the lorde; and as for the meit offering, I will no*ch*t accept It at ʒour hand. For frome þe rising vp of þe sone onto þe gangin doun of þe samyn my name Is grit amang þe gentylis: ʒe, in everie place
30 sall þair sacrifice be done and ane clene oblatioun offerit vp onto my name. For my name Is grit amangis þe gentyllis." Mark the word*is* of þe p*ro*phet, *and* ʒe sall persaif þat þai ar nocht spokkin of þe sacrifice of þe lord*is* body offerit vp apon þe croce. For quhy, þe sacrifice of þe lord*is* body on þe croce was onelie in Hierusalem, *and* þe word*is* of þe prophet speikis of ane
35 sacrifice offerit vp in everie place. Als þe word*is* of þe prophet can no*ch*t be vndirstand of þe sacrifice of þe Iewis, becaus þe word*is* planelie declaris þat all þair sacrifices war repudiat be þe lorde God fra þe tyme þat þe lord*is* body was offerit vp on þe croce. Nor ʒit þe word*is* of þe prophet can be vnderstand of þe sacrifice of oratioun, prayer, and almous deid. For in
40 diuers places ar diuerss oratiouns and prayer, and þe prophet speik*is* of ane

156

sacrifice in all places. Quhairfoir we ar compellit to say þat þir wordis war
spokkin onelie of þe sacrifice of þe mess, quhair into þe maist clene sacrifice
of þe precious body and blude of Iesus Christ hes evyr beyn offerit vp vnder
þe formis of breid *and* wyne [f. 4v.] in all places professand Iesus Christ,
5   sen þe tyme of Christ to þir oure dayes. For lyk as þe prophet*is* <Gen. 49.,
Esa. 7., Baruch. 3., Esa. 53.> prophecit of þe cum*in* of Christ, of his
natiuite, of his marvellous werk*is and* deyt*h*, Sua did þe prophet Malachie
<Mala. 1.> prophecie of ane clene sacrifice to be offerit vp oure all þe
warld, quhilk is þe precious blude *and* body of Iesus Christ offerit vp be þe
10 minister in the sacrifice of þe mess <B.>.

And to be assurit þat þis is þe trew interpretatioun *and* declaratioun of
þe word*is* of þe latter supper *and* als of the prophet Malachie, I will certifie
ʒou þat þis is þe declaratioun of thais quha war disciplis to þe ap*ost*lis *and*
all vtheris godlie interpreto*uris* of Goddis word, bayt*h* Grek*is* and
15 Latinistis, to gidder w*it*h þe vniuersale consent and deliberatioun of þe
maist anceant *and* godlie generale consellis quhilkis evir hes bene sen þe
tyme of Christ <[Ale]x*ander*, Ep*ist*ol*a* 1.; [Iren]eus, lib. 4., [ca.] 32.;
[Da]mascenus, [lib.] 4. De Fide [Ort]hodoxa., ca. [14.]; [Au]gust., lib. 8.
[De] Ciuitate Dei., [ca.] 35. Et lib. [19], ca. 23; [Ru]p*er*tus, in [Com]menta.
20 [su]p*er* Exod.; [C]oncili*um* Nicenu*m*.; [C]oncili*um* Ephesinu*m*.; … na of
þe …st consell*is* >.

I. In case all þe generale consellis *and* all þe writaris quhilk*is* evir hes
bene sen þe tyme of Iesus Christ had Interpret þe word*is* of þe latter supper
as ʒe haif done, It is ane fals and ane vngodlie interpretatioun expres aganis
25 þe scripture.

Q. ʒe suppone þe thing quhilk Is Impossible, ascrywand Ignorance *and*
wickitnes to þe Interpretatioun of þe disciplis of þe ap*ost*lis *and* all vther
fayt*h*full ministeris quhilk*is* evir hes bene sen þe tyme of Christ to þir oure
dayes. Thairfoir I am desyrous to heir ʒou how ʒe will preif þair Inter-
30 pretatioun to be expres aganis þe scripture.

I. I will preif It on þis maneir: The ap*ost*le sanct Paull in diu*er*ss places
testifeis þat Iesus Christ oure salueour sufferit anis for vs *and* is nevir to
suffir agane, quhairby we ar assurit þat oure salueoure was offerit vp anis
ane <fo. 5.> sacrifice on þe croce for ma*n*nis redemptioun and is nevir to
35 be offerit vp agane; *and* ʒe say he is offerit vp daylie in þe sacrifice of þe
mess. How can þir tua stand? <[He]b. 9. et 10>

Q. It is treut*h* þat Christ was offerit vp apon þe croce and is nevir to be
offerit vp agane eftir þat maner as ane bludy sacrifice <A. 1.>, and It is
treut*h* þat þe lord*is* body is offerit vp eftir ane vther maner in þe sacrifice of
40 þe mess, conforme to Christis com*m*andiment, as ane vnbludy sacrifice.

157

Forquhy, ane verite makis no*ch*t ane vther verite fals <A. 2.>.

I. ʒour ans*er* and ressoning apperis to me to be sump*art* obscure and diffice. Þairfoir I wald ʒe maid ʒour saying*is* maid plane.

5 **Q.** To þe effect þat ʒe may þe mair easelie vnderstand my sayingis, ʒe sall mark þe difference betuix þe sacrifice of þe lord*is* body on þe croce *and* þe sacrifice of þe mess, quhilk*is* in sumparte aggreis *and* in sump*art* differis <A. 3.>.

First, þai aggre in safer as It is þe sam self body in substance þat is offerit vp In þe sacrifice of þe mess þat was offerit vp apon þe croce, con-
10 forme to Christis awin word*is*, sayand <Luc. 22.>: ,,This Is my body, quhilk Is gevin for ʒou''.

Secundlie, It Is co*m*mwne to þe sacrifice of þe croce *and* þe sacrifice of þe mess þat, lyk as þe p*ro*phetis prophecit of þe sacrifice of þe croce, Sua did þai <Daniel. 12.> prophecie of þe sacrifice of þe mess, and specialie þe
15 p*ro*phet Malachie <Mala. 1.>, as I haif all reddy declarit.

Thridlie, þai aggre þ*at*, lyk as þe sacrifice of þe croce, was prefigurate be mony diuers figuris *and* signis <Nu. 21.>, Sua was þe sacrifice of þe mess prefigurate be þe preistheid *and* oblatioun of Melchisedech <A. 4.; Gen. 14.>.

20 **In** sump*art*is thay differ, þat þe lordis body was offerit vp apon the [f. 5v.] croce in þe awin forme, visible and sensible; And þe lordis body in þe sacrifice of þe mess is offerit vp vnder þe formis of breid *and* wyne, Invisible and Insensible. Sua þai differ in maner *and* forme of offering vp, and nocht in substance.

25 **Feirdlie,** þai differ consideratioun beand had of þe caus quhairfoir þe lordis body was offerit vp apon þe croce, And þe caus quhairfoir þe lord*is* body is offerit vp in þe sacrifice of þe mess. The lordis body was offerit vp apon þe croce to þe effect þat we my*ch*t obtene eu*er*lastand lyf, satisfactioun for syn, redemptioun fra þe captiuite and serwitude of þe devill <B. [1.]>.
30 The sacrifice of þe mess was institute be oure salueo*ur* in þe latter supper, no*ch*t as ane new satisfactioun or redemptioun, bot as ane new sacrifice In commemoratioun *and* reme*m*berance of Christis dey*th* *and* passioun <B. [2.]>, be þe vse of þe q*uhi*lk we ar maid parttakaris of þe fructe of þe dey*th* and passioun of Iesus Christ oure salueo*ur*.

35 **I.** It apperis þat þe sacrifice of þe mess dois obscure *and* diminiss þe gloir of þe sacrifice of þe croce. For gif þe sacrifice of þe croce was p*er*fyt in þe self, quhat suld mister ane new sacrifice or ony may sacrifices?

Q. ʒe sall consider þat þe gloir of þe sacrifice of þe croce Is na wayes obscurit nor diminissit be þe sacrifice of þe mess, bot rather advansit
40 <B. [3.]> insafer as þe mess Is bot ane sacrifice of commemoratioun

158

quhairby ar applyit þe fructis off Christis deyth *and* passioun obtenit be þe
sacrifice of þe croce <[He]b. 10.; [I]o. 3.>, quhilk is þe sacri[fo. 6.]fice of
redemptioun. And albeit þe sacrifice on þe croce was in þe self all wayes
perfyte, nocht þeles It is necessar þat þe fructis of þe samyn be daylie
5   renewit *and* applyit, as be þe sacrament of baptyme <Io. 3.>, þe supper
of þe lorde <Io. 6.; Luc. 22.>, þe sacrifice of þe mess <1. Cor. 11.>, *and*
diuers vtheris maners off wayes, as þe scripture planelie techis vs, quhilk
argumentis na Imperfectioun to be in þe sacrifice of the croce. For lyk as,
ane perfyte medycyne beand applyit be diuers instrumentis proper þairfoir,
10 þe instrumentis dois nocht argwne þe Imperfectioun of þe medicyne, nor
ȝit obscure þe gloir of þe samyn bot rather advansis, sua þe sacrifice of þe
croce (quhilk is þe onelie medycyne of oure redemptioun) Is na wayes
obscurit nor diminissit be þe sacrifice of þe mess, be supper of þe lorde,
þe sacrament of baptyme *and* diuerss vþeris, bot rather advansit. For quhy,
15 Christis deyth is þe medicyne <Ephe. 5.; Rom. 5.; 1. Cor. 15.>, þe
sacramentis *and* þe sacrifice of þe mess ar þe instrumentis, cheif menis, *and*
way quhairby þe fructis of Christis deyth and passioun is daylie renewit *and*
applyit. And lyk as men ar daylie subiect to þe hevy seiknes of syn, sua
It is necessar þat þe medicyne of redemptioun be daylie applyit þairto,
20 quhilk is nocht be renovatioun of Christis deyth and passioun, bot be þe
applicatioun of þe fructis of þe samyn in maner abone rehersit.

I. All wayis I think ȝe quha vsis þe mess dois nocht as Christ did in þe
latter supper. For Christ in þe latter supper conmwnicate to þe multitude,
and ȝe tak all to ȝour self.

25 **Q.** Be þe samyn argument I will cut ȝour throte with ȝour awin suorde.
Forquhy, Christ commwnicate eftir supper <1. Cor. 11.>, *and* ȝe of þe
new learnyng communicatis [f. 6v.] vther tymes of þe day; Christ commwnicate to þe tuelf apostlis in þe latter supper allanerlie <Marc. 14.>,
and ȝe communicate till all men and wemen of þe congregatioun indiffer-
30 entlie. Sua do ȝe nocht as Christ did in þe latter supper. Forquhy, þe
scripture makis na mentioun þat þair was only wemen at þe commwnioun
in þe latter supper.

Treulie, brother, *and* ȝe be sua scrupulows scripturaris þat ȝe will do na
thing bot as Christ did towart þe vse of þe sacramentis, ȝe will subwert oure
35 haill fayth *and* condemp ȝour awin doingis. For quhair find ȝe þat Christ
evir appoynctit ane man to hald his awin barne to be baptizate? I dar
bauldlie say þis ordinance was nevir of þe evangell, nor ȝit of þe kirk of
God nor na vther haifand iust authorite older of God or man.

I. I persaif be ȝour ressoning It is expedient þat þair be diuers ceremoniis *and* customes vsit in ministratioun of þe sacramentis, *and* als In þe sacrifice of þe mess, quhilkis ar no*c*ht contenit In scripture <B.>.

Q. Treu*t*h it is, albeit Iesus Christ oure salueo*u*r hes appoinctit, be his worde *and* scripture, all thingis necessar for ma*n*nis saluatioun as towart þe
5 substance *and* effect, No*c*ht þeles, as towart þe cerimoniis *and* maner how thais thingis salbe vsit q*u*hi*l*k*i*s he has appoinctit for ma*n*nis saluatioun, he referrit to his kirk *and* ministeris, to quhom he p*r*omisit þe spreit of verite to þe end of þe warld <[Io.] 14.>. As be exemple, o*u*r salueo*u*r, quhen he institute þe sacrament of baptyme, he co*m*mandit his apo*s*tlis <[Ma]th.
10 28.; Marc. vlt.> þat þai suld baptize in the name of þe Father, þe Sone, *and* þe halie Gaist. He <fo. 7.> appoynctit nolder tyme, nor place, nor quha suld beir witnes to thais þat war baptizate; schortlie, he appoinctit na kynd of cerimoniis concerning þe vse of þis sacrament. Lykwyse, quhen oure salueo*u*r institute in þe latter supper þe sacrifice of the mess (as towart
15 þe substance *and* effect), he appoinctit nolder tyme, place, nor multitude þat suld co*m*municate. Forquhy, in case þair war ane p*er*sone disposit to co*m*municate, It war nocht ressone þat p*er*sone suld be frustrate of þe communioun onto þe tyme þe rest of þe congregatioun war disposit to co*m*municate.

20 *And* sua þe preist, albeit he co*m*municate onelie, he Iniuris na wayes þe ordinance of Christ, considering he Is reddy at all tymes to co*m*mwnicate to all vtheris beand disposit.

I. I wald ʒe maid me to vndirstand mair p*er*fytlie how oure salueo*u*r appoinctit be his worde all thingis necessar for ma*n*nis saluatioun *con*-
25 cerning þe effect *and* substance, *and* schew no*c*ht be his worde þe cerimoniis *and* maner how thais thingis suld be vsit, bot referrit to his kirk.

Q. For þe vnderstanding of þe samyn I will geif ʒou ane rude *and* familiar exemple. Ane potent prince beand of purpose to send his com*-*missionaris and ambassato*u*ris to ane vther realme, he geiffis þame þair
30 commissioun *con*tenand certane heydis and articles beirand in substance and effect þe purpose of þair commissioun. No*c*ht þeles, It is no*c*ht *con*tenit in þair co*m*missioun quhat tyme thai sall present þair co*m*missioun, nor quhat [f. 7v.] garmontis þai salbe cled wi*t*hall þat day þai vse þair com*-*missioun, nor ʒit na vther kynd of cerimoniis quhilkis ar necessar and
35 expedient to set furt*h* *and* decoir þair commissioun. Sua Iesus Chryst oure potent prince, he left his co*m*missioun in his worde and scripture *con*-tenand þe effect *and* substance of all thingis necessar for ma*n*nis saluatioun. And as towart þe cerimoniis *and* maner how thais thingis ar to be vsit, he referrit onto his kirk. *And* quhasumeuir will vse ony vþ*er* cerimoniis towart
40 þe ministratioun of þe sacrame*n*tis nor þe kirk hes obseruit evir be p*er*-

160

petuall successioun of tyme, sen þe tyme of the apostlis to þir oure dayes,
þai ar worthy to be cryit out on be all gude christiane men, according to þe
doctryne of sanct Paule, sayand <[1.] Cor. 11.>: "Gif þair be ony man
þat apperis to be contencious, we haif nocht sic ane consuetude, nor ʒit þe
5 kirk of God." – As he wald say: gif ony pryvate man wald steir vp scisme,
diuisioun, and discorde amangis christiane men, vseand ony vther cerimoniis or customes vther nor þe kirk of God hes evir vsit, he is nocht to
be hard. Quhairfoir ʒour mischeant ministeris ar to be explodit and repellit
be all gude christiane men, with þair new cerimoniis and customes quhilkis
10 war nevir obseruit nor vsit in þe kirk of God amangis na christiane men
sen þe fayth first began.

I. I am neirby satiffeit with ʒour ansueris towart all þe argumentis movit
be me <fo. 8.> incontrar þe mess. Bot I am nocht ʒit sufficientlie persuadit
þat oure salueour offerit his body and blude in sacrifice at his latter supper.

15 Q. And ʒe will mark diligentlie þe diffinitioun and declaratioun of þe
mess all reddy declarit, ʒe haif iust occasioun (conforme to þe scripturis) to
be persuadit þairwith. Nocht þe les, to geif ʒou ferther persuasioun, ʒe sall
consider þat oure salueoure In þe latter supper institute ane sacrament,
quhilk ʒe call þe commwnioun, and als þe sacrifice of þe new testament,
20 callit þe mess. Sua in þe latter supper he Institute bayth ane sacrament and
ane sacrifice <A.>.

I. I vndirstand þat oure salueour institute þe commwnioun in þe latter
supper, bot I can nocht vndirstand þat he institute þe sacrifice of þe mess.

Q. For þe vnderstanding þairof ʒe sall consider þat þe preistheid and
25 sacrifice of Aaron (quhilk was ane bludy sacrifice) ceissit be þe bludy
sacrifice of oure salueoure on þe croce, quha was þe fyne of þe law <Ro.
10.>. Now man ʒe consider þat Iesus Christ oure salueour, knawand þat þe
preistheid and sacrifice of Aaron (beand þe sacrifice of þe auld testament)
was to ceiss and tak ane end be his deyth and passioun, Institute ane new
30 sacrifice of þe new testament according to þe ordour of Melchisedech.

I. I vndirstand þat all þe sacrifices of þe auld testament ceissit be þe
sacrifice of oure salueour on þe croce. Bot I do nocht ʒit consider þat oure
salueour institute ane new sacrifice of þe new testament in þe latter supper.

Q. To geif ʒou iust occasioun to consider þe samyn, I will ʒit as of befoir
35 call to rememberance þe wordis of þe latter supper, quhair oure salueour
gaif command to his apostlis, sayand: "Do þis in rememberance of me",
be þe quhilkis wordis he commandit his apostlis nocht onelie to eit his
body [f. 8v.] and drink his blude, bot als to mak oblatioun of the samyn.

I. I vndirstand þat oure salueour gaif command to his apostlis to eit his
40 body and drink his blude, bot I beleif ʒe will nocht preif propirlie be þe

wordis of þe latter supper þat he *com*mandit to mak oblatioun of his body *and* blude.

Q. I will preif propirlie þat he maid oblatioun of his body and blude in þe latter supper: be þe word*is* of þe samyn, sayand <Luc. 22.>: "Tak ȝe, eit ȝe; This is my body, q*uhi*lk Is gevin for ȝou", – or offerit for ȝou, bayth Is ane in effect.

I. It apperis to me ȝe rehers the text wrang, for þe text sayis <[1.] Cor. 11.>: "This is my body, q*uhi*lk salbe gevin for ȝou". Þair is ane grit difference betuix "salbe gevin for ȝou" *and* "Is gevin for ȝou".

Q. ȝe sall be assurit þat þir wordis ar spokkin in þe present tyme (as testifeis þe excellent clerk Erasmus) according to þe Greik text, quhilk Is þe naturale text of þe new testament for þe maist p*ar*t.

I. Gevand þat thir word*is* war spokkin in þe present tyme, ȝit þair Is ane difference betuix þir word*is*: "This is my body, q*uhi*lk Is gevin for ȝou", and "offerit for ȝou".

Q. Thay will na man of Iugement or learning mak difference betuix þir word*is* "gevin for ȝou" *and* "offerit for ȝou" as towart þe effect, albeit þe phrase *and* maneir of speche differis.

I. In case þair be na difference, quhat will ȝe infer of þat?

Q. I will infer my intent, q*uhi*lk Is þat our lorde maid oblatioun of his body and blude in þe latter supper, *and* gaif conmand to his ap*ost*lis to do þe samyn. Forquhy, gif our salueo*ur* in þe latter supper had institute onelie þe conmwnioun, *and* no*ch*t ane sacrifice, than had he sayd: "Tak <fo. 9.> ȝe, eit ȝe; This is my body, quhilk is gevin to ȝou", *and* no*ch*t "for ȝou", becaus "gevin to ȝou" includ*is* onelie þe co*m*mwnioun, and "gevin for ȝou" includ*is* nocht onelie þe co*m*mwnioun bot als ane sacrifice, as þe phrase of þe word*is* planelie declaris.

Attour, þe oblatioun *and* sacrifice maid be oure salueo*ur* in þe latter supper Is ane mair propir *com*memoratioun *and* reme*m*berance of þe sacrifice of þe croce nor Is þe co*m*mwnioun, quhairfoir þe sacrifice of þe mess is callit ane sacrifice of commemoratioun. *And* sua ȝe may persaif be þe *com*mand q*uhi*lk oure salueour gaif to his ap*ost*lis, sayand "Do þis in reme*m*berance of me", þat he rather appoinctit þe sacrifice of þe latter supper to be ane co*m*memoratioun of his dey*th* *and* passioun nor þe commwnioun.

And þis may ȝe cleirlie p*er*saif þat oure salueo*ur* in þe latter supper institute ane sacrament, quhilk Is callit þe co*m*mwnioun, *and* als ane sacrifice of commemoratioun callit þe mess. And sua he institute ane sacrament *and* ane sacrifice in þe latter supper.

I. I pray ȝou mak ȝo*ur* argument formalie, þat I may p*er*saif gif sua be.

162

Q. I will mak my argument on þis maneir:

The lorde gaif *com*mand to his ap*ost*lis in þe latter supper to do as he did. The lorde maid oblatioun of his body and blude in þe latter supper (as Is sufficientlie pr*ov*in be þe plane text). It followis weill þat þe lorde gaif
5 command to his ap*ost*lis to do þe samyn, sayand: "Do þis in reme*m*berance of me" <Luc. 22.>.

And to be assurit þ*at* þis conclusioun is trew *and* propir, aggreand with þe word*is* of þe latter supper, I will mak ʒou to vndirstand þe samyn be conferrence of scriptur*is*, [f. 9v.] as eftir followis.
10 The psalmist <[ps]al. 109.> and als þe ap*ost*le sanct Paull <[He]b. 7.> affirmis oure salueour to be ane preist for evir according to þe ordour of Melchisedech, quha maid sacrifice and oblatioun of breid *and* wyne onto God, as þe scripture planelie techis vs <Gen. 14.>. Now will I ressone on þis maneir: Reid all þe evangell quha pleissis, he sall find in na place of þe
15 evangell quhair oure salueoure vsit þe preistheid of Melchisedech, declarand him self to be ane preist according to þe ordour of Melchisedech, bot in þe latter supper, quhair he maid oblatioun of his precious body and blude vnder þe forme of breid *and* wyne prefigurate be þe oblatioun of Melchisedech <[Cy]prian*us*, lib. [2.] Ep*isto*la 3.; [A]mbros., lib. [4.] De
20 Sacrame*ntis*, [c]a. 3.; [A]ugust., lib. [1]7. De Ciuita. [D]ei, ca. 17.; [L]utherus in [p]sal. 109.>. Than ar we co*m*pellit to affirme þ*at* oure salueo*u*r maid oblatioun of his body and blude in þe latter supper, or ellis he was nocht ane preist according to þe ordo*u*r of Melchisedech, quhilk Is expres aganis þe scripture <[P]sal. 109.; Heb. 7.>.
25 **I.** Sua beand þ*at* Melchisedech maid oblatioun of breyd *and* wyne onto God, ʒo*u*r argument hes grit apperence.

Q. The scripture declaris þe samyn sua planelie as It leiffis na place of dout <Gen. 14.; [H]ierom. in Psal. 109.; Aug., lib. 16. De Ciuitate Dei, ca. [2]2.; [T]heophilac., [de] Ep*isto*la ad Heb., [c]a. 5.; [A]rnobius in [P]sal.
30 109.; Beda in [M]arc. lib. [4.] ca. 14.; ... sa. 26.>. Ferther ʒe sall consider þat, lyk as ane tre haiffand þe leiffis dilatate *and* spred, þe sone schynand þ*air*apon, everie leif of þe tre castis ane vmbre correspondent þairto, And everie vmbre of þe tre has ane leyf correspondent to It, Sua It is þ*at* everie figure of þe auld testament has sum place of þe new testament correspondent
35 þairto, and eu*er*y misterie of þe new testame*n*t has sum place of þe auld testament correspondent to It. As be exemple, Thair is na dout bot þe sacrifice of þe paschale lamb was ane figure of þe sacrifice of þe lord*is* body on þe croce <B.>. Nocht þeles, þat figure was no*ch*t [fo. 10.] correspondent in all p*art*is to It þ*at* was done apon the croce, bot rather
40 to It þ*at* was done in þe latter supper. For quhy, we reid <Exod. 1[2.]>

þat þe lamb was offerit in sacrifice be þe Hebreanis in recordatioun of þe
benefice be þe quhilk þe peple of Israell war deliuerit fra þe seruitude of
Pharao *and* þe bringin out of Egipt. Bot þe sacrifice of the croce was nocht
ane recordatioun of ony benefice, bot It was þe self benefice, þe samyn self
5   liberatioun fra syn, þe samyn self redemptioun fra þe captiuite of þe devill.
Quhairfoir It was necessar þat be þe Immolatioun of þe paschale lamb
ane vþer Immolatioun, besydis It done on þe croce, suld be signifeit, þe
quhilk in þe latter supper was done <Luc. 22.; 1. Cor. 1[1.]>.

Than man we *conclude* (*conforme* to þe scripturis) þat, lyk as þe sacrifice
10 of þe paschale lamb was ane commemoratioun of þe benefice and gudenes
of almychtie God towart þe peple of Israell, quhair þai war deliuerit fra þe
seruitude *and* tyrannie of Pharao, Evin sua Is þe sacrifice of þe lordis body
in þe latter supper, callit þe mess, ane perpetuall commemoratioun *and*
rememberance of þe grit gudenes of almychtie God, quhair he deliuerit þe
15 haill warld fra þe tyrannie and seruitude of þe devill be þe sacrifice on þe
croce. And sua þe sacrifice of the croce and þe sacrifice of þe mess in all
partis ar correspondent to þe figure *and* sacrifice of þe paschale lamb.

Attour, It is sure þat Iesus Christ our salueour come to fulfill þe law,
nocht to brek þe law <Math. 5.>. It was commandit be þe law <Exod.
20 1[2.]> to mak oblatioun of the paschale lamb afoir It was eittin. Sua It was
necessar þat oure salueour had first maid oblatioun of [f. 10v.] his body
afoir he gaif þe samyn to be eittin, to þe effect þat þe verite suld correspond
to þe figure. Quhairfoir we ar compellit to affirme þat oure salueour maid
oblatioun of his body in þe latter supper afoir he gaif þe samyn to be eittin,
25 or ellis þe verite was nocht correspondent to the figure, quhilk is aganis all
verite. And þis may ȝe cleirlie persaif þat þe paschale lamb was nocht onelie
ane figure of þe sacrifice of þe croce, bot ane mair expres figure of þe sacrifice of þe mess <B.1.>, as is sufficientlie provin.

I. I think þat þe figuris of þe auld testament ar nocht sufficient *con-*
30 firmatioun of materis of fayth concerning þe new testament <B. 2.>.

Q. ȝe think all wrang, becaus ȝour thocht Is aganis þe scripture. Dois
nocht oure salueour <Math. 12.> confirme his bureing till indure thre
dayes *and* thre nychtis be þe figure of Ionas þe prophet? Dois nocht Peter
<[1.] Pet. 3.> preif baptym necessar be þe figure of þe Ark of Noe,
35 affirmand all þame to haif perissit quhilkis war out of It? Lykwyse Paull
<[G]alat. 4.> callis to rememberance þe tua sonnis of Abraham to haif
signifeit þe tua testamentis. This we may persaif þe speciall materis of oure
fayth contenit in þe new testament to be confirmit be þe figuris of þe auld
testament.

40   **I.** I am sufficientlie satisfeit with ȝour conferrence of scripturis, bayth

164

auld testament *and* new, and think*is* þame *p*ropir to þe purpose. No*cht*-
þeles, I am desyrous to knaw be quhat vther menis *and* way ȝe will *p*ersuade
þat oure salueo*u*r institute þe sacrifice of þe mess in þe latter supper.

Q. I will *p*ersuade þe samyn be þe vniu*er*sale doctryne, interpretatioun,
5   and consent of þe auld anceant fatheris Interpretouris of þe scripturis of
almy*ch*tie God, bay*th* Greik*is and* Latinist*is*, <fo. 11.> to gidder w*ith* þe
deliberatioun of þe maist anceant and notable generall *con*sellis quhilk*is*
evir hes beyn sen þe fay*th* began.

I. Think ȝe þat þe doctryne and Interpretatioun of þe auld wrytaris *con*-
10   cerning þe misterie of þe supper of þe lorde Is sufficient to *p*ersuade þe
sacrifice of þe mess?

Q. Treulie, I am perswadit be invincible ressouns, quhilkis ar aggreable
w*ith* þe scripturis of almy*ch*tie God <Luc. 24.; Io. 16.>, þat þe auld
wrytaris (specialie thais quhilk*is* war disciplis to þe ap*ost*lis) had þe trew
15   mynd *and* vnderstanding of þe misteriis of þe scripture, specialie of þe
word*is* of þe latter supper, quhairby þai vnderstude þe sacrifice of þe
mess <A.>.

I. I pray ȝou lat me heir ȝo*u*r ressonis.

Q. ȝe sall consider þat eftir þe ascentioun of oure salweo*u*r þe spreit of
20   verite enterit in þe hartis of the ap*ost*lis <Luc. 24.; Io. 16.>, gevand þame
full instructioun of all places of scripture quhair oure salueo*u*r had spokkin
in parabolis, and all vtheris misteriis of þe scripturis *con*cerning oure fay*th*
and trew vndirstanding of þe samyn <Irene*us*, [lib.] 3., ca. 3.>. Now man
ȝe vnderstand þat, lyk as þe spreit of verite gaif instructioun to þe ap*ost*lis
25   of all þe misteriis of þe scripturis, Sua did þe ap*ost*lis geif instructioun to
þair disciplis of all þe misteriis of þe scripturis necessar to be knawin for
ane christiane ma*n*nis saluatioun: quha war þe prymatywe kirk (as I wald
say), þe begynnaris of þe fay*th*full *con*gregatioun Immediatlie nixt to þe
ap*ost*lis. Quhairfoir, quhen sumeuir questioun is for þe vndirstanding of
30   þe misteriis of þe scripture, specialie þe sacramentis *and* þe ry*ch*t [f. 11v.]
vse of þame (quhilk*is* but dout ar þe maist *p*rofund misteriis in all þe
scripturis), It is ane assurit way to haif recours to þe auld anceant wrytaris,
specialie thais q*uhi*lk*is* war disciplis to þe ap*ost*lis *and* martyris for þe fay*th*
of Iesus Christ, to haif trew instructioun bay*th* of þe sacramentis *and* of þe
35   ry*ch*t vse of þame, as þe kirk of God has evir techit vs be perpetuall
successioun of tyme, sen þe tyme of þe ap*ost*lis to þir oure dayes, conforme
to þe doctryne *and* interpretatioun of þe scripture maid be þame quha war
disciplis to þe ap*ost*lis, *and* als *con*forme to þe deliberatioun of þe generale
*con*sellis (dewlie *con*venit), to quhom It appertenis to tak ordo*u*r In all
40   materis doutsum concerning þe fay*th*, *con*forme to þe scripture.

I. I think it (treulie) in my conscience to be of verite þat þe disciplis of þe apostlis had þe trew vndirstanding of all þe misteriis of þe scripturis necessar to be knawin for ane christiane mannis saluatioun, specialie of þe profund misterie of þe supper of þe lorde, quhair of Is gadderit the sacrifice of þe mess. Quhairfoir I am desyrous to knaw þe sayingis of þe auld writaris (specialie of thais quhilkis war disciplis to þe apostlis) towart the mess, and gif þai mak mentioun of It into þair werkis. <B.>

Q. Ignacius (quha was sanct Iohnis disciple) sayis <[Ig]nacius, [Episto-] la ad [Sm]irnenses.> : "It is nocht leifful to offer, nor to mak sacrifice, nor say mess, without þe bischopis authorite or consent." Hidderto Ignacius.

Clemens (quha was sanct Peters disciple) wrytis on þis maneir <Clemens, [E]pistola 2. ad [Ia]cobum Fra[tr]em Dominj.> : "Nane of þe preistis sall say mess in his parrochin, nor baptize, nor do ony vther thing, without per-[fo. 12.]missioun of þe bischop. Thir sayingis þe apostlis ressauit of þe lorde and gaif to ws, and we teche þe samyn to ȝou, and commandis ȝou to hald and teche þe samyn to all men without reprehensioun." Hidderto Clemens. – Mark how þir disciplis of þe apostlis makis mentioun of þe mess.

Alexander (quha was martyrit for þe fayth of Iesus Christ fouretene hundreth thretty nyne ȝeiris bypast) writis on þis maneir <Alexander, 4., [Ep. 1.]> : "Oure lordis passioun is to be rehersit in all solemniteis of þe mess. With sic sacrifice þe lorde is delytit and pacifeit <A. 1.>, and will forgeif grit synnis. For amangis all sacrifices þair can be na thing gretar þan oure lordis body and blude; þair is na sacrifice bettir nor þis. This excellis all vtheris, quhilk man be offerit onto þe lorde with ane pure conscience and ressauit with ane cleyn mynd and worschippit with all men." <A. 2.> Hidderto Alexander. – Mark how þis godlie martyr affirmis þe mess to be ane sacrifice for syn, and als to be worschippit with all men.

Ireneus (Polycarpus disciple, quha was disciple to sanct Iohne þe evangelist, and martyrit for þe fayth of Iesus Christ threttene hundreth fourescore fywe ȝeiris bypast) writis on þis maneir <Ireneus, [lib.] 4., ca. [17.]> : "Christ tuke breid and gaif thankis, sayand 'This is my body', and tuke þe chalice of wyne and confessit it to be his blude <Luc. 22.; 1. Cor. 11.>, and techit ane new sacrifice of þe new testament, quhilk þe kirk rasaifand of þe apostlis offerit onto God in all þe haill warld." Hidderto Ireneus. – Mark how this godlie marthir affirmis þat oure salueour in þe latter supper techit ane new sacrifice of þe new testament, quhilk þe kirk ressauit of þe apostlis.

Cypriane (quha was martyrit for þe fayth of Iesus Christ tuelf [f. 12v.]

166

hundreth fourescoir sextene ʒeiris bypast) wrytis on þis maneir <Cypria[ne,] Ep*isto*la [3.], lib. 2.>: "Gif oure lorde Iesus Christ – and God him self – be þe hie preist of God þe Father and be him self did first offer ane sacrifice to God þe Father, and has co*mm*andit þe samyn to be done in reme*mber*-
5 ance of him <[Lu]c. 22.; [1.] Cor. 11.>, þat preist is veralie Chris*tis* vicare quhilk dois follow þat thing quhilk Christ hes done." Hidderto Cypriane. And als he affirmis þat Christ Is þe authour *and* techear of þe sacrifice of þe mess.

   Chrisostome, ane anceant Greik wrytar *and* doctour Alevin hundreth
10 fiftie >*and*< sevin ʒeiris bypast, writis on þis maneir <[C]hrisosto., [Ho]m. 2. [in] 2. Timoth. [ca.] 1.>: "Christ has preparit ane mekle mair wondirfull and magnificent sacrifice, bay*th* quhen he changeit þe sacrifice It self and als quhen he did *com*mand him self to be offerit in sted of brutale beistis, quhilk*is* war offerit in þe auld law." <[Lu]c. 22.; [1.] Cor.
15 11.> Hidderto Chrisostome. He wrytis in ane vther place <[ca.] 4. De [Di]gnitate [Sac]erdotali, [lib.] 3>, sayand: "O grit gude will of God towart vs! O miracle! He þat sittis apon þe ry*ch*t hand of þe Father in hevin abuif is *con*tenit in me*nn*is hand*is* in tyme of þe sacrifice." Alsua he sayis in ane vther place: "Do we no*ch*t offer sacrifice daylie? We do offer,
20 bot doing it in reme*mber*ance of Christis dey*th* <[Lu]c. 22.; [1.] Cor. 11.>. And þis hoist is ane, no*ch*t mony <[He]b. 9. et [10].>. How is it ane, *and* no*ch*t mony? And þat oblatioun was anis offerit in to hevin. Bot þis sacrifice is ane exemple of þat. We do offer þe samyn self thing. We offer no*ch*t þe day ane lamb (Christ) and þe morne ane vther, bot evir þe samyn
25 self thing. Quhairfoir þis sacrifice is ane; or ellis, be þat ressone þat it is offerit in mony places, ar þai mony Christis? Na thing les, bot thair is ane Christ oure all quhair, being heir all haill and thair all haill: ane body. For as þat quhilk is offerit In everie place is ane body, evin sua it is ane sacrifice. <fo. 13.> Bot he is oure bischop, quhilk offerit ane sacrifice
30 makand vs cleyn. We do offer þe samyn, *and* þat quhilk was than offerit can no*ch*t be now *con*swmat." Hidderto Chrisostome, oute of quhais word*is* mony notable lessouns may be collectit In contrar þe railling ressoning *and* mischeant mokrie off vane men in þir dayes aganis þe mess.

   Ambrose, ane anceant doctour approvin be þe kirk of God, Alevin
35 hundre*th* threscoir and sextene ʒeir*is* bypast, wrytis on þis maneir <Ambrosius, [in] Psal. 38.>: "We haif seyn þe prince of princis cum onto vs, we saw him *and* hard him offer for wss his blude. Lat vs, preistis, follow as we may offer sacrifice for þe peple, altho*ch*t we be waik be oure deserving, ʒit we ar honorable throu*ch*t þe sacrifice <A. 1.>. For albeit
40 Christ is no*ch*t seyn to be offerit, nevir þeles he is offerit apon þe erth quhen

his body is offerit. ʒe, he is declarit planelie to offer it in vs, quhais word*is*
makis halie þe sacrifice q*uhi*lk Is offerit. Hidder to Ambrose.

Augustyne, ane excellent docto*ur* approvin be þe kirk, alevyn hundret*h*
fiftie sex ʒeir*is* bypast, reprevit Aerius as ane heretyk <August., li[b. de]
5   Heres. Heres. [53.]>, becaus he said (as mony sayis now of sobir knawlege)
þat men suld no*ch*t pray for þe deid nor offir sacrifice for þame. He wrytis
þis concerning þat mater <In Enchirid[ion], ca. 110.>: "It is no*ch*t to be
denyit þat þe saullis of men dep*ar*tit ar relevit throu*ch*t þe godlines of þair
freynd*is* on lyf, quhen þe sacrifice of oure mediatour Christ Is offerit for
10   þame." Hidderto Augustyne. He wrytis in ane vþir place <Sermo 11, De
Sacra...>, sayand: "Quhen þe sacrifice of þe altare or almous is offerit
for þe deid quhilkis war baptizate, þai ar thankis gevin for þame þat be
verray gude peple; and for þame quhilkis ar no*ch*t verray evill, þai ar
propiciatiouns or purchasing*is* of m*er*cy *and* favour of God." He writis in
15   ane vther place <A. 2.; Sermo 32, De V*er*bis A[post*o*li.]>, sayand: "It is
nocht [f. 13v.] to be douttit bot þe saullis dep*ar*tit ar helpit be þe halie
kirk*is* prayeris *and* þe sacrifice of saluatioun *and* almous, quhen þai ar
gevin for þame at God suld deill mair mercifullie w*ith* þame þan thair
synnis had deserwit". Hidderto Augustyne. – Mark how þis godlie docto*ur*
20   *and* bischop affirmis þe sacrifice of þe mess to be propiciatorie and helplyk
for thais þat be dep*ar*tit.

According to þe samyn wrytis ane excellent *and* anceant father, **Tertu-**
liane, thretteyn hundreth fourescoir *and* sexteyn ʒeir*is* bypast <[Ter]tulia-
nus, [C]orona Milit*is*.; [O]bet mess.>: "We mak oblatioun, for thais
25   q*uhi*lk*is* ar departit, ʒeirlie þe day of þair dep*ar*ting." <B.> Hidderto
Tertuliane.

Gregour, ane godlie docto*ur* approvin be þe kirk of God, nyne hundret*h*
threscoir ʒeir*is* bypast, writis on þis maneir <Gregorius Magnus, Hom.
[37]. in Evang.>: "Lat ws send (brethir) onto God oure messingeris be
30   weiping, gevin almous, *and* offering of þe halie hoistis. For þe sacrifice of
þe halie altare, offerit vp w*ith* weiping *and* devotioun of mynd, dois singularie help onto oure absolutioun fra sin. For als oft tymes as we offer onto
him þe sacrifice of his passioun, sua oft do we repair *and* apply to vs his
passioun for oure absolutioun." Hidderto Gregou*r*. – Mark how þis godlie
35   docto*ur* dois affirme þe fructis of Christis deyt*h* *and* passioun to be applyit
be þe sacrifice of þe mess.

Gif I wald call to reme*m*berance all þe saying*is* of þe godlie father*is*
quhilkis treittis according þis purpose, **oure colloquium** *and* ressoning suld
exceid þe bound*is* *and* grow to ane grit werk. Quhairfoir, will we now
40   schortlie reherss þe saying*is* of þe maist notable generale consellis towart
<fo. 14.> this purpose.

168

The consel Nicene, quhylk was þe first generale concell eftir þe tyme of þe apostlis, approvin in all ageis, tuelf hundreth tuenty sex ʒeiris bypast <Histo. Trip., [lib.] 2., ca. 1.>, writis and sayis on þis maneir: "Disponand oure selfis onto þe godlie table, lat vs nocht luke sclendirlie apon þe breid
5 and coupe set befoir vs, bot lat vs lift vp our mynd be fayth, vndirstanding in þat halie table to be þe lamb of God taikand away þe synnis of þe warld, offerit be þe preistis without blude. And we, ressaifand veralie his preciouse body and blude, aucht to beleif þame to be þe plege of oure resurrectioun." <A.> Hidderto þe concell.
10   **The generall** concell haldin at Ephesus alevin hundreth tuenty aucht ʒeiris bypast (quhair into wass condempnit þe errour of Nestorius) wrytis on þis maner <Concilium Ephesin[um]>: "We do offer ane vnbludy sacrifice. Alsua we cum onto þe halie sacrament, and ar maid halie beand part takaris of þe halie body and blude of Iesus Christ, quhilk wass maid
15 redemar of vs all: nocht ressaifand It as conmwne flesche (God forbid þat), nor as þe flesche of ane man maid halie and Iwnit onto þe Sone of God be ane vnite of worthines or ellis as being ane mansioun of God, bot as þat quhilk veralie geifis lyf onto mennis saull and was maid propir onto Goddis awin Sone him self." Hidderto þe concell. – Mark how þir tua anceant
20 concellis dois appreif þe sacrifice of þe mess, and als þe reale presence of þe lordis body in þe sacrament of þe altare.
    I. Treulie, þe sayingis of þe auld wrytaris, and als þe sayingis of þe generale concellis ar verray [f. 14v.] propir for ʒour purpose concerning þe sacrifice of the mess. Quhairfoir I wald pray ʒou þat ʒe will mak ane
25 schorte rehers of þe effect and substance of ʒour ressoning, specialie declarand þe forme of ʒour confirmatiouns, quhilk wilbe ane grit eiss for my memorie.
    Q. For satisfactioun of ʒour desyr, ʒe sall consider þat þe markispoinct of oure ressoning is to knaw gif þe mess be ane sacrifice Institute be Iesus
30 Christ oure salueour in þe latter supper. For þe mair perfyt vnderstanding of þe samyn I diffinit þe mess; and to preif þe diffinitioun þairof, I groundit me apon þe wordis of þe latter supper, quhair oure salueour gaif command to his apostlis – and all vtheris faythfull ministeris in his kirk – to offer his body and blude in sacrifice, sayand <Luc. 22.>: "Do þis in remember-
35 ance of me." And to be assurit þat þis is þe trew mynd and vndirstanding of þe wordis In the latter supper:
    First I callit to rememberance the sayingis of þe prophet Malachie <Mala. 1.>, quhairby we ar instructit þat þe sacrifice of þe auld testament (quhilk was according to þe ordour of Aaron) ceissit and ane cleyn sacrifice
40 succedit in þe place of It, institute be oure salueour in þe latter supper,

quhilk is þe sacrifice of þe new testament according to þe ordour of Melchisedech, callit þe mess.

Secundlie, I confirmit þe wordis of þe latter supper *and* als þe saying*is* of
þe pr*oph*et Malachie to be vndirstand as said is be þe word*is* of the ap*ost*le
5   sanct Paull <Heb. 7.>, *and* als þe sayingis of þe pr*oph*ete Dauid <Psal.
109.>, quhair þai do affirme oure salueo*ur* to be ane preist according to
þe ordo*ur* of Melchisedech, be quhais <fo. 15.> sayingis we ar co*m*pellit
to affirme þ*at* oure salueo*ur* offerit his body and blude vnder þe formes of
breyd *and* wyne in þe latter supper, or ellis he was no*ch*t ane preist accord-
10   ing to þe ordo*ur* of Melchisedech.

Thridlie, we confirmit þe mess to be ane sacrifice be þe figure of þe
paschale lamb <Exod. 12.>, quhilk was no*ch*t onelie ane figure of þe
sacrifice of redemptioun maid on þe croce, bot als ane figure of þe sacrifice
of co*m*memoratioun institute be oure salueo*ur* in þe latter supper <Math.
15   26.>.

Feirdlie, we confirmit be diuers testimoniis of þe new testament <1.
Pet. 3.; Galat. 4.> þe figuris of þe auld testament to be sufficient co*n*firmatioun of þe sacrifice of þe mess, lyk as þai ar sufficient confirmatioun
of vtheris misteriis co*n*cerning þe fay*th*.

20   Fiftlie, we confirmit þe sacrifice of þe mess be þe Interpretatioun of þe
scripturis according to þe doctryne of þe auld fatheris.

Sextlie, be Invincible ressouns aggreable w*ith* þe scripture <Luc. 24.;
Io. 10; Ireneus, [lib.] 3., ca. 3.> we previt þe interpretatioun of þe auld
fatheris towart þe supper of þe lorde to be sufficient confirmatioun *and*
25   preif of þe sacrifice of þe mess.

Last of all, we *co*nfirmit þe sacrifice of þe mess be þe deliberatioun *and*
sayingis of þe maist notable generall co*n*cellis <Concili[um] Nicenum,
Concili[um] Ephesin[um]> quhilkis evyr hes bene sen þe tyme of þe
ap*ost*lis, to quhome It appertenis (deulie *co*nvenit) to tak ordo*ur* in all
30   materis doutsum concerning þe fay*th*.

And sua I beleif þat þir confirmatiouns ar sufficient to preif þat þe mess
Is ane sacrifice according to þe ordinance *and* institutioun of Iesus Christ
oure salueour in þe latter supper. Gif [f. 15v.] þair be ony man offendit
w*ith* þir sayingis *and* ressouns, lat þame mark þe place or testimonie of
35   scripture allegeit or applyit be me Impropirlie for *co*nfirmatioun of þis
caus, *and* mak þe redar to vndirstand þe samyn be oþeris scripturis *and*
ressouns pr*o*pirlie allegeit *and* applyit in þe contrar.

I. I persaif, quha evir will Impung ʒo*ur* saying*is* towart þe *co*nfirmatioun
of þe sacrifice of þe mess, thai sall no*ch*t haif ʒou onelie to þair partie, bot
40   als þai sall haif thais quhilkis war disciplis to þe ap*ost*lis, to gidder w*ith* þe

170

rest of þe anceant fatheris *and* generale concellis to be in þair contrar, quhilk
is na litle mater to ony pryvate man to attempt, specialie quhair questioun
is for þe vndirstanding of þe profund misteriis of þe scripture. Nochtþeles,
I will speir ʒit ane questioun at ʒou, albeit It be Impertinent to þe purpose,
5   sua ʒe will nocht be offendit.

      Q. Treulie, brother, I lyk nocht digressiouns, specialie in sa wechtie ane
mater as we haif in hand. Nochtþeles, I will heir ʒour questioun.

      I. Quhat is þe caus of þis grit variance of opinioun quhilk is rissyn
laitlie amangis christin men for maters of the faytʜ? <B.>

10   **Q.** ʒour questioun is mair difficle to anser to nor ony questioun ʒit
proponit; It comprehendis sua mony heidis.

      I. I heir say þat preistis, monkis *and* freiris, *and* ʒe abbottis, priouris, *and*
bischoppis hes bene þe first Inventaris of þis dangerous danse cumin
amangis vs temporale men, sua þat ʒe kirkmen has þe haill wyte of all þe
15   cummyr amangis vs temporale men for þe fayth.

      Q. ʒe sall wit þat thare Is kirkmen evin as Iudas was ane apostle, sua
þat þe [fo. 16.] speciall caus, eftir my Iugement, of all kynd of variance in
religioun *and* mischeif amangis christiane men for þe faytʜ, Is þat princis
has vendicat dispositioun of benefices, disponand þame to vnqualifeit men
20   ass temporale revarde. Haif we nocht seyn in oure dayes Ane bletour stert
vp to be ane bischop, Ane awn to be ane abbote, Ane pultroun to be ane
priour, ane þelour to be ane persone, Ane veill to be ane vicar, Ane kow
to be ane curate? Quhen sic monstruous ministeries, blindit in Ignorance,
drownit in lustis, ar appoinctit to haif authorite in þe kirk of God, quhat won-
25   der is it þat þe warld be confundit with hereseis, factioun, *and* opinioun as it
is? For I dar bauldlie say: sua lang as we haif sic pestilent precheouris to
be oure pastouris, sic Ignorant awns to be oure abbottis, sic prowd pultrouns to be oure priowris – quha, vnder þe pretense of þe liberte of þe
evangell, seikis onelie þe liberte of þair flesche, takand na thocht to subuert
30   þe haill ordour, policie, *and* religioun of christindome sua þai may suage
þair insaciable sensualite –, sa lang sall þair nevir be gude ordour nor
quietnes in þe kirk of God. As to me, I will say na thing, bot thankis to God
þair is nane sic in þis realme, as þe experience daylie techis vs. Lat vs þairfoir returne to oure purpose.

35   **I.** I can say na ferther to þis purpose pertenand to þe mess presentlie.
Bot I pray God, gif all thais in þis realme quhilkis ar perturbate with
factioun and opinioun had harde *and* vnderstude oure ressoning, þan, I
think, þair suld nocht be sa mony criaris oute aganis þe blissit sacrifice of
þe mess, calland It Idolatrie, nocht knawand quhat þe mater menis.

40   **Q.** I will geif ʒou ane persuasioun contenand thre heidis, [f. 16v.] quhair-

by ȝe salbe assurit þat þe mess is nocht Idolatrie. **The** first heid salbe
groundit on þe auld testament. **The** secund heid on þe new testament. **The**
thrid on ane notable doctryne set furth be ane anceant wrytar callit
Vincentius Lirinensis, alevin hundreth ȝeir syne and mair.

5   **As to þe first heid,** reid all þe auld testament quha pleissis, he sall evir
find þat þe peple of Israell (quha leiffit vnder þe bondage *and seru*itude of
circu*m*cisioun, in expectatioun of Christis cu*ming*) beand abusit w*ith*
Idolatrie þe space of fourtie ȝeiris, or at þe maist þe space of ane ma*n*nis
lyftyme, bot anis in þat tyme, be þe provisioun of God, þai war brocht to
10   þe trew knawlege *and* worschipping of þair lorde God. And als þai war
nevir vniuersalie gevin to Idolatrie. How, than, is it possible þat all christiane man – beand baptizate in þe name of Iesus Christ, beleifand surelie
þat he is all reddy cu*min* salueoure *and* redemar of þe warld – has levit
vniuersalie in p*er*petuale Idolatrie, thir fyftene hundret*h* ȝeir *and* mair,
15   w*ith*out repwgna*n*ce or ganestanding be þe provisioun of God? Be this
argument we ar co*m*pellit to say and affirme þat þe mess is nocht Idolatrie,
or ellis þat þe lorde God hes moir sclendirlie furthschawin his benevolence,
mercy, and grace to thais qwhilkis war baptizate In þe name *and* blude of
Iesus Christ oure lorde nor he did to þe Iewis, quhilk is expres aganis þe
20   scripture <[T]it. 3.>.

       As to þe secund heid, It is writtin in þe eva*n*gell <[Io]. 14.; [M]ath. 18.>,
þe promyse q*uhi*lk oure salueo*ur* maid to his apos*t*lis *and* to all vtheris
fayt*h*full ministeris in þe kirk of God to þe end of þe warld, on þis maneir:
"I sall pray þe Father, and he sall geif ȝou ane vther co*n*fortar þat may
25   <fo. 17.> byd w*ith* ȝou for evir: þe spreit of verite." Quhen was this
promise fulfillit of oure lorde Iesus Christ, towart þe spreit of verite, to his
kirk *and* fayt*h*full ministeris, gif all þe ministeris of þe samyn and all
vtheris of Christis kirk hes leiffit vniuersalie in p*er*petuale Idolatrie, sen
þe tyme of Christ to þir oure dayes? Treulie, I dar bauldlie say be þis
30   argument we ar co*m*pellit to affirme þat þe mess is nocht Idolatrie, or ellis
þat þe lord*is* promyse hes nocht bene fulfillit according to þe scripturis. For
we ar assurit be all writar*is* þat þe mess hes bene vniuersalie approvin In
all ageis, ȝeiris, *and* tymes, evir sen þe tyme of Iesus Christ oure lorde onto
þir oure miserable dayes. Quhairfoir It Is als fals as God is trew to affirme
35   þe mess Idolatrie. <A.>

       As towart the third heid, we will collect off ane godlie doctryne set furt*h*
be ane anceant father Vincentius Lirine*n*sis <Vincenti[us] Lirine*n*s[is]>,
quhair he makis me*n*tioun, in his laudable werk, of thre notis *and* propirteis be þe quhilk*is* all godlie doctryne co*n*cerning þe fayt*h* may be assuritlie
40   knawin and tryit be ane fals *and* vngodlie doctryne.

172

The first note *and* propirtie quhairby we sall ken ane godlie doctryne Is antiquite <Antiquite>, þat is to say þat It has had þe fundament of þe auld, *and* nocht laitlie Inventit be þe brane of man.

The secund note *and* propirte of ane gude *and* godlie doctryne concerning
5 þe fayth is vniuersalite <Vniuersa[lite]>, þat is to say þat It be approvin vniuersalie be all regiouns, all natiouns professand þe fayth of Iesus Christ, quhilk can nocht be bot ane gude *and* godlie doctryne becaus þe lorde at na tyme permittis his kirk vniuersalie to be abusit with Idolatrie, according to his promyse.

10 **The thrid** propirtie Is consent <Consen[t]>, [f. 17v.] þat is to say aggreabilnes in ane doctryne without factioun or diuisioun.

As to þe laudable sacrifice of þe mess, It has all thir thre propirteis requyrit to ane godlie doctryne. <B. [1.]>

First, it has antiquite. Forquhy, as towart þe substance and effect It had
15 þe begynning and was institute be Iesus Christ oure salueour, as is suf-ficientlie provin. As towart þe terme, we ar certifeit þat it was vsit be þe apostlis and þair disciplis. And as towart þe cerimoniis or oratiouns set furth be þe kirk to decoir þe laudable sacrifice of þe mess, the laittest is ane thousand ʒeir and mair. This may we be assurit þat þe mess has antiquite
20 alwayes.

Secundlie, þe mess has evir had vniuersalite. Forquhy, þe mess hes beyn approvin vniuersalie be all regiouns, all natiouns professand þe fayth of Iesus Christ. <B[. 2.]>

Thridlie, þe mess has had evir consent. Forquhy, þe mess hes bene evir
25 approvin be all martyris, all virgynis, all confessouris, all doctouris, schortlie be all thais baptizate in þe name of Iesus Christ, learnit *and* lawit, hie degre *and* law, be perpetuall successioun of tyme >sen þe tyme of Christ to þir our dayes<. And þis may we persaif þat þe laudable sacrifice of the mess has evir had all þir propirteis requyrit to ane godlie doctryne.

30 **Be** þe contrar, ʒe salbe assurit þair is na Idolatrie nor wickit doctryne aganis þe trew fayth þat had þir thre propirteis, þat is to say: approvin at all tymes, in all places, and be all christiane men professand þe fayth of Iesus Christ. Treuth it is, þe wickit opinioun of Arrius <Arrius> aganis þe trew fayth was verray auld *and* was approvin in diuers regiouns;
35 nochtþeles, It had nevir consent. Forquhy, þe speciall ministeris [fo. 18.] quhilkis war in þe kirk of God for þe tyme, planelie ganestude his errour. Als we reid of thre diuerss sectis *and* factiouns quhilkis war amangis þe Arrianis <Hist. Ecclesiasti[ca,] ca. 25., lib. [6.]>.

As to þe wickit heresie and opinioun aganis þe mess, It has nevir had
40 ane of þir thre propirteis requyrit to ane godlie doctryne. <A. 1.>

First, it wantis antiquite. Forquhy, þe first þat evyr ganestude þe mess was ane callit Wicleff <Wicleff>, nynescoir ʒeiris syne bypast, quhilk was threttene hundret*h* fourescoyr ʒeiris eftir þe birth of Christ. <A. 2.> And eftir him þis heresie aganis þe mess ceissit to þe dayes of Luther, quha
5   sayis In ane of his werkis þat þe devill forbad him to vse þe mess. <A. 3.> Thair is anew now þ*at* followis þe devilliss doctryne and consell.

Secundlie, þe wickit heresy and doctryne aganis þe mess was nevir vniuersalie approvin be all regiouns, all natiouns professand þe fayt*h* of Iesus Christ, bot planelie ganestand be all men of godlie learning *and* gude
10 lyff. Treut*h* It is, now laitlie in þir dayes þair is in dyuers regiouns sum miserable peple, blindit in Ignorance, drownit in avarice, desyrous of novelte, q*uhilkis* mwrmwriss aganis þe mess.

Thridlie, þe wickit heresie *and* opinioun aganis þe mess had nevir consent. Forquhy, Thai ar diuidit in diuers sectis *and* opiniouns þat ganestude þe
15 mess. This may we cleirlie persayf þat þe wickit opinioun aganis þe mess, affirmand þe mess to be Idolatrie, is rather ane devillische opinioun nor ane godlie doctryne.

Now, brother, for co*n*clusioun I desyr noc*h*t ellis of ʒow bot þat ʒe will [f. 18v.] stand be þis persuasioun ay and quhill þe samyn be sufficientlie
20 co*n*futate be scripturis treulie *and* propirlie allegeit, or ellis be sum sufficient ressone. Sua beand, I obliss my self be þis my hand wryte to renu*n*ce my religioun, *and* subiect my self to ʒoure factioun, quhilk I rekkin na les in my conscience nor to renu*n*ce my God *and* subiect my self to evirlastand deyt*h* and damnatioun: quhairfra þe lorde mot preserwe ʒow
25 and me *and* all christiane men for evir and evir. Amen.

Appendex

I. Sen we ar certifiit be Goddis worde, bayt*h* auld testament *and* new (according to þe interpretatioun, doctryne, *and* iugement of thais q*uhilkis* war disciplis to þe ap*ost*lis *and* martyris for þe fayt*h* of Iesus Christ in þe
30 primatywe kirk) þat þe mess (as towart þe substance *and* effect) was institute be Iesus Christ oure salueour in the latter supper, Now will I pray ʒou, In favouris off thais quhilkis ar vnlearnit, to mak manifest quhom be þe oratiouns *and* cerimoniis vsit in þe mess ar institute.

26. G] Ane appendix In maner off collocutione *and* resoning betwyxe Quhintyne, co*m*mendator off Corsraguell, *and* his browthir Iames Kennate: set fwrth be þe sayd co*m*mendator. 27. *worde*] G grace *and* worde. 28. *interpretatioun*] G interpretationes. 29. *martyris*] G martyrit. 31. *the*] G his. 33. *oratiouns and cerimoniis*] G orationes; *ar*] G war.

174

Q. To cum to þe vndirstanding of þe samyn, ȝe sall consider þat albeit þe mess (as towart þe substance and effect) was institute be Iesus Christ oure salueour, [fo. 19.] Nochtþeles, as towart þe cerimoniis *and* oratiouns, thai war institute be þe ap*ost*lis and þair disciplis, *and* thais godlie fatheris
5 succedant in þair rowme.

The first þat evir institute ony cerimonie or oratioun to decoyr the laudable sacrifice of þe mess was sanct **Peter,** quha appoinctit þat þe prayer of þe lorde (callit þe 'P*ater* n*oster*') suld be vsit in þe sacri[fi]ce of þe mess. Albeit þe scripture dois no*ch*t testifie þe samyn, nochtþeles It is to be
10 belevit, becaus þai ar diuers thing*is* to be belevit quhilkis ar no*ch*t *con*tenit in scripture: as is þ*at* þe evangell of sanct Iohne is attentik scripture, quhilk can no*ch*t be p*ro*vyn attentict scripture be na vþ*er* scripture – becaus It was writtin eftir all þe rest of þe scripturis –, mair nor þat Peter appoinctit þe dominicall prayer to be said in the tyme of þe mess, as ferther þe redar
15 salbe assurit be þe werk of Dionisius Ariopagita (quha was sanct Paullis disciple), callit Hierarchia Eccl*es*iastica <parte [3.], ca. 3.>.

The secund þ*at* institute ony oratioun or cerimonie to decoir the laudable sacrifice of þe mess was þe godlie father **Alexander,** quha was þe fift þat succedit in þe place of Peter and was martyrit for þe fayt*h* fouretene
20 hundret*h* threttynyne ȝeiris bypast, quha appoinctit þir word*is* following to be said in þe sacrifice of þe mess: 'Qui pridie qu*am* pateretur' (et cetera). Lykwyse he institute halie watter to be maid everie Sonday, accordyng to the laudable custome obseruit in þe kirk of God, conforme to þe scripture <Leui. 16.; Heb. 9.>.

25 The thrid þ*at* appoinctit oratiouns or cerimoniis to be vsit in þe sacrifice of þe mess [f. 19v.] was ane godlie father callit **Sextus,** quha was þe sext eftir Peter, *and* martyrit for þe fayth fouretene hundret*h* thretty ane ȝeir bypast. He appoinctit 'Sanctus, Sanctus, Sanctus, d*omin*us Deus sabaoth' to be said in þe tyme of þe mess, and als þ*at* þe corporale, chalice, *and*
30 patene suld no*ch*t be tuichit be laick men, according to þe scripture <[Nu.] 4.; [2. Re]g. 6.>.

Telesphorus, quha was sevint eftir Peter *and* martyrit for þe fayt*h* fouretene hundret*h* tuentie sex ȝeir*is* bypast, statute þat in þe ny*ch*t of þe natiuite of oure salueour þe angelicall hympne (callit 'Gloria in excelsis
35 Deo') suld be soung solempnitlie in þe mess. And als he appoinctit thre

1. *þat albeit*] G albeit. 5. *rowme*] G rowmes. 13. *scripturis*] G scripture. 19. *Peter*] G sanct Peter. 19. *martyrit*] G martyr; *fayth*] G fayth of Iesus Chryst. 20. *threttynyne*] G thretty *and* nyne. 20–21. *to be said in þe sacrifice of þe mess*] *omitted in* G. 26. *quha*] *omitted in* G. 27. *martyrit*] G sufferit martyrium; *fayth*] G fayth off Iesus Cryst; *thretty ane ȝeir*] G thretty *and* ane ȝeir*is*. 29. *þe corporale*] G corporall. 30. *scripture*] G scriptures. 33. *statute*] G he statut.

messis to be said þe day of þe Natiuite of our lorde be everie preist: The
first mess to be said in þe myddis of þe nycht – quhilk we call þe vknyng –,
In rememberance *and* thankis gevin þat Christ Iesus, þe Sone off God,
was borne in Bethleem in to þe nycht <[Lu]c. 2.>; The secund mess was
5   appoinctit to be said in þe dawin of þe day, In rememberance þat þe
pastouris *and* hirdis come in the mornyng to Bethleem, instructit be þe
angell, to se þe barne þat was borne <[Lu]c. 2.>; The thrid mess was statute to be said on fair day lycht eftir þe sone rysing, In rememberance of his
natiuite quha was þe lycht, redemar, and iustifear of þe haill warld <[Io].
10   1.; [G]ala. 3.>.

     Damasus appoynctit tuelf hundreth ʒeir syne, or þair by, þe 'Confiteor'
and als 'Credo in vnum Deum' to be said in þe tyme of þe mess, and be þe
consell of sanct Hierome appoinctit þe epistole and þe evangell to be red in
þe mess throucht all þe haill ʒeir.

15   **As to þe canone** of þe mess, I find it vsit of auld abuyf alevyn hundreth
and fiftie ʒeiris be Ambrose <[Am]bros., lib. De [Sac]ra., ca. 6.> *and*
Augustyne <[Au]g., Epist. 59., [ad P]aulinum>. Lykwyse we reid
'Sursum corda; Habemus ad dominum' vsit be Chrisostome <Chrisost.,
Hom. [de] Enceniis.> *and* Augustyne <Aug., Sermo. ... De Tempore.>.
20   [fo. 20.].

     The godlie father **Gelasius** abuif ane thousand ʒeir bypast appoinctit þe
preface of þe mess. The godlie father **Gregour** appoinctit nyne hundreth
threscoir ʒeiris syne bypast 'Kyrie eleyson' and 'Alleluya' to be said in þe
mess. The godlie father **Sergius** nyne hundreth ʒeiris syne, or þairby,
25   appoinctit 'Agnus Dei' to be said in þe tyme of þe mess. **Ite missa est** was
appoinctit to be said be þe preist, quhylk dois signifie þat þe godlie sacrifice
of þe mess was finissit *and* done, *and* þat þe peple mycht departe.

     I. I persaif þe oratiouns contenit in þe mess to be institute be þe godlie

---

1. *þe day of þe Natiuite of our lorde*] G þe sayd day. 2. *we call*] G is commonlye callit. 3. *Christ
Iesus*] G Iesus Chryst. 4. *was*] G he. 6. *in the mornyng to Bethleem*] G In to Bathleem In
þe morning. 7. *borne*] G borne, and fande hym, his mother Marye, *and* Iosephe his foster
fathir; *was statute*] G he statut. 9. *was þe lycht*] G was *and* is þe inextinguabill lycht off þe
warld. 11. *Damasus ... Confiteor*] G Damasus xijᵗ ʒeiris syne or þairby appontit þe generall
confessione, callit þe confiteor. 13. *appoinctit ... to be red*] G þe epistill *and* evangill war
appontit to be red. 17. *we reid*] G to be rede. 18. *vsit be Chrisostome*] omitted in G. 21. *The
godlie father*] omitted in G; *ʒeir bypast*] G ʒeiris bypastis. 22–23. *appoinctit ... Alleluya*] G nyne
hundretht *and* threscoir ʒeiris syne appontit 'kyrie elysone, xpe eliesone' *and* 'halleluia'. 25.
Agnus Dei] G the Angnus Dej. 26. *appoinctit*] G appontit be þe ancient faderes, godlie men
off lewing, *and* kyrk of Gode; *signifie*] G signifye and aduertess þe pepill. 27. *þe mess ...
departe*] G þe mes (quhilk is þe sacrifice off þe newe testament) is finesset *and* for þat tyme endit,
swa þat þe pepill may depart to þair lesum vder besyness.

176

fatheris of auld. Nochtþeles, I harde sum of oure precheouris preche þat
þe papistis will say mess for ane kow *and* als for ane sow. I pray ʒou certify
me gif þair be sic ane thing or no*ch*t.

Q. Lorde God! Quhat christiane man may pacientlie thoill sic In-
5 tollerable mokkis *and* leys! I sall call to reme*m*berance þe oratioun vsit
in þe tyme of þe mess quhairpon þai gaddir þis mokrie *and* dispyt, and ʒe
salbe iuge gif þai haif iust occasioun to do þe samyn or no*ch*t. Thir ar þe
wordis eftir following: "O lorde God, quhilk has subrogate *and* ordanit
solace *and* releif to þe lawbo*uris* of men be dwm beistis: we pray þe
10 hwmelie, lat þame no*ch*t periss fra oure vse, wi*th*out þe quhilk*is* þe conditioun *and* stait of man is no*ch*t sustenit." – Quhat is heir *con*tenit worthy
to be mokkit *and* scornit? Did no*ch*t Dauid pray bayt*h* for man *and* beist,
sayand <Psal. 35.>: "Man *and* beist þow sall preserwe, O lorde", as he
wald say: þou sall preserwe man fra evirlastand deyt*h* *and* dampnatioun,
15 *and* beyst fra Inco*n*venient, to þe vtilite *and* profet of man?

I. [f. 20v.] I beleif þair will na ressonable man find falt wi*th* þis oratioun.
Nochtþeles, I will speir at ʒou geif It was leifsum to þe foirfatheris to eik sa
mony oratiouns *and* cerimoniis to þe mess, it beand þe ordinance of God.

Q. Quhat did þe fatheris in þis case quhilk Is nocht conforme to þe
20 scripturis? Did no*ch*t Dauid *and* Salamon <[1. Par]a. 6., 24., [2]6., et
[2. P]ara. 4.> eik hympnis *and* sangis *and* magnific ornamentis to be vsit
in þe temple to þe gloir of God, No*ch*t wi*th*standing þat þe lorde be Moyses
had appoinctit þe ryte *and* ordo*ur* of making of sacrifices? Sua Iesus Christ
oure lorde Institute þe sacrifice of þe mess (concernyng þe effect and
25 substance); *and* as towart þe oratiouns *and* cerimoniis expedient to decoir
þe sacrifice *and* als þe sacramentis, he referrit to his kirk, as I haif all reddy
declarit.

---

1. *precheouris preche*] G newe p*r*echeou*ris* say *and* preche. 2. *and als*] G *and; I pray*] G þairfor
I pray. 3. *ane thing*] G thyng. 4. *Lorde*] G O lorde. 6. *þai gaddir*] G thay pestilent p*r*echores
gadd*er*. 8–9. *ordanit solace ... be dwm beistis*] G ordan*n*it for solace ... dwme beist*is*. 11. *sustenit*] G sustenit, &c; *heir*] G heir in. 12. *Dauid*] G sanct Dauid. 13. *Man ... lorde*] G O lorde,
þo*w* sall p*r*eserff ma*n* *and* best. 16. *with*] G to. 17. *was*] G war. 18. *cerimoniis*] G prayares.
20. *Dauid and Salamon*] G Salomon *and* Dauid. 21. *hympnis and sangis*] G hymnes, sange.
23. *appoinctit*] G appo*n*tit expreslie; *ordour of making of sacrifices*] G custome off making
off sacrifice, *and* ordor þair off. 24. *lorde*] G lorde *and* faythtfull teychair off verite; *concernyng*] G as concerning. 26. *sacrifice*] G sacrifice off þe mess; *sacramentis*] G remane*n*t sacrame*n*t*is*; *referrit*] G referrit þat; *kirk*] G deirly belowit kyrk (bow*ch*t wi*th* his p*r*ecius
blowd), q*uh*ilk is þe pillair Immovabill *and* grwnd off trewtht wndesawabill, trewlie treitand
and inte*r*pretand þe worde *and* will off Gode for edificatio*n*e þairoff, as þe occasio*n*e req*ui*res,
gouernit be þe halye Spreit send þairfor fra tyme to tyme *and* ayge to aige, quha is off na less
dignite þa*n* þe redemair off ma*n*kynd bot equaill wi*th* hy*m* in diuinite: and swa is his doctry*n*e
semblabill trewlie instructand his belowitt*is* (quhat is expedie*n*t to be teychit *and* obser*u*it, and
quhat to be rebuitit *and* detestit).

I. We of þe new learning ar hiechtlie offendit wi*th* ʒour cerimoniis, sic as bekking, kneylling, blissing, crocesing, gapyng, glowring, lyftyn vp of ʒour hand*is*, and knokking on ʒour breist.

Q. I wait no*ch*t quhat ʒe call gaiping *and* glowring, bot þe psalmist
5 desyrit þe lorde to oppin his lippis, and his mouth suld furthschaw his
loving <[Ps]al. 50.>. Lykwyse we ar techit be oure salueour no*ch*t onelie
to elevate oure hartis *and* mynd*is* In tyme of oratioun *and* prayer, bot als
oure corporale eyn <[Io.] 11.; [Io.] 17.; [M]ar. 7.>. Ar we no*ch*t lykwyse
instructit be oure salueoure no*ch*t onelie to fall doun on kneis bot alsua on
10 growf in tyme of prayer? Did no*ch*t oure salueo*ur* bliss þe breid and als his
ap*ost*lis <[Lu]c. 22.; [M]arc. 14.; [Lu]c. 24.>? Attour we ar instructit be
þe godlie fatheris to vse þe signe of þe croce in reme*m*berance þat be þe
sacrifice on þe croce oure deidlie Inimie was ourcumin <[Ter]tuli., De
Co[ron]a Milit.; [Chr]isost., Ho. 55. [in] Matheum.>. Did no*ch*t sanct
15 Paull <[1. T]imoth. 2.> appoinct to lift vp oure hand*is* in tyme of
prayer? Lykwyss þe scripture <[E]xod. 17> testifeis, sua lang as Moyses
held vp his hand*is* *and* prayit, sa lang had þe peple of God victorie; *and*
quhen his hand*is* declynit, the Inimeis had victorie.

As concerning [fo. 21.] þe knokking on þe breist, I will ask at ʒow: quhat
20 falte fand oure salueo*ur* with þe publicane þat did þe samyn <Luc. 8.>?
Treulie, gif ʒe war trew followaris of Christ, ʒe wald no*ch*t be offendit
þair*with* mair nor he was. This may ʒe persaif þat all þe cerimoniis vsit
be þe kirk in þe tyme of þe sacrifice of þe mess ar aggreable wi*th* Goddis
worde. For þe outwarte cerimoniis testifeis þe Inwarte fervour *and* de-
25 votioun, *and* geifis gude exemple to vther*is*, as did oure salueo*ur* quhen he
wische his disciplis feit <Io. 13.>. Lykwyse be outwarte cerimoniis we ar
bro*ch*t to þe mair perfyt knawlege of God, conforme to þe doctryne of all

---

3. *breist*] G brest*is*, *and* sic lyk thyng*is*. 4. *psalmist desyrit*] G psalmist (gentill Dauid) ferventlye desirit. 5. *þe lorde*] G his lorde Gode; *and his mouth*] G promittand þa*n* þat his mowtht. 6. *loving*] G godlie lowing. 7. *In tyme of oratioun and prayer*] G þe tyme off prayair *and* oratione. 9. *oure salueoure*] G hy*m*; *kneis*] G our kneis. 10. *prayer*] G our prayar*is*. 11. *From 'Attour' onwards G continues as follows:*
Attou*r* we ar Instructit be þe godlye fatheres to vss þe signe of þe croce oft syss *and* ay, maist freque*n*tlye in tyme off appera*n*d pe*r*ill or da*n*ger, In reme*m*brance þat be þe sacrifice off þe croce ou*r* deidlie Inimye Satane was o*ur*cumin. And to aboless þe fructfull memorye þairoff he steiris vpe his awne bawbeis *and* sowklingis No*ch*t only to detest þe samy*n* – becauss he, þair father, was þairby vncust *and is* daly fra godlie p*er*sones be þat sing *and* calling vpone þe merites off þat deit for þa*m* þairone rebuttit –, Bot allsua to downe cast þe samy*n* singe quhair evir þaj may be maist*er*, othir in pairt *and* ... haweand þe sam in na less disdayne *and* ignomiiniusnes nor þe theyff hes þe gallois or þe brygant þe gybet or þe rowe: as þair wark*is* wytnesses; *and* oure eyne dowes o*ur* larglie hawe occasione to testifye þair vnbrydlit deformatione, proude pratling, *and* rakless railling, entisand to seditione *and* lawless liberte.Godlie Augustyne affirmes that thynge q*uhi*lk þe vniu*er*sall kyrk of God obs*er*ues *and* hes bene off þe ancient

178

men of godlie learning; sua þat, gif ʒe tak away þe cerimoniis *and* vther
godlie customes vsit in þe kirk for to decoir þe *s*er*v*ice of God be proces of
tyme þe peple in þe warld sall forʒet þair is ane God, quhilk Is þe markis-
poynct þat þe devill schutis at be heretykis, his Instrumentis, in þir miser-
5 able dayes vnder þe colo*u*r of godlines.

    I. Thair is ane vse *and* custome vsit in þe mess quhilk grevis ws abuif all
þe rest: þat Is þe elevatioun *and* adoratioun of þe sacrament.

    Q. As to þe elevatioun, It is vsit in reme*m*berance of Christ*is* elevatioun
apon þe croce. As towart þe adoratioun: treulie, quhairsumeuir Christ is
10 (as he is assuritlie in þe sacrament), thair is bayt*h* God *and* man; *and*
quhairsumeuir God is, he is to be adorit. No*ch*t þat christiane men gevis
Goddis gloir to þe formis of breid *and* wyne, quhilkis þai se with þair
corporale eyn, bot to þe blissit body of þe lorde, quhilk Is contenit invisiblie
vnder þe formis of breid *and* wyne *and* is seyn w*ith* þe eyn of oure fayt*h and*
15 vnderstanding, as Christis awin worde techis vs, sayand <Luc. 22.>:
"This is my body". Lyke as þe thre wyse men quhilk*is* come fra þe orient
<Math. 2.> gaif no*ch*t adoratioun to oure salueo*u*r in respect of his man-
[f. 21v.]heid, quhilk þai saw onelie w*ith* þair corporale eyn, bot be ressone
of his godheid, quhilk be fayt*h* þai saw cled with his hwmanite.
20 **I,** We think ʒoure mess clayt*his* and arrayment plane dissagysing proper
for ane farss.

    Q. ʒe think evin as þai tho*ch*t quha crucifeit Christ. For þair is na
arrayment apon þe preist in þe tyme of þe mess quhilk dois no*ch*t represent
sump*ar*t of þe arrayment quhilk was apon oure salueo*u*r þe day of his
25 deyt*h and* passioun. As be exemple, **the amict** signifeis the clayt*h* quhair-
wit*h* oure salueo*u*ris face was cled quhen he was mokkit and scornit
<[M]arc. 14.>.

---

fatheris actorisit past memor, of q*uhi*lk*is* þe fyrst appo*n*tme*n*t þairoff is no*ch*t *con*stitut in þe
generall *con*sales, the samy*n* rychtuslye is to be belewit Institu*t* be þe auctorite off þe ap*os*tlis
of Iesus Cryst. Swa one forss (be resone þe Institutione þairoff is of sic *an*tiquite þat it hes past
memor) sic as will p*re*tende to raill þairvpone, mo*n* schawe þe traditione þairoff, be quhome,
and quho*w* lang passit, or ellis w*ith* þe godlye saying*is* abowne reheirsit apprayss þe sa*m*ing as
gewein *and* Institu*t* be Chryst*is* ap*os*tlis, Instructit þair*to* be þe Spreit off verite, q*uhi*lk þaj had
abu*n*dlye resauit.
Iames: Assuritlie, I thynk ʒo*ur* saying wonder*us* godlie, *and* I þairby am p*er*swadit no*ch*t onlye
to hawe þe sam in reverence *and* admiratione, bot þairwith þe rest off þe approving ceromonies
obser*u*it vniu*er*salie in þe kyrk off God, albeit as ʒyte my rudness *and* lak off knawlege be
no*ch*t sufficie*n*tlye instructit to w*n*d*er*stand þe misteres þairoff, lyk as I was heirin afor ʒo*ur*
declaratione heiroff: desiring ʒo*w* in my maist hartlye maner no*ch*t to be misco*n*tentit w*ith* me
illuminat w*ith* ʒo*ur* doctryne *and* accuregit w*ith* ʒo*ur* worthy resolutiones, albeit I dema*n*d
farthair.
Q.: Say one, browthir. For he þat refuses to ra*n*dir cowmpt (ʒae, albeit it be off his faytht, to
all ma*n* askand þairoff in dewe tyme *and* place) quhair by þe ignora*n*t may be Instructit, he **is**

The alb signifeis þe clayth quhairwith he was cled, send fra Herode to Pylate <[Lu]c. 23.>.

The belt signifeis þe scurge quhairwith he was scurgit <[M]arc. 15.>.

The stoill signifeis þe corde quhairwith Christ was bound to þe pillare
5 quhen he was scurgit <[M]ath. 27.>.

The fannon signifeis þe corde quhairwith he was bound quhen he was drawin to þe fals iugeis <[Io]. 18.>.

The chesabill signifeis þe purpure clayth þat he was cled withall quhen þe croun of thorne was pressit down apon his heid <[Io]. 19.>. – And þir ar
10 þe vestimentis concerning þe sacrifice of þe mess, quhair with ʒe haif na iust occasioun to be offendit.

Attour, ar we nocht certifeit be Goddis worde <[Ex]od. 28.> þat þe ministeris of þe auld law had gorgeous *and* costlie reparaling (quhilkis war dedicate onelie to þe seruice of God) quhen þai war in þe temple þe tyme of
15 þe sacrifice, It beand bot þe schaddow and figure? How mekle mair is It aggreable with all gude ressoun, conforme to Goddis worde, þat [fo. 22.] þe ministeris of þe new law haif þair reparaling decent for to decoir þe maist hevinlie, pure, and clene sacrifice of þe lordis body, quhilk is þe verite, prefigurate be þe oblatioun of Melchisedech <Gen. 14.> and propheceit
20 be þe prophet Malachie <Mala. 1.>!

I. Gif þe mess be gude, quhat is þe caus ʒe will nocht say it in oure awin langage, þat we may all vndirstand It?

Q. The mess is said in þe Latyne toung, quhilk is ane vniuersale toung, becaus It is ane vniuersale sacrifice, as testifeis þe prophet <Mala. 1.>.
25 Als þe minister in þe tyme of þe sacrifice had evir ane distinct prayer propir þairfoir <Luc. 1.>. Attour, It is mair decent (as sayis Erasmus) þat þe peple haif þe profund misteriis of oure religioun In admiratioun, nor

---

accusabill off þe misvsing off Godis talent grantit to hym. And farthair, I belewe hym vnabill to gewe his gudis and hasard his body for þe weill off þe flok off Chryst Iesus, þat refuses to gewe his gude consall to his carnall browthtar, and speciallie in thyngis belangand faytht *and* religione.

Iames: I persawe diuerss persones, quhilkis I esteyme to be werray godlie (be resone þaj, as gude fructfull treis, bryngis fwrtht gude fructis), off quhilkis sum makis þe sing off þe croyss vpone þair foirheyd, sum one breyst, sum one þair bak, sum one þair mowtht, *and* vderes ane greit croyss our all þair body: and twychin þe motyves heiroff I wald be instructit. For, albeit my selff be Ignorant off þe mistereis þairoff, I suppone na less bot þe haly kyrk catholik, quhilk hes sufferit þe samyn be vsit off sic antiquite as it hes bene, can dewlie intrepte þe samyn, quhilk I belewe to hawe bene Institut be þe Instructione off þe haly Spreit, quha fullfillis þe haill warld.

Quintinus: Blyssit be þe Sone off Gode, borne off þe permanent virgen and moder meyk, Mary, quha, be þe haly Spreit promisset to be send, nocht onlye hes steirrit vpe ʒour wnderstanding for eruditione to be had þairin (and nocht off waine curiosite to demand sic questione), bot þairwith hes kyndlyt my hart with his birnand fyr off cherite *and* illuminat my Ingyne to

180

þat þai suld be commwne *and* vulgare, becaus þe peple oft tymes contempnis that thing quhilk is maist commwne *and* vulgare to þame.

    I. I am sufficientlie satisfeit, no*ch*t onelie w*ith* þe effect and substance
of þe mess, bot als w*ith* þe oratiouns, cerimoniis, vestimentis, *and* all þe
5 rest. Bot ʒit remanis ane questioun – quhairw*ith* gif I war satisfeit, I wald
think my self at rest in my co*n*science with all maneir of thing co*n*cerning
þe mess –, quhilk Is Gif deidlie syn be remittit be þe sacrifice of the mess.

    Q. ʒe sall vnderstand þat Christis deyth Is þe onelie medicyne for syn
<Rom. 5.>, quhilk medicyne (according to Christis co*m*mandiment
10 <Math. vlti.; Marc. vlti.; Io. 20.; Luc. 13.; Ezechie. 1.>) man be applyit
diuers maners of way, be diuers sacrame*n*tis as instrume*n*tis propir þairfoir, sua þat þe sacrament of baptyme and þe sacrament of pennance ar
þe sacramentis *and* instrume*n*tis quhairby Iesus [f. 22v.] Christ has appoinctit þe fructis of his deyt*h* and passioun to be applyit concerning
15 remissioun of originall *and* deidlie syn.

    I. How, þan, ar þe wordis of Alexander þe martyr to be vndirstand,
sayand þat God will forgeif grit synnis be þe sacrifice of þe mess, quhairapon ʒe infer þ*at* þe mess is ane sacrifice for syn?

    Q. ʒe sall vnderstand þ*at*, albeit deidlie syn be nocht remittit be þe sacri-
20 fice of þe mess, no*ch*tþeles þai ar grit co*m*moditeis of þe fruct*is* of Christis
deyt*h* and passioun applyit be þe sacrifice of þe mess for saluatioun of man
helplyk for syn, Lyk as thais quhilk*is* ar in deidlie syn be þe sacrifice of þe
mess ar supportit (it beand offerit for þame) In safer as grace is obtenit, be
þe vse of þe quhilk he quha is in deidlie syn is maid þe mair hable to cum to
25 pe*n*nance, quhilk is þe instrument quhairby ar applyit þe fructis of Christis
deyt*h* and passioun co*n*cerning remissioun of deidlie syn. Als grit paynis
ar diminissit, quhilk*is* ar deserwit for syn. Atto*u*r we ar strent*h*it, confortit,

schawe to ʒow sic pr*o*funde misterye þairoff and godlie meninge off þe samy*n* as for þis pr*e*sent
tyme off seditione *and* vproir may be sufficient to pecefye þe hart *and* co*n*science off ane gude
chrystiane ma*n*. Fyrst, sic as vsis to mark þa*m* self *is* w*ith* þat worthty sing vpone þair foirheyd:
remem*b*rand quhow þaj *and* þair pare*n*tis sum tyme Inimes to God foirfaltit off þair heretage
be þe greyfus sine of Ada*m* exilit arthtly p*ar*radis, be þat owtwart sing (to þe eruditione off
vd*er*es *and* humiliatione off þe rebelland flesche, q*u*hi*l*k was þe causs off þat pestiferus misbelewe
and hurtfull rebellione off ou*r* fyrst [MS. fyst] pare*n*tis, co*n*fessand in hum*l*ie maner w*ith* ane
sonlye reuerence *and* co*n*stance off ane strange soldior wnd*er* þe baner *and* charge off Iesus
Chryst þair capitane – quha vincust þair awld inimye vpone ane croyss *and* restorit ma*n*kynd
to his foirfaltit heretage (evirlestand lyffe) – þam self*is* oppinlie to be off his retenwe *and*
falloschype, takand þis bauge vpone sic p*ar*t off þair body as is maist co*m*mo*n*lye ay vncoverit
(viz.) þe foirheyd, and þat þaj sall thynk na lak nor schaym þairoff, bot wailʒeantlye tewlʒae
wnd*er* his baner, quhe*ir*to þaj ar sworne þe day off þair baptyme, quhe*n* þaj fyrst resavit þe
sayd sing in place abowne exp*re*mit.
Iames: Quhydder gyff ony sic sing or cerimonye was vsit afoir þe passione off Chryst.
Q.: ʒae, off trewetht.

and grace is augmentit be þe sacrifice of þe mess, quhairby we ar maid
mekle mair hable to resist all kynd of syn, with vtheris Innumerable commoditeis helplyk for syn, quhilkis to rehers war our prolixt.

    According to þis wrytis þe apostoll <Heb. 7.>, sayand: "For euery hie
5 preist þat Is takin frome amangis men Is ordanit for men in thingis pertenand to God, to offer giftis *and* sacrifice for syn." Quhairfoir, sen be
Goddis worde we ar certifeit þat sacrifice was offerit in þe auld law for syn
(quhilk was þe vmbre *and* schaddow), how mekle [fo. 23.] mair is þe maist
clene and pure sacrifice of þe new law (quhilk is þe verite) to be offerit vp
10 daylie for syn considerand we syn daylie? – quhilk hevinlie sacrifice Is ane
cheif instrument, moyane, and way, quhairby ar applyit (according to
Christis commandiment) þe fructis of his deyth and passioun helplyk for
syn. Conforme to þis wrytis þe prophet <Mala. [1.]>, sayand: "In euery
place sall þair sacrifice be done, and ane clene oblatioun offerit vp onto
15 my name." Hiddirto þe prophete.

    This sall ȝe consider þat þair war evir thre thingis concurrand þe gidder:
The law, þe preist, *and* þe sacrifice; – The law, quhilk was þe conditioun
betuix God *and* þe peple; The preist, to quhom It appertenit to interpret þe
law and offir vp sacrifice for þe synnis of þe peple; þe sacrifice, quhilk was
20 þe oblatioun *and* offering offerit onto God be þe preist. And eftir þis maneir
Is the godlie martyr Alexander to be vndirstand, and all vtheris quhilkis
treulie dois affirme þe mess to be ane sacrifice for syn.

    I. We belevit þat þe papistis had Inventit þe mess of þair awin brayn, as
ane new satisfactioun and redemptioun for syn.

25   **Q.** It is nocht þe first lesing þat heretykis has falslie Imputate on to thais
quhilkis þai call papistis, howbeit þai menit nathing less bot þat þe mess is

---

Iames: Sum part off scriptur hawe I red, *and* be my Iugment I can nocht call to memory
quhow þe samyn may be scriptur be provin. Nocht þe less, I will raythtair attribut þe misknawin þairoff to my negligence in reding þairoff withowt circumspectione *and* dewe attendance þairto nor vderwyss.

Q.: Browthir, ȝour gentill resoning *and* godlie mening þairoff provokis me with þe haill pytht
off my Ingyne to schawe gud will to satyfye ȝour rationabill desyris. And I am assurit þat he
quhilk hes promissit to be in þe mydis off twa or thre convenit in his nayme (as we ar wndowtitlie) sall performe þis purpoyss dewlie.

Iames: Gode grant.

Quintinus: The godlie propheit Ezechiell makis mensione þat, þe wraytht *and* greyfus vengence
off God beand in radyness to be powrit vpone þe Inhabitantis off Iherusalem for þair abbo-
minationes (be þe angelis his ministeres send þairfor) withowt ony miseratione, that þe pesefullness off God causit hym command ane off þaj angelis to pass *and* mark all sic within þat
towne quhair þe plage was to cum as lamentit *and* gayne stud þe vngodlie [MS. vndoglie]
with þat letter tau in þair foirheyd: quhilk is þe figure off þe croce mayd one þis maner 'T', and
is þe last lettre off þe Hebrues.

[*At this point the text is discontinued.*]

182

þe sacrifice of þe new law institute be Iesus Christ in þe latter [supper]
<Luc. 22.>, callit þe sacrifice of commemoratioun, be þe vse of þe quhilk
ar applyit þe fructis of Christis deyth *and* passioun, obtenit be þe sacrifice
of redemptioun [f. 23v.] for saluatioun of man, helplyk for syn in maneir
5 abone rehersit.

And þis may ȝe cleirlie *per*saif þat no man has iust occasioun to be
offendit w*ith* the doctryne of þe kirk of God towarte þe vse and vndirstanding of þis profund misterie of þe sacrifice of þe mess, conforme to
Goddis worde, bayt*h* auld testament and new <[Ge]n. 14.; [M]ala. 1.;
10 [L]uc. 22.; [1.] Cor. 11.>. Quhairfoir þe lorde mot Illuminat ȝo*ur* hartis
w*ith* his Spreit, þ*at* peace *and* verite mot be in oure dayes. Amen.

Fiat pax et veritas in diebus nostris.

<[4.] Reg. 20.>.

Title page. The title page is in the same free hand as the body of the tract. The first letter is considerably bigger, the remaining letters of the first two words are slightly bigger than the rest.

deniand. Small hole in the MS affecting the bracketed letters. The appended transcript of this title page, in Constable's hand, has *deniend.* No other *-end* forms occur, and on the supposition that the exact original spelling was illegible in Constable's time, *-and* is definitely to be preferred.

p. 112, line 1. *The first cheptour.* Only the first word (and the first two letters of *The* in the next line) have slightly more than normal size in the MS.

p. 112, 2. *redar.* Top right hand corner torn off. The suggested reading is supported by *benevolent reader* in 132, 6 and by the opening words of the first chapter of the *Compendius Tractiue:* "*The nerrest, and onelie way, (benevolent Redare,) to be satifiit and establischeit in all materis brought in debait,*" &c. (*Wodrow Misc.,* p. 99).

p. 112, 7f. Note the emphasis created by *ma, aucht, suld – contentacione, contenment, satisfaccione.*

p. 112, 19. *caput 1.* Not the first chapter of the tract, but the first principal section covering chapters I–V; cp. the opening passage of ch. VI.

p. 112, 21–23. *cheif testimonyis ... þe kirk ... þe opinione.* Top left hand corner torn off; reading *cheif* supported by line 24.

p. 112, 23. *Ecolampadius.* From this instance onwards the flourish indicating the nasal marks the end of the name.

p. 112, 24f. Marginal text partly cropped. It will have read: *þis (? his) maner sal appreif his vickit opinione.* It is the only marginal comment in Kennedy's tract of the sort which forms such a prominent feature in Knox's edition of the *Maybole Ressoning.*

p. 112, 28. *caput 2m.* i.e. chapter VI; cp. first sentence of ch. VII.

p. 112, 30f. The text of Mr. fforde's MS (F) begins with *þat Interpretatioun quhilk is.*

p. 113, 1. *þat.* Relative supported by 115, 13.

p. 113, 4f. *S. Mathow. of* omitted. Since the marginal comment of 112, 24f. proves a considerable original margin, the chapter numbers may well have been preceded by the abbreviated forms of the evangelists' names, as elsewhere.

p. 113, 6. F *quhilk salbe sched for ȝow and mony.* Additional words supported by 114, 14.

p. 113, 7. *vriting.* i.e. 'written'.

p. 113, 9. F *And quhen.* Conjunction supported by Vulgate *et gratias agens fregit.* But the Latin text may have been a reason for supplying an originally absent word.

brak. r obliterated by stain; other letters of the word and scriptural reference in the margin barely legible.

p. 113, 11–14. Reading supported by Vulgate. Note, however, that line 10 omits Vulgate *hoc facite in meam commemorationem.*

p. 113, 14f. *Quhasumeuer.* Reading supported by Vulg. *quicumque.*

p. 113, 15. F *of þe lord.* Reading supported by Vulg. *Domini;* but see comment to line 9.

p. 113, 16. F *þe lord.* Reading supported by Vulg. *Domini.*

p. 113, 20. *testimonyis of scripturis.* Apparently a contamination of *scripturis* ('scriptural texts') and *testimonyis of scripture;* cp. line 31.

p. 113, 22. F *quhilkis.* Scribal slip.

p. 113, 23. *our saluiour, Sayand.* F reading indicates haplography.

p. 113, 24. *be ane figure and similitude.* i.e. 'figuratively'.

p. 113, 28. *and in ane oþer place.* Perhaps a scribal addition to avoid the impression that the two quotations occur in the same place.

p. 113, 29. *with ʒow.* Cp. Vulg. *me autem non semper habetis* and Smith's translation (*Confutation*, p. 44r) *but me ye shal not euer haue*, both supporting F reading.

p. 113, 30f. Possibly meant to quote places like *1 Thess.* 4, 15; *2 Tim.* 4, 1; *1 Pet.* 3, 22 and 4, 5. The margin opposite these lines contains traces of writing which have become illegible through a stain.

p. 114, 3. *Mark diligently, gud redar.* With such connective phrases, compare Fisher's frequent *attende lector, vides lector, aduerte lector, hic aduertis lector, diligenter considerate,* &c.

p. 114, 12. *nor þir.* F reading supported by more common syntax; cp. line 5; 115, 2f; 115, 4, &c. For instances where the subject is no demonstrative pronoun, cp. 116, 14f. (verb absent in both MSS) and 125, 14 (verb absent in A).

p. 114, 17. *vas.* Cp. *is* in 113, 2. The teaching that *Cristis real body and bluid* in the Eucharist, even though separately represented by the outward form of bread and wine, formed an inseparable unit, would easily lead to considering it a grammatical unit as well. However, *ar* in line 16 shows that the A text is not consistent in this respect. The singular form may well have been influenced by *it vas.*

p. 114, 18f. *Lat ane man exame hyme self, and swa lat hyme eit.* Reading supported by Vulg. *probet autem seipsum homo, et sic de pane illo edat* and by line 24.

p. 114, 20. *cwpe.* Last two letters obliterated by stain.

p. 114, 27. *it beand bot ane syng or takine only.* i.e. because the other sacraments did not at the same time contain the spiritual reality signified; cp. 117, 25f., where Kennedy says that the Eucharist is at once sign and reality.

p. 114, 29f. *The circumstance of the text.* F *Thaireftir* would correspond to *First* in line 24, but a copyist may well have considered it an inaccuracy which ought to be corrected (cp. *1 Cor. 11, 27–29*). See, however, next note.

p. 114, 32f. *þe body and bluid of þe lord.* Haplography.
it folowis. If F *Thaireftir* is taken to present the original reading, this can only refer to logical connection, not to sequence. If, on the other hand, *First* is taken in the sense of 'firstly' and it is further supposed that, instead of continuing with *secundlie*, Kennedy considered is better to bring in the omitted verse 27 *(The circumstance of þe text)*, the word *folowis* denotes sequence as well as consequence.

p. 115, 1. *Gud redar.* F reading supported by 125, 2 and *Compendius Tractiue, Wodrow Misc.*, p. 167 *(Lorde God, gude Redare);* cp. 137, 10; 137, 22; 177, 4.

p. 115, 2. *real presens ... to be realy in.* Apparently a contamination of *þe real body ... to be present* (title page) and *þe real presens of þe body ... in* (line 6). The A text has the same tautology in 116, 26f. and 126, 23f. It presupposes that in connection with the Eucharist *þe real presens* and *þe body and bluid of Christ* were felt to be synonymous. Cp. C. Lattey, ed., *Catholic Faith in the Holy Eucharist* (Cambridge Summer School of Catholic Studies, 1922), 3rd edition, Cambridge, 1927, pp. 155ff., where phrases like *the Reserved Eucharist, the Abiding Presence* and *the Presence abiding with man* are used as synonymous with *Christ in the Holy Eucharist.*

p. 115, 3. *ask at.* Preposition invariably added.

p. 115, 12. *scripturis of inferrens.* i.e. scriptural texts interpreted beyond the obvious literal meaning.

p. 115, 17–19. *sal ve ... to mak.* Cp. 117, 29 *(vil we ... to mak)*, where F again omits *to*. It is not used when the infinitive immediately follows *sal (sal ve raherss).*

p. 115, 19. *mak ... to onderstand.* Normal construction; cp. 117, 29; 118, 28 (F reading); 119, 13; 126, 4f.; 128, 12 (F reading); 134, 9; 138, 24.

p. 115, 25. *for mony.* Mathew and Mark have *pro multis*, Luke *pro vobis*. But the interlinear insertion of *ʒow and* in F is probably due to a copyist's attempt to give the words of consecration in the Latin rite *(pro vobis et pro multis).*

p. 115, 26. *to be spokin.* Similarly in 116, 11, 14, 15 and 18; 117, 1 and 4; 120, 25f.; *haue bene* in 118, 17f. and 135, 11.

p. 115, 27f. *thrawine ... ramemberance.* Bracketed letters all but completely obliterated by stain in top right hand corner.

p. 115, 30. *dure.* Last two letters all but completely faded.

p. 115, 31–33. *lik as ... vas ... Swa ... was.* F reading supported by 139, 37f.

p. 116, 1. *þis.* Reading supported by 140, 1.

Inpropir. Prefix at the end of a line.

p. 116, 1f. *seruis of nocht to þair intent.* Also in 117, 12; 118, 10f.; 126, 10f. The expression corresponds to Fisher's *tuae causae nihil omnino prosunt* and, more significantly, Smith's *which doe nor serue for that purpose (Confutation,* p. 95v.; cp. 84r *maketh not for your purpose).* The Scots expression will be based on OF syntax (see Ducange, s.v. *servire).*

p. 116, 2–4. *For quhy ... confundit.* F reading supported by 140, 2–4.

p. 116, 4. *As be ane exempil.* Corresponds to Fisher's *sicut per exemplum.* The use of the article is peculiar to A; cp. 129, 6.

p. 116, 4–8. Simpler A reading must be due to scribal interference with the text, as in the preceding lines.

p. 116, 10. *rehersit* MS *reher//harsit,* with the last two syllables on a new line.

p. 116, 14. *suld.* Small hole in MS; *u* completely, *s* and *l* partly absent.

figure. Only *g* distinguishable, other letters obliterated by stain in top left hand corner.

p. 116, 16f. *nother befoir nor ʒit þat efter folowis, giffand.* The alternative *precedand and efter folovand* (line 23 and p. 133, 14f.) supports *þat.* The structure of the sentence, which runs parallel with that of line 12, does not admit of F *and:* 'there is no scriptural context *(dependens of scripture)* which gives'. Cp. *praecedentia sequentiaque* (Fisher, *o.c.,* lib. v, cap. xxvi).

p. 116, 21. *þe roik.* Definite article in both A and F; cp. 113, 26; 115, 29; 139, 37; 140, 23.

p. 116, 25–27. *dois ... thrawand.* F reading supported by structure and content of the sentence.

p. 116, 28. *Arrius.* The anti-trinitarian heretic condemned at the Council of Nicea (A.D. 325). His name was normally thus spelled.

Marcione. Second-century heretic who denied the reality of Christ's humanity (see next paragraph).

damnable heretikis. F reading supported by Kennedy's usual distinction between *damnable hereseis* and *deplorit heretikis;* cp. 138, 26; 139, 4.

p. 116, 29. *fortify.* Reading supported by, e.g., 115, 27; 118, 1; 139, 35; 140, 10.

p. 117, 3. *flesche and.* Bracketed letters absent through small hole in the MS. F reading clearly required by sense and regular syntax.

On the comparison of Oecolampadius with Marcion and Arius, see for example Fisher, *De Veritate,* lib. ii, cap. 1f.

p. 117, 5. *eftervart.* See chapters VII–IX.

p. 117, 9. *þe sacrament.* F reading supported by usual contrast of *figure* and *real body;* cp. 113, 22; also lines 16 and 25.

altare. Bracketed letters illegible through small ink blot.

p. 117, 14–16. *verraly God, ane with þe Fader in substance ... þe invisible God, equal and ane with þe Fader.* Probably a theological touching up of the simpler F reading.

p. 117, 17. *formis.* i.e. the outward appearance, which forms a *figure* in as far as it points to the presence of *þe sam self body.* In the *Oratioune* Kennedy illustrated it as follows: *"Thar is sum signis, callit effectuis signis, quhilkis nocht onely dois signify bot als ar the samyn thing quhilk thai do signify, as breid in ane baxtaris buyth wyndo signifys breid to be saulde, and is brede the self quharwith menne ar corporalie refreschit"* (Laing, *Works,* vi, p. 164).

p. 117, 20. *paschal lam.* Cp. *"Nunquid agnus ille recenter occisus et assus non multo expressior figura mortis Christi fuerat quam panis? Et tamen hunc, non illum, pascha suum, hoc est Christi proprium, Tertullianus appellat. Et qua ratione (precor) panem istum potius quam agnum illum pascha Christi cognominat, nisi quia Christum in hoc sacramento vere contineri credidit? verum-que corpus in hoc edi verumque sanguinem potari? Fuit vtique figura mortis Christi tam agnus ille quam duplex ista panis et vini species"* (Fisher, *De Veritate,* lib. ii, cap. xxi).

p. 117, 22. F *þe bluid of þe lambe þe bluid of Christ.* Perhaps omitted in A through recurrence of *Christ.*

p. 117, 23. *lame.* Omitted word added in margin.

186

þe quhilk. Probably a scribal simplification of F *be þe quhilkis* ('for which reasons').

p. 117, 26. *vordis.* Bracketed letters all but completely faded.

p. 117, 28 f. From this chapter heading onwards the headings themselves and the first letter(s) of the first word in the next lines stand out among the writing of the MS through size and thickness. For the presumable source of the first part of this chapter, see pp. 100f., above.

p. 117, 29. *it.* Cp. 126, 4 *(As hes pleasit God to gif vs grace)* and 138, 14 *(as it hes plesit God to gif vs grace).* Equivalent expressions occur in 151, 9f.: *be Goddis grace and favour* and *God willing.*

p. 118, 3. *Ane.* Reading supported by 141, 18.

p. 118, 4. *vord.* Cp. 141, 21.

p. 118, 8. *onprofitable.* Reading supported by context.

p. 118, 12. *to quhome þir vordis var spokin.* Probably a scribal simplication of the longer F text.

p. 118, 15. *imperfit.* Additional *in þe fayth* in F supported by 120, 18.

lenit to. i.e. 'leaned, relied on'.

p. 118, 17 f. *quha belewit þat our saluiour wald hef giffin his flesche to hef beine couponit.* Cp. *quhilkis [belewit] our saluiour to gif his flesche to be eaten* (120, 18 f.), which rather supports the F reading.

p. 118, 20. *profeit.* i.e. 'profited'.

p. 118, 23. *indifferently.* i.e. 'without differentiation, in general'.

p. 118, 27 f. *To mark … And þat þa ma be.* F reading supported by context and by other instances of *mak … to;* see note to p. 115, 19.

p. 118, 29. *þe testimonyis.* F reading supported by context.

p. 118, 30. *anciant authouris.* Cp. the passage from Fisher, p. 100, above, which mentions Chrysostom and Augustine.

p. 118, 31. *vritin.* i.e. 'writing'; cp. 121, 21.

p. 119, 1. *persaif.* Additional words in F supported by similar phrases elsewhere (e.g. 154, 21) and the frequent *þis may þow persaif.*

p. 119, 3 f. *as flesche is þat is deuidit one þe skamles.* F reading supported by *in macello venditur;* cp. 118, 19 and 120, 19. Phrases like *flesche deuidit fra þe spreit* and *flesche Iunit to þe spreit* would easily suggest a similarly structured *flesche deuidit one þe skamles.* In fact, the A reading is a better rendering of St. Augustine's *quomodo … in macello venditur,* but it would appear that the repeated F reading can only be explained as a faithful reproduction of Kennedy's original.

p. 119, 8–11. *þe first … The secund … Thayrbye.* This last word has been touched up from what appears to have been *thirlye.* This, and similar enumerations elsewhere (see 151, 26 ff.; 158, 8 ff.; 169, 37 ff.; 174, 1 ff.), support the reading in F.

p. 119, 10. *bodie.* First instance of change in the spelling of A; see pp. 104f., above.

p. 119, 12 f. *quhilk beand Iunit to his manheid makis hyme to be bayth God and man.* The construction of the F reading is not uncommon in Kennedy's tracts (e.g. 120, 8: *he beand in his mortale liff he ves subieckit*) and is probably original.

manheid. MS *man//manheid* (first syllable at the end of a line).

p. 119, 14–20. *Now … flesche.* A reading hopelessly corrupt. The general structure of the sentence must be: *consider þat lik as it vas nocht … Inlikmaner it is nocht,* as in F; cp. e.g. 115, 31 ff.

p. 119, 21 f. *part takar of his diuine nature.* Cp. *1. Pet.* 1, 4.

p. 119, 22. *Iwnit inseperatlie to his flesche and is.* Probably a scribal interpolation to drive home the point; cp. 118, 22.

p. 120, 1 f. *nor ʒit of ony maner of vay.* Double negation as in F would be normal native syntax; cp. 122, 24 *(nor ʒit can noch be).*

p. 120, 3. F *þe separatioun.* Obviously a scribal slip.

p. 120, 4. *as þe scriptoure plainlye techis ws.* Kennedy probably means that Scripture testifies to Christ's death and, as he says in the next sentence, that he rose from death *be verteu of his godheid.*

p. 120, 9. *hundyr.* Scribal slip for *hungyr.*

p. 120, 10. *lik as in his death.* i.e. just as it remained united to his manhood during the period when he was dead.

p. 120, 11. *in twa natures.* F reading supported by parallel construction in line 13.

p. 120, 18. *vas.* Cp. 118, 15.

F *quhilkis belewit.* Supported by 118, 17.

p. 120, 26. *spiritual manducacione.* This is not the same as the eating of *spirituall fuid* (line 21); unlike this latter phrase it connotes the exclusion of Christ's real presence in the eucharistic bread. Also see note to p. 130, 5–14.

p. 120, 27. *anciaunt.* F reading supported by 124, 14 and 133, 16.

p. 120, 28. *Chrisostom, Homelia 46 super Ioannem.* See notes to 133, 17 and 156, 13, which suggest that F *Homilia 48* may be the more correct reading; but cp. Migne, *PG,* vol. lix, cols. 261 ff.

p. 120, 28f. *Augustine, tractatu 26 super Ioannem.* See Migne, *PL,* vol. xxv, cols. 1606 ff..

p. 120, 29. *Hilarius, li. 8 De Trinitate.* See Migne, *PL,* vol. x, cols. 234 ff. Tunstal (*o.c.,* pp. 21r ff.) has a long quotation with commentary.

p. 120, 29f. *Cirillus, super Ioannem sexto.* Cyril of Alexandria's commentary on the sixth chapter of St. John, which had been quoted by Tunstal (*o.c.,* pp. 19v ff.). See Migne, *PG,* vol. lxxiii, cols. 559 ff. and 602 f.

p. 120, 30. *Theophilactus, super Ioannem 6.* See Migne, *PG,* vol. cxxiii, cols. 1282 ff. It contains a denial of mere *figuratio* which is almost *verbatim* the same as that quoted in 133, 25 ff. (see the respective note, below): col. 1307.

p. 120, 30f. *Ambrosius, li. 6 De Sacramentis, ca. primo.* See Migne, *PL,* vol. xvi, cols. 453 ff. It is probable that Kennedy had especially the last sentence in mind: "*Quia idem Dominus noster Jesus Christus consors est et divinitatis et corporis, et tu qui accipis carnem divinae ejus substantiae in illo participaris alimento*" (col. 455).

p. 120, 31. *Gregorius, super Ioannem ca. 6.* Since Gregory the Great has left no commentary on the fourth gospel, the F reading is presumably correct. See Migne, *PL,* vol. lxxv, cols. 765 ff. The sixth chapter of St. John is quoted in col. 771, but its context is not particularly clear.

p. 120, 31f. *Ciprianus, super Exposicione Oracionis Dominice.* See Migne, *PL,* vol. iv, cols. 519 ff. Kennedy will have thought of clauses like the following: "*manifestum est eos vivere qui corpus ejus attingunt et Eucharistiam jure communicationis accipiunt*" (cols. 531 f.). Cp. Tunstal, *o.c.,* pp. 60v f.

p. 120, 32. *Origenis, Homilia 7 super Numeros.* See Migne, *PG,* vol. xii, cols. 611 ff. Fisher (*De Veritate, prooemium quarti libri, trecenarivs primvs*) quotes from it at some length (col. 613).

p. 120, 32f. *Ireneus, li. 5 Aduersus Hereses.* See Migne, *PG,* vol. vii, cols. 1117 ff. Also quoted by Fisher (*l.c.*) and Tunstal (*o.c.,* p. 59r).

p. 121, 5. *vas.* F reading supported by numerous other instances.

diuers. Last two letters cropped with the margin.

p. 121, 7. *Marye Magdalene.* Cp. lines 14 and 17 and 122, 17. The use of the definite article would presumably depend on the extent to which *Magdalene* was felt to be a qualifying adjective, as in *þe concell Nicene.* Unlike F and B, A also prefers to speak of *the counsall of Nece.*

disdanit. i.e. 'regarded with disdain'.

p. 121, 9. *with ʒow.* F reading supported by Vulg. *me autem non semper habetis.*

p. 121, 15. *þe same selffe ... quhilk ... and þat quhilk.* The F reading is a not uncommon MSc confusion of comparison of equality and inequality and may well be authentic.

p. 121, 26–28. The infinitive *cleith* instead of *be clede with* (as in line 30; 122, 8; 128, 15, 19 and 29) suggests that the additional words in A are a scribal interpolation.

p. 121, 29. *luffis.* Perhaps indicative of phonetic approximation of /i/ and /ü/.

p. 121, 30. F *agane.* Supported by Vulg. *rursum circumdabor pelle mea.*

188

p. 122, 1. *Treulye.* This fits better in the context than F *trewþt it is*, 'true enough', and the use of the thorn in that position is exceptional. It would appear that a small *l* had been mistaken for the last stroke of *w* and that the common symbol for scribal *þ* and *y* had further misled the (a) copyist of F.

p. 122, 3. *efter diuerse respeckis.* i.e. 'from different points of view'. *Efter* here represents Latin *secundum*, as in *efter þis maner* (cp. *one þis maner*, Lat. *hoc modo*).

p. 122, 9. *subieckit.* Omission of the additional F text probably connected with the insertion of 121, 26–28.

p. 122, 10. *þat.* F *Than* corresponds to *quhen* (line 7) and is a better parallel to *efter þat maner* in the preceding sentence.

p. 122, 12. *nochtþe lese.* The context requires 'although', i.e. F *nocht the les þat*, but *þat* was frequently omitted in MSc conjunctional groups.

p. 122, 14f. *Sua in lik maner þat albeit.* Probably inverted order of the last two words. It is difficult to suppose that a copyist would thus alter an original *Sua albeit* (F). Tautological *Sua in lik maner* is not abnormal.

p. 122, 16. *hauand.* i.e. 'as if it had'.

p. 122, 19ff. Cp. 140, 27ff. and Smith, *Confutation*, pp. 105v ff.

p. 122, 25. *artikil.* F reading supported by 123, 9 and 140, 31.

p. 122, 26f. *as ar al þe artikles of our beleif.* Cp. Smith, *Confutation*, p. 60v: "*Are not lyke wyse al the articles of our faith against both reason and natural operation?*" It is clear from the context that both Smith and Kennedy mean 'beyond' rather than 'against' human reason; cp. the note to 125, 8.

p. 122, 28. *vordes.* The plural form may be explained as comprising the two different 'words' mentioned in the next lines.

almychty. F. reading supported by 123, 21; 127, 5 and 8; 131, 16; 146, 23.

p. 123, 2f. *þe same selff bodye in substance.* But with a different mode of existence. In its thirteenth session, October 1551, the Council of Trent had expressed it as follows: "*Neque enim haec inter se pugnant, ut ipse Salvator noster semper ad dextram Patris in coelis assideat iuxta modum exsistendi naturalem, et ut multis nihilominus aliis in locis sacramentaliter praesens sua substantia nobis adsit, ea exsistendi ratione, quam etsi verbis exprimere vix possumus, possibilem tamen esse Deo cogitatione per fidem illustrata assequi possumus et constantissime credere debemus*" (Mansi, vol. xxxiii, col. 80). Kennedy does not speak of a 'sacramental (mode of) existence' as distinct from a 'natural' one. Instead of proving the possibility (or non-impossibility) of a sacramental but real presence in the Eucharist simultaneous with Christ's natural presence in heaven, Kennedy argues from Scripture that Christ's glorified body is governed by different laws from those governing an ordinary human body. It has *the propirteis and qualiteis of ane spreit* and is present in the Eucharist *be ane supernatural maner*. Also cp. Fisher (*De Veritate*, lib. v, cap. xxvi): "*Nam iuxta substantiam idem corpus est, at iuxta modum existendi non idem. Neque enim dimensiue est et visibiliter in Eucharistia, sicut erat in cruce aut sicut iam est in coelo, sed spiritualiter et inuisibiliter.*"

p. 123, 3. *vertue.* Reading supported by 127, 18.

p. 123, 5f. *quhat phrais and maner of spekynge menis þir vordes.* A contamination of *quhat menis þir vordes* (9f.) and *quhat maner of spekynge is þis*, but no exceptional use of either *phrais* or *maner of spekynge* (cp. 124, 8; 141, 11; 162, 18). The confusion of the two constructions may have been Kennedy's own.

p. 123, 11f. *power ... power.* Probably haplography in F.

p. 123, 12. *to.* F reading supported by what must have been the original structure of the sentence: 'it follows much better (in accordance with the doctrine of the church) that he is not confined to one place ...., than that he is ...' The correlation *better ... nor* (*nocht*, line 15) apparently escaped the copyist's attention.

p. 123, 15. *astrickit.* F reading required by parallelism.

p. 123, 19f. *astrickand ... to remane.* i.e. 'compelling ... to remain'.

p. 123, 21 f. *nocht … but also.* F reading supported by contrastive pattern. Note the exceptional spelling *but* instead of *bot.*

p. 123, 22. *expresse.* Note the absence of adverbial *-ly.*

p. 123, 25. *epistle.* F reading a scribal slip.

p. 123, 26. *Iesus our saluiour.* F reading supported by all other instances in Kennedy's tracts.

p. 123, 26 ff. Cp. Smith, *Confutation*, p. 9 v: "*paule saw hym bodily vpon earth after his ascension (as he testifieth), and by that sight he proued that he was risen againe bodily from death to lyf, which he could not haue done, yf that seinge of hym had bene but a spiritual vision.*"

p. 123, 31. *as did the laif of þe apostlis.* i.e. with his true body, as the other apostles had seen him before his ascension.

p. 123, 32. *it vas.* F reading makes no sense in the context.

resurreccione. The qualification *corporall* is essential to the meaning.

p. 124, 2 f. *tretaris … to be.* It would appear that both MSS are corrupt here. The construction of 123, 19 f. suggests that the original reading was either *all sik astrictaris* or *all sik as strictis* (with an aphetic verbal form).

p. 124, 7. *to.* F reading supported by preceding *sik.*

p. 124, 17. *Psalm. 89.* Kennedy refers to St. Augustine's commentary *one the 89. psalme* in 132, 16, where he actually quotes from that on psalm 98 (see respective note). In the present instance the quotation is from *Enarr. in Ps. 33* (Migne, *PL*, vol. xxxvi, col. 306). The passage is paraphrased by Smith (*Confutation*, p. 52 r) and quoted by both Fisher (*De Veritate*, lib. i, cap. viii) and Tunstal (*o.c.*, p. 99 r). In the latter's reading: "*… manibus aliorum potest portari homo, manibus suis nemo portatur. … in Christo autem inuenimus. Ferebatur enim Christus in manibus suis, quando commendans ipsum corpus suum ait, Hoc est corpus meum.*" Note the freedom of Kennedy's rendering, which appears to be based on Smith's paraphrase rather than the Latin.

p. 124, 18. *bot Iesus Christ.* F reading suggested by Smith's *bare his own body (l.c.).*

p. 124, 22. *in ane tyme.* F reading supported by other instances (e.g. line 15 and 15, 12); also cp. 125, 29 (A *in*).

in ane other place. If the rendering is equally free as that of the preceding quotation, the reference may be to *Epist. clxxxvii (ad Dardanum)*, where St. Augustine says: "*Noli itaque dubitare ibi nunc esse hominem Christum Jesum unde venturus est …. nec aliunde quam inde venturus est ad vivos mortuosque judicandos*" (Migne, *PL*, vol. xxxiii, col. 835). This letter is actually discussed in Fisher's *De Veritate*, lib. v, cap. xxxii.

p. 124, 29. *to. 5.* Presumably a particular edition used by Kennedy or a copyist to check the text.

p. 124, 30. *Hom. 50 ad Populum Antiochenum.* In Migne *Homilia 2 ad Populum Antiochenum, De Avaritia* (*PG*, vol. xlix, col. 46).

p. 124, 30 ff. F reading supported by Smith, *Confutation*, pp. 43 r f.: "*Helias the prophete ascendyng vp lefte his mantel vnto his disciple, but the sone of god ascending vp in to heauen hath lefte vnto vs his oune flesh. As for helias leauing his mantel vnto his disciple, lefte it from him selfe, but our sauiour christ hath both left his fleash with vs, and also taken it with hymselfe in his ascension*" (reference to *Hom. 2 ad Antiochenum populum*). It would appear that the (a) copyist of the A text checked the quotation and made a more literal translation.

p. 125, 6. *dispar and … be in doute.* The juxtaposition shows that *dispare* in 126, 22 f. has the meaning 'disbelieve'.

p. 125, 8. *Nochtþeles þat.* If, as usual, the F reading is correct, the new sentence must begin here rather than with *Is it nocht* in the next line.

agane þe ordour of nature. Represents scholastic *praeter (contra) ordinem naturae* or *praeter naturam.* Elsewhere Kennedy has *abone* instead of *agane;* cp. 126, 2 (Latin *praeter naturam*) with 135, 23.

p. 125, 14. *saiand … saynge.* F reading presumably original; cp. the similarly structured sentence in 122, 29 ff.

p. 125, 18. *to luke for þe ordre of nature.* i.e. to suppose that divine things are governed by the same laws as human things.

190

p. 125, 19ff. Among the reasons why Christ should have instituted the Eucharist as explained by him, Smith mentions "*that man mygt* [sic.] *merite beleuing against his senses iudgementes, which hath no merite (as Saynt Gregorie sayeth) when he hath prouffe of the thinge*" (*Confutation*, p. 57v.) There is nothing in the A text that might not be Kennedy's own (cp. e.g. the absolute construction *durris and vindokkis beand closit* with 129, 8 and 22f.). The passage may have been omitted in F because *faith hes na merit* was considered misleading.

Hom. super Ioannem, 20 cap. i.e. on the 20th chapter of the fourth gospel. Smith *(l.c.)* refers to *Hom. 28 in Evang.;* in Migne it is *Hom. xxvi in Evangelia (PL*, vol. lxxvi, col. 1197). The Latin text shows what is translation and what is not: "*Prima lectionis hujus evangelicae quaestio animum pulsat, quomodo post resurrectionem corpus dominicum verum fuit, quod clausis januis ad discipulos ingredi potuit. Sed sciendum nobis est quod divina operatio si ratione comprehenditur, non est admirabilis; nec fides habet meritum, cui humana ratio praebet experimentum. Sed haec ipsa nostri Redemptoris opera, quae ex semetipsis comprehendi nequaquam possunt, ex alia ejus operatione pensanda sunt, ut rebus mirabilibus fidem praebeant facta mirabiliora. Illud enim corpus Domini intravit ad discipulos januis clausis, quod videlicet ad humanos oculos per nativitatem suam clauso exiit utero Virginis.*"

p. 125, 23f. *mervalus* and *miracle. vark* omitted; cp. preceding line.

p. 125, 24. *for.* i.e. *quhair;* see p. 84, above.

p. 125, 26. *considderit and wyit be.* Same use of *be* as in 127, 3f. *(mesure … be); 172, 40 (knawin and tryit be)* and 154, 21–23 *(ane grit difference … to do … be to do).* It indicates comparison.

p. 125, 33. *S. Ambrouse.* viz. *Liber de Mysteriis,* cap. ix (Migne, *PL*, vol. xvi, col. 407). Smith gives two different translations (*Confutation*, pp. 37r and 63r), the latter of which is copied by Kennedy: "*Why doest thou seake here yn the sacrament the ordre of nature yn christes body, seyng Christ our savyour was borne of the vyrgen against the ordre of nature?*" – Cp. *Quhy dois þow seik* with *Quhy diffidis þow* (127, 20).

p. 126, 13. *quhat blindnes, quhat ignorance, fure and vodnes.* F reading supported by *Compendius Tractiue (Wodrow Misc.,* p. 124): "*Quhat blindnes, quhat ignorance, quhat furie and wodnes.*" Smith has similar exclamations: "*What madnes is it*" (*Confutation*, p. 100v); "*What is this, yf it be not playne blyndnes and ignoraunce*" (p. 159r).

p. 126, 22. *theme.* Obviously not the Jews; F *men* avoids the ambiguity.

p. 126, 26. *bot.* i.e. *bot þat,* as in F.

p. 126, 29. *vse.* Practically equivalent to 'live'.

p. 127, 12. *vitnes.* F *ws* probably represents an abbreviated form of the same word.

p. 127, 14ff. Cp. "*Si Moyses potuit vertere virgam in serpentem et iterum serpentem in virgam commutare, quare non valebit sacerdos verbo Domini panem et vinum in Christi corpus et sanguinem permutare?*" (Bunderius, *Detectio Nugarum Lutheri,* 1551, p. 22v). It is not at all necessary, however, that this was Kennedy's source.

p. 127, 20–26. A copyist might object to this passage in as far as, speaking of an entirely different kind of change, it is rather confusing than illustrative. As an interpolation it would be a very successful imitation of Kennedy's style, but an unfortunate example.

p. 127, 27. *is.* Omission in F can only be a scribal slip.

p. 127, 30. *als.* F reading required by context; *þe sammyne* may represent an attempt of a subsequent copyist to correct the resulting anomaly.

p. 127, 33f. *vnit to his godhede in ane persone.* Cp. 124, 10 and 125, 13. But 128, 6 supports the F reading in this instance.

p. 128, 1–4. Cp. "*Nos autem, etsi non dicamus panem continere corpus, aut in pane corpus esse, tamen asserimus ipsum corpus et sanguinem esse sub speciebus panis et vini*" (Fisher, *De Veritate,* lib. ii, cap. xiii). Kennedy's own mode of expression in 129, 19 and 132, 30 might further appear to support the F reading. In this case, however, Kennedy merely gives his adversaries' supposed view of the real presence by way of introduction to a more accurate statement and defence of catholic teaching. The A reading appears to echo a similar sentence of Smith's: "*where it appeareth straunge, that Christe beynge of infinite magnitude or greatnes, can be, and* *is conteyned in so small a rowme or place, as is the hoste, and the leste sensible parte therof, in dede yf Christes body were sayde to be here in the sacrament of the aulter naturally, and locally, as occupyenge a place, lyke as mortal and common bodyes do, it were not onely straunge and wonderfull, but also incredible and impossible.*" Smith goes on to explain that Christ is present "*supernaturally and sacramentally, vnder the visible fourme of breade*" (*The Assertion and Defence of the Sacramente of the Aulter*, London, 1546, pp. 239v f.).

p. 128, 7. F reading supported by context; cp. 129, 1.

p. 128, 10 ff. *ane vayne inuentit thinge be Imaginacione ... of man.* The rest of the sentence suggests that here, too, F has the authentic reading. *To onderstand þe sammyne* begins with a capital and is preceded by a double dot in A, which indicates the beginning of a new sentence. In F, on the other hand, the new sentence begins with *First*, which gives a not uncommon pattern to the preceding sentence (cp. e.g. 115, 14 ff.).

p. 128, 13. *hauand.* Concessive.

p. 128, 16. *quhow.* Clearly preferable to F *þow.*

p. 128, 17. *savine ane naturall body.* Reading supported by Vulg. *seminatur corpus animale, surget corpus spiritale (1 Cor. 15, 44).* F *is* may represent a scribal slip for *as.*

p. 128, 18. *nocht.* F *ar* suggests haplography: *... spirituall bodyis.* [*He sayis nocht þat our bodyis*] *ar changet In spiritis (God forbeid þat), bot þat our bodyis salbe claid than with spirituall giftis and qualiteis.* This would certainly mean an improvement of the latter part of the sentence in A.

p. 128, 24. *to.* F reading supported by next line.

p. 128, 30. *as the scriptour plainly techis vs.* Kennedy is probably thinking of *Heb.* 1, 4 ff.

p. 129, 2. *vsit and communicat.* Cp. *ʒe quha vsis þe mess* (159, 22).

p. 129, 3. *chengene, alteracione, nor is diuidit.* Probably an interpolation of a copyist who did not first read the entire sentence.

p. 129, 5. *impassible, occupeand na place therin.* In scholastic parlance, Christ's body is really present in the Eucharist, though not *per modum quanti* but *per modum substantiae,* i.e. with its quantity *(hauand flesche, bluide and bonis)* but without *contactus quantitatis (impassible; clede with spirituall giftes and qualiteis).* This implies that there is no local relationship between the different parts of Christ's body *(occupeand na place therin;* not so much *contenit in sa litle ane quantite of bread and vyne* as *contenit onder þe formes of breade and vyne).* Also see note to 132, 3.

p. 129, 10. *mair nor.* Cp. *mair nor quhen* (line 3) and *mair then quhen* (line 21).

p. 129, 16. See *Luc.* 24, 39.

p. 129, 21. F *mair than nor quhan.* Not exceptional in MSc.

p. 129, 23. *is as sufficient.* F reading clearly required.

þe ane as the other. Haplography.

p. 129, 26. *faith.* Scribal slip (*f* and *s* as well as *t* and *c* were often barely distinguishable and an excrescent *t* was freely added to final *th,* whilst *cht* often became *ch*).

p. 129, 31. *quhat is the cause.* Kennedy does not here inquire into the nature of Christ's presence, which is the immediate cause of his invisibility, but into the reason why Christ should have chosen this particular mode of presence.

p. 129, 31 f. F *we see ... and felis.* Normal MSc syntax. The F reading may be considered to be supported by the frequent combination *sene, felit and grapit* (cp. 130, 11 f., 18, 20 and 28).

p. 130, 3 f. *Damascen, Theophilactus, and others of the anciant fathers.* Cp. Smith: "*... least we shold abhorre to drinke it, yf it did appeare bloud, as S. Damascene, Theophilacte, Euthymius, and many other learned men do wytnesse*" (*Confutation,* p. 57v). For Damascene he refers to *Lib. 4, ca. 14* (i.e. *De Fide Orthodoxa,* see Migne, *PG,* vol. xciv, cols. 1142 f.), for Theophilact to *in Marci 14* (i.e. *Enarr. in Evangelium Marci, cap. xiv,* see Migne, *PG,* vol. cxxiii, col. 650), whilst he gives no reference to the writings of Euthymius or the *many other learned men.* That Kennedy actually used Damascene and Theophilact for lines 5–14 is suggested by the following passages: "*Panis porro vinumque adhibentur quia, cum Deo explorata sit imbecillitas humana, quae ut plurimum ea aversetur quae usu minime trita sunt, hinc fit ut pro solita sua erga nos* *indulgentia per ea quae naturae familiaria sunt res natura sublimiores efficiat. ... quia hominum consuetudo fert ut panem edant vinumque et aquam bibant, idcirco conjuncta cum illis sua divinitate haec corpus et sanguinem suum fecit, uti per usitata et naturae consentanea assurgamus ad ea quae supra naturam sunt"* (Damascene, *l.c.*). *"O homo, propter nostram infirmitatem istud fit. Quia enim panis quidem et vinum ex his sunt quibus assuevimus, ea non abhorremus: sanguinem vero propositum et carnem videntes non ferremus, sed abhorreremus; idcirco misericors Deus nostrae infirmitati condescendens, speciem quidem panis et vini servat, in virtutem autem carnis et sanguinis transelementat"* (Theophilact, *l.c.*).

p. 130, 5–14. F reading clearly corrupt in latter half of the passage. The general structure of the A reading is clear enough: *Iesus Christ ... conuertit and chengit ... and is resauit and remanis.* Its line of thought may be paraphrased as follows. Christ wished to be present with his followers in a manner which would symbolize that he is their spiritual sustenance. They would have been horrified at the thought of having to eat a visible human body; in that supposition, moreover, Christ would cease to exist. In order that they should not be deprived of his salutary presence he therefore chose to be with them in a way which would not interfere with his continued presence in heaven and in which he could be their spiritual sustenance without any suggestion of cannibalism. But it necessarily involved the impossibility of feeling or seeing his presence, except by faith. – The idea of Christ as spiritual nourishment which is not digested in the body of the receiver, is principally expressed in the word *remanis* and may, as far as Kennedy is concerned, derive from Fisher's *De Veritate* (e.g. lib. ii, cap. xxx and lib. v, cap. xxvii), which devotes much space and energy to the accusation of supposed cannibalism.

p. 130, 11. *quhilkis ar nocht necessar to.* i.e. 'which need not'.

p. 130, 12f. *(nocht ...) bot onely be faith in þe forme and quantite of bread and vyne.* Reading supported by contrastive arrangement. In the context, *quantite* fits much better than *qualite* as a qualification of *forme*. Also cp. Fisher, quoting St. Augustine: *"Nihil vtique praeter similitudinem panis aut cernitur aut gustatur: veruntamen sub illa forma panis quiddam aliud inuisibiliter intelligitur (De Veritate,* lib. v, cap. xxvi).

p. 130, 21. F *declarand.* Scribal slip.

p. 130, 22. *to make his body.* F reading supported by *hauand ane immortal ... body.*

insensible. i.e. not perceptible to the human senses; cp. lines 24f.

hauand. i.e. 'now that he has'.

p. 130, 23. F *mortall.* Scribal slip.

p. 130, 24f. *vithout persauynge of there senses and vittis.* F reading supported by line 22.

p. 130, 25. *hauand.* i.e. 'when he had'.

p. 130, 26. *grosse gospellaris.* Cp. the similar alliteration in *scrupulows scripturaris* (159, 33).

p. 130, 28. *Quhy dar.* F reading supported by *speir ane questione; or nocht* would naturally be omitted after the alteration.

p. 131, 2. *na vay to knaw.* i.e. 'no way of knowing'.

p. 131, 6. *techis vs ane man to haue.* Cp. 130, 30 and 131, 3.

p. 131, 13f. *satifyet and ... at þe rest of our conscience.* Cp. *satifeit in conscience* (112, 2f), which may be considered to support the F reading.

p. 131, 14. *pertenand til.* Preposition supported by *to* or *til* in all other instances.

p. 131, 17. *Chrisostome.* Quotation from *Hom. 82 in Math.* (see Migne, *PG*, vol. lviii, col. 743). Kennedy's translation is copied from Smith (*Confutation*, pp. 67r f.): *"Let vs beleue god in euery thing, and not say against hym, yea althoughe the thing that he sayeth doth appeare an inconuenience both vnto our senses, thought, and vnderstandyng, and doth also excede our sense, capacyte, and reason. Let vs, I besech yow, beleue his wordes in al thinges, but chyefely in the sacramentes, not loking only vpon those thinges which lye before vs, but considering also his woordes. For by his wordes we can not be disceaued, but our senses are moost easy to be disceaued. His wordes can not be false, our senses are very often tymes disceaued. Wherefore seing christ hath sayed: This is my body, let vs nothing doubte therof, but beleue, and perceaue it wyth the eies of our vnderstandyng. Hyther to this holy doctour."*

p. 131, 18. *in God euery thynge.* F reading supported by Smith, *l.c.*

agane saynge. F reading supported by Smith, *l.c.*

p. 131, 19. *althouch the thynge þat he say nocht appere and be.* F reading supported by Smith, *l.c.* Note that *inconuenient* was freely used as a noun in MSc.

p. 131, 20. *our senses, boith thouch and onder-. capacite and resone:* lat vs I bese between *senses* and *boith*, but erased by the copyist when he noticed that he had continued with the text following upon the second *senses*. *onder[standing]* is not completed on the new page.

Smith's translation is based on a Latin text different from that in Migne but used by Tunstal (*o.c.*, p. 71r). Smith's *both vnto our senses, thought, and vnderstandyng* corresponds to *sensui et cognitioni*. The copyist of A did not realize that *thouch* and *onderstanding* formed appositional synonyms and he accordingly moved *boith* to a position where it appeared to make better sense.

p. 131, 20 f. *senses capacite and reasone.* Cp. *et sensum et rationem nostram* (Tunstal, *l.c.*). Smith's printed text has a comma after *sense.* The form A *senses* is a genitive plural.

p. 131, 21. *lat vs, I beseik ȝow, beleif in his vorde in al thingis.* F reading supported by Smith, *l.c.* Cp. Tunstal, *l.c.*: "*quaeso ipsius uerbum quod in omnibus faciamus*". For different Latin renderings, see Fisher, *De Veritate*, lib. i, cap. xxv; lib. iv, cap. xxvii; and the *Prooemium Tertii Libri.*

p. 131, 22. *and cheifly in the sacrament of þe altare.* F reading supported by Smith, *l.c.*, with the exception of the singular form *sacrament.* Cp. Tunstal, *l.c.*, "*et praecipue in mysteriis*".

p. 131, 24. *dissauit.* Haplography. For syntax of F, cp. 130, 11.

p. 131, 25. *begilit and.* Probably a scribal interpolation.

p. 131, 28. *1100 and more ȝeres sene.* Cp. 107, 9 f.

p. 132, 2. *of.* F reading suggests haplography in A.

p. 132, 3. *ane atome.* The F reading may have been occasioned by Antonio di Adamo's *Anatomie de la messe et du missel* (French editions in 1555 and 1561). *Atome* must be the correct reading. Cp. Fisher, *De Veritate*, lib. ii, cap. xiii: [Oecol.] "*Eo enim tandem sermo ducet, vt et in atomo panis, si dari posset, integrum poneretis corpus*". After defining the word 'atom', Fisher answers as follows: "*Sed haec apud eos qui in scholis exercitati sunt habentur dilucida, neque repugnantiae quicquam infert vt corpus Christi totum sacramentali modo sit sub minima panis specie, non tamen sub puncto atomo*". He has similar statements elsewhere, as in lib. v, cap. xxviii: "*Nam sicut anima propter eius spiritualitatem est tota in qualibet parte corporis quod animatur ab ea, ita Christi corpus totum est sub quauis particula speciei panis. At istud ipse non capis.*"

p. 132, 7. *abone.* Or *aboue;* no distinctive mark in the MS.

p. 132, 9. *to be* omitted after *sacrament.*

p. 132, 11. *quha* or *quhilkis* omitted after *others.* F reading probably better in the other details where the two MSS differ.

p. 132, 15. *S. Augustine.* Quotation from *Enarr.* in *Ps. 98* (see Migne, *PL*, vol. xxxvii, col. 1264). Smith's translation is different from Kennedy's (*Confutation*, pp. 145v f.). Fisher deals with it at some length (*De Veritate*, lib. v, cap. xxvi); a comparison with his Latin text illustrates Kennedy's simplification. "*Suscepit enim de terra terram, quia caro de terra est, et de carne Mariae carnem accepit. Et quia in ipsa carne hic ambulauit, et ipsam carnem nobis manducandam ad salutem dedit. Nemo autem illam carnem manducat nisi prius adorauerit; inuentum est quemadmodum adoretur tale scabellum pedum Domini, et non solum non peccemus adorando, sed peccemus non adorando.*"

p. 132, 16 ff. The F reading of lines 20 f. is clearly supported by the Latin as well as by 133, 2 and 179, 17, which suggests that it also gives the better text for 16–18.

one the 89. psalme. Scribal error for *98;* see above.

p. 132, 25 ff. Same passage in 179, 9 ff.

p. 132, 27. *formes.* Reading supported by 179, 12.

p. 132, 28–30. *nor ȝit ... conteint.* F reading supported by 179, 14. Interpolation probably introduced to complete parallelism with 133, 3 f. Also cp. Fisher, *De Veritate*, lib. iii, cap. v: "*Neque enim adoramus ipsam externam speciem panis et vini, sed Christum sub vtriusque specie.*"

194

p. 132, 31. *faith and onderstandyng.* Reading supported by 179, 14f.

p. 133, 2. *gef.* Reading supported by 179, 17.

p. 133, 4. *they saw be faith vnite.* F reading supported by 179, 19.

p. 133, 6. *It is nocht onknavin to me quhow þair is sum.* This need not necessarily imply that Kennedy was familiar with contemporary protestant literature. Oecolampadius' appeal to these words, together with Fisher's answer, is to be found in the same chapter of the *De Veritate* from which St. Augustine's previous words have been quoted. And it is precisely on this point that, in the *Compendius Tractiue*, he refers his readers to Fisher's work (*Wodrow Misc.*, pp. 167f., with St. Augustine's commentary on psalm 98 expressly mentioned).

p. 133, 6f. *the vordes of S. Augustine.* "*Non hoc corpus quod uidetis manducaturi estis, et bibituri illum sanguinem quem fusuri sunt qui me crucifigent*" (*l.c.*).

p. 133, 10. F *we newir eate ... nor drink.* Absence of sibilant suffix proves omission of *sal.*

p. 133, 10–13. Cp. Fisher, *l.c.*: "*Nam iuxta substantiam idem corpus est, at iuxta modum existendi non idem: Neque dimensiue est et visibiliter in Eucharistia, sicut erat in cruce aut sicut iam est in coelo, sed spiritualiter et inuisibiliter.*"

p. 133, 14. *þe true menynge.* Definite article obviously preferable.

p. 133, 14f. *þe hail sentence precedand and efter folovand.* i.e. as explained by Fisher.

p. 133, 17. *Chrisostome.* Same quotation in 156, 13ff. and in the *Oratioune* (Laing, *Works*, vi, p. 163), with reference to *Hom. 48 in Ioannem* in both cases. In Migne it may be found in *Hom. 1 de Proditione Iudae* (*PG*, vol. xlix, col. 380). Kennedy's translation is copied from Smith, *Confutation*, p. 51v: "*It is not man that maketh our lordes body and bloud of the thinges, set furth vpon the table to be consecrated, but it is Christ, that was crucified for vs. The wordes are pronounced of the priest, and the thinges (bread and wyne) are consecrated by gods pouer and grace; he sayed: This is my body, Hoc verbo proposita consecrantur, the bread and wyne, which are set furth, be consecrated by this word*" (reference to *Hom. 45 in Ioannem*). For a corresponding Latin text, different from that in Migne, see Fisher, *De Veritate*, Prooemium Quarti Libri, trecenarius secundus.

ane man. Article in both MSS; cp. 156, 14.

p. 133, 18. *thynge.* Singular form in both MSS.

p. 133, 19. *crucifyet.* F reading supported by Smith, *l.c.*, and 156, 15.

Thir. Demonstrative pronoun in both MSS; cp. 156, 16.

p. 133, 20. *ane preist.* F reading supported by Smith, *l.c.*, and 156, 16.

þe breade and vyne. Note that Kennedy substitutes Smith's explanation for his translation of *proposita.*

Goddes vord. F *þis* presupposes that *vord* is authentic.

Damascene. Quotation from *De Fide Orthodoxa*, lib. iv, cap. xiii (see Migne, *PG*, vol. xciv, cols. 1147ff.). Kennedy's translation is copied from Smith's *Confutation*, p. 51r: "*The bread, and wyne are not a figure of the body and bloud of christ (god forbidde that) but our lordes body it selfe, ioyned vnto the godhead, our lord hymself sayng: This is my bodye, not a figure of my bodye, but my bodye.*"

p. 133, 21. *vritis.* MS *vrtis.*

p. 133, 22. *Christis bodye and bloude.* Original reading presumably as in Smith, *l.c.*

it is made. F reading supported by Smith, *l.c.*

p. 133, 23. *to.* F reading supported by Smith, *l.c.*

p. 133, 23f. *vorkand be his vord ... pronuncit be þe preiste.* F reading supported by Smith, *l.c.*

p. 133, 24. *Theophilact.* Quotation from *Enarr. in Evangelium Marci, cap. xiv* (see Migne, *PG*, vol. cxxiii, col. 650. Kennedy's translation is almost certainly altered from Smith's *Confutation*, p. 121r: "*For the bread is not a figure and a certen exemplar of our lordes bodye, but it is chaunded* [sic.] *in to the selfe same bodie of christ. For oure lord sayeth, the bread which I wil gyue is my flesh. He sayed not, it is a figure of my flesh, but it is my flesh.*"

vritand. F reading supported by lines 17, 21, 28 and 30.

p. 133, 27. *he said nocht: it is a figure of my flesche.* Reading supported by Smith, *l.c.*, but words omitted through repetition of *flesche*.

S. Ambrouse. Quotation from *De Sacramentis*, lib. iv, cap. iv (see Migne, *PL*, vol. xvi, col. 439). Kennedy's translation is copied from Smith's *Confutation*, p. 51r; "*Afore it be consecrated, it is bread, but after christes wordes are come vnto it, it is christes body.*" – Note that the passages from Chrysostom, Damascene and Ambrose occur together in Smith, but in reversed order.

p. 133, 28. *in this maner.* F reading supported by lines 17, 21, 24 and 30, and numerous other instances.

p. 133, 28 f. *Affore þat ... efter þat. þat a*dded both times in both MSS; cp. e.g. 113, 11 and 114, 24.

p. 133, 29. *till it.* F reading supported by *Oratioune* (Laing, *Works*, vi, p. 163).

Cipriane. Latin text, without reference, in Fisher's *De Veritate, Prooemium secundi libri: Panis iste, quem Dominus discipulis porrigebat, non effigie sed natura mutatus, omnipotentia verbi factus est caro.* Smith (*Confutation*, p. 94v) refers to *de coena dom.*, but the passage does not occur in Migne, *PL*, vol. iv, cols. 925 ff. Kennedy's translation, repeated in the *Oratioune* (Laing, *Works*, vi, p. 163), appears to be copied from Smith: *The bread, which our lord gaue vnto his disciples, not chaunged in forme, but in nature by the almyghty power of the worde is made flesh. (l.c.).*

p. 133, 30. *The breade.* F reading supported by *Oratioune, l.c.*

p. 133, 31. *efter.* F reading supported by *Oratioune, l.c.*

þe nature. F reading supported by *Oratioune, l.c.*

p. 133, 31 f. *be the almychty power of the vorde is made flesche.* F reading supported by *Oratioune, l.c.*

p. 134, 4 f. *the transsubstanciacione and chaungene of the substance.* In 1551 the Council of Trent had called transubstantiation a convenient and most apt term to express the change of the substance of bread and wine into Christ's body and blood (*Sessio xiii, cap. iv and canon 2;* see Mansi, vol. xxxiii, cols. 80 ff.). For Kennedy, the real presence of Christ in the Eucharist means that the bread and wine cease to be bread and wine and this *chaungene of the substance* is synonymous with *transsubstanciacione*. His answer to the objection that catholic teaching on the real presence of Christ in the Eucharist was of comparatively recent origin is, therefore, to produce quotations from the fathers which teach or imply a change of the bread and to conclude that they held transubstantiation. The following extract from Knox's *Apology for the Protestants in Prison in Paris* illustrates the necessity of clarification on the point: "*And thair Transsubstantiatioun, that horribill ydoll thair god of bread, was be tirannie establissit, first in the dayis of Pope Nycolas the Secund (sum say the Third), who, in the Consall of Lateran, compellit Berengarius to recant, and schamefullie to abrenunce his former doctrine of the Lordis Supper (by thame callit the Sacrament of the Altar), and to affirme that blasphemous and dampnabill errour of Transsubstantiation, confessing that that Consall did teache him, that efter the wordis whilk thai call of consecratioun, thair resteth na mair bread and wyne, but that Chrystis verie bodie and blude is thair not onlie sacramentallie, but also sensibillie (that is to say, that it may be sene and felt, brokin and eattin with the handis and teith of the preistis). This blasphemous doctrine was unknawn to the Primative Kirk, yea, to the auncient wrytteris and fatheris, as thair doctrine and wryttingis do witnes*" (Laing, *Works*, iv, pp. 314 f.). Cp. Calvin's *Institutio*, lib. iv, cap. xvii, n. 12.

p. 134, 6. *this is and euer hes bene.* Apparently a contamination of *this is the doctrine of the fathers* and *this hes bene the doctrine of the kirk*. Cp. 135, 32 f.

p. 134, 7. *plaine.* F *planlye* and *manifestlye* clearly preferable.

p. 134, 8. *þe sicht of.* Cp. the *Compendius Tractiue:* "*Be the contrar, wyll thou consider the jugement and doctryne of all sic factius and curius men, as disdanis ... and thow sall easilie persaue, that not allanerlie ar thay repugnant...*" (*Wodrow Misc.*, pp. 156 f.), which may be considered to support the F reading.

p. 134, 11. *his.* Clearly better than F *þir*.

p. 134, 11–25. With this section compare the remarkably similar passages in Fisher's *De Veritate, Prooemium tertii libri, corroboratio xiii*, and *Praefatio primi libri, tertia ratio*. Kennedy's

196

indebtedness to sentences such as the following, from the latter source, seems obvious: "*Lutherus constanter docet in Eucharistia verum Corpus Christi vna cum substantia panis contineri. Oecolampadius aperte negat illic adesse Christi corpus. ... Quicquid enim Lutherus aduersus Oecolampadium affert vt euincat in Eucharistia uerum esse corpus Christi, id (quis non perspicit) ecclesiae partes corroborat? Et rursum, quicquid Oecolampadius profert vt statuat hunc panem haudquaquam esse corpus Christi, mirifice confirmat ecclesiae decretum.*"

p. 134, 13. *reprevis.* Reading supported by context.

p. 134, 20. One leaf missing from F after the page ending with *settis furtht þe reall presence contrar.*

p. 134, 30. Cp. Smith's *Confutation:* "*... the church, agaynst whom hel gates, that is to say, synne and heresie, neuer could nor neuer shal preuaile*" (p. 16v).

p. 134, 34. *þe first hede and part.* Cp. 112, 19 ff.

p. 135, 4. *restes to considder.* Same phrase in similarly structured sentence in 144, 6.

p. 135, 4 ff. Contamination of three sentence patterns: *considder quhidder þe doctrine of the kirk giffis glore; considder quhidder the opinione of Ecolampadius giffis glore as dois the kirk; considder þat Ecolampadius and operis giffis les glore, becaus they expone.* It is not excluded, however, that the text is corrupt.

p. 135, 14. *the sacramentes and figures of þe auld lawe.* Cp.: "*... in the Sacrament we receive Jesus Christ spiritually, as did the fathers of the Old Testament*" (Knox, *The Lord's Supper, called the Sacrament of the Body and Blood of Our Saviour Jesus Christ*, in Laing, *Works*, iii, p. 75).

p. 135, 21. F text resumed at *And þow sall clierlye perceaue.*

p. 135, 22 f. *conforme to his vorde.* Note that Kennedy here presupposes the correctness of his own interpretation of Scripture.

p. 135, 23. *abone.* Or *aboue.*

ordour. F reading supported by lines 29 and 30.

p. 135, 26. *disciples.* Cp. 125, 29 and 129, 7.

p. 135, 28. *abone.* Or *aboue.*

p. 135, 29. *abone.* Or *aboue.*

p. 135, 32. *the godlye doctrine and vonderfull beleif.* The two groups are synonymous, i.e. *beleif* is used in the sense of 'truth believed'.

p. 135, 33 f. *þe mair vonderful ... the maire it is to þe glore of God.* Cp. Fisher, *De Veritate*, lib. iii, cap. iv: "*... sed nec gloriam eius minuit quicquam, imo potius auget, quandoquidem ita credere non solum eius supernaturalem potestatem, verum etiam ineffabilem ipsius amorem erga nos haud mediocriter extollit, nihilque Christo tribuit aut indignum aut a solita sua erga nos benignitate alienum.*"

p. 136, 2 f. *mekil mair profitable to þe resauar.* F reading probably authentic; as in 135, 22 f., the argument presupposes Kennedy's interpretation of Scripture. It also presupposes that God will have chosen the means which are most profitable to mankind. Kennedy's teaching would imply greater profit. Cp. Fisher's *De Veritate*, lib. iii, cap. iv: "*Per istam vtique praesentiam ineffabilem exercetur nostra fides ad meritorum incrementum. Nam fides nisi magna fuerit nihil meretur. ... Christus igitur, vt fidei nostrae periculum faceret, seipsum praesentem inuisibiliter in hoc sacramento praebuit.*"

p. 136, 3. *quha sa euer.* F *quhat sumeuir* must be a scribal slip.

p. 136, 4. *profeit.* The F reading corresponds to Latin *ex parte recipientis ratione fidei ... ex parte ipsius sacramenti ratione praesentiae Christi.* It seems very unlikely that a copyist would thus alter an original A reading.

p. 136, 5–7. *Christis ... inseparatlye ... restis.* Top right hand corner torn off. The reading *restis* is conjectural, but makes good enough sense in A. It is doubtful, however, whether the A reading of the sentence is authentic. In view of 137, 1, F *mekle mair abundance* seems preferable to A *mekil mair aboundantlye*, and parallelism would then require the F reading *far gretar assurite.* The noun *assurite* may have been mistaken for a past participle (with silent final *e*) and the rest of the sentence would then have to be adjusted.

p. 136, 11 ff. F reads as follows: "*þow sall consider þat þar Is greys In þe Receawing of þe*

197

lordis body, lyk as In þe Receawing of þe gifftis of þe haly Gaist. We ar assuret þat the apostolis ressauit þe gift of þe haly Gaist diuers wayis at diuers tymes, mair abundantlye at ane tyme nor ane vthir. For trewlye þe apostolis ressauit þe gift of þe haly Spreit; notheles þar Is na doubt bot þe apostolis ressauit þe gift of þe haly Gaist mair abundantlye eftir þe ascentione of oure salueour be ane visible figure. Sua sum tymes we ar ..." (no punctuation at all in this part of the MS.).

The lucid style of this passage is much more like Kennedy than the A reading and says exactly what the context requires, viz., that there is a difference between a worthy reception of the eucharistic bread and a purely spiritual communion, which may be compared with the way in which the apostles received the Holy Spirit at Pentecost and the way in which they had received Him before.

p. 136, 29–p. 137, 2. F reading presumably authentic.

p. 137, 4. *apperaunce of.* F reading supported by 140, 21 and 142, 14, as well as the second part of the sentence.

p. 137, 10f. *christiane hartis of men.* F reading supported by frequent occurrence of *christiane men/man;* cp. 138, 1.

p. 137, 11f. *Goddes menynge.* F reading supported by numerous instances.

p. 137, 17. *interpretacione.* Singular form supported by context.

p. 137, 19. *fleschly in Iugement.* Cp. 129, 14.

p. 137, 24. *euellis.* Evidently from Latin *evellere*, 'tear out'. F *annoillis* has a mark over the first *i* indicating that it was meant to be *u* ('annul'). Cp. note to 181, 7.

fauour. Context requires *fervour;* cp. 138, 2 (F) and 9f.

p. 137, 27f. F reading supported by following lines; cp. 113, 16 and 114, 24.

p. 137, 28. *Quhow.* MS *qhuow.*

p. 137, 30. *fleschlye.* F reading supported by contrast with *truely* in 138, 3.

p. 137, 31f. *in ane figure ... of the lordis body.* One preposition superfluous. F reading supported by other instances.

p. 138, 1–5. Cp. Smith's *Confutation:* "*Or may we say wel, that he is gyltie of mysse intreating of a kynges oune person, when he doth abuse only his image or picture?*" (p. 32r). As in Kennedy's case, this is said in connection with *1 Cor. 11.*

p. 138, 2. *sterit vp to.* Preposition supported by context; cp. line 10 and 142, 31.

fauour. F reading supported by context.

p. 138, 2f. *sik ... his.* Top right hand corner torn off. *sik ... as gif he thouch.* The interpretation required by preterite *thouch* is: Who could thus dispose himself for the reception of a mere similitude as if he were to receive his lord in person? But the MS has present tense *cane*, and the parenthetic clause of 4f. would be meaningless. It would appear that the (a) scribe overlooked the correlation *sik ... as.* The F reading fits perfectly in the context: Who can be stirred up to the same degree of fervour when he (wrongly) thinks that he is to receive a similitude of his lord as when he (correctly) thinks that he is to receive his lord in person? The word *gif* suggests a contamination of *such (the same) ... as* with *only ... if.*

p. 138, 4. *crear.* Regularly formed from original verb stem with native suffix.

p. 138, 10. *to þe rigour.* F reading suggests haplography in A.

p. 138, 13ff. Cp. the similar recapitulations in the *Compendius Tractiue*, last part of ch. xiv (*Wodrow Misc.*, p. 153) and concluding passage of the tract (p. 173).

p. 138, 15. *interpretaciones.* F reading supported by *the twa interpretaciones* of line 17.

p. 138, 20. *concluid and reasonynge.* The *ing*-form in both MSS is presumably authentic, but it may well stand for an infinitive which, together with *concluid and*, would mean 'offer a final argument'. Cp. the loss of the past participle ending after nasals in *bound, cum, funde, soung,* and *onderstand.* F *ane* probably represents an attempt to give meaning to the gerundial form.

p. 138, 25. *abone.* Or *aboue.*

p. 138, 27f. *this maner and conforme to þe procedynge.* F reading supported by context.

p. 138, 28. *adieckit.* Cp. *Compendius Tractiue:* "*mony in thir dayis, that folischelie followis, and addictis thame selfis to the wickit opinioun of sum private factius men*" (*Wodrow Misc.*, p. 105), which supports F *addictet.*

198

p. 138, 30. After the page ending with *Be quhat scriptoure propirlye and trewlye* two leaves missing from F.

p. 139, 2. *resauit and approvyne true.* Line 6 shows that *as* has been omitted before *true.*

p. 139, 3. *Macedonius.* Anti-trinitarian heretic, condemned at the first Council of Constantinople (A.D. 381).
Nestorius. Heretic who held a human as well as a divine personality in Christ and who was condemned at the Council of Ephesus (A.D. 431).

p. 139, 5f. Perhaps *Ecolampadius and Calvine to be resauit and approvyne true and godlye doctrine, And the opinione of* in lines 2f. had been erroneously copied from the continuation of the text.

p. 139, 6. Part of a sentence may have been omitted before *bot.*

p. 139, 11. *þe vark of Hilarius.* i.e. *De Trinitate,* by Hilary of Poitiers; see Migne, *PL,* vol. x, esp. cols. 100ff.

p. 139, 12. *the vorke of Athanasius.* This might refer to a large number of writings by or attributed to Athanasius; see Migne, *PG,* vols. xxv–xxviii.

p. 139, 24. *ve vil nocht curiouslye do the sammyne.* i.e. he will draw a parallel between the Arians and Oecolampadius, but not out of *cursit curiosite* to find out how strong the individual arguments of the Arians were as compared with those of Oecolampadius.

p. 139, 26. *it is.* MS *is is.*

p. 139, 26ff. *ve vill conterfate …* Cp. *Maybole Ressoning,* where Kennedy says that he is "*willing to contrafit the wisdome and prudence of the wise and prudent medicinar …, for lyke as the prudent medicinar dois expell ane vennome or poysone be contrapoysone, Swa wald I expel the damnable herisies of the Caluinistes, Lutherians, and Aecolampadians, be conferrence with the damnable herisies of the Arrians, quha did alledge ten testimonies of scripture for ane, geuand mair appearance to preif that Christ was not ane substance with the Father nor dois the Caluinistes, Lutherians, and Aecolampadians to preif that the messe is idolatrie*" (Laing, *Works,* vi, p. 214).

p. 139, 27. *persauand.* MS *persuand.*

p. 139, 28. *lik as ve intend.* Anacoluthon.

p. 139, 31. *vrityne.* Top right hand corner torn off.
for. i.e. *quhair;* cp. 115, 21.

p. 139, 37. *allegeand.* Cp. 115, 31 *(allegeand þat).*

p. 139, 38. *swa sais Ecolampadius.* Same construction as in 115, 32, F reading. The brackets there indicate a parenthesis, although the following *þat* leaves the construction anacoluthic.

p. 140, 2. *in the first chaptour.* See 116, 1ff.

p. 140, 6. *The kirk.* If the reading of these lines is correct, the new sentence must begin with *as* (instead of *als*) in line 4. But the copyist put a double dot after *persaue* in line 5 and began the following article with a capital, indicating that in his opinion the new sentence started with *The kirk.* In that case he must have omitted the continuation of the sentence after *I and þe Father ar boith ane* or erroneously substituted *allegeand* for *allegit.* The last suggestion suits the context perfectly; cp. *alleget* in line 12.

p. 140, 9. *þir vordes of our saliuour folouand.* Probably a scribal error for *þir vordes and þe vordes of our saliuour folouand;* cp. John 10, 30ff.

p. 140, 17. Haplography. The omitted words will have read something like: *swa the Father and the Sone ar nocht ane in substance, bot be concord of mynd and vyll.*

p. 140, 19. *suld … hed place.* The only example of this Scots syntax. Cp. e.g. Burns, *Tam O'Shanter:* "The wind blew as 'twad blawn its last."

p. 140, 28. *vsis.* i.e. 'employ'.

p. 140, 28ff. F text resumed at *þe trew doctrine of þe kirk.*

p. 140, 31. *for.* This may be construed into evidence for an earlier North-Eastern copy. If Alexander Wood understood *for* to be a co-ordinating conjunction, he would naturally omit *as.*

p. 141, 1. *as said Arrius.* Reading supported by context.

p. 141, 9f. *suld be … suld be.* F reading supported by present tense in line 13.

p. 141, 11. *spekin.* Gerund.

p. 141, 13. *Or quhow can there be.* F reading supported by context.

p. 141, 21. *vord.* Cp. 118, 4.

our. Top right hand corner torn off.

sayand. F reading supported by 118, 4.

p. 141, 23. *applyis.* F reading supported by lines 25f.

p. 141, 24. *This is my bodye.* F reading supported by absence of preceding *sayand.*

p. 141, 33. *Inlykvise.* Reading supported by *lyke as* in line 32.

p. 142, 1. *þe flesche.* F reading supported by 119, 5.

p. 142, 2. *as Christes flesche.* F reading supported by 119, 5.

p. 142, 2f. *all reddelye declarit.* See chapter ii.

p. 142, 3–6. F reading supported by characteristic parallelism.

p. 142, 7. *confer þe scriptouris quha plesis, they sal.* F reading supported by Latin prototype of the syntax: "*legat quisquis velit Homiliam 83 Chrysostomi ..., et perspicue cernet ...*" (Fisher, *De Veritate*, lib. ii, cap. xxx).

p. 142, 8. *þe conferrens.* F. reading supported by context.

p. 142, 9. *perceaue.* Reading supported by following *rather.*

p. 142, 10. *heresye.* Small hole in MS.

p. 142, 15. *maist propir.* Reading supported by context, which requires the meaning 'least improper'.

p. 142, 26. *counsall of Nece.* F reading supported by other instances in *Compendius Tractiue* and *Compendious Ressonyng.*

vas. F reading supported by singular.

p. 142, 30. *quhare.* F reading supported by context.

disput. Preterite.

p. 142, 32. *this counsal of Rome and diuerse others.* Berengarius was condemned at councils held at Rome (1050), Vercelli (1050), Florence (1055) and Rome (1059, 1078 and 1079); see Mansi, vol. xix, cols. 759ff., 773ff., 837f., 900; vol. xx, cols. 516 and 524.

p. 143, 1ff. The purpose of this passage is clearly to give an additional reason for the equalization Arius-Oecolampadius. This is plainly introduced by the F reading, which has every appearance of authenticity.

p. 143, 2. *other.* Scribal errour for *otheris.*

p. 143, 8. *And sa far as.* Scribal errour for *in sa far as.*

p. 143, 9. *to site anent.* F reading supported by its characteristic Kennedy wording.

p. 143, 9f. *mistery of.* Small hole in MS.

p. 143, 12. *determyt as efter folowis.* Some phrase like this had to follow after *And sa far as* instead of *in sa far as,* whilst it would make no sense after *in sa far as.* But this latter phrase is clearly preferable in the context, viz. as introducing the explanation of the statement that the Council of Nicea had condemned Oecolampadius. – For the Latin text, see the note to 169, 3ff.

p. 143, 13f. *and onderstandan.* Top right hand corner torn off.

p. 143, 14. *myndis.* F reading supported by 169,5.

p. 143, 15. *takar.* F reading supported by 169, 6.

p. 143, 16. *preist.* F reading supported by 169, 7.

p. 143, 25. *alse the grete.* F reading supported by context: *the same ... as* and *as grete ... as.*

p. 144, 7f. *þat the ane ... and the other.* Hole in MS.

p. 144, 10–12. *quhilk ... quhar ... denyand.* Top left hand corner torn off.

p. 144, 19. *aige, ʒeire, and tymes.* F reading supported by 143, 24f.

p. 144, 22. *in ane opinione of.* Words omitted through repetition of *opinione;* cp. line 24.

p. 145, 1. *sik.* F reading supported by context.

p. 145, 6. *faitfull.* Thus in the MS.

clenget. Reading supporting by context.

p. 145, 7. *approvin be so mony.* Hole in MS; auxiliary apparently omitted.

p. 145, 12. *now trowbles ... the scriptouris.* Top right hand corner torn off.

200

p. 145, 15. *considder, lik as.* F reading supported by context.

p. 145, 18. *termes.* F reading supported by lines 20f.

p. 145, 27. *colleckit for þe sammyne.* F reading supported by context. *abone.* Or *aboue.*

p. 145, 30. *abone.* Or *aboue.*

p. 146, 2–4. *reasone ... aucht and suld ... vp.* Hole in MS.

p. 146, 4. *one.* Reading supported by line 6.

p. 146, 7f. *alik baith ... onderstandit.* Top left hand corner torn off.

p. 146, 9. *deſeruis.* Present tense supported by context.

p. 146, 10. *equall.* i.e. 'equally'.

p. 146, 12ff. Cp. the final passage of the *Oratioune:* "*And thus we conclude ...* [and] *with all my hart exhortis ... pestilent precheouris, puffit vp with vane glore, quhilkis rackinnis thaim-selfis of gretar knawlege nor Christis haill kirk, cumand but authorite, subuertand, subornande, and circumuenande the simple peple, cersande thair pray like the deuillis rachis, barkcand bauldly like bardis aganis the blissit sacrament of the altare, the sacrifice of the mess, and all vther godlie ordinance of Jhesus Christ and his kirk, to preiss thair wittis and inginis, and to streik all thair pennis in my contrar ...*" (Laing, *Works*, vi, p. 165). Also cp. *Compendius Tractiue, Wodrow Misc.*, p. 139. – The structure of the F reading is exactly that of the above extract; *exhortand þe pestilent precheouris ... to preiffe all thair wittis ... and defend be scriptour ....* The word *preiffe* represents a slight slip of *ff* for double medial *s*, but apart from that the F reading may be presumed to offer the original text.

p. 146, 21ff. *because ... nocht onelye ... bot alse.* The correlation is that with *bot alse* of line 25, not with that of 24.

p. 146, 26f. Cp. Smith's *Confutation:* "*... Vnto whom with the father and the holy goost be honour and glory for euer. Amen.*" (p. 166r).

Title page. The Latin quotation (Acts 5, 39 completed from verse 38) is in a more formal style of writing, the rest of the page, with the exception of the decoration, is in the same hand as the tract. The first letter of the title is elaborately decorated with flower designs and a bearded human face in black and red. The upper strokes of two ordinary *b*'s and the first letter of the Latin quotation are likewise decorated in black and red, for the sake of symmetrical layout as well as the decoration itself.

The meaning of the Latin text after the title is obvious: if the Mass is of divine institution, it will be impossible to eradicate it.

p. 149, 1. *Ane.* Initial elaborately decorated in black and red, second and third letters written in larger and bolder type than the remainder of the page.

p. 149, 5. *fo. 2.B.* The foliation meant is that which begins on p. 153. The *B* stands for the *verso* of the leaf indicated. If there are more references than one to the same page, the number of the reference is added to the capital (see e.g. line 10). This latter number and capital *A* (for the *recto*) and *B* are in red ink both in this table and in the margin of the respective page.

p. 149, 31. *and nevyr to be offerit vp. is* omitted; cp. 157, 37.

p. 150, 32f. Note that *trew* and *new* are rhymes.

p. 151, 1. *To.* Capital *T* elaborately decorated in black.

p. 151, 5. *Haifand.* Capital *H* very elaborately decorated in black and red; the remaining letters are in bold black.

p. 151, 13. *To.* In bold black. This also holds for the other words printed in heavy type in this preface.

p. 151, 26. *Schir.* In imitation of the Latin *Dominus* this title was applied to priests, especially those with an academical training but without the Master's degree. On Knox's priesthood, see M. R. Adamson, J. H. Burns, W. J. Anderson and R. McLaren, "The Ordination of John Knox. A Symposium," *Innes Review*, vol. vi (1955), pp. 99ff.

p. 151, 26f. *quia est sacerdos Dei altissimj secundum ordinem Caluini.* Cp. *Gen.* 14, 18 *(sacerdos Dei altissimi)*, Psalms 110 (109), 4 and *Heb.* 7, 11 *(secundum ordinem Melchisedech)*. The point of the remark seems to be that Knox must justify his defection from the order of Melchisedech to that of Calvin.

p. 151, 29. *father Willock.* A bishop was normally addressed as 'father in God' and Kennedy uses the appellation here in as far as Willock, as Superintendent of the West, lived as bishop of Glasgow. See G. Donaldson, *The Scottish Reformation*, Cambridge, 1960, pp. 102ff.

p. 151, 29f. *quia multa contingebant illi in figuris quhen he was ane freir.* Cp. *1 Cor.* 10, 11: *Haec autem omnia in figura contingebant illis.* Willock had been a friar in Ayr and Kennedy states that his life then had been only a 'figure' compared with his present life. It may refer to the state he kept; cp. Donaldson, *o.c.*, p. 127.

p. 151, 32. *Magister noster.* Title of a university professor. John Winram (1492–1582), doctor of divinity and subprior of St. Andrews, had become superintendent of Fife.

p. 151, 37, *doctour Gudeman.* Christopher Goodman (c. 1520–1603), an Englishman, who had been Knox's fellow-minister of the Puritan congregation at Geneva and had joined him in Scotland not long after Knox's own return in 1559. For a time he was minister in Ayr.

p. 152, 1. *doctour Douglas.* John Douglas (c. 1494–1574), provost of St. Mary's College, St. Andrews, and Rector of the university from 1550 onwards, who was to become the first 'tulchan' archbishop of St. Andrews.

Qui de nulla non re dubitat. Rather cheap jesting based on the alliteration *Douglas-dubitat.*

p. 152, 4. *Hereot.* Adam Heriot (d. 1574), a canon of St. Andrews, who had become minister at Aberdeen.

Qui adhuc hesitat. Alliteration *Hereot-hesitat.*

p. 152, 8. *Spottiswod.* John Spottiswoode (1510–1585), parish priest of Calder, who had become superintendent of Lothian.

p. 152, 9. *tak nocht þat spot to him.* i.e. accept charge over that district. The pun contains an insinuation that there had been *wodnes* on the part of Spottiswood to be appointed to the *spot* in question.

p. 152, 13. *my lorde of Athenis.* Alexander Gordon, bishop-designate of Galloway and titular archbishop of Athens who had been a supporter of the Reformation movement from before the parliament of 1560. See G. Donaldson, "Alexander Gordon, Bishop of Galloway (1559–1575)," *Transactions of the Dumfriesshire and Galloway Natural History and Antiquarian Society*, 3rd series, vol. xxiv (1947), pp. 111–128, and A. Ross, "More about the Archbishop of Athens," *Innes Review*, vol. xiv (1963), pp. 30–37.

p. 152, 15. *mature and constant in all his deliberatiouns.* Probably a hint at Gordon's efforts for ecclesiastical preferment.

p. 152, 22f. Cp. 174, 24f.

p. 152, 24–26. More formal style of writing, as for the Latin sentence on the title page. First letter of *Hodie* decorated in black ink. Cp. *Psalms* 95 (94), 7f.

p. 153, 1. *Ane.* Capital *A* very elaborately decorated in black and red.

p. 153, 6. *Iames Kennedy of Vchtwallure.* Quintin Kennedy's youngest brother, who held the lands of Ochtrelour (also spelled *Ochterlour, Ochtrolure, Auchterlure* and *Auchtralure*), about one mile S.W. of Stranraer and belonging to the barony of Soulseat abbey; cp. *Ailsa Papers*, section i, nos. 536f., 594 and 631.

p. 153, 7f. Capitals *Q* and *I* elaborately decorated in black and red. The first letter of *Broder* is decorated in black ink with some red and is smaller in size. The remaining letters of *Quintinus, Iacobus* and *Broder* are in a fat black type, about three times the size of the ordinary text. See *Plate XXIX* in *Essays*, facing p. 400.

p. 153, 8. *stand with.* Cp. *stare (male) cum aliquo* (Ducange, *s.v. stare*).

p. 153, 10f. *cleyth me ... þe ... personage.* Cp. *Induite vos ... benignitatem* (Coloss. 3, 12); but it seems probable that the preposition *with* has been omitted because of *tak apon me.*

p. 153, 13. *I contentit.* Scribal slip for *I am contentit.*

p. 153, 16–18. Apparently Kennedy was being accused of sophistry and a lack of honesty.

p. 153, 20. *vndeserwit.* Note the post-position, even after the prepositional adjunct.
I stand nocht þairby. Cp. *iuri stare;* hence 'I do not accept that verdict'.

p. 153, 20–22. *bot þat ... in þat case.* Probably short for *bot swa beand þat ... in þat case.*

p. 153, 22. *I renunce Goddis mercy.* George Hay comments as follows: "*such imprecations, as they proceed of an obstinate and contumatious heart, so they be altogether Deuillish, to deceaue and draw back the simple ignorant and vnskilful Reader, vnto vtter distruction*" (*Confutation,* p.4r).

p. 153, 33. *ascriuit ... to be.* i.e. 'reckoned'; cp. line 28.

p. 153, 36. *fo. 2.* Upward stroke of *f* cropped.

p. 154, 2. *He is ane evill Iuge condempnis or he knawis.* Same expression, but with relative *that*, in the Kennedy-Knox correspondence (Laing, *Works*, vi, p. 178).

p. 154, 4. *tane ... on hand.* i.e. 'taken in hand', 'undertaken'.

p. 154, 6–9. The syllogism is taken from Knox's *Vindication of the Doctrine that the Mass is Idolatry;* see Laing, *Works*, iii, p. 34. The first proposition is subsequently defended as follows: "*And that is principall Idolatrie when our awn inventionis we defend to be rychteous in the sycht of God, becaus we think thame gude, laudable, and pleasant. We may not think us so frie nor wyse, that we may do unto God, and unto his honour, what we think expedient. No! the contrarie is commandit by God, saying, 'Unto my Word sall ye add nothing; nothing sall ye diminische thairfrom, that ye mycht observe the preceptes of your Lord God:' Whilk wordis ar not to be understand of the Decalogue and Law Morall onlie, but of statutis, rytis, and ceremonyis; for equall obedience of all his Lawis requyreth God*" (*ibid.*, pp. 37f.).

p. 154, 19. *1 Reg. 15., 1 Reg. 13.* Both instances quoted by Knox (*l.c.*, pp. 35f.).

p. 154, 21–23. *it is ane grit difference ... to do ... be to do.* i.e. 'there is a great difference ... between doing ... and doing'.

p. 154, 23. *of godlie zeill.* i.e. 'out of godly zeal'; cp. *on ane gude zeill* in 29 f.

p. 154, 25. *Cornelius centurio.* Knox had cited this case in connection with the decision of the Council of Jerusalem *"that the Gentilles sall not be burdenit with the law"* (*l.c.*, pp. 43 ff.).

p. 154, 27. *þis subtyle ressonar.* i.e. Knox. Kennedy apparently forgets that he has just referred to *sum prophane precheouris.*

p. 154, 33. *As.* In thicker and larger black type, as before.

p. 154, 34. *þe effect and substance of þe mess.* Cp. *I desyre to be certifeit what thai call thair Masse? Whether the haill actioun, with all ceremonies, useit now of olde, or a pairt thairof? ... But thai say, All theis ceremonies ar not of the substance of the Masse, but ar addit for gude caussis. What commandement haif thai ressavit to add any thing to the ordinance of God, for any cause apeiring to thame?* (Knox, *l.c.*, pp. 48 f.).

p. 154, 39. *Luc. 22.* Capital cropped at outer edge. The same holds for all letters of marginal entries placed within square brackets.

p. 155, 8. *þair is nocht sic ane terme in all þe new testament.* Cp. *My question is, Yf the Spreit of God hath inventit and pronuncit this dictioun Missa to signifie a sacrifice for the synnis of the quick and the deid?* (Knox, *l.c.*, p. 47). Kennedy does not permit James to bring in this point till a later page.

fo. 3. Upward stroke of *f* cropped.

p. 155, 11f. *Clemens, Epistola 3. ad Iacobum fratrem Dominj.* Kennedy probably refers to the words ascribed to Clement of Rome in the *Decretum de Consecratione*, dist. i, cap. xiv, with their mention of *missas celebrare* (Migne, *PL*, vol. clxxxvii, col. 1710).

p. 155, 13. *Ignacius, Epistola ad Smirnenses.* See note to 166, 8. Hay comments: *"Ignatius writeth in Greik ... The ignorance of this language, deceaueth thee glorious Doctor, howsoeuer thou be puft vp in thy owne consaite and playes King harrad amongest thy owne companions, lyke vnto thy self"* (*Confutation*, p. 10 v).

p. 155, 16 ff. Cp. the similar passage in Smith's *Confutation*, pp. 59 v f., which also distinguishes between the terms and *the thing signified.*

p. 155, 21 f. *Hist. Trip., lib. 5., ca. 42.* i.e. the *Historia Ecclesiastica Tripartita* of Cassiodorus, the medieval textbook of church history in the West; the relevant passage may be found in Migne, *PL*, vol. lxix, cols. 1020 f.

p. 155, 24. *Platina, Vigili p.* i.e. the life of Pope Vigilius in Battista Platina's *Opus de vitis et gestis summorum pontificum* (Venice, 1518, p. xxxvi v.). It is noteworthy that Kennedy refers to the life of a sixth-century pope, which does not mention Nestorius himself. Its mention and brief explanation of the term *theotokos* must have been the only reason.

p. 155, 25 f. *nevir ane of þir thre termes is expreslie contenit in þe new testament.* Hay comments: *"What if I shal deny this, vnto this new start vp Doctor of Carrick? How is he able to proue it, if he vnderstandeth not the language, that the Scriptures were first written in, by the finger of the holy Goste?"* (*Confutation*, p. 11 r).

p. 155, 34–40. This definition, more complete than that of the previous page, contains the following elements: the bread and wine are consecrated in accordance with Christ's institution, offered to the Father of Heaven by way of mystical re-enactment of Christ's passion and death, and received as the source and sustenance of the spiritual life. Note that Kennedy generally speaks of Christ's *deyth and passioun*, in this order.

p. 156, 3. *Or ellis I wald think my labouris in vane.* Cp. *"But in vane, will sum think, that all this labour I have takin; for na man of haill judgement any part of this wold haif denyit; nor yit doith it prove any thing of myne intent"* (Knox, *l.c.*, p. 47). Kennedy appears to be using the very words of his opponent.

p. 156, 12. *þou.* Note the singular.

p. 156, 13. *Chrisostom., Homil. 48. In Ioahan.* See note to 133, 17. The form *Ioahan.* must be a case of dittography.

p. 156, 14. *þe lordis body and blude.* Hay's copy had a possessive pronoun (*Confutation*, p. 15 r), which is supported by 133, 17.

þe breid and wyne. Supported by quotation in Hay, *l.c.;* cp. note to 133, 17.

p. 156, 21. *fo. 4.* Upward stroke of *f* cropped.

and brokin. Having argued that what had been common bread was now the body of Christ, Kennedy goes on to say that the breaking and distribution was meant to represent in some mystical way the death of Christ. When James remains unconvinced, he points out to him that Christ uses the preposition 'for' instead of 'to' (162, 3–27). From other scriptural passages and from tradition he further argues that his interpretation is the correct one.

p. 156, 40. *oratiouns and prayer.* The juxtaposition requires a plural *prayeris*, as in the quotation given by Hay (*Confutation*, p. 25v.).

p. 157, 5f. *Gen. 49., Esa. 7., Baruch. 3., Esa. 53.* The references correspond to the four points enumerated in the text.

p. 157, 15. *Latinistis.* Smith uses the term *latinis* (*Confutation*, p. 148v).

p. 157, 17–21. *Alexander, Epistola 1.* See Migne, *PG*, vol. v, col. 1064; cp. the quotation in 166, 21 ff.

Ireneus, lib. 4., ca. 32. i.e. of his *Adversus Haereses;* see Migne, *PG*, vol. vii, col. 1023 (cap. 17, formerly 32; cp. the quotation in 166, 33 ff.).

Damascenus, lib. 4. De Fide Orthodoxa, ca. 14. See Migne, *PG*, vol. xciv, cols. 1150 f. (cap. 13, formerly 14; cp. the quotation in 133, 21 ff., which Smith assigns to cap. 14).

August., lib. 8. De Ciuitate Dei., ca. 35. Hay remarks: *"thou cyteth Augustine in the eight boke. 33. Chap. the whole boke being conteined and deuided in. 27. Chapiters"* (*Confutation*, p. 26v). The reference must be to lib. 18, cap. 35; see Migne, *PL*, vol. xli, col. 594.

Et lib. 19, ca. 23. See Migne, *PL*, vol. xli, col. 655.

Rupertus, in Commenta. super Exod. i.e. the commentary on Exodus by Rupert of Deutz. The reference is probably to Book iii, chapter xiv; see Migne, *PL*, vol. clxvii, col. 664.

Concilium Nicenum.; Concilium Ephesinum. Perhaps Kennedy is thinking of the passages he quotes in 169, 3–19. They support his interpretation of the words of institution, but, unlike the other passages referred to, do not mention *Malachy* by way of illustration or proof.

... na of þe ...st consellis. The letters *na* (*? ua*) stand free. At the extreme edge there is just a trace that some writing has been cropped. The conjectural reading *Tua of þe first consellis* has the disadvantage that the capital *T* would stand at an unusually long distance from the other two letters.

p. 157, 31–35. Same argument used by Knox (Laing, *Works*, iii, pp. 55 f.); also cp. *Confessio Scotica*, art. xxii.

p. 157, 34. *fo. 5.* Upper part cropped.

ane sacrifice. Probably scribal slip for *in sacrifice*, as in 149, 30 and in the MS used by Hay (see *Confutation*, p. 27r).

p. 157, 37 ff. Knox had anticipated such a reply in the following way: *"I knaw ye will say, it is none uther sacrifice, but the self same, save that it is iteratit and renewit. But the wordis of Paule bind you more straitly than that so ye may eschaip: for in his haill disputation, contendeth he not onlie that thair is no uther sacrifice for sin, but also that the self same sacrifice, anis offerit, is sufficient, and nevir may be offerit againe"* (Laing, *Works*, iii, p. 56). Kennedy's answer is that the Mass does not imply any derogation of the sacrifice of the cross, so that the objection from the words of St. Paul is beside the mark. Instead, the difficulty is a purely human one, viz. to see the harmony between the oneness of Christ's sacrifice and Christ's own institution of the sacrifice of the Mass.

p. 158, 8. *in safer as.* *as* written through *þat*, or *þat* through earlier *as;* cp. line 40.

p. 158, 14. *Daniel. 12.* The reference is undoubtedly to the sacrifice mentioned in verse 11.

p. 158, 17. *Nu. 21.* i.e. chapter 21 of the Book of Numbers. The reference is to the brazen serpent as a figure of the crucified Christ.

p. 158, 31. *nocht as ane new satisfactioun or redemptioun.* Knox had said: *"heirin is the Masse blasphemous unto Chryst and his Passioun. For in so far as it offereth or permitteth remissioun of synnis, it imputeth imperfectioun upon Chryst and his sacrifice, affirmyng that all synnis wer not remittit by his death"* (Laing, *Works*, iii, p. 65). Cranmer had made the same objection; see Smith, *Confutation*, p. 21v.

p. 158, 33. *we ar maid parttakaris of þe fructe.* Smith speaks of application of these fruits unto remission of sin (*Confutation*, pp. 22r, 25r, 148v). Kennedy must be consciously avoiding such terminology; cp. 159, 18–21.

p. 159, 2. *fo. 6.* Completely cropped.

p. 159, 5. *renewit and applyit.* i.e. "applied anew', not 'merited anew and applied'; cp. lines 20f. and 158, 31.

p. 159, 9. *ane perfyte medycyne.* The image was far from original and Knox had effectively turned it to his own advantage: "*Thay say it is Sacrificium applicatorium, a sacrifice whairby thai do and may apply the merittis of Chrystis passion unto synneris. Thay will be layaris to of plaisteris! but I feir the wound be not weill rypit, and thairfoir that the plaisteris be unprofitable*" (*l.c.*, p. 58).

p. 159, 22. *nocht.* Cp. Hay, *Confutation*, p. 37r.

p. 159, 23. *conmwnicate.* Prefix at the end of a line.

p. 159, 25. *I will cut ȝour throte with ȝour awin suorde.* Cp. Smith: "*may it not be wel sayed here, that my lord is slayne with his owne swerd, as they saye commonlye?*" A marginal caption reads: "*Episcopus iste sua iugulatur (ut aiunt) gladio*" (*Confutation*, p. 87r). The Latin expression occurs several times in Fisher's *De Veritate*. In Kennedy's tract it sounds much too personal (worse so in Hay's copy, which had twice *thy* instead of *ȝour*: *Confutation*, p. 37r).

p. 159, 26f. Cp. "*Then let your communion be celebrated at nyght, my lord, when Christ did institute it*" (Smith, *Confutation*, p. 28r).

p. 159, 33–38. Hay cites this passage as follows: "*Trewly brother and ȝe be sa scrupulus Scripturares, that ȝe will do nothing but (but is not in my Text) as Christe did, towardes the vse of the Sacramentes, ȝe will subuert our haile Faith, and commend our awin doinges (so I ride it: our own doinges or commonly I can not tell which should be red, or if there be any other thing yet) For quhair find ȝe that Christe euer appointed ane man to be Baptised. I dar bauldlie say this ordinance wes neuer of the Euangell, nor ȝit of the Kirk of God, nor of ony vther haueand iuste authoritie, ather God or man*" (*Confutation*, pp. 37r f.). It is one of the instances which show that Hay's copy, which does not appear to have included the table and preface, was far from perfect. *Condemp ȝour awin doingis* fits exactly in the context. The reading *ane man to be Baptised* is certainly corrupt (cp. 160, 8–11). Instead, one would expect a remark on the baptism of children (as in the *Compendius Tractiue*, *Wodrow Misc.*, pp. 168f., and in Smith's *Confutation*, p. 27r: "*What saye ye then, my lord, vnto the baptisme of children?*"). But the reading of MS B may well be correct. One of the charges against Adam Wallace, a native of Failford, Kyle, had been that he had baptized his own child, in contempt of a priest's services, that is (Laing, *Works*, i, p. 239). And the council of 1559, after discussing the validity of such baptisms according to a rite introduced by the Sacramentarians, had decreed that, except in danger of death, children were to be baptized by priests only (see *Statuta*, ii, no. 293, pp. 174f.).

p. 160, 6f. *he referrit to his kirk.* Absence of *it* normal; cp. e.g. 115, 22.

p. 160, 11. *fo. 7.* Only downward strokes remaining, rest cropped.

p. 160, 13–22. The answer to 159, 23f.

p. 160, 30. *beirand.* MS *beirand beirand*, first word subsequently erased with red ink.

p. 161, 12ff. Note the successful dialogue of the following page. At the same time it is a skillful introduction to the argument from the references to Melchisedech: James is given full opportunity to voice his basic objection so that his ultimate submission to Quintin's arguments will be the more impressive.

p. 162, 10f. *as testifeis þe excellent clerk Erasmus.* See his commentary on *1. Cor.* 11, 24 (pp. 620f. in *Annotationes, of Aanteekeningen op 't Nieuwe Testament ... volgens des Schrijvers vijfde en leste vermeerdering*, Amsterdam, 1663).

p. 162, 23. *conmwnioun.* Prefix at the end of a line.

p. 163, 10–19. Cp. Fisher: "*His accedit quod in Scripturis plerunque de sacerdotio nouo secundum ordinem Melchisedech mentio facta sit, et quod Christus secundum ordinem illum sacerdos fuerit saepius asseritur. Quod si verum sit, oportuit aliquando Christum in pane et vino sacrificasse, quemadmodum et Melchisedech in eis sacrificasse traditur. At nusquam id fecisse legitur*

206

praeterquam in coena quando sub specie panis et vini sacramenta sui corporis et sanguinis instituit. Quamobrem et in coena uere sacrificauit, verumque patri suo sacrificium obtulit" (*Assertionvm Regis Angliae de Fide Catholica adversvs Lvtheri Babylonicam Captivitatem Defensio*, cap. vi, par. 9).

p. 163, 19. *Cyprianus, lib. 2, Epistola 3.* i.e. *Epistola ad Caecilium;* see Migne, *PL*, vol. iv, cols. 375–377.

p. 163, 19f. *Ambros., lib. 4. De Sacramentis, ca. 3.* See Migne, *PL*, vol. xvi, cols. 438f.

p. 163, 20. *August., lib. 17. De Ciuita. Dei, ca. 17.* See Migne, *PL*, vol. xli, col. 550f.

p. 163, 21. *Lutherus in psal. 109.* The name *Lutherus* is uncertain; the first *u* may have to be *n*. If the reading is correct, Kennedy may have wished to show that the Reformer's interpretation differed from the other authors rather than adduce him as an additional witness.

p. 163, 25f. Hay introduces a somewhat different reading in the following way: "*Hereby, Sire, ye may vnderstand sufficiently that to be a preist, after the ordour of Melchisedech, is not to offer vp bread and wyne, as ye falsly alledge Melchisedech to haue done, but this to be referred to the stabilitie of Christes preisthead, and eternitie of the same, as I haue declared at large, so that we may collect the dout of James to be moste reasonable, douting 'Gif he maid oblation of bread and wyne, for vther wayis (As he sayeth) ȝour argument can haue na apperence'* (*Confutation*, p. 57r).

p. 163, 28. *Hierom. in Psal. 109.* See Migne, *PL*, vol. xxvi, col. 1165.

p. 163, 28f. *Aug., lib. 16. De Ciuitate Dei, ca. 22.* See Migne, *PL*, vol. xli, col. 500.

p. 163, 29. *Theophilac., de Epistola ad Heb., ca. 5.* See Migne, *PG*, vol. cxxv, col. 242.

p. 163, 29f. *Arnobius in Psal. 109.* See Migne, *PL*, vol. liii, col. 496.

p. 163, 30. *Beda in Marc. lib. 4. ca. 14.* See Migne, *PL*, vol. xcii, col. 272.

... *sa. 26.* Perhaps *et Psa. 26*, i.e. in Bede's *In Psalmorum Librum Exegesis*, Migne, *PL*, vol. xciii, col. 613.

p. 163, 33–36. Cp. the first chapter of the *First Book of Discipline:* "*By preaching of the Evangell we understand nott onlie the Scripturis of the New Testament, bot also of the Auld; to wit, the Law, Propheittis, and Histories, in quhilk Christ Jesus is no les conteaned in figure, then we have him now expressed in veritie*" (Laing, *Works*, ii, p. 185).

p. 163, 38. *fo. 10.* Completely cropped.

p. 164, 6–8. In other words, in as far as it was a commemorative sacrifice, the sacrifice of the paschal lamb did not so much prefigure that of the cross as that of the last supper.

p. 164, 22. *þe verite.* i.e. the New Testament event or truth prefigured in the Old Testament; cp. 182, 8f.

p. 165, 23. *Ireneus, lib. 3., ca. 3.* i.e. of his *Adversus Haereses;* see Migne, *PG*, vol. vii, cols. 848ff.

p. 166, 8f. *Ignacius, Epistola ad Smirnenses.* Cp. Migne, *PG*, vol. v, cols. 714 and 851. Kennedy's translation is undoubtedly copied from Smith's *Confutation:* "*Ignatius, S. Ihons scholer sayeth: It is not leful to offre, nother make sacrifice, nor to celebrate masses without the byshops autorite or consent*" (p. 160v).

p. 166, 11f. *Clemens, Epistola 2. ad Iacobum Fratrem Dominj.* The Latin text may be found in the *Decretals* of Isidore Mercator: "*Quoniam in aliis locis sacrificare et missas celebrare non licet, nisi in his in quibus episcopus proprius jusserit, aut ab episcopo regulariter ordinato tenente videlicet civitatem ubi consecratus fuerit. Aliter enim non sunt haec agenda, nec rite celebranda, docente nos Novo et Veteri Testamento. Haec apostoli a Domino acceperunt et nobis tradiderunt, haec nos docemus, vobisque et omnibus absque reprehensione tenere et docere quibus agendum est mandamus*" (Migne, *PL*, vol. cxxx, col. 50).

p. 166, 14. *fo. 12.* Completely cropped.

p. 166, 20f. *Alexander, 4., Ep. 1.* i.e. par. 4 of the first letter; see Migne, *PG*, vol. v, cols. 1064f. Kennedy's translation is not quite the same as that of Smith: "*Our lordes passion must be recited in al solennites of masses, ... With such sacrifices our lord wil be delited and pacified, and wil for gyue great synnes, for emonge sacrifices there can be nothinge greater than oure lordes bodie and bloud. There is no sacrifice better than this, but this excelleth al other, which must be* *offered vnto our lord with a pure conscience and receaued with a cleane mynde, and worshipped of al men"* (Confutation, p. 163v).

p. 166, 28. *ane sacrifice for syn.* Kennedy returns to this point in the last pages of the tract.

p. 166, 32. *Ireneus, lib. 4., ca. 17.* i.e. of his *Adversus Haereses;* see Migne, *PG,* vol. vii, col. 1023. Kennedy's translation is copied from Smith: "*Christ toke bread and gaue thankes sayinge, This is my body. And toke the chalice of wyne, and confessed it to be his bloud, and he taught a newe sacrifice of the newe testament, which the church receauinge of the apostles, offereth vnto god in al the whole world* (Confutation, p. 158v, with reference to *lib. 4, ca. 32,* which may also have been the reading in Kennedy's margin.

p. 167, 1f. *Cypriane, Epistola 3., lib. 2.* i.e. *Epistola ad Caecilium;* see Migne, *PL,* vol. iv, cols. 383f. Kennedy's translation and the concluding sentence of the paragraph are copied from Smith: "*If our lord iesus christ, and god hymselfe be the highe priest of god the father, and he hymselfe did first offre a sacrifice vnto god the father, and hath commaunded that same to be done in remembraunce of hym, that priest is verily christes vicar, which doth folowe that thynge that christ hath done. ... And in the begynnynge of that epistle he sayeth that Christ is the authour and teacher of this sacrifice of the masse ...*" (Confutation, p. 159r).

p. 167, 10f. *Chrisosto., Hom. 2. in 2. Timoth. ca. 1.* George Hay complains that he has not been able to find the passage in the 2nd homily on *2 Tim. 1* (Confutation, p. 76r). Kennedy had copied the translation from the same page from which he had taken the Cyprian text, and Smith's reference is to *Hom. 24. in 1 Cor. 10:* "*But Christ hath prepared a much more wounderful, and a magnificent sacrifice, both when he chaunged the sacrifice it selfe, and also when he did commaunde hym selfe to be offered in the steade of brute beastes, which were offered in the old lawe*" (Confutation, pp. 159v f.). See Migne, *PG,* vol. lxi, col. 200.

p. 167, 15f. *ca. 4. De Dignitate Sacerdotali, lib. 3.* See Migne, *PG,* vol. xlviii, col. 642. Kennedy's translation is from Smith's *Confutation:* "*O great good wyl of god towardes vs, o miracle. He that sitteth vpon the right hand of his father in heauen aboue, is conteined in mennes handes in the tyme of the sacrifice*" (p. 43r, with a reference to *Lib. 4, cap. 3 de dign. sacerd.,* which Kennedy may have checked and corrected).

p. 167, 19. *in ane vther place.* After the above text from Chrysostom, Smith continues with: "*Also he sayeth in an other place,*" and goes on to quote from *Hom. 17. in epist. ad Heb.* Kennedy copies the connecting sentence and then turns to pp. 156v f., where Smith gives a longer quotation from the same homily: "*Do we not offre sacrifices daily? We do offre, but doinge it in remembraunce of christes death. And this hoost is one, not manye. Howe is it one and not many? And that oblation was ones offered in to heauen, but this sacrifice is an example of that, we do offre the selfe same thinge. Whe [sic.] offre not to daye one lambe (Christ) and twoo [sic.] morowe an other, but euer the selfe same thynge. Wherfore this sacrifice is one, or els by that reason that it is offered in many places, are they many christes? Nothinge lesse, but there is one christ euery were [sic.], beynge both here ful and there ful, one body. For as that which is offered in euery place, is one body, and not many bodies, euen so it is also one sacrifice, but he is oure bysshop, which offered a sacrifice makinge vs cleane, we do offre the same, and that which then was offered can not nowe be consumed. Hytherto chrysostom, out of whose wordes many notable lessons may be gathered for the confutation of al your raylinge reasonynge, my lord.*" Cp. Migne, *PG,* vol. lxiii, col. 131.

p. 167, 36. *Ambrosius, in Psal. 38.* See Migne, *PL,* vol. xiv, cols. 1051f. Kennedy's translation is from Smith's *Confutation:* "*We haue seene the prince of priestes cominge vnto vs. We sawe hym and hard him offeringe for vs his bloud. Lette vs priestes folowe, as we may offre sacrifice for the people, althoughe we be weake by oure deseruinge, yet we are honorable throughe the sacrifice, for albeit Christ is not seene to be offered, neuerthelesse he is offered vpon the earth, when his bodie is offered. Yea, he is declared plainly to offre it in vs, whose word maketh holie the sacrifice, which is offered*" (pp. 161v f.). The reading *prince of princis* also occurred in Hay's copy of Kennedy's tract (see Confutation, p. 77v); the Latin has *Principem sacerdotum.*

p. 168, 4f. *August., lib. de Heres. Heres. 53.* i.e. no. 53 of his *De Haeresibus ad Quodvultdeum;* see Migne, *PL,* vol. xlii, cols. 39f. Kennedy's words are from Smith's *Confutation,* which con-

208

continues as follows immediately after the words last quoted: "*Saint Austen reproued Aerius for an heretike, as also Epiphanius did, because he sayed (as my lord and his secte doth) that men should not praye for the dead, nor offre sacrifice for them, and S. Austen sayed thus in that matter*" (*l.c.;* the text continues with the quotation given in the next note).

p. 168, 7. *In Enchiridion, ca. 110.* See Migne, *PL*, vol. xl, col. 238. Kennedy's translation is copied from Smith's *Confutation:* "*It is not to be denyed, that the souls of men departed are relieued throughe the godlynes of their frendes aliue when the sacrifice of oure mediatour Christ is offered for them or els almes be geuen for them in the church. But these thingis do profite them, which did deserue, when they lyued, that they might afterward profite them. Anon after he sayeth thus. Therfore when sacrifices, either of the aulter, or els of any maner of almasses are offered for al the dead, wich* [sic.] *were baptized, they are thankes geuinge for them, that be very good people, and for them which are not very badde, they are propitiations, or purchasinges of mercy and fauour of god*" (pp. 162r f.).

p. 168, 10 f. *Sermo 11, De Sacra.* There can be no doubt that at least the copyist saw this as a reference for lines 11–14. But, as Smith indicates (see above), the words are from the *Enchiridion* and occur a few lines after the preceding quotation.

p. 168, 15. *Sermo 32, De Verbis Apostoli.* See Migne, *PL*, vol. xxxviii, col. 938. Kennedy's translation is copied from Smith's *Confutation:* "*Austen sayeth also serm. 32. de verb. apost. It is not to be doubted but the souls departed are helped by the holy churches prayers, and the sacrifice of saluation, and almes, when they are geuen for them, that god shold deale more mercyfully with them, than their synnes had deserued*" (p. 163r).

p. 168, 23 f. *Tertulianus, Corona Militis.* See Migne, *PL*, vol. ii, col. 79: "*Oblationes pro defunctis pro natalitiis annua die facimus.*"
Obet Mess. i.e. Mass for the dead, *in* or *pro die obitus*.

p. 168, 28 f. *Gregorius Magnus, Hom. 37. in Evang.* See Migne, *PL*, vol. lxxvi, col. 1279. Kennedy's translation is from Smith's *Confutation:* "*S. Gregorie, which was aboue Dccccxl yeares passed, writeth thus also against your doctrine. Let vs send, brethren, vnto god our embassadours, by weapinge, gyuinge of almes, and offeringe of holy hoostes. For the sacrifice of the holy aulter, offered wyth weapinge and deuotion of mynde, doth syngularly helpe vnto oure absolution from synne. For as often tymes as we offre vnto hym the sacrifice, or hoost of his passion, so often we do repare vnto vs his passion, for our absolution*" (pp. 164v f.). Note Kennedy's *repair and apply* (Latin *reparamus*).

p. 168, 38. *oure colloquium.* In the more formal style of writing used for the Latin quotations elsewhere.

p. 168, 41. *fo. 14.* Upward stroke of *f* cropped.

p. 169, 2. *tuelf hundreth tuenty sex ʒeiris bypast.* Hay's copy had the same number (*Confutation*, p. 84r), so that it is difficult to admit a scribal error of twenty instead of thirty. Kennedy probably copied the number from a work which had been written some ten years before he wrote his own tract. Cp. line 10; the Council of Ephesus took place in A.D. 431.

p. 169, 3. *Histo. Trip., lib. 2., ca. 1.* i.e. the *Historia Ecclesiastica Tripartita;* see Migne, *PL*, vol. lxix, cols. 919 ff., *De praesulibus Ecclesiarum qui interfuerunt Nicaeno concilio.*

p. 169, 3–8. Tunstal gives the following Latin translation: "*Iterum etiam hic in diuina mensa, ne humiliter intenti simus ad propositum panem et poculum, sed attollentes mentem, fide intelligamus situm in sacra illa mensa agnum illum Dei, tollentem peccata mundi, incruente a sacerdotibus immolatum, et preciosum ipsius corpus et sanguinem nos uere sumentes, credere haec esse nostrae resurrectionis symbola*" (*De ueritate Corporis et Sangvinis Domini Nostri Iesu Christi in Eucharistia*, p. 40v).
I have not come across an English translation in Smith.

p. 169, 12. *Concilium Ephesinum.* See pp. 71f., above.

p. 171, 17. *fo. 16.* Completely cropped.

p. 171, 18 f. *princis has vendicat dispositioun of benefices.* Kennedy had denounced the prevailing system of provision to benefices in the fourteenth chapter of the *Compendius Tractiue*, in language which suggests that he was indebted to the preface of Smith's *A brief treatyse* *settynge forth diuers truthes necessary both to be beleued of chrysten people, and kepte also, whiche are not expressed in the scripture but left to the church by the apostles tradition* (London, 1547). John Major had used equally strong and bold language before them (see *History of Greater Britain*, Scottish History Society, 1892, pp. 136 f.). Also cp. Winzet's *Certain Tractates*, ed. J. B. Gracie, pp. 7 f.

p. 171, 16–34. See p. 100, above.

p. 171, 32 f. *As to me, I will say na thing, bot thankis to God þair is nane sic in þis realme, as þe experience daylie techis vs.* Kennedy owed his abbacy to the same system, so that he would at least create an impression of hypocrisy if his own case would be passed over in silence. Kennedy declares himself the worst of his class, no doubt confident that his readers will know him to be an exception the other way.

p. 172, 5–10. The structure of this passage is irregular and the reading may well be corrupt. It confuses two different constructions: *sall evir find þat þe peple of Israell ... war brocht* and *sall nevir find þat þe peple ... war abusit ... bot anis ... þai war brocht.* Hay's copy had a variant of this latter construction, and in this particular case it may have the correct reading: *sall neuer read the people of Israell ... till haue bene abused ... but anes thai war broght* (*Confutation*, p. 89r). The meaning of the passage is that however much idolatry there may have been in the less perfect Old Testament times, God never allowed it to last longer than a lifetime.

p. 172, 22 f. *þe promyse ... þe warld.* A peculiar kind of apposition, probably reflecting some Latin original; cp. Smith, *Confutation*, pp. 11r ff.

p. 172, 25. *fo. 17.* Upper half cropped.

p. 172, 38. *in his laudable werk.* i.e. *Commonitorium;* see Migne, *PL*, vol. 1, esp. col. 640. Smith quotes the 'Vincentian canon' on p. 15r of his *Confutation:* "*In ipsa catholica ecclesia magnopere curandum est vt id teneamus quod vbique, quod semper, quod ab omnibus creditum est. Sequenda est nobis antiquitas, vniuersitas, et consensus.*" Cp. chapter xviii of the *Confessio Scotica:* "*The nottis, signes, and assured tokenis whairby the immaculat spous of Christ Jesus is knawin from that horrible harlote the Kirk malignant, we affirme ar neyther antiquitie, title usurped, lineall discente, place appointed, nor multitude of men approving ane errour*" (Laing, *Works*, ii, p. 109).

p. 173, 3. *and nocht laitlie Inventit.* Perhaps *is* omitted.

p. 173, 35. *fo. 18.* Completely cropped.

p. 173, 38. *Hist. Ecclesiastica, ca. 25., lib. 6.* Perhaps copied from the *Compendius Tractiue:* "*as we reid of divers sectis amangis the Arrianis, Anabaptistes, and Manacheis,*" with marginal reference to *Hist. Eccl. cap. 25, libro 10* (Wodrow *Misc.*, p. 160). If, which seems most likely, this reference is to the *Historia Tripartita*, the reading *lib. 6* would appear to be better than *lib. 10;* cp. Migne, *PL*, vol. lxix, cols. 1046 and 1182.

p. 174, 5. *In ane of his werkis.* viz. in his *Von der Winkelmesse und Pfaffenweihe;* see the Weimar *Kritische Gesamtausgabe* of Luther's *Werke*, vol. xxxviii, pp. 183 ff. Bunderius refers to it in a way similar to Kennedy's and may well have been the latter's source; see *Detectio Nugarum Lutheri*, Louvain, 1551, pp. 8v and 23v.

p. 174, 32. *quhom be.* Like *quhairof*, &c.

p. 175, 3. *fo. 19.* The leaves if the *Appendex* are not foliated. Since there are no references to them in the table, it cannot be established whether an original foliation has been cropped.

p. 175, 7. *sanct Peter.* Since Kennedy mentions Platina's work elsewhere, it may well have constituted Kennedy's immediate source for much of the historical information proposed in this and the following paragraphs: "*In celebratione uero mandauit: ut sanctus sanctus deus sabahot cantaretur. Nudo primo haec erant et omnia simpliciter tractabantur. Petrus enim ubi consecrauerat: oratione Pater noster usus est.*" (*Opus de vitis et gestis summorum pontificum*, Venice, 1518, p. viii v).

p. 175, 8. *sacrifice.* MS *sacrice*.

p. 175, 11. *þat þe evangell of sanct Iohne is attentik scripture.* Kennedy means that supposing there were scriptural warrants for all the other books of Scripture, it would still be impossible thus to prove the divine character of the book which was written after all the others. Cp.

210

Compendius Tractiue, Wodrow Misc., p. 172, and Smith's *Confutation*, p. 19v.

p. 175, 15. *Hierarchia Ecclesiastica, parte 3., ca. 3.* Perhaps *parte 2.;* see Migne, *PG*, vol. iii, cols. 426ff. The reference is not given in proof of the statement that St. Peter ordered the Lord's Prayer to be said, but of the statement implied by the sentence as a whole that even in apostolic times there had been a quite elaborate Mass ceremonial not to be found in the scriptural account of the last supper. A statement to this effect, with a reference to Denis, is actually underscored on p. 246v of Kennedy's copy of Gagneius, *Clarissima et facillima ... scholia* (see p. 68, footnote 54, above).

p. 175, 18. *Alexander.* Cp. Platina's life of Alexander: "*At uero Alexander Romanus pontifex primus ob memoriam passionis Christi in sacrificio addidit: qui pridie quam pateretur usque ad hanc clausulam: hoc est corpus meum. Instituit item ut aqua quam sanctam appellamus sale admixta interpositis sacris orationibus et in templis et in cubiculis ad fugiendos daemones retineretur*" (*o.c.*, pp. viiir f.). If this was Kennedy's source, it is worthy of note that he makes Alexander the fifth successor of St. Peter, whilst he is the sixth in Platina's series. This may mean indebtedness to the *Decretum de Consecratione:* see Migne, *PL*, vol. clxxxvii, col. 1787.

p. 175, 26. *Sextus.* Cp. Platina's life of Sixtus I: "*Sixtus autem rei diuinae ut par erat curam gerens constituit: ne a quoquam nisi a ministris sacrorum mysteris et uasa sacra tangerentur: maxime uero a foeminis: neue quod sacerdotes corporale uocant ex alio quam ex lineo panno et quidem purissimo fieret. ... In celebratione uero mandauit: ut sanctus sanctus deus sabahot* [sic.] *cantaretur*" (*o.c.*, p. viii v.).

p. 175, 32. *Telesphorus.* Cp. Platina's life of Telesphorus: "*Telesphorus autem quem diximus Sixto successisse constituit: ut ... in natali Iesu Christi noctu tres missae celebrarentur: prima in dimidio noctis: quo Christus in Betleem nascitur: secunda illuscescente aurora quando a pastoribus cognitus est: tertia eadem hora diei qua nobis dies redemptionis et ueritatis illuxit. ... Constituit item ut ante sacrificium hymnus ille caneretur: Gloria in excelsis deo*" (*o.c.*, p. viii r.).

p. 176, 11. *Damasus.* Cp. Platina's life of Damasus: "*Primus etiam Hieronymi scriptis auctoritatem dedit cum prius .lxx. interpretum scripta tantummodo in precio essent. Nam et biblia Hieronymi legi coepta est. ... Mandauit item: ut in principio celebrationis quam missam uocant: confessio diceretur ut hodie fit*" (*o.c.* p. xxxix v.). In his life of Sixtus I he had said: "*missae dedit ... Epistolam et Euangelium Hieronymus*" (*o.c.*, p. viii v.).

p. 176, 16. *Ambros. lib. De Sacra., ca. 6.* i.e. *lib. 4*, where a passage from the canon of the Mass is cited; see Migne, *PL*, vol. xvi, cols. 445f.

p. 176, 17. *Aug., Epist. 59., ad Paulinum.* In Migne's edition *Epistola 149: PL*, vol. xxxiii, col. 636.

p. 176, 18f. *Chrisost., Hom. de Enceniis.* It is rather odd, and perhaps significant of Kennedy's knowledge of history, that he should cite Chrysostom as an authority for the antiquity of the Roman rite. He may have been struck by a quotation in Smith's *Confutation*, with a marginal reference to *Hom. de euch. in enceniis:* "*Didest not thowe promyse to the priest, which sayed, lyft vp your myndes and hartes: and thowe didest answeare, we lyfte them vp vnto the lord?*" (p. 103r). The words are in reality from *Hom. 9 de Poenitentia* (Migne, *PG*, vol. xlix, col. 345).

p. 176, 19. *Aug., Sermo ... De Tempore.* Probably *Sermo 227;* see Migne, *PL*, vol. xxxviii, cols. 1100f.

p. 176, 21. *Gelasius.* Cp. Platina's life of Sixtus I: *missae dedit ... Collationes Gelasius primus* (*o.c.*, p. viii v.).

p. 176, 22. *Gregour.* Cp. Platina's life of Gregory the Great: "*Eius quoque inuentum est: ut nouies Kyrieleison caneretur: et alleluia: interpositis septuagesimae diebus usque ad pascha*" (*o.c.*, p. xxxix r.).

p. 176, 24. *Sergius.* Cp. Platina's life of Sergius I: "*Constituit praeterea: ut in fractione dominici corporis caneretur Agnus dei qui tollis peccata mundi: miserere nobis*" (*o.c.*, p. xlviii r.).

p. 177, 1. *sum of oure precheouris.* Cp. Knox's *Vindication of the Doctrine that the Mass is Idolatry:* "*... dyvers Massis celebratit for dyvers caussis: sum for peace in tyme of war; sum for raine; sum for fair weather; yea, and (allace, my hart abhorreth sic abominatioun!) sum for sicknes of bestiall. Thay will say, thay severallie take prayeris for obteanyng sic thingis; and that* *is all whilk I desire thay say; . . . to pray that the tuthe-acke be takin away from us; that oure oxen suld not tak the lowing ill, oure horse the spavin or fersie, and so of all maner of diseassis for oure cattell. Yea, what was it whairfoir ye wald not say Masse, perversit Preistis?*" (Laing, *Works*, iii, p. 65; Knox takes a different view of prayer in his *Declaration What Trew Prayer Is*, printed in the same volume: "*Who will pray, must knowe and understand that Prayer is ane earnest and familiar talking with God, to whome we declair oure misereis, whois support and help we implore and desyre in our adversiteis, and whome we laude and prais for our benefittis received*": p. 83).

p. 177, 7f. *þe wordis eftir following.* The prayer *pro peste animalium*, which may be found in the Arbuthnott Sarum Missal (printed at Burntisland, 1864, p. 458) as well as in the *Missale Romanum* (no. 19 of the *orationes diversae*): "*Deus, qui laboribus hominum etiam de mutis animalibus solatia subrogasti: supplices te rogamus ut, sine quibus non alitur humana conditio, nostris facias usibus non perire.*"

p. 178, 1. *We of þe new learning.* Cp. Knox's *Vindication:* "*In the Papisticall Masse, the congregation getteth nothing except the beholding of your jukingis, noddingis, crossingis, turnyng, uplifting, whilk all ar nothing but a diabolicall prophanation of Chrystis Supper. Now, juke, cross, and nod as ye list, thai ar but your awn inventionis. And finallie, Brethrene, ye gat nothing, but gaseit and beheld whill that one did eat and drink all*" (Laing, *Works*, iii, p. 67).

p. 178, 13f. *Tertuli., De Corona Milit.* i.e. cap. iii; see Migne, *PL*, vol. ii, col. 80: "*Ad omnem progressum atque promotum, ad omnem aditum et exitum, ad calciatum, ad lavacra, ad mensas, ad lumina, ad cubilia, ad sedilia, quaecumque nos conversatio exercet, frontem crucis signaculo terimus.*"

p. 178, 14. *Chrisost., Ho. 55. in Matheum.* See Migne, *PG*, vol. lviii, col. 537: "*Crucem Christi quasi coronam circumferamus; per eam enim omnia quae ad nos spectant perficiuntur. Si regenerari oporteat, crux adest; si mystico illo cibo nutriri, si ordinari, et si quidvis aliud faciendum, ubique nobis adest hoc victoriae symbolum. Idcirco et domi, et in parietibus, et in fenestris, et in fronte et in mente, illam cum multo studio depingimus.*"

p. 179, 9–19. Copied from *Litil Breif Tracteit:* 132, 24ff.

p. 179, 20f. Cp. Knox's *Vindication: In the Papisticall Masse, the preistis . . . ar cled in disagysit garmentis* (Laing, *Works*, iii, p. 66).

p. 179, 24f. *þe arrayment quhilk was apon oure salueour þe day of his deyth and passioun.* Although direct indebtedness cannot be demonstrated with certainty, there is a striking similarity between the wording of these and the following lines and that of the *Opusculum super Missam* of the thirteenth-century Franciscan William of Middleton, who "*inter primos fuisse videtur qui sistematice omnia paramenta explicat tanquam symbola Christi passionis*" (A. van Dijk, "De Fontibus *Opusculi super Missam* Fr. Gulielmi de Melitona, Ord. Min.", *Ephemerides Liturgicae*, liii (1939), p. 312, footnote 10). The text may be given for comparison: '*Item sex paramenta sacerdotis . . . significant secundum litteram quaedam quae fuerunt facta Christo tempore passionis suae. . . . Imprimis ergo sacerdos volens celebrare Missam ponet sibi in capite primum paramentum quod dicitur amictus et significat velamen quod fuit positum ante faciem Christi tempore passionis in derisionem, sicut dicunt Evangelistae. Secundum paramentum dicitur alba vel camisium quod significat vestem albam qua fecit Herodes Christum indui in derisionem. Item ponit cingulum, manipulum et stolam sive orarium quasi tria vincula, quia Christus tribus vicibus fuit ligatus tempore passionis: primo quando captus est in die Coenae et ligatis manibus ductus ad principem sacerdotum, secundo ductus fuit in die Veneris sancti in mane ligatis manibus ad praetorium Pilati; tertio nudus fuit ligatus ad columnam et flagellatus. Ultimum paramentum vocatur planeta vel casula et significat chlamydem purpuream qua induerunt Christum in derisionem milites Pilati*" (*l.c.*, pp. 312f.).

p. 180, 2. *Luc. 23.* MS *29.*

p. 180, 26. *as sayis Erasmus.* Reference not identified. The following words from the *Praefatio in Mattheum* shows that, if Kennedy's statement is correct, Erasmus must have had different views on the subject at different times: "*indecorum vel ridiculum potius videtur quod idiotae et mulierculae, psittaci exemplo, psalmos suos et precationem dominicam immurmurant, cum ipsae quod sonant non intelligant*" (H. and A. Holborn, *Des. Erasmus Roterodamus. Ausgewählte*

212

Werke, Munich, 1933). Less than a year after Kennedy wrote his tract, the argument that the use of Latin ensured greater decorum was voiced by a Spanish theologian at the Council of Trent *(Diariorum, Actorum, Epistularum, Tractatuum nova Collectio*, Görres Society, vol. viii, p. 744: *"ne vulgo arcana Dei publicentur et ludibrio habeantur."*).

p. 181, 7. *Gif deidlie syn be remittit be þe sacrifice of the mess.* Cp. Knox's *Vindication:* "*But now let us heir yf unto the Masse be joynit a wickit opinioun. It hath bene haldin in commoun opinioun, It planelie hath bene taught, by law it is decreit, and in the wordis of the Masse it is expressit, That the masse is a Sacrifice and oblatioun for the synnis of the quick and the deid: so that remissioun of synnis undoubtedlie was belevit by that same actioun and work presentlie done by the Preist*" (Laing, *Works*, iii, p. 54). In January 1560/61, during their disputation with Alexander Anderson and John Lesley, the Protestant ministers had likewise "*affirmed the actioun of the Messe to be expressedlye repugnyng unto the last Supper of the Lord Jesus; the sayar of it to committ horrible blasphemye, in usurping upoun him the office of Christ* [i.e. in presuming to offer for the sins of men]; *the hearers to committ damnable idolatrie, and the opinioun of it conceaved to be derogatioun, and as it war, disanulling of Christis death*" (Knox's *History*, in Laing, *Works*, ii, p. 139). Kennedy disavows the imputed derogation of Christ's sacrificial death and briefly explains that, though the Mass may lead to repentance, it is not the Mass but the sacraments of baptism and penance which have been instituted for a particular person's reconciliation with God. Also see p. 221, below.

p. 181, 16. *þe wordis of Alexander.* See 166, 19ff. Kennedy does not recall the words of St. Augustine and Tertullian or explain in what sense the Mass profits the dead; cp. p. 168.

p. 182, 17. *conditioun.* Apparently in the literal sense of Latin *condicio*, 'agreement', 'covenant'.

p. 182, 18f. Cp. *Compendius Tractiue*, ch. iii (*Wodrow Misc.*, pp. 107f.).

p. 183, 1–5. Cp. 158, 40ff.

Note on the text of MS G. The style of the text from p. 178 onwards is clearly different from that of Kennedy, much less polished that is. The rather abrupt ending may mean that Greenlaw intended to continue his digression on the sign of the cross, perhaps along the lines of Smith's *Bryefe treatyse of the sygne of the Crosse, and of the Crucifyxe* (pp. 49r–78r of *A bouclier of the catholike fayth of Christes church*). With the last lines of Greenlaw's text, compare: "*God said to the angel (good christen reader): passe thorow þe middest of þe citye Hierusalem, and make þe signe of Thau, vpon þe foreheades of men, mourning and sorowing kil not al them, vpon whom ye shall se, Thau. S. Hierome expoundyng that text of þe prophete, writeth thus: 'Thau litera, crucis habet similitudinem, quae in christianorum frontibus pingitur, et frequenti manus inscriptione signatur'* " (p. 50r).

TEXT OF CONSTABLE'S EXPLANATORY LETTER [1]

This Manuscript by Quintin Kennedy, abbot of Crosraguell, "vritine and endit the thyrde day of august ā 1561", belonged to Sir Robert Gordon of Gordonstoun, Baronet, Son of Alexander the fifteenth Earl of Sutherland, was MS 36 in the Catalogue of his Library, and came into my possession in the year 1803, in a manner of which it may not be uninteresting to relate the particulars.

I purchased the Library of the Gordonstoun family in November 1801, for One hundred and fifty pounds, from a Bookseller in Edinburgh, who had himself obtained it from Mr William Gordon, (natural) Son of the last Baronet of that name, at some very low price. I made the purchase without having had time to examine the Books particularly, having indeed transacted the business at first sight on a Saturday evening. On the Monday following, when I came to take possession of them, I found a number of volumes had in the meantime been abstracted; much concerned at this circumstance, I immediately waited upon Mr John Clerk, Advocate, to advise with him as to the best means of obtaining redress. Mr Clerk, who was at this time making a Library, proposed to relieve me of the bargain, to take the collection as it then was, and to give me a profit of One hundred Guineas. As I was at this time a young Man, having received many civilities from Mr Clerk, and seeing also the difficulty of proving the extent of the dilapidation, I agreed to Mr Clerk's terms and he accordingly got the Books. I afterwards spent some days in going over the Collection, which proved a truly curious one containing many valuable articles of Old English Literature – Such as the Chronicles of Fabian, Grafton, Holinshed and others, works of Gascoigne, Heywood, &c. &c., but above all a most valuable Collection of Tracts in 4to, collected by Sir Robert Gordon in the early part of the seventeenth Century, all with a few exceptions in old vellum binding, as clean as the day they were put together. The more modern part of the Collection was of little value, consisting chiefly of Civil Law, old medicine, and other articles collected (I think) by a Patrick Gordon in the Reign of Charles IId. One of the rarest Books in the Collection, and perhaps in Scotland at this day, is "Chrysoloras Erotemata Linguae Graecae 1507". Sir Robert Gordone wrote his Name on the title page of almost every Book thus [signature reproduced in facsimile], by which means the Books collected by him are the more easily distinguished. Of so little value had this Collection upon the whole been considered, however, [2] For in the Family Catalogue made up in the year 1743, and now in Mr Clerk's hands, there is the following document:

„At Gordonstoun the tenth day of September one thousand sevenhundred and
„seventy seven years I Mr John Bell Bookseller in Edinburgh having now and formerly
„examined this Catalogue of Books, and a separate List of Books on a paper apart
„marked by me as relative to this report and having also in consequence of the
„Commissionary of Murray's warrand of this date, examined the Books themselves:
„Do Report and say that I consider and esteem the whole Books in the Library at this

---

[1] See p. 51, above.
[2] Here the fair copy probably omits a line of an earlier draft.

,,place and contained in this Catalogue, and foresaid separate list to be worth Fifty
,,pounds sterling and no more. In witness whereof these presents wrote by Alexander
,,Shepherd Clerk to Sir William Gordon of Gordonstoun Baronet, are subscribed by
,,me place and date foresaid before these witnesses Mr John Innes writer to the signet
,,and the said Alexander Shepherd.

Signed

John Innes Witness

Alex^r Shepherd Witness

John Bell''

About two years after my transaction with Mr Clerk I had occasion to visit the
warehouse of the Bookseller (whose name I forbear to mention), when I found this
Manuscript and some others of the missing articles; and having got it restored as far as
possible and carefully bound up, it can no where be placed with such propriety as in
the Library at Cleveland House, and is now most respectfully offered to the Marchioness of Stafford,[3] with this History of the dispersion of the Library of the Historian
of Her Ladyship's Illustrious House.

[signed] Arch. Constable

Edinburgh, February 15. 1809.

---

[3] Elizabeth, Countess of Sutherland, 1765–1839. In 1785 she married Viscount Trentham,
subsequently second Marquess of Stafford (1803) and Duke of Sutherland (1833); see *The
Complete Peerage, or a History of the House of Lords and all its Members from the Earliest
Times*, new edition by Geoffrey H. White, vol. xii, pt. I (London, 1953), pp. 563 f.

THE MAYBOLE DISPUTATION.

Accounts of the three-days' disputation between Kennedy and Knox[1] must of necessity be based on Knox's *Maybole Ressoning*. It contains the only first-hand information not merely on the debate itself, but also on the circumstances which led up to this marathon encounter. Moreover, the difference between Knox as a disagreeably mocking editor and Knox as debater, combined with the general impression that the logical manipulations indulged in did not give either contestant reason for boasting of anything like an important triumph, lends an unmistakable air of veracity to the record, which was meant to prove that the victory belonged to Knox instead of Kennedy.[2] It thus constitutes an important historical document, of particular interest in that it shows Kennedy at last engaged in a public disputation.

The correspondence which preceded the disputation, and which started with a letter dated September 6th, presupposes at least one earlier letter, viz. one addressed to Knox by the Earl of Cassillis. This letter is not extant and it is not known when it was written, but the essence – or what appears to have been the essence – of this earlier communication can be gleaned from allusions to it in the surviving correspondence.

As one of the catholic magnates Cassillis was evidently anxious not to endanger his position by unduly antagonizing the 'Congregation' or by exposing himself to the accusation of having contravened the queen's proclamation respecting the religious situation. If Knox wished "to preach the trew word, conform to the consuetude of the realme," the Earl would give him a safe conduct in Carrick and receive him in his own house.[3] But he was unwilling to allow a disputation between his uncle and Knox unless the latter would take the first step towards it.

The letter may well have been written on the occasion referred to by Kennedy as "the last tyme ze come in this cuntrie,"[4] i.e. either during an earlier visit of Knox to Ayrshire (but after August 1561), or on an earlier visit to Carrick during his present trip to the West. On that occasion Cassillis had apparently dissuaded Kennedy from an encounter with Knox, and had in fact forbidden it "in name and behalf of the counsel", not improbably because it was the abbot who had taken the initiative. Kennedy accused Knox of having imputed to him the unwillingness which had been the Earl's only.[5]

Knox had set out to the West in the second half of August,[6] and had concentrated his efforts on the Ayrshire districts during the first weeks of his campaign. Kennedy,

---

[1] See e.g. Thomas M'Crie, *Life of Knox*, 1855 edition, pp. 193ff.; James Patterson, *History of the County of Ayr*, 2 vols., Ayr, 1847, vol. i, pp. 69ff.; F. C. Hunter Blair, *Crossraguel Charters*, vol. i, pp. 128ff.; Hugh Watt, *John Knox in Controversy*, London, 1950, pp. 51ff.

[2] See Laing, *Works*, vi, pp. 174f. and 219f.

[3] *Ibid.*, p. 181 ("as I wrait to zow of before") and p. 176 ("ze haif my Lord of Cassillis promes").

[4] *Ibid.*, p. 183.

[5] *Ibid.*, pp. 176 and 183.

[6] See letters by Randolph of August 16th and 31st in Laing, *Works*, vi, p. 143.

'perceauing the great perturbation, controuersie, and debate ... stirred vp laitlie in all Christen realmes for the cause or religion, ... and als being remembred of the terrible sentence conteined in scriptures toward all negligent pastors," preached to his flock at Kirkoswald on Sunday, August 30th, in order to make them "enarmed against all wicked and decetfull preachers." His sermon was especially on the Mass and before leaving the pulpit Kennedy announced that, presuming there would be no danger of public disturbance, he would continue his instructions on the following Sunday, i.e. September 6th.[7]

On the Friday of that week, however, seventy-seven lairds of Kyle, Cunningham and Carrick gathered round Knox at Ayr to sign the solemn 'Band' in which they promised to assist and defend with common effort the preaching of the reformed religion.[8] The day after the signing of this 'Band' Knox, accompanied by "fewer then tuentie" and presumably aware that the Earl of Cassillis was away from the district, came down to Maybole,[9] within two miles to the north of Crossraguel – about as far as Kirkoswald was to the south of the abbey. Early on the Sunday morning a delegation led by "the Laird of Caprinton elder"[10] presented itself at Kennedy's door with the proposal that he should

"either ... come and teach according to his promes and so ... suffer his doctrine in "audience of suche as he named his owne flock, to be tryed, or els ... come and heare "doctrine, and with sobrietie and gentilnes, to oppon at his pleasure,"[11]

Kennedy subsequently claimed that he had made it quite clear that he would not be present, and that he had considered himself exonerated from his promise because Knox was to appear "conuoied with v. or vj. scoir of strangers;"[12] he had also handed the messenger a refutation of Knox's syllogism against the Mass, to be presented to Knox.[13] The latter afterwards greatly wondered that Kennedy should allege that he had duly informed him of his absence. He, Knox, had gone to Kirkoswald and, when

---

[7] *Ibid.*, pp. 179 and 185. – Kennedy's first speech at Maybole had "sonday the aucht day of September", whence Paterson speaks of "Sabbath the 8th September" (*o.c.*, p. 70), whilst Hugh Watt assigns the 29th to a Sunday: "Knox must have felt it a singularly unprofitable Sunday, but, though nothing is said about adjournments for services, the comparative brevity of the recorded debate suggests that there were intermissions" (*o.c.*, p. 61). Actually, the disputation took place on the last Monday, Tuesday and Wednesday of September. On the day to which he referred back at Maybole Kennedy wrote his first recorded letter to Knox, which is dated "this Sonday, the sext of September". After receiving Knox's reply he wrote again on "this monunday the seuint of September" (Laing, *Works*, vi, pp. 177 and 178). Cp. A. Giry, *Manuel de Diplomatique*, Paris, 1894, p. 203.

[8] See p. 39, above.

[9] See Laing, *Works*, vi, pp. 176, 179 and 181.

[10] William Cunningham of Caprington, a relative of the Earl of Glencairn. Two persons of the name had signed the 'Band' at Ayr, one of them styled "younger" (Laing, *Works*, ii, pp. 348f.).

[11] *Ibid.*, vi, p. 193.

[12] *Ibid.*, pp. 185 ("being certefied that I might [i.e. 'could'] not be present") and 179.

[13] *Ibid.*, p. 176. This refutation will have been the same as in the *Oratioune* (Laing, *Works*, vi, p. 159) and the *Compendious Ressonyng* (p. 154, above).

the abbot failed to appear, preached to the people; it was after this sermon that Kennedy's letter had been given to him by "a seruand of the abbotes".[14]

"The abbotes first letter" begins with the tactical supposition that Knox had come to Carrick in order to oppose Kennedy. The latter gladly accepted this challenge on condition that the debate was to take place at Maybole, in any house of Knox's choice, and that it would be conducted in an orderly fashion with at most twenty witnesses on both sides. He also stipulated a postponement of eight days. He had had to promise the Earl of Cassillis not to engage in debates with the protestant ministers till the Earl's return but, although he was anxious to have his nephew as one of his witnesses, Kennedy would apply for written permission in case the Earl should not be back in eight days' time. If Knox refused to agree to the necessary conditions for an orderly procedure, it would be clear that he was only after creating disturbance; in that case Kennedy would not consider himself bound to appear. But if he would give the abbot's messenger a signed statement that he agreed to the conditions, Kennedy would at once inform the Earl. He would also send Knox the 'artickles' of his instructions, so that there would be no misunderstanding as to what he was to attack. In other words, Kennedy was anxious to have a written admission that Knox had taken the first step towards the disputation and that Kennedy was the defendant. His letter was not to be interpreted as a first challenge, but as the conditional acceptance of a challenge.[15]

Knox did not reply till the next day, when he had repaired to Ayr and, presumably, consulted with his followers. His first concern was to re-interpret his presence at Kirkoswald. He had not come to Ayrshire to seek disputation but to preach salvation through Jesus Christ and the fruit thereof. Accordingly, it was Kennedy's 'blasphemous artickles' that had provoked him, not the other way about. He gladly accepted an orderly disputation as proposed by Kennedy and was even willing to yield to the unreasonable demand of a maximum number of forty witnesses. But he stipulated that the disputation was to be held in St. John's church, Ayr, and that "Noters and Scribes" would be present to register the proceedings. Moreover, some delay would be necessary on account of his promised visit to Nithsdale and Galloway; if Kennedy would send his 'artickles' to the bailies of Ayr before the 15th, Knox would appoint a day on his return.[16]

That same day Kennedy wrote a reply, in which he made it quite clear that he was not going to Ayr. And in a letter which is not recorded Knox also yielded on this point.[17] Strangely enough, the 'Noters and Scribes' are not mentioned in the abbot's letter.

The next recorded letter is that of the Earl of Cassillis, dated "of Sainct Johnes chapell, the xxiij. of September". Before this date Knox and Kennedy had agreed on

---

[14] *Ibid.*, pp. 193 and 182. This shows that Kennedy communicated twice with his opponent on the Sunday morning, first through the Laird of Caprington and afterwards through his own servant. The first communication is not recorded by Knox. The second informs us that Kennedy had given Knox's messenger at least a written answer to his syllogism against the Mass, but there is no way of definitively ascertaining whether or not he had let Knox know that he would absent himself.

[15] *Ibid*, pp. 176 f.

[16] *Ibid.*, pp. 177 f.

[17] *Ibid.*, pp. 178 ff.

the 28th as the day for their debate, and the Earl's letter looks like yet another attempt to induce Knox to shoulder the responsibility for the conference. Briefly, Cassillis repeated that he was willing to receive Knox at his house if he wished to "preach the trew word, conform to the consuetude of the realme", but that he would not allow a disputation "except it cum of zour occasion."[18] Knox replied at once that "the occasion did procead of the abbote", who had provoked him by publicly declaring that he would maintain his "deceauable doctrine" against any person who might oppose him, and who had "required disputation" when Knox had actually presented himself at Kirkoswald.[19] Now that they had agreed on a definite date, Knox had no intention of backing out and humbly requested the Earl not to forbid his uncle to be present, but rather to "prouoke and encurage" him.[20]

The next letter published by Knox is one by the abbot, written on the 24th and presupposing that, at least in its writer's opinion, Knox was interpreting the Earl's letter as prompted by Kennedy and as an attempt to have the disputation cancelled. Kennedy vigorously protested that he would adhere to the terms of the agreement "in cace I sould do the samin with the haissart on my lyfe", and that he would hold Knox to his promise as well; if Knox intended to withdraw, he was not to think that he could use the Earl's letter as an excuse.[21] The next day Kennedy wrote a brief note to inform Knox and the bailies of Ayr that the Earl had come round and that the conference could take place.[22]

It is not known when and by whom "some other letters", omitted by Knox as of less importance, were written. At least two, exchanged about the 20th, must have related to the day on which the debate was to be held. In any case, Knox was at Maybole on Sunday the 27th. On that day he and Kennedy signed an official document in which they declared their agreement as to day, place, hour and conditions of the debate. Each disputant was to appear with his witnesses, scribes and "learned men", but no notaries were mentioned.[23]

At eight o'clock next morning the two parties convened in the house of Andrew Gray, provost of the collegiate church of Maybole.[24] In accordance of the final agreement of the previous day, the Earl of Cassillis admitted as many people as he deemed the house would hold. An incident threatened when Knox demanded attention for an opening prayer and Kennedy strongly objected. But when Knox had ended his prayer,

---

[18] *Ibid.*, p. 181.

[19] In his first letter Kennedy had written: "I will not refuse disputation with zow but maist ernistlie and effectuouslie couatis the samin ... lyke as I haif the rest of the ministers quhilk hes bene heir, and culd haif nane." Knox's answer might be interpreted as admitting a distinction: "ye haue required disputation of the ministers ... ye offer vnto me ... reasoning." Kennedy had insisted that he had in vain "required disputation of John Willock and als of maister George Hay," but had continued to consider himself challenged by Knox: "zit will I not refuse gif ony man will mak impugnation." To Cassillis Knox wrote: "as he had required disputation of the other ministers, so did he of me." (*Ibid.*, pp. 176, 177, 179, 180 and 182 respectively).

[20] *Ibid.*, p. 182.

[21] *Ibid.*, p. 183.

[22] *Ibid.*

[23] *Ibid.*, p. 184. It would appear that each side made its own report of the debate. There is no indication that Kennedy and Knox signed each other's reports.

[24] See Paterson, *o.c.*, p. 70. The "Prouestis place", which was opposite the church, was demolished in recent years.

"the abbote said be my faith it is weil said." The debate, which was to a large extent a continuation of the preliminary fencing of the correspondence, started when Kennedy requested one of his scribes to read out his opening address.[25]

After a brief review of the circumstances and events which had led up to the conference, Kennedy declared that for him the matter to be discussed had been settled by the church in general council and that, therefore, he considered it disputable only in a restricted sense. He had come to Maybole "to affirme the saides artickles as they ar written, beginning at the artickle concerning the masse." Knox was welcome to attack his propositions, as he had offered to do at Kirkoswald on September 6th. Kennedy then produced his scriptural justification for the sacrificial character of the Mass, which may be summarized as follows: In the *Psalms* and the *Letter to the Hebrews* Christ is called priest according to the order of Melchisedech; but what is known about Melchisedech's priesthood is limited to his offering a sacrifice of bread and wine; therefore there was question of a sacrifice at the last supper.[26]

The argument was an ingenious one in that it appeared to be based on, if not to consist of, two scriptural warrants for analogous sacrifices by Melchisedech and Christ. What strength it had as a scriptural argument lay in its appeal to psalmist and apostle. For that reason it is extremely strange that these two authorities are no more mentioned in Knox's account. As the hours – and the days – passed, Knox managed to shift the discussion to the literal text of Genesis and successfully defied Kennedy to point out a 'plain' reference to a sacrifice. The latter, apparently unaware of how much his argument was patristic instead of scriptural[27] and without again naming *Psalms* or *Hebrews*, took up the position that the sacrifice was 'plainly' implied by the words of *Genesis* and that it was Knox's task to prove from the words in question that Melchisedech had offered no sacrifice.

When Kennedy's argument had been read out, Knox asked for the text,[28] so that he might study it and give a detailed answer. But before proceeding to "familiar, formall, and gentill reasoning" Knox held a lengthy and rather too vigorous discourse, in which he drew a parallel between the false prophets and pharisees of the Old and New Testaments who had resisted the true prophets of God and, on the other side, Kennedy

---

[25] Laing, *Works*, vi, p. 184.

[26] *Ibid.*, pp. 185f.

[27] i.e. in its application of the analogy between Melchisedech and Christ to the last supper; the marginal references in the *Compendious Ressonyng* (p. 163, above) show that he was fully aware of the fathers' interpretation. What he did not realize was that the analogy could not be used as a strict proof against a person who did not believe in the sacrificial nature of the Mass. On the other hand, the argument was not Kennedy's own, as is supposed by Hugh Watt ("so far as I can find, he is its 'onlie begetter'. ... I could find nothing in the least resembling Quintin Kennedy's argument": *o.c.*, pp. 64f.). If from no other source, he might have it from Fisher (extensively in his *Sacri Sacerdotii Defensio contra Lutherum*, congressus II, decimum axioma). – Ten days before the Maybole disputation the council of Trent had incorporated the traditional analogy in its decree on the Mass without making it a strict proof (Mansi, vol. xxxiii, cols. 128f.).

[28] This may imply that Kennedy had not sent Knox his 'artickles' as he had offered to do in his first letter. In the absence of part of the correspondence one ventures to surmise that Knox may have repudiated such assistance, feeling that it would too much limit the scope of his arguments. The beginning of the disputation bears out that Knox had in fact anticipated a programme based on chapter xxii of the *Confessio Scotica*, and the struggle about the question with whom lay the *onus* of proof continued till the end of the third day.

and "the whole rable of the horned Bischoopes" with their "supersticion, idolatrie, pride, vaine glorie, ambition, vniust possessions, superfluous rentes and filthy liuing." In answer to Kennedy's earlier protestation, he then declared that for him the "plaine worde of God" was the only final and certain norm of truth.[29]

At this moment he was interrupted by Kennedy, who had been offended by several details in his opponent's discourse. He saw matter for later discussion in the question of the authority of councils and church fathers, and requested Knox to reply to his scriptural argument for the Mass.[31]

Knox answered that he would like to know what Kennedy understood by the Mass, although he was clear enough himself about "that which is cropin in into the kirk visible", which had a "name, a forme and action, an opinion conceaued of it, and an actor of the same". But Kennedy did not give him a chance to resume his denunciations. He referred him to the definition contained in the *Compendious Ressonyng* and sent to Knox the previous February and, at his request, had it again read out, adding that he meant to defend no other Mass than that which had been substantially instituted by Christ.[31]

This was not quite what Knox wanted. He wished to know whether or not Kennedy could produce any scriptural justification for the four aspects of the Mass which he, Knox, had distinguished, viz. "name, action, opinion and actor". Kennedy repeated that for the time being he insisted on having the discussion limited to the one crucial point whether Christ had substantially instituted the Mass, and when Knox answered that the ceremonies had been considered to belong to the substance, he retorted that he had not come to defend opinions of men but the institution of Christ, although once the main point were settled, he would gladly show that additional elements were not inconsistent with Scripture.[32]

Knox then pointed out that Kennedy's definition was not quite in accordance with the rules of scholastic argumentation, so would he make it clear whether he held the Mass to be a propitiatory sacrifice or some other kind of oblation? Apparently Kennedy felt this to be another attempt to shift the discussion away from his syllogism, and his answer was an evasion of what Knox appeared to be aiming that. He held the sacrifice of Calvary to be the one sacrifice of redemption and the Mass the sacrifice of commemoration of Christ's death and passion. Knox tried to construe this into a denial of the propitiatory nature of the Mass,[33] or at least an admission of inability to produce arguments for it, but Kennedy protested that he had admitted nothing and once more invited Knox to restrict himself for the time being to his syllogism.[34] To this Knox replied that if Kennedy considered Melchisedech's sacrifice a scriptural justification of the Mass, he, Knox, simply denied that there had ever been such a

---

[29] Laing, *Works*, vi, pp. 187–194.

[30] *Ibid.*, p. 194.

[31] *Ibid.*, pp. 195f.

[32] *Ibid.*, pp. 196ff.

[33] In the course of the disputation held at Edinburgh in January 1560/61 Knox had, according to his *History*, disconcerted Alexander Anderson and John Lesley by first drawing from them a denial that the Mass is a propitiatory sacrifice and then producing the Canon of the Mass as well as offering to show that "a hundreth places of your Papisticall Doctouris" defended that position (Laing, *Works*, ii, pp. 138ff.). Actually, Kennedy had answered the difficulty in his *Compendious Ressonyng* (pp. 181f., above).

[34] Laing, *Works*, vi, pp. 198f.

sacrifice. Kennedy failed to point out at this juncture that it was not accurate to imply that his syllogism exclusively appealed to the literal text of *Genesis*. Instead, he merely reminded his opponent that it was his task not merely to deny but to prove, adding that, as for himself, he took the text for his warrant.

Knox, who was to remember and make much of Kennedy's slip when he published the report,[35] had the relevant passage in the fourteenth chapter of *Genesis* read and pointed out that there was no mention of a sacrifice. Kennedy insisted that the sacrifice was clearly implied; if Knox chose to deny it, he would have to show what else had been done with the bread and wine. Knox answered that he could not accept a sacrifice for the simple reason that the text made no mention of it; and as to the purpose of the bread and wine, Melchisedech might well have brought them with him in order to refresh Abraham and his company, as authors like Flavius Josephus and Chrysostom had interpreted the text.[36]

Thus before the end of the first day the two disputants had arrived at the deadlock where they would not finally admit to have landed until another two even less interesting days had passed. Kennedy had several opportunities of correcting his slip of the first day, as when Knox said that, considering the importance of the matter, the vague text of *Genesis* did not give sufficient ground for admitting an oblation of Melchisedech's bread and wine.[37] But he failed to take them. The report of the second day of the disputation centres entirely round the possibility of the conjecture that Melchisedech had offered refreshment to an Abraham who had at his disposal the spoils of all the vanquished kings. Knox repeatedly said that he did not really care what Melchisedech had done with the bread and wine, provided he was not expected to admit a sacrifice, but that he saw no real objection to the refreshment-theory. Kennedy with like repetition argued that this was no adequate explanation, and thus his own interpretation still stood undefeated.[38] At the beginning of the third day he took occasion to review the principal points of the previous day's debate and yet again requested Knox to produce proper arguments if he still wished to refute Kennedy's position. Knox had never explicitly admitted Kennedy's sole right of demanding proofs. He replied that it was up to Kennedy to prove the sacrificial nature of the last supper, because he had not justified it so far with his appeal to an alleged sacrifice of Melchisedech. He denied that Scripture anywhere affirmed such a sacrifice, stressed yet again that the reasons actually brought forward by Kennedy lacked the clear support of the text and added that he, Knox, was still waiting for a scriptural justification of Kennedy's affirmation.[39]

With an appeal to "the haile warld" Kennedy protested that "formall ressoning" required him to defend and Knox to impugn, but that he would afterwards give as much scriptural justification of the Mass as Knox would be able to adduce in support of the incontested consubstantiality of Christ with God the Father.[40] Knox declared himself scandalized at this attempt to put "the greatest mysterie" on a par with "damnable idolatrie", but was prepared to prove the consubstantiality of Christ with

---

[35] See *ibid.*, pp. 200 and 218.

[36] *Ibid.*, pp. 199ff.; cp. Flavius Josephus, *Antiquitates*, lib. i, cap. x, and Joannes Chrysostomus, *Homilia xxxv in Cap. XIV Gen.* (Migne, *PG*, vol. liii, cols. 327f.).

[37] *Ibid.*, p. 205; cp. pp. 210–213.

[38] *Ibid.*, pp. 202–208.

[39] *Ibid.*, pp. 209ff.

[40] Cp. above, p. 142.

the Father. Kennedy, however, did not relent; Knox would first have to produ e solid arguments against the Mass, or admit defeat on that point.[41]

As neither of the disputants was willing to give in, it was decided to break off the debate. Knox proposed moreover to have the conference adjourned to Ayr "because the noble men heir assembled, were altogether destitute of all prouision, bothe for hors and man." Kennedy refused to comply and Knox had lost all desire to continue the disputation at Maybole. Thereupon Kennedy suggested applying for permission from the Queen and the Privy Council to fight it out at Edinburgh in their illustrious presence. It was agreed that Kennedy was to approach the Queen on the matter, and Knox the Privy Council.[42]

The disputation was in fact never resumed. Knox may have been proclaimed victor by his following,[43] whilst Kennedy is certain to have claimed that the Mass had been vindicated. Less than a year afterwards Knox complained of "the common brute ... that ye my Lorde, your flatterers, and collateralles brag greatlie of your victorie, obteined in disputation against John Knox."[44] And it was to counteract the influence of such rumours that Knox published his report of the disputation.

After some introductory pages in which he scoffs at "this great God of bread", he proposes the criterion for his readers to make out whether victory is to be attributed to himself or to "M. Quintyne that great patron of the Masse": if Kennedy had put forward his 'artickles' as doubtful matter, he would have been free to adhere to them until they were proved false; but as long as he proposed them as divine truth, he would have to produce arguments that they were more than human inventions.[45]

Although he never expressed it that way, this was precisely the reason why Kennedy had insisted that Knox was the 'impungnar' and he himself the 'defendar'. In his own, still largely Catholic, Carrick where he had explained the traditional belief to his flock, Knox, one of the "wicked and decetfull preachers quhilk gaes about not knowing quherefra they come, nor by quhat ordre,"[46] had appeared with novel doctrines. Knox, therefore, was the assailant, and Knox had not succeeded in proving his point. If Kennedy claimed the victory on this ground – and everything points to it that it was on this ground – it was at most a victory of a very dubious nature. When he began the disputation with a syllogism that included the transition from priesthood to a very particular sacrifice, it was but natural that Knox should demand a closer argumentation. Kennedy denied him the right to do so, but he had already given him an opportunity of putting it to the world that he, Kennedy, had shirked the issue – an opportunity which Knox did not fail to exploit.

---

[41] Laing, *Works*, vi, pp. 212ff.

[42] *Ibid.*, pp. 216f.

[43] "It is said, perhaps erroneously, that the books brought for reference by the Abbot, amounting to several wain loads, were seized by the mob, and consigned to the flames on the green of Maybole, in celebration of the assumed triumph of Knox" (Paterson, *o.c.*, p. 73). This might have happened at Ayr, but hardly at Maybole.

[44] Laing, *Works*, vi, p. 220. According to Lesley even Knox's own followers were none too pleased with his performance: "ut ... ipsi sectarii Knoxio infensi redderentur, quod provinciam quam susceperat Calvinismi defendendi melius non exornasset." (*De Rebus Gestis Scotorum*, quoted in *Crossraguel Charters*, i, pp. 129f.; Scots translation, edited for S.T.S. by E. G. Cody, vol. ii, 1895, pp. 468f.).

[45] *Ibid.*, p. 175.

[46] *Ibid.*, p. 185.

At the beginning of the third day Kennedy had attempted to turn Knox's own handling of Scripture against him. Knox held that no interpretation of Scripture was to be accepted unless it was absolutely plain from the words of Scripture itself; therefore "be his awin iudgement" Knox's explanation of Melchisedech's bread and wine was to be rejected.[47] Knox had asked leave to answer at leisure, and when the disputation broke up later that day, Kennedy made this argument a kind of symbol of Knox's failure to substantiate his charges against the Mass. In reality it gave his opponent a chance to publish a carefully prepared answer to which Kennedy had no opportunity of replying. Knox was not quite fair when he stated that Kennedy had made Melchisedech's sacrifice "the ground and cause why it behoued Christe Jesus to haue made oblation of his bodie and blood, vnder the formes of bread and wine, in his latter Supper," and that, therefore, "the masse standeth groundless". But if Knox had success in claiming that "the greatest patrone thereof, for all his sicker riding, hath ones loste his stirropes, yea, is altogether set besydes his sadil," Kennedy's purely defensive and none too brilliantly maintained tactics were at least partly to blame.[48]

---

[47] *Ibid.*, pp. 208f.
[48] *Ibid.*, pp. 217–220.

BIBLIOGRAPHY

1. History and Literature

Acts and Proceedings of the General Assemblies of the Kirk of Scotland From the Year M.D.LX., 3 vols., Edinburgh, Bannatyne Club, 1839.

AGNEW, A., *The Hereditary Sheriffs of Galloway*, 2nd ed., 2 vols., Edinburgh, 1893.

Ailsa Papers; MSS with inventory, kept at H.M. General Register House, Edinburgh (pressmark *GD. 25*).

AINSLIE, J. L., "The Scottish Reformed Church and English Puritanism", *Records of the Scottish Church History Society*, vol. viii (1944), pp. 75 ff.

AITKEN, J. M., *The trial of George Buchanan before the Lisbon Inquisition*, Edinburgh and London, 1939.

ALDIS, H. G., *A List of Books Printed in Scotland before 1700*, Edinburgh, 1904.

ALLEN, J. W., *A History of Political Thought in the Sixteenth Century*, 2nd ed., London, 1941.

ANDERSON, J. MAITLAND (ed.), *Early Records of the University of St. Andrews: the Graduation Roll 1413–1579, and the Matriculation Roll 1473–1579*, Edinburgh, Scottish History Society, 1926.

ANDERSON, W. J., "Narratives of the Scottish Reformation, II: Thomas Innes on Catholicism in Scotland, 1560–1653," *Innes Review*, vol. vii (1956), pp. 112 ff.

BAIN, J. (ed.), *Calendar of State Papers Relating to Scotland and Mary Queen of Scots 1547–1603*, Edinburgh, 1898 ff.

BARCLAY, A., *The Protestant Doctrine of the Lord's Supper. A Study in the Eucharistic Teaching of Luther, Zwingli and Calvin*, Glasgow, 1927.

BARRETT, M., *The Scottish Monasteries of Old*, Edinburgh and London, 1913.

BARROW, G. W. S., "Scottish Rulers and the Religious Orders," *English Historical Review*, iii (1953), pp. 77 ff.

BARRY, J. C., "William Hay of Aberdeen. A Sixteenth Century Scottish Theologian and Canonist," *Innes Review*, ii (1951), pp. 82 ff.

BATIFFOL, P., *L'Eucharistie, la présence réelle et la transsubstantiation* (Etudes d'histoire et de théologie positive, série II), Paris, 1920.

BELLESHEIM, A., *History of the Catholic Church of Scotland*, translated, with notes and additions, by D. Oswald Hunter Blair, O.S.B., 4 vols., Edinburgh and London, 1887–90.

BENNETT, H. S., *English Books and Readers 1475 to 1557*, Cambridge University Press, 1952.

BENNETT, J. A. W. (ed.), *Devotional Pieces in Verse and Prose*, S.T.S., Edinburgh and London, 1955.

BENOIST, R., *Renatus Benedictus, Verbi Dei Professor, disertissimo Ioanni Knox atque aliis eruditissimis viris apud antiquitatem nobilem Scotiae vocatis Ministris* [1561], in J. Lee (ed.), *Tracts by David Fergusson*, Edinburgh, Bannatyne Club, 1860.

BENOIST, R., *Necessarius atque certus modus tollendae Religionis Discordiae* [1561], Paris, 1562.

BENOIST, R., *Stroma de obedientia vere fidelium et rebellione infidelium haereticorum* [1561] and *Stroma de Idololatria Coenae Caluinicae* [1561 or 1562], appended to *Locorum praecipuorum sacrae scripturae ... conquisitio, et Catholica expositio*, Paris, 1575.

BLAIR, F. C. HUNTER (ed.), *Charters of the Abbey of Crosraguel*, 2 vols., Edinburgh, Ayrshire and Galloway Archaeological Association, 1886.

BONAVENTURE, BROTHER, "The Popular Theology of John Ireland," *Innes Review*, xiii (1962), pp. 130 ff.

BOSWELL, A. (ed.), *Ane Oratioune set furth be Master Quintine Kennedy, Commendatour of Corsraguell, ye zeir of Gode 1561*, and *Heir followeth the Coppie of the Ressoning which was betuix the Abbote of Crossraguell and John Knox, in Mayboill concerning the masse, in the yeare of God, a thousand fiue hundreth thre scoir and two yeares*, Edinburgh, 1812.

BRESCH, F., *Strasbourg et la Querelle Sacramentaire, ou rapports de Bucer à ce propos avec Luther, Zwingle et Calvin*, Montauban, 1902.

BRIE, F., *Die nationale Literatur Schottlands von den Anfängen bis zur Renaissance*, Halle, 1937.

BROWN, P. HUME, *George Buchanan: Humanist and Reformer*, Edinburgh, 1890.

BUNDERIUS (J. van den Bundere), *Detectio Nugarum Lutheri, cum declaratione veritatis catholicae et confutatione dogmatum Lutheranorum*, Louvain, 1551.

BURLEIGH, J. H. S., "The Scottish Reforming Councils, 1549 to 1559," *Records of the Scottish Church History Society*, xi (1951–53), pp. 189ff.

BURLEIGH, J. H. S., *A Church History of Scotland*, Oxford University Press, 1960.

BURNS, J. H., "Three Scots Catholic Critics of George Buchanan," *Innes Review*, i (1950), pp. 92ff.

BURNS, J. H., "The Scotland of John Major," *Innes Review*, ii (1951), pp. 65ff.

BURNS, J. H., "John Ireland and 'The Meroure of Wysdome'," *Innes Review*, vi (1955), pp. 77ff.

BURNS, J. H., "The Political Ideas of the Scottish Reformation," *Aberdeen University Review*, xxxvi (1956), pp. 253ff.

BURNS, J. H., "John Knox and Revolution, 1558," *History Today*, viii (1958), pp. 565ff.

BURNS, J. H., "The Conciliarist Tradition in Scotland," *Scottish Historical Review*, xlii (1963), pp. 89ff.

BURTON, J. H., and MASSON, D. (eds.), *The Register of the Privy Council of Scotland, First Series, 1545–1625*, 14 vols., Edinburgh, 1877–98.

BURTON, J. H., *The History of Scotland*, 8 vols., Edinburgh, 1876.

CAMERARIUS (D. Chalmers), *De statu hominis simul et novae Ecclesiae et de sanctis Regni Scotiae*, Chalons, 1627.

CAMERARIUS, *De Scotorum Fortitudine*, Paris, 1631.

CAMERON, A. I. (ed.), *The Scottish Correspondence of Mary of Lorraine*, Edinburgh, Scottish History Society, 1927.

CANT, R. G., *The College of St. Salvator, its Foundation and Development*, Edinburgh, 1950.

CHAMBERS, R. W., "The Continuity of English Prose from Alfred to More and his School," pp. xlv–clxxiv in the E.E.T.S. edition of *Harpsfield's Life of More*, London, 1932 (also published separately by the Oxford University Press).

CHRISTIE, G., *The Influence of Letters on the Scottish Reformation*, Edinburgh, 1908.

CLARK, F., *Eucharistic Sacrifice and the Reformation*, London, 1960.

CLIFFORD, A. (ed.), *The State Papers and Letters of Sir Ralph Sadler*, 2 vols., Edinburgh, 1809.

COCHLEUS, J., *In causa religionis miscellaneorum libri tres*, Ingolstadt, 1545 (fol. 65r–96v *Dialogus de tollenda in fide et religione discordia per concilium generale*).

CODY, E. G. (ed.), *Leslie's Historie of Scotland*, S.T.S., 4 vols., Edinburgh and London, 1884–95.

CONAEUS (George Conn), *De Duplici Statu Religionis apud Scotos Libri Duo*, Rome, 1628.

COUTTS, A., "Ninian Winzet: Abbot of Ratisbon, 1577–1592," *Records of the Scottish Church History Society*, xi (1951–53), pp. 240ff.

COWAN, H., *John Knox. The Hero of the Scottish Reformation*, New York, 1905.

COX, J. E. (ed.), *Writings and Disputations of Thomas Cranmer ... Relative to the Sacrament of the Lord's Supper*, Cambridge, Parker Society, 1844.

CRANSTOUN, J. (ed.), *Satirical Poems of the Time of the Reformation*, S.T.S., Edinburgh and London, 1891.

DAVIDSON, D., "Influence of the English Printers on the Scottish Reformation," *Records of the Scottish Church History Society*, i (1926), pp. 75ff.

DEMPSTER, T., *Menologium Scoticum*, Bologna, 1622.

DEMPSTER, T., *Historia Ecclesiastica Gentis Scotorum: sive, De Scriptoribus Scotis*, Bologna, 1627.

DICKINSON, W. CROFT (ed.), *John Knox's History of the Reformation in Scotland*, 2 vols., London, 1949.

226

DICKINSON, W. CROFT, *Scotland from the Earliest Times to 1603*, London, 1961.

DICKINSON, W. CROFT, DONALDSON, G., and MILNE, I. A. (eds.), *A Source Book of Scottish History*, 2nd ed., 3 vols., London, 1958.

DICKSON, R., and EDMOND, J. P., *Annals of Scottish Printing*, Cambridge, 1890.

DILLON, W. J., "The Origins of Feudal Ayrshire," *Ayrshire Archaeological and Natural History Society Collections*, 2nd series, iii (1950–54), pp. 65 ff.

DIX, G., "Dixit Cranmer et non timuit," *Church Quarterly Review*, 1948, nos. 290 and 291.

DONALDSON, G. (ed.), *Accounts of the Collectors of Thirds of Benefices, 1561–1572*, Edinburgh, Scottish History Society, 1949.

DONALDSON, G., *The Scottish Reformation*, Cambridge University Press, 1960.

DOWDEN, J., *The Bishops of Scotland*, Glasgow, 1912.

DUGMORE, C. W., *The Mass and the English Reformers*, London, 1958.

DUNLOP, A. I., *The Life and Times of James Kennedy, Bishop of St. Andrews*, Edinburgh and London, 1950.

DURKAN, J., "Robert Wauchope, Archbishop of Armagh," *Innes Review*, i (1950), pp. 48 ff.

DURKAN, J., "John Major: After 400 Years," *Innes Review*, i (1950), pp. 131 ff.

DURKAN, J., "The Beginnings of Humanism in Scotland," *Innes Review*, iv (1953), pp. 5 ff.

DURKAN, J., *The Scottish Universities in the Middle Ages*, Ph.D. thesis (unpublished), Edinburgh University, 1959.

DURKAN, J., and ROSS, A., *Early Scottish Libraries*, Glasgow, 1961.

EASSON, D. E., "The Collegiate Churches of Scotland: Part I, Their Characteristics; Part II, Significance," *Records of the Scottish Church History Society*, vi (1938), pp. 193 ff. and vii (1941), pp. 30 ff.

EASSON, D. E., *Medieval Religious Houses: Scotland*, London, 1957.

EVENNETT, H. O., *The Cardinal of Lorraine and the Council of Trent*, Cambridge University Press, 1930.

FERGUSSON, J., "The Protocol Book of Henry Prestoun" (with abstracts of instruments), *Ayrshire Archaeological and Natural History Society Collections*, 2nd series, iii (1950–54), pp. 46 ff.

FERGUSSON, J., *The White Hind and Other Discoveries*, London, 1963.

FISHER, JOHN, *Opera quae hactenus inueniri potuerunt omnia*, Wurzburg, 1597.

FLEMING, D. HAY, *Mary Queen of Scots, From her Birth to her Flight into England*, 2nd ed., London, 1898.

GARRETT, C. H., *The Marian Exiles, a study in the origins of Elizabethan Puritanism*, Cambridge, 1938.

GILLOW, J., *A Literary and Biographical History, or Bibliographical Dictionary of English Catholics, from the breach with Rome ... 1534, to the present time*, 5 vols., London, 1898.

GRACIE, J. B. (ed.), *Certain Tractates for Reformation of Doctrine and Manners in Scotland, by Ninian Winzet, MDLXII–MDLXIII*, Edinburgh, Maitland Club, 1835.

HANCOCK, P. D., *A Bibliography of Works Relating to Scotland, 1916–1950*, 2 vols., Edinburgh, 1959–60.

HANNAY, R. K., *The Statutes of the Faculty of Arts and the Faculty of Theology at the Period of the Reformation*, St. Andrews, 1910.

HANNAY, R. K., and HAY, D. (eds.), *Letters of James V*, Edinburgh, 1954.

HAY, GEORGE, *The Confutation of the Abbote of Crosraguels Masse*, Edinburgh, 1563.

HAY, RICHARD AUGUSTINE, *Scotia Sacra: Ane Account of The most renowned churches, Bishopricks, monasteries, and other devote places from the first introducing of Christianity into Scotland, To the disturbances occasioned in that nation by the severall reformations of Religion*, MS (National Library of Scotland), 1700.

HENDERSON, T. F., *Scottish Vernacular Literature*, 3rd ed., Edinburgh, 1910.

HERFORD, C. H., *Studies in the Literary Relations of England and Germany in the Sixteenth Century*, Cambridge, 1886.

HEWAT, K., *Makers of the Scottish Church at the Reformation*, Edinburgh, 1920.

227

HEWISON, J. KING ed.), *Certain Tractates, together with the Book of Four Score Three Questions and a Translation of Vincentius Lirinensis,* by Ninian Winzet, S.T.S., 2 vols., Edinburgh and London, 1888–90.

HOLINSHED, R., *The Scottish Chronicle, or, A Complete History and Description of Scotland,* (reprinted) 2 vols., Arbroath, 1805.

HOPF, C. L. R. A., *Martin Bucer and the English Reformation,* Oxford, 1946.

HUGHES, P., *The Reformation in England,* 3 vols., London, 1950–54.

JAMOULLE, E., "Le Sacrifice Eucharistique au Concile de Trente," *Nouvelle Revue Théologique,* lxvii (1945), pp. 513 ff.

JUNGMANN, J. A., *The Mass of the Roman Rite: Its Origins and Development,* English translation by F. A. Brunner (from German revised edition of *Missarum Solemnia,* 1949), 2 vols., New York, 1951–55.

KEITH, R., *History of the Affairs of Church and State in Scotland, from the Beginning of the Reformation to the Year 1568,* reprinted for the Spottiswoode Society, 3 vols., Edinburgh, 1844.

KENNETH, BROTHER, "Sir David Lindsay, Reformer," *Innes Review,* i (1950), pp. 79 ff.

KIDD, B. J., *Documents of the Continental Reformation,* Oxford, 1911.

KRAPP, G. P., *The Rise of English Literary Prose,* New York, 1915.

LAING, D. (ed.), *The Miscellany of the Wodrow Society,* Edinburgh, 1844.

LAING, D. (ed.), *The Works of John Knox,* 6 vols., Edinburgh, Wodrow Society and Bannatyne Club, 1846–64.

LANG, A., *John Knox and the Reformation,* London, 1905.

LAW, T. GRAVES (ed.), *Hamilton's Catechism,* Oxford, Bannatyne Club, 1884.

LAW, T. GRAVES (ed.), *Catholic Tractates of the Sixteenth Century: 1573–1600,* S.T.S., Edinburgh and London, 1899–1900.

LEE, J. (ed.), *Tracts by David Fergusson,* Edinburgh, Bannatyne Club, 1860.

LEITH, W. FORBES, *Narratives of Scottish Catholics under Mary Stuart and James VI,* London, 1889.

LEITH, W. FORBES, *Pre-Reformation Scholars in Scotland in the Sixteenth Century,* Glasgow, 1915.

LESLAEUS, IOANNES, *De Origine, Moribus et Rebus Gestis Scotorum,* Rome, 1578.

LEWIS, C. S., *English Literature in the Sixteenth Century Excluding Drama* (vol. iii of *Oxford History of English Literature*), Oxford University Press, 1944.

LIVINGSTONE, M., and others (eds.), *Registrum Secreti Sigilli Regum Scotorum. The Register of the Privy Seal of Scotland,* Edinburgh, in progress, 1918–.

LORIMER, P., *Precursors of Knox,* Edinburgh, 1857.

LORIMER, P., *John Knox and the Church of England,* London, 1875.

M'CRIE, T., *Life of John Knox,* new ed., Edinburgh and London, 1855.

MACDONALD, G., "The Mint of Crosraguel Abbey," *Proceedings of the Society of Antiquaries of Scotland,* liv (1920), pp. 20 ff.

McDOWALL, J. KEVAN, *A Genealogical History in Cartographic Form Pertaining to Galloway and its Ancient Division of Carrick,* Chart, 9′ × 2′8″, Glasgow, 1938.

McEWEN, J. S., *The Faith of John Knox,* London, 1961.

McGARRY, L., *The Holy Eucharist in Middle English Homiletic and Devotional Verse,* Washington, 1936.

MACKAY, A. J. G., *Memoir of John Major of Haddington ... 1469/70–1550. A Study in Scottish History and Education,* Edinburgh, 1892.

MACKENZIE, A. MURE, *An Historical Survey of Scottish Literature to 1714,* London, 1933.

MACKENZIE, G., *The Lives and Characters of the most Eminent Writers of the Scots Nation; with an Abstract and Catalogue of their Works, their various Editions, and the Judgment of the Learn'd concerning them,* Edinburgh, 1722.

MACKENZIE, W. M. (ed.), *The Poems of William Dunbar,* Edinburgh, 1932.

McROBERTS, D. (ed.), *Essays on the Scottish Reformation, 1513–1625,* Glasgow, 1962.

MAJOR, JOHN, *History of Greater Britain*, translated for the Scottish History Society by A. Constable, Edinburgh, 1892.

MATHESON, C., *A Catalogue of the Publications of Scottish Historical and Kindred Clubs and Societies, 1908–1927*, Aberdeen, 1928.

MATHIESON, W. LAW, *Politics and Religion. A Study in Scottish History from the Reformation to the Revolution*, 2 vols., Glasgow, 1902.

MAXWELL, M., *John Knox's Genevan Service Book*, London, 1931.

MAYOR, J. E. B., and BAYNE, R. (eds.), *Bishop Fisher's English Works*, E.E.T.S., extra series, 2 vols., 1876 and 1915.

MEIKLE, H. W., *Scotland*, Cambridge, 1950.

MESSENGER, E. C., *The Reformation, the Mass and the Priesthood*, 2 vols., London, 1936–37.

MEZGER, A., *John Knox et ses Rapports avec Calvin*, Montaubon, 1905.

MILL, A. J., *Mediaeval Plays in Scotland*, St. Andrews, 1927.

MILLAR, J. H., *A Literary History of Scotland*, London, 1903.

MITCHELL, A. F. (ed.), *The Catechism set forth by Archbishop Hamilton, together with the Two-Penny Faith*, Edinburgh, 1882.

MITCHELL, A. F. (ed.), *A Compendious Book of Godly and Spiritual Songs, Commonly Known as 'The Gude and Godlie Ballatis'*, S.T.S., Edinburgh and London, 1897.

MITCHELL, A. F., and FLEMING, D. HAY, *The Scottish Reformation*, Edinburgh, 1900.

MURISON, W., *Sir David Lyndsay: Poet and Satirist of the Old Church in Scotland*, Cambridge University Press, 1938.

OECOLAMPADIUS, J., *De genuina verborum Domini 'Hoc est corpus meum' iuxta vetustissimos auctores expositione liber*, Basle, 1525.

OWST, G. R., *Preaching in Mediaeval England*, Cambridge University Press, 1926.

OWST, G. R., *Literature and Pulpit in Medieval England*, Cambridge University Press, 1933.

PASQUIER, E., *René Benoist, le 'Pape des Halles' (1521–1608)*, Paris, 1913.

PATERSON, J., *History of the County of Ayr: with a Genealogical Account of the Families of Ayrshire*, 2 vols., Ayr, 1847.

PATRICK, D. (ed.), *Statutes of the Scottish Church, 1225–1559*, (translation of Robertson's collection), Scottish History Society, 1907.

PAUL, JAMES BALFOUR, *The Scots Peerage, Founded on Wood's Edition of Sir Robert Douglas's Peerage of Scotland*, Edinburgh, 9 vols., 1904–1914.

PERCY, LORD EUSTACE, *John Knox*, London, 1937.

PITCAIRN, R. (ed.), *Historical and Genealogical Account of the Principal Families of the Name of Kennedy, from an original MS, with Notes and Illustrations*, Edinburgh, 1830.

PITCAIRN, R. (ed.), *Criminal Trials in Scotland*, Edinburgh, 1833.

PITCAIRN, R. (ed.), *Memorials of Transactions in Scotland A.D. MDLXIX–A.D. MDLXXIII. By Richard Bannatyne, Secretary to John Knox*, Edinburgh, Bannatyne Club, 1836.

POLLARD, A. W., and REDGRAVE, G. R., *A Short-Title Catalogue of Books printed in England, Scotland, and Ireland, And of English Books Printed Abroad 1475–1640*, London, Bibliographical Society, 1946.

POLLEN, J. H., *Papal Negotiations with Mary Queen of Scots, 1561–67*, Edinburgh, Scottish History Society, 1901.

POLMAN, P., "La méthode polémique des premiers adversaires de la Réforme," *Revue d'histoire ecclésiastique*, xxv (1929), pp. 471 ff.

POLMAN, P., *L'Élément historique dans la controverse réligieuse du XVIe siècle*, Gembloux, 1932.

POLMAN, P., "Religieuze Polemiek en Historische Kritiek in de XVIe Eeuw," *Studia Catholica*, x (1933–34), pp. 421 ff.

QUINN, E., "Bishop Tunstall's Treatise on the Holy Eucharist," *Downside Review*, li (1933), pp. 674 ff.

REID, W. STANFORD, "Clerical Taxation: The Scottish Alternative to Dissolution of the Monasteries, 1530–1560," *Catholic Historical Review*, xxiv (1948), pp. 129 ff.

RICHARDSON, C. C., *Zwingli and Cranmer on the Eucharist: Cranmer dixit et contradixit*, Evanston, Illinois, 1949.

ROBERTSON, J. (ed.), *Concilia Scotiae: Ecclesiae Scoticanae Statuta tam Provincialia quam Synodalia quae supersunt*, 2 vols., Edinburgh, Bannatyne Club, 1866.

ROBERTSON, W., *Ayrshire. Its History and Historic Families*, 2 vols., Kilmarnock and Ayr, 1908.

ROBINSON, H. (ed.), *Original Letters Relative to the English Reformation*, 2 vols., Cambridge, Parker Society, 1846–47.

ROBINSON, H. (ed.), *The Zurich Letters*, 2 vols., Cambridge, Parker Society, 1842–45.

ROGERS, C., *Three Scottish Reformers*, London, English Reprint Society, 1874.

ROSS, J. M., *Scottish History and Literature to the Period of the Reformation*, Glasgow, 1884.

SCOTT (OF PERTH), J., *A History of the Protestant Reformers in Scotland*, Edinburgh, 1817.

SMALL, J. (ed.), *Poems of Walter Kennedy*, S.T.S., Edinburgh and London, 1893.

SMELLIE, A., *The Reformation in its Literature*, London, 1925.

SMITH, G. G., *Scottish Literature: Character and Influence*, London, 1919.

SMITH, G. G., *The Transition Period* (in *Periods of European Literature*), Edinburgh, 1900.

SMITH, RICHARD, *The assertion and defence of the sacrament of the aulter*, London, 1546.

SMITH, RICHARD, *A Defence of the Sacrifice of the masse ... Wherein are diuerse doubtes opened ouer and aboue the principal matter*, London, 1547.

SMITH, RICHARD, *A brief treatyse settynge forth diuers truthes necessary both to be beleued of chrysten people, and kepte also, whiche are not expressed in the scripture but left to the church by the apostles tradition*, London, 1547.

SMITH, RICHARD, *Of vnwryten verytyes*, London, 1548.

SMITH, RICHARD, *A Confutation of a certen booke, called a defence of the true and Catholike doctrine of the sacrament ... sette fourth of late in the name of Thomas Archebysshoppe of Canterburye*, n.p., 1550.

SMITH, RICHARD, *A bouclier of the catholike fayth of Christes church conteynyng diuers matiers now of late called into controuersy, by the new gospellers*, n.p., n.d. –*The seconde parte of the booke called a Bucklar of the Catholyke fayeth, conteyninge seuen chapiters*, London, 1555.

SOUTHERN, A. C., *Elizabethan Recusant Prose 1559–1582*, London and Glasgow, n.d. [1950].

SPEIRS, J., *The Scots Literary Tradition*, 2nd ed., London, 1962.

SPINGARN, J. E., *A History of Literary Criticism in the Renaissance*, New York, 1912.

SPOTTISWOODE, J., *History of the Church of Scotland*, 3 vols., Edinburgh, Spottiswoode Society, 1851.

STURGE, C., *Cuthbert Tunstall*, London, 1938.

TAVARD, G. H., *Holy Writ or Holy Church: The Crisis of the Protestant Reformation*, New York, 1959.

TAYLOR, M., *The Doctrinal Defence of Mass and the Sacraments during the Scottish Reformation (1549–1564)*, Rome, Gregorian University thesis (unpublished), 1954.

TERRY, C. SANFORD, *A Catalogue of the Publications of Scottish Historical and Kindred Clubs and Societies, 1780–1909*, Glasgow, 1909.

THOMSON, J. MAITLAND, and PAUL, J. BALFOUR (eds.), *Registrum Magni Sigilli Regum Scotorum. The Register of the Great Seal of Scotland*, 6 vols., Edinburgh, 1882–90 (vol. i revised 1912).

THOMSON, T. (ed.), *Diurnal of Remarkable Occurrents*, Edinburgh, Bannatyne and Maitland Clubs, 1833.

THOMSON, T., and INNES, C. (eds.), *The Acts of the Parliaments of Scotland A.D. MCXXIV–MDCCVII*, 12 vols. in 13, Edinburgh, 1814–75.

TIMMS, G. B., "Dixit Cranmer," *Church Quarterly Review*, 1947, nos. 286 and 287.

TOWNSEND, G. (ed.), *The Acts and Monuments of John Foxe: With a Life of the Martyrologist, and Vindication of the Work*, 8 vols., London, 1843–49.

TUNSTAL, CUTHBERT, *De ueritate Corporis et Sanguinis Domini nostri Iesu Christi in Eucharistia*, 2nd ed., Paris, 1554.

230

VERMIGLI, PETER MARTYR, *De Sacramento Eucharistiae in celeberrima Angliae schola Oxoniensi habita tractatio*, (1549), Zurich, 1552.

WILDBOLZ, E., *Biblical Exegesis in the Writings of John Knox and his Scottish Contemporaries*, Ph.D. thesis (unpublished), Edinburgh University, 1952.

WILLIAM OF MIDDLETON, *Opusculum super Missam*, ed. A. v. Dijk, *Ephemerides Liturgicae*, liii (1939), pp. 291ff.

WITTIG, K., *The Scottish Tradition in Literature*, Edinburgh and London, 1958.

2. Language

BALD, M. A., "The Anglicisation of Scottish Printing," *Scottish Historical Review*, xxiii, pp. 107ff.

BALD, M. A., "The Pioneers of Anglicised Speech in Scotland," *Scottish Historical Review*, xxiv, pp. 179ff.

BALD, M. A., "Contemporary References to the Scottish Speech of the Sixteenth Century," *Scottish Historical Review*, xxv, pp. 163ff.

BAUGH, A. C., *A History of the English Language*, 2nd ed., London, 1962.

BERGSTEN, N., *A Study on Compound Substantives in English*, Uppsala, 1911.

BJÖRKMAN, E., *Scandinavian Loanwords in Middle English*, Studien zur Englischen Philologie, VII), Halle, 1900–02.

BOSWORTH, J., and TOLLER, T. N., *An Anglo-Saxon Dictionary*, Oxford, 1882–98; *Supplement* by T. N. Toller, Oxford, 1908–21.

BRUNNER, K., *Die Englische Sprache. Ihre geschichtliche Entwicklung*, 2 vols., Tubingen, 1960–62.

CALLAWAY, M., *Studies in the Syntax of the Lindesfarne Gospels*, Baltimore, 1918.

COLVILLE, J., *Studies in Lowland Scots*, Edinburgh and London, 1909.

CRAIGIE, J. (joint editor with H. W. Meikle and J. Purves), *The Works of William Fowler*, S.T.S., Edinburgh and London, vol. iii (study on the language) 1940.

CRAIGIE, J. (ed.), *Thomas Hudson's Historie of Judith*, S.T.S., Edinburgh and London, 1941.

CRAIGIE, J. (ed.), *The Basilicon Doron of King James VI*, S.T.S., Edinburgh and London, vol. ii (with study on the language) 1950.

CRAIGIE, W. A. (ed.), *Livy's History of Rome: The First Five Books; Translated into Scots by John Bellenden (1533)*, S.T.S., 2 vols., Edinburgh and London, 1901–03.

CRAIGIE, W. A., "Older Scottish and English. A Study in Contrasts," *Transactions of the Philological Society*, London 1935, pp. 1ff.

CRAIGIE, W. A., "Scottish Language," *Chamber's Encyclopedia*, 1950, vol. xii, s.v.

CRAIGIE, W. A., and AITKEN, A. J. (eds.), *A Dictionary of the Older Scottish Tongue*, University of Chicago Press, in progress, 1937–.

CURME, G. O., "A History of English Relative Constructions," *Journal of English and Germanic Philology*, xi (1912), pp. 10ff., 180ff. and 355ff.

DANIELSON, B., *Studies in the Accentuation of Polysyllabic Latin, Greek and Romance Loan Words in English* (Stockholm Studies in English, III), Stockholm, 1948.

DELLIT, O., *Über lateinische Elemente im Mittelenglischen*, Marburg, 1905.

DIETH, E., *A Grammar of the Buchan Dialect (Aberdeenshire)*, vol. i, Phonology–Accidence, Cambridge, 1932.

DOBSON, E. J., *English Pronunciation 1500–1700*, 2 vols., Oxford, 1957.

DU CANGE, C., and FAVRE, L., *Glossarium Mediae et Infimae Latinitatis*, 10 vols., London, 1884–87.

ECKHARDT, E., "Der Übergang zur germanischen Betonung bei den Wörtern französischer Herkunft im Mittelenglischen," *Englische Studien*, lxxv (1942), pp. 9ff.

ELLIS, A. J., *On Early English Pronunciation*, E.E.T.S., Extra Series, 5 vols., London, 1867–89.

FLOM, G. T., *Scandinavian Influence on Southern Lowland Scots* (Columbia University Germanic Studies, I), New York, 1900.

231

FRANCISQUE-MICHEL, *A Critical Enquiry into the Scottish Language*, Edinburgh, 1882.

FRIES, C. C., "On the Development of the Structural Use of Word-Order in Modern English", *Language*, xvi (1940), pp. 199 ff.

GADDE, F., *On the History and Use of the Suffixes -ery (-ry), -age and -ment in English*, Lund, 1910.

GEDDIE, W. A., *A Bibliography of Middle Scots Poets*, S.T.S., Edinburgh and London, 1912.

GILES, P., "The Making of our Mother Tongue," *Transactions of the Buchan Field Club*, viii, pp. 185 ff.

GIRVAN, R. (ed.), *Ratis Ravyng and Other Early Scots Poems on Morals*, S.T.S., Edinburgh and London, 1939.

GRANT, W., and DIXON, J. M., *A Manual of Modern Scots*, Cambridge, 1921.

GRANT, W., and MURISON, D. (eds.), *The Scottish National Dictionary*, Edinburgh, in progress, 1931–.

GROOT, A. W. DE, "Subject-Predicate Analysis," *Lingua*, vi (1956–57), pp. 301 ff.

HENSCHEL, P., *Darstellung der Flexionslehre in John Barbour's Bruce*, Leipzig, 1886.

HOLTHAUSEN, F., "Negation statt Vergleichungspartikel beim Komparativ," *Indogermanische Forschungen*, xxxii, pp. 339 f.

JAMIESON, J., *An Etymological Dictionary of the Scottish Language*, new edition, revised and collated by J. Longmuir and D. Donaldson, 4 vols., Paisley, 1879–82.

JESPERSEN, O., *Growth and Structure of the English Language*, 9th ed., Oxford, 1952.

JONES, R. F., *The Triumph of the English Language*, London, 1953.

JORDAN, R., *Handbuch der mittelenglischen Grammatik*, I. Lautlehre, 2nd edition, revised by H. C. Matthes, Heidelberg, 1934.

KELLER, W., *Skandinavischer Einfluss in der englischen Flexion*, Heidelberg, 1925.

KELLNER, L., "Abwechselung und Tautologie: zwei Eigenthümlichkeiten des alt- und mittelenglischen Stiles," *Englische Studien*, xx (1895), pp. 1 ff.

KELLNER, L., *Historical Outlines of English Syntax*, London, 1924.

KNOPFF, P., *Darstellung der Ablautsverhältnisse in der schottischen Schriftsprache, mit Vergleichungen in Bezug auf Abweichungen der anderen mittelenglischen Dialekte*, Wurzburg, 1904.

KNÜPFER, H., "Die Anfänge der periphrastische Komparation im Englischen," *Englische Studien*, lv (1921), pp. 321 ff.

KÖKERITZ, H., *Shakespeare's Pronunciation*, Yale University Press, 1953.

KURATH, H., and KUHN, S. M. (eds.), *Middle English Dictionary*, Ann Arbor, University of Michigan Press, in progress, 1952–.

LENZ, K., *Zur Lautlehre der französischen Elemente in den schottischen Dichtungen von 1500–1550* (G. Douglas, W. Dunbar, D. Lyndesay, Clariodus), Marburg, 1913.

LUICK, K., *Untersuchungen zur englischen Lautgeschichte*, Strassburg, 1896.

LUICK, K., *Studien zur englischen Lautgeschichte*, Vienna, 1903.

LUICK, K., *Historische Grammatik der englischen Sprache*, Leipzig, 1921–40.

McDOWALL, J. KEVAN, *Carrick Gallovidian*, Ayr, 1947 (on place-names in Kennedy area).

McINTOSH, A., *Introduction to a Survey of Scottish Dialects*, Edinburgh, 1961.

MENDENHALL, J. C., *Aureate Terms*, Lancaster, Pa., 1919.

METZGER, E., *Zur Betonung der lateinisch-romanischen Wörter im Neuenglischen* (Anglistische Forschungen, XXV), Heidelberg, 1908.

MÜLLER, P., *Die Sprache der Aberdeener Urkunden des sechzehnten Jahrhunderts*, Berlin, 1908.

MURRAY, J. A. H. (ed.), *The Complaynt of Scotland*, E.E.T.S., extra series, 1872.

MURRAY, J. A. H., *The Dialect of the Southern Countries of Scotland*, London, 1873.

MURRAY, J. A. H., and others (eds.), *A New English Dictionary on Historical Principles*, Oxford, 1888–1928.

MUSTANOJA, T. F., *A Middle English Syntax*, Helsinki, 1960.

MUTSCHMANN, H., 'A Phonology of the North-eastern Scotch Dialect," *Bonner Studien zur englischen Philologie*, i (1909), pp. 1 ff.

POPE, M. K., *From Latin to Modern French with Especial Consideration of Anglo-Norman*, Manchester University Press, 1956.

POUND, L., *The Comparison of Adjectives in English in the XV. and the XVI. Century* (Anglistische Forschungen, VII), Heidelberg, 1901.

PRICE, H. T., "A History of Ablaut in the Strong Verbs from Caxton to the End of the Elisabethan Period," *Bonner Studien zur englischen Philologie*, iii (1910), pp. 1 ff.

REEVES, W. P., *A Study in the Language of Scottish Prose before 1600*, Baltimore, 1893.

SCHMIDT, K. H., *Präfixwandlungen im Mittelenglischen und Neuenglischen bei Verben, Substantiven und Adjektiven*, Strassburg, 1909.

SHEPPARD, E. A., *Studies in the Language of Bellenden's Prose*, University of London thesis (unpublished), 1936.

SIEVERS, A., and BRUNNER, K., *Altenglische Grammatik*, Halle, 1942.

SINCLAIR, I. G., *The Thistle and Fleur de Lys: a Vocabulary of Franco-Scottish Words*, Edinburgh and London, 1904.

SKEAT, W. W. (ed.), *Barbour's Bruce*, S.T.S., 3 vols. (introduction in vol. iii), Edinburgh and London, 1893–94.

SKEAT, W. W. (ed.), *The Kingis Quair, together with a Ballad of Good Counsel*, S.T.S., Edinburgh and London, 1911.

SKEAT, W. W., *An Etymological Dictionary of the English Language*, 4th ed., reprinted, Oxford, 1961.

SMITH, G. G., *Specimens of Middle Scots*, Edinburgh and London, 1902.

SPROTTE, O., *Zum Sprachgebrauch bei John Knox*, Berlin, 1906.

STEINKI, J., *Die Entwicklung der englischen Relativpronomina in spätmittelenglischer und frühneuenglischer Zeit*, Breslau, 1932.

STRATMANN, F. H., and BRADLEY, H., *A Middle English Dictionary*, Oxford, 1891.

SWEET, H., *A History of English Sounds from the Earliest Period*, Oxford, 1888.

TEICHERT, F., *Über das Aussterben alter Wörter im Verlaufe der englischen Sprachgeschichte*, Kiel, 1912.

VISSER, F. T., *A Syntax of the English Language of St. Thomas More*, 3 vols., Louvain, 1946–1956.

VISSER, F. T., *An Historical English Syntax, Pt. I: Syntactical Units with One Verb*, Leiden, 1963.

WARRACK, A., *A Scots Dialect Dictionary*, London, 1911.

WESTERGAARD, E., "Verbal Forms in Middle Scotch," *Anglia*, xliii (1919), pp. 95 ff.

WESTERGAARD, E., *Studies in Prefixes and Suffixes in Middle Scottish*, Oxford University Press, 1924.

WILLIAMS, O. T., "The Development of ai and ei in Middle Scotch," *Transactions of the Philological Society*, 1907–10, pp. 285 ff.

WILLIAMS, O. T., "On OE a, ā and æ in the Rimes of Barbour's Brus and in Modern Scotch Dialects," *Transactions of the Philological Society*, 1911–14, pp. 7 ff.

WOOLLEY, J. S., *Bibliography for Scottish Linguistic Studies*, Edinburgh, 1954.

WRIGHT, J., *The English Dialect Dictionary*, 6 vols., London, 1898–1905.

WRIGHT, J., *The English Dialect Grammar*, Oxford, 1905.

ZOEGA, G., *A Concise Dictionary of Old Icelandic*, Oxford, 1910.

Gordon, Alexander, Titular Archbishop of Athens, Bishop Designate of Galloway, 54, 59n.

Gordon, George, 4th Earl of Huntly, Chancellor of Scotland after Card. Beaton's death, 20n, 39.

Gordon, Sir Robert, 51.

Goudanus, 37n, 38.

Greenlaw, John, 51, 54, 71, 88, 101, 102, 106, 108, 109.

Gregory of Nanzianzen, St., 68.

Gropper, John, 18.

Guerrero, Archbishop of Granada, 66n.

Guise, Mary of, 1, 2. 4, 6, 9, 10, 15n, 19, 20, 23, 29, 34n, 60n, 61.

Hamilton, James, 2nd Earl of Arran, Duke of Châtelherault, 1, 4, 6, 9, 10, 13, 19, 20n, 28, 29.

Hamilton, Jean, Arran's daughter, 28f.

Hamilton, John, Abbot of Paisley and Archbishop of St. Andrews, 1, 5, 19, 21, 26, 29, 38.

Hamilton, Patrick, protestant martyr, 12.

Hamilton's Catechism, 17f.

Harlaw, William, 19, 21.

Hay, Archibald, 3.

Hay, George, 2, 26, 39n, 40, 44, 55, 67f.

Hay, Richard Augustine, 48.

Henry II, King of France, 1, 23n.

Henry VIII, 1, 9, 10, 12, 18, 28, 64.

Heriot, Adam, 54, 59n.

Hilary of Poitiers, 68.

Holinshed, 45.

Hosius, Stanislaus, 68.

Huntley, Earl of, see Gordon.

Ignatius of Antioch, St., 67.

Innes, Thomas, 43.

Irenaeus, St., 68.

James V, 1, 4, 5, 6, 9, 11, 12, 13, 15n, 66, 102.

Jerome, St., 68.

John Damascene, 68.

Keith, Bishop Robert, 49, 56.

Kennedy, Archibald, Brother to Quintin Kennedy, 25n.

Kennedy, David, 1st Earl of Cassillis, 25.

Kennedy, David, Brother to Quintin Kennedy, 25n.

Kennedy, Gilbert, 1st Lord K., 25.

Kennedy, Gilbert, Provost of Maybole collegiate church, 8.

Kennedy, Gilbert, 2nd Earl of Cassillis, Quintin's father, 25.

Kennedy, Gilbert, 3rd Earl of Cassillis, Quintin's brother, 1, 4n, 13, 15, 19, 20n, 25, 27, 28, 29, 30, 32, 61.

Kennedy, Gilbert, 4th Earl of Cassillis, Quintin's nephew, 2, 9, 25, 30, 32, 33, 35, 39, 41, 42, 49, 60, 62n.

Kennedy, Henry, Cinneadais, 25n.

Kennedy, Hugh, Brother to Quintin K., 8, 25n.

Kennedy, James, Son-in-law to Robert III, 25.

Kennedy, James, Bishop of St. Andrews, 5, 25.

Kennedy, James, Vicar of Maybole, 8.

Kennedy, James, Vicar of Dunscore, 8.

Kennedy, James, Vicar of Penpont, 8.

Kennedy, James of Ochtrelure, Brother to Quintin K., 25n, 41n, 54f.

Kennedy, John, 2nd Lord K., 8.

Kennedy, John, Maybole prebendary, 8.

Kennedy, Quintin, Abbot of Crossraguel, *passim.*

Kennedy, Thomas, Brother to Quintin K., 8, 25n, 26.

Kennedy, Walter, Parson of Douglas, Poet, 8, 25.

Kennedy, Walter, Parson of Douglas, Canon of Glasgow, Poet's son, 8.

Kennedy, William, Abbot of Crossraguel, Quintin's uncle, 7, 8, 26, 27, 28, 29.

Kilmaurs, Lord, see Cunningham.

Knox, John, 1, 2, 3, 10, 11, 13n, 15, 17, 18, 19, 20, 23, 31, 37ff., 47, 48, 53, 55, 57, 58n, 59n, 61, 63, 65, 68, 69, 75, 84.

Leich, Andrew, O.P., 69.

Leo X, 5.

Lesley, John, Bishop of Ross, 44ff., 48n, 71n.

Lollards, 10f., 13n.

Luther, 69, 102.

Lyndsay, Sir David, 4.

Mackenzie, George, 47, 48.

Major, John, 10n, 26, 65, 66.

Malcolm IV, 25n.

Marshall, Richard, 18.

Methuen, Paul, 21.

Micheas, Crossraguel monk, 69n.

Moray, Earl of, see Steward, James.

Montgomerie, Hugh, 3rd Earl of Eglinton, 27, 33, 35.
Mure, John, Sub-prior of Crossraguel, 69n.
Myln, Walter, 10.

Nestorius, 53.
Nisbet, Murdoch, 33n.

Oecolampadius, 52, 53, 62ff., 69, 101, 102.
Origen, 68.

Philip II, King of Spain, 10n, 19.
Pius IV, 41.
Pinkie Cleuch, Battle of, 1, 8, 15.
Platina, Battista, 68.

Randolph, English Ambassador, 32n, 37, 38, 40, 41, 42n.
Robert III, 25, 27.
Robert the Bruce, 26.

Sadler, Sir Ralph, 9, 12.
Sichardus, 70.
Scot, John, printer, 49.
Smith, Richard, 1, 64, 71, 72, 101.
Solway Moss, Battle of, 1, 13.
Sophocardius, *see* Wishart, George.
Spottiswoode, John, Superintendent of Lothian, 54, 59n.
Stewart, James, Earl of Moray, 19, 41n, 51.
Stewart, John, Duke of Albany, 1, 5.

Stewart, Mary, Queen of Scots, 1, 2, 10, 13, 15, 21, 23n, 25, 32n, 35.
Suffolk, Duke of, 12.

Tertullian, 68.
Theophilact, 68.
Thin, Francis, 55.
Tudor, Mary, 2, 10, 19, 21.
Tunstal, Cuthbert, Bishop of Durham, 32, 65.

Vermigli, Peter, 64.
Vincent of Lerins, 70.

Wallace, Adam, 17.
Wauchope, Robert, Archbishop of Armagh, 17n.
Wedderburn, James, 14.
Wedderburn, John, 14.
Wedderburn, Robert, 14.
William the Lion, 25n.
Willock, John, Superintendent of Glasgow, 2, 12, 19, 21, 33, 34, 39n, 47, 54, 56, 57, 59n, 63, 64, 65, 68, 69n.
Winram, John, Superintendent of Fife, 54, 59n.
Winzet, Ninian, 32, 37, 44, 49, 58n, 62, 67, 74, 75.
Wishart, George, 1, 12, 14, 15, 47, 61, 63.
Wood, Alexander, Chaplain at Old Aberdeen, 51, 104.
Wycliff, John, 33n, 65.

Abbreviations used: *adj.* = adjective, adjectival; *adv.* = adverb(-ial); *comp.* = comparative; *conj.* = conjunction(-al group); *gen.* = genitive; *inf.* = infinitive; *num.* = numeral; *pl.* = plural; *p.p.* = past participle; *prep.* = preposition(-al group); *pret.* = preterite; *pron.* = pronoun; *pr. p.* = present participle; *rel.* = relative; *sb.* = substantive; *sg.* = singular; *superl.* = superlative; *vb.* = verb.

237

venient (to), 112,26; aggreabill: 123,8;
agreabil: 123,19; aggreable: 132,9;
149,16; 155,1; 155,27; 165,12; 170,22;
178,23; 180,16; agreable: 124,13; 132,
13; 134,1; 135,3; 138,16; 143,19;
145,26; 130,14; 137,16; 141,12.
aggreabilnes, *sb.*, agreement, consent,
173,11.
Agnus Dei, 176,25; Angnus Dej: 176,25G.
aige, *sb.*, age, 144,19; fra ayge to aige:
177,26G; *pl.* ayges: 143,24; aegis:
144,19F; ageis: 169,2; 172,33 (OF
aage).
alb, *sb.*, id., 180,1 (OF albe).
albeit, *conj.*, although, 120,19; 121,12;
122,15; 122,26; 129,2; 129,19; 137,14;
140,2; 155,28; 159,3; 160,3; &c.
ald, *adj.*, old, 133,16; auld: 135,14; 147,2;
148; 149,14; 149,22; 150,33; 151,13,
151,33; 151,35; &c.; awld: 181G; ald
anciant: 133,16; auld anciant: 124,14;
ayld anceante: 120,27F; auld anceant:
165,5; 165,32; of auld: 176,15; 177,1
(OE eald, ald).
alevin, *num.*, eleven, 167,9; 167,34; 169,10;
172,4; alevyn: 168,3; 176,15.
alik, *adj.*, similar, 146,7 (OE onlic and
Scand. alikr).
alikvise, *adv.*, similarly, 121,5 (OE on lice
wise). *See* inlikvis.
al(l), *adj.*, = all: 112,4; 112,8; 113,1;
114,9; 115,12; 115,13; &c.; = every:
112,14; 149,18; 152,23; 154,6; 154,10;
164,25; &c.; = entire: 131,5; 157,8;
151,3; 155,8; 163,14; &c.; *sb.*, = all:
120,33; 132,13; 135,26; 136,23; 140,24;
144,22; 144,23; 144,24; &c.; = everything: 159,24; *adv.*, = entirely: 164,31;
last of all: 152,13; 170,26; oure all
quhair = everywhere: 167,27; all (þe)
hail(l), *adj.*, entire, 141,16, 166,36;
176,14; all haill, *adv.*, in its entirety,
167,27.
allanerlye, *adv.*, only, solely, 120,26; 124,3;
136,10; 137,2; allanerlie: 159,28 (all +
anerly).
allege, *vb.*, a) adduce, 115,5; 139,18;
allage; 139,7; allegis: 133,6; alleges:
139,9; 139,10; *pret.* alleget: 140,12;
p. p. allegit: 112,21; 112,24; 114,4;
114,6; 114,7; 115,8; 115,11; 115,18;
&c.; alleget: 139,15; 139,16; 139,17;
139,20; 139,21; 139,22; allegeit: 151,38;

170,35; 170,37; 174,20; b) affirm, 117,
2F; allegis: 115,25; 116,31; *pr. p.*
allegeand: 115,30; 139,37; *pret.* allegit:
117,3F; alleget: 140,9; (AN alegier).
allegeance, *sb.*, a) citation, 142,22; allegeans: 142,9; b) allegation, 115,27.
all reddy, *adv.*, already, 154,32; 158,15;
161,16; 172,13; 177,26; al(l) reddelye:
124,28; 137,8; 140,1; 131,9; 142,2.
almous, *sb.*, alms, 168,11; 168,17; 168,30
(OF almosne).
almous deid, *sb.*, almsgiving, 156,39.
almychty, *adj.*, almighty, 122,28; 127,23;
133,32; 134,32; 135,13; 135,20; almichty: 125,3; 135,22; almychtie: 148;
151,11; 164,11; 164,14; 165,6; 165,13;
almychtyne: 145,5; almychthing: 133,
32F.
als, *adv.*, also, 112,23; 113,26; 116,21;
117,14; 117,17; 117,22; &c.; alss: 113,7;
alse: 122,5; 132,24; 139,12; 143,21;
143,25; &c.; alsse: 134,7; also: 123,22;
131,20; 134,27; 136,5; alsua: 131,23;
134,25; 167,18; 169,13; 178,9.
Correlation: als ... as: 125,9–11; 125,15–
16; 142,11; 150,32; 172,34; alse ... as:
127,31–32; 129,23–25; 130,21; 131,5;
137,6; 141,9–10; 141,14–15; as ... as:
125,14; 129,23; 130,21–23; 134,19–20.
Also see sa, sik, lik.
altare, *sb.*, altar, 112,4; 113,2; 113,22;
114,2; 114,5; 168,11; 168,31; 169,21;
&c. (OE altar, Lat. altare).
alteracione, *sb.*, alteration, 129,3.
alteris, *vb.*, alters, 137,25 (Lat. alterare).
althouch, *conj.*, although, 131,19; althocht:
167,38 (al + Scand. þauh).
alvay, *adv.*, always, 125,17; alvais: 112,33;
137,6; al vais: 141,31; alwayis: 125,17F;
all wayis: 159,22; all wayes: 153,10;
159,3.
am, *vb.*, *see* be, *vb.*
amang, *prep.*, among, 156,29; among:
126,29; amonge: 125,21; 125,29; amangis: 150,23; 156,31; 161,6; 161,10;
166,23; 171,9; 171,14; 171,15; 171,18;
173,32 (OE onmang).
ambassatouris, *sb.*, *pl.*, ambassadors, 160,
29 (cp. Lat. ambassiata).
amict, *sb.*, amice, 179,25 (OF amit).
anatomie, *sb.*, anatomy, 132,3F.
anciant, *adj.*, ancient, old, 113,1; 118,30;
124,29; 125,32; 126,16; 130,4; &c.; an-

238

ciaunt: 120,27; anceant: 149,28; 151,15; 151,17; 152,17; 156,12; 157,16, &c.; ancient: 176,26 G (OF ancien + t). *Also see* ald.

and, *conj.*, a) and, *passim;* b) if, 123,5; 125,23; 129,27; 132,21; 139,23; 153,18; 154,21; 155,32; 159,33; 161,15.

ane, *article, passim; num.*, one, 117,14; 117,16; 118,3; 120,12; 120,13; 123,13; &c.; one: 125,15; in ane, *adv.*, as one, 120,33; anis, *adv.*, once, 120,1; 149,30; 157,32; 157,33; 167,22; 172,9; *correlation:* the ane ... the other: 116,17–18; 125,7–8; 125,15–16; 130,21; 138,7–8; 154,30–31; ane ... ane other: 136,16; 127,24.

anent, *prep.*, concerning, 136,21; 143,9 (OE an-efen + t).

anew, *pron.*, sufficient, enough, 174,6 (OE ȝenoȝe).

angell, *sb.*, angel, 176,7; *pl.* angellis: 128,24; 128,25; 128,26; 128,29; 129,1; angelis: 182 G.

angelicall, *adj.*, of the angels, 175,34.

ansuer, *sb.*, answer, 125,22; ansuere: 130,3; anser: 158,2; *pl.* ansueris: 161,12 (OE and-swaru).

anser, *vb.*, answer, 153,17; 171,10; *pr. p.* ansuerynge: 125,19; *pret.* ansuerit: 128,22 (OE and-swarian).

antiquite, *sb.*, antiquity, 173,2; 173,14; 174,1; *pl.* antiquiteis: 145,1.

apon, *prep.*, on, upon, 149,30; 151,13; 151,28; 152,2; 152,5; 152,16; 153,10; 156,15; &c.; apone: 121,8; 127,29; 127,32; 130,16; 131,22; 133,18; 143,13 (OE upp-on).

apostle, *sb., id.*, 128,16; 131,11; 137,25; 139,36; 157,31; 163,10; 170,4; apostil: 113,7; 113,26; 114,18; 114,28; &c.; apostol: 182,4; *pl.* apostles: 123,27; apostlis: 123,31; 125,21; 125,29; 129,11; 129,26; 130,1; &c.; apostolis: 153,33.

appeir, *vb.*, appear, 154,22; appere: 131,19; apperis: 121,23; 155,9; 158,2; 158,35; 161,4; 162,7; *pr. p.* apperand: 178 G (OF aperer).

appendix, *sb., id.*, 174,26 G; appendex: 174,26.

apperance, *sb.*, support, 116,17; apperaunce: 137,4; 139,21; 140,21; 142,14; 144,26; apperence: 163,26 (Lat. adparere).

appertenis, *vb.*, pertains, 151,19; 165,39; 170,29; *pret.* appertenit: 182,18 (OF apartenir).

appetitis, *sb., pl.*, inclinations, 117,7 (OF apetit, Lat. appetitus).

applaude (to), *vb.*, applaud, support, 144,11 144,14; *pr. p.* applaudand: 144,12 (Lat. applaudere + dat.).

applicacione, *sb.*, application, 140,18; applicatioun: 159,21.

apply, *vb., id.*, 118,3; 120,27; 141,26; 168,33; applyis: 133,7; 141,23; *pr. p.* appliand: 145,12; *p. p.* applyit: 112,21; 112,24; 115,20; 118,1; 121,5; 122,19; &c. (OF aplier).

appoinct, *vb.*, appoint, ordain, 178,15; *pret.* appoinctit: 160,12; 160,15; 160,24; 162,33; 175,7; 175,13; &c.; appoynctit: 159,36; 160,11; 176,11; appontit: 176, 11 G; *p. p.* appoinctit: 160,3; 160,6; 171,24; 176,5; 177,23; 181,13; appontit: 176,13 G (OF apointer).

appontment, *sb.*, ordinance, 179 G.

apprayss, *vb.*, esteem highly, 179 G (OF a-preiser).

appreif, *vb.*, prove, approve, 112,25; 156,1; 169,20 appreue: 112,22; apprevis: 134, 11; 134,14; *p. p.* approvin: 150,27; 167, 34; 168,3; 168,27; 169,2; 172,32; &c.; approvine: 112,15; approvyne: 139,2; 145,13; approwyne: 142,19 approwine: 143,24; approving: 179 G (OF apreuver).

ar, *vb., see* be, *vb.*

argument, *sb., id.*, 117,12; 122,19; 139,8; 140,27; 141,18; 154,10; 154,33; &c.; *pl.* argumentis: 118,3; 161,12; argumentes: 134,16 (Lat. argumentum).

argumentis, *vb.*, argues, proves, 117,9; 155,17; 155,29; 159,8; argumentes: 140,3 (Lat. argumentare).

argwne, *vb.*, argue, prove, 159,10 (OF arguer).

ark, *sb., id.*, 164,34 (Lat. arca).

arrayment, *sb.*, raiment, 179,20; 179,23 (OF arei-ment).

arthtly, *adj.*, earthly, 181 G.

article, *sb., id.*, 141,5; 141,7; 141,16; artikil: 115,3; 122,25; *pl.* articles: 123,9; 125,9; 140,31; 160,30; artikles: 122,26; (OF article).

as, *conj. and rel. particle*, as, such as, just as, 112,7; 116,9; 116,28; 117,5; 118,16; 118,18; 121,14; 122,4; 122,5; 122,21;

239

&c.; *correlation:* as ... sua: 131,6f.; as ... In þis sammyne maner: 145,5–8. *Also see* als, equal, exemple, far, inlikmaner, lik, sa, sik.

ascendit, *vb., pret.,* ascended, 122,30; 124,5; 125,2; 140,31; ascendite: 122,22; *pr. p.* ascendand: 124,30; 124,31.

ascensione, *sb.,* ascension, 123,29; 124,3; 136,18; 136,20; ascentioun: 165,19.

as concerning, *prep., id.,* 177,24G; 178,19; as concernynge: 133,30.

ascriuit, *vb., pret.,* ascribed, judged, 153,33; *pr. p.* ascrywand: 157,26 (OF ascriver).

as for, *prep.,* respecting, 156,27.

ask (at), *vb.,* ask, 115,3; 178,19; aske: 127,14; *pr. p.* askand: 179G (OE ascian, *with Northern* /k/).

assurit, *p. p. and adj.,* assured, 119,31; 124,11; 126,9; 128,30; 136,8; 136,14; 157,33; 162,10; 163,7; 165,32; &c.; assuritly, *ad.,* 131,3; assuirtly: 132,25; assuritlie: 179,10; 179G (OF aseurer).

as to, *prep.,* concerning, respecting, 153,19; 154,10; 154,33; 155,34; 171,32; 172,5; 172,21; 173,12; 173,39; 176,15; 179,8.

as tovart, *prep.,* respecting, 112,34; as towart: 160,4; 160,5; 160,38; 162,17; 172,36; 173,14; 173,16; 173,17; 174,30; 175,2; 175,3; 177,25.

astrickit (to), *vb., p. p.,* confined (to), 123, 13; 123,15; astrictet: 123,15F; *pr. p.* astrickand + obj. + to + inf. (binding, compelling) 123,19; *perhaps similarly in* 124,2 (Lat. astrictus).

at, *conj.,* that, 144,23; 168,18; *prep.,* 113, 30; 115,33; 122,22; 122,30; 123,6; 124,15; 125,12; 127,28; 128,1; 129,4; 131,10; 156,28; &c.; *also see* ask *and* speir. (Scand. at OE æt).

atome, *sb.,* atom, 132,3 (OF atome).

attempt, *vb.,* 171,2.

attendance, *sb., id.,* 182G.

attentik, *adj.,* authentic, 175,11; attentict: 175,12 (OF autentique).

attour, *adv.,* moreover, 119,31; 124,5; 130,15; 136,1; 142,7; 143,1; 144,19; 164,18; 178,11; 180,12; 180,26; 181,27 (at + over).

attribut, *vb.,* attribute, 182G.

aucht, *vb.,* ought, 112,7; 142,24; 143,17; 146,3; 146,5; 169,8; auch: 141,15 (OE ahte).

aucht, *num.,* eight, 151,21; 151,22; 151,23; 169,10; aucht: 140,26 (OE æhta).

auchtene, *num.,* eighteen, 142,27.

augmentit, *vb., p. p.,* augmented, 182,1 (OF augmenter, Lat. augmentare).

authorite, *sb.,* authority, 126,18; 144,2; 159,38; 166,10; 171,24; authoritie: 134,15; 139,1; 142,18; 143,25; 143,26; 143,28; 145,31; 146,3; 146,14; 146,18; auctorite: 179G (Late Lat. authoritas).

authour, *sb.,* author, 167,7; *pl.* authouris: 118,30 (Late Lat. author).

avansyt, *vb., p. p.,* advanced, 135,17; advansit: 158,39; 159,14; advansis: 149, 36; 159,11 (OF avancer).

avarice, *sb., id.,* 174,11 (OF avarice).

avay, *adv.,* away, 143,15; away: 169,6 (OE on + weg).

awin, *adj.,* own, 120,7; 124,18; 125,7; 131,5; 158,10; 158,21; &c.; avin: 113,18; 114,21; 117,7; 119,19; 127,12; &c.; awne: 178G (OE agen).

awn, *sb.,* ass, 171,21; *pl.* awns: 171,27 (OF asne, âne).

ay, *adv.,* always, 116,2; 174,19; 178G (Scand. ey).

bair, *adj.,* mere, 137,31 (OE bær).

baith, *pron. and adv.,* both, 122,3; 134,23; 139,20; 145,8; 146,7; bayth: 119,13; 148; 149,22; 150,33; 151,33; 154,31; &c.; boith: 125,7; 125,13; 125,15; 126,26; 128,6; 129,18; &c. *in MS A.*

bak, *sb.,* back, 180G (OE bæc).

baldely, *adv.,* boldly, 125,17; bauldlie: 153,30; 159,37; 171,26; 172,29; baldy: 144,11; baldye: 139,17; 141,11; 146,16 (OE bald).

baptize, *vb., id.,* 160,10; 166,43; *p. p.* baptizate: 159,36; 160,12; 168,12; 172,12; 172,18; 173,26 (OF baptiser, Lat. baptizare).

baptym, *sb.,* baptism, 164,34; baptyme: 159,5; 159,14; 160,9; 181,12; 181G (OF baptesme).

bardis, *sb., pl.,* bards, 146,16 (Gaelic bard).

barkand, *vb., pr. p.,* barking, 146,16 (OE beorcan).

barne, *sb.,* child, 159,36; 176,7 (OE barn).

bauge, *sb.,* badge, 181G (OF bage).

bawbeis, *sb., pl.,* babes, 178G (ME babe).

be, *prep.,* by, by means of, from, *passim* (OE big).

be, *vb.*, *id.*, *passim; present tense:* am, ar, art (119,21 *only*), is, be *(subjunctive); pret.*: was, vas, ves, war, var, ver; *pr. p.*: beand, being (167,27; 169,17); *p. p.*: bein, beine, bene, beyn.

because, *conj.*, *id.*, 139,7; 140,20; 146,6; 146,21; becaus: 113,18; 114,21; 114,34; &c.; becauss: 178G (hybrid).

before, *prep.*, *id.*, 119,12; 131,23; 143,14; befoir: 169,5; *conj.*, 137,25; *adv.*, befoir: 116,16; 118,25; of before: 133,13; 136,18; of befoir: 161,34; of befoire: 121,19 (OE be-foran).

begilit, *vb.*, *p. p.*, beguiled, 131,25 (OF guiler).

begine, *vb.*, begin, 132,15; *pret.* began: 151,19; 161,11; 165,8; begane: 138,26; 144,20; 146,21 (OE be-ginnan).

begynnaris, *sb.*, *pl.*, beginners, 165,28.

begynnning, *gerund*, 173,15; begynnyng: begynnynge: 119,12.

beir, *vb.*, bear, 160,12; beres: 127,12; *pr. p.* beirand: 160,30; *pret.* buir: 124,18; *p. p.* borne: 126,1; 176,4; 176,7; 180G (OE beran).

beis, *sb.*, *pl.*, bees, 127,20 (OE beo).

beist, *sb.*, beast, 177,12; 177,13; beyst: 177,15; best: 177,13G; *pl.* beistis: 131,3; 167,14; 177,9 (OF beste).

bekking, *gerund*, making gestures, 178,2 (ME beknen).

belangand, *pr. p.*, *prep.*, pertaining, concerning, 180G (cp. Dutch belangen, *vb.*).

beleif, *vb.*, believe, 130,19; 130,27; 131,4; 131,18; 131,21; 131,26; &c.; beleue: 125,27; 130,28; 140,13; 141,5; 141,15; belewe: 180G; beleiff; 125,10: beleiffe: 143,17; beleius: 130,30; *pr. p.* beleuand: 129,12; beleifand: 172,12; *pret.* belevit: 182,23; belewit: 118,17; *p. p.* beleuit: 121,24; belevit: 175,10; belewit: 179G (OE be-lefan).

beleif, *sb.*, belief, 115,3; 118,20; 122,25; 122,27; 135,15; 135,32; 136,1; 140,31; 145,3; beleue: 123,9; 141,5; beleiff: 141,7; 141,16; beleiffe: 125,9.

belt, *sb.*, girdle, 1803 (OE belt, Lat. balteus).

beluffit, *adj.*, beloved, 116,5; belowit: 177,26G; *sb.*, *pl.* belowittis: 177,26G (OE be-lufian).

benefice, *sb.*, benefit, 130,7; 164,2; 164,4; 164,10; *pl.* benefices (= benefices): 171,

14 (ME benefice, Lat. beneficium).

benevalent, *adj.*, benevolent, 112,2; 132,6.

benevolence, *sb.*, *id.*, 172,17.

beseik, *vb.*, beseech, 131,21 (OE be-secan, *with Northern* /k/).

besid, *prep.*, beside, 139,21; besydis: 146,7 (OE be sidan).

besyness, *sb.*, occupation, 176,27G (OE bisig-nes).

bettir, *adj.*, *comp.*, better, 166,24; *adv.* 153,18; better: 123,12.

betuix, *prep.*, between, 135,13; 153,3; 158,5; 182,18; betwyxe: 174,26G (OE betweohs).

biddis, *vb.*, bids, 114,24; 114,28 (OE biddan).

birnand, *vb.*, *pr. p.*, burning, 180G (OE byrnan).

birth, *sb.*, *id.*, 125,30; 174,3 (Scand. byrþ).

bischop, *sb.*, bishop, 164,14; 167,29; 168, 20; 171,21; bischope: 131,27; 132,15; bischoppe: 132,22; byschope: 139,13; byschoppe: 125,32; *gen.* bischopis: 166, 10; *pl.* bischoppis: 171,13 (OE biscop).

bletour, *sb.*, bleater, sheep, 171,20 (OE bletan).

blindit, *vb.*, *p. p.*, blinded, 171,23; 174,11 (OE blind).

blindnes, *sb.*, blindness, 126,13.

bliss, *vb.*, bless, 178,10; *gerund* blissing: 178,2; *pret.* blissit: 115,22; 115,32; blessit: 139,32; *p. p. (adj.)* blissit: 112,4; 113,8; 114,2; 114,25; 118,2; 119,10; &c.; blist: 129,25; blessit: 145,23; blesset: 120,13; 125,31; 128,5; 137,26; 146,16; blessed: 122,23; 123,14; 125,30; 129,15; blyssit: 180G (OE bletsian).

blude, *sb.*, blood, 128,5; 155,38; 156,9; 156,14; 157,3; 157,9; &c.; bluid: 113,3; 113,6; 113,12; 113,16; 113,25; 114,1; &c.; bluide: 128,13; 133,10; 133,12; 134,3; bloud: 119,30; 127,14; bloude: 121,25; 122,1; 122,4; 122,7; 122,8; &c.; blud: 115,24 (OE blod).

bludy, *adj.*, bloody, 157,38; 161,25.

body, *sb.*, *id.*, 111; 113,3; 113,5; 113,10; 113,16; 113,19; 113,23; &c.; bodie: 119,10; bodye: 121,10; 121,13; 121,15; 121,17; 121,27; &c.; *pl.* bodeis: 128,18; bodies: 129,2; *gen.* bodyes: 121,24 (OE bodig).

bondage, *sb.*, *id.*, 1726 (AN bondage).

bonis, *sb.*, *pl.*, bones, 128,6; 128,13; 129,11;

129,16; 135,27; 135,31 (OE ban).

bosume, *sb.*, bosom, 135,24; bosoume: 125,31 (OE bosm).

bot, *adv.* (only), *prep.* (except), *conj.* (but), 113,22; 113,29; 114,27; 115,11; 115,33; 116,2; 117,26; 119,2; 119,5; 119,6; &c.; bot þat, *conj.*, except that, 120,20; 123, 11; 174,18; *also see* but (OE butan).

bound, *vb.*, *p. p.*, *id.*, 180,4; 180,6 (OE bunden).

boundis, *sb.*, *pl.*, bounds, limits, 168,39 (OF bonne, bonde).

bowcht, *vb.*, *p. p.*, bought, 177,26G (OE boht).

brane, *sb.*, brain, 154,6; 154,11; 154,34; 173,3; brayn: 151,8; 154,7; 155,9; 182,23; braine: 128,10; brayne: 148 (OE brægen).

breid, *sb.*, bread, 113,9; 113,13; 113,15; 113,17; 114,19; &c.; breyd: 163,25; 170,9; bread: 127,18; 127,25; 128,3; 130,13; 135,30; breade: 124,19; 127,7; 127,13; 129,20; 130,10; &c.; (OE bread).

breif, *adj.*, brief, 111; breifly, *adv.*, 112,17 (OF brief).

breist, *sb.*, breast, 178,3; 178,19; breyst: 180G; *pl.* brestis: 178,3G (OE breost).

brek, *vb.*, break, 164,19; *pret.*, brak: 113,9; *p. p.* brokin: 156,21 (OE brecan, bræc, brocen).

broder, *sb.*, brother, 153,8; 153,13; brother: 159,33; 174,18; browthir: 174,26G; 179G; 182G; browthtar: 180G; *pl.* brethir: 153,3; 168,29; brether: 128,22 (OE broþor, *dat. sg.* breþer).

brutale, *adj.*, of beasts, 167,14 (Lat. brutalis).

brygant, *sb.*, brigand, 178G (ME bregaund).

bryngis, *vb.*, brings, 180G; *gerund* bringin: 164,3; *p. p.* brocht: 172,9; 178,27 (OE bringan, broht).

bureing, *gerund*, state of being buried, 164,32 (OE byrgan).

but, *prep.*, without, 144,28; 165,31; *conj.*, but, 123,22 (OE butan).

by, *prep.*, against, beyond, 126,6; 133,7; 137,11; 139,18; 142,4; 154,16 (OE big).

byd, *vb.*, abide, 172,25 (OE bidan).

bypast, *adj.* (postposition), past, ago, 151,7; 166,20; 166,32; 167,1; &c.; *pl.* bypastis: 176,21G (*vb.* pass).

calamiteis, *sb.*, *pl.*, calamities, 120,10; 122, 14; 129,1.

cald, *sb.*, cold, 120,9; calde: 122,16; cauld: 122,14; caulde: 122,5 (OE cald).

call, *vb.*, *id.*, 142,11; 154,35; 161,19; 161, 35; 168,37; &c.; cal: 115,28; 121,4; 133,16; 139,36; 145,1; callis: 113,25; 128,18; 154,1; 164,36; *pr. p.* calland: 171,39; caand (= driving): 146,15; *pret.* callit: 169,37; *p. p.* callit: 112,12; 142,34; 149,38; 150,1; 150,29; &c. (Scand. kalla).

can, *vb.*, *id.*, 117,11; 118,20; 119,5; 122,24; 125,25; &c.; cane: 120,2; 126,30; 128,3; 134,31; 138,1; 141,16; *pret.* culd: 114,11; 115,1; 125,3; 142,11 (OE can, cuþe).

canone, *sb.*, canon, (of the Mass), 176,15 (Lat. canon).

capacite, *sb.*, capacity, 131,21.

capitane, *sb.*, captain, 181G (OF capitaine).

captiuite, *sb.*, captivity, 158,29; 164,5.

carnall, *adj.*, carnal, 180G (Lat. carnalis).

case, *sb.*, *id.*, 153,22; 177,19; in case, *conj.*: 157,22; 162,19; in cace: 173,3; in caiss: 118,7 (OF cas).

castis, *vb.*, casts, 163,32 (Scand. kasta).

catholike, *adj.*, catholic, 134,22.

cause, *sb.*, *id.*, 129,31; caus: 114,30; 116,12; 119,15; 149,38; 150,1; &c.; causs: 119, 16; 181G (OF cause).

cause, *vb.*, *id.*, 140,28; *p. p.* causit: 182G.

ceiss, *vb.*, cease, 161,29; *pret.* ceissit: 161, 25; 161,31; 169,39 (OF cesser).

celestial, *adj.*, *id.*, 146,25 (OF celestiel).

cerimonie, *sb.*, ceremony, 175,6; 175,17; cerimonye: 181G; *pl.* cerimoniis: 150,5; 155,4; 159,34; 160,5; 160,25; &c.; ceromonies: 179G (OF ceremonie).

certane, *adj.*, certain, 118,14; 154,40; 155,4; 160,30 (OF certein).

certify, *vb.*, *id.*, inform, 114,11; 177,2; certifye: 123,25; certifie: 153,27; 157,12; certifyes: 144,30; *p. p.* certifyet: 123,2; 144,2; certifeit: 149,16; 173,16; 180,12; 182,7; certifiit: 174,27 (OF certifier).

chalice, *sb.*, *id.*, 166,34; 175,29 (OF chalice).

chaplane, *sb.*, chaplain, 147,2 (ME chapelein).

chaptour, *sb.*, chapter, 117,28; 120,24; 121,3; 126,3; 134,32; 140,2; chaptor: 129,30; 138,12; 140,26; 144,1; cheptour: 112,1; (OF chapitre).

charge, *sb.*, command, 181G (OF charger).

chaunge, *vb.*, change, 127,18; 127,21; 127, 24; 127,25; *pret.* chaunged: 127,16; 127,17; changeit: 167,12; chengit: 130, 10; *p. p.* chaunged: 147,14; 128,15; changed: 133,31; changit: 128,18; *gerund* chaungene: 134,5; chengene: 129,3 (OF changier).

cheif, *adj.*, chief, 112,21; 112,24; 115,18; 118,3; 119,15; &c.; cheiff: 141,18; cheiffe: 122,19; 140,27; *adv.* cheifly: 131,22 (OF chief).

cherite, *sb.*, charity, 119,1; 119,2 (OF charitet).

christian, *adj.*, *id.*, 131,29; christiane: 121, 24; 123,25; 125,17; 130,7; &c.; chrystiane: 181G; christin: 171,9; christine: 119,23; 146,11 (Lat. christianus).

christindome, *sb.*, christendom, 142,29; 171,30 (OE cristendom).

circumcisioun, *sb.*, circumcision, 172,7 (Lat. circumcisio).

circumspectione, *sb.*, attention, 182G (Lat. circumspicere).

circumstance, *sb.*, surroundings, 114,30 (AN circumstance).

circumveyn, *vb.*, circumvent, 153,16; *pr. p.* circumuenand: 146,15; *p. p.* circumvenit: 151,7 (Lat. circumvenire).

clayth, *sb.*, garment, 179,25; 180,1; 180,8; *pl.* claythis,: 179 20 (OE claþ).

cleirly. *adv.*, 115,4; 115,14; 115,19; 116,25; 117,5; &c.; cleirlye: 111; 123,20; 124,1; 135,18; &c.; cleirlie: 119,24; 164,26; 174,15; clearly: 120,14 (OF cler).

cleith, *vb.*, be clothed with, clothe oneself, 121,27; 121,28; 153,10; *p. p.* cled: 128, 15; 128,29; 160,33; 179,19; 179,26; 180,1; 180,8; clede: 121,30; 122,8; 128,19 (OE clæþan).

clene, *adj.*, clean, 156,30; 157,2; 157,8; 180,18; 182,9; 182,14; cleyn: 166,26; 167,30; 169,39 (OE clene).

clenget, *vb.*, *pret.*, cleansed, 145,6; *p. p.* clengit: 136,22 (OE clænsian).

cloik, *sb.*, cloak, 124,31 (OF cloque).

closit, *vb.*, *p. p.*, closed, 125,22; 125,29; 125,31; 129,8; 129,23; 130,2; 135,26 (OF clos).

collect, *vb.*, gather, 112,17; 172,36; *p. p.* colleckit: 112,32; 145,27; collectit: 149, 20 (OF collecter).

collocutione, *sb.*, dialogue, 174,26G.

colour, *sb.*, *id.*, 179,5 (OF colour).

command, *vb.*, *id.*, 167,13; commaund: 137,26; commandis: 166,15; *pret.* commandit: 156,6; 160,9; 161,37; 162,1; *p. p.* commandit: 164,19; 167,4 (OF commander).

command, *sb.*, *id.*, 154,7; 154,8; 154,11; 154,14; 154,23; &c.

commandiment, *sb.*, command(-ment), 154,21; 154,22; 157,40; 181,9; 182,12.

commemoratioun, *sb.*, commemoration, 150,1; 155,35; 158,32; 158,40; 162,34; &c. (Lat. commemoratio).

commendatour, *sb.*, commendator, 148; 153,4; commendator: 174,26G (Lat. commendatarius).

commiseratioun, *sb.*, pity, 151,5.

commissionaris, *sb.*, *pl.*, envoys, 160,28.

commissioun, *sb.*, mandate, 160,30; 160, 31; 160,32; 160,33; 160,35; 160,36 (Lat. commissio).

communicate, *vb.*, *id.*, 159,29; 160,16; 160,17; 160,19; 160,20; conmunicatis: 159,27; *pret.* commwnicate: 159,26; 159,27; conmwnicate: 159,24; *p. p.* communicat: 129,2 (Lat. communicare).

commwne, *adj.*, common, 157,12; 181,1; 181,2; conmwne: 169,15; *adv.* commonlye: 137,17; 176,2G; 181G (OF commun).

commwnioun, *sb.*, communion, 155,5; 159,31; 160,18; 161,19; 161,22; &c.; conmwnioun: 162,23; commwnioune: 155,4.

compellit, *vb.*, *p. p.*, compelled, 114,15; 114,22; 123,27; 157,1; &c. (OF compeller).

compendious, *adj.*, *id.*, 148 (OF compendieux).

complesit, *adj.*, pleased, 116,6 (OF plesir).

comprehendis, *vb.*, comprehends, 171,11; *p. p.* comprehendit: 125,25; 125,25 (Lat. comprehendere).

concerning, *prep.*, *id.*, 152,7; 153,9; 153, 21; 160,24; 164,30; &c.; concernyng: 149,15; 150,24; 177,24; concernynge: 125,18. *Also see* as concerning.

conclude, *vb.*, *id.*, 164,9; concluid: 138,20; 146,12; *pr. p.* concludand: 144,22; *pret.* concludit: 144,24 (Lat. concludere).

conclusioun, *sb.*, conclusion, 151,34; 163,7; 174,18.

concord, *sb.*, *id.*, 140,16 (OF concorde).

concurrand, *vb.*, *pr. p.*, concurring, 182,16 (Lat. concurrere).

condame, *vb.*, condemn, 143,6; 143,7; 143,27; condemp: 159,35; condempnis: 154,2; *pret.* condamnit: 142,27; 144,28; *p. p.* condamnit: 112,13; 142,25; 142,32; 143,3; 143,26; 146,7; 146,19; condamnet: 144,25F; condempnit: 169,11 (OF condempner, Lat. damnare).

condamnable, *adj.*, condemnable, 138,26; 144,5; 145,32.

conditioun, *sb.*, condition, state, 153,13; 177,10; 182,17 (OF condicion).

confer, *vb.*, *id.*, 118,29; 139,23; 142,6; confere: 121,19; *gerund* conferrynge: 139,29 (Lat. conferre).

conferrens, *sb.*, comparison, consultation, 112,18; 116,1; 138,20; 142,8; 145,30; confferrens: 140,1 conferrence: 163,9; 164,40.

confessand, *pr. p.*, confessing, 181G; *pret.* confessit (= declared): 166,34 (OF confesser).

confessione, *sb.*, confession, 176,11G.

confessouris, *sb.*, *pl.*, confessors, 173,25.

confirmacione, *sb.*, confirmation, affirmation, 120,25; 126,11; 134,29; 139,10; 140,22; 142,14; 142,22; confirmatioun: 149,14; 151,27; 151,30; 151,34; 152,2; &c.; *pl.* confirmatiouns: 151,21; 151,23; 151,38; 152,18; 169,26; 170,31 (Lat. confirmatio).

confirme, *vb.*, confirm, assert, 164,32; *pret.* confirmit: 170,3; 170,11; 170,16; 170, 20; 170,26; *p. p.* confirmit: 164,38; confermit: 136,22 (OF confermer, Lat. confirmare).

confiteor, *sb.*, *id.*, 176,11 (Lat.).

conforme to, *prep.*, in conformity with, 112,7; 112,10; 112,15; 112,30; 113,1; &c. (OF conforme).

confortar, *sb.*, comforter, 172,24.

confortit, *vb.*, *p. p.*, comforted, 129,25; 129,26; 181,27 (OF conforter).

confund, *vb.*, destroy, confuse, 116,9; 140,5; *p. p.* confundit: 116,4; 140,4; 171,25 (OF confondre, Lat. confundere).

confusione, *sb.*, confusion, 134,28.

confutate, *vb.*,*p.p.*,174,20(Lat.confutatus).

confutatioun, *sb.*, confutation, 151,27; 151,30; 151,34; 151,37; &c.; *pl.* confutatiouns: 151,23.

congregacione, *sb.*, congregation, 112,30; 112,32; 145,6; 145,9; congregatioun: 151,4; 159,29; 160,18; 165,28; *pl.* congregaciones: 129,24 (Lat. congregatio).

consauit, *vb.*, *p. p.*, conceived, 135,23; 135,35 (OF conceiv-).

conscience, *sb.*, *id.*, 112,3; 131,14; 137,30; 138,30; 152,20; &c. (OF conscience).

consecrate, *vb.*, *id.*, 156,7; *p. p.* consecrate: 133,28; 155,36; 156,15; 156,18; consecrat: 133,19; 133,20 (Lat. consecrare).

consecratioun, *sb.*, consecration, 150,25; 156,8; 156,20.

consent, *sb.*, *id.*, 157,15; 165,5; 166,10; 173,10; 173,35; 174,13 (OF consentir).

consider, *vb.*, *id.*, 154,34; 158,38; 161,18; 161,25; &c.; considder: 112,25; 119,7; 119,11; 119,14; &c.; *pr. p.* considderand: 127,1; *p.p.* considderit: 125,26; 126,12; 142,22 (OF considerer).

consideratioun, *sb.*, consideration, 154,28; 158,25; *pl.* consideratiouns: 149,34; consideraciones: 122,3; 141,33.

considering, *conj.*, *id.*, 160,21; considerand: 123,17; 155,8; considderinge: 151,5; 135,34; considderrynge þat: 121,24; considderynge þat: 125,7; 125,12; consydderinge þat: 130,20; *gerund* considdering: 119,7.

constance, *sb.*, constancy, 181G.

constant, *adj.*, *id.*, 145,2; 152,15 (OF constant).

constitut, *vb.*, *p. p.*, decreed, 179G (Lat. constitutus).

constreine, *vb.*, compel, 139,29; constrenis: 132,2 (OF constreign-).

consuetude, *sb.*, *id.*, 161,4 (Lat. consuetudo).

conswmat, *vb.*, *p. p.*, consummated (as sacrifice), 167,31 (Lat. consummatus).

contempnis, *vb.*, holds in contempt, 181,1 (OF contemner).

contenand, *vb.*, *pr. p.*, containing, 160,30; 160,36; 171,40; *p. p.* contenit: 112,4; 113,2; 114,2; 114,16; 114,23, &c. (OF contien-).

contencious, *adj.*, contentious, 161,4 (OF contentieux).

contenment, *sb.*, satisfaction, 112,8; 137,12 (OF content).

contentacione, *sb.*, satisfaction, 112,8.

contentit, *adj.*, content, 153,13.

conterfate, *vb.*, imitate, 139,26 (OF contre-
fait).

continual, *adj.*, *id.*, 112,18 (OF continuer).

contrar, *adj.*, contrary, 123,9; *sb.*, the contrary, 114,6; 115,8; 132,12; 134,19;
170,37; 171,1; *prep.*, contrary to, 111;
114,10; 115,10; 115,12; 115,16; &c.;
contrar to: 154,29; *also see* incontrar.

contrarius to, *prep.*, contrary to, 112,11;
118,25; 145,29; 146,24 (Lat.).

contrauersie, *sb.*, controversy, 153,9 (AN
controversye).

conuenant, *vb.*, *pr. p.*, convening, 144,22;
pret. conuenit: 143,9; 144,23; *p. p.*
conuenit: 142,26; 142,29; 143,23; convenit: 151,19; 165,39; 170,29 (OF con-
venir).

conuertit, *vb.*, *pret.*, changed (substantially), 130,10 (OF convertir).

corde, *sb.*, chord, 180,4; 180,6 (OF corde).

corporal, *adj.*, *id.*, 120,5; 130,12; corporall:
123,30; 133,3; corporale: 132,28; 178,8;
179,13; 179,18; *adv.* corporally: 123,31;
124,4; 136,25 (OF corporal).

corporale, *sb.*, corporal, 175,29; corporall:
175,29 G (Latin corporalis).

correspond (to), *vb.*, *id.*, 164,22; correspondent (to): 163,32; 163,33; 163,34;
163,36; 163,39; 164,17; 164,25 (OF
correspondre).

corrupcione, *sb.*, corruption, 122,6 (Lat.
corruptio).

corruptible, *adj.*, *id.*, 122,8; corruptable:
121,27.

costlye, *adj.*, costly, 121,8; costlie: 180,13.

counsall, *sb.*, counsel, 131,17; consall:
180 G; consell: 174,6; 176,13; *pl.* consellis: 152,15; 165,7; 165,39; 168,40 (OF
conseil).

counsall, *sb.*, council, 142,26; 143,6; 143,9;
143,18; &c.; counsal: 142,29; 142,32;
143,7; 143,22; cunsal: 145,21; consell:
155,19; concell: 169,1; 169,9; 169,10;
169,19; *pl.* consales: 179 G; consellis:
149,28; 151,18; 152,17; 157,16; 157,21;
157,22; concellis: 169,20; 169,23; 170,
27; 171,1 (OF councylle).

couponit, *vb.*, *p. p.*, cut to pieces, 118,18
(F coupon).

cowmpt, *sb.*, account, 179 G (OF accomp-
ter).

craft, *sb.*, ability, craft, 127,21; 127,23;
139,27; 153,21 (OE cræft).

crear, *sb.*, creator, 138,4.

creat, *vb.*, *p. p.*, created, 119,10; (Lat.
creatus).

creatour, *sb.*, creator, 138,4 F.

creature, *sb.*, *id.*, 136,24.

criaris oute, *sb.*, *pl.*, those who cry out,
171,38.

croce, *sb.*, cross, 114,17; 149,12; 149,31;
149,36; 149,38; &c.; croyss: 180 G (OE
cros).

crocesing, *gerund*, crossing, 178,2.

cropin, *vb.*, *p. p.*, crept, 126,14 (OE creo-
pan).

croun, *sb.*, crown, 180,9 (OF corone).

crucifyis, *vb.*, crucifies, 133,9; *pret.* crucifeit: 179,22; *p. p.* crucifyet: 133,19;
crucifeit: 156,15 (OF crucifier).

cryit out, *vb.*, *p. p.*, decried, 143,4; 146,10;
146,19; 161,2 (OF crier).

cum, *vb.*, come, 113,14; 155,32; 169,13;
175,1; 181,24; cumis: 136,21; *pr. p.*
cumand: 126,18; 146,14; *pret.* come:
125,30; 126,19; 133,2; 164,18; 176,6;
179,16; *p. p.* cumin: 133,29; 171,13;
172,13; cum: 129,12; *gerund*: cuming:
172,7; cumin: 157,7 (OE cuman,
cwom, cumen).

cummyr, *sb.*, grief, trouble, 171,15 (cp.
Dutch kommer).

cuntre, *sb.*, country, 153,18; 153,19 (OF
contree).

curate, *sb.*, *id.*, 171,23 (Lat. curatus).

curiositie, *sb.*, curiosity, 132,2; curiosite:
180 G.

curiouse, *adj.*, curious, 132,1; 139,23;
curyouse: 142,11; *adv.* curiouslye: 139,24
(OF curios).

curis, *vb.*, cures, 139,28 (OF cure).

cursit, *adj.*, cursed, 132,2 (OE cursian).

custome, *sb.*, custom, 175,23; 177,24 G;
179,6; *pl.* customes: 160,1; 161,7; 161,9;
179,2 (OF costume).

cut, *vb.*, *id.*, 159,25 (Scand.).

cwpe, *sb.*, cup, 113,11; 113,14; 113,15;
113,17; 114,20; 143,14; cowpe: 114,32;
cupe: 115,24; coupe: 169,5 (OE cuppe).

damnable, *adj.*, *id.*, 116,28; 146,21; damnabil: 116,29.

damnacione, *sb.*, condemnation, 113,18;
114,21, 114,25; 114,33; 137,28; damnatioun: 174,24; dampnatioun: 152,21;
117,14 (OF damner *and* dampner).

danger, *sb.*, *id.*, 178 G (OF dangier).

dangerous, *adj.*, *id.*, 171,13.

danse, *sb.*, dance, 171,13 (OF danser).

dar, *vb.*, dare, venture to, 125,17; 130,28; 139,17; 141,11; 144,11; &c.; darn: 141,11 F; 144,11 F (OE dar).

dawin, *gerund*, dawning, 176,5 (ME dawen, *vb.*).

day, *sb.*, *id.*, 113,31; 120,6; 122,23; 123,20; 124,4; &c.; daye: 121,30; *pl.* days: 126,6; 126,14; 134,9; 145,15; dais: 111; 115,15; 116,31; 117,19; 118,1; &c. (in MS A); dayes: 149,29; 149,36; 157,5; 157,29; &c. (in MS B); þe day, *adv.*, to-day: 167,24 (OE dæg).

daylie, *adv.*, daily, 149,32; 157,35; 159,4; 159,17; &c.; daly: 126,29; 178 G; dalye: 129,2; *adj.* daly: 130,14.

day lycht, *sb.*, day-light, 176,8.

debate, *sb.*, *id.*, 153,9 (OF debatre).

decent, *adj.*, *id.*, 180,17; 180,26 (OF decent).

declair, *vb.*, declare, 115,1; 138,14; 153,16; declayr: 153,26; declare: 128,11; declaris: 116,23; 133,15; 135,22; 156,36; 162,27; 163,27; *pr. p.* declarand: 114,7; 145,23; 149,2; 149,5; &c.; *pret.* declarit: 156,22; *p. p.* declarit: 112,7; 117,5; 120,22; 124,28; &c. (OF declairier).

declaracione, *sb.*, declaration, 112,10*I* 112,16; 112,19; 141,3; 143,19; 144,30; 146,24; declaratioun: 151,17; 155,32; 155,34; 156,1; &c.; declaratione: 179 G.

declynit, *vb.*, *pret.*, were lowered, 178,18 (OF decliner).

decoir, *vb.*, add lustre to, 155, 1; 155,4; 160,35; 173,18; decoyr: 175,6 (OF decorer).

dedicate, *vb.*, *p. p.*, dedicated, 180,14 (Lat. dedicatus).

defend, *vb*, *id.*, 153,15 (OF defendre).

deformatione, *sb.*, deformation, 178 G (Lat. deformatio).

degre, *sb.*, degree, rank, 145,8; 173,27 (OF degre).

deid, *sb.*, deed, *adv.* in deid (= really): 115,29; 117,11; 139,37; 154,20; *pl.* dedis: 146,23 (OE ded).

deid, *sb.*, (the) dead, 113,31; 168,6; 168,12 (OE dead).

deidlie, *adj.*, deadly, 178,13; 181,7; 181,15; 181,19; &c.

deill (with), *vb.*, deal (with), 168,18 (OE dælan).

deirly, *adv.*, dearly, 177,26 G (OE deore).

deith, *sb.*, death, 152,21; 154,19; 154,38; 155,36; 156,24; &c.; deitht: 117,11; deth: 120,2; 144,15; deit: 178 G; death: 120,2; 120,10; deid: 113,14 (OE deaþ *and* Scand. död).

deliberatioun, *sb.*, deliberation, 149,27; 151,17; 152,16; 157,15; &c.; *pl.* deliberatiouns: 152,15 (Lat. deliberatio).

deliuer, *vb.*, deliver, 145,9; *pret.* deliuerit: 145,6; 164,14; *p. p.* deliuerit: 164,2; 164,11 (OF delivrer).

delytit, *vb.*, *p. p.*, delighted, pleased, 150,11; 166,22 (OF deliter).

demand, *vb.*, request, 179 G; 180 G (OF demander)

deny, *vb.*, *id.*, 154,27; denyis: 115,9; 116,26; 135,6; denyes: 134,12; 134,13; 134,14; 134,21; *pr. p.* denyand: 137,23; 138,21; 143,2; 144,3; &c.; deniand: 111; *pret.* denyit: 128,20; 140,8; *p. p.* denyit: 168,8 (OF denier).

depart, *vb.*, *id.*, 176,27 G; departe: 176,26; *p. p.* departit: 150,14; 168,8; 168,16; 168,21; 168,25; *gerund* departing: 168,25 (OF departir).

dependens, *sb.*, context, 116,16 (Lat. dependentia).

deplorit, *p. p.*, *adj.*, deplored, 138,26; 139,4; 144,25 (Lat. deplorare).

derogacione, *sb.*, derogation, 120,16 (Lat. derogatio).

deseruis, *vb.*, deserves, 146,9; *p. p.* deserwit: 168,14; 181,27; *gerund* deserving: 167,39 (OF deservir).

desyr, *vb.*, desire, 151,26; 151,29; 151,37; 152,4; &c.; *pr. p.* desiring; 179 G; *pret.* desyrit: 178.5; desirit: 178,5 G (OF desirer).

desyr, *sb.*, desire, 169,28; *pl.* desyris: 182 G.

desyrous, *adj.*, desirous, 157,29; 165,2; 166,5; 174,11.

determyt, *vb.*, *pret.*, determined, 143,12 (OF determiner, cp. exame).

detest, *vb.*, *id.*, 178 G; *p. p.* detestit: 177, 26 G (OF detester).

detestable, *adj.*, *id.*, 138,22.

devill, *sb.*, devil, 150,31; 153,32; 158,29; 164,5; &c.; *gen.* devillis: 146,16 (OE deofol).

devilliss, *adj.*, devilish, 174,6; devillische: 174,16; deuillische: 146,22 F; dewillye: 146,22.

devotioun, *sb.*, devotion, 168,31; 178,24; deuocione: 136,28 (OF devotion).

dewe, *adj.*, due, 179G (OF deu).

dewite, *sb.*, duty, 125,17.

dewlie, *adv.*, properly, 151,19; 165,39; 180G; dewly: 142,29; dewlye: 142,26; 143,9.

differ, *vb.*, *id.*, 158,20; 158,23; 158,25; differis: 150,4; 158,7; 162,18 (OF differer).

difference, *sb.*, *id.*, 135,13; 154,21; 158,5; 162,9; &c.; make na difference (differens) of (=fail to distinguish): 113,19; 114,21; 114,34 (OF difference).

difficle, *adj.*, difficult, 158,3; 171,10 (Lat. difficilis).

diffidis, *vb.*, be diffident, 127,20 (Lat. diffidere).

diffinit, *vb.*, *pret.*, defined, 169,31 (OF definer).

diffinitioun, *sb.*, definition, 149,5; 154,36; 161,15; 169,31.

dignite, *sb.*, dignity, 177,26G (OF dignité).

digressiouns, *sb.*, *pl.*, digressions, (Lat. digressio).

dilatate, *vb.*, *p. p.*, spread, 163,31 (OF dilater, Lat. -atus).

diligently, *adv.*, *id.*, 112,25; 114,3; 114,22; 132,6; diligentlye: 123,5; 126,20; 139,19; diligentlie: 154,27 (OF diligent).

diminiss, *vb.*, diminish, derogate, 149,35; 149,35; 158,35; diminucis: 123,21; 135,12; 146,23; dyminucis: 135,19; *p. p.* diminissit: 158,39; 159,13; 181,27 (ME menusen, Lat. diminuere).

disciple, *sb.*, *id.*, 124,31; 155,12; 166,8; 166,11; 166,30; *pl.* disciples: 120,18; 123,27; 124,19; 129,7; &c.; disciplis: 149,17; 149,23; 150,8; 151,15; &c.; discipulis: 115,22; 115,33; 118,14; *gen. pl.* discipliss: 178,26 (OF disciple, Lat. discipulus).

discorde, *sb.*, discord, 161,6 (OF discord).

discouerit, *vb.*, *pret.*, uncovered, took off his cloak, 125,1 (OF descovrir).

disdanit, *vb.*, *pret.*, considered with disdain, 121,7 (OF desdegnier).

disdayne, *sb.*, contempt, 178G.

dispare, *vb.*, despair, 126,22; 126,23; dispar: 125,6 (OF despeir-).

dispone, *vb.*, dispose, prepare, 137,29; disponis: 138,10; *pr. p.* disponand: 143,12; 169,3; 171,19 (=disposing of);

p. p. disposit: 160,16; 160,18; 160,22 (Lat. disponere).

dispositioun, *sb.*, (right of) bestowal, 171, 19; disposicione (= preparation): 137,25.

disput, *vb.*, *pret.*, (or *p. p.*), discussed, 142,30 (OF desputer).

disputacione, *sb.*, discussion, 132,7; 134,33.

dispyt, *sb.*, contempt, 151,25; 177,6 (OF despit).

dissagysing, *gerund*, disguising, 179,20 (OF desguisier).

dissaitfull, *adj.*, deceitful, 151,7.

dissauit, *vb.*, *p. p.*, deceived, 131,24 (OF deceiv-).

dissimwlatioun, *sb.*, dissembling, 153,21 (OF dissimulation).

distinct, *adj.*, *id.*, 180,25 (OF distinct).

distinguit, *p. p.*, distinguished, distinct, 141,13 (OF distinguer).

distres, *sb.*, distress, 129,1; 129,8 (OF destresse).

diuers, *adj.*, divers, diverse, 113,20; 154,13; 154,25; 154,40; &c.; diuerse: 120,23; 122,3; 123,16; 124,15; &c.; diuerss: 111; 112,6; 115,15; 116,10; &c.; diuersse: 136,12; dyuers: 174,10 (OF divers).

diuersite, *sb.*, diversity, 154, 28.

diuidit, *vb.*, *p. p.*, divided, 118,18; 120,19; 129,3; 141,6; 141,33; 174,14; deuidit: 118,18; 118,19; 118,21; 119,4 (Lat. dividere).

diuine, *adj.*, divine, 119,19; 119,22; 123,11; 123,13; &c. (OF divin).

diuinite, *sb.*, divinity, 118,22; 119,31; 120,3.

diuisioun, *sb.*, division, disagreement, 161, 6; 173,11.

do, *vb.*, *id.*, (*also auxiliary*), 113,12; 129, 23; 131,20; 139,24; &c.; dois: 115,5; 116,25; 118,16; 120,24; &c.; doise: 127,3; 134,19; dowes: 178G; *pr. p.* doing: 167,20; *pret.* did: 116,10; 116,28; 117,2; 123,31; &c.; dide: 140,12; 143,7; 143,27; 144,14; dyde: 143,6; *p. p.* done: 128,28; 154,28; 154,29; 156,30; &c.; *gerund pl.* doingis: 159,35 (OE don, dyde, gedon).

doctour, *sb.*, doctor, learned person, 124, 21; 124,32; 131,28; 132,22; &c.; *pl.* doctouris: 173,25 (OF doctour).

doctrine, *sb.*, *id.*, 112,6; 112,11; 112,15; 112,23; &c. (*in MS A*); doctrin: 117,8; 134,2; doctryne: 144,8; 149,23; 150,19; 150,21; &c. (*in MS B*).

dominicall, *adj.*, of the Lord, 175,14 (Lat. dominicalis).

doute, *vb.*, doubt, 131,26; douteis: 153,26; *pr. p.* douttand: 145,5; *p. p.* douttit: 168,16 (OF douter).

doute, *sb.*, doubt, 125,6; 136,17; 144,28; dout: 152,1; 163,28; 163,36; 165,31; dowt: 112,30; 114,9.

doutsum, *adj.*, doubtful, 165,40; 170,30.

down, *adv.*, *id.*, 180,9; doun: 156,29; 178,9; (OE of-dune).

downe cast, *vb.*, cast down, 178G (Scand. kasta).

drawin, *vb.*, *p. p.*, drawn (OE dragen).

dremis, *vb.*, dream, 117,19; dreymis: 149, 36 (OE dream).

drink, *vb.*, *id.*, 113,12; 113,13; 113,15; 113,17; &c.; drinke: 129,28; 133,10; drinkis: 113,18; 113,19; 114,20; 114,32; &c. (OE drincan).

drownit, *vb.*, *p. p.*, drowned, intoxicated, 171,24; 174,11 (ME druncnen).

duellinge place, *sb.*, dwelling (-place), 119, 28.

duellis, *vb.*, dwells, 119,30 (OE dwelan).

dwm, *adj.*, dumb, 177,9; dwme: 177,9G (OE dumb).

dysseuer, *vb.*, dissever, separate, 136,24; *p. p.* disseuerit: 136,24 (OF dessevrer).

easy, *adj.*, *id.*, 139,23; *adv.* easelie: 158,4; easaly: 136,11; 139,11; easalye: 121,18; 123,7; esaly: 114,3; 116,22; 118,12; 118,28 (*see* ese).

edificatione, *sb.*, edification, 176,26G.

edifyis, *vb.*, edifies, 119,1; 119,3 (OF edifier).

effeccione, *sb.*, affection, sentiment, 139,26 (Lat. affectus).

effect, *sb.*, *id.*, 112,17; in effect: 143,7; 162,6; substance and effect (=*scholastic* effectus formalis): 160,5; 160,15; 160,25; 160,31; &c.; to þe effect þat, *conj.*, 115,14; 118,11; 121,18; 128,9; 136,11; 164,22 (AN effect, Lat. effectus).

effectuislye, *adv.*, effectively(?), 143,3 (Lat. effectuosus; *perhaps* affectuose, strongly).

effore, *prep.*, before, 136,26 (*see* afoir).

efter, *prep.*, after, 113,10; 118,19; 122,3; 123,29; 125,28; &c.; eftir: 165,19; 171,17; 174,3; 174,4; &c.; *adv.* 116,17; 116,23; 133,15; 143,12; eftir: 163,9; 177,8; efter þat, *conj.*: 113,11; 123,26; 133,29 (OE æfter; Scand. efter).

eftervart, *adv.*, afterwards, 117,5; eftervard: 120,21 (OE æfterweard).

eik, *vb.*, eke, add, 177,17; 177,21; *pret.* eikit: 156,20 (OE ecan).

eit, *vb.*, eat, 113,10; 113,13; 113,15; 113,17; &c.; eat: 130,9; eate: 129,27; 132,20; 133,8; eittis: 113,17; 113,18; 114,20; 114,31; 114,33; ettis: 118,26; eatis: 119,29; 129,29; *p. p.* eittin: 118,19; 164,20; 164,22; 164,24; eaten: 120,19; 120,20 (OE etan, eten).

elevate, *vb.*, *id.*, 178,7 (Lat. elevatus).

elevatioun, *sb.*, elevation, 179,7; 179,8.

ellis, *adv.*, else, in addition, 174,18; or ellis (=otherwise): 151,24 156,3; 163,22; 164,25; &c.; or elss: 114,16 (OE elles).

end, *sb.*, *id.*, 124,23; 156,24; 160,8; 161,29; 172,23 (OE ende).

endit, *vb.*, *p. p.*, ended, 147,1; 176,27G.

ennimeys, *sb.*, *pl.*, enemies, 134,8 (OF enemi).

entisand, *vb.*, *pr. p.*, enticing, 178G (OF enticier).

entyr, *vb.*, enter, 153,14; *pret.* enterit: 125,21; 125,28; 129,7; 130,1; 135,25; 165,20 (OF entrer).

epistle, *sb.*, *id.*, 123,25; epistill: 176,13G; epistole: 176,13 (OF epistle, Lat. epistola).

equal, *adj.*, *id.*, 138,6; 141,32; equall: 141,32; 146,9; equal ... with: 117,16; 141,31; equall ... with: 123,11; 123,12; 123,17; 123,22; 125,10; equal ... as: 137,4f.; *adv.* (=equally): 146,10 (Lat. equalis).

equalite, *sb.*, equality, 124,8; 141,29; 141,30; 144,15.

equiualent, *adj.*, equivalent, 146,7 (Lat. equivalens).

erbis, *sb.*, *pl.*, herbs, 127,21 (OF herbe).

ernistly, *adv.*, earnestly, 114,28; 116,20; ernistlye: 134,19; 138,6 (OE eorneste).

errour, *sb.*, error, 139,14; 140,12; 140,22; 143,27; &c.; *pl.* errouris: 139,29; 140,11; 142,6 (OF errour).

erth, *sb.*, earth, 153,24; 167,40; earth: 123,29 (OE eorþe).

eruditione, *sb.*, instruction, 180G; 181G (Lat. eruditio).

ese, *sb.*, ease, 137,12; eiss: 169,26 (OF aise).

establisit, *vb.*, *p. p.*, made sure, 112,2 (OF establiss-).

esteyme, *vb.*, esteem, 180G (OF estimer).

estimacione, *sb.*, estimation, 135,7.

euellis, *vb.*, destroy, 137,24 (Lat. evellere).

euentuir, *sb.*, event; in euentuir, *conj.*, lest, 139,24 (Lat. aventura, eventura).

euer, *adv.*, ever, 113,1; 115,13; 116,19; 117,6; &c.; evir; 149,28; 150,27; 150,29; 151,18; &c.; evyr: 157,3; 170,28; 174,1 (OE æfre).

euerlestand, *adj.*, everlasting, 131,30; euerlestyng: 118,26; euerlestynge: 129,29; euerlastand: 158,28; evir lastand: 152,21; evirlastand: 174,24; 177,14; 181G (OE læstan).

euery, *adj.*, every, 131,29; 163,35; 182,13; everie: 156,29; 156,35; 163,32; 163,33; &c.; euery thynge, *adv.*, in every respect: 131,18.

evangell, *sb.*, gospel, 128,20; 130,15; 139, 31; 159,37; &c.; evangel: 116,4; euangell: 129,6; evangill: 176,13G; *pl.* evangelis: 113,4; 115,21 (OF evangille, Lat. evangelium).

evangelist, *sb.*, *id.*, 166,30.

evill, *adj.*, evil, 154,2; 155,26; 168,13 (OE yfel).

evin, *adv.*, even, 144,15; 164,12; 167,28 (OE efne).

exame, *vb.*, examine, 113,16; 114,19; 114, 24; 114,30; exeme: 137,27; 137,29 (OF examiner).

excede, *vb.*, exceed, 131,20; exceid: 168,39 (OF exceder).

excellent, *adj.*, *id.*, 115,16; 122,21; 126,8; 126,17; &c. (OF exceller).

excellis, *vb.*, excels, 166,25.

exempil, *sb.*, example, 118,30; exemple: 160,28; 167,23; as be (ane, *MS A*) exempil, exemple: 116,4; 129,6; 160,8; 163,36; 179,25 (OF exemple).

exilit, *vb.*, *p. p.*, exiled, 181G (OF exiler).

exort, *vb.*, exhort, 138,6; *pr. p.* exhortand: 146,12 (OF exhorter).

expectatioun, *sb.*, expectation, 172,7 (Lat. expectatio).

expedient, *adj.*, *id.*, 150,5; 159,39; 160,35; 177,25 (Lat. expediens).

expell, *vb.*, expel, 139,30 (Lat. expellere).

experience, *sb.*, *id.*, 125,24; 171,33 (OF experience).

explodit, *vb.*, *p. p.*, decried, 146,10; 146,19; 161,8 (OF exploder).

expone, *vb.*, explain, interpret, 135,10; exponis: 139,34 (Lat. exponere).

expremit, *vb.*, *p. p.*, expressed, 181G (Lat. exprimere).

express, *adj.*, *id.*, 154,24; 154,26; 154,30; expres: 149,12; 154,6; 154,8; 154,11; 154,14; expresse: 124,2; 127,26; *adv.* expres (= distinctly): 154,12; 154,20; 154,22; 154,29; &c.; expresse: 123,22; 141,4; expresly: 115,3; 137,26; expreslye: 132,22; 145,20; expreslie: 155,25 (OF expres).

eyn, *sb.*, *pl.*, eyes, 178,8; 179,13; 179,14; 179,18; eyne: 130,12; 131,27; 132,28; 132,31; 133,4 (OE egan).

faccionaris, *sb.*, *pl.*, adherents of faction, 145,10.

faccione, *sb.*, faction, 141,1; 141,2; 142,23; 146,6; factioun: 152,20; 171,25; 171,37; 173,11; 174,22; *pl.* faccions: 140,28; factiouns: 173,37 (OF faction).

faccious, *adj.*, factious, 126,18; facciouse: 121,1.

face, *sb.*, *id.*, 179,26 (OF face).

fader, *sb.*, father, 113,30; 116,5; 117,4; 117,13; &c.; fadir: 116,15; father: 121,28; 122,22; 122,30; 123,7; &c.; fathir: 176,7G; *pl.* faderis: 113,1; faderes: 176,26G; fatheris: 151,15; 154,40; 165,5; 168,37; &c.; fatheres: 120,27; 178G; fathers: 124,14; 126,16; 130,4; 132,13; &c. (OE fæder).

fair, *adj.*, *id.*, 176,8 (OE fæger).

faith, *sb.*, *id.*, 120,18; 125,19; 125,24; 129, 26; &c. (*MS A*); fayth: 116,4; 116,9; 149,15; 149,24; &c. *(in MS B);* faytht: 175,19G; 175,27G; 179G (OF fei, feid).

faithfull, *adj.*, faithful, 145,9; faitfull: 145,6; faythfull: 157,28; 165,28; 169,33; 172,23; &c.; faythtfull: 177,24G.

fall, *vb.*, *id.*, 139,25; 178,9 (OE fallan).

falloschype, *sb.*, company, 181G.

fallowis, *sb.*, *pl.*, fellows, 126,18 (Scand. felagi).

false, *adj.*, *id.*, 131,24; 131,25; 132,10; 137,6; fals: 140,8; 149,33; 150,32; 157,24; &c.; *adv.* falslye: 111; 116,25; 145,12; falslie: 151,8; 182,25 (OF fals).

falt, *sb.*, fault, 177,16; falte: 155,3; 178,20; fault: 145,16; 145,19; 145,22; 145,25 (OF faute, Lat. fallere).

familiar, *adj.*, *id.*, 116,18; 117,6; famyliar: 142,18 (Lat. familiaris).

famous, *adj.*, *id.*, 152,14; famows: 151,3; 151,22 (OF famos).

fannon, *sb.*, maniple, 180,6 (Fr. fanon).

far, *adv.*, *id.*, 128,29; 135,28; 139,22; 140,21; *correlation*, in sa far (...) as: 119,15; 131,3; 132,29; 143,8 F; als far (...) as: 125,9; 125,15; 127,31; 141,9; *comp.* farthair: 179 G; 180 G; ferther: 155,16; 163,30; 175,14; 171,35; 161,17 *(adj.); also see* forder (OE feor).

farss, *sb.*, farce, 179,21 (Fr. farce).

fauour, *sb.*, favour, 136,8; 137,24; 138,2; favour: 151,9; 168,14; *pl.* favouris: 153,8; 174,32 (OF favour).

fauouris, *vb.*, favour, 140,28; 141,1; *pr. p.* fauourand: 142,23; *pret.* fauourit: 141,2.

feill, *vb.*, feel, touch, 130,28; *pret.* feld: 131,1; *p. p.* feld: 130,18; feild: 130,20; felit: 131,7; 131,8 (OE felan).

feit, *sb.*, *pl.*, feet, 178,26 (OE fet).

ferde, *num.*, fourth, 126,3; *adv.* feirdlie: 151,37; 158,25; 170,16 (OE feorþa).

feruentlye, *adv.*, fervently, 138,9 ferventlye: 178,4 G (OF fervent).

fervour, *sb.*, *id.*, 178,24; feruor: 138,2 F (OF fervor).

feyr, *sb.*, fear, awe, 138,2 (OE fær).

fift, *num.*, fifth, 129,30; 175,18 *(sb.); adv.* fiftlie: 152,1; 170,20; 176,16 (OE fifta).

fiftie, *num.*, fifty, 167,10; 168,4 (OE fiftig).

figure, *sb.*, figure, type, 113,24; 115,26; 115,32; 115,33; &c.; *pl.* figuris: 149,14; 151,31; 162,6; 158,17; &c. *(in MS B);* figures: 135,14; 135,15 (Fr. figure, Lat. figura).

find, *vb.*, *id.*, 155,3; 159,35; 163,14; 172,6; &c.; fynd: 145,9; fynde: 139,20; 144,21; fyndis: 145,16; *pret.* fand: 145,22; 178,20; fande: 176,7 G; *p. p.* funde: 120,27 (OE findan, fand, funden).

finissit, *vb.*, *p. p.*, finished, 176,27 (OF finiss-).

first, *adj.*, *adv.* and *sb.*, first, firstly, 112,1; 112,19; 114,24; 128,12; 119,8; 138,27; &c.; fyrst: 179 G; 181 G (OE fyrst).

fleand, *vb.*, *pr. p.*, fleeing, 139,24 (OE fleon).

flesche, *sb.*, flesh, 113,27; 116,8; 118,5; 118,9; &c.; flesch: 129,11 (OE flæsc).

fleschly, *adj.*, fleshly, 118,20; 127,27; 129,1; 129,14; &c.; fleschlye: 120,17; 122,4; 122,9; 122,13; &c.

flok, *sb.*, flock, 180 G (OE flocc).

floureseis, *sb.*, *pl.*, flowers, 127,22 (OF flour).

foirfaltit, *vb.*, *p. p.*, forfeited, 181 G (OF forfait).

foirfatheris, *sb.*, *pl.*, forefathers, 177,17.

foirheyd, *sb.*, forehead, 180 G, 181 G; 182 G.

follow, *vb.*, *id.*, 167,6; 167,38; followis: 154,8; 163,4; 163,9; 174,6; folowis: 114,33; 116,17; 123,12; 143,12; *pr. p.* folovand: 116,23; 133,15; folouand: 133,7; 140,9; following: 175,20; 177,8; *p. p.* folowit: 137,7 (OE folgian).

folowaris, *sb.*, *pl.*, followers, 178,21.

for, *conj.*, *id.*, 112,30; 113,17; 114,10; 114,20; &c.

for, *prep.*, *id.*, 112,5; 113,6; 113,10; 114,13; &c.

for, *adv.*, where, 125,24; 139,31; 140,31.

forbeid, *vb.*, forbid, 133,22; forbid: 169,15; *pret.* forbad: 150,31; 174,5 (OE forbeodan).

forder, *comp.*, further(-more), *adj.*, 119,7; *adv.*, 120,6; 124,13; 130,26 (OE furþra).

forgeif, *vb.*, forgive, 166,23; 181,17.

formalie, *adv.*, formally, 162,40 (Lat. formalis).

forme, *sb.*, form, appearance, 127,6; 130,12; 133,31; 158,21; 158,23; *pl.* formis: 117,17; 155,38; 156,10; 157,4; &c.; formes: 129,19; 132,27; 132,30; 135,30; 170,8; formys: 154,37 (OF forme).

forquhy, *adv.*, on which account *(used in sense of Lat.* 'etenim'*)*, 162,22; 173,14; 173,21; 173,24; &c.; *in MS A* for quhy: 114,6; 116,2; 117,12; 122,29; &c. (OE for hwig).

forth, *adv.*, *id.*, 125,30 (OE forþ).

fortify, *vb.*, strengthen, 115,27; 116,29; 118,1; fortifye: 121,7; 126,10; 139,35; 140,10; &c.; fortifie: 154,17 (OF fortifier).

forʒet, *vb.*, forget, 179,3 (OE forgetan).

foster fathir, *sb.*, foster-father, 176,7 G (OE fostor).

fourescoir, *num.*, eighty, 167,1; 168,23; fourescoire: 166,31; fourescoyr: 174,3 (Scand. skor).

fouretene, *num.*, fourteen, 166,19; 175,19; 175,29; 175,33 (OE feowertene).

fourtie, *num.*, forty, 172,8 (OE feowertig).

fouth, *sb.*, fulness, 136,21 (OE full-þu).

fra, *prep.*, from, 118,19; 118,21; 120,3; 120,4; &c. (Scand. fra).

freir, *sb.*, friar, 151,30; *pl.* freiris: 171,12 (OF freire).

frelie, *adv.*, freely, 153,10 (OE freo).

frequentlye, *adv.*, frequently, 178 G (Fr. frequent).

freyndis, *sb.*, *pl.*, relatives, 168,9 (OE freond).

frome, *prep.*, from, 156,28; 182,5 (OE from).

fructe, *sb.*, fruit, 158,33; *pl.* fructis: 159,1; 159,4; 159,17; 158,21; &c. (OF fruit; Lat. fructis).

fructfull, *adj.*, fruitful, 178 G; 180 G.

frustratis, *vb.*, deprives, 146,25 F; *p. p.* frustrate: 160,17; frustrat: 130,7 (Lat. frustratus).

fude, *sb.*, food, 146,25; 155,39; fuid: 120,21; fwid: 120,12 (OE foda).

fulfill, *vb.*, fulfil, 164,18; fullfillis: 180 G; *p. p.* fulfillit: 172,26; 172,31 (OE fulfyllan).

fundament, *sb.*, foundation, 173,2 (OF fondement, Lat. fundamentum).

fure, *sb.*, fury, 126,13; 126,21; (OF furie).

furth, *adv.*, forth, 133,18; 148; 151,9; 156,15; &c.; fwrth: 174,26 G; fwrtht: 180 G.

furthschaw, *vb.*, show forth, proclaim, 113,14; 178,5; *p. p.* furthschawin: 172,17 (OE sceawian).

fyftene, *num.*, fifteen, 172,14 (OE fiftene).

fyne, *sb.*, end, 161,26 (Lat. finis).

fyr, *sb.*, fire, 180 G (OE fyr).

fywe, *num.*, five, 148; 166,32; fiwe: 144,23.

gaddir, *vb.*, gather, 177,6; *p. p.* 142,28; 149,20; 151,21; 166,4 (OE gaderian).

gaist, *sb.*, ghost, 160,11; goist: 119,9; 145,4; 146,27 (OE gast).

gallois, *sb.*, *pl.*, gallows, 178 G (OE galga).

ganestude, *vb.*, *pret.*, withstood, 150,29; 150,30; 173,36; 174,1; 174,14; gayne stud: 182 G; *p. p.* ganestand: 174,9; *gerund* ganestanding: 172,15 (OE gegn + standan).

gange, *vb.*, go, 127,32; *gerund* gangin: 156,28 (Scand. ganga).

gapyng, *gerund*, gaping, opening the mouth, 178,2; gaiping: 178,4 (Scand. gapa).

garmontis, *sb.*, *pl.*, garments, 160,33 (OF garnement).

geif, *vb.*, give, 160,27; 161,17; 161,34; 165,25; &c.; gewe: 180 G; gif: 117,29; 120,19; 120,20; 126,4; &c.; gyfe: 133,27; geiffis: 160,29; geifis: 169,18; 178,25;

giffis: 113,28; 118,5; 118,7; 118,22; &c.; gevis: 179,11; giffes: 142,14; *pr. p.* gevand: 165,20; 162,13; *(conj.,* supposing); giffand: 116,12; 116,17; *pret.* gaif: 161,36; 161,39; 162,21; 162,32; &c.; geue: 139,40; gef: 115,22; 115,33; 124,19; 132,19; &c.; *p. p.* gevin: 162,5; 162,8; 162,9; 162,14; &c.; gewein: 179 G; giffin: 113,6; 113,9; 113,10; 114,13; 114,17; &c.; *gerund* gevin: 168,12; 168,30; 176,3 (OE gifan).

geif, *conj.*, if, 177,17; gif: 114,22; 116,3; 116,9; 117,18; &c.; gife: 141,6; giff: 142,11; gyff: 181 G; giffe: 134,16.

general, *adj.*, *id.*, 142,29; generall: 142,25; 143,23; 165,7; 169,10; 170,27; generale: 149,28; 151,18; 152,17; 157,16; &c.; in generale, *adv.*, 151,1 (OF general).

generat, *vb.*, *p. p.*, generated, 125,10 (Lat. generatus).

gentill, *adj.*, gentle, 178,4 G; 182 G (OF gentil).

gentyll, *sb.*, gentile, 154,25; *pl.* gentyllis: 156,31; gentylis: 156,29.

gift, *sb.*, *id.*, 136,26; 136,29; *pl.* giftis: 182,6; giftes: 128,16; 128,19; 136,14; 136,15; 136,17; geftis: 128,29 (OE gift).

gilty, *adj.*, guilty, 113,15; 114,32; gilteous: 114,32 F (OE gyltig).

glaid, *adj.*, glad, 153,8 (OE glæd).

glore, *sb.*, glory, honour, 112,29; 112,31; 132,27; 135,7; &c.; *(in MS A);* gloir: 149,35; 158,35; 158,38; 159,11 (OF glorie).

glorifyet, *vb.*, *p. p.*, glorified, 125,13; 127,33; 128,5; 129,17; 129,21; 130,23; glorifiet: 129,1 (OF glorifier).

gloriouse, *adj.*, glorious, 132,18; 136,18.

glowring, *gerund*, glowering, moving of the eyes, 178,2; 178,4.

go, *vb.*, *id.*, 152,14; 153,27 (OE gan).

God, *id.*, *passim; also* Gode; *gen.* Goddis, Goddes, Godis (180 G).

godheid, *sb.*, godhead, 119,11; 119,16; 120,5; 120,7; godhede: 125,11; 127,33; 128,6; 133,4; &c.

godly, *adj.*, *id.*, 114,10; 115,10; 115,13; 115,16; &c.; godlye: 112,23; 122,20; 124,21; 124,29; &c.; godlie: 121,28; 150,18; 150,21; 154,16; &c.

godlines, *sb.*, godliness, 168,8; 179,5.

gorgeous, *adj.*, *id.*, 180,13.

gospellaris, *sb., pl.,* 'gospellers', 130,26 (OE godspell).

gouernit, *vb., p. p.,* governed, 177,26G (OF governer).

grace, *sb., id.,* 117,29; 121,26; 126,4; 130, 10; &c. (OF grace).

grant, *vb., id.,* 182G; *p. p.* grantit: 180G (OF graunter).

graipe, *vb.,* feel, 130,28; *pret.* grapit: 131,1; *p. p.* grapit: 121,14; 130,12; 130,18; 130,20 (OE grapian).

grete, *adj.,* great, 130,6; 130,7; 134,28; 135,16; &c.; grit: 150,22; 151,5; 154,21; 156,29; &c. *(in MS B);* greit: 180G; *comp.* gretar: 117,23; 136,7; 166,23; gretare: 139,21; greater: 140,21; 146,13; *adv.* gretarlye: 136,7; *superl.* gretast: 144,16 (OE great).

grevis, *vb.,* grieves, 179,6 (OF grever).

greyfus, *adj.,* grievous, 182G.

grosse, *adj.,* gross, 130,26 (OF gros).

ground, *vb., id.,* 151,13; *pret.* groundit: 169,31; *p. p.* groundit: 151,28; 151,31; 151,34; 152,2; 172,2; groundyt: 152,5; grundit: 152,11; 152,16.

grow, *vb., id.,* 168,39 (OE growan).

growf, *adj.,* flat, on growf (= prostrate): 178,10.

grwnd, *sb.,* ground, 177,26G (OE grund).

gude, *adj.,* good, 125,2; 131,13; 134,1; 138,14; &c.; guid: 112,8; 125,33; 146, 20; gud: 112,14; 114,3; 115,1; 126,4; &c.; guide: 146,10 (OE god).

gudenes, *sb.,* goodness, 164,10; 164,14; gudnes: 130,5; 145,5.

gudis, *sb., pl.,* goods, 180G.

gybet, *sb.,* gibbet, 178G (OF gibbet).

hable, *adj.,* able, 156,1; 181,24; 182,2; (OF able, Lat. habilis).

haif, *vb.,* have *(also auxiliary),* 151,9; 151,21; 152,1; 153,20; &c.; haue: 112,5; 113,29; 120,27; 121,8; &c. hawe: 178G; 179G; 180G; 182G; haf: 113,28; hef: 112,14; 114,11; 115,1; 118,17; has: 149,28; 150,17; 154,27; 155,3; &c.; hes: 112,7; 113,1; 115,13; 117,6; &c.; *pr. p.* haifand: 151,5; 159,38; haiffand: 163, 31; hauand: 122,16; 126,29; 128,5; 128,13; &c.; *pret.* had: 149,17; 157,23; 178,17; 178,18; &c.; hed: 113,9; 113,11; 117,9; 117,23; &c.; hede: 128,22; hade: 123,30; *p. p.* hed: 134,32; 140,18; 140,19;

had: 140,25; 150,9; 158,25; hed rather + *infin.:* 137,11 (OE habban).

hail, *adj.,* whole, 116,9; 132,6; 133,14; 135,27; &c.; haill: 159,35; 171,14; 171, 30; 176,9; &c. (OE hal).

hailsoume, *adj.,* wholesome, 131,29.

hald, *vb.,* hold, 159,36; 166,16 (OE haldan).

haly, *adj.,* holy, 112,29; 112,32; 115,17; 117,8; &c.; holy: 124,15; 125,4; 132,15; 136,14; &c. *(in MS A);* holye: 140,14; 146,24; halie: 160,11; 168,16; 168,30; 168,31; &c. (OE halig).

hand, *sb., id.,* 113,30; 122,22; 122,30; 123,6; &c.& *pl.* handis: 167,18; 178,3; 178,15; 178,17; handes: 124,18 (OE hand).

handelit, *vb., p. p.,* handled, 130,11; handlet: 121,13 (OE handlian).

hand wryte, *sb.,* hand-written document, 152,19; 174,21 (OE ge-writ).

hart, *sb.,* heart, 131,30; 138,1; harte: 153, 13; *gen.* hartes: 137,24; *pl.* hartis: 137,11; 165,20; 178,7; 183,10; hartes: 162,14; 138,10; 143,8 (OE heorte).

he, *pron., id., passim* (OE he).

he, *adj.,* high, 145,8; hie: 153,17; 167,3; 173,27; 182,4; *adv.* hiechtlie: 178,1 (OE heh-e).

hede, *sb.,* heed, 141,22 (OE hedan).

hede, *sb.,* head, section, 126,30; 134,33; heid: 112,19; 112,28; 112,34; 172,1; &c.; *pl.* hedis: 112,17; heidis: 171,11; 174,40; heydis: 160,30 (OE heafod).

heir, *vb.,* hear, 157,28; 165,18; 171,7; 171, 12; *pret.* hard: 167,37; harde: 177,1; *p. p.* hard: 116,5; 161,8; harde: 171,37 (OE heran).

heir, *adv.,* here, 125,33; 132,13; 167,27; 177,11; here: 121,4; 124,20; 128,24 (OE her).

hellis, *sb., gen. sg.,* hell, 134,30 (OE hel, *gen.* helle).

help, *vb., id.,* 168,32; *p. p.* helpit: 168,16 (OE helpan).

helplyk, *adj.,* helpful, 168,20; 181,22; 182,3; 182,12; 183,4.

heresy, *sb., id.,* 111; 117,19; 132,10; 137,20; &c.; heresye: 138,20; 138,25; 142,10; 142,16; &c.; herese: 116,29; haresy: 134,30; heresie: 174,4; 174,13; *pl.* hereseis: 138,23; 171,25; hereseys: 137,18; 138,26; heresis: 112,13 (OF heresie).

heretage, *sb.,* heritage, 181G (OF heritage).

heretyk, *sb.*, heretic, 168,4; *pl.* heretykis: 179,4; 182,25; heretikis: 116,10; 116,18; 117,6; 139,4; &c. (OF heretique).

hevin, *sb.*, heaven, 124,27; 128,23; 128,26; 129,1; &c.; hevine: 124,26; 125,7; hewine: 122,27; 122,30; 123,3; 123,20; 124,11; hewyne: 140,32; heawin: 124,5; heawyn: 122,22; heavin: 124,3; heawine: 121,23; 122,1; 122,2; &c.; heawyne: 121,25 (OE heofon).

hevinlie, *adj.*, heavenly, 155,39; 180,18; 182,10.

hevy, *adj.*, heavy, 159,18 (OE hefig).

heycht, *sb.*, height, 130,16 F (OE hehþu).

hidderto, *adv.*, hitherto, 156,18; 166,16; 166,27; &c. hidder to: 168,2; hitherto: 131,27; hithertil: 143,18 (OE hider).

hill, *sb.*, *id.*, 130,16 (OE hyll).

him, *pron.*, *id.*, 150,31; 152,9; 167,5; hym: 113,12; 125,13; 130,28; hyme: 112,24; 114,19; 117,10; 119,13; &c.; *reflexive* him self, hym self, hyme self *and* hyme selff *invariably two words*: 167,1; 114,24; 113,11; 130,30, &c.

hindmest, *adj.*, last., 152,14.

hirdis, *sb.*, *pl.*, herds, 176,6 (OE hirde).

his, *pron.*, *id.*, passim.

hoist, *sb.*, host, 167,21; *pl.* hoistis: 168,30 (Lat. hostia).

honor, *sb.*, honour, 146,27 (AN honur).

honorable, *adj.*, *id.*, 152,13; 167,39.

honorit, *vb.*, *p. p.*, honoured, 150,12.

how, *adv.*, *id.*, 160,5; 160,23; 160,38; 166,17; &c.; *also see* quhow (OE hu).

howbeit, *conj.*, although, 182,26.

hows, *sb.*, house, 125,21; house: 125,28; 129,7; 129,22; 130,2; 135,25 (OE hus).

humanite, *sb.*, humanity, 119,31; 120,3; 120,8; humanitie: 133,5 (OF humaniteit).

humiliatione, *sb.*, humiliation, 181G (Lat. humiliatio).

humilye, *adv.*, humbly, 138,6; hwmyllie: 152,13; hwmelie: 177,10; humlie: 181G (OF humble, Lat. humilis).

hunder, *num.*, hundred, 144,14; 144,23; hundreth: 142,27; 148; 150,15; 153,36; &c.; hundretht: 176,22G (OE hund-red; Scand. hundraþ).

hungyr, *sb.*, hunger, 122,5; 122,13; 122,16; hunger: 120,9 F (OE hungor).

hurtfull, *adj.*, hurtful, 181G (OF hurter).

hwny, *sb.*, honey, 127,22 (OE hunig).

hyid, *vb.*, hide, 135,12; hydis: 146,22; hyddis: 135,19 (OE hydan).

hympne, *sb.*, hymn, 175,34; *pl.* hympnis: 177,21; hymnes: 177,21 G (OF hymne).

hypocrysie, *sb.*, hypocrisy, 135,21 (OF hypocrisie).

I, *pron.*, *id.*, passim.

idolatrie, *sb.*, idolatry, 150,31; 150,32; 151,8; 153,28; &c. (Fr. idolatrie).

ignominiusnes, *sb.*, dishonour, 178G (Fr. ignominie).

ignorance, *sb.*, *id.*, 126,13; 126,21; 134,29; &c. (OF ignorance).

ignorant, *adj.*, *id.*, 153,19; 153,31; 171,27.

illuminat, *vb.*, enlighten, 183,10; *p. p.* illuminat: 179G; 180G (Lat. illuminatus).

image, *sb.*, *id.*, 117,15 (OF image).

imaginacione, *sb.*, imagination, 112,33; 128,10; 135,35.

immediately, *adv.*, *id.*, 165,28 (Fr. immediat).

immolatioun, *sb.*, immolation, 164,6; 164,7 (Fr. immolation).

immortal, *adj.*, *id.*, 130,23; 130,29; 131,1; &c.; immortall: 127,33; 130,30 (Fr. immortel, Lat. immortalis).

immortalitie, *sb.*, immortality, 121,28; 122,9.

immovabill, *adj.*, immovable, 177,26G.

impassible, *adj.*, *id.*, 129,5; impassable: 129,5 F (Fr. impassible).

imperfeccione, *sb.*, imperfection, 132,3; imperfectioun: 159,8; 159,10; *pl.* imperfecciones: 122,4; 122,10; 122,13; 130,8.

imperfit, *adj.*, imperfect, 118,15 (OF imparfait).

impertinent (to), *adj.*, not pertaining (to), 171,4 (Lat. impertinens).

impossible, *adj.*, *id.*, 127,23; 128,2; 157,26 (OF impossible).

imprent, *vb.*, *id.*, 131,29 (OF empreindre).

impropir, *adj.*, improper, 118,10; 118,13; 140,1; &c.; inpropir: 116,1; *adv.* impropirly: 113,25; 115,12; 115,20; 115,28; &c.; impropirlye: 132,12; 135,9; 139,35; &c.; impropirlie: 170,35 (OF impropre).

impung, *vb.*, impugn, 170,38 (OF impugner).

imputate, *vb.*, *p. p.*, imputed, 182,25 (Lat. imputatus).

in, *prep.*, in, into, at, *passim.*

incarnacione, *sb.*, incarnation, 132,18; 138,23 (OF incarnation).

incline, *vb.*, lay down, 126,30 (OF incliner).

includis, *vb.*, includes, 162,25; 162,26 (Lat. includere).

incomprehensible, *adj.*, *id.*, 131,12 (OF incomprehensible).

incontrar, *prep.*, against, 139,33; 141,19; 141,24; 142,13; &c.; incontrare: 125,4; 126,7; in contrar: 112,23; 118,3; 167,32; incontra: 122,20; 141,27; 142,15; 145,24 (Fr. en contraire).

inconuenient, *adj.*, inconvenient, 131,19 (OF inconvenient).

inconuenient, *sb.*, inconvenient thing, 139, 25; 177,15.

incorrupcione, *sb.*, incorruptibility, 121,27; 122,9 (Lat. incorruptio).

indifferently, *adv.*, without specification, discrimination, 118,23; indifferentlie: 159,29 (Lat. indifferenter).

indurite, *adj.*, obdurate, 126,26 (Lat. induratus).

induritnes, *sb.*, obduracy, 134,31.

inextinguabill, *adj.*, inextinguishable, 176, 9 G (Fr. inextinguible).

infer, *vb.*, *id.*, 118,5; 122,23; 181,18; 162, 19; 162,20; inferris: 113,31; 121,10; *pret.* inferrit: 140,15 (Fr. inferer).

inferrens, *sb.*, inference, 115,12; 118,10; 118,13; 123,18.

infinite, *adj.*, *id.*, 130,5; 130,9; 145,5 (OF infinit).

infundit, *vb.*, *p. p.*, infused, 136,22 (Lat. infundere).

ingine, *sb.*, mind, wit, 138,28; ingyne: 153,15; 182 G; *pl.* ingynis (OF engin).

inhabitantis, *sb.*, *pl.*, inhabitants, 182 G (Fr. inhabiter).

inimie, *sb.*, enemy, 178,13; inimye: 178 G; *pl.* inimeis: 178,18; inimes: 181 G; *also see* ennimeys (OF enemi, Lat. inimicus).

iniures, *sb.*, *pl.*, injuries, 129,3 (AN injurie).

iniuris, *vb.*, disobeys, 160,20.

iniust, *adj.*, unjust, 153,15 (Fr. juste).

inlik maner, *adv.*, similarly, 145,22; inlikmaner as (just as): 119,17; in lik maner ... as (in such a way that): 112,13.

inlikvis, *adv.*, likewise, 114,18; 115,24; 116,7; 117,3; 118,1; inlikvise: 130,19; 143,29; lyke as ... inlykvise (just as ... so): 141,33.

innocence, *sb.*, *id.*, 117,20 (Fr. innocence).

innumerable, *adj.*, *id.*, 182,2 (Fr. innumerable).

insaciable, *adj.*, insatiable, 171,31 (Fr. insatiable).

insafer (as), as far (as): 158,40; in safer (as): 158,8; 181,23.

insensible, *adj.*, not perceptible to the senses, 130,22; 131,10; 158,23 (Lat. insensibilis).

inseparatly, *adv.*, inseparably, 120,7; inseparatlye: 119,20; 124,10; 128,7; 132, 29; inseperatlie: 119,22; inseperatlye: 119,20 F; inseperablelye: 124,10 F (Lat. in-separatus).

inspiracione, *sb.*, inspiration, 145,3.

instinccione, *sb.*, instinct, 127,21; 127,23 (Lat. instinctio).

institute, *vb.*, *pret.*, instituted, 156,8; 160,9; 160,14; 161,18; &c.; *p. p.* institute: 148; 154,37; 162,22; 169,29; &c.; institut: 179 G (Lat. institutus).

institutioun, *sb.*, institution, 150,17; 155,7; 155,37; 170,32; &c.; institutione: 179 G.

instructand, *vb.*, *pr. p.*, instructing, 177, 26 G; *p. p.* instructit: 169,38; 176,6; 178,9; 178,11; &c. (Lat. instructus).

instructioun, *sb.*, instruction, 150,9; 165, 21; 165,24; &c.

instrument, *sb.*, *id.*, 119,26; *pl.* instrumentis: 159,9; 159,10; 159,16; &c.; instrumentes: 134,27 (Fr. instrument).

intend, *vb.*, *id.*, 139,28 (Fr. entendre, Lat. intendere).

intent, *sb.*, purpose, 116,2; 118,11; 126,11.

interpret, *vb.*, *id.*, 182,18; *pr. p.* interpretand: 177,26 G; *pret.* interpreit: 142,4; *p. p.* interpret: 157,23 (Fr. interpreter).

interpretacione, *sb.*, interpretation, 112,22; 112,31; 115,13; &c.; *pl.* interpretaciones: 112,26; 112,28; 138,7; 138,15; 138,17.

interpretouris, *sb.*, *pl.*, interpreters, 157,14; 165,5.

in til, *prep.*, unto, 136,18.

in to, *prep.*, in, into, 113,12; 115,15; 125,20; 127,25; into: 155,36.

intolerable, *adj.*, *id.*, 134,28; intollerable: 151,24; 177,5 (Fr. intolerable).

intoxicat, *vb.*, *p. p.*, poisoned, 139,27 (Lat. intoxicatus).

inuent, *vb.*, invent, 145,25; *pr. p.* inuentand: 145,18; *pret.* inuentit: 125,20; 125,23; inventit: 154,13; 155,20; 155,22; *p. p.* inuentit: 128,10; inventit: 148; 151,8;

154,6; &c. (Fr. inventer).

inventaris, *sb.*, *pl.*, inventors, 171,13.

invicible, *adj.*, *id.*, 134,16; 149,16; 165,12; 170,22 (Fr. invincible).

invisible, *adj.*, *id.*, 117,15; 130,22; 131,10; 136,29; *adv.* 130,24; 132,30; invisiblie: 179,13 (Fr. invisible).

inwarte, *adj.*, inward, 178,24 (OE inneweard).

inwnctit, *vb.*, *p. p.*, anointed, 121,6; 121,14; 121,16; 122,17 (OF enoint, Lat. unctus).

is, *vb.*, *see* be.

it, *pron.*, *id.*, passim; *reflex.* it self: 133,23.

iuge, *sb.*, judge, 138,6; 153,17; 154,2; 177,7; *pl.* iugeis: 180,7 (Fr. juge).

iuge, *vb.*, judge, 113,31.

iugement, *sb.*, judgment, 115,13; 118,15; 153,17; 153,19; &c.; *pl.* iugementis: 120,33; iugements: 124,6.

iunit, *vb.*, *p. p.*, joined, 119,2; 119,5; 119, 12; ionit: 119,10; 120,1; iwnit: 119,16; 119,20; 119,22; 169,16; iounit: 128,7; 132,29; 142,1; iounyt: 120,7 (OF joint).

iust, *adv.*, just, 112,14; 116,12; 134,22; 144,30; *adv.* iustlye: 142,27; 142,32; iustlie: 154,4 (Fr. juste).

iustifear, *sb.*, justifier, 176,9.

iustifie, *vb.*, justify, prove, 156,1 (Fr. justifier).

keip, *vb.*, keep, 140,14 (OE cepan).

ken, *vb.*, know, 173,1 (Scand. kenna).

king, *sb.*, *id.*, 154,18; 154,19 (OE cyning).

kingdome, *sb.*, kingdom, 121,25; kyngdome: 121,23; 122,1; 122,2; &c.

kirk, *sb.*, church, 112,6; 112,11; 112,15; &c.; kirke: 126,15; 134,23; 135,3; 139, 34; kyrk: 126,7; 176,26G (OE cirice, *with Northern* /k/).

kirkmen, *sb.*, *pl.*, churchmen, ecclesiastics, 171,14; 171,16.

knaw, *vb.*, know, 131,2; 134,9; 153,23; &c.; knawe: 121,29; knawis: 131,1; 154,2; *pr. p.* knawand: 161,27; 171,39; knavand: 130,5; knowand: 126,18; *p. p.* knawin: 149,18; 165,26; 166,3; 172,40; knavin: 112,5 (OE cnawan, cnawen).

knawlege, *sb.*, knowledge, 146,14; 168,5; 172,10; 178,27.

kneis, *sb.*, *pl.*, knees, 178,9 (OE cneo).

kneylling, *gerund*, kneeling, 178,2 (OE cneowlian).

knokking, *gerund*, beating, 178,3; 178,19 (OE cnocian).

kow, *sb.*, cow, 171,22; 177,2 (OE cu).

kynde, *sb.*, kind; all kynd of: 171,17; 182,2; na kynd(e) of: 160,13; 160,34 (OE cynd).

kyndlyt, *vb.*, *p. p.*, kindled, 180G (Scand. kynda).

laick, *adj.*, lay, 175,30 (Lat. laicus).

laif, *sb.*, rest, 123,31; 151,3 (OE laf).

laitlie, *adv.*, recently, 150,22; 155,9; 155, 14; &c. (OE læt).

laittest, *superl.*, *sb.*, most recent one, 173,18.

lak, *sb.*, lack, 179G (ME lak).

lak, *sb.*, blame, 181G (*cp. Dutch* laken).

lam, *sb.*, lamb, 117,20; 117,21; 117,22; lame: 117,23; 143,15; lamb: 149,11; 151,31; 163,37; &c. (OE lamb).

lamentit, *vb.*, *pret.*, lamented, 182G (Fr. lamenter).

langage, *sb.*, language, 155,25; 180,22 (Fr. langage).

lang, *adj.*, long, 151,6; lange: 144,18; *adv.*, 171,26; 171,31; 178,16; 178,17; lange: 130,18; 145,7 (OE lang).

lat, *vb.*, let, 113,16; 114,18; 114,19; &c. (Scand. lata).

laubouris, *sb.*, *pl.*, exertions, 156,3; lawbouris: 177,9 (OF labour).

laudable, *adj.*, *id.*, 143,9; 155,1; 172,38; 173,12; &c. (Lat. laudabilis).

law, *adj.*, low, 145,8; 173,27 (Scand. lagr).

law, *sb.*, *id.*, 150,12; 161,26; 164,18; &c.; lawe: 135,14 (OE lagu).

lawit, *adj.*, unlearned, 144,14; 173,26 (OE læwede).

lawless, *adj.*, *id.*, 178G.

learnit, *p. p.* and *adj.*, learned, 130,3; 144,22; 144,23; &c.; learnet: 139,27; 145,8; *gerund* learning: 162,16; 174,9; 178,1; 179,1; learnyng: 153,12; 159,27; learnynge: 125,32; lernynge: 142,28 (OE leornian).

led, *p. p.*, led, 153,31 (ME ledde).

left (hand), *id.*, 124,7 (OE lef-t).

leif, *sb.*, leaf, 163,32; leyf: 163,33; *pl.* leiffis: 149,2 (OE leaf).

leif, *vb.*, leave, 114,9; leiffis: 163,37; levis: 124,26; *pret.* left: 124,30; 124,31; 125,1; 160,36; *p. p.* left: 113,20 (OE læfan).

leifful, *adj.*, permitted, 166,9.

leifsum, *adj.*, permitted, 177,17; lesum: 176,27 G (OE ge-leaf-sum).

lene to, *vb.*, lean on, trust in, 127,8; 131,16; *pr. p.* lenand: 127,4; *pret.* lenit: 118,15; 126,27 (OE hleonian).

lerit, *adj.*, learned, 144,14 (OE læran).

lesing, *gerund*, calumny, 182,25 (OF leser).

less, *adv.*, *adj.* and *sb.*, less, 177,26 G; 182, 26; 180 G; lesse: 142,20; lese: 120,20; 141,28 (OE læs-sa).

lesse nor, *conj.*, unless, 130,27.

lessouns, *sb.*, *pl.*, 167,32 (OF lecon).

lettar/er, *adj.*, *comp.*, latter, last, 113,30; 115,21; 115,33; &c.; latter: 159,28; 159,30; 159,32; &c.; *superl.* last: 113,23 *(adj.)*; 116,24 *(adv.)*; last of all (finally): 122,5; 152,13; 170,26; *also see* laittest (OE læt).

letter, *sb.*, id., 182 G; lettre: 182 G (Fr. lettre).

lewis, *vb.*, lives, 121,29 F; luffis: 121,29; *pr. p.* levand (the living): 113,31; leving: 116,7; *pret.* leiffit: 172,6: 172,6; *p. p.* leiffit: 172,28; levit: 172,13; *gerund* lewing: 176,26 G (OE libban).

leys, *sb.*, *pl.*, lies, 177,5 (OE lige).

liberatioun, *sb.*, liberation, 164,5.

licht, *sb.*, light, 125,30; lycht: 176,8; 176,9 (OE leoht).

lift vp, *vb.*, lift up, 169,5; 178,15; lyft vp: 143,14; *gerund* lyftyn vp: 178,2 (Scand.

lik, *prep.*, like, 146,16; lyke: 146,16; lik as, *adv.* (just as): 115,31; 116,31; 119,14; 120,10; &c.; lyke as: 120,12; 141,32; 179,16; like as: 135,23; 140,15; lyk as: 157,5; 158,13; 158,16; &c.; lik to, *adj.* (similar to): 128,24; lik onto: 128,25; lyk maneir (in the same way): 155,22; lykwyse: 160,13; 164,35; 175,22; 176,17; &c. (OE lic).

litil, *adj.*, *sb.* and *adv.*, little, 111; 118,25; litle: 128,3; 135,13; 135,15; 149,4; litell: 146,12 (OE lytel).

logik, *sb.*, logic, 153,16 (OF logique).

lord(e), *sb.*, lord, *passim; gen.* lordes and lordis (OE hlaford).

lordeschip, *sb.*, lordship, 152,14.

loving, *gerund*, praise, 178,6; lowing: 178,6 G (OE lofian).

luf, *sb.*, love, 136,24; luff: 136,23 (OE lufu).

luke, *vb.*, look, 125,18; 143,13; 169,4; *pr. p.* lukand: 131,22 (OE locian).

lustis, *sb.*, *pl.*, lusts, 171,24 (OE lust).

lyf, *sb.*, life, 158,28; 169,18; lyff: 174,10; lyffe: 181 G; lif: 113,28; 118,5; 118,7; &c. *(MS A);* liff: 119,23; 120,8; 120,15; &c. *(MS A);* liffe: 120,5; 122,5; 122,11; &c. *(MS A);* on lyf (alive): 168,9 (OE lif).

lyftyme, *sb.*, lifetime, 172,9.

lyis, *vb.*, lie, 131,23 (OE licgan).

lyk, *vb.*, like, 171,6 (OE lician).

ma, *vb.*, may, 112,7; 115,4; 115,14; &c.; may: 123,14; 124,10; 124,20; &c.; *pret.* mich: 125,23; 136,23; mych: 136,24; 142,11; mycht: 158,28; 176,27 (OE mæg).

ma, *adj.*, more, 142,12; may: 158,37 (OE ma, *adv.*).

magnific, *adj.*, beautiful, 177,21 (Lat. magnificus).

magnificent, *adj.*, id., 167,12 (Lat. magnificent-).

mair, *comp.*, *adv.* and *adj.*, more, 114,4; 115,3; 116,14; 116,18; &c.; maire: 135,34; 136,15; 137,1; more: 125,27; 128,8; 131,28; *superl.* maist: 112,26; 112,29; 112,31; &c.; mast: 112,16; 122,21; 132,18; 138,9; most: 125,30; 126,8; 126,16 (OE mara, mæst).

maister, *sb.*, master, 148; 153,4; master: 111; 138,3; 138,4 (OF maistre).

mak, *vb.*, make, 115,19; 117,29; 120,15; &c.; make: 130,22; 132,3; makis: 113,8; 113,18; 114,21; &c.; *pr. p.* makand: 167,30; makande: 135,13; *pret.* maid: 160,23; 162,20; 163,3; mayd: 182 G; *p. p.* maid: 111; 115,21; 116,8; 117,3; &c.; made: 119,28; 128,26; 131,25, &c.; *gerund* making: 177,23 (OE macian).

man, *vb.*, must, 124,6; 124,8; 134,17; 155, 32; &c. (Scand. mun).

man, *sb.*, id., *passim;* mane: 127,6; *gen.* mannis: 112,33; 119,4; 119,17; &c.; *pl.* men, *passim; gen.* mennis: 112,5 (OE mann).

manducacione, *sb.*, eating, 120,26 (Lat. manducatio).

maner, *sb.*, manner, 112,24; 113,4; 113,11; &c.; maneir: 162,18; 163,1; 163,14; 166,11; *pl.* maneris: 136,12; maners: 159,7; 181,11 (OF maniere).

manhede, *sb.*, manhood, human nature, 120,10; 128,7; 133,3; &c.; manheid: 119,12; 119,16; 124,10; 179,17.

manifest, *adj.*, *id.*, 114,7; 114,27; 115,5; &c.; *adv.* manifestly: 116,23; manifest-lye: 134,7; 134,22 (OF manifeste).

manifestacione, *sb.*, manifestation, 134,28; 145,25.

mankynd, *sb.*, mankind, 177,26G; 181G.

manly, *adj.*, human, 122,26; 137,17; man-lye: 141,17; manlie: 119,14; 119,17.

mansioun, *sb.*, mansion, 169,17 (OF man-sion).

mantemares/is, *sb.*, *pl.*, supporters, 129,24; 146,4 (OF maintenir).

marckispoinct, *sb.*, aim, mark, 169,28; 179,3.

mare, *vb.*, marry, 128,23; *p. p.* mareit: 128,22 (OF marier).

mariage, *sb.*, marriage, 128,24 (OF maria-ge).

mark, *vb.*, *id.*, note, 112,19; 112,22; 112,28; &c.; marke: 114,19; *p. p.* markit: 154,28; 155,19 (OE mearcian).

martyr, *sb.*, *id.*, 166,27; 181,16; 182,21; *pl.* martyris: 149,24; 151,16; 165,33; &c. (OE martyr).

martyrit, *vb.*, *p. p.*, martyred, 166,19; 166, 31; 166,40; 175,19.

marvell, *vb.*, marvel, 153,35; 153,36; *p. p.* mervalit: 125,5; 126,13; (Fr. merveille).

marvellous, *adj.*, *id.*, 157,7; mervalus: 125,23; mervalous: 125,25; 125,27; mervalouse: 125,27.

mater, *sb.*, matter, 112,13; 135,16; 140,25; *pl.* maters: 137,14; 171,9; materis: 149, 14; 150,23; 152,6; &c. (OF matere).

mateyme, *miswritten for* manteyme, *vb.*, maintain, 144,14 (OF maintenir).

mature, *adj.*, *id.*, 152,15 (Lat. maturus).

me, *pron.*, *id.*

mediatour, *sb.*, mediator, 168,9 (Lat. mediator).

medicinaris, *sb.*, *pl.*, medical practitioners, 139,27.

medicyne, *sb.*, *id.*, 159,10; 159,15; 159,19; 181,8; medycyne: 159,9; 159,12 (OF medecine).

meit offering, *sb.*, meat offering, 156,27 (OE mete).

mekil, *adv.*, much, 114,4; 123,8; 123,12; &c. *(in MS A)*; mekle: 151,33; 153,36; 167,11; &c. *(in MS B)*; mekill: 132,9; 139,9 (OE micel, Scand. mikill).

memorie, *sb.*, memory, 131,30; 169,27; memory: 182G; memorye: 178,10G

(AN memorie).

mencione, *sb.*, mention, 113,8; 115,21; 121,22; 139,31; mentioun: 154,17; 159, 31; 166,7; 166,17; 172,38; mensione: 182G (OF mention).

menis, *vb.*, means, 123,6; 123,9; 125,50 &c.; *pret.* menit: 182,26; meanit: 120,20; *gerund* menyng: 114,10; 115,16; 116,29; 154,16; menynge: 126,7; 133,8; 133,14; &c.; meanynge: 139,33; 142,4; 145,13 (OE mænan).

mercy, *sb.*, *id.*, 121,25; 130,9; 153,22; 168,14; 172,18 (OF mercit).

merit, *sb.*, *id.*, 125,24; *pl.* merites: 178G OF merite).

merite, *vb.*, merit, 146,9.

mess, *sb.*, Mass, 148; 149,5; 149,7; &c.; *pl.* messis: 176,1.

messingeris, *sb.*, *pl.*, messengers, 168,29 (ME messager).

mesure, *vb.*, measure, 127,3 (OF mesure).

meynis, *sb.*, *pl.*, means, 154,13; menis: 159,16; 165,2 (OE meien).

michty, *adj.*, mighty, 123,21; mychty: 127,5; 127,8; 127,20; 131,16; 146,23 (OE mihtig).

minister, *sb.*, *id.*, 157,10; 180,25; *pl.* minis-teris: 134,27; 156,23; 157,28; &c.; ministeres: 182G (OF ministre).

ministratioun, *sb.*, (ad-)ministration, 150,6; 160,1; 160,40.

miracle, *sb.*, *id.*, 125,24; 127,11; myracle: 125,23; *pl.* miracles: 127,1 (Fr. miracle).

misbelewe, *sb.*, misbelief, 181G.

mischeant, *adj.*, wicked, 161,8; 167,33 (Fr. mechant).

mischeif, *sb.*, mischief, 171,18 (OF mes-chief)).

miserable, *adj.*, *id.*, 115,15; 172,34; 174,11; miserabil: 111; 126,14; *adv.* miserable: 137,19; 145,12; miserabillie: 151,6 (Fr. miserable).

miseratione, *sb.*, commiseration, 182G (Lat. miseratio).

misery, *sb.*, *id.*, 127,2; miserye: 126,31; *pl.* miseryes: 122,14; miseries: 120,10 (OF miserie).

misknawin, *gerund*, ignorance, 182G.

mister, *vb.*, need, 158,37 (Scand. mista).

mistery, *sb.*, mystery, 112,3; 112,7; 118,2; &c.; mystery: 122,21; misterie: 152,11; 153,2; 155,20; misterye: 120,11; 127,2; 137,5; &c.; *pl.* misteryis: 112,4; 125,18;

137,5; &c.; mysteryis: 145,25; mistereis: 131,14; 180 G; misteriis: 149,18; 151,20; 152,10; &c. (Lat. mysterium).

moder, *sb.*, mother, 145,24; 155,23 (OE moder).

mokkis, *sb.*, *pl.*, mockery, 177,5.

mokkit, *vb.*, *p. p.*, mocked, 177,12; 179,26 (OF mocquier).

mokrie, *sb.*, mockery, 151,24; 167,33; 177,6.

monkis, *sb.*, *pl.*, 171,12 (OE munec).

monstruous, *adj.*, monstrous, 153,27; 171, 23 (OF monstrueus).

montane, *sb.*, mountain, 130,16 F (OF montaine).

mony, *adj.* and *sb.*, many, 114,14; 115,25; 118,16; 122,19; &c. (OE monig).

morne, *sb.*, morrow; þe morne (to-morrow): 167,24 (OE morgen).

mornyng, *sb.*, morning, 176,6.

mortal, *adj.*, *id.*, 121,27; 122,8; 127,32; 130,17; mortall: 122,11; 122,17; 130,25; mortale: 120,8; 122,4 (OF mortal).

mot, *vb.*, may, 152,22; 174,24; 183,10; 183,11 (OE mot).

mouth, *sb.*, *id.*, 178,5; mowtht: 180 G (OE muþ).

mowis, *vb.*, moves, 126,15; 126,22; *pret.* mowit: 126,21; 126,25; *p. p.* mowit: 125,19; movit: 161,12; (OF movoir).

moyane, *sb.*, means, 182,11 (OF moien).

multitude, *sb.*, *id.*, 130,16; 130,24; 159,23; 160,15 (OF multitude).

mwrmwr, *sb.*, murmur, 153,19 (Fr. murmure).

mwrmwriss, *vb.*, murmurs, 174,13.

my, *pron.*, *id.*, *passim;* my self: 152,19; 152,21; 153,23.

myddis: in þe myddis of (in the middle of): 176,2; in þe mydis off: 182 G.

mynd, *sb.*, mind, 131,30; 140,17; 165,15; &c.; *pl.* myndis: 143,14; 178,7 (OE gemynd).

na, *adj.*, no, 113,19; 114,9; 114,21; 116,12; &c. (OE na).

name, *sb.*, *id.*, 140,14; 156,29; 156,30; &c.; nayme: 182 G (OE nama).

nane, *sb.*, none, 130,29; 166,12; 171,33 (OE nan).

nathing, *sb.* and *adv.*, nothing, 182,26; na thing: 113,27; 117,18; na thyng: 118,5; 118,10; na thinge: 120,20; 127,9; na

thynge: 120,15; 135,16; no thing: 154,35 (OE na + þing).

natiouns, *sb.*, *pl.*, nations, 150,28; 173,6; 173,22; 174,8 (ME nation).

natiuite, *sb.*, nativity, 157,7; 175,34; 176,1 (ME natiuitee).

natural, *adj.*, *id.*, 119,8; 127,30; 130,17; &c.; naturall: 120,20; 125,23; 125,24; 128,17; naturale: 162,12; *adv.* naturally: 130,8; 142,30.

nature, *sb.*, *id.*, 119,14; 119,18; 119,19; &c.; *pl.* natures: 119,13; 120,11; 120,13; 135, 25 (Fr. nature).

na vay, *adv.*, in no way, 125,17; 128,31; 142,7; 142,18; na vais: 124,3; no vays: 122,28; na wayes: 159,12 (OE nanes weges).

necessar, *adj.*, necessary, 112,5; 129,24; 129,26; 130,11; &c. (OF necessaire).

negligence, *sb.*, *id.*, 182 G (Fr. negligence).

neir, *adv.*, 144,13; neirby: 161,12; *superl.* nerrest, *adj.:* 112,2; nixt, *sb.:* 150,30; nixt to: 165,28 (OE near).

neuer, *adv.*, never, 114,26; 118,20; 118,21; nevir: 150,20; 154,30; 157,32; nevyr: 149,3; nevir ane (not one): 155,25; nevir sa gude (ever so good): 154,22 (OE næfre).

new, *adj.*, *id.*, 113,6; 113,12; 114,13; &c.; newe: 176,27 G (OE neowe).

nocht, *adv.*, not, *passim;* noch: 122,12; 122,24; 129,13; 145,20 (OE nawiht).

nochtvithstandynge þat, *conj.*, although, 128,8; 134,24; 136,25; 139,17; nochtvithstandinge þat: 129,10; nochtwithstanding: 153,23 (*? adv.).*

nochtþeles, nocht þe les(se), *adv.* and *conj.*, although, 112,10; 117,14; 117,15; 125,8; &c.

nor, *conj.*, neither, than, 115,11; 116,12; 114,5; 114,12 (OE nahwæþer).

notable, *adj.*, *id.*, 134,9; 149,3; 151,17; &c.

note, *sb.*, mark, 173,1; 173,4; *pl.* notis: 172,38 (Fr. note, Lat. nota).

note, *vb.*, *id.*, 112,25.

nother (... nor), neither, 116,16; 128,23; nolder: 160,11; 160,15.

novelte, *sb.*, novelty, 174,12 (OF noveliteit).

now, *adv.*, *id.*, 117,29; 119,14; 129,13; &c.; nowe: 142,21; 146,12 (OE nu).

nowmer, *sb.*, number, 143,4; 144,21 (OF nombre).

nycht, *sb.*, night, 175,33; 176,2; 176,4; *pl.*

nychtis: 164,33 (OE niht).

nyne, *num.*, nine, 176,22; 176,24; *ordinal* nint: 144,1 (OE nigon).

nynescoir, *num.*, a hundred and eighty, 174,2.

obet mess, *sb.*, Mass for the dead, 150,15; 168,24 (OF obit).

oblatioun, *sb.*, oblation, 149,9; 149,10; 151,28; &c.; oblacione: 117,23 (Fr. oblation).

oblis, *vb.*, oblige, 152,19; obliss: 174,21 (OF obliss-).

obscure, *adj.*, *id.*, 158,2 (Fr. obscur).

obscure, *vb.*, derogate, 135,12; 149,35; 158,35; 159,11; obscuris: 123,21; 135,19; *p. p.* obscurit: 158,39; 159,13.

obscuriteis, *sb.*, *pl.*, obscurities, 151,20 (Fr. obscurité).

obserues, *vb.*, observes, 178G; *p. p.* obserwit: 150,15; obseruit: 160,40; 161,10; 175,23; 177,26G (OF observer).

obtene, *vb.*, obtain, 158,28; *p. p.* obtenit: 159,1; 181,23; 183,3 (OF obtenir).

occasione, *sb.*, occasion, 112,14; 116,12; 134,32; &c.; occasioun: 161,16; 161,34; 177,7; 180,11 (Fr. occasion).

occupeis, *vb.*, occupies, 128,7; 129,21; 135,31; *pr. p.* occupeand: 129,5; *pret.* occupeit: 129,9; 135,27 (Fr. occuper).

of(f), *prep.*, of, from, *passim;* by: 129,6; 133,19; 156,16 (OE of).

offendar, *sb.*, offender, 153,23.

offendit, *vb.*, *p. p.*, offended, 127,15; 127, 27; 127,29; 171,5; &c. (Fr. offendre).

offense, *sb.*, offence, 153,11 (OF offense).

offer, *vb.*, *id.*, 166,9; 167,3; 167,19; 167,23; offir: 182,19; *pret.* offerit: 161,14; *p. p.* offerit: 143,16; 149,30; 149,31; *gerund* offering: 117,24; 156,27; 158,23; 168, 30; 182,20; offerynge: 143,22 (OE offrian).

oft, *adv.*, often, 112,6; 168,33; sa oft as euer (as often as): 113,12; quhow oft þat euer: 113,13; oft tymes: 131,25; 168,32 (OE oft).

omnipotent, *adj.*, *id.*, 123,4; 123,23; 124, 12; &c. (Fr. omnipotent).

on, *prep.*, on, in, 128,16 *and passim in MS B;* one: *passim in MS A* (OE on).

onder, *prep.*, under, 114,25; 127,6; 129,19; &c. *in MS A* (OE under).

onderstand, *vb.*, understand, 112,34; 115, 19; &c.; onderstande: 121,18; 138,24; 143,5; *pr. p.* onderstandand: 127,8; 143,14; *pret.* onderstude: 126,27; *p. p.* onderstand: 144,30; onderstandit: 146, 8; *gerund* onderstanding: 112,3; 112,11; 112,16; &c.; onderstandinge: 121,12; 122,20; 132,8; &c.; onderstandyng: 132,31; onderstandynge: 131,27; 135,1; 136,2; &c. (OE understandan).

one defendit, *p. p.*, undefended, 146,17 (OF defendre).

one to, *prep.*, unto, 121,7; 124,4; 124,23; 143,12; onto: 128,25; 160,18; 160,39; &c.

one true, *adj.*, untrue, 139,5; *adv.* one truely: 139,16; ontruelye: 135,9 (OE untreowe).

onforce, *adv.*, necessarily, 134,17; one forss: 179G (Fr. en force).

ongodly, *adj.*, ungodly, 144,8; ongodlye: 135,9; 139,5; 143,29; &c.

onknavin, *p. p.*, unknown, 133,6.

onlearnet, *adj.*, unlearned, 145,8.

only, *adv.* and *adj.*, *id.*, 112,2; 113,23; 114,27; onlye: 120,17; 123,20; onely: 126,24; 130,12; 133,3; onelye: 135,15; 135,17; 136,27; &c.; onelie: 159,12; 160,20; 161,37; &c.; nocht on(e)ly(e) … bot als: 117,25; 131,22; 132,23; &c. (OE anlic).

onprofitable, *adj.*, unprofitable, 118,8; 119,2; 119,4 (OE un + Fr. profitable).

onpropirlye, *adv.*, improperly, 139,17; cp. impropir.

onvorthely, *adv.*, unworthily, 113,15; 113, 18; 114,32; onworthely: 114,20 (OE weorþ).

ony, *pron.*, any, 114,26; 116,9; 116,12; &c. (OE ænig).

operacione, *sb.*, operation, 119,9 (Fr. operation).

opinione, *sb.*, (heterodox) opinion, 111; 112,22; 112,25; &c.; opinioun, 150,20; 154,17; 171,8; &c. (Fr. opinion).

oppin, *vb.*, open, 178,5 (OE openian).

oppinlie, *adv.*, openly, 181G.

or, *conj.*, before, 154,2 (OE ar, ær).

or, *conj.*, or, 114,26; 116,14; 116,16; &c. (OE oþþe, ME other).

oratioun, *sb.*, prayer, 156,39; 175,6; 175, 17; &c.; oratione: 178,7G; *pl.* oratiouns: 154,40; 155,4; 156,40; &c.; orationes: 174,34G (Lat. oratio).

259

ordanit, *vb.*, *p. p.*, ordained, 177,8; 182,5; ordannit: 177,8 G (AN ordeiner).

ordinance, *sb.*, regulation, 159,37; 160,21; 170,32; 177,18 (OF ordenance).

ordour, *sb.*, arrangement, 125,8; 125,9; 125,16; &c.; ordoure: 149,2; ordor: 177,23 G; ordre: 125,18 (Fr. ordre).

orient, *sb.*, (the) east, 133,2; 179,16 (Fr. orient).

originall, *adj.*, original, 181,15 (Lat. originalis).

ornamentis, *sb.*, *pl.*, ornaments, 177,21 (Fr. ornement; Lat. ornamentum).

other ... or, *conj.*, either ... or, 124,7; older ... or: 153,20; 159,38 (OE oþþe ... oþþe).

our, *pron.*, *id.*, *passim in MS A;* our *and* oure *in MS B; reflex.* our selfis: 114,28; our selues: 143,12 (OE ure).

our, *adv.*, excessively, too, 129,14; 132,13; 178 G (OE ofer).

ourcumin, *p. p.*, overcome, 178,13.

oure, *prep.*, over, 157,8.

oute, *prep.*, out, 167,31 (OE ute).

outvart, *adj.*, outward, external. 126,28; 131,15; 133,31; 137,16; outvard: 127,4; outwart: 118,16; outwarte: 178,24; 178, 26 (OE ute-weard).

oþer, other, *adj.* and *sb.*, other, *passim in MS A;* othir: 178 G; *pl.* oþeris *(also* 170,36) *and* others (OE oþer).

pacient, *sb.*, patient, 137,28 (OF patient).

pacientlie, *adv.*, patiently, 177,4.

paine, *sb.*, pain, 114,25; payne: 137,28; *pl.* paynis: 181,26 (OF peine).

papistis, *sb.*, *pl.*, papists, 177,2; 182,23; 182,26 (Lat. papista).

parabolis, *sb.*, *pl.*, parables, 165,22 (OF parabole).

parentis, *sb.*, *pl.*, parents, 181 G (Fr. parent).

parradis, *sb.*, paradise, 181 G (Fr. paradis).

parrochin, *sb.*, parish, 166,13 (Lat. paroecia).

part, *sb.*, *id.*, 133,16; 134,33; 141,1; 144,16; parte: 151,5; 154,10; 154,33; pairt: 178 G; *pl.* partis: 163,39; 164,17; partes: 142,29 (Fr. parf).

part takar, *sb.*, partaker, 114,25; 119,21; *pl.* partakaris: 119,26; 138,10; parttakaris: 137,27; 158,33.

paschal, *adj.*, *id.*, 117,20; paschale: 149,11; 151,31; 163,37; &c. (Fr. paschal).

pass, *vb.*, *id.*, 182 G; pase: 130,23; *pret.*

passet: 130,16; *p. p.* passit; 179 G; past: 179 G; *gerund* passyng: 129,9; 129,10; passynge: 135,28 (Fr. passer).

passage, *sb.*, passing, 129,9 F; 129,10 F; 135,28 F (Fr. passage).

passe, *sb.*, passage, section, 131,5 (Lat. passus).

passioun, *sb.*, passion, 154,38; 155,36; 158,32; &c.; passione: 136,25; 181 G (Fr. passion).

pastouris, *sb.*, *pl.*, pastors, 171,27; 176,6 (Lat. pastor).

patene, *sb.*, paten, 175,30 (OF patene).

pecefye, *vb.*, put at rest, 181 G (*contamination of* peace *and* pacify).

pelour, *sb.*, thief, 171,22 (Fr. piller).

pennance, *sb.*, penance, 181,12; 181,25 (OF penance).

peple, *sb.*, people, 153,31; 164,2; 164,11; &c.; pepill: 176,26 G; people: 146,15 (AN people).

perchance, *adv.*, *id.*, 129,31; perchaunce, 142,00 (ME parchaunce).

perfeccion, *sb.*, perfection, 128,26 (Fr. perfection).

perfurnys, *vb.*, perform, 154,4; performe: 182 G (OF parfournis-).

perfyt, *adj.*, perfect, 169,30; perfyte: 159,4; 159,9; *adv.* perfytlie: 160,23 (OF parfit).

perill, *sb.*, peril, 178 G (OF peril).

perissit, *vb.*, *p. p.*, perished, 164,35 (Fr. periss-).

permanent, *adj.*, *id.*, 180 G (Fr. permanent).

permittis, *vb.*, permits, 173,8 (Lat. permittere).

perpetuall, *adj.*, perpetual, continuous, 161,1; 164,13; 165,35; perpetuale: 172, 14; 172,28 (Fr. perpetuel).

persaif, *vb.*, perceive, 116,22; 116,25; 117,6; 117,25; &c.; persayf: 174,15; persaw: 124,20; persawe: 180 G; persaue: 114,3; 115,4; 115,10; &c.; perceaue: 126,21; 128,24; 131,26; &c.; *pr. p.* persauand: 139,27; *p. p.* persauit: 118,12; 123,7; 139,11; 140,18; &c.; perceauit: 141,16; *gerund* persauynge: 130,24 (OF perceiv-).

personage, *sb.*, character, 153,11 (Fr. personnage).

persone, *sb.*, person, 119,13; 120,12; 120, 13; 171,22 (= parson); *pl.* personis: 141,7; 141,10; 141,14; parsonis: 125,11 (OF persone).

persuade, *vb. id.*, make accept, 165,2; 165,4; 165,10; perswade: 124,25; 142, 24; 143,28; 143,29; perswaide: 139,1; persuadis: 142,18; persuades: 144,26; 145,31; 145,33; perswades: 139,8; 144,3; *pr. p.* persuadand: 151,7; *p. p.* persuadit: 144,7; 161,13; 161,17; perswadit: 165,12 (Fr. persuader).

persuasione, *sb.*, persuasion, persuasive argument, 143,1; persuasioun: 161,17; 171,40.

pertenis, *vb.*, belongs, pertains, 137,21; *pr. p.* pertenand: 131,14; 137,21; 171,35; 182,5 (OF partenir).

perturbate, *p. p.*, perturbed, 171,36 (Lat. perturbatus).

peruersit, *adj.*, perverse, 115,27; 126,17; *adv.* peruerstly: 114,9; 115,12; 115,16; &c.; peruerstlye: 139,18 (Fr. pervers+t).

pesefullness, *sb.*, peacefulness, 182G (OF pais).

pestiferus, *adj.*, pestiferous, 181G (Lat. pestiferus).

pestilent, *adj., id.*, 146,12; 171,26 (Fr. pestilent).

phrais, *sb.*, phrase, 123,5; 124,8; phraise: 141,11; phrase: 162,18; 162,26 (Fr. phrase).

pictour, *sb.*, picture, 138,2 (Lat. pictura).

piete, *sb.*, pity, 151,5 (OF pite).

pillare, *sb.*, pillar, 180,4; pillair: 177,26G (OF piler).

place, *sb., id.*, 113,28; 114,9; 123,14; &c.; *pl.* places: 116,3; 123,16; 124,15; &c. (Fr. place).

plage, *sb.*, plague, 182G (OF plage).

plain, *adj., id.*, 115,5; 134,29; 135,4; plaine: 112,27; 114,4; 114,7; &c.; plane: 134,2; 149,21; 149,26; &c.; playne: 124,14; 126,11; 142,10; *comp.* planar: 114,10; 115,1; 125,2; *adv.* plainly: 115,3; 115,5; 134,29; 135,4; plainlye: 120,4; 123,25; 125,8; &c. (Fr. plain).

plege, *sb.*, pledge, 169,8; plaege: 143,17 (OF plege).

pleis, *vb.*, please, 117,29; 152,14; pleissis: 163,14; 172,5; plesis: 123,15; 131,11; 142,7; pleasis: 123,16; *pret.* plesit: 130, 18; 143,8; *p. p.* plesit: 138,14; pleasit: 126,4 (OF plesir).

plesour, *sb.*, pleasure, 139,26; 156,27.

policie, *sb.*, polity, 171,30 (OF policie).

possesse, *vb.*, possess, 121,23; 121,25; 122,1; &c.; *p. p.* possessit: 153,32 (Lat. possessus).

possible, *adj., id.*, 127,6; 137,29; 172,11 (Fr. possible).

potent, *adj.*, powerful, 160,28; 160,36 (Lat. potens).

pouerte, *sb.*, poverty, 126,31; 127,2 (OF poverte).

powar, *sb.*, power, 120,7; 156,10; pover: 123,17; 127,17; 129,5; power: 122,29; 123,11; 123,12; &c. (OF poer).

powrit, *vb., p. p.*, poured, let loose, 182G (OF purer).

poysone, *sb.*, poison, 139,28 (OF puison).

poysont, *vb., p. p.*, poisoned, 139,28.

praye, *sb.*, prey, 146,15 (OF praie).

praye, *vb.*, pray, 140,12; pray: 131,29; 140,23; 162,40; 165,18; 169,24; *pr. p.* prayand: 151,22; *pret.* prayit: 140,16; 178,17 (OF preier).

prayer, *sb., id.*, 156,39; 156,40; 175,7; &c.; prayair: 178,7G; *pl.* prayeris: 168,17; prayares: 177,18G.

pratling, *gerund*, prattling, 178G (prate + -le).

precedand, *pr. p.*, preceding, 116,23; 133, 14 (Fr. preceder).

preche, *vb.*, preach, 177,1 (OF prechier).

precheouris, *sb., pl.*, preachers, 151,3; 151,22; 154,16; &c.; prechores: 177,6G; preacheouris: 146,12.

precious, *adj., id.*, 114,12; 128,28; 157,3; 157,9; 163,17; preciouse: 121,13; 123,13; 126,23; &c. (OF precios).

preferrit, *vb., p. p.*, preferred, 121,1 (OF preferer).

prefigurate, *vb., pret.*, prefigured, 149,9; *p. p.*: 158,16; 158,18; 163,18; 180,19 (Lat. prefiguratus).

pregnant, *adj., id.*, 138,28 (OF pregnant).

preif, *vb.*, 113,25; 114,4; 114,6; 115,5; &c.; preiffe: 146,17F; preife: 123,24; 128,11; preiff: 132,12; preuis: 123,29; 134,15; *pr. p.* prevand: 111; *pret.* previt: 170,23; *p. p.* provin: 149,21; 149,26; 163,4; &c.; provyn: 175,12 (ME preuen).

preif, *sb.*, proof, 170,25; preiffe: 123,32.

preissand, *vb., pr. p.*, sharpening, 153,15; *p. p.* pressit (pressed): 180,9 (Fr. presser).

preist, *sb.*, priest, 133,20; 143,16; 160,20; 163,11; preiste: 133,19; *pl.* preistis: 166,12; 167,37; 169,7; 171,12; preistes: 143,22 (OE preost).

preistheid, *sb.*, priesthood,149,9;151,28,&c.

prepair, *vb.*, prepare, 114,28; *p. p.* preparit: 146,25, 167,11 (Fr. preparer).

presence, *sb.*, *id.*, 132,8; 134,3; 134,11; &c.; presens: 114,4; 114,8; 114,11; &c. (OF presence).

present, *adj.*, *id.*, 128,9; 162,10; 162,13; *adv.* presently: 156,22 (at the same time); presentlie: 171,35 (just now).

present, *vb.*, *id.*, 160,32 (OF presenter).

preserwe, *vb.*, preserve, 152,22; 177,13; 177,14; preserff: 117,13G; *pret.* preserwit: 154,19 (OF preserver).

pretende, *vb.*, presume, 179G.

pretense, *sb.*, pretence, 171,28 (Lat. praetensus).

prevaile, *vb.*, prevail, 134,31 (OF prevail).

prince, *sb.*, *id.*, 160,28; 160,36; 167,36; *pl.* princis: 167,36; 171,18 (Fr. prince).

principall, *adj.*, principal, 141,5 (Fr. principal).

priour, *sb.*, prior, 171,22 *pl.* priouris: 171, 12; priowris: 171,28 (OF priour).

prise, *sb.*, praise, 135,8; pryise: 146,27 (OF prisier).

priuate, *adj.*, private, 121,1; priuat: 125,4; 126,18; pryvate: 161,5; 171,2 (Lat. privatus).

procede, *vb.*, proceed, 146,4; 146,5; *gerund* procedynge: 138,28 (Fr. proceder).

proces, *sb.*, process, 179,2 (OF proces).

processioun, *sb.*, procession, 152,14.

profeit, *sb.*, profit, 112,29; 112,31; 130,6; &c. (Fr. profit).

professand, *vb.*, *pr. p.*, professing, 150,28; 157,4; 173,6; &c. (OF profes).

profitable, *adj.*, *id.*, 119,3; 119,6; 119,24; &c.

profitis, *vb.*, profits, 113,27; 118,5; 118,11; &c.; *pret.* profeit: 118,20 (Fr. profiter).

profund, *adj.*, profound, 112,3; 119,7; 149,18; &c.; profunde: 125,18; 127,3; 136,2; &c.; *adv.* profundlie: 152,9 (Fr. profond).

prolixit, *adj.*, prolix, 132,14 (Fr. prolix+t).

promise, *sb.*, *id.*, 172,26; promyse: 172,22; 173,9; promesse: 136,19; 138,13 (Fr. promesse).

promittand, *vb.*, *pr. p.*, promising, 178,4G; *pret.* promisit: 160,7; promissit: 182G; promisset: 180G (Lat. promittere).

pronuncit, *vb.*, *p. p.*, pronounced, 133,19; 133,24; 156,16 (Fr. prononcer).

prophane, *adj.*, profane, 154,15 (Fr. profane).

prophecie, *sb.*, prophecy, 152,2 (OF prophecie).

prophecie, *vb.*, prophesy, 157,8; 158,14; *pret.* prophecit: 149,8; 157,6; 158,13; *p. p.* prophecit: 180,19.

prophet, *sb.*, *id.*, 149,8; 156,26; 156,31; &c.; prophete: 170,5; 182,15; propheit: 182G; *pl.* prophetis: 157,5; 158,13 (OF prophete).

propir, *adj.*, proper, 112,26; 114,4; 117,20; &c.; proper: 159,9; 179,20; propyre: 126,11; *adv.* propirly: 112,32; 115,11; 118,20; propirlye: 138,30; 139,16; 142, 21; propyrlye: 145,26; propirlie: 148; 149,20; 154,35; &c. (Fr. propre).

propirte, *sb.*, property, 150,20; 173,4; propirtie: 173,1; 173,10; *pl.* propirteis: 129,17; 131,9; 150,17; &c.

propitiatorie, *adj.*, propitiatory, 168,20 (Lat. propitiatorius).

proponit, *vb.*, *p. p.*, proposed, 171,11 (Lat. proponere).

protest, *vb.*, *id.*, 153,14 (Fr. protester).

proud, *adj.*, *id.*, 119,1; proude: 179G; prowd: 171,27 (OF prud).

providand, *conj.*, providing, 153,10 (Lat. providere).

provisioun, *sb.*, provision, 172,9; 172,15 (Fr. provision).

provokis, *vb.*, provokes, 182G (Fr. provoquer).

pruyf, *sb.*, proof, 152,6.

prymatywe, *adj.*, primitive, 149,24; 151,14; 165,27 (Fr. primitif).

psalme, *sb.*, psalm, 132,16 (Lat. psalmus).

psalmist, *sb.*, *id.*, 163,10; 178,4.

publicane, *sb.*, publican, 178,20 (Lat. publicanus).

puft vp, *p. p.*, puffed up, 146,13 (ME puffen).

pultroun, *sb.*, poltroon 171,21; *pl.* pultrouns: 171,27 (Fr. poltron).

punishment, *sb.*, *id.*, 146,3; 146,10 (Fr. punisser).

purchasingis, *gerund*, *pl.*, obtaining, 168,14 (OF purchacer).

pure, *adj.*, *id.*, 166,25; 180,18; 182,9 (Fr. pur).

purpos, *sb.*, purpose, 113,21; purpose: 120, 25; 145,2; 160,28; &c.; purposse: 134,9 (OF pourpos).

purpure, *adj.*, purple, 180,8 (OF porpre).

put, *vb.*, *pret.*, *id.*, 129,4 (OE putian).

puyr, *adj.* and *sb.*, poor, 113,28; pwir: 126, 28; pwire: 121,8 (OF povre).

pytht, *sb.*, pith, 182G (OE piþa).

qualiteis, *sb.*, *pl.*, qualities, 122,12; 122,17; 128,19; &c. (Fr. qualité).

quantite, *sb.*, quantity, 127,7; 128,3; 130,13 (Fr. quantite).

questione, *sb.*, question, 125,19; 130,3; 130,26; 135,2; questioun: 165,29; 171,4; 171,7; 171,10 (Fr. question).

quha, *rel. pron.*, who, 114,31; 115,9; 118, 15; &c,; quho: 127,15; quhais: 120,33; 127,17; 128,21; 131,11; &c.; quhom: 151,19; 160,7; 165,39; 174,32; quhome: 116,6; 118,12; 137,21; &c.; the quhome: 146,26; *indefinite* quhasumeuir: 113,14; quhasumeuir: 160,39; quha sa euer: 136,3 (OE hwa).

quhair, *adv. pron.*, where, 113,7; 114,12; 115,21; 118,4; &c.; quhar: 123,24; quhare: 128,1; 128,12; 130,2; &c.; *compounds* quhairapon: 149,19; 177,6; 181, 18; quharby; 119,26; quharbe: 123,2; 128,30; 130,30; &c. *in MS A;* quhairby: 151,9; 154,21; 155,14; &c. *in MS B;* quhar euer: 123,15; 144,11; quhare euer: 139,9; quhairfoir: 154,27; 157,1; 158, 25; &c.; quhairfor: 114,27; 114,30; 116,13; 116,17; quharfor: 117,11; quhar-fore: 127,14; 127,28; 131,25; quhairfra: 174,24; quhair fra: 126,19; quharin: 119,27; 136,29; quhare in: 135,16; quhar into (= wherein): 142,26; quhair into: 157,2; quhair of: 151,21; 166,4; quhar-sumeuer: 118,21; quhair sum euer: 132, 25; quhair sumeuer: 132,26; quhair-sumeuir: 179,9; 179,11; quheirto: 181G; quhairthrow: 156,20; quhairwith: 155,2; 179,25; 180,1; &c.; quhair with: 180,10 (OE hwar).

quhat, *pron.*, *adj.* and *sb.*, what, 114,10; 115,1; 123,9; 125,5; &c. (OE hwæt).

quhen, *adv.*, when, 122,7; 122,17; 123,16; &c.; quhene: 113,9; *indefinite* quhen-sumeuer: 116,19; 119,20; quhen sumeuir: 165,29 (OE hwænne).

quhidder, *conj.*, whether, 135,2; 135,4; 138,14; quhethir: 130,28 F; quhydder: 181G (OE hwæþer).

quhilk(is), *rel.* and *interr. pron.*, which, who, *passim;* quhylk: 169,1; 176,26; qwhilkis: 172,18; þe quhilk: 117,23; 152,22 (OE hwilc).

quhill, *prep.* and *conj.*, until, 123,20; 113, 14; 174,19 (OE hwile).

quhow, *adv.*, how, 113,13; 115,19; 116,25; 117,30; &c.; quhowe: 124,13; *also see* how (OE hu).

quhy, *adv.*, why, 125,33; 127,20; 127,22; &c. (OE hwi).

quickly, *adv.*, *id.*, 134,19 (OE cwic).

quietnes, *sb.*, quietness, 171,32 (Lat. quietus + nes).

rachys, *sb.*, *pl.*, scenting dogs, 146,16 Scand. racke).

raill, *vb.*, rail, 179G; *pr. p.* railling: 151,24; 167,32; ralling: 148 (Fr. railler).

randir, *vb.*, render, 179G (Fr. rendre).

rather, *adv.*, *id.*, 126,12; 137,7; 137,11; &c.; raythtair: 182G (OE hraþor).

rationabill, *adj.*, reasonable, 182G (Lat. rationabilis).

real, *adj.*, *id.*, 111; 113,2; 114,4; &c.; reall: 123,28; 125,6; 125,20; &c.; reale: 169, 20; *adv.* realy: 114,2; 114,23; 115,2; &c.; realye: 121,11; 128,31; 135,29; really: 123,14; 130,19; reallye: 127,6; 136, 28; realie: 119,18; 154,37; reallie: 136,9 (Lat. realis).

realme, *sb.*, realm, 160,29 (OF realme).

rebelland, *vb.*, *pr. p.*, rebelling, 181G (Fr. rebelle).

rebellione, *sb.*, rebellion, 181G (Fr. rebellion).

rebuittit, *vb.*, *p. p.*, rebutted, rejected, 177, 26G (OF rebouter).

recant, *vb.*, *id.*, 151,24 (Lat. recantare).

recordatioun, *sb.*, commemoration, 164,1; 164,4 (Lat. recordatio).

recours, *sb.*, recourse, 112,5; 165,32 (Fr. recours).

redar, *sb.*, reader, 114,3; 115,1; 115,19; &c.; redare: 120,14, 121,18; readar: 126, 20; reader: 124,1; 125,2; 126,5; &c.; *pl.* redaris: 117,29; readaris: 134,9.

reddy, *adj.*, ready, prepared, 116,9; 160,21 (OE ræde).

rede, *vb.*, read, 120,8; 128,20; 144,16; reid: 154,24; 155,11; 163,14; &c.; reide: 144, 23; reade: 139,11; *p. p.* red: 176,13; 182G; *gerund* reding: 182G (OE rædan).

redemar, *sb.*, redeemer, 126,31; 138,5; 169,15; &c.; redemare: 120,29; redemair: 177,26G (Fr. redimer).

redempcione, *sb.*, redemption, 119,16; 119, 17; 120,11; redemptioun: 149,38; 157, 34; 158,31; &c. (Fr. redemption).

referrit, *vb.*, *pret.*, referred, left, 160,7; 160,26; 160,39; 177,26 (OF referer).

refuise, *vb.*, refuse, 126,15; 131,15; refuses: 179G; 180G; *p.p.* refusit: 139,4 (OF refuser).

regard, *sb.*, *id.*, 140,18 (Fr. regarder).

regiouns, *sb.*, *pl.*, regions, 150,27; 173,6; 173,22; &c. (Fr. region).

rehers, *sb.*, repetition, 169,25.

rehers, *vb.*, repeat, recall, 162,7; 182,3; reherss: 168,40; reherse: 132,13; rahers: 113,21; raherss: 115,18; *p.p.* rehersit: 116,10; 132,7; 138,25; &c.; rahersit: 116,24; rehersyte: 145,27; reheirsit: 179G (OF reherser).

rekkin, *vb.*, reckon, 153,28; 174,22; rekkyn: 152,20; rakynnis: 146,13; *p.p.* rekkynnit: 138,27 (OE ge-recenian).

releif, *sb.*, relief, 177,9 (OF relef).

relevit, *vb.*, *p.p.*, relieved, 168,8 (Fr. relever).

religioun, *sb.*, religion, 150,24; 152,19; 171,18; 171,30; religione: 180G (Fr. religion).

remane, *vb.*, remain, 123,20; remanis: 122, 19; 130,13; 181,5; *pr.p.* remanand: 120, 9; 125,31; remanent: 177,26G (OF je remain).

rememberance, *sb.*, remembrance, 133,16; 154,38; 155,35; &c.; ramemberance: 113,25; 115,28; 117,10; ramemberans: 113,13; rememberaunce: 142,12; 145,1; remembrance: 139,36; 178G; ramembrance: 121,4 (Fr. remembrance).

remembrand, *vb.*, *pr.p.*, remembering, 181G (OF remembrer).

remissioun, *sb.*, remission, 181,15; 181,26 (Fr. remission).

remittit, *vb.*, *p.p.*, remitted, 181,7; 181,19 (Lat. remittere).

remowe, *vb.*, remove, 124,6 (OF removoir).

renovatioun, *sb.*, renovation, repetition, 159,20 (Fr. renovation).

renow, *vb.*, renew, 112,13; *p.p.* renewit: 159,5; 159,17 (re + OE neowe).

renunce, *vb.*, renounce, 152,19; 152,21; 153,22; 174,22; 174,23 (Fr. renoncer).

repair, *vb.*, apply, 168,33 (Lat. reparare).

reparaling, *gerund*, apparel, vestments, 180,17 (OF pareiller).

repellit, *vb.*, *p.p.*, repelled, 139,5; 144,8; 161,8 (Lat. repellere).

reprehensioun, *sb.*, blame, 166,16 (OF reprehension).

reprevis, *vb.*, reproves, 134,13; *pret.* reprevit: 168,4 (OF repreuve).

repudiat, *p.p.*, repudiated, 156,37 (Lat. repudiatus).

repugnant, *adj.*, *id.*, 122,26; 122,28; 124, 24; 134,24 (Fr. repugnant).

repwgnance, *sb.*, repugning, intervention, 172,15 (Fr. repugnance).

requyr, *vb.*, require, 153,14; requiris: 137, 25; requires: 177,26G; *p.p.* requirit: 114,26; 138,10; 150,17; requyrit: 173,13; 173,29; 173,40 (OF requerre).

resauar, *sb.*, receiver, 136,3; 137,8; *pl.* resauars: 138,18.

resaue, *vb.*, receive, 136,9; 136,20; 136,27; &c.; rasaue: 114,29; 114,31; 136,7; rasaif: 112,15; receaue: 137,26; 137,31; 138,2; 138,4; resauis: 136,4; rasauis: 119,20; 136,5; *pr.p.* resauand: 136,8; 137,1; 143,16; rasaifand: 166,35; ressaiffand: 169,7; 169,15; *pret.* resauit: 136,15; 136,16; resavit: 181G; ressauit: 166,14; 166,38; *p.p.* resauit: 119,18; 129,25; 130,13; &c.; rasauit: 112,33; ressauit: 155,39; *gerund* resauynge: 119, 27; 136,12; 136,14; resauyng: 114,26 (AN receivre).

resist, *vb.*, *id.*, 182,2; *pret.* resistit: 139,14 (OF resister).

resolut, *p.p.*, assured, 134,33 (Lat. resolutus).

resolutiones, *sb.*, *pl.*, assurances, 179G.

respect, *sb.*, *id.*, 133,3; 141,29; 141,31; *pl.* respeckis: 122,3; 141,33; respectis: 149, 34 (Fr. respect).

ressonar, *sb.*, one who reasons, 154,27.

ressone, *sb.*, reason, 116,12; 122,26; 160, 17; &c.; reasone: 125,23; 125,24; 131, 21; &c.; resone: 179G; 180G; ressoun: 180,16; *pl.* ressonis: 165,18; reasones: 134,16; ressouns: 165,12; 170,22; 170, 34; 170,37; *conj.*, be ressone þat: 112,10; 117,21; 167,25; be resone: 179G; 180G; *prep.* be ressone (reasone) of (= because of): 117,22; 120,5; 124,9; 133,4; 136,5 (OF reson).

264

ressone, *vb.*, reason, 112,13; 153,8; 163,13;
  p. p. reasonit: 138,17; *gerund* ressoning:
  153,14; 158,2; 159,39; &c.; ressonyng:
  148; &c.; resonyng: 112,17; reasonynge:
  138,20 *(see note);* 141,15.
rest, *sb.*, rest, peace, 131,13 (OE rest).
rest, *sb.*, rest, remainder, 117,30; 123,27;
  138,30; &c. (Fr. reste).
restis, *vb.*, remains, 136,7; restis/es to considder (it remains to consider): 135,4;
  144,6; 145,15 (Fr. rester).
restorit, *vb.*, *pret.*, restored, 181G (OF
  restorer).
resurreccione, *sb.*, resurrection, 121,22;
  123,30; 123,32; &c. (OF resurrection).
retenwe, *sb.*, retinue, 181G (OF retenue).
returne, *vb.*, return, 113,30; 122,23; 140,
  32; 171,34 (Fr. retourner).
revarde, *sb.*, reward, 171,20 (OF reward).
reverence, *sb.*, *id.*, 179G; reuerence: 181G
  (OF reverence).
rewil, *sb.*, rule, 116,19 (OF reule).
richt, *adj.*, right, 124,7; rycht: 112,3; 113,
  30; 165,30; 165,35; rich: 123,6; 124,6;
  140,32; rych: 122,22; 122,30; 123,10;
  adv. rychtuslye: 179G (OE riht, rihtwis-
  lice).
rigorous, *adj.*, *id.*, 153,25; rigorouse: 137,
  30; *adv.* rigourislye: 114,31 (Fr. rigo-
  reux).
rigour, *sb.*, *id.*, 138,10 (OF rigour).
roik, *sb.*, rock, 113,26; 115,29; 115,31;
  116,21; roike: 139,37; 140,23 (OF
  roque).
rowe, *sb.*, wheel (as instrument of execut-
  ion), 178G (Fr. roue).
rowme, *sb.*, room, place, 175,5; *pl.* rowmes:
  175,5G (OE rum).
rude, *adj.*, ignorant, 130,29 (Fr. rude).
rudness, *sb.*, ignorance, 179G.
ryise, *vb.*, rise, 121,29; 128,17; *pret.* rais:
  120,6; *p. p.* rissin: 150,22; rissyn: 171,8;
  gerund rising: 156,28; rysing: 176,8 (OE
  risan).
ryngis, *vb.*, reigns, 126,14; rengis: 137,10;
  pret. range: 145,7 (OF regner).
ryte, *sb.*, rite, 177,23 (Lat. ritus).

sa, *vb.*, say, 114,15; 118,7; say: 114,18;
  116,8; 116,9; &c.; sais: 114,12; 116,8;
  117,9; &c. *in MS A;* sayis: 150,31; 153,
  18; 156,27; &c. *in MS B; pr. p.* saiand:
  122,29; 125,14; 141,7; sayand: 113,5;

113,8; 113,11; &c.; saynge: 119,29; 124,
  30; 125,14; sainge: 140,6; sayng: 127,26;
  pret. said: 113,10; 116,6; 118,25; &c.;
  p. p. said: 114,11; 115,1; 118,20; &c.;
  sayd: 162,23; 174,26G; 176,1G; *gerund*
  saynge: 121,26; sainge: 121,28; *pl.*
  saingis: 134,1; sayingis: 156,12; 158,3;
  158,4; &c. (OE secgan, sægde).
sa, *adv.*, so, 114,28; 114,31; 127,24; &c.;
  so: 125,8; 126,26; 132,1; 145,7; 145,12;
  correlation: sa ... as: 113,12; 130,18;
  131,3; &c.; so ... as: 119,15; sa ... þat:
  114,7; 116,3; 143,3 (OE swa).
sacrament, *sb.*, *id.*, *passim in MS A; pl.*
  sacramentes: 135,14 (Lat. sacramentum).
sacrifice, *sb.*, *id.*, *passim in MS B; pl.* sacrifices: 156,37; 158,37 (Fr. sacrifice).
sal *(MS A)*, sall *(MS B)*, salbe, *vb.*, shall
  (be), *passim; pret.* suld, sulde (127,32).
  (OE sceal, sceolde).
saluacione, *sb.*, salvation, 112,5; 119,4;
  127,2; &c.; salvatioun: 149,19; 160,4;
  160,6; &c. (OF salvation).
saluiour, *sb.*, saviour, *passim in MS A;*
  saluioure: 121,6; salueour: *passim in
  MS B;* salueoure: 157,33; 161,26; 163,
  15; 172,13; salweour: 165,19; *gen.* saluiouris: 139,39 (OF salveor).
sam, *adj.* and *sb.*, same, 142,9; 179G;
  same: 126,21; 133,12; 143,25 sammyne:
  passim in MS A; samyne: 125,2; sammyn: 127,9; 135,35; 140,11; samyn:
  passim in MS B; saming: 179G; sam(e)
  self (= selfsame): 117,17; 117,26; 121,15;
  122,11; &c.; samyn self: 164,4; sam
  verray (= very same): 156,22 (OE same,
  Scand. samr).
sanct, *adj.*, saint, 155,12; 155,13; 157,31;
  &c. (AN seint; Lat. sanctus).
sangis, *sb.*, *pl.*, songs, 177,21 (OE sang).
satifeit, *vb.*, *p. p.*, satisfied, 112,2; satifyet:
  131,13; 134,33; satiffeit: 161,12; satisfeit: 181,3; 181,5 (OF satifier).
satisfaccione, *sb.*, satisfaction, 112,8; satisfactioun: 158,28; 158,31; 169,28 (Fr.
  satisfaction).
saul, *sb.*, soul, 119,10; 120,21; 130,30; &c.;
  saull: 119,19; 119,23; 120,4; &c.; *pl.*
  saulis: 130,29; 136,22; saullis: 168,8;
  168,16 (OE sawol).
savine, *vb.*, *p. p.*, sown, 128,17 (OE sawen).
schawe, *vb.*, show, 179G; 181G; 182G;
  schawis: 114,30; *pret.* schew: 160,25;

p. p. schawin: 126,4; schavin: 133,13; 138,14 (OE sceawian).

schaym, *sb.*, shame, 181G (OE sceamu).

sched, *vb.*, shed, 133,9; *p. p.* sched: 114,14; 114,17; 115,25; 133,12 (OE sceadan).

schir, *title*, sir, 147,1; 151,26 (AN sire).

scho, *pron.*, she, 128,21.

schorte, *adj.*, short, 169,25; *adv.* schortly (briefly *and* soon): 115,17; 140,21; schortlye: 133,7; schortlie: 160,12; 168, 40; 173,26 (OE sceort).

schutis, *vb.*, shoots, aims, 179,4 (OE sceotan).

schynand, *vb., pr. p.*, shining, 163,31 (OE scinan).

science, *sb., id.*, 119,1; 119,2 (Fr. science).

scisme, *sb.*, schism, 161,5 (Fr. scisme).

sclendirlie, *adv.*, slightly, slightingly, 169,4; 172,17; sklenderly: 143,13 (OF esclendre).

scornit, *vb., p. p.*, mocked at, 179,26 (OF escorner).

scripturaris, *sb., pl.*, 'gospellers', 159,33.

scripture, *sb.*, scripture, scriptural passage, 112,27; 112,32; 115,3; &c.; scriptur: 114,10; scriptour: 120,24; 123,19; 124, 20; &c.; scriptoure: 120,4; 121,4; 126, 27; &c.; *pl.* scripturis: 112,4; 112,18; 112,21; &c.; scriptures: 126,9; scriptouris: 120,27; 121,19; 124,14; &c. (OF escripture).

scrupulows, *adj.*, scrupulous, 159,33 (Fr. scrupuleux).

scurge, *sb.*, scourge, 180,3; (AN scourge).

scurgit, *vb., p. p.*, scourged, 180,3; 180,5.

se, *vb.*, see, 121,31; 129,16; 129,31; &c.; *pr. p.* seand: 126,28; *pret.* saw: 123,28; 123,29; 123,32; &c.; *p. p.* sene: 123,26; 123,27; 123,30; 130,12; seyne: 130,18; seyn: 167,36; 167,40; 171,20; &c.; seine: 131,7; 131,8; 133,11; sein: 130,20; *conj.* seand þat: 126,1 (OE seon).

sect, *sb., id.*, 154,1; 154,4; *pl.* sectis: 173,37; 174,14 (Fr. secte).

secund, *num.*, 112,28; 117,28; 119,9; &c.; *adv.* secundlie: 151,29; 158,12; 170,3; 173,21; 174,7 (Fr. second).

seditione, *sb.*, sedition, 178G; 181G (OF sedition).

see, *sb.*, sea, 127,29; 127,32 (OE sæ).

seik, *vb.*, seek, 125,33; seikis: 171,29; *pr. p.* sekand: 137,12 (OE secan).

seiknes, *sb.*, malady, 159,18 (OE seoc).

seirsynge, *gerund*, searching, 132,1 (AN sercher).

self: *see* sam *and the various pronouns;* in þe self (= in itself): 159,3.

semblabill, *adj., (probably)* gathered in council, 178G (OF asembler).

seme, *vb.*, seem, 140,28 (OE seman).

sene, *prep.*, since, 124,3; 138,23; 144,19; sen: 149,28; 157,5; 157,23; &c.; *conj.*: 126,11; 131,25; 134,32; &c.; sen: 151, 18; 161,11; 165,8; *adv.*: 131,28 (OE siþþan).

send, *vb., id.*, 160,28; 168,29; *p. p.* send: 180,1; 180G (OE sendan).

sensible, *adj.*, perceptible to the senses, 158,21 (Lat. sensibilis).

sensis/es, *sb., pl.*, senses, 118,16; 126,28; 127,4; 130,24; &c. (Lat. sensus).

sensualite, *sb.*, sensuality, 171,31 (Fr. sensualité).

sentence, *sb., id.*, 133,14 (Fr. sentence).

separacione, *sb.*, separation, 120,3 (Fr. separation).

separate, *p. p.*, separated, 120,1; separat: 120,2 (Lat. separatus).

serpent, *sb., id.*, 127,16 (Fr. serpent).

seruand, *sb.*, servant, 127,16 (Fr. servant).

seruis, *vb.*, serves, 116,1; 117,12; 118,10; 126,10 (Fr. servir).

seruice, *sb.*, service, 179,2; 180,14 (OF service).

seruitude, *sb.*, servitude, 164,2; 164,12; 172,6; serwitude: 158,29 (Fr. servitude).

set furth, *vb.*, proclaim, produce, 160,35; settis furth: 134,18; 134,20; *p. p.* set furth: 133,18; 134,8; 148; &c. (OE settan).

sevin, *num.*, seven, 128,22; 167,10; *ordinal* sevint: 138,12; 175,32; *adv.* sevintlie: 152,8 (OE seofon).

sex, *num.*, six, 168,4; 169,2; 175,33; sax: 142,12; *ordinal* sext: 175,26; saxt: 120, 24; 134,32; *adv.* sextlie: 152,4; 170,22 (OE six and sæx).

sextene, *num.*, sixteen, 167,1; 167,35; sexteyn: 168,23.

seyllie, *adj.*, simple, 126,29 F (OE sælig).

sic, *adj.* and *sb.*, such, 155,16; 161,4; 166, 22; 171,26; &c.; sik: 120,10; 122,14; 126,31; &c.; *correlation* sic (...) as: 148; 153,31; 155,8; &c.; sik (...) as: 114,14; 120,28; 122,17; &c. (OE swilc).

sicht, *sb.*, sight, vision, 134,8; sich: 123,29

(OE ge-siht).

signe, *sb.*, sign, 138,9; 178,12; sygne; 136, 10; 137,2; sing: 178 G; syng: 113,22; 114,27; 114,29; *pl.* signis: 158,17 (OF signe).

signifie, *vb.*, signify, 176,26; signifye: 176, 26 G; signifeis: 179,25; 180,1; 180,3; 180,4; &c.; *pret.* signifyit: 117,22; *p. p.* signifeit: 155,18; 164,7; 164,37 (Fr. signifier).

similitude, *sb.*, *id.*, 113,24; 115,26; 115,32; &c.; *pl.* similitudes: 135,15 (Fr. similitude).

simpil, *adj.*, simple, 126,29; sympil: 127,15; symple: 146,15 (Fr. simple).

singularie, *adv.*, singularly, 168,32 (Lat. singulariter).

site, *vb.*, sit, 143,9; sittis: 113,30; 122,22; 122,30; &c. (OE sittan).

skamles, *pl.*, shambles, 118,18; 119,4; skambles: 120,19 (OE scamel).

skyne, *sb.*, skin, 121,30 (Scand. skinn).

small, *adj.*, *id.*, 127,24 (OE smæl).

sobyr, *adj.*, small, little, 127,7; sobir: 168,5 (Fr. sobre).

solace, *sb.*, *id.*, 177,9 (OF solaz).

solempnitlie, *adv.*, solemnly, 175,35 (OF solempne;.

sone, *sb.*, sun, 156,28; 163,31; 176,8 (OE sunne).

sone, *sb.*, son, 116,7; 116,15; 117,4; &c.; son: 116,5; 116,8; *pl.* sonnis: 164,36 (OE sunu).

sonlye, *adj.*, filial, 181 G.

sophistrie, *sb.*, sophistry, 153,16 (Fr. sophisterie).

sorcerie, *sb.*, sorcery, 153,28; 153,33 (OF sorcerie).

sort, *sb.*, sort, manner, 142,3 (OF sorte).

soung, *vb.*, *p. p.*, sung, 175,35 (OE sungen).

sow, *sb.*, *id.*, 177,2 (OE sugu).

sowklingis, *sb.*, *pl.*, sucklings, 178 G (OE sucan).

space, *sb.*, *id.*, 172,8 (Fr. espace).

speche, *sb.*, speech, 162,18 (OE spræc).

special, *adj.*, *id.*, 121,4; speciall: 134,8; 164,37; 171,17; 173,35; *adv.* in special: 132,14; in speciall: 139,26; 151,2; 151, 22; specialie: 149,19; 151,15; 153,9; &c.; speciallie: 180 G (OF especial).

speikis, *vb.*, speaks, 156,34; 156,40; spekis: 116,2; speakis: 140,3; *pr. p.* spekand: 132,17; 136,19; *pret.* spak: 116,3; *p. p.*

spokin: 113,24; 115,26; 116,11; &c.; spokine: 117,1; 120,26; 125,3; spoken: 135,11; 139,35; 140,9; spokkin: 156,32; 157,2; 162,10; &c.; *gerund* spekynge: 123,5; 124,8; spekin: 141,11 (OE sprecan).

speir, *vb.*, ask, 130,26; 130,30; 138,28; &c.; spere: 129,31; *pret.* sperit: 128,21 (OE spyrian).

spendynge, *gerund*, spending, 121,7 (OE spendan).

spiritual, *adj.*, *id.*, 120,26; 128,12; 128,27; &c.; spirituall: 120,21; 123,31; 124,1; &c.; *adv.* spiritually: 136,8; 136,25; spiritualye: 136,27; 136,28; 137,1 (Fr. spirituel).

spot, *sb.*, *id.*, 152,9 (ME spot).

spred, *vb.*, *p. p.*, spread, 163,31 (OE sprædan).

spreit, *sb.*, spirit, 113,27; 118,5; 118,7; &c.; sprite: 128,8; 128,15; *pl.* sprites: 128,19 (OF esprit).

stait, *sb.*, state, condition, 177,11 (OF estat).

stand by (be), *vb.*, abide by, 153,20; 174,19.

stand with, *vb.*, be reconciled with, 140,30; 153,8; 154,30; 157,36.

statute, *vb.*, *pret.*, ordained, 175,33; statut: 175,33 G; *p. p.* statute: 176,7; statut: 176,7 G (Lat. statutus).

sted, *sb.*, stead; in sted of: 167,13 (OE stede).

steir vp, *vb.*, stir up, 143,8; 161,5; steiris vpe: 178 G; *p. p.* sterit vp: 138,2; 142,31; steirrit vpe: 180 G (OE styrian).

steraris vp, *sb.*, *pl.*, those who stir up, 146,4; 146,6.

stert vp, *p. p.*, suddenly promoted, 171,20 (ME sterten).

still, *adv.*, *id.*, 130,13 (OE stille).

stoill, *sb.*, stole, 180,4 (Lat. stola).

strange, *adj.*, *id.*, 121,24; 127,9; 128,2; 129,19 (OF estrange).

sua, *adv.*, so, thus, 115,4; 117,16; 119,3; &c.; swa: 113,16; 114,19; 116,25; &c.; *correlation* (lik) as ... sua/swa: 115,32; 117,2; 131,7; &c.; *conj.* sua beand þat: 163,25; sua (=if): 171,5; 171,30 (OE swa; Scand. sva).

suage, *vb.*, assuage, 171,30 (OF asouager).

subiect, *vb.*, *id.*, 152,19; 152,21; 174,22; 174,23; subieke: 126,17; *p. p.*, *adj.* subiect: 159,18; subieckit: 120,8; 122,4; 122,9; &c. (Lat. subiectus).

subiectis, *sb.*, *pl.*, subjects, 151,5.

subornand, *vb.*, *pr.p.*, suborning, 146,15 (Fr. suborner).

subrogate, *vb.*, *p.p.*, ordained, 177,8 (Lat. subrogatus).

substance, *sb.*, *id.*, 117,8; 117,9; 121,15 (Fr. substance).

subtyle, *adj.*, subtle, 154,27 (OF sutil, Lat. subtilis).

subuert, *vb.*, subvert, 171,29; subwert: 159, 34; *pr. p.* subuertand: 146,14; *p. p.* subuertit: 144,17 (Fr. subvertir).

succedant, *vb.*, *pr.p.*, succeding, 175,5; *pret.* succedit: 169,40; 175,19 (Fr. succeder).

successioun, *sb.*, succession, process, 154, 40; 161,1; 165,36; 173,27 (Fr. succession).

sufficient, *adj.*, *id.*, 123,32; 127,12; 129,23; &c.; *adv.* sufficiently: 112,6; sufficientlye: 142,30; 179G; sufficientlie: 149,21; 149,26; 155,30 (Lat. sufficiens).

sufficis, *vb.*, suffices, 141,14 (Fr. suffis-).

suffir, *vb.*, suffer, 157,33; sufferis: 129,3; *pret.* sufferit: 129,8; 157,32; *p. p.* sufferit: 180G (OF suffrir).

sukkin, *sb.*, what is sucked from flowers, nectar, 127,21 (OE sucan).

sum, *adj.*, and *sb.*, some, 112,20; 112,24; 117,9; 133,16; &c. (OE sum).

sumpart, *adv.*, somewhat, 112,13; in sumpart/e/is (= partly): 150,3; 150,4; 158,6; 158,20.

sumtyme, *adv.*, sometimes, 116,2; 140,3; sum(e) tymes: 136,27; 136,28.

suorde, *sb.*, sword, 159,25 (OE sweord).

superflowis, *adj.*, extra, 143,1 (Lat. superfluus).

superintendent, *sb.*, *id.*, 152,8 (Fr. superintendant).

supernatural, *adj.*, *id.*, 113,3; supernaturall: 120,21 (Fr. supernaturel).

suppar, *sb.*, supper, 113,23; 115,21; 115, 33; 117,10; supper: 124,18; 139,31; 140, 30; &c. (OF soper).

suppone, *vb.*, suppose, 157,26; 180G (Lat. supponere).

supportit, *vb.*, *p. p.*, supported, helped, 181, 23 (Fr. supporter).

supprese, *vb.*, suppress, 120,17 (Lat. suppressus).

sure, *adj.*, *id.*, 164,18; *adv.* surelie 172,12 (OF sur).

sustenit, *vb.*, *pret.*, suffered, 127,1; *p.* (= sustained): 177,11 (AN sustein-).

sworne, *vb.*, *p. p.*, sworn, 181G (OE sworen).

swpit, *vb.*, *p. p.*, supped, 113,11 (OE supan).

syde, *sb.*, side, 129,4 (OE side).

syne, *adv.*, ago, 150,16; 172,4; 174,2; 176, 11; 176,23 (OE siþþan).

syne, *sb.*, sin, 122,5; 122,13; 134,30; 136, 22; syn: 158,29; 159,18; 164,5; &c.; sin: 168,32 *pl.* synnes: 143,15; synnis: 166,23; 168,19; 169,6; 181,17 (OE synn).

syne, *vb.*, sin, 132,21; sine: 132,20; 181G (OE syngian).

synnar, *sb.*, sinner, 153,24.

table, *sb.*, *id.*, 133,18; 143,13; 143,15; &c. (Fr. table).

tak, *vb.*, take, 113,10; 137,21; 151,19; &c.; takis: 153,22; *pr. p.* taikand: 169,6; takand: 171,29; *pret.* tuk: 113,11; tuik: 119,9; tuke: 119,18; 124,19; 132,18; 166,33; *p. p.* tane: 119,11; 154,4 (Scand. taka).

takar avay, *sb.*, one who takes away, 143,15.

takin, *sb.*, token, sign, 113,23; 114,29; takine: 114,27; taken: 126,25; 135,18 (OE tacn).

talent, *sb.*, *id.*, 180G (Fr. talent).

teche, *vb.*, teach, 136,21; 166,15; 166,16; techis: 120,4; 125,7; 127,30; &c.; *pret.* techit: 166,35; 166,38; *p. p.* techit: 127, 11; 165,35; 178,6; teychit: 177,26G (OE tæcean).

techear, *sb.*, teacher, 167,7; teychair: 177, 24G.

temple, *sb.*, *id.*, 180,14; tempil: 119,28 (OE tempel).

temporale, *adj.*, temporal, secular, 171,15; 171,20 (OF temporal).

terme, *sb.*, term, word, 145,18; 145,20; 145,23; &c.; *pl.* termes: 145,18; 145,25; 155,25; 155,27 (Fr. term).

testament, *sb.*, *id.*, 113,6; 113,12; 114,13; &c.; *pl.* testamentis: 164,37 (Fr. testament).

testifie, *vb.*, testify, 175,9; testifye: 178G; testifeis: 157,32; 162,11; 178,24; 180,24 (Fr. testifier)

testimony, *sb.*, *id.*, 127,26; 139,10; testimonye: 121,4; testimonie: 149,21; 149, 27; 170,34; *pl.* testimonyis: 112,21; 112,24; 113,20; &c.; testymonyis: 120,

24; testymoniis: 139,7; testimoniis: 152,5 (Lat. testimonium).

tewlȝae, *vb.*, toil, 181G (AN toiler).

text, *sb.*, 112,27; 114,30; 115,11; &c. (Fr. text).

þa, *pers. pron.*, they, 114,9; 115,20; 115,28; 118,7; þaj: 122,23; þai: 156,32; 158,8; 158,14; &c.; thay: 158,20; they: 126,27; 126,30; 128,23; &c.; thai: 160,32; 174, 14; 175,4 (Scand. þeir).

þa, *dem. pron.*, those, 115,12; þaj: 145,27; þai: 153,31; they: 131,22: 133,9 (OE þa).

þair/thair, *poss. pron.*, their, 115,11; 115, 20; 115,27; &c.; there: 130,8; 130,24; 132,28; &c. *in MS A* (Scand. þeirra).

þair/thair, *adv.*, there, 116,12; 116,16; 118, 22; &c.; þare: 136,23; thare: 134,16; 171,16; there: 128,9: 129,12; 130,29; &c. *in MS A;* ther: 139,21; 144,13; thay: 162,16; þai: 154,15; *compounds* þairapon: 163,32; þairby: 153,20; thayrbye: 119, 11; thairefter: 112,22; therefter: 139,17; þairfoir/thairfoir: 153,27; 154,8; 158,3; &c.; þairfor/thairfor: 118,22; 177,26G; therfore: 142,16; 146,9; therfor: 126,11; 129,11; 137,18; þairin: 117,18; 180G; therin: 129,6; 130,20; 135,31; þairof(f): 161,26; 169,31; 178G; therof: 131,26; þairone: 178G; þairto: 159,19; 163,32; 163,35; therto: 124,29; þair- throcht: 115,18; þairvpone: 179G; þairwith: 112, 23; 161,17; 178,22; þarwith: 123,19: therwith: 127,15; 127,29; 132,13.

thais, *dem. pron.*, those, 149,17; 149,23; 150, 14; &c. *in MS B;* thays: 151,15 (OE þas).

þam, *pers. pron.*, them, 115,11; 115,18; 126,10; &c.; þame: 129,15; 160,29; 164, 35; &c.; them: 126,15; 133,7; 139,22; theme: 126,22; 126,29; 136,24; &c.; *reflex.* þam(e) selues/is: 125,26; 126,17; 130,28; them(e) selues: 137,28; 138,29; 146,13; (Scand. þeim).

þan/than, *adv.*, then, 117,20; 118,24; 123, 11; &c.; thane: 112,25; 132,1; 140,24 (OE þanne).

þan/than, *conj.*, than, 115,4; 116,18; 132, 10; &c.; then: 129,21; (OE þonne).

thankis, *sb.*, *pl.*, thanks, 113,9; 166,33 (OE þanc).

thankis, *vb.*, thank, 171,32 (OE þancian).

thankis gevin, *gerund*, thanksgiving, 168,12; 176,3.

þat/that, *conj.* and *pron.*, *passim.*

þe/the, *article*, *passim;* in þe self (= itself): 158,36; 159,3.

theyf, *sb.*, thief, 178G (OE þeof).

thing, *sb.*, 157,26; 166,13; 167,23; thinge: 128,10; thyng: 116,19; 177,10G; thynge: 131,19; 133,18; *pl.* thingis: 119,8; 131, 21; 160,4; &c.; thyngis: 180G (OE þing).

think, *vb.*, *id.*, 124,7; 126,24; 127,9; 153, 30; &c.; thynk: 128,9; 129,19; 139,25; thynke: 127,27; 128,14; thinkis: 127,22; 128,1; 137,30; &c.; *pr. p.* thinkand: 126, 26; 127,5; 154,18; *pret.* thocht: 179,22; thouch: 126,30; 138,3; *p. p.* thocht: 112,11; 116,13; thouch: 140,25 (OE þencean).

þir/thir, *dem. pron.*, these, *passim (origin obscure)*.

þis/this, *dem. pron.*, this, *passim* (OE þis).

þis/this, *adv.*, thus, 117,6; 117,25; 119,24; &c.; thys: 137,3; 145,28 (OE þus).

thocht, *sb.*, thought, 164,31; 171,29; thouch: 131,20 (OE þoht).

thoill, *vb.*, thole, endure, 177,4 (OE þolian).

thorne, *sb.*, thorn, 180,9 (OE þorn).

thousand, *num.*, *id.*, 148; 173,19; 176,21 (OE þusend).

þow/thow, *pers. pron.*, *passim (in MS A);* *poss.* þj (= thy): 140,14; *obj.* þe/the (= thee) 115,3; 113,13; 140,34 (OE þu).

thraw, *vb.*, twist, distort, 114,9; 117,7; 137,11; thrawis: 154,16; *pr. p.* thrawand: 116,27; *pret.* threw: 142,4; *p. p.* thrawin: 115,12; 115,16; thrawine: 115,27; 137, 23; 139,35; thravin: 126,10 (OE þrawan, þreow, þrawen).

thre, *num.*, three, 119,8; 133,1; 139,10; &c.; *ordin.* thrid: 172,3; 173,10; 175,25; 176,7; third: 121,3; 172,36; thyrd(e): 120,6; 147,1; *adv.* thridlie: 151,32; 158, 16; 170,11; 173,24; 174,13 (OE þreo).

threscoir, *num.*, sixty, 148; 167,35; 168,28; 176,23.

threttene, *num.*, thirteen, 166,31; 174,3; thretteyn: 150,15; 168,23 (OE þreotene).

thretty, *num.*, thirty, 142,12; 166,20; 175,27 (OE þrittig).

thrist, *sb.*, thirst, 120,9; 122,5; 122,13; 122,16 (OE þirst).

throte, *sb.*, throat, 159,25 (OE þrote).

throuch, *prep.*, through, 130,7; 132,3; 150, 12; throucht: 167,39; 168,8; 176,14; throw: 130,23 (OE þurh).

til(l), *prep.*, to, unto, 112,21; 114,9; 126,30;

&c. (Scand. til).

to, *prep.*, *id.*, *passim.*

to gidder, *adv.*, together, 112,20; 120,1; 120,12; &c.; þe gidder: 182,16 (OE togædere).

toung, *sb.*, tongue, 180,23 (OE tunge).

tovart, *prep.*, concerning, 112,3; 112,15; 112,20; &c.; tovarte: 143,21; towart: 151,19; 159,34; 160,4; &c. (OE toweard, *adj.*).

towne, *sb.*, town, 182 G (OE tun).

tracteit, *sb.*, tractate, 111; 138,13; (Lat. tractatus).

tractiwe, *sb.*, tractate, 146,12 (Lat. tractivum).

traditione, *sb.*, tradition, 179 G (Lat. traditio).

traist, *vb.*, trust, 130,29 (Scand. treysta).

traist, *sb.*, trust, 153,25.

transsubstanciacione, *sb.*, transubstantiation, 134,4; 134,12; 134,15; &c. (Fr. transubstantiation).

tre, *sb.*, tree, 115,30; 115,31; 116,22; 163, 31; *pl.* treis: 180 G (OE treo).

treittis, *vb.*, treat, 168,38; *pr. p.* treitand: 177,26 G (ME treten).

tretaris, *see note to* 124,2.

trew, *adj.*, true, 112,11; 112,16; 122,3; &c.; true: 122,29; 123,1; 125,14; &c.; *adv.* treuly: 112,7; 114,15; 116,1; &c.; treulye: 121,29; 122,1; 122,6; truely: 122,26; 123,30; 125,1; &c.; truelye: 123,18; 124,31; 125,5; &c.; treulie: 148; 149,19; 151,10; &c.; trewlie: 177,26 G (OE treowe).

trewtht, *sb.*, truth, 177,26 G; treuth: 149, 30; 149,32; 153,17; &c.; trewetht: 181 G; trueth: 133,10; 134,26; truetht: 124,22 (OE treowþu).

trinite, *sb.*, trinity, 119,10; 155,25; (OF trinite).

triumphe, *vb.*, triumph, 140,25 (OF triumphe).

trowbles, *vb.*, troubles, 145,12 (OF trubler).

tryis, *vb.*, tries, tests, 134,26; *p. p.* tryit: 172,40 (Fr. trier).

tua, *num.*, two, 153,3; 157,36; 164,37; 169, 19; twa: 112,17; 112,26; 112,28; &c. *in MS A;* two: 125,11 (OE twa).

tuelf, *num.*, twelve, 159,28; 166,40; 169,2; 176,11 (OE twelf).

tuenty, *num.*, twenty, 169,2; 169,10; tuentie: 175,33 (OE twentig).

tuichit, *vb.*, *p. p.*, touched, 175,30; *pr. p.* twychin (*prep.*, relating to): 180 G (Fr. toucher).

tyme, *sb.*, time, 119,9; 119,12; 120,2; &c.; *pl.* and *adv.* tymis/es: 112,6; 117,7; &c. (OE tima).

tyrannie, *sb.*, tyranny, 164,12; 164,15 (Fr. tyrannie).

vaik, *adj.*, weak, 118,15; 120,18; waik: 167,38 (Scand. veikr.)

vaiknes, *sb.*, weakness, 130,8.

vald, *see* will.

vand, *sb.*, wand, rod, 127,16 (Scand. vöndr).

vane, *adj.*, vain, 119,25; 149,36; 167,33; vayne: 128,10; waine: 180 G; *adv.* in vane: 156,3 (Fr. vain).

vanite, *sb.*, vanity, 125,4 (Fr. vanite).

var/ver, *see* be.

vardle/vordle, *see* warld.

variance, *sb.*, difference, disagreement, 150, 22; 171,8; 171,17 (OF variance).

vark, *see* werk.

vas/ves, *see* be.

vater, *see* watter.

vax, *sb.*, wax, 127,22 (OE weax).

vay, *see* way.

vayne glore, *sb.*, vainglory, 146,13.

vder, *see* vþer.

vderwyss, *adv.*, otherwise, 182 G.

ve, *see* we.

veil, *sb.*, and *adv.*, *see* weill.

veill, *sb.*, calf, 171,22 (OF veël).

vendicat, *vb.*, *p. p.*, vindicated, claimed, 171,19 (Lat. vindicatus).

vengebel, *adj.*, vengeful, 137,10 (OF vengier).

vengence, *sb.*, vengeance, 182 G.

verite, *sb.*, verity, truth, 136,21; 149,33; 158,1; &c., veritie: 136,19; 141,7 (Fr. verité).

verkis, *see* werk.

verray, *adj.* and *adv.*, true, very, 113,2; 114,1; 116,1; 118,10; &c.; veray: 125,6; very: 123,28; werray: 180 G; *adv.* (=truly) veralye: 143,16; verraly: 117, 14; 127,10; veralie: 167,5; 169,7; 169,18 (OF verai).

verse, *sb.*, *id.*, 132,16 (Lat. versus).

verteu, *sb.*, virtue; *prep.* be (þe) verteu, vertue, of: 120,7; 123,3; 127,18 (Fr. vertu).

vestimentis, *sb.*, *pl.*, vestments, 181,4 (OF

vestement).

vicare, *sb.*, vicar, locum tenens, 167,5 (Lat. vicarius).

vice, *sb.*, *id.*, 122,5; 122,13; 134,30 (Fr. vice).

vickit, *see* wickit.

victorie, *sb.*, victory, 178,17; 178,18 (OF victorie).

vif, *sb.*, wife, 128,21 (OE wif).

vil(l), *see* will.

vincust, *vb.*, *pret.*, vanquished, 181G; *p. p.* vncust: 178G (OF veinquiss-).

vine, *see* wyne.

vindokkis, *sb.*, *pl.*, windows, 125,22; 125, 29; 129,8; &c. (Scand. vindauga).

virgine, *sb.*, virgin, 119,9; 119,15; 119,18; virgyne: 155,23; virgen: 180G (OF virgine).

visdome, *sb.*, wisdom, 130,5; 131,11; 136, 19 (OE wisdom).

vise, *adj.*, wise, 133,2; wyse: 179,16 (OE wis).

visible, *adj.*, *id.*, 158,21 (Fr. visible).

visione, *sb.*, vision, sight, 123,31; 124,1 (Fr. vision).

vith(-out), *see* with(-out).

vitnes, *see* witnes.

vittis/es, *see* wit, *sb.*

vknyng, *sb.*, wake, vigil, 176,2 (*cp.* Icel. vakna-skeiþ).

vmbre, *sb.*, shadow, 163,32; 163,33; 182,8 (Fr. ombre).

vnabill, *adj.*, unable, 180G.

vnbludy, *adj.*, unbloody, not involving the shedding of blood, 156,23; 157,40; 169, 12.

vnbrydlit, *p. p.*, unbridled, 178G (OE bridlian).

vncoverit, *p. p.*, uncovered, 181G (OF covrir).

vnctment, *sb.*, ointment, 121,8 (OF oignement, Lat. unct-us).

vnder, *prep.*, under, 154,37; 155,38; 156, 10; &c., wnder: 181G (OE under).

vnderstand, *vb.*, understand, 155,34; 158,4; 165,24; &c.; vndirstand: 160,23; 161,22; 161,23; 161,31; wnderstand: 179G; *pr. p.* vndirstanding: 169,5; *pret.* vnderstude: 165,16; 171,37; *p. p.* vnderstand: 156,36; 156,39; vnderstanding: 118, 28F; *gerund* vnderstanding: 149,17; 153,22; 153,26; &c.; vndirstanding: 151, 20; 165,23; 165,29; &c.; wnderstanding: 180G (OE understandan).

vndeserwit, *p. p.*, undeserved, 153,20 (OF deservir).

vngodlie, *adj.*, ungodly, 153,19; 154,20; 157,24; &c.

vnit, *p. p.*, united, joined, 120,12; 124,10; 127,33; &c.; vnite: 133,4 (Lat. unitus).

vnite, *sb.*, unity, 169,17; vnitie: 132,29 (AN unite).

vniuersale, *adj.*, universal, 157,15; 165,4; 180,23; 180,24; vniuersall: 178G; *adv.* vniuersalie: 172,11; 172,14; 172,28; &c. (Fr. universel).

vniuersalite, *sb.*, universality 173,5; 173,21 (Lat. universalitas).

vnknawyne, *p. p.*, unknown, 120,23; vnknawin: 154,15.

vnlearnit: *adj.*, unlearned, 174,32.

vnqualifeit, *adj.*, unqualified, 171,19 (Fr. qualifier).

voce, *sb.*, voice, 116,5 (OF vois).

vodnes, *sb.*, madness, 126,13; 137,10 (OE wod).

vonder, *see* wonder.

vonderris, *vb.*, wonder, 129,13; *pret.* vonderit: 129,12 (OE wundrian).

vord, *see* worde.

vork, *sb.*, *see* werk.

vork, *vb.*, work, 127,2; *pr. p.* vorkand: 133,23; *pret.* vrocht: 120,11 (OE wyrcan).

vorth, *adj.*, worthy of, 131,30; worthy *(adj., id.):* 161,2; 177,11; 179G; worthy: 181G; *adv.* vorthely(e): 119,27; 136, 4; 136,28 (OE wyrþe, wyrþig).

vp, *adv.*, up, 138,2; 140,31; 143,14; &c.; vpe: 178G; 180G (OE up).

vpone, *adv.* and *prep.*, upon, 178G; 180G; 181G; 182G (OE uppon).

vproir, *sb.*, uproar, 181G (Dutch oproer).

vristit, *vb.*, *p. p.*, wrested, twisted, 135,11 (OE wræstan).

vritis, *see* writis.

vs, *pers. pron.*, us, 114,17; 120,25; 124,31; &c.; ws: 114,11; 114,28; 117,29; &c. (OE us).

vse, *sb.*, use, 130,14; 158,33; 159,34; 160,13 (OF us).

vse, *vb.*, use, practice, 126,29; 150,31; 160, 33; vsis: 140,28; 159,22; 181G; *pr. p.* vseand: 161,6; *p. p.* vsit: 129,2; 150,5; 150,8; &c., *gerund* vsyng: 114,26 (Fr. user).

vþer/vther, *adj.* and *sb.*, other, 149,33; 150,

23; 154,31; 160,39; &c.; vþir: 168,10; vder: 176,27G; *pl.* vþeris/vtheris: 153, 36; 154,13; 154,40; 159,14; &c.; vderes: 180G; 181G (OE oþer).

vther wayes, *adv.*, otherwise, 153,23 (*cp* vderwyss).

vtilite, *sb.*, utility, 130,6; 177,15 (Fr. utilité).

vulgare, *adj.*, common, 181,1; 181,2 (Fr. vulgaire).

waik, *see* vaik.

wailȝeantlye, *adv.*, valiantly, 181G (Fr. vaillant).

waine, *see* vane.

wantis, *vb.*, lacks, 174,1 (Scand. vanta).

war/was, *see* be.

warld, *sb.*, world, 156,24; 157,9; 160,8; vardle: 124,23; 125,30; 126,31; &c.; vordle: 145,12 (OE woruld).

watter, *sb.*, water, 175,22; vater: 127,17 (OE wæter).

way, *sb.*, *id.*, 159,17; 165,2; 165,32; 182,11; vay: 112,2; 116,9; 120,2; &c.; *gen.* and *pl.* wayis/es: 154,13; 159,3; 159,7; 159, 12; &c.; vais/vays: 122,28; 124,3; 136,15 (OE weg).

we, *pers. pron.*, *id.*, rare in MS A, passim in MS B; ve: *passim in MS A* (OE we).

wechtie, *adj.*, important, 171,6 (OE ge-wiht).

weill, *adv.*, well, 154,8; veil: 116,6 (OE wel).

weill, *sb.*, weal, good, 180G; veil: 112,29; 112,31; 138,18 (OE wela).

weiping, *gerund*, weeping, 168,30; 168,31 (OE wepan).

wemen, *sb.*, *pl.*, women, 159,29; 159,31 (OE wifmen, wimmen).

werk, *sb.*, work, 149,4; 151,9; 154,18; work: 154,20; 154,22; 154,23; vork: 125,27; 135,22; vorke: 135,12; 135,19; 139,12; vark: 125,22; 139,11; *pl.* werkis: 154,28; 154,29; 157,7; 174,5; workis: 153,33; 154,25; warkis: 178G; verkis: 125,25; vorkis/es: 125,27; 134,11 (OE werc).

werray, *see* verray.

wichecraft, *sb.*, witchcraft, 153,28; 153,31; 153,33 (OE wiccecræft).

wickit, *adj.*, wicked, 150,20; 154,17; 155, 21; &c.; vickit: 111; 115,11; 115,20; &c.; vicket: 134,27; *adv.* wickitlie: 151,8; vickitly(e): 116,25; 142,4 (OE wicode).

wickitnes, *sb.*, wickedness, 157,27.

will, *sb.*, *id.*, 167,16; vil(l): 126,4; 131,10; 138,14; vyll: 140,17 (OE willa).

will, *vb.*, *id.*, *passim in MS B;* vil: *passim in MS A;* wil: 139,15; vyl: 139,10; wilbe: 169,26; *pret.* wald: 118,17 *and common in MS B;* vald: *regular form in MS A; pr. p.* (God) willing/villing: 112,14; 115, 19; 117,5; 151,10; &c.; *adj.*, villing: 112, 12; *adv.* villingly: 127,1; 130,9 (OE willan, wolde).

wine tre, *sb.*, vine, 115,30; vine tre: 115,31; 116,22.

wische, *vb.*, *pret.*, washed, 178,26 (OE wox, wosc).

wit, *vb.*, know, 171,16; *pret. present* wait: 178,4 (OE witan, wat).

wit, *sb.*, *id.*, 153,15; *pl.* vittes: 146,17 (= wits); vittis/es: (= senses): 118,16; 126,28; 127,4; &c. (OE witt).

with, *prep.*, *id.*, *passim;* vith: *less frequent form in MS A* (OE wiþ).

withall, *adv.*, with, 160,33; 180,8.

within, *prep.*, in, 182G.

without, *prep.*, *id.*, 112,30; 119,2; 119,3; &c.; vithout: 130,26; 136,17; withoutin: 119,12F (OE wiþutan).

witnes, *sb.*, witness, 160,12; vitnes: 127,12 (OE witnes).

wnder, *see* vnder.

wndesawabill, *adj.*, undeceivable, infallible, 177,26G.

wndouttitlie, *adv.*, undoubtedly, 182G.

wonder, *sb.*, *id.*, 171,24; vonder: 127,11 (OE wundor).

wonderus, *adv.*, wondrous, wonderfully, 179G (wonder-s).

wondirfull, *adj.*, wonderful, 167,12; vonder-ful(l): 127,1; 135,12; 135,34; &c.; *adv.* wondirfullie: 151,6; wonderfullie: 151, 32; vonderfullye: 134,26.

worde, *sb.*, word, *passim in MS B;* vord(e): *passim in MS A; pl.* wordis: 114,22; 115,28 *and in MS B;* vordis/es: *passim in MS A* (OE word).

worschip, *vb.*, worship, hold in honour, 154,14; *p. p.* worschippit: 150,10; 166, 26; 166,28; *gerund* worschipping: 154,6; 154,11; 172,10 (OE weorþscipe, *sb.*).

worthy, *see* vorth.

worthines, *sb.*, worthiness, 169,17.

wrang, *adv.*, wrong, 162,7; 164,31 (OE wrang).

wraytht, *sb.*, wrath, 182G (OE wræþo).

wrechit, *adj.*, wretched, 153,24 (ME wrecched).

writis, *vb.*, writes, 166,20; 167,10; 168,14; 168,28; wrytis: 156,26; 166,11; 167,1; &c.; vritis: 124,17; 124,23; 124,29; &c. *in MS A; pr.p.* wrytand: 156,13; vritand: 131,17; 132,16; 134,13; 139,12; vriting: 113,7; vritynge: 121,21; vritin: 118,31; *p.p.* writtin: 172,21; 175,13; vritin: 113,4; 115,21; 116,5; &c. *in MS A;* vriten: 123,25; vritine: 147,1; vrityne: 139,31 (OE writan, writen).

wrytar, *sb.*, writer, 167,9; 172,3; *pl.* wrytaris: 165,9; 165,14; 165,32; 169,22; writaris: 157,22; 172,32.

wryte, *sb.*, *see* hand wryte.

ws, *see* vs.

wyit, *vb.*, *p.p.*, weighed, compared, 125,26 (OE wegan, wegen).

wyne, *sb.*, wine, 154,37; 155,36; 155,38; &c.; vine: 117,17; 117,19; 117,26; &c. *in MS A;* vyne: 127,13; 127,17; 127,18; &c. *in MS A* (OE win).

wyse, *adj.*, *see* vise.

wyte, *sb.*, blame, 171,14 (OE witan).

wytnesses, *vb.*, witness, 178G.

zeill, *sb.*, zeal, 154,22; 154,23; 154,29; 154, 30 (Fr. zele).

ȝe, *pers. pron.*, ye, you, *passim in MS B; poss.* ȝour(e): 151,7; 151,24; 152,20; &c.; *obj.* ȝou; ȝow; 151,22; 152,22; 153, 15; &c.; *reflex.* ȝour self: 159,24 (OE ȝe).

ȝe, *particle*, yea, 156,29; ȝea: 120,2; 128,2; 131,29; 144,15; ȝae: 179G; 181G (OE ȝea).

ȝeid, *vb.*, *pret.*, went, 127,29 (OE ge-eode).

ȝeir, *sb.*, year, 148; *pl.* ȝeir: 150,16; 172,4; 172,14; &c.; ȝeres/is: 131,28; 143,24; ȝeiris: 148; 166,20; 166,32; &c. (OE ȝer).

ȝeirlie, *adv.*, annually, 168,25.

ȝettes, *sb.*, *pl.*, gates, 134,30 (OE ȝeat, ȝatu).

ȝit, *adv.*, yet, 121,19; 122,19; 129,8; &c.; not ȝit *(after negation);* 116,16; 120,1; 122,24; &c.; as ȝyte: 179G (OE ȝit).

SAMENVATTING

Quintin Kennedy behoorde tot een voorname familie in Z.W. Schotland. Aan de universiteiten van St. Andrews en Parijs werd hij opgeleid voor een kerkelijk ambt. Door de invloed van zijn oudste broer, de Earl van Cassillis, werd hij in 1548 abt van Crossraguel, een klooster in het zuidelijke deel van Ayrshire. Hij stierf op 22 augustus 1564, toen hij nog niet ver in de veertig was maar, volgens Thomas Dempster en andere auteurs na hem, niet dan nadat hij een respectabel aantal polemische werken zou hebben geschreven tegen de Schotse hervormers.

Indien Kennedy de twaalf verhandelingen had geschreven die hem door Dempster worden toegekend, zou hij werkelijk een uitzonderlijke plaats innemen in de Schotse geschiedenis van de zestiende eeuw door zijn literaire productiviteit in een kritieke periode waarin er door zijn Schotse geloofsgenoten niet of nauwelijks aan gedacht werd de pen op te nemen ter verdediging van hun Kerk. Bovendien zou zijn werk van groot belang zijn voor de kennis van het zestiende eeuwse literaire Schots. In feite wordt Kennedy in studies of overzichten van het midden der zestiende eeuw wel vermeld als een uitzonderingsfiguur, om de integriteit van zijn persoon zowel als om zijn literaire activiteiten. Tot op heden heeft het evenwel ontbroken aan voldoende gegevens voor een kritische beoordeling van zijn leven en werk. In de bekende bronnen van zijn tijd komt zijn naam slechts sporadisch voor. Van zijn geschriften waren er tot voor kort niet meer dan twee bekend, nl. de *Compendius Tractiue*, een korte verhandeling over het gezag van de Kerk, gepubliceerd in 1558, en de *Oratioune*, een pamflet dat in 1812 voor het eerst in druk verscheen. Verder wist men dat er in de negentiende eeuw nog een handschrift had bestaan van de *Compendious Ressonyng*, een korte verhandeling over de H. Mis. Van zijn overige oeuvre kende men alleen de titels in de lijst van Dempster.

Het zoekgeraakte handschrift van de *Compendious Ressonyng* werd twaalf jaar geleden teruggevonden. In 1960 verscheen er op een Londense veiling bovendien een handschrift van een ongeveer even lange verhandeling over de tegenwoordigheid van Christus in de Eucharistie. Hiermee is het aantal van de bekende geschriften van Kennedy toegenomen tot vier. En er is reden om aan te nemen dat, indien er niet meer gevonden zullen worden, dit niet komt doordat er verloren zouden zijn gegaan, maar eenvoudig omdat Kennedy er nooit meer geschreven heeft.

De twee verhandelingen die in dit proefschrift voor het eerst gepubliceerd worden, bevatten samen Kennedy's Eucharistieleer. Tegelijkertijd vormen zij de meest complete verklaring die de Middelschotse taal te bieden heeft omtrent dit onderwerp. Zij zijn van belang voor de historicus in zover zij het katholieke antwoord vertegenwoordigen op de uitdaging van de Reformatie in Schotland, voor de filoloog in zover dit antwoord wordt gepresenteerd in zestiende eeuws Schots. Zij blijken het midden te houden tussen een uitgebreide schoolkatechismus en een theologische verhandeling. Beter gezegd, zij zijn een vereenvoudiging van de laat-Middeleeuwse theologie, afgestemd op een publiek dat weinig of geen theologische scholing bezat maar dat wel geconfronteerd werd met de bezwaren tegen de traditionele Eucharistieleer en -viering. En er zijn aanwijzingen dat Kennedy zich in het bijzonder richtte tot de hogere en lagere adel.

Naast verdediger van de traditionele leer tegen die van de Reformatie was Kennedy ook voorvechter van hervorming binnen de Katholieke Kerk. Van een rol die hij gespeeld mag hebben tijdens de Schotse synoden die de Reformatie probeerden af te wenden, is niets bekend. Uit zijn geschriften blijkt evenwel dat hij het succes van de Reformatie toeschreef aan de misbruiken op het gebied van de kerkelijke benoemingen en de verslapping van de kerkelijke discipline die er het gevolg van was. De nadruk van zijn geschriften ligt echter op de uitleg en verdediging van de Katholieke leer. En ofschoon men vaak aantrekkelijke passages tegenkomt, is hij over het algemeen geneigd te abstract te zijn in dit opzicht.

Een eerste onderzoek toont verder aan dat Kennedy geen oorspronkelijk denker of schrijver geweest is. Er is geen reden om met een van zijn tegenstanders aan te nemen dat hij de Kerkvaders alleen uit de citaten in andere polemische verhandelingen kende. Anderzijds is het zeker dat hij vrij gebruik maakte van de werken van andere auteurs, voornamelijk de Engelsen John Fisher en Richard Smith.

De citaten die Kennedy van deze laatste overschrijft geven enig beeld van het verschil tussen zestiende eeuws Schots en Engels. Kennedy schreef in de literaire taal van zijn eigen land. In tegenstelling tot b.v. die van zijn tijdgenoot en tegenstander John Knox, die verscheidene jaren in Engeland had vertoefd, bevatten zijn geschriften slechts weinig specifiek Engelse elementen. In de meeste gevallen beperken ze zich bovendien tot de spelling. En omdat de bestaande handschriften copieën zijn, moeten die wellicht aan anderen worden toegeschreven. Veel opvallender is het Latijnse element in zijn taal, voornamelijk in zijn vocabulaire maar ook in de zinsbouw en rhetorische stijl. Het is de voornaamste reden waarom zijn Schots betrekkelijk gemakkelijk te lezen is voor de twintigste eeuwse lezer.